UNFREE LABOR

UNFREE LABOR

American Slavery and
Russian Serfdom

PETER KOLCHIN

The Belknap Press of
Harvard University Press
Cambridge, Massachusetts
and London, England

Library of Congress Cataloging-in-Publication Data

Kolchin, Peter.
Unfree labor.

Bibliography: p.
Includes index.
1. Slave labor—Cross-cultural studies. 2. Slavery—
United States—History. 3. Serfdom—Soviet Union—
History. I. Title.
HD4861.K65 1987   306'.362'0973   86-14909
ISBN 0-674-92097-X (alk. paper) (cloth)
ISBN 0-674-92098-8 (paper)

For Anne

Contents

MAPS

TABLES

Preface

THIS BOOK has three principal subjects: Russian serfdom, American slavery, and the comparative study of unfree labor. With all three, I build upon a substantial body of recent historical scholarship. Among historians of the United States few subjects—perhaps none—have received more sustained attention or reinterpretation during the past quarter-century than southern slavery; among historians of imperial Russia the volume of works focusing on some aspect of serfdom has been equally impressive. At the same time a growing number of scholars have been approaching slavery, labor systems, and race relations—especially in the Americas—from a comparative perspective. I am deeply indebted to all of these scholars, without whose work this volume could not exist in its present form.

Because of its novelty, the comparative aspect of this work deserves a brief elaboration. At the simplest level the comparative approach reduces the parochialism inherent in single-case studies by showing developments to be significant that would not otherwise appear so. The approximate tripling of the American slave population during the half-century after the cutting off of legal slave imports in 1808, for example, did not strike historians as especially noteworthy until they realized that elsewhere in the New World the slave population grew only so long as importation of fresh slaves from Africa continued. At a higher level comparison allows scholars to formulate and test hypotheses. Some scholars have concentrated on explaining historical differences or peculiarities, while others have sought to recognize common patterns and make generalizations, but functionally the process is the same: comparison enables one to weigh the impact of different variables and hence to distinguish the specific or incidental from the general or inherent.

Although in this volume I build upon the work of other scholars, in a number of important respects my approach differs from theirs. Most basic, by comparing Russian and American bondage, I expand the geographic (and hence the substantive) scope of comparative studies, which with a couple of notable exceptions have been confined to New World slave societies. American slavery and Russian serfdom exhibited fundamental similarities and significant differences. Both were systems of unfree labor that emerged on the periphery of an expanding Europe in the sixteenth and seventeenth centuries; both lasted into the second half of the nineteenth century, with one abolished in 1861 and the other in 1865. They were also similar as systems of bondage; Russian serfdom had by the second half of the eighteenth century become essentially a variant of slavery, much closer to American chattel slavery than to the serfdom of, say, medieval France. They existed, however, in strikingly different historical environments, which helped to shape them differently. Because Russian serfdom emerged within a historical context that was in many ways fundamentally unlike that of the New World—and for all their differences New World slave societies all operated within the same context—comparing it with American slavery proves especially revealing.

Unlike American slavery, for example, Russian serfdom was a largely nonracial system. That serfdom developed essentially "racial" features—the distinction between nobleman and peasant came to seem as inherent as that between white and black in America—suggests the degree to which race is socially rather than biologically determined. Still, comparison illustrates how race was important in shaping the nature of southern slavery. Both masters and slaves blurred the master-slave, white-black distinction and came to see class relationships in racial terms; as a result, race, no matter how artificial, became an essential component of *American* master-slave relations.

In two additional respects this book takes a broader focus than most recent comparative studies. First, I cover a wide temporal span, beginning with the establishment of Russian and American bondage and concentrating on the century preceding their abolition. Such a perspective clearly reveals how much both slavery and serfdom evolved over time. The lives of antebellum southern slaves, for example, differed in many ways from the lives of their forebears a century earlier, from religious beliefs to material standards of living; over that century Russian serfs experienced increasing division of labor and constituted a declining proportion of the population. In both

Russia and America the masters' attitudes toward bondage underwent significant alterations. Revelation of these and other changes demands attention to chronology as well as a focus on a broad stretch of time. Second, I deal with an expanded cast of characters. Although American historians have during the past two decades subjected the lives of antebellum southern slaves to close scrutiny, comparative scholars have generally been slow to follow their lead, looking instead primarily at the masters, their ideologies, and the overall systems they directed. I believe that it is time for comparative history to join the mainstream of recent slavery scholarship by paying as much attention to the bondsmen as to their owners, for only such an approach can reveal the full complexity of relations between masters and bondsmen. Although the former supposedly were in charge, the latter were far from passive and never conformed entirely to the masters' wishes or expectations. Their relationship therefore represented an uneasy equilibrium, a compromise with which no one was entirely happy. If the masters had the upper hand, the slaves and serfs played major roles in shaping—and setting limits to—their own bondage.

A final way in which this volume differs from much existing comparative history lies in its organization. I have sought to avoid writing what might be termed parallel history, in which two stories are essentially juxtaposed and the comparison left largely to a conclusion, or even to the reader. Of course, in some sections of this book I describe what happened in either Russia or the American South, but I interweave these with comparative sections organized around themes or questions and dealing with both countries. Each chapter, as well as the book as a whole, is thus fully comparative.

Although this book is long, its structure is relatively simple. An introductory chapter sets the stage for the rest of the volume, covering the origins, establishment, consolidation, and development of unfree labor in Russia and the United States to the middle of the eighteenth century. Despite their specific differences, Russian serfdom and American slavery both emerged under conditions of widespread labor scarcity and became entrenched as systems of agricultural production based on forced labor.

In Part I, I examine the world of the masters, detailing the management, treatment, and defense of unfree labor and revealing a basic contrast between the two countries. Although serfholders and slaveholders shared certain characteristics as beneficiaries of the forced labor of human property, historical conditions produced two very dif-

ferent master classes, whose nature reflected two very different environments. The rural United States South was a slaveowner's world;
rural Russia was a peasant world.

In Part II, I turn to the bondsmen. Here too, despite important
similarities in their experiences, a crucial distinction emerges: the
masters—and bondage in general—impinged less on the everyday
lives of the serfs than on those of the slaves. In both countries the
bondsmen's lives differed from those prescribed for them, but the serfs
found it easier than the slaves to maintain at least partial communal
autonomy. Because the bondsmen's values were most clearly revealed
when they resisted what they regarded as mistreatment, a central feature of Part II is an analysis of the causes, consequences, and patterns
of this resistance.

In a brief epilogue I draw together the book's main themes and
examine the crises that unfree labor faced in Russia and the United
States South by the middle of the nineteenth century. The crises,
though different, both led to emancipation. I conclude by looking
ahead to this emancipation and the legacy of bondage that survived
it.

I have omitted some subjects for reasons of space and thematic
unity. Urban slavery and serfdom, for example, although worthy subjects of study, are clearly peripheral to bondage as a whole, which in
both countries was an overwhelmingly rural phenomenon. More important, I have slighted such major topics as the economics of forced
labor and opposition to slavery and serfdom, because I intend to deal
with them in a sequel in which I will examine the abolition of bondage in the United States and Russia.

A couple of technical matters deserve clarification. Many (but not
all) of the Russian population figures are for males only. Since only
males were subject to the soul tax that Peter I first imposed on most
of the population, women were usually ignored in the ten national
censuses conducted between 1719 and 1858. Sources frequently refer
to the number of "souls" or "male souls," which means quite simply
the number of males (of all ages); to arrive at a rough population
estimate for both sexes, one can double this figure. (Noblemen and
clergymen, however, were exempt from the soul tax and not referred
to as souls.) To avoid misunderstanding, a reference in the following
pages to the number of serfs or peasants should be understood to
include *both* sexes unless the term *souls* or *male souls* is specifically
used.

With minor modifications I have followed standard Library of

Congress guidelines in transliteration and use of Russian terms. I have translated most Russian terms but have transliterated a few terms that lack precise English equivalents (see the list of frequently used Russian terms). I have translated the names of well-known people and places for which English names exist; thus I use Nicholas I, not Nikolai I, and Moscow, not Moskva. Similarly, I have used conventional English-language spelling for the names of a few prominent individuals (Tolstoy, not Tolstoi). I have dropped final soft signs for well-known proper names (Gogol rather than Gogol' and Riazan rather than Riazan'). Finally, I have retained the original spelling in transliterating names and titles of works cited.

*   *   *

DURING THIS BOOK'S decade-and-a-half gestation period I have built up a large number of intellectual debts that it is now my pleasure to acknowledge. Generous institutional support enabled me to take time off from teaching for research and writing. This support includes fellowships from the National Endowment for the Humanities, the John Simon Guggenheim Memorial Foundation, the Institute of Southern History at Johns Hopkins University, and the Charles Warren Center for Studies in American History at Harvard University. Additional financial assistance came from the University of New Mexico in the form of a one-semester sabbatical and a grant-in-aid to facilitate travel for research.

I have presented some of my ideas in preliminary form in talks at the Charles Warren Center, Clark University, Alfred University, Princeton University, the University of Chicago, and the University of Pennsylvania, and in papers given at the American Historical Association's annual conventions in 1978 and 1983. Numerous comments by readers and listeners helped me refine my arguments. Portions of Chapter 5 were published in somewhat different form as "The Process of Confrontation: Patterns of Resistance to Bondage in Nineteenth-Century Russia and the United States," *Journal of Social History*, 11 (Summer 1978), 457–90; and portions of Chapter 3 were published in somewhat different form as "In Defense of Servitude: American Proslavery and Russian Proserfdom Arguments, 1760–1860," *American Historical Review*, 85 (Oct. 1980), 809–27. I am grateful to these journals for permission to republish this material. Some of the ideas developed in Chapters 4, 5, and 6 were also tested in "Reevaluating the Antebellum Slave Community: A Comparative Perspective," *Journal of American History*, 70 (Dec. 1983), 579–601.

Although he has not read this manuscript and bears no responsibility for its faults, David Herbert Donald deserves a special word of thanks and acknowledgment. As my mentor in graduate school at Johns Hopkins University, he trained me to think critically and analytically, and in subsequent years he has continued to take an active and supporting interest in my work. He will probably not agree with all of my interpretations in this book, but in a very real sense he made its existence possible.

Editors at Harvard University Press—Aida D. Donald, Elizabeth Suttell, and Peg Anderson—helped transform a rough manuscript into a finished work. It was a pleasure to work with them. The fine maps are the handiwork of Lisa T. Davis.

Numerous friends, colleagues, and experts read portions of this book and offered helpful comments and suggestions. I would especially like to thank John T. Alexander, Ira Berlin, Nancy F. Cott (who suggested this volume's title), Drew Gilpin Faust, Michael Flusche, George M. Fredrickson, D. Barry Gaspar, Robert A. Gilmour, James Henretta, Steven Lukashevich, Theda Skocpol, R. Jackson Wilson, and Raymond Wolters.

A smaller number of scholars read all or most of the manuscript; these include Daniel Field, Eugene D. Genovese, Kenneth S. Greenberg, Richard Hellie, and especially Howard N. Rabinowitz, whose friendship and intellectual discourse helped make my nine years at the University of New Mexico as enjoyable as they were. None of these scholars agreed with everything I wrote, nor did I follow all of their suggestions, but their extensive and thoughtful criticisms saved me numerous errors and helped make this a much better book than it otherwise would have been. I am grateful for their service, which far exceeded the call of professional duty.

Finally, my greatest debt is to Anne M. Boylan, my wife. Anne has served as my best—I will not say severest—critic. She has read and discussed with me two drafts of this manuscript, as well as numerous preliminary talks, papers, and articles and has provided penetrating comments and suggestions for improvement. Because her field of expertise is neither slavery nor serfdom, she has been able to read my work with the kind of detachment and breadth of vision difficult to find in a specialist; because she is a professional historian, she has been able to read it with an eye to far more than matters of style and common sense.

UNFREE LABOR

FREQUENTLY USED RUSSIAN TERMS

Barshchina	Corvée, dues paid in labor
Desiatskii	Tenth (peasant designated to keep order on a large estate)
Dvorovye	House serfs
Ispravnik	Noble police chief in each provincial district
Kholop	Slave (pre–eighteenth century)
Mir	Peasant communal organization (also world, peace)
Obrok	Quitrent, dues paid in money or kind
Obshchina	Peasant commune
Otkhodnik	Departer, peasant with a pass temporarily working away from his estate
Pomeshchik	(1) Noble landowner, planter; (2) conditional landholder (pre–eighteenth century)
Sotskii	Hundredth (peasant designated to keep order on a large estate)
Starosta	Elder, chief peasant communal official
Volnenie	Minor peasant rebellion or strike; disturbance, agitation

The Origin and Consolidation
of Unfree Labor

AT APPROXIMATELY the same time two systems of human bondage, American slavery and Russian serfdom, emerged on Europe's borders. Although specific and sharply differing historical conditions dictated their establishment, their origins were more closely linked than was readily apparent. Both provided by compulsion what could not be adequately secured without it: agricultural labor. Both were preeminently systems of forced labor.

Over the course of generations these labor systems became consolidated and entrenched. By the middle of the eighteenth century they had reached a level of maturity; class lines hardened, and relationships that had once been tentative came to seem inherent and immutable. Russian serfdom and American slavery were by no means identical, but as systems of unfree labor they played similar social and economic roles in the development of the two countries.

*   *   *

THE ESTABLISHMENT of these labor systems can be approached on two levels, the specific and the general. Concrete historical circumstances produced serfdom in Russia; a different set of concrete historical circumstances produced slavery in America. One may legitimately explain each without reference to the other or indeed to slavery or serfdom anywhere else. At the same time, because neither American slavery nor Russian serfdom emerged in isolation, a full understanding of the significance of their introduction requires placing it in the context of similar developments elsewhere.

The geographic and economic expansion of Europe in the sixteenth and seventeenth centuries brought with it the emergence—in some cases the reemergence—of forced labor on both its eastern and western borders. Portuguese, Spanish, Dutch, French, and English colonists resorted to varying forms of peonage and indentured servitude before settling on slavery as the institution most suitable to developing the economic potential of newly acquired lands in the Americas. At the same time, an upsurge of economic activity and internal colonization in eastern European countries from the Baltic to the Ukraine led to the reenserfment of a peasantry that had recently acquired a limited degree of freedom and in Russia the enserfment of a population most of which had been juridically free all along. This remarkable growth in the use of unfree labor along the periphery of an expanding Europe stood in marked contrast to its continuing decline in the more economically advanced nations of western Europe.[1]

Shortage of labor provides the essential link between the specific delineation of how bondage emerged in particular locations and the general explanation of its widespread simultaneous appearance. Wherever slavery and serfdom arose on the borders of early-modern Europe, it was a response to a pervasive scarcity of agricultural labor. Examination of developments in Russia and the American South thus reveals both the specific events producing bondage in each country and the way in which those events were part of a general trend.

The enserfment of the Russian peasantry was a drawn-out process spanning some three hundred years and developing in three basic stages, the first and third of which were long and the second of which was relatively short. During the second half of the fifteenth and most of the sixteenth centuries the peasants' freedom was gradually limited; then, during the last two decades of the sixteenth century and the first decade of the seventeenth, a sudden and complete prohibition of their right to move occurred; finally, in the seventeenth and the first half of the eighteenth century, the new arrangement became solidified and codified, and Russian serfdom came increasingly to resemble chattel slavery.

Before the establishment of serfdom there already existed a significant group of unfree Russians known as *kholopy* and usually denominated *slaves* in English.[2] Constituting perhaps 10 percent of the population, they were a diverse group: among them were high-status persons who served in administrative capacities as well as more numerous domestic servants, artisans, and agricultural laborers. Some were allotted land to work on their own and lived like peasants, but most lived in or near the households of their owners and served to increase their prestige and comfort rather than to augment their incomes. Over the course of the sixteenth century changes occurred in the nature of this slavery. The number of high-status slaves decreased, and hereditary slavery increasingly gave way to "limited service contract slavery," under which individuals or small groups sold themselves into theoretically temporary bondage that almost always lasted for life. This modified slavery often served essentially a welfare function, with those on the margins of society voluntarily going into slavery in hard times in exchange for subsistence. During the seventeenth century kholopy and serfs gradually merged, and in 1723 Peter I transferred all remaining slaves into the ranks of serfs.[3]

Although there were slaves in Russia in the first half of the sixteenth century, Russia was not at the time a slave society in the sense of having an economy based on slave labor. Not only were most kholopy not engaged in agriculture, but the great bulk of the population consisted of juridically free peasants. They were not an undifferentiated mass: indeed, there were numerous partially overlapping designations, both legal and descriptive, for people whose status sometimes differed only slightly or not at all, and there were significant variations in actual status as well.[4] Some peasants, especially in the more remote areas of the north and northeast, had their own land and lived self-sufficient lives practicing subsistence agriculture.

The great majority of peasants, however, were dependent on people richer and more powerful than themselves. They lived on someone else's land—the holder could be an individual, a monastery, or the tsar himself—and paid rent in exchange for use of this land. The form of rent varied, but there were three basic types (which continued under serfdom as well). Peasants might perform labor obligations, known as *barshchina,* cultivating seigneurial land as well as their own rented allotments. They could also pay for their use of land with quitrent payments, known as *obrok;* these could be either in kind—grain, eggs, butter, meat, and the like—or in cash. Although all three forms of rent coexisted, sometimes on the same landholding, obrok in kind remained the prevalent form of rent into the sixteenth century; the amount of land under direct seigneurial cultivation was small, and money transactions played a limited role in the countryside.

Although peasants were dependent, they remained free and were able—in theory and often in practice—to move in search of better conditions. Such movement usually meant trading dependence on one source for dependence on another; for example, peasants would leave one landlord to rent from another who promised better terms. Still, the very ability to move in a time of relative labor scarcity served as an important safeguard to the peasants and a major annoyance to landholders. The latter, therefore, strove to limit their dependents' ability to move. They loaned peasants money and refused to allow them to leave without paying their debts; they required the payment of exit fees; and they pressed the government, which had a fiscal interest of its own in the presence of the peasants and hence their ability to pay taxes, to come to their aid. In 1497 the new legislative code for the first time made general a provision that had occasionally been applied during the previous half-century on a local level: peasants could move only during a two-week period extending from one week before to one week after the autumn St. George's day (26 November), when the harvest was in and migration would be least disruptive. Furthermore, they had to pay an exit fee, which increased with the number of years (up to four) they had lived on the land they were leaving. These provisions, reiterated in the code of 1550, confirmed a principle that was apparently already widely accepted in fact: peasants who were long-term residents "belonged" where they were, but those who had lived somewhere for a relatively short period had less of a commitment to stay put. Nevertheless, peasants of all categories continued to move, both legally at St. George's day and illegally through flight. The St. George's day provision did not so much stop movement as regulate its timing, and landlords hungry for laborers would often pay peasant loans and exit fees, provoking bitter charges of labor stealing. Peasant freedom of movement was thus gradually curtailed, but by no means abolished, during a period of more than a century.[5]

One of the basic factors leading to this erosion of peasant freedom was the centralization and expansion of the Russian state. Between the middle of the fifteenth and the middle of the sixteenth century Muscovy, originally one of several Russian principalities, became the center of a far-flung empire; from 1462 to 1533 the area controlled by the Muscovite state increased about sevenfold, and during the remainder of the sixteenth century it doubled again. This geographic expansion was accompanied by a corresponding growth in the power of the tsars, who made themselves masters of Russia through a combination of policies that included military conquest, land expropriation, extermination of some political rivals, forcing others to come to Moscow and enter the tsar's service, and creation of a new group of state servitors who owed their position—and hence their allegiance—to the tsar.

As the state expanded and the power of the tsar grew, a revolution in the system of landholding contributed substantially to the emergence of serfdom. Determined to secure the loyalty of their noble subordinates, Ivan III (1462–1505) and his successors rewarded them with conditional grants of land known as *pomest'ia* (singular *pomest'e*), to be kept as long as the holders (known as *pomeshchiki*) remained in good graces. The process involved widespread violence and confiscation of hereditary landholdings (*votchiny*). In the 1470s and 1480s, for example, when Ivan III annexed Novgorod, he executed scores of local landowners, deported about eight thousand others to distant regions, and settled some two thousand men loyal to him on their lands. The new pomeshchiki, whose principal obligation to the tsar was to fight in his wars, were to be supported by the peasants who lived on their estates, and land grants typically listed the villages or resident peasants and instructed them to "obey" their new landlord, "cultivate his land and pay him grain and money obrok." Because these landholders, who were absent in military service much of the time, depended for their livelihoods on "their" peasants, the new system brought the labor question to the fore.[6]

The establishment and spread of the pomest'e system coincided with a marked economic upturn that accelerated during the first half of the sixteenth century. Agricultural production increased, new cities burgeoned, trade and small-scale artisanry flourished. A strong, centralized government facilitated commerce, and territorial expansion was accompanied by a concomitant growth in the area of land tilled as a result of both internal colonization of previously unused land and cultivation of newly occupied territory, especially in the south and east where many pomeshchiki were situated. Although these were also boom years in the rest of Europe, western European travelers, rarely prone to exaggerate the prosperity or happiness of Russia, were impressed by the bustling agricultural economy they found there. "The country betwixt [Moscow and Iaroslavl]," wrote one in 1553, "is very well replenished with small villages, which are so well filled with people, that it is wonder to see them: the ground is well stored with corne which they carrie to the citie of Mosco in such abundance that it is wonder to see it."[7]

This economic upturn was accompanied by an increase in seigneurial production. If in the fifteenth century most peasants had paid rent in kind for land they then used as they wished, during the first two-thirds of the sixteenth century a rising demand for agricultural products, especially grain—stimulated in part by a growing urban population and in part by military needs—led many landholders to introduce barshchina obligations and raise their own goods for market. In many cases peasants who had formerly been exclusively on obrok continued to make obrok payments but also found themselves burdened with tilling seigneurial ploughland as well as their "own." In selected parts of the Novgorod region, for example, the proportion of land under seigneurial cultivation increased threefold between 1500 and 1539, from about 5 percent to 15 percent of the total cultivated. Farther south, where land was more fertile and the climate milder, the proportion of land under seigneurial cultivation was substantially greater. Historians disagree over whether this increase was achieved primarily through encroachment on land that obrok-paying peasants used or through cultivation of previously untilled soil, although there is no doubt that both occurred. Unlike the situation in other countries of eastern Europe, however, in Russia seigneurial production increased to meet domestic needs; regions along the western periphery of Russia—some of which were incorporated into the Russian empire in the eighteenth century—engaged in substantial exports of grain to western Europe, but Russia proper exported very little in the sixteenth century.[8]

The ultimate effect of increased seigneurial production, however, was the same: the peasants were the main losers. The rising market for grain, the spread of the pomest'e system, the increase in seigneurial cultivation—together with a very sparse population—created a pervasive labor shortage.[9] Peasants found their work loads increased; at the same time, competition for workers became more acute, and landlords, concerned with protecting their labor supply from neighbors, took an increasingly proprietary interest in what they were coming to regard as "their" peasants.

An abrupt reversal of this long-term boom ushered in the second stage of enserfment. Beginning in the 1560s a series of profound shocks plunged Russia into a period of social chaos and economic crisis that lasted a half-century and fundamentally altered relations between landlords and peasants. The Livonian war, a twenty-five-year struggle with Lithuania, Poland, and Sweden launched by Ivan IV (1533–84) in 1558, cost Russia dearly in manpower, resources, and human suffering. Even more devastating was the internal war he waged against his political enemies, which wreaked havoc and destruction on much of the countryside between 1565 and 1572. A temporary lull in the late 1580s and early 1590s was followed by a series of dynastic quarrels beginning in 1598 that plunged the country into a succession of civil wars that did not end until after the founding of the Romanov dynasty in 1613. Add to this the armed intervention of Polish and Swedish forces, three successive crop failures creating widespread famine and epidemics during the years 1601–3, and the uprising led by Ivan Bolotnikov in 1606–7, and one can begin to imagine how cataclysmic these years were for Russia. The consequences of these events were most devastating for the peasants.[10]

The most immediate result was economic collapse. Agricultural production declined sharply, and large numbers of people were simply unable to support themselves. Foreign travelers who until the 1560s had described a prosperous society now told a very different story. A Vatican envoy who arrived in 1581 to mediate between protagonists in the Livonian war described Russia as a "harsh land . . . much of it uncultivated and uninhabited." Other visitors told of a country "sore visited by the hand of God with the plague" and spoke of the devastation caused by Ivan IV's henchmen, who "murdered everyone they encountered" and "ransacked the entire countryside."[11]

Peasants responded to the crisis in a variety of ways. Some sold themselves into slavery. Others resorted to crime; records from the period show a marked rise in vagabondage, theft, and brigandage, and a general collapse of the social order. The most characteristic peasant response, however, was flight. Hundreds of thousands of desperate villagers left their homes, often in families or groups of families, in search of food, livelihood, and security. Some joined roving bands that foraged and pillaged throughout the countryside, and others eventually wound up on the lands of nearby magnates or monasteries. Many, however, fled the central part of Russia altogether for the newly opened lands in the south and southeast, eventually joining the cossacks or settling on the estates of frontier pomeshchiki who, desperately short of labor, were all too happy to shelter the fugitives. Peasants also sought refuge in the far north, along the desolate borders of the White Sea, and across the frontiers of Sweden, Lithuania, and Poland.

Documents from the 1570s and 1580s reveal an extraordinary depopulation of central Russia. In the Moscow district 84 percent of the land lay fallow in the 1580s, and farther north the figure approached 90 percent. For peasants who remained, conditions worsened dramatically as landlords sought increased labor and obrok payments from them to compensate for the loss of those who fled. In many cases whole villages were entirely deserted. Estate inventories, surveys, and land grants typically described villages as either underpopulated or abandoned; over and over one comes across entries such as "there are no households on this land," or this village is "empty, and in it two empty households, the ploughland fallow." Some documents listed the reasons for such depopulation, as in a village "empty from plague and from hunger for 4 years," and others suggested the ultimate fate of the fugitives: "from these households the inhabitants left for who knows where, and some died." British ambassador Giles Fletcher wrote in 1588 of "many villages and towns . . . uninhabited, the people being fled all into other places by reason of the extreme usage and exactions done upon them."[12]

Landlords faced a crisis as well, although of a different nature. For them the problem was one of labor: there had been a shortage before, but now the shortage was critical. The situation was complicated by the intraclass character that the struggle for peasants often assumed, with would-be employers squabbling over the dwindling supply of laborers, striving to keep their "own" peasants and lure others away from their neighbors. In the newly opened lands of the south, such as Orel, Tula, and Elets, pomeshchiki and government authorities frequently welcomed fugitives from the center and therefore tended to favor the continuation of free peasant migration. Large landowners and monasteries, who could afford to offer peasants better terms and who had the muscle to defend their interests by force if necessary, were often successful in stealing peasants from their less fortunate neighbors. Those who suffered most were the mass of relatively poor pomeshchiki; each of them depended for his livelihood on the labor of only a few peasant families, whose departure threatened not only monetary loss but total ruin. It was these pomeshchiki, therefore, who clamored most for relief, although no landlord was immune from the havoc wrought by the labor shortage, and all looked to the government to restore order and defend their interests.[13]

The solution was obvious: if peasant departures were causing such trouble, why not forbid them? Beginning in 1581 a succession of tsars issued decrees declaring certain years "forbidden years" during which peasants could not legally move, even in the two-week St. George's day period. Although the forbidden years were at first temporary measures and probably applied only to particular areas, by 1592 departure was forbidden throughout the country. In conjunction with the prohibition of movement, the government undertook to register the population in a series of local cadasters, so that in case of dispute a peasant's proper residence could be determined. Using its police powers for the first time to track down and return fugitives to their rightful masters, the government also established a five-year search period during which missing peasants could be hunted; those who eluded capture for more than five years were for the time being safe.

The prohibition of peasant movement, together with the return of peace, led to a partial economic recovery in the 1590s, but the early years of the seventeenth century brought renewed crisis when the famine of 1601–3 led to widespread flight and an upsurge of social violence. The government of Boris Godunov wavered. In 1601 and 1602 he issued decrees once again allowing peasant departures, probably in part to relieve growing popular restiveness and in part to curry favor with the richest magnates who, confident of their ability to attract laborers, had never been so enthusiastic about the forbidden years as the majority of pomeshchiki. The result was disastrous. Massive flight, brigandage, and social chaos once again engulfed the countryside, and the population suffered from three successive crop failures. In 1603 the government restored the forbidden years, and thereafter *every* year was a forbidden year. From then on, despite turmoil, revolt, and warfare against foreign and domestic enemies, the Russian government remained firm in maintaining and gradually strengthening the prohibition on peasant movement.[14]

The first full legal codification of serfdom did not take place until half a century later in the legislative code of 1649. Some Soviet historians, seeking to explain this delay, argue that Ivan Bolotnikov's uprising of 1606–7 frightened the government into pursuing a cautious policy to avoid creating further social unrest. This explanation is both unconvincing and unnecessary. I shall deal with Russia's "peasant wars" later in this book; suffice it to say here that none of them resulted in a more moderate government policy toward the peasantry. As for the delay in codifying serfdom, it was only because urban riots in 1648 led to an extraordinary convening of the Assembly of the Land that a new legal code was drafted in 1649. In any case, peasant departures continued to be illegal after the reimposition of the forbidden years in 1603. Whatever wavering there was on the issue resulted from the conflicting interests of wealthy landowners and frontier authorities on the one side, who favored maintenance of the short, five-year search period, and the more numerous small and medium-size holders on the other, who pressed for tighter restrictions on peasant movement. In 1637 a large number of the latter collectively petitioned the tsar, complaining of "Moscow strong people" who stole their peasants, "relying on your royal time limit of five years." The petitioners noted their desperate poverty and begged the monarch for help, "so that our service lands and hereditary lands will not be laid waste and the rest of the peasants and bondsmen will not leave us, and so that we . . . will not perish completely." In response to such pressure the government extended the search period to nine years in 1637 and to ten years in 1642, except for peasants spirited away by landlords, for whom the new search period was fifteen years. The code of 1649 finally abolished the search periods altogether; henceforth a serf could not escape from his owner no matter how many years had elapsed.[15]

The essence of the enserfing legislation, as enacted from the code of 1497 to that of 1649, was the restriction and finally the prohibition of movement. It should be pointed out that the serfs, although by far the most numerous, were not the only segment of the population affected by this legislation; the code of 1649 also forbade movement without permission for peasants who resided on court and government lands and for taxpaying urban residents. In this sense the entire Russian population, legally categorized into estates or orders, was bound except for the nobility (and even it was "bound" to government service). What distinguished the serfs from others whose movement was restricted was that serfs were subject to the authority of the individual or monastery on whose land they lived. They were thus bound not only to their residence but also in effect to their landlords, who became for all practical purposes their owners. During the century following the enactment of the code of 1649, in the third and final stage of serfdom's creation, prohibition of movement would cease to be its defining characteristic, and the institution would come more and more to resemble chattel slavery.

*   *   *

A SHORTAGE of laborers also plagued English settlers in the American colonies, and there, as in Russia, this situation led to the use of physical compulsion to secure workers. A vast abundance of virgin land together with a paucity of settlers defined the problem in all the mainland colonies; everywhere, land was plentiful and labor scarce. To attract laborers, the colonists consequently found it necessary to pay wages that in Europe would have been considered exorbitant. "Poor People (both men and women) of all kinds, can here get three times the wages for their Labour they can in *England* or *Wales*," reported an observer from Pennsylvania in 1698. In all the colonies complaints were rampant about the high cost of labor and about the resulting lack of submissiveness among the much-sought-after workers. The law of supply and demand rendered unsuccessful the early efforts of several colonial governments to legislate maximum wages, and both skilled and unskilled labor continued to command wages up to twice those prevalent in England.[16]

The payment of high wages proved inadequate, however, to secure a sufficient number of workers, and in every colony highly paid free labor was supplemented by forced labor of one type or another. Like the Spaniards to the south, although with less success, the English forced Indians to work for them. Indian slavery was most prevalent in South Carolina, where in 1708 the governor estimated that there were 1,400 Indian slaves in a population of 12,580, but Indians also served as house servants and occasional laborers in the other colonies: New Jersey wills reveal the continued presence of small numbers of Indian slaves in that colony as late as the middle of the eighteenth century.[17]

For a variety of reasons, however, Indian slavery never became a major institution in the English colonies. The proximity of the wilderness and of friendly tribes made escape relatively easy for Indian slaves. The absence of a tradition of agricultural work among East Coast Indian males—women customarily performed the primary field labor—rendered them difficult to train as agricultural laborers. Because they were "of a malicious, surly and revengeful spirit; rude and insolent in their behavior, and very ungovernable," the Massachusetts legislature forbade the importation of Indian slaves in 1712. Finally, there were not enough Indians to fill the labor needs of the colonists. In New England, for example, most of the natives present when the Puritans arrived died from illness and war during the next half-century. The policy of eliminating the threat of Indian attack by eliminating the Indians themselves proved in the long run incompatible with the widespread use of Indians as slaves and necessitated the importation of foreign laborers.[18]

For the greater part of the seventeenth century the colonists relied on the most obvious source for their labor: other Europeans. Although more prevalent in some colonies than in others, indentured servants were common everywhere in seventeenth-century America. Most served between four and seven years in exchange for free passage from Europe to America, although some were kidnapped and others transported as criminals. All found themselves highly prized commodities. In many colonies, such as Virginia, settlers received a headright—often fifty acres—for every person they imported. But even without such incentives, colonists eagerly snapped up newly ar-

riving stocks of servants, who performed vital functions as agricultural laborers, domestics, and artisans. These immigrant servants, as
well as colony-born Americans bound out for poverty, debt, or crime,
were virtually slaves during their periods of indenture, bound to do
as their masters ordered, subject to physical chastisement, forbidden
to marry without permission, and liable to be bought and sold. Like
slaves, some were forcibly separated from their relatives. Although a
few servants became prosperous and influential in later life, for most
the future was decidedly less rosy. In the mid-seventeenth century
close to half the servants in Virginia and Maryland died before their
terms of indenture were complete; once freed, many males continued
to labor for others, living in their households and often—because of
the excess of men over women—remaining unmarried.[19]

Finally, the colonists turned to Africa for labor. As early as 1619
the forced labor of blacks supplemented that of whites in Virginia,
and by the middle of the seventeenth century blacks were to be found
in all the existing English colonies. Nevertheless, what is most striking
about the early American labor force is the length of time it took for
slavery to replace indentured servitude: throughout most of the seventeenth century white laborers, not black, prevailed in the English
mainland colonies, and it was only between 1680 and 1730 that
slaves became the backbone of the labor force in the South (see Table
1). This pattern raises two interrelated questions: why, despite the
presence of some slaves, did the colonists continue for so long to rely
primarily on indentured servants, and why, during the half-century
beginning in the 1680s, did African slaves replace European servants
in most of the colonies?

Despite the prevailing labor shortage, there were certain limitations
on the colonists' demand for slaves. Very few could afford to buy
them during the first three-quarters of the seventeenth century. Most
early settlers were people of fairly modest means for whom the purchase of a servant—at one-third to one-half the price of an African
slave—represented a substantial investment. Even if one could afford
the initial outlay, the high mortality rate among the inhabitants of the
early southern colonies made the purchase of slaves risky, and servants who were held for only a few years may have represented a
better buy. Not only were servants cheaper than slaves, but their successful management required smaller investments of time and effort.
They usually spoke the language—at least in the seventeenth century,
when most of them came from the British Isles—and were at least
partially familiar with the agricultural techniques practiced by the set-

tlers. Given the circumstances, as long as European servants were readily available, their labor continued to make sense to most colonists.[20]

Precisely such conditions prevailed during the first three-quarters of the seventeenth century, when the population of the colonies was small and the number of Englishmen anxious to come as servants was large. Readjustments in the English economy during the late sixteenth and early seventeenth centuries worked serious hardships on many British subjects, who suffered through periodic depressions and famines. Vagabondage, crime, and destitution all increased markedly, as did public awareness of these problems. Increased concern was expressed both by greater attention to charity and by savage repression of the criminal, the rowdy, and the idle. Impoverished Britons were only too anxious to start anew in America, where radically different conditions promised some hope of success and where they were actually wanted rather than regarded as a burden, but so too were many skilled and semiskilled workers who saw their opportunities decline at home. Recent studies of servant immigrants in the seventeenth century suggest that they were overwhelmingly young and male but represented a wide diversity of occupations with perhaps as many as one-half having some skill.[21] The tide of immigration reached its peak in the third quarter of the seventeenth century when, spurred by a series of ten crop failures, political dislocations at home, and a strong colonial demand for labor, close to forty-seven thousand Englishmen came to Virginia alone.[22]

If the supply of servants seemed abundant during most of the seventeenth century, that of slaves was limited at best. The English were latecomers to the African slave trade which, throughout the first two-thirds of the century, was primarily in Portuguese and then Dutch hands. Only after the Anglo-Dutch war of 1664–67 was English naval superiority established; shortly thereafter, in 1672, the Royal African Company, with a (theoretical) monopoly of the English slave trade, was formed. Even then, the supply of Africans remained limited. Despite the anguished cries of British planters in the West Indies (where the most lucrative colonies were located), the Royal African Company was unable to supply a sufficient quantity of slaves. West Indian planters mounted a vigorous attack on the company's monopoly, and even before 1698, when the monopoly was formally lifted, private traders illegally supplied a large portion of the islands' laborers. If there were not enough Africans for the West Indies, where the need was greatest, the number available for export to the mainland, which was of relatively small economic importance, was small indeed. Until the last third of the century, most of the slaves imported to the mainland colonies were probably bought from Dutch and other private merchants, so it is not surprising that New York, where the Dutch had early encouraged the importation of slaves, had a higher proportion of blacks in its population than any other English mainland colony except South Carolina as late as 1680.[23]

During the half-century from 1680 to 1730 these conditions impeding the importation of slaves changed radically. The growing prosperity of many colonists meant that an increasing number of them were able to afford slaves. The growth in the number and wealth of large holdings was especially significant, because large planters, who could afford to make the initial investment and whose need for labor was greatest, were the principal purchasers of slaves. In Maryland, for example, the average net worth of the richest 10 percent of probated estates increased 241 percent between 1656–83 and 1713–19, far more than the increase among smaller estates; as a consequence the proportion of all wealth owned by the richest 10 percent increased from 43 to 64 percent.[24]

Since servants were only temporarily bound and did not produce new servants, as the colonial population grew the number of servants imported would have had to increase sharply in order for them to form a constant proportion of the population. The 10,910 headrights issued in Virginia between 1650 and 1654 were the equivalent of more than 57 percent of the colony's estimated population in the former year; the 10,390 issued between 1665 and 1669 were only equal to about 29 percent of the population in 1670. Even if the number of immigrants had remained constant, they would have represented a continually decreasing percentage of the population and would soon have become inadequate to meet the colonies' labor needs.[25]

In fact, the supply of English servants declined sharply at just the time that the demand for labor was increasing in many of the colonies. As the English social situation stabilized following the restoration of 1660 and the British government adopted a strongly mercantilist policy, Englishmen no longer complained, as they had formerly, about an excess population; instead, with increasing economic productivity and well-being, a large population now seemed an asset in Britain's struggle for supremacy with other European powers. Although conditions for the poor remained hard, they no longer experienced the continual crises, famines, and unemployment of the early and middle seventeenth century. Conditions within the colonies also acted to discourage immigration. By the late seventeenth century land was no longer so easily acquired as it had been earlier; furthermore, generally declining tobacco prices may have led merchants to reduce intentionally their importation of servants to Maryland and Virginia.[26]

The result was a rather abrupt decline in the number of British immigrants to the colonies. In no five-year period between 1650 and 1674 did the number of headrights issued for whites in Virginia fall below 7,900; in none between 1675 and 1699 did it rise above 6,000:

1650–54:	10,910	1675–79:	3,991
1655–59:	7,926	1680–84:	5,927
1660–64:	7,979	1685–89:	4,474
1665–69:	10,390	1690–94:	5,128
1670–74:	9,876	1695–99:	4,251

The number of English servants thus declined precisely when more were needed. Although Britain continued to transport convict laborers to Maryland and a growing number of German and Irish servants settled in Pennsylvania, there simply were not enough Europeans willing to sell themselves into indentured servitude in America to continue filling the labor needs of the colonies.[27]

At the same time that the supply of servants was decreasing, that of enslaved Africans was increasing, and it was this changing relative supply (and hence price) of labor in the face of high (indeed growing) demand that most simply explains the shift in the nature of the colonial labor force. With the founding of the Royal African Company in 1672, Britain became the foremost slave-trading country in the world. In 1713, by the Treaty of Utrecht, the English won the *asiento* or monopoly awarded by the Spanish government to supply the Spanish colonies with slaves. The eighteenth century was the golden era of the English slave trade, when British merchants provided slave labor for most of the world's colonies.[28]

Given the heightened demand for labor and the new availability of Africans, planters who needed large, stable labor forces had good reason to prefer slaves to indentured servants even had the supply of the latter not begun to dwindle. For one thing, slaves were held permanently—as were their children—while servants were freed after a definite term. As a consequence, although slaves required a larger initial investment, a plantation using slaves became a self-perpetuating concern, especially by the early eighteenth century, when slave fertility rates increased markedly, mortality rates declined, and the black population began to grow through natural reproduction as well as importation. A plantation using indentured servants, however, required the continual replenishment of the labor force.[29]

Equally important, servants tended to disrupt the efficient working of a farm or plantation by running away. Although slaves too attempted to escape, it was more difficult for them to succeed. Their color made them easily identifiable and naturally suspect. White servants, on the other hand, had little trouble pretending to be free, and the shortage of labor rendered it easy for fugitives to find employment. As a result, the flight of indentured servants was a common and widely lamented occurrence. The colonies adopted stringent penalties for fugitives, usually involving their serving additional time and, for subsequent offenses, branding or mutilation. Newspaper advertisements for fugitives give evidence of both the scope of the problem and the treatment of servants. A typical notice in the Pennsylvania *Gazette* of 18 June 1752 offered a five-pound reward for the return to his West Jersey master of "an Irish servant man, named Thomas Bunn, a thick well set fellow, of middle stature, full faced, a little pock mark'd, and his hair cut off; he speaks pretty good English, and pretends to be something of a shoemaker, he has a scar on his belly, and is mark'd on the upper side of his right thumb with TB."[30]

A comparison of the number of slaves and servants from New Jersey listed in newspaper advertisements with the number of slaves and servants listed in New Jersey wills suggests how much more often indentured servants escaped than did slaves. Although more than four times as many slaves as servants were listed in the wills of 1751–60, in 1753 and 1754 there were fifty-four notices of fugitive servants and only seventeen of slaves. In other words, servants were apparently escaping at a rate about thirteen times as high as that of slaves. For planters this kind of discrepancy must have been a powerful argument in favor of using slaves.[31]

Discontent with white laborers was not confined to the problem of fugitives. The prevalent labor shortage together with the availability of land encouraged an independent mode of thought on the part of supposedly subordinate white workers—who knew they would have little trouble finding employment no matter what their behavior—that was extremely distasteful to employers. After complaining about the high price of blacks, New York planter-politician Cadwallader Colden noted that "our chief loss is from want of white hands . . .

The hopes of having land of their own & becoming independent of Landlords is what chiefly induces people into America, & they think they have never answer'd the design of their coming till they have purchased land which as soon as possible they do & begin to improve ev'n before they are able to mentain [sic] themselves." That slavery did not allow for the development of this kind of independence among the laboring class was one more consideration in its favor.[32]

* * *

RECENTLY there has been renewed interest among social scientists in forming generalizations about the causes of slavery in particular and forced labor in general. The most persistent theory has been one that sees a shortage of labor produced by a high land-to-population ratio (low population density) as the crucial ingredient leading people to force others to work for them. One of the earliest systematic proponents of this theory was H. L. Nieboer, who developed it at the turn of the twentieth century in a book called *Slavery as an Industrial System*. Noting that slavery rarely existed where a population was dense, Nieboer argued that it could only develop where there existed what he called "open resources," by which he meant primarily unused land. "Among people with open resources," he explained, "everybody is able to provide for himself; therefore free labourers do not offer themselves . . . If therefore a man wants others to perform the necessary drudgery for him . . . he must compel other men to serve him." Since Nieboer's day other scholars have developed and elaborated on his thesis. Eric Williams put it in perhaps the simplest and most starkly economic-determinist form when he argued that slavery remained profitable only until "the population has reached the point of density and the land available for appropriation has already been apportioned." When this occurred, as it had in the British West Indies by the early nineteenth century, emancipation inevitably followed. More recently, Evsey D. Domar has once again suggested that a high land-to-population ratio is the key to the emergence of forced labor and has applied his theory specifically to Russia and the United States.[33]

This approach has not, however, gone unchallenged. Examining and categorizing slave societies around the world, Orlando Patterson found little evidence that it is "labor scarcity resulting from the man/land ratio that accounts for the presence or absence of slaves in a society" and concluded that slavery "developed for entirely different reasons in different kinds of social systems." Frederic L. Pryor reached a similar conclusion, and Igor Kopytoff and Suzanne Miers have recently argued that in Africa slavery usually served political or social, not economic, needs and have rejected "unstated assumptions that slavery has to do primarily with labor, and that labor has to do with agriculture." Finally, Eric Williams's thesis that increasing population density rendered British West Indian slavery unprofitable and led to its abolition in the 1830s has been persuasively refuted.[34]

The reader of this chapter will have little trouble recognizing that my account of the origins of forced labor in Russia and America is generally compatible with the Nieboer thesis and its subsequent modifications. Indeed, I believe there is reason to refrain from celebrating the demise of the idea that shortage of labor in general and population sparseness in particular were crucial elements in the emergence of unfree labor in the modern Western world. The attack on Williams's economic interpretation has focused largely on the abolition of slavery, not its establishment. One may readily concede that profitable institutions are sometimes abolished, that unprofitable ones may be maintained for noneconomic reasons, and that ideology played a powerful role of its own in the debate over abolition, without making any concessions concerning the reasons for the original introduction of slavery. In order to argue that scarcity of labor produced slavery one need not hold that a plentiful supply of labor overthrew it.

As for the other criticisms, they amount to the assertions that slavery and unfree labor have existed in many different kinds of societies, serving varying functions, and that it is risky to abstract from slavery of particular societies with which scholars are most familiar. This argument certainly has some validity. Slavery *has* served a variety of economic and noneconomic functions. There have been high-status slaves who served as administrators, government officials, warriors, and scholars in societies as diverse as ancient Greece, traditional Africa, and fifteenth-century Russia. Some slaves in almost all slaveholding societies have been domestic servants, lending their owners comfort and prestige rather than earning them money. Slaves have been used for ritual sacrifice to placate the gods, and others have been held in sexual bondage. In none of these cases do labor scarcity and land-to-population ratios explain the imposition of slavery. In short, there is a problem with excessively broad levels of generalization. One cannot isolate the "cause" of bondage in the history of the world, because in different eras and social systems it has fulfilled different functions.

Such generalization does make sense, however, if we confine our attention to the modern Western world—that is, European and European-derived societies since the sixteenth century. This was a world in which, despite innumerable cultural, social, and economic variations, people shared basic axioms about what life was all about, from an emphasis on the desirability of economic gain to assumption of a hierarchical order and a belief in Christianity. And this was a world that saw the widespread emergence of forced labor on its periphery as it entered the modern era. One can generalize about the causes, character, and consequences of this forced labor because it did serve a common function whether it occurred in North America, the Caribbean, South America, Russia, or other countries of eastern Europe.

Wherever this modern Western bondage occurred in the sixteenth and seventeenth centuries, shortage of labor *was* the most basic element. Whatever purpose slavery may have served in other times and places, here we are talking about a system of agricultural labor: people were compelled to work for others because there were not enough agricultural workers. The shortage was in turn made possible by the low population density—what has variously been termed open resources and high land-to-population ratio. But low population density cannot in itself create a labor shortage or a demand for forced labor: slavery made little headway in colonial New England, nor did serfdom in seventeenth-century Siberia. Demand for labor is rarely excessive on a desert. A low population density, then, made possible but did not guarantee the emergence of a labor shortage.

Any number of factors can contribute to a demand for labor in a region of population scarcity. I have described several in this chapter. A decrease in the existing labor supply, caused in Russia by massive flight and depopulation and in the English colonies by the decline in the number of Europeans willing to come to America as indentured servants, led to efforts to regularize a new labor arrangement. In Russia, the establishment of the pomest'e system and the consequent need to support pomeshchiki servitors had a similar effect. But the most general ingredient was the expansion of agricultural production, whether stimulated by growing foreign or domestic demand. When land was plentiful and labor scarce, such increased production was feasible only under conditions of physical compulsion.[35]

In the American colonies, efforts of landholders to take advantage of the growing foreign demand for agricultural staples played the key role in the growth of unfree labor. Of course, colonial cities—especially Philadelphia and New York—served as outlets for farmers in

Table 1

Estimate of blacks as a percentage of the population in thirteen American colonies, 1680–1770

Colony	1680	1690	1700	1710	1720	1730	1750	1770
New Hampshire	3.6	2.4	2.6	2.6	1.8	1.8	2.0	1.0
Massachusetts	0.4	0.8	1.4	2.1	2.3	2.4	2.2	1.8
Rhode Island	5.8	5.9	5.1	4.9	4.7	9.8	10.1	7.1
Connecticut	0.3	0.9	1.7	1.9	1.9	1.9	2.7	3.1
New York	12.2	12.0	11.8	13.0	15.5	14.3	14.3	11.7
New Jersey	5.9	5.6	6.0	6.7	7.7	8.0	7.5	7.0
Pennsylvania	3.7	2.4	2.4	6.4	6.5	2.4	2.4	2.4
Delaware	5.5	5.5	5.5	13.6	13.2	5.2	5.2	5.2
Maryland	9.0	9.0	10.9	18.6	18.9	19.0	30.8	31.5
Virginia	6.9	17.6	27.9	29.5	30.3	26.3	43.9	41.9
North Carolina	3.9	4.0	3.9	5.9	14.1	20.0	25.7	35.3
South Carolina	15.7	38.5	42.9	37.7	70.4	66.7	60.9	60.5
Georgia	—	—	—	—	—	—	19.2	45.5

Source: Compiled from *Historical Statistics of the United States: Colonial Times to 1957* (Washington: Government Printing Office, 1960).

surrounding areas, but these cities remained very small until the late eighteenth century, and by far the largest share of products raised for sale was for export abroad. These exports were dominated by a small number of staple crops in great demand in Europe; indeed, during the first half of the eighteenth century two of these products alone—tobacco and rice—contributed about three-quarters of the value of all goods exported to England.[36]

The key determinant of the kind of labor system that emerged in the American colonies was the degree to which agriculture was geared to market. Although the increased availability of Africans made *possible* the widespread adoption of slave labor after 1680, slavery became the backbone of the economy in some colonies while in others it made little or no advance (see Table 1 and Map 1). Where a basic subsistence agriculture was practiced (as in most of New England), farms were small, the labor of a farmer and his family—and perhaps one or two extra hands at harvest time—was quite sufficient, and there was little need for forced labor. Where crops were grown for export, planters sought to maximize their production and extend the acreage planted. In such areas, which included much but not all of the southern colonies, the demand for labor was great, and the inden-

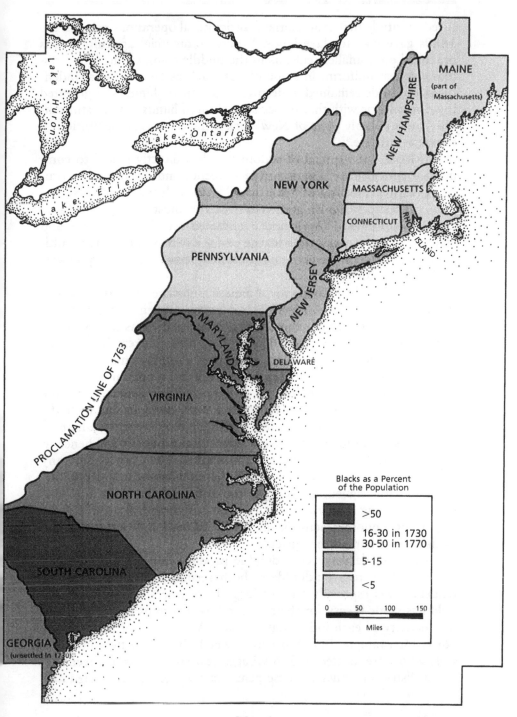

Map 1
Blacks as a percentage of the population in the American colonies,
1730 and 1770.

tured servitude that characterized agricultural operations prior to the 1680s gave way to slave labor. Where commercial agriculture was practiced on a smaller scale, as in the middle colonies, the labor system was less uniform: in some places, such as Pennsylvania, indentured servitude remained widespread; in others, families augmented their own labor with that of occasional hired hands; and in still others—most notably parts of New York—slavery was an institution of some importance.[37]

In Russia, the spread of serfdom was less directly linked to commercial agriculture. Exports in the sixteenth and seventeenth centuries consisted mostly of "precocities" such as leather and furs, and even domestic sale of grain—rye was the most widely cultivated crop—was limited. Agricultural techniques remained primitive and yields low, and it was only because of the extensive area under cultivation and the low level of peasant consumption that any surplus was available for sale.[38]

Nevertheless, in Russia as in America, shortage of labor was fundamentally a product of growth and expansion. Even more important in this process than the burgeoning urban market was the introduction of the pomest'e system. Under conditions of extremely low agricultural productivity the need to support a significant number of pomeshchiki as servitors fighting for the tsar put a premium on labor in much the same way that foreign demand did in America. After the establishment of serfdom, its spread went hand in hand with the spread of commercial agriculture, with landholders striving wherever conditions permitted to increase seigneurial production and hence to increase as well their own access to market. Thus, Soviet (and many non-Soviet) historians have linked the establishment and growth of serfdom with seigneurial production and barshchina. As V. I. Koretskii, the leading modern authority on enserfment, put it, "the most important economic factor in the final formation of serfdom was the institution of barshchina agriculture."[39]

There is evidence of considerable production for market among seventeenth-century landholders, both secular and monastic. This tendency was especially true of large landowners, whose extensive holdings made it easy for them to produce a surplus despite the low productivity of each individual peasant. At the time of his death in 1661, for example, B. I. Morozov owned about fifty-five thousand serfs who were located in 336 villages scattered across nineteen different districts of Russia. These peasants owed extremely varied and multifarious obligations. Many paid money obrok, and they sent a wide variety of food items—butter, eggs, chickens, geese, sheep, fish, and the like—to the nobleman's table in Moscow. Most of his serfs, however, spent part of their time performing barshchina on his seigneurial holdings, cultivating his rye and oats, making potash, and carting his goods to market. He even had a substantial number of peasants who had no allotments of their own and performed exclusively seigneurial labor. Of course, the size of Morozov's operations was unusual, but smaller landowners and monasteries as well often directed part of their product to market.[40]

The prevalence of seigneurial production in the seventeenth century has been systematically documented in recent years by historian Iu. A. Tikhonov. He found that although the forms of peasant obligations varied widely and on many estates barshchina coexisted with money and natural obrok, some degree of seigneurial cultivation existed almost everywhere: of the 365 seventeenth and early eighteenth-century estates he studied, barshchina was present on 324 (or 89 percent).[41]

A brief examination of the geographic distribution of slaves and serfs illustrates the close connection between agricultural expansion and the spread of forced labor. In the British mainland colonies large-scale commercial agriculture developed first in the Chesapeake Bay region. As early as 1617 tobacco was grown "in the streets, and even in the market-place of Jamestown"; a Dutch traveler reported of Maryland and Virginia in 1679 that "tobacco is the only production in which the planters employ themselves, as if there were nothing else in the world to plant." Spurred by a seemingly insatiable European demand for the new weed and blessed with good soil, a mild climate, and an excellent system of water routes, Chesapeake Bay planters produced increasing quantities of tobacco throughout the seventeenth century; the 20,000 pounds exported in 1619 swelled to 175,590,000 in 1672 and 353,290,000 in 1697, after which, despite annual fluctuations varying with tobacco prices, average yields stabilized for the next generation.[42]

With an abundance of land and a shortage of labor, the amount of tobacco a planter could raise depended primarily on the number of workers he could command. Relying throughout most of the seventeenth century on a continual supply of fresh indentured servants, beginning in the 1680s, when the number of white immigrants had begun to decline sharply and African slaves had become more readily available, planters turned to slave labor. Wesley Frank Craven's computation of slave imports into Virginia, based on the number of black headrights granted, shows a marked increase beginning in 1690:

1650–54:	162	1675–79:	115
1655–59:	155	1680–84:	388
1660–64:	280	1685–89:	231
1665–69:	329	1690–94:	804
1670–74:	296	1695–99:	1,043

He suggests, however, that "the greatly expanded number of black headrights in the 1690s ... is substantially representative of postponed claims for Negroes reaching the colony somewhat earlier." Corroborative evidence comes from a calculation that in York county, Virginia, the ratio of servants to slaves plummeted from 1.90 in 1680–84 to 0.27 in 1685–89 to 0.07 in 1690–94; within a decade servants had virtually stopped coming to the county. By 1700, when more than one-quarter of Virginia's population was black, the revolution in the composition of the colony's labor force had been largely completed. In Maryland, too, the number of slaves increased markedly, although because large parts of Maryland were unsuited for tobacco growing and because the colony continued to receive substantial shipments of convict servants, the change occurred slightly later than in Virginia and was less dramatic.[43]

Even more heavily dependent on slave labor, although later in development, was South Carolina. First settled by Europeans in the 1660s, it grew slowly as colonists sought in vain to find a staple that would play for them the same role that tobacco did in Virginia. They raised cattle and hogs for sale to the West Indies and also exported deerskins and naval stores. Because of the large role played by West Indian planters in the settling of South Carolina, the colony from the beginning had a higher percentage of slaves than the other mainland colonies, although as elsewhere from Pennsylvania south most of the early immigrants were white indentured servants.

Then, in the 1690s, Carolinians discovered rice, a crop that within a few years became as much a staple for them as tobacco was to planters of the Chesapeake. American rice shipments to England— almost all of which came from South Carolina (and from the middle of the eighteenth century, Georgia)—increased from less than 1 percent of the total value of American shipments to England in 1697–

1705 to 12 percent in 1721–30 and 24 percent in 1766–75. Even more than in Virginia, South Carolina's commercial orientation created a society in which most heavy labor was coerced. With a population of only a little more than a thousand in 1680, the colony by 1740 claimed forty thousand residents, of whom approximately two-thirds were slaves.[44]

Slavery was much less central in the northern colonies and consequently proved relatively easy to abolish without serious social dislocations in the late eighteenth and early nineteenth centuries; in the rest of this book I shall deal very little with slavery in the North. Nevertheless, it is worth noting that unfree labor was of some importance in parts of the North as late as the middle of the eighteenth century. In Pennsylvania, spurred in part by an active propaganda campaign waged by William Penn and his agents who sought to convince impoverished Europeans of the boundless opportunities that awaited them in the colony, tens of thousands of indentured servants, many of them German, continued to perform a significant share of the agricultural labor. By far the largest concentration of slaves outside the southern colonies, however, was located in New York: as late as 1760 about one of every seven New Yorkers was a black slave.[45]

Although both the Dutch, who ruled the colony as the New Netherlands until 1667, and the British who came after them actively promoted the importation of Africans, this policy would have met with little success had not conditions there been conducive to their employment. Wherever water transportation was available, especially on Long Island, Staten Island, and along the banks of the Hudson River, large planters—beneficiaries of huge land grants from both the Dutch and the English—grew a variety of crops for sale. The most important of these was wheat. "Wheat is the staple of this Province . . ." explained New York's governor in 1734; "it's generally manufactured into flower [sic] and bread, and sent to supply the sugar collonys." Slaves appeared wherever large quantities of wheat or other crops were raised for export; on Long Island, for example, they increased from 14 percent of the population in 1698 to 21 percent in 1738. Of course, some New Yorkers, especially in the city, employed slaves as house servants, and others possessed slaves who performed various trades. The typical owner, however, was a farmer with one to five slaves, who used them to supplement his family's labor and increase the amount of its product available for sale.[46]

Slavery was least important in New England, where small farms and a largely self-sufficient agriculture required little labor that a farmer's family could not provide. In the seventeenth century the New England colonies contained relatively few indentured servants, and those few more often served as domestics and artisans than as agricultural laborers. In the early eighteenth century blacks constituted about 2 percent of the population in Connecticut, Massachusetts, and New Hampshire, and few of them were farm workers. They were a luxury for those who could afford them rather than an essential part of the economy.[47]

The one area of New England where extensive use of slaves prevailed nicely illustrates the impact of commercially oriented agriculture on the labor system of colonial America. In the fertile flatlands of the Narragansett region of Rhode Island there arose a system of large-scale stock raising and dairy farming. There, on soil ideally suited for grazing, planters bred the famed Narragansett racehorses, raised herds of sheep and dairy cows, and developed an aristocratic life-style similar to that of Virginia and Carolina planters. Estates of hundreds and sometimes thousands of acres required a large, steady laboring population, and it is no accident that "slavery, both negro and Indian, reached a development in colonial Narragansett unusual in the colonies north of Mason and Dixon's line." In 1730 about 10 percent of Rhode Island's population was black, but this figure conceals widespread variations. In the Narragansett country townships of South Kingston and Jamestown from one-fifth to one-quarter of the inhabitants were black, and including Indians about one-third were slaves; in many other areas of Rhode Island blacks constituted no more than 3 or 4 percent of the population. As elsewhere in the colonies, slavery in Rhode Island was strong only where there was substantial market-oriented agriculture.[48]

In Russia, too, serfdom became more prevalent in some areas than in others. Most peasants (the overwhelming majority of the population) were serfs, but there were others who had escaped enserfment and later came to be known as state peasants. They had no immediate owner and consequently enjoyed much more freedom than the serfs; their status was thus in some respects similar to that of free blacks in the slaveholding United States, like whom they were "slaves without masters." Peasants owned by the tsar—known as court peasants— occupied an intermediate position between serfs and state peasants, although they were often grouped with the latter.[49]

Although population statistics for seventeenth-century Russia were until recently even more problematical than those for the seventeenth-century American colonies, historical demographer Ia. E. Vodarskii has done exhaustive work on the incomplete census of 1678, making corrections for obvious errors and checking data against one another for the most plausible appraisals. As a result of his work we now have what appear to be fairly accurate population estimates, by category and geographic region, for 1678. Together with the census of 1719—the first of ten nationwide censuses held periodically between 1719 and 1858—the 1678 material provides a good picture of the distribution of the population during the early years of serfdom.[50]

In 1678, according to Vodarskii's estimates, the male population of Russia, excluding the newly acquired Left-bank Ukraine and the Baltic region, was about 4.8 million. (Russian censuses, whose main purpose was fiscal, usually counted only males, since only they were subject to the "soul tax"; sources frequently refer to the number of "souls" or "male souls," which means quite simply the number of males. One can double these figures to get a rough approximation of the total population.) Nine-tenths of these people, or 4.3 million, were peasants. This peasant population was composed of the following groups:

Privately held peasants	2.3 million (53.5%)
Clerical peasants	0.7 million (16.3%)
Court peasants	0.4 million (9.3%)
State peasants	0.9 million (20.9%)

Thus, serfs (privately held and clerical) made up about seven-tenths of the peasant population.[51]

But they were not evenly distributed across Russia. In general, serfdom spread into areas most suitable for agricultural development. A region could be attractive either because of its good soil and relatively mild climate or because its location—for example, proximity to Moscow—provided a market for agricultural goods. Areas where the soil was poor or the climate harsh, and where a sparse population produced no significant demand, were usually left to the state peasants, who eked out a living through subsistence farming and handicrafts. As Englishman Joseph Marshall noted, "Peasants in this empire are in general happy in proportion to the neglect under which the country lies; in the midst of vast wastes and forests they seem to be tolerably easy; but any tracts well cultivated are done at their expence, and they appear very near on the same rank, as the blacks in our sugar colonies."[52]

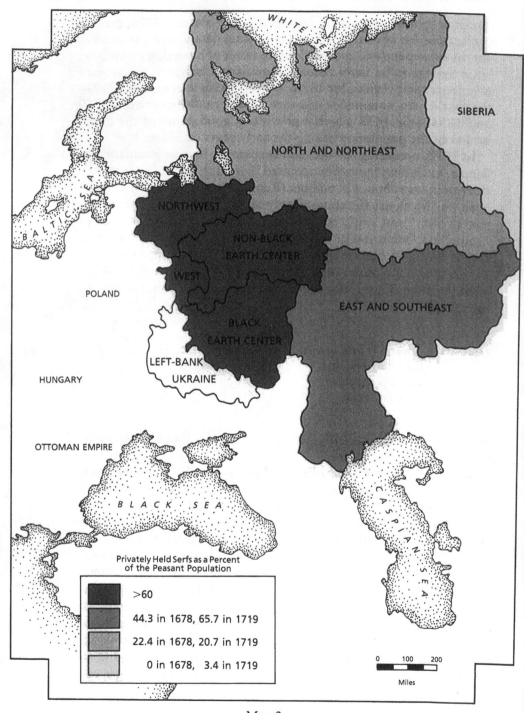

WHITE SEA

SIBERIA

NORTH AND NORTHEAST

NORTHWEST

NON-BLACK
EARTH CENTER

BALTIC SEA

WEST

POLAND

EAST AND SOUTHEAST

BLACK
EARTH CENTER

LEFT-BANK
UKRAINE

HUNGARY

OTTOMAN EMPIRE

BLACK SEA

CASPIAN SEA

Privately Held Serfs as a Percent
of the Peasant Population

>60

44.3 in 1678, 65.7 in 1719

22.4 in 1678, 20.7 in 1719

0 in 1678,   3.4 in 1719

0   100   200

Miles

Map 2
Regions of Russia, with privately held serfs as a percentage
of the peasant population, 1678 and 1719.

Using a slight modification of standard Soviet geographic categorization, Vodarskii divided Russia into seven major regions (see Map 2). Three of these regions, the Non–black earth center, the Northwest, and the West, had long been settled and were the most populated areas of the Russian empire. The climate was relatively harsh, and later, with the development of regional specialization and a national market for grain, agriculture there would increasingly give way to handicrafts and small-scale manufacturing. In the seventeenth and early eighteenth centuries, however, they remained largely agricultural, with production stimulated by the presence of major cities, especially Moscow in the Non–black earth center, but also Novgorod and Pskov in the Northwest and Smolensk in the West.

The other four regions were to one extent or another frontier territory. Still, they differed sharply from one another in other respects. The Black earth center, lying directly to the south of the Non–black earth center, enjoyed fertile soil and a relatively good climate and was destined to become the breadbasket of Russia. The northern part of this region was already settled in the seventeenth century, but the southern part was an area of new colonization, as was the East and southeast region, much of which was also ideally suited for agriculture and livestock raising. In contrast, the wooded North and northeast region and Siberia, although areas of sparse settlement, were inhospitable to agriculture because of their harsh climate. (An eighth region, the newly acquired Left-bank Ukraine, not covered by the census of 1678 and hence not included in this regional breakdown, was similar in many respects to the neighboring Black earth center.)[53]

In only two of these regions were state peasants in the majority: Siberia, where there were virtually no privately held serfs at all, and the North and northeast, where less than one-quarter of the peasants were privately held. Elsewhere, the great majority of the population were serfs, and with some variations about two-thirds of the peasants were privately owned (see Table 2). In the Non–black earth center, the Northwest, and the West there were no state peasants at all. Farther to the south and east, in fertile lands newly opened to settlement, serfdom quickly came to prevail, despite the flood of fugitives from the north seeking to escape bondage. Thus, in the East and southeast the number of privately held serfs more than tripled between 1678 and 1719 and increased from 44 to 66 percent of the peasant population. Pomeshchiki similarly appropriated the bulk of the land in the fertile southern part of the Black earth center; from 1700 to 1737 the number of pomeshchik holdings there quadrupled, and the number

Table 2
Percentage distribution of peasant population by category in seven regions
of Russia, 1678 and 1719

Region	Year	Category of peasant			
		Privately held	Clerical	Court	State
Non–black earth center	1678	62.6	20.8	16.6	0.0
	1719	67.8	21.2	11.1	0.0
Northwest	1678	62.7	28.0	9.2	0.0
	1719	62.3	26.3	11.3	0.0
West	1678	64.1	6.8	29.1	0.0
	1719	78.3	6.3	15.5	0.0
Black earth center	1678	62.3	8.4	10.8	18.6
	1719	62.2	7.1	7.6	23.2
East and southeast	1678	44.3	12.7	19.9	23.1
	1719	65.7	11.8	14.4	8.4
North and northeast	1678	22.4	15.5	5.0	57.1
	1719	20.7	11.9	12.1	55.4
Siberia	1678	0.0	8.2	0.0	91.8
	1719	3.4	9.5	0.0	88.2

Source: Computed from Ia. E. Vodarskii, Naselenie Rossii v kontse XVII–nachale
XVIII veka (Moscow: Izdatel'stvo "Nauka," 1977), 151–52.

of male serfs more than tripled, from 49,200 to 151,800. In short, serfdom quickly expanded to the south and southeast, as Russia did, permeating all areas of the country conducive to productive agriculture.[54]

In the broadest sense, then, serfdom in Russia and slavery in America were part of the same historical process, despite the vastly differing societies in which they emerged. Both were products of geographic and economic expansion in areas of sparse settlement. In both countries there had been a long-term trend toward forced labor and experimentation with various forms of it: these included kholopstvo and the restriction of peasant movement in Russia and indentured servitude and Indian slavery in America. In both countries a crisis in the labor supply finally forced landholders and the governments that depended on them to make arrangements that led to the spread and institutionalization of new systems of unfree labor. Neither of these was an isolated development; both occurred in other areas of the Americas and eastern Europe.

There was one other, subsidiary, precondition for the introduction of bondage: the prevalence of a system of values compatible with its existence. (It is unlikely that should a shortage of labor improbably materialize next year in the United States, slavery would emerge as the solution.) Until the middle of the eighteenth century, however, slavery and serfdom created few moral problems for anyone. Russians, Englishmen, and Americans were already familiar with unfree labor in various guises, and the notion that it was wrong for some to live off of the labor of others—even under physical compulsion—was virtually nonexistent among them.[55]

* * *

OVER THE COURSE of the seventeenth and first part of the eighteenth centuries unfree labor gradually became entrenched and solidified in Russia and the American South. If at first serfdom and slavery had emerged as institutions designed to help landholders cope with specific problems of labor shortage, by the middle of the eighteenth century they appeared part of the natural order, as God-given as government or agriculture itself. A central feature of this process of entrenchment was the hardening and clarification of class lines, so that in both countries the welter of overlapping groups that still prevailed in much of the seventeenth century had coalesced by the eighteenth into well-delineated classes, the masters and their bondsmen. Of course, there remained intermediate groupings, people who did not fit into either of these major classes; these two, however, dominated society and gave shape to the social order.

It was not at first obvious that this would be so. In the English mainland colonies, class lines were still fluid during most of the seventeenth century, and a variety of laborers, ranging from slave through semifree to free, rubbed shoulders. Indentured servants continued to arrive and in some colonies—most notably Pennsylvania—continued to provide a large share of agricultural laborers well into the eighteenth century. There were still Indian slaves. Criminals and debtors were routinely bound out to work as servants, as were children learning a trade. Nor was the status of all blacks immediately clear: there were some who served as indentured servants, especially during the first two-thirds of the seventeenth century, and for several decades the notion persisted among some colonists that the conver-

sion of African slaves to Christianity might necessitate their manumission. The very term *slave* lacked precision and was sometimes
used for someone only temporarily deprived of freedom. In 1639, for
example, a white man, "John Kempe, for filthy, uncleane attempts
with 3 yong girles, was censured to bee whiped . . . very severely,
and was committed for a slave." In this case and several others from
the same period the slavery imposed was only temporary, but it is
significant that the nature of slavery and freedom could remain so ill
defined in the 1630s and 1640s. The early colonists were familiar
with a continuum of unfree and semifree statuses and did not yet set
the black slaves off from other laborers as an entirely separate class.
Of course, the Africans were different and perceived as such, but so
too were they differentiated from one another on the basis of national
origins; among Carolina planters, for example, "Coromantes and
Whydahs, because of their greater hardiness, were supposed to be
especially desirable as field hands, whereas Ibos, Congos, and Ango-
las, allegedly weaker, were said to be more effective as house servants." The rigid dichotomy of later years between black and white,
slave and free, did not yet exist.[56]

A flexibility was evident in South Carolina slavery as late as the
early years of the eighteenth century when, although blacks were already a majority of the labor force, there was considerable leeway in
what was expected of them. Until the 1720s "servants and masters
shared the crude and egalitarian intimacies inevitable on a frontier."
Because of the lack of white manpower in this frontier environment,
slaves performed a multitude of jobs that would later be considered
inappropriate and that sometimes involved considerable initiative, independence, and free association with whites. Thus, slaves served as
hunters, trappers, guides, sailors, and fishermen; they were even used
to fight Indians, as in the Yamassee war of 1715.[57]

In Virginia, where until shortly before the turn of the century
blacks were still a small proportion of the population and most unfree
workers were white, racial lines seemed even less firmly drawn. Black
and white agricultural laborers often worked together; in his 1705
description of Virginia Robert Beverley noted that "the male servants,
and slaves of both sexes, are employed together in tilling and manur-
ing the ground" although "some distinction indeed is made between
them in their clothes, and food" and white women were no longer
assigned field work. Black and white laborers also fraternized with
one another, shared living accommodations, and sometimes ran away
together. Indeed, black and white, slave, servant, and often ex-servant

as well were all part of a general underclass, a "giddy multitude" that in the third quarter of the seventeenth century showed growing restiveness and caused considerable unease among the well-to-do.[58]

Just how fluid class alliances still were was demonstrated by Bacon's Rebellion, a conflict that erupted in 1676 when Nathaniel Bacon led an uprising against the government of Governor William Berkeley, an uprising that achieved momentary success before its leader caught ill and died of the "bloody flux" and his forces disintegrated. One of a series of violent upheavals that shook the colonies in the 1670s and 1680s, Bacon's Rebellion seemed destined to bear out all the worst fears about the "giddy multitude." Although historians have disagreed sharply over the nature of the rebellion, what is significant here is not Bacon's goal so much as the composition of his forces, which cut across racial and class lines. Enlisted in Bacon's ranks was an incongruous medley of disaffected Virginians: slaves, indentured servants, debtors, ex-servants, frontiersmen chafing under Berkeley's restrained Indian policy, and political enemies of the governor. That such an alliance was possible and that the governor's supporters did not make an issue of the participation of blacks on the side of the rebels indicate how little slavery had yet shaped class attitudes.[59]

Such a configuration of forces as was seen in Bacon's Rebellion would have been impossible in the southern colonies by the early eighteenth century. The rapid spread of slavery and the decline in the number of servant immigrants meant that blacks, instead of constituting one element of a complex, turbulent underclass, were now the backbone of the labor force. Class lines were coming more and more to approximate racial lines. The change was not just one of numbers: the social distance between blacks and whites increased too. As plantation labor came to be associated with slaves, there was a perceptible rise in the status, treatment, and economic well-being of most white colonists. Not only were fewer whites coming over as indentured servants, but those who did tended to be from a somewhat higher social rank, often possessing mechanical skills much in demand in the colonies. David W. Galenson, after examining the backgrounds of 2,955 servants leaving England for Jamaica, Maryland, Pennsylvania, and Virginia between 1718 and 1759, found that most were skilled, 65 percent of the men were literate, and only 6 percent listed their occupations as "laborers."

Equally important were the changed conditions they met in the colonies. As fewer servants arrived, the colonists felt stronger pressure to treat them tolerably, because only by convincing prospective immigrants that they faced a bright future in America could the colonists generate continued immigration. Of course, even at the height of the immigration in the 1650s and 1660s the need to attract laborers had militated against treatment so harsh as to discourage other would-be servants from indenturing themselves; here is one reason, as Edmund Morgan has suggested, that indentured servants were never actually reduced to slaves. But when the economic and political dislocations leading Englishmen to flee their country had largely disappeared, the need to offer positive incentives to potential immigrants was much greater. The relatively few immigrants who continued to perform agricultural labor were increasingly differentiated from slaves, as Beverley noted in stressing differences in food, clothing, and treatment of women. The economic well-being of white immigrants in the colonies also improved. Not only were they employed more often in skilled trades, but as the general economic level of the colonies improved they were more able to translate the heavy demand for their services into better material conditions.[60]

There was no such improvement in the status of blacks, who came to America involuntarily and did not have to be lured by attractive conditions. In fact, as the ranks of indentured servants diminished and as their condition improved, the blacks seemed increasingly different and threatening, and there was a decrease in the fraternization and sense of common cause that had once existed between black and white in the laboring underclass. Contributing to this growing isolation of black slaves was the fact that whereas previously most had spent time in the West Indies, where they had already been "seasoned" before coming to the United States, from the 1680s the majority were imported directly from Africa, spoke no English on arrival, and consequently seemed more alien to white Americans. By the turn of the century the pervasive fear of the "giddy multitude" had disappeared. Southern colonists of the eighteenth century dreaded rebellion too, but their fear was of a "servile insurrection," an uprising by black slaves against whites. The growing tide of slave imports and the changed relations between whites and blacks led to a sharp rise in white racial consciousness and widespread expressions of fear that too large a slave population threatened the peace of the community. As Virginia planter William Byrd—himself a large slaveowner—wrote to the Earl of Egmont in 1736, congratulating him on the (temporary) prohibition of slavery in the new colony of Georgia, "They import so many Negros hither, that I fear this Colony will some time or other be confirmed by the Name of New Guinea . . . The farther Importation of them in Our Colonys should be prohibited lest they prove as troublesome and dangerous everywhere, as they have been lately in Jamaica."[61]

The result was a rash of colonial legislation designed to regulate slaves. Codification of slavery lagged well behind its actual establishment. In Virginia blacks "had an uncertain legal status" until 1661, and it was only in 1664 that a Maryland law spelled out that "all Negroes and other slaves . . . shall serve Durante Vita"; so long as there were relatively few blacks in the colonies there seemed little need to pass elaborate legislation defining their status and regulating their behavior. During the late seventeenth and early eighteenth centuries, however, the southern colonies passed a series of laws designed to set blacks off from whites, legitimize slavery, and protect society from potential servile insurrections. These laws ranged from reassurances that conversion to Christianity did not require manumission, as in Virginia's act of 1667 and Maryland's of 1671, to measures prohibiting free blacks from voting, testifying in court against whites, or marrying whites, to the establishment of slave patrols to guard against suspicious behavior and the passage of duties in part designed to stem the importation of Africans and thus safeguard public security.[62]

By the middle of the eighteenth century slavery was solidly entrenched as the labor system of the southern colonies, from Maryland to Georgia. Whereas a century earlier freedom was a vague concept, and the lot of most laborers, white and black, was to one extent or another unfree, now the assumption was practically universal among whites that slavery was the natural state of blacks and freedom that of whites. Blacks were simply different: "Kindness to a Negroe by way of reward for having done well is the surest way to spoil him although according to the general observation of the world most men are spurred on to diligence by rewards," wrote Virginia planter Landon Carter in 1770. Eight years later he expressed the same sentiment more bluntly: blacks "are devils," he proclaimed, "and to make them otherwise than slaves will be to set devils free."[63]

* * *

A SIMILAR PROCESS of clarification of class lines occurred in Russia. There, too, a confused medley of social groups continued to exist in the early seventeenth century. There were serfs held by individual landholders, those owned by monasteries, court peasants, and several kinds of peasants who had so far escaped enserfment; there were various categories of slaves, of whom the most numerous were now limited service contract slaves; there were cotters (or *bobyli*), who were usually poor landless peasants but might on occasion be quite prosperous. And various judicial terms—for example, those distinguishing newly arrived peasants from the long-term residents—continued to be used even though they had lost most of their significance. Meanwhile, fugitives from the center of the country swarmed south, where local authorities often welcomed them with open arms; vagabonds roamed much of the countryside; and in the southern borderlands cossacks, their ranks swelled by fresh fugitives, served as a buffer between Russia and the Tatars, sometimes cooperating with the Russian government but usually left free to live their own seminomadic lives.[64]

Among landholders there was equal confusion. The very term *nobleman* (*dvorianin*), derived from what had previously been one service rank, did not come into general use to describe all privileged landowners until the eighteenth century. Numerous aristocratic ranks existed—within the boiar elite who sat in the Boiar Duma, for example, were (in descending order of exaltation) the ranks of *boiarin, okol'nichii, dumnyi dvorianin,* and *dumnyi d'iak*—but these magnates had little sense of belonging to the same privileged landed class as lesser servitors of the tsar. The terms *votchinnik* and *pomeshchik* persisted, even though over the course of the seventeenth century they lost almost all distinction. Southern pomeshchiki continued to welcome fugitives from the north and until 1649 favored maintenance of a short search period, whereas landlords in the center pressed for the abolition of search periods altogether; labor stealing was rampant. In short, absence of the term *nobleman* reflected an equally prevalent absence of the concept, even though an estate of state servitors with a monopoly on secular landownership in fact existed.[65]

Although the seventeenth century brought the consolidation of the Russian population into two dominant classes, it was a gradual process that the participants themselves at first only dimly recognized. This is made clear by a brief examination of alliances formed in the uprising led by Ivan Bolotnikov in 1606–7. What is known by Soviet historians as the First Peasant War amounted to a civil war in which Bolotnikov's rebel forces sought to overthrow Tsar Vasilii Shuiskii in favor of one of a series of pretenders who claimed to be the rightful tsar, Dmitrii. Whether they actually believed that Dmitrii lived—the original Tsar Dmitrii had died in 1591 and a first, briefly successful, pretender had been murdered by Shuiskii's supporters in 1606—

those opposed to Shuiskii's rule now rallied around Bolotnikov's rebels. The insurgents captured much of Russia and laid siege to Moscow
itself before they were finally routed and Bolotnikov was tortured and
drowned.[66]

What is of interest here is the nature of class alliances formed in
Bolotnikov's uprising. His forces consisted of an unlikely coalition of
groups opposed to Shuiskii's rule. Bolotnikov himself was a former
slave—probably of elite military status—who had run away, joined
the cossacks, and endured capture by Crimean Tatars and bondage to
a succession of Tatar, Turkish, and German masters before escaping
in Venice and making his way back to Russia. Behind him rallied an
assorted collection of the disaffected: slaves, cossacks, fugitives, peasants, brigands, poor townsmen—in short, something close to the
kind of "giddy multitude" taking part in Bacon's Rebellion. In this
sense, as one scholar has written, "This was a cry for vengeance for
the have-nots . . . against those that thrived on their misery and enslavement." Yet fighting along with these were men of a very different
stripe: landholders, especially relatively minor pomeshchiki from the
south, who were opposed to the Shuiskii government—although not
to serfdom and slavery—for their own reasons. These privileged rebels included Bolotnikov's former owner, Prince Andrei Teliatevskii.

Like Bacon's Rebellion, then, this was a war of the outs against the
ins and of the frontier against the settled heartland that took place at
a time when class lines were so muddy that antagonistic social groups
could participate on the same side of the struggle. In Russia, as in
America, this was a short-lived phenomenon, and fear of servile insurrection soon precluded a repetition of these interclass alliances.
Russia's future "peasant wars," most notably those led by Stepan Razin in 1670–71 and by Emelian Pugachev in 1773–74, saw increasing
class consciousness on both sides, and one looks in vain for noblemen
fighting in the ranks of the insurgents. The entrenchment of serfdom
and consolidation of class lines over the course of the seventeenth and
early eighteenth centuries made inconceivable the combination of
forces present in Bolotnikov's war.[67]

As serfdom spread and became recognized as the fate of most peasants, the multiplicity of divisions that differentiated the laboring population became meaningless and gradually evaporated. Although it
would be unnecessarily long and tedious to trace this process for each
group, a look at how slaves slowly merged with serfs is instructive.
Kholopy had long served a variety of functions, usually acting as
house servants but sometimes performing agricultural labor like most

peasants. The main distinction between kholopy and serfs was that whereas the latter were usually self-supporting, growing their own food on allotted plots of land, the former were usually maintained by their owners; instead of living in a village with the peasants, they lived in or near their owners' residences. During the seventeenth century, therefore, terms signifying the slaves' living patterns became prevalent: slaves were *zadvornye liudi* (people who lived behind the *dvor* or household of their owner), or *dvorovye liudi* (people who lived in the owner's household). Many of these people continued to be house servants, and in the eighteenth century *dvorovyi* became the general term for a serf house servant.

As the seventeenth century progressed, the terms *zadvornye liudi, dvorovye liudi, delovye liudi,* and *kholopy* were often used interchangeably to describe people virtually indistinguishable from serfs, who performed agricultural labor for their owners and sometimes even received their own landed allotments to support themselves. Because slaves were used for agricultural labor and serfs could be assigned to housework, the actual distinction between them became increasingly artificial. For example, nobleman A. I. Bezobrazov used the terms *delovye liudi* and *dvorovye liudi* interchangeably in the 1670s and 1680s, to describe people of varying occupations. Some were servants in his Moscow household, but such servants also included peasants removed from their home villages and brought to Moscow; others lived in villages, performed agricultural labor, supported themselves with their own allotments, and were for all practical purposes indistinguishable from serfs. The enserfment of the peasantry thus reduced the distinctiveness of the kholopy. The distinction between slaves and serfs was fully abolished in 1723, and kholopy became serfs, when Peter I ordered them to pay the "soul tax" he imposed on all male peasants.[68]

A different kind of simplification occurred during the first two-thirds of the eighteenth century with secularization of the clerical serfs. For centuries the government had been suspicious of the wealth and power of various clerical bodies—especially the monasteries—which in 1678, in addition to their vast landholdings, owned some 149,000 peasant households equal to more than 16 percent of the peasant population. Between 1701 and 1720 Peter I instituted what amounted to partial secularization of clerical holdings, putting many of them under government control and appropriating to the state a large share of the income they generated. Although Peter's immediate successors wavered in their policies toward ecclesiastical estates, the monasteries and churches never regained full control of their serfs, and in 1764 Catherine II ordered the complete secularization of clerical property in Russia (the same process followed in the Ukraine in 1785), with monks and high church officials henceforth to be supported by the state. The former clerical serfs now joined the ranks of state peasants (although they were temporarily put in a category of their own, "economic peasants").[69]

By the middle of the eighteenth century the peasantry had coalesced into two broad groups, serfs and state peasants. Serfs, now owned almost exclusively by noblemen, constituted more than half the peasant population. The remainder, the state peasants, consisted of a variety of peasant groups that had escaped enserfment or had recently been freed. In addition to the former clerical serfs, they included the so-called taxpaying (*chernososhnye*) peasants who lived in the north on land few wanted; the *odnodvortsy* or single-homesteaders, descendants of the lowest level of servicemen who had been settled on the southern and eastern frontier in the seventeenth century and had gradually sunk into the peasantry; and the non-Slavic nationalities of the east who came under Russian authority as the state expanded in the sixteenth and seventeenth centuries. Court peasants, although formally a distinct category, are often grouped with the state peasants because like them they were free of an immediate owner and hence subject to less supervision than privately held serfs. Although state peasants were certainly in a more favored position than serfs, they were never secure; over the course of the eighteenth century hundreds of thousands of them had the misfortune of being converted into serfs as part of huge grants of land and peasants made by the tsars to favored noblemen.[70]

This consolidation of the peasantry was mirrored by a similar process among the nobility. By the middle of the eighteenth century the word *dvorianstvo,* derived from what had previously been one service rank, came to be applied to the nobility as a whole. Several features helped cement the nobility and contributed to their self-consciousness as an estate. For one thing, they constituted a landowning class. During the course of the seventeenth century conditional pomest'ia gradually merged with hereditary votchiny, and the government formally acknowledged this merger in 1714. Henceforth, *pomeshchik* came simply to mean a noble landowner, and the reader who encounters the term in the rest of this book can think of it as the rough equivalent of *planter* in the United States. Second, they and they alone formed a serfowning class. A series of laws enacted between 1730 and 1762 effectively limited the ownership of settled estates to members of the nobility, although wealthy merchants repeatedly sought the right to acquire serfs (and were able from the early eighteenth century to employ "assigned" peasants in their manufacturing establishments, the most important of which were mining and metallurgical plants in the Urals). Third, they were a service class: all male noblemen shared the obligation—legal until 1762, moral thereafter—of state service, either military or civil. There was, in fact, a close connection between this service obligation and serfdom linking the peasantry, the nobility, and the state in a bond of universal service: serfs served their owners, who in turn served either in the military or in the government. Finally, with Peter I's establishment of the Table of Ranks in 1722, they became a clearly defined class with carefully spelled out privileges and duties. The table established a hierarchy of fourteen service ranks, with promotion theoretically based entirely on merit and length of service and nobility awarded to commoners reaching the eighth civil rank. Entirely separate was Peter's creation of the hereditary honorific titles *count* and *baron*—*prince* had been an old Russian title—with which he and his successors rewarded special favorites.[71]

Nobles remained a tiny fraction of the population, although not so tiny as in countries like England, where shortage of land necessitated reserving noble status to firstborn sons. In Russia all children of noblemen were noblemen, and it was established practice to divide landed property among all noble children as well. At the time of the fourth census, in 1782, there were 108,155 male noblemen, who formed 0.79 percent of the male population. (That figure grew sharply in subsequent years because of the acquisition of Polish territory containing a much higher proportion of noblemen, but in the interior of Russia noblemen continued to constitute less than 1 percent of the population.) Whatever their weakness in numbers, their wealth and power were extensive: although enormous variations existed within the nobility, as a class they held most of Russia's land, owned almost all of its serfs, and dominated its government.[72]

Just as the gap between white and black increased in the American colonies, so too did that between nobleman and peasant in Russia. The gap was widened by Peter I's insistence that noblemen shave their beards and adopt western European manners, but it was essentially a product of a natural cultural division between the two very different social classes that had emerged. During the eighteenth century noblemen and peasants came to inhabit such different worlds that the distinction between them seemed as inherent as that between white and black. "Nature herself . . . furnished different talents to different people, wisely allotting some to be rulers and leaders, others good executers, and finally the third blind actors," explained Prince M. M. Shcherbatov, the most persistent ideologue of noble rights in the 1760s to 1780s. Whereas those who were well born were natural leaders, bringing glory to their country, the peasants were lazy, crude, and totally unfit for freedom. Because of their wild nature, as demonstrated in Pugachev's rebellion, "any breach of the ancient seigneurial authority over the peasants," he warned, "could bring great ruin and destruction to the state."[73]

*   *   *

AS CLASS LINES HARDENED, the serfs' status deteriorated to the extent that they became in most respects indistinguishable from slaves. If the original earmark of Russian serfdom as defined in the decrees of the 1590s and the legislative code of 1649 had been prohibition of movement, noblemen wasted little time in behaving as if they actually owned the peasants who lived on their lands. A series of acts passed in the late seventeenth and early eighteenth centuries made it clear that in fact they did. The debasement of the serfs was essentially a linear process; virtually every Russian monarch was responsible for some piece of legislation that further reduced the serfs' rights, with some of the most important acts being passed during the reigns of the reforming monarchs Peter I (1682–1725) and Catherine II (1762–96). By the middle of the eighteenth century the formal power of the pomeshchik over his serfs was as great as that of the American slaveowner over his chattel—almost total, short of deliberate murder.[74]

Russian serfdom thus departed significantly from the serfdom that had existed in medieval Europe, the most salient feature of which was binding the peasants to the land. Even in the code of 1649 landholders with more than one estate were allowed to move their serfs from one pomest'e or votchina to another, although they could not transfer them from a pomest'e to a votchina, because pomest'ia and therefore the serfs living on them were in theory conditional grants. With the merger of these two forms of landholding, however, serfowners were able to move their peasants wherever they wished. During the second half of the seventeenth century, probably in the 1660s, noblemen began buying and selling serfs without land, and by the eighteenth century the practice had become commonplace. By the end of Peter I's reign any idea that serfdom meant simply prohibition of movement or that serfs were tied to the land was long since gone. Serfs could be bought and sold, traded, won and lost at cards. They were, in short, personal property.

Over this property serfowners had almost total control, although they did not always choose to exercise it. Such control extended to the serf's "possessions," which in fact belonged to his master. Thus, although it was common practice to provide serfs allotments of land by which they would support themselves and to recognize as theirs whatever they earned on their own time, this was simply a custom that noblemen could and sometimes did violate. Serfs could be taken away from their landed allotments and made into house servants, or into day laborers entirely supported by their owners and performing barshchina for them six days per week. The control also extended to the bodies of the serfs, who could be corporally punished as an owner saw fit, removed from their loved ones at his whim, and denied his permission to marry. About the only right serfs had that slaves in many countries did not was that of being sent into the army. (Kholopy, too, had served in the Muscovite army.) Under the recruit system established by Peter I in 1700 peasants were subjects to periodic military levies, in which a given number of young men from each village would be taken into the army. Military service hardly constituted a privilege, however, and was usually looked upon more as a death sentence than as a release from serfdom; service was for life until 1793, when it was reduced to a twenty-five-year term. Peasants taken into the army could expect never to see their homes or families again.[75]

Given the position that serfs had reached by the eighteenth century, it is hardly surprising that contemporaries, both Russian and foreign, considered them in fact to be slaves. Russians themselves sometimes used the traditional word for slavery (*rabstvo*)—the same word they applied to the American institution—to describe the condition of their serfs, whom they referred to as slaves (*raby*). Most foreign travelers who commented on the nature of serfdom also equated it with slavery. Thus, Englishman William Richardson wrote in 1784 that "the peasants in Russia . . . are in a state of abject slavery; and are reckoned the property of the nobles to whom they belong, as much as their dogs or horses." Almost forty years later Frenchman M. P. D. de Passenans, who spent much of his youth in Russia, explained that although peasants were often called serfs, they were really slaves. "The words serfs and vassals connote dependence, but not property," he wrote, "and cannot be applied to the Russian subjects, who are condemned at the same time to both real and personal servitude."[76]

Historians of widely varying persuasions have generally concurred in this judgment, describing eighteenth-century and nineteenth-century serfdom as essentially slavery. Whatever differences they have had on this point revolve around the hairsplitting determination of whether serfdom "very closely approached" slavery or in fact *was* slavery, a dispute more of semantics than anything else. Thus, like many other Soviet scholars, A. V. Predtechenskii cites Lenin to support his assertion of "the disappearance in serfholding Russia of any difference in fact between a slave and a serf," and Jerome Blum notes that "by the last part of the eighteenth century the Russian serf was scarcely distinguishable from a chattel slave." Even more absolute is Alexander Gerschenkron's declaration that "the term serfdom to characterize the peasants' condition in Russia, although conventional, is quite misapplied. With the strong centralized government guarding the rights of the landowners serfdom had long degenerated into outright slavery."[77]

It would be foolish to contest a verdict that has achieved such historical consensus, especially since it is one with which I agree. Nevertheless, it is important to point out that although Russian serfdom was indeed a form of slavery, it was a form that differed in two basic respects from the slavery that existed in the southern part of the United States. Because these differences are important, it is necessary to introduce them at the start of this volume.

First, American slaves were aliens, taken from their homes in Africa against their will and deposited in a strange land among people they did not know. As a consequence, slavery in America entailed a number of basic relationships other than that of master and slave. Master and slave were, at first, of different nationality, race, and cultural background; they spoke different languages and practiced different religions. Over the course of several generations, some of these differences were reduced or entirely overcome, as the Africans and their descendants adjusted to their new homes, acquired and modified some elements of their masters' culture, and in turn influenced the civilization of white America. But blacks remained in an important sense outsiders living in an alien white America. White southerners always so regarded them; no matter how affectionately a slaveowner might speak of "my people," "*the* people" was a term always reserved for whites who formed the body politic.

This was not the case in Russia, where with few exceptions masters and serfs were of the same nationality. True, in the western provinces of the Russian empire there occurred the interaction of different religions and nationalities; in the right-bank Ukraine, for example, Orthodox Ukrainian peasants frequently had Polish Catholic owners, and in the Baltic region Orthodox peasants had German Lutheran owners. Similarly, as the empire spread to the south and east, conquered nationalities were absorbed into the serf population. In the great interior of Russia, however, peasants and noblemen shared the same race, religion, and cultural roots. Nor were the peasants outsiders the way American blacks were, removed from their native land and placed in a strange new world. They constituted the lowest level of society rather than outcasts from it. Many Americans advocated a United States without blacks, but to imagine a Russia without the peasants was inconceivable; they were the essence of it—and 90 percent of its population. When Russians spoke of "the people," they meant precisely the peasants.

Of course, national, religious, or racial distinction between master and bondsman is not an intrinsic element of slavery; in his survey of slave societies around the world Orlando Patterson found that in about one-quarter, some or all of the slaves were of the same ethnic group as their masters. Nevertheless, the Russian case flies in the face of assertions made by some scholars that slaves must, by their very nature, be outsiders, that no people would enslave their own compatriots. "What sets the slave apart from all other forms of involuntary labor is that, in the strictest sense, he is an outsider," wrote Moses I. Finley. "He is brought into a new society violently and traumatically; he is cut off from all traditional human ties of kin and nation and even his own religion; he is prevented, insofar as that is possible, from creating new ties, except to his masters, and in consequence his descendants are as much outsiders, as unrooted, as he was." Finley's statement is an exaggeration: slaves in the Americas *did* form ties—familial and other—and subsequent generations of slaves were hardly as unrooted as the original African imports. Still, the Russian enserfment of other Russians is unusual—Patterson noted "a universal reluctance to enslave members of one's own community"—and produced consequences that in important ways differentiated Russian serfdom from American slavery.[78]

Historians have hardly dealt with the question of how Russians were so easily able to contradict the general rule that slaves must be outsiders. Richard Hellie plausibly suggests the importance of kholopstvo as a precedent, noting that "Russians for centuries [had] been accustomed to enslaving their own people" and suggesting that early Russian enslavement of insiders was facilitated by a "fundamental lack of ethnic identity and cohesion among the inhabitants of Muscovy." What appears to have been crucial in serfdom—in addition to the legacy of kholopstvo—was its gradual degeneration into slavery, so that there was no one point in time when Russians actually took the step of enslaving their fellow countrymen. By the time serfdom had fully developed, in the eighteenth century, nobleman and peasant seemed as different from each other as white and black, European and African. Russian noblemen were thus able to create the kind of social distance between themselves and their peasants necessary for the maintenance of serfdom.[79]

The second major difference between American slavery and Russian serfdom was in part a consequence of the first. Although juridically the powers of a nobleman over his serfs were as extensive as those of a planter over his slaves, because serfdom emerged gradually and because the peasants were not outsiders but for the most part members of the same community as their parents, grandparents, and earlier ancestors, the role of tradition in limiting the total control of masters over the lives of their bondsmen was greater in Russia than in the United States. This was especially true of the bondsmen's economic lives. Although serfs did not legally own any landed property, most received from their owners allotments of their "own" that they used to support themselves. Unlike most American slaves, who worked for their masters all the time and received sustenance in exchange, most serfs worked only part of the time for their owners, received no support from them, and were expected to maintain themselves. There was thus a dual economy in Russia: the peasants cultivated their owners' seigneurial land, but they also cultivated their "own" land and were free to use its product as they saw fit.

The contrast was not absolute and legally it was nonexistent. Not all serfs had their own allotments. A small number of agricultural laborers and much larger number of house serfs worked full-time for their owners and received sustenance from them. Furthermore, any serf could be transferred to house status, and noblemen could ultimately dispose of their peasants' property as they saw fit. In America, too, most slaves had small garden plots with which they supplemented their food allowances, and a few were permitted to hire their own time, giving their owners the equivalent of obrok payments; in a few areas—most particularly the South Carolina and Georgia lowlands—something approaching Russia's peasant economy existed. (This was even more true in Jamaica and some other Caribbean slave societies, where the slaves *were* self-supporting; see Chapter 4.) In neither country, then, did the legal rights of the bondsmen necessarily define their actual condition. Still, the role of custom in shaping master-bondsman relations was greater in Russia than in the United States, where both slave and slaveowner were relative newcomers and tradition weighed less heavily in shaping social relations.

I will elaborate on these two distinctions, and on their most important consequences, in much of this book. The most fundamental consequence concerns the relationship between the masters and bondsmen; on the whole, Russian serfs were able to lead lives that, although circumscribed by the authority of their owners, were much more independent than those of American slaves. Russian serfdom was a very particular type of slavery, with features that in many ways resembled those of America's "peculiar institution" but in other respects differed sharply from them. It is precisely because both the similarities and differences were so marked that the comparison of these two institutions is so fruitful.

PART I

The Masters and Their Bondsmen

1

Labor Management

THE LIFE SPANS of the unfree labor systems spawned by European expansion proved to be remarkably uniform. Born during the sixteenth and seventeenth centuries, these systems survived for more than two hundred years and then came under attack as barbarous relics of an unenlightened past. As the following timetable of emancipation shows, they expired over a relatively short period from the American Revolution to the 1880s, the vast majority during the first two-thirds of the nineteenth century:[1]

1774–1804	Northern United States (gradual in some cases)
1804	Haiti
1807	Prussia, Poland
1813–14	Argentina, Colombia (gradual)
1816–19	Baltic provinces of Russian empire
1823–42	Central America, Mexico, Bolivia, Uruguay, Chile
1833–38	British colonies
1848	German states, Austrian empire, French and Danish colonies
1851–54	Ecuador, Peru, Venezuela
1853	Hungary
1861	Russia
1863	Dutch colonies
1864	Romania
1865	Southern United States
1873	Puerto Rico
1886	Cuba
1871–88	Brazil

Emancipation came in varying ways. Often it was gradual and compensated, as in the British colonies, Russia, and most of the northern United States. Sometimes it was sudden and uncompen-

49

sated, as in Haiti and the southern United States. In several countries, including some of the Spanish possessions and the northern United States, it was a consequence of wars for independence, while in others, such as Russia, Prussia, and Brazil, it was decreed by monarchs over the grumbling of local landowners. In only one case, however—that of Haiti—did abolition come from "below," as a result of the much dreaded servile insurrection. Elsewhere, emancipation came from "above," the consequence of decisions by established authorities that for one reason or another human bondage was inappropriate. This was true in both the United States and Russia.[2]

In other respects, however, the process of emancipation differed sharply in Russia and the American South. Southern slaveowners vehemently resisted all proposals to interfere with their authority over their slaves and finally, in 1861, took their states out of the Union rather than tolerate the election of a president committed to stopping the spread of slavery into new territory. The result was civil war, the defeat of the "slave power," and an emancipation conceived and administered by northerners who held little sympathy for the slaveowners or their interests. In Russia emancipation came peacefully, the result of a decision by Tsar Alexander II and his advisors that serfdom was an anachronism and an impediment to progress that could no longer be tolerated. Although many noblemen were unhappy with this decision, there was no overt resistance, no threat to take up arms as southern planters did in the United States. What is more, these noblemen played a major role in formulating and executing the emancipation provisions. Emancipation in the United States South was violent and part of a conscious effort to destroy the power of the slaveowning class; emancipation in Russia was peaceful and carried out with the interests of noblemen in mind.[3]

This contrast in the manner of emancipation had important consequences concerning the new social arrangements established in the two countries. More to the point here, it also reflected the sharp divergence between the lives of American slaveowners and those of Russian serfowners during the decades preceding emancipation. If emancipation in America, unlike that in Russia, occurred only over the armed resistance of those most directly threatened by it, this contrast represented the culmination of a growing gap between the two countries with respect to the masters' commitment to forced labor. That gap became fully apparent, however, only gradually, during the first half of the nineteenth century. For numerous reasons southern planters were in a far stronger, more independent position than Russian pomeshchiki in relation to both their government and their property and hence were better able to resist changes foisted upon them. In this and the next two chapters I shall explore the contrasting worlds of the masters, showing how despite basic similarities between Russian serfdom and American slavery, the master class in the southern United States was able to build for itself a much more secure, autonomous, and defensible existence than was that in Russia.

* * *

IT IS APPROPRIATE to begin with some simple statistics, because the composition of the population everywhere helped to define the nature of bondage. These statistics, drawn from censuses of 1795 and 1858 in Russia and 1790 and 1860 in the United States, are neither entirely uniform over time nor fully reflective of earlier conditions. In the South the proportion of slaves increased substantially between the late seventeenth and late eighteenth centuries and then remained more or less constant; in Russia the proportion of serfs peaked during the second half of the eighteenth century and then declined broadly.[4] The following figures, however, provide good introductory glimpses of Russian serfdom and American slavery as mature institutions during their last seventy-five years; what is more, despite some demographic changes the basic trends that these statistics illustrate prevailed during the preceding seventy-five years as well.[5]

In both countries the bondsmen formed roughly similar proportions of the total population: about one-third in the United States South and one-half in Russia. The difference was in the number of owners. In Russia serfowning noblemen represented a tiny fraction of the population, whereas in the South about one-quarter of all whites—or one-sixth of the population as a whole—were members of slaveowning families. As a consequence the balance of forces was strikingly different: in Russia in 1858 there were 24.4 male serfs for every male nobleman, whereas in the slaveholding United States in 1860 there were only 2.1 slaves for every member of a slaveowning family. The contrast is even sharper if one widens the scope by including state peasants and free Negroes. For every male nobleman there were 51.8 male peasants in Russia; for every white southerner there were 0.5 blacks. Russian noblemen thus lived in an overwhelmingly peasant world; white southerners did not live in a correspondingly black world (see Tables 3 and 4).

It is therefore not surprising that Russian serfs were usually held in much larger units than were American slaves. The great majority of

Table 3
Male population of Russia, 1795 and 1858

	1795		1858	
	No. males	% of population	No. males	% of population
Serfs	9,787,802	53.9	11,338,042	39.2
State peasants[a]	6,534,182	36.0	12,677,609	43.8
Total peasants	16,321,984	89.8	24,015,651	83.0
Noblemen	362,574	2.0	463,968	1.6
Other	1,484,016	8.2	4,455,571	15.4
Total population	18,168,574		28,935,190	
Serfs/noblemen	27.0		24.4	
Peasants/noblemen	45.0		51.8	

Sources: V. M. Kabuzan, *Izmeneniia v razmeshchenii naseleniia Rossii v XVIII- pervoi polovine XIX v.* (Moscow: Izdatel'stvo "Nauka," 1971), appendix 2; V. M. Kabuzan and S. M. Troitskii, "Izmeneniia v chislennosti, nadel'nom vese i razme- shchenii dvorianstva v Rossii v 1782–1858 gg.," *Istoriia SSSR*, 1971, no. 4, 164.
   a. Includes court peasants.

southern slaveowners had only a few slaves each: more than two-thirds held 9 or fewer and more than four-fifths held 19 or fewer. The proportion of large slaveowners was tiny (see Table 5). The Russian contrast was striking: more than one-half of all serfowners owned 21 or more male souls (i.e., 42 or more serfs) and more than one-fifth had 101 or more souls (202 or more serfs) (see Table 6). Although the 1860 census listed only one American slaveowner with more than a thousand slaves, the 1858 census in Russia counted 3,858 such own-ers. Traditional criteria for categorizing the wealth of Russian po-meshchiki seem ludicrous by American standards. The leading expert on the census of 1858, for example, defined noblemen with 100 or fewer male souls as small holders, those with 101 to 500 as middle, and those with more than 500 as large. Southerners, however, reck-oned someone with 50 slaves a very substantial slaveowner, and own-ership of 20 slaves was often used to separate planters from farmers.[6]

The contrast in size of holdings is even greater if one focuses on the bondsmen themselves rather than on their owners. The great majority of all serfs belonged to noblemen owning more than 100 males, and almost one-half belonged to those with more than 500. Of course, when noblemen owned thousands of serfs they usually did not all live together on one estate; in 1851, for example, the prominent Voron-

Table 4
Population of the United States South, 1790 and 1860[a]

	1790		1860	
	No.	% of population	No.	% of population
Slaves	657,538	33.5	3,950,511	32.3
Free blacks	32,246	1.6	254,054	2.1
Total blacks	689,784	35.2	4,204,565	34.4
Individual owners			383,637	
Owner family members[b]			1,918,185	15.7
Other whites			6,118,514	50.0
Total whites	1,271,390	64.8	8,036,699	65.7
Total population	1,961,174		12,241,264	
Slaves/owner family members				2.1
Blacks/whites		0.5		0.5

Sources: U. S. Census Office, *Population of the United States in 1860* (Washington, 1864), 592–95; U. S. Census Office, *Agriculture of the United States in 1860* (Washington, 1864), 247; Donald B. Dodd and Wynelle S. Dodd, comps., *Historical Statistics of the South, 1790–1970* (University, Ala.: University of Alabama Press, 1973).

a. 1790 figures are for eight southern states only; 1860 figures exclude Washington, D.C., and federal territories.

b. Estimate, based on assumption of five persons per family.

tsov family held 37,702 male souls distributed among numerous estates scattered across sixteen different provinces. Still, it was not at all unusual for individual estates to contain hundreds of serfs. Such concentrated holdings were rare in the United States, where almost half of all slaves were held in units of fewer than 20 and three-quarters were held by owners with fewer than 50. In Russia 80.8 percent of the serfs had owners with more than 200 bondsmen each; in the United States 2.4 percent of the slaves had such owners (see Tables 5, 6).[7]

Of course, in both countries there were regional variations. Slaves formed a much higher proportion of the population—typically about one-half—in the deep South, where cotton was grown in the nineteenth century, than in the upper South (see Map 3), and in some counties more than four-fifths of the population were slaves. In such

Table 5
Distribution of American slaveowners and slaves by size of holdings, 1860

	Number of slaves owned				
	1–9	10–19	20–49	50–199	>199
Percentage of slaveowners	71.9	16.0	9.3	2.6	0.1
Percentage of slaves	25.6	21.6	27.9	22.5	2.4

Sources: U. S. Census Office, Agriculture of the United States in 1860, 247; Lewis Cecil Gray, History of Agriculture in the Southern United States to 1860 (Washington: Carnegie Institution of America, 1933), I, 530.

Table 6
Distribution of Russian serfowners and serfs by size of holdings, 1858

	Number of male serfs owned			
	1–20	21–100	101–500	>500
Percentage of serfowners	43.6	33.9	18.9	3.6
Percentage of serfs	3.3	15.9	37.2	43.6

Source: A Troinitskii, Krepostnoe naselenie v Rossii, po 10–i narodnoi perepisi (St. Petersburg, 1861), 45.

areas slaveholdings were unusually large. Thus, whereas half the South's slaves lived on holdings of more than 23 slaves, in the deep South the median was 32.5, in Louisiana it was 49.3, and in Concordia parish, Louisiana it was 117; in the western Kentucky tobacco region, by contrast, the median figure was only 14. In Russia the proportion of serfs varied from well over half the population in the central provinces to an insignificant number in Siberia and the north (see Map 4). The size of holdings also varied widely: in Saratov province, in the southeast, more than half the serfs were held by owners with more than 500 male souls each, but in Olonets province in the north none was. The proportion of noblemen varied too: although in the Russian empire as a whole they formed 1.6 percent of the population in 1858, this figure is inflated by inclusion of territory acquired from Poland in the late eighteenth century, where noblemen constituted about 5 percent of the population; in Russia proper, noblemen continued to form less than 1 percent of the population.[8]

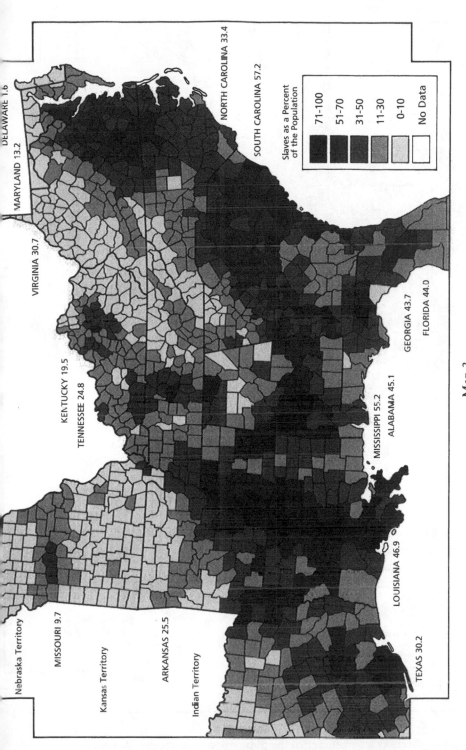

Map 3

Slaves as a percentage of the population in the United States South, by county and state, 1860.

DELAWARE 1.6
MARYLAND 13.2
VIRGINIA 30.7
NORTH CAROLINA 33.4
SOUTH CAROLINA 57.2
KENTUCKY 19.5
TENNESSEE 24.8
GEORGIA 43.7
FLORIDA 44.0
MISSISSIPPI 55.2
ALABAMA 45.1
LOUISIANA 46.9
Nebraska Territory
MISSOURI 9.7
Kansas Territory
ARKANSAS 25.5
Indian Territory
TEXAS 30.2

Slaves as a Percent
of the Population

71–100
51–70
31–50
11–30
0–10
No Data

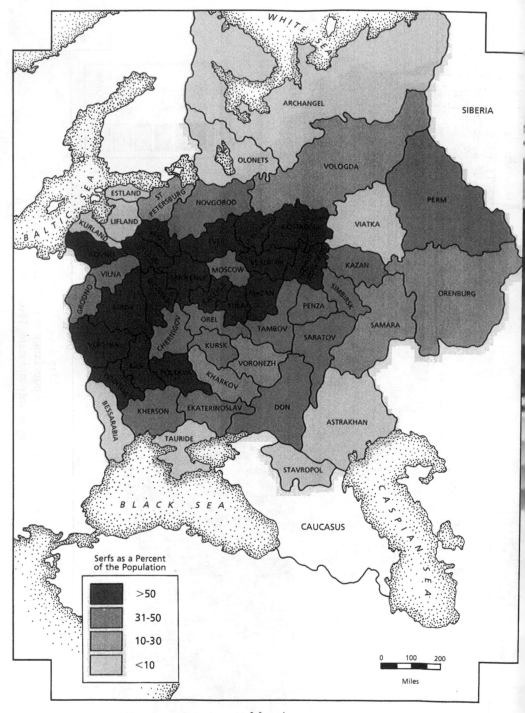

Serfs as a Percent
of the Population

>50

31-50

10-30

<10

Map 4
Serfs as a percentage of the population in European Russia,
by province, 1858.

Whatever the regional variations, however, holdings were almost everywhere much larger in Russia than in the United States, and the ratio of bondsmen to their owners was much greater. Even in the north of Russia, where there were few serfs, holdings were large by American standards; in Olonets province, for example, only 4 percent of the population were serfs in 1858, but three-quarters of them belonged to pomeshchiki with more than 20 males and two-fifths of them belonged to owners with more than 100 males. Similarly, areas with the largest slaveholdings in the United States would hardly have seemed exceptional in Russia. Ascension parish, Louisiana, had an unusually high concentration of slaves even for Louisiana; half lived on holdings of 175 or more. In Russia, however, four-fifths of all serfs lived on holdings of more than 200. Regional variations, then, were significant, but they did not alter the basic contrast between the distribution of bondsmen in Russia and in the United States. In the latter ownership of slaves was broadly based among the white population and typical holdings were small; in the former ownership of serfs was confined to a tiny privileged group, and holdings were usually quite large. In this respect Russia and the slave South were at opposite ends of a broad continuum, with other modern Western slave societies falling in between. In Jamaica in the eighteenth and early nineteenth centuries, for example, the ratio of blacks to whites was about 10, far in excess of the 0.5 ratio in the southern United States but well short of the 51.8 ratio of peasants to noblemen in Russia. Jamaican plantations were generally considerably larger than American—they typically contained hundreds of slaves—but even the largest Jamaican slaveowners were dwarfed by wealthy Russian pomeshchiki who owned thousands and sometimes tens of thousands of serfs.[9]

This contrast in size of holdings and in the balance of forces between owners and owned had important consequences for both the bondsmen and their masters. For the bondsmen it meant that they would come in contact with outsiders much less often in Russia than in the United States and have correspondingly more opportunity to lead their own lives with a minimum of interference. It thus reinforced the contrast between Russian peasants living in their traditional villages and American blacks uprooted from their homes and deposited in an alien environment. White America impinged on the lives of the slaves much more than noble Russia did on the lives of the serfs (see Part II). For the masters it meant that their relationships both with their laborers and with each other would differ in important ways in the two countries. These differences ranged from methods of running their estates to the social cohesion of their civilization.

*   *   *

RELATIONS BETWEEN master and bondsman were in general far more impersonal in Russia than in America. The majority of serfs rarely saw their owners; they dealt instead with a hierarchy of administrators who in theory—and sometimes in practice—represented those owners and promoted their interests. To such serfs the pomeshchik was typically a remote, faceless figure, an ultimate authority to be feared or appealed to in time of duress. Most slaves, by contrast, dealt with their masters on a regular basis. Slaveowners were familiar with the names, appearance, and outward behavior of their slaves, in whose careers, for better or worse, they took a lively interest.

For two principal reasons the Russian nobility displayed a strong absentee orientation. Most obvious, they continued to be a service class. The service requirement, which dated from the establishment of the pomest'e system and was reinforced and regularized when Peter I created the Table of Ranks as a service hierarchy, was gradually relaxed during the second half of the eighteenth century, and in a series of measures culminating with acts of Peter III in 1762 and Catherine II in 1785 noblemen won their freedom from compulsory state service. Nevertheless, both government and noblemen continued to regard service as the norm. Although most noblemen resented the compulsory nature of service under Peter I and therefore rejoiced at its abolition, they continued to consider themselves as members of a service class, whose main loyalty was to tsar and country, not to region or locality. The very wealthy usually spent most of their lives far removed from their peasants, in Moscow, St. Petersburg, or abroad, and retired to one of their country estates only as old men. Count S. R. Vorontsov, for example, one of the most illustrious noblemen of his era, lived in London from 1785 to 1832, where he served as ambassador and felt far more comfortable than in provincial Russia. "My principal object and that which is closest to my heart is to achieve the education of my son, which I can only completely finish here, where I have begun it," he explained to his brother in 1797, "especially on account of mathematics, for which he has a penchant and even, says his instructor, much talent." He remained in London, however, for several decades after his son's education was completed. Less prosperous pomeshchiki, although lacking the cultural pretensions of Vorontsov, often needed their service salaries to supplement the incomes from their estates. The "emancipation" of the nobility thus did not alter its essentially serving nature and mentality.[10]

Even had the nobility not possessed this service character, the very size and number of their estates would have meant that most serfs rarely saw their owners. Wealthy pomeshchiki almost always owned more than one estate, and even owners of fairly modest proportions often had two or three holdings rather than a solitary estate containing all their serfs. Because many lesser noblemen were also away from their holdings in service, it is safe to assert that a majority of pomeshchiki were absent much of the time and that the vast majority of serfs belonged to absentee owners.

Information on the residence of pomeshchiki in three districts of Saratov province in 1836 reveals how rarely these noblemen lived "at home." Of 624 pomeshchiki with estates in at least one of the three districts, 421—slightly more than two-thirds—did not live in the district. Very wealthy noblemen were almost always absent: of 13 pomeshchiki with more than 1,000 souls, only one was resident. But even among lesser noblemen absence was the norm: two-thirds of the pomeshchiki with 20 or fewer souls did not live in the district. What is more, such figures clearly understate the degree of absenteeism: some noblemen listed as living in the district doubtless lived in the district capital rather than in the countryside, and those having more than one estate were absentee owners to many of their serfs even if they lived on one of their estates. And since the largest owners were almost all absent, far more than two-thirds of the serfs had absentee owners. Although not all provinces had an absentee rate equal to Saratov's—those near Moscow and St. Petersburg, for example, appeared more desirable places to live than those that were remote—there is little doubt concerning the overall tendency to absentee relations that existed almost everywhere.[11]

The small size of American holdings, by contrast, made possible—indeed encouraged—the residence of the owner and close contact between master and slaves. Very few slaveowners had holdings so extensive that they themselves could not exercise direct management of them. Unlike pomeshchiki, few planters had multiple holdings and were thus forced to be absentee proprietors for at least some of their slaves.[12]

Of course there were exceptions. In colonial Virginia and Maryland it was a common practice to place newly imported blacks on holdings known as "quarters," isolated from the main plantation, where they could be trained for their new lives in small groups averaging eight hands per quarter. In addition, the largest eighteenth-century planters usually had several plantations; among the one hundred wealthiest Virginians in 1778–88, for example, ninety held land in at least two counties, and the very richest had holdings scattered across the state. In colonial South Carolina, too, the wealthiest planters were often absentee lords for at least part of the year; as a British officer noted in 1764, "almost every family of note have a Town residence [in Charleston], to which they repair on publick occasions, and generally for the three Sickly months in the fall." [13] In the antebellum period absentee proprietorship continued, especially but by no means exclusively among very rich planters, most notably on the coastal rice lands of South Carolina and Georgia and on the large cotton and sugar estates along the lower Mississippi River. Pressing business could also keep a slaveowner away from home, as in the case of politician and eventually President James K. Polk, whose career kept him in Washington, far from his Tennessee and Mississippi plantations, throughout most of the 1830s and 1840s. Or a planter could be an absentee owner out of inclination, as was George Noble Jones, who owned two adjacent estates near Tallahassee, Florida, but lived most of the year in Savannah. [14]

Nevertheless, it is important to keep such absenteeism in perspective. It was always the exception, not the rule, in the United States South. The overwhelming majority of slaveowners possessed only one farm or plantation, on which they lived. Similarly, because most slaves lived on relatively small holdings and even large slaveowners usually lived on their plantations, the great majority of slaves had resident masters.

As important as the contrast in the actual residence of owners was that in their mentality. If the Russian nobleman had a serving mentality and typically felt trapped or isolated on his provincial estate, the southern planter was torn from his roots when away from his plantation. (Contrast the refrain in Anton Chekhov's play *Three Sisters*—the sisters' dream to escape from the boredom of country life and "go to Moscow"—with that of Margaret Mitchell's novel *Gone with the Wind:* "I can't let Tara go. It's home. I won't let it go. Not while I've got a breath left in me!" declares Scarlett. The thought of her home plantation continually revives her: "I'm going home . . . Yes, yes! To Tara! . . . I will go home! . . . I will! I will!") This self-perception of southern planters as a resident class developed early, persisted throughout the slave regime, and was one of the most important characteristics that distinguished the southern United States from most other modern slave societies. Already in the eighteenth century, when West Indian slaveowners saw their estates as speculations to be milked to the utmost so that they could retire in luxury in England, Virginia planters regarded themselves "at home" in Virginia. When Thomas Jefferson referred to Virginia as "my country," he was expressing a sentiment unusual in either a Russian pomeshchik or a West Indian planter. Even when a southern planter was unable to be present on his plantation, that plantation was still home, and its management constituted his main social duty. Being a planter, South Carolina's Reverend Charles C. Jones lectured his son in 1854, is a full-time occupation, and *you can never succeed and attain to any eminence in your profession* [law] *if you have anything at all to do with the management of negro property. No man in any profession* within my knowledge ever has—" he modestly continued, "and for the obvious reason that no man can succeed in either profession who follows *two.*" [15]

Differences in the size, residence, and mentality of landowners dictated equally important differences in their methods of labor management. Most pomeshchiki relied on various intermediaries to run their estates. The wealthiest noblemen, who were relatively few but who owned a substantial share of the serfs, had elaborate, three-tier administrative apparatuses to control their far-flung holdings. The top level, usually located in Moscow or St. Petersburg, consisted of a central or home office under the authority of a manager. With the help of various assistants he would keep track of developments on the various estates, transmit orders to them from the owner, receive detailed reports back, keep voluminous records, and direct the pomeshchik's overall operations. In some cases the owner himself exercised control over the central office, but often he chose to delegate to it most or all of his day-to-day authority. Such was the case, for example, with Count S. R. Vorontsov, who had two home offices, one in Moscow and one in St. Petersburg, each with control over a specific geographic area. Each of these offices was headed by a chief manager who was assisted by a manager and a substantial staff including two or three clerks. As was often the case, the manager, clerks, and other assistants were usually house serfs owned by Vorontsov, but the chief manager was a free man and indeed nobleman himself, as befitted the position of someone coordinating the administration of sixteen estates containing more than thirty thousand male souls. [16]

Although anyone with more than five hundred souls was likely to own several estates and need some sort of administration to manage them, not all such pomeshchiki made use of elaborate and bureaucratically organized central offices. Some, especially if their serfs numbered no more than two or three thousand, preferred to exercise authority over them more directly. Such was the case with A. I. Bezobrazov, owner of about eleven hundred male souls in the late seventeenth century, who dispensed with a home office and personally corresponded with authorities on his individual estates. Since these estates were spread over eleven districts, however, he needed some way of checking up on them and enforcing his authority over them. His solution was to keep a group of four specially trained kholopy in Moscow, where he employed them as head stewards to act as intermediaries between himself and the estate administrators and serve as troubleshooters in whatever capacity he deemed necessary.[17]

The second level of administration, which for pomeshchiki without home offices was the top level, was composed of stewards[18] who ran the individual estates, and their various assistants. It was the responsibility of the steward to manage an estate's day-to-day operations, supervise seigneurial labor, ensure that peasants performed their obligations and behaved properly, oversee the collection of obrok fees, watch over the keeping of estate records, and send constant reports to the central office or pomeshchik. A resident owner might assume some of these supervisory functions himself, but only the smallest estate could do without a steward altogether. Stewards were usually serfs themselves, although in the nineteenth century there was an increasing tendency among noblemen who considered themselves forward-looking to hire free men—often Germans—who would supposedly be more professional in running estates. Except on very small holdings, the steward would have a number of assistants, all of whom were serfs. The most important was usually the clerk who, because he kept records and handled correspondence, was in a position of strategic importance. On large estates stewards often appointed one peasant for every hundred households (called a *sotskii* or "hundredth") to help in preserving order; under his authority might be "tenths" (*desiatskie*) and "fiftieths" (*piatidesiatskie*). Serfs who were members of the estate administration—especially stewards—occupied precarious positions, because their heightened responsibility brought with it proportional risks should they displease their owners. Pomeshchiki, upon appointing stewards, typically warned them of "cruel punishment without mercy" should they fail in their assigned tasks.[19]

The lowest level of estate administration belonged to the peasants themselves. The degree of authority that this level enjoyed varied widely, but it was common for pomeshchiki to allow the peasant commune and its elected representatives—the most important of whom was the *starosta* or elder—a considerable role in self-administration (see Chapter 4). Peasant representatives helped stewards in their administrative tasks, ranging from the collection of obrok to administering justice and selecting military recruits, but they were also active in the internal world of the peasants. Peasant officials thus played a dual role: on the one hand they were members of the estate administration, serving as assistants to the steward and working for the interests of their owner; on the other they were representatives of the peasants themselves, expressing their interests to the estate administration.[20]

The functioning of this lowest level of estate administration depended in part on the method by which serfs performed their seigneurial obligations. The basic forms of these obligations remained what they had been before. Serfs owed their owners either barshchina or obrok—although there was a tendency, as the economy became more commercial in the second half of the eighteenth century, for obrok in kind to give way to money obrok—or some combination of the two. There were other obligations as well: serfs had to cart seigneurial products to market and, equally important, cart provisions to their owners' homes, which were sometimes hundreds of miles away; they had to perform various construction and maintenance jobs; they had to provide military recruits (or money to buy substitutes); and like most of the population they had to pay the government a soul tax for each male. The most onerous obligation, however—and the one that shaped much of their relations with their owners—was the serfs' basic obrok or barshchina.

On estates where serfs were exclusively on obrok, they often enjoyed a considerable degree of freedom from day-to-day seigneurial interference, and the authority of the peasant commune was often correspondingly great. Occasionally, such an arrangement was the result of a nobleman's deliberate reform proclivities. In the late eighteenth century, for example, I. M. Khreptovich abolished all barshchina requirements on his estates in Belorussia, renting out the seigneurial land to his peasants and allowing them largely to manage their own affairs. His son Adam, who continued the reform administration in the nineteenth century, boasted that without seigneurial compulsion his serfs worked better and his income increased because "the people work assiduously, since they are working for themselves." Usually, however, whatever peasant freedom existed on obrok estates was less a consequence of the owners' reform ideology than of their convenience. So long as they received their obrok payments, many such pomeshchiki cared relatively little about the lives of their serfs and found it easier not to worry about their day-to-day existence. It is not surprising, therefore, that serfs strongly preferred obrok to barshchina and often vigorously pressed their owners to convert the latter to the former.[21]

It was precisely because obrok seemed to permit peasants an excessive degree of freedom that most pomeshchiki insisted that barshchina was preferable. Peasants were naturally lazy and improvident, they argued, and hence needed the supervision of steady seigneurial labor. Such arguments were especially prevalent during the last third of the eighteenth century, when the "peasant question" and the proper manner of estate management first came to the fore as subjects of debate. Noble ideologues found most disturbing the tendency of some landowners to allow a number of their serfs to leave their estates to engage in handicrafts, small-scale trading, factory work, and odd jobs in cities, thus escaping seigneurial supervision in exchange for their annual obrok payments. Noblemen blamed this practice for a widely perceived agricultural crisis marked by crop failures, hunger, and inflation in the price of grain, but they took the practice so seriously primarily because they saw it as merely the tip of a dangerous iceberg representing the failure of pomeshchiki properly to supervise their serfs. Noblemen who debated the causes of rural problems almost always identified inadequate supervision as a central concern and advised pomeshchiki to put their peasants on barshchina and make sure their stewards were performing their tasks properly. Some went further: Count Roman Vorontsov, alarmed by the proliferation of laziness among the peasantry, suggested that "such idlers should be put to work even on holidays," on which peasants were usually given the day off, "for God demands from people virtue, truth, and labor, not idleness."[22]

More concrete factors than ideology, however, usually determined the relative prevalence of barshchina and obrok. Owners were entirely free to establish both the nature and size of their serfs' obligations, and the particular inclinations of individual pomeshchiki no doubt influenced the decisions of many. Some enjoyed managing the labor of their charges, either directly or through intermediaries, but others wanted nothing from them except the income they produced. On estates with resident owners barshchina was almost universal. It was also thought that barshchina was easier to manage on relatively small estates. Large owners, who tended to be absent, often preferred to leave their serfs on obrok rather than worry about the supervisory abilities of their stewards. (At least one author, however, made the opposite argument, pointing out that where tiny villages were scattered far from each other, seigneurial supervision was all but impossible and each peasant "cultivates his field when he feels like it," taking time out to loaf, harbor thieves and fugitives, and trade with wandering Jews.)[23]

But the most important factors in determining whether pomeshchiki would have their serfs on barshchina or obrok were the quality of the land and the capacity for producing crops for market. Where such production was widespread, landowners strove to take advantage of it by putting their serfs on barshchina and maximizing seigneurial output; elsewhere it was easier to extract money from the peasants and let them fend for themselves. During the second half of the eighteenth century a regional division of labor became more and more noticeable, with the fertile lands to the south and southeast becoming the main agricultural areas of Russia, exporting grain to the less climatically favored north. This trend, which was accentuated still further during the first half of the nineteenth century, led to a similar regional division in the method of exploiting serf labor, with pomeshchiki in rich agricultural areas increasing the proportion of their serfs on barshchina, while those in the north transferred most to obrok. In the provinces bordering on Moscow and St. Petersburg many serfs were allowed to abandon agriculture altogether and seek urban employment; in Bogorodskii district of Moscow province in 1834, for example, 2,819 serfs were on barshchina and 21,720 on obrok, with many of the latter evidently working in Moscow.[24]

Throughout the last century of serfdom a majority of serfs were on barshchina, but this overall majority masked increasing regional variations. In the 1850s 71.5 percent of the serfs in the country as a whole were on barshchina and 28.5 percent on obrok. The former system prevailed throughout most of Russia; in some regions, such as the Left-bank Ukraine and the southern steppes, virtually all serfs were on barshchina. Two regions of European Russia, however, were exceptions to this pattern: two-thirds of the serfs in the Non–black earth center and five-sixths of those in the North were on obrok.[25]

American slaveowners did not need the elaborate administrative structures found in Russia to manage their plantations. One looks in vain for any equivalent of the home offices of wealthy pomeshchiki or the kind of complex bureaucratic hierarchy that prevailed among their administrative staffs. A few very rich slaveholders had head overseers—sometimes called *stewards* or *managers*—to supervise the administration of several plantations, but such men coordinated the management of at most hundreds, not thousands, of slaves and required only rudimentary staffs—if any at all—in order to perform their duties.[26]

At the head of a large plantation was often—although by no means always—an overseer. His task was similar to that of the Russian steward: to manage plantation operations, maximize agricultural production, and supervise the slaves both in their labor and in their private lives—making sure that order was maintained while caring for the master's property. If the slaveowner was an absentee proprietor the overseer had total charge of the plantation, but with a resident owner he often amounted to little more than an assistant who executed policies set on a daily basis by his employer. Unlike the Russian steward, however, the overseer was not ordinarily a slave, for southern racial prejudice strongly militated against placing blacks in positions of semi-independent authority (although even here there were exceptions). He was, rather, a freely hired white man who usually fell into one of three categories: the son or other relative of a planter, a poor white who lived in the vicinity, or—most likely—a professional who made a career of supervising plantations.[27]

The relationship between overseers and planters was usually extremely delicate. On the one hand, overseers were conscious of their equality, as free white men, with their employers, but on the other, their dependent position and lower social status required them to show a proper degree of deference and respect. The overseer, noted South Carolina planter-politician James H. Hammond, "will be expected to obey strictly all instructions of the Employer." Not only must he abstain from alcoholic beverages—upon pain of immediate dismissal—but his whole life must revolve around caring for the slaveowner's property; "as the Employer's business will require his whole attention," explained Hammond, "he is expected to see but little company." This juxtaposition of equality and subservience proved an impossible combination for many overseers and planters. Illustrative of the delicacy of this relationship was the case of John Evans, overseer on one of George Noble Jones's two absentee plantations in central Florida. In 1854, after overseeing eight years for Jones, Evans finally got up the courage to ask for a raise to $600 per year, which he claimed was the going rate, promising that if it were granted "I never shall ask you to Raise my wages any more." He also cautiously broached the possibility of marrying, explaining that "I dont noe that I shall Ever marry but I mearly mention this so wee will noe what to depend a pon," and reassuring the planter that "I would not think of getting a wife without your Consent." Shortly thereafter Evans married, but Jones soon became disturbed by what he considered the excessive entertaining of friends by the new couple. Now assertion of rights replaced humility. "I have always been accustomed to having my friends to see me and the indulgence of it never for a moment caused me to neglect the business committed to my charge," protested the overseer, who announced he was quitting. Although Evans later returned to work for Jones, the exchange illustrated the complex mixture of subservience and self-assertion typical of overseers in their dealings with planters.[28]

Whether or not they had overseers, large plantations lacked the substantial administrative staffs common in Russia. There was no need for much division of managerial labor in order to administer estates containing fifty or one hundred persons. Planters' wives often performed much of the household management, supervising the dairy and garden, presiding over the distribution of food, and caring for sick slaves. The functions of clerk, treasurer, and most other subsidiary administrators were performed directly by either the slaveowner or his overseer. Among the slaves the driver was the only management figure of widespread prevalence and importance. Every large plantation would be likely to have one or more slave drivers—a very big plantation might have a head driver—appointed for their strength, responsibility, loyalty, and intelligence, whose task was to assist the planter or overseer in all matters of slave supervision from field work to punishment. Like peasant officials in Russia, they were in an extremely ambiguous position, at the same time slaves and instruments of planter authority. Often drivers earned extraordinary trust and confidence of their owners, and on some plantations they were virtually indistinguishable—except by their color—from overseers. Driver authority reached its highest level in the atypical, absentee-held rice estates of the South Carolina and Georgia lowlands, where head drivers often ran plantation affairs on a day-to-day basis and were subject to only loose supervision by white stewards.[29]

It is important, however, when discussing American plantation management, to keep its limited nature in mind. Farms and small plantations with fewer than thirty slaves almost never had overseers, and even on large holdings they were by no means universal. In 1860 fewer than one slaveowner in ten employed an overseer, and a recent scholar has estimated that "no more than one-third and possibly only one-fourth of the rural slaves worked under overseers"; since many of these also had resident planters, the proportion of slaves under the direct authority of an overseer was quite small.[30] Perhaps half of all slaves labored under the watchful eye of a driver, but these drivers were not part of elaborate administrative bureaucracies, and management hierarchy was virtually nonexistent. For the substantial number of slaves who lived on farms and small plantations, the organization of work and leisure was likely to be highly informal, with the owner personally directing their labor, working alongside them, and treating them with an easy familiarity that came as much from close contact as from social superiority. Even on larger plantations, the problems of organization were minuscule compared with those faced by medium-size Russian pomeshchiki. And whether they lived on farms or plantations, the great majority of American slaves—unlike Russian serfs—had resident owners who undertook the main chores of running plantation affairs themselves.

*   *   *

THE CONCERNS of pomeshchiki are clearly revealed in the instructions they sent their stewards on how to run their estates. These instructions spanned the seventeenth through the first half of the nineteenth centuries, but they were most numerous in the eighteenth, in part because pomeshchiki were in the process of regularizing their systems of estate management and in part because in the second half of the century the question of proper relations between landlords and their serfs was for the first time a subject of serious debate among noblemen. Although the instructions varied widely, over the course of the eighteenth century they tended to become more detailed and more concerned with regulating peasant behavior. Those drafted in the nineteenth century were often only slight modifications of earlier instructions, and the decline in their number probably reflected the diminished need to establish basic principles of estate management as well as the continued use of instructions composed earlier. Of course, these instructions do not describe actual so much as idealized behavior; they are valuable, however, in indicating attitudes of pomeshchiki concerning how they wished to organize their estates and relate to their serfs.[31]

Many of the instructions were issued upon the appointment of new stewards, and they typically began with directions on taking over from previous stewards, taking inventory of the estates, and putting affairs in order. Frequently the new appointee was ordered to assemble the serfs and read them a seigneurial directive to obey him, and sometimes the owner sent a special message to peasant representatives informing them of the change. Often the new steward was told to seek the assistance of peasant officials and a select group of "good peasants" in familiarizing himself with conditions.[32]

Since landowners were vitally concerned with the income generated by their estates, it is hardly surprising that the extraction of this income occupied a central part of almost all the instructions. When serfs were on barshchina, pomeshchiki directed their stewards on the routine of agricultural operations and on their organization and supervision of the peasants' labor. As dictated by accepted custom, noblemen usually told their stewards to have serfs do three days of seigneurial labor per week and three days of work on their own allotments, leaving Sunday as a day of rest. It was not at all unusual, however, for barshchina in practice to occupy four or five days' labor, and a few noblemen actually stipulated that their serfs should perform more than three days' barshchina. Seigneurial labor could be organized in several ways. One popular method was to have two members of a household work "brother for brother," with one engaged in seigneurial cultivation six days per week while the other was released to work full time on the family allotment. Other pomeshchiki had each individual work on barshchina the designated time period. Still others, especially in the nineteenth century, resorted to the task system, whereby a serf who had completed his assigned work for the day was free to do what he wanted, under the belief that this created a powerful incentive for the laborer to work diligently.

Whatever system was used, noblemen were especially concerned that stewards on barshchina estates exercise the utmost possible control over peasant laborers in order to overcome their natural tendency to laziness. "If any of the peasants arrive late for my work," seventeenth-century pomeshchik A. I. Bezobrazov instructed one of his stewards, he should beat the miscreants "mercilessly in front of all the peasants." Eighteenth and nineteenth-century landowners were likely to go into considerably more detail. According to Count P. A. Rumiantsev's elaborate provisions, each Sunday the steward would go over what work was to be done the following week, with the sotskie issuing lots to determine who received what assignment. To make sure that the peasants worked well, each would receive a receipt at the end of every month certifying satisfactory performance, but to ensure that the steward did not overwork them, peasant representatives would give him a monthly receipt as well. The steward supervised seigneurial labor with the help of a field starosta and the sotskie. Not all instructions were so complicated, but almost always stewards were told to maintain close control of peasants engaged in seigneurial labor.[33]

The concern of pomeshchiki for the revenues produced by their obrok estates was equally great, although direct control of peasant labor was unnecessary. Here instructions stressed the prompt collection of obrok payments, the forwarding of money and provisions to the owners, and the punishment of those who would not or could not pay on time. Some instructions to stewards on obrok estates were confined almost exclusively to this task of extracting income. Peasants were designated to collect the obrok sums and others to store them. Money was usually forwarded to noblemen two or three times per year, but provisions had to be sent periodically to avoid spoiling. Whatever the arrangement, it was a constant struggle for pomeshchiki to exact the requisite sums on time, and a good deal of correspondence was devoted to this issue. In 1652, for example, one of B. I. Morozov's stewards reported that he could not send the fish obrok demanded by the owner because the peasants insisted that the river was too low and there were no fish. Morozov, however, was not satisfied with this ploy. There had been plenty of fish, he noted, when his peasants had belonged to the tsar, but now all of a sudden there were none; "the Oka river flows as always—why are there no fish?" he enquired, warning that if the fish were not forthcoming he would impose an obrok three times as great on the peasants and remove the steward from his command. Often serfs found themselves unable to pay their obrok fees and built up hefty arrears. Although on special occasions pomeshchiki sometimes accepted peasant excuses for such delays, usually they assumed that negligence or fraud was at the root of the problem and threatened dire consequences should the serfs continue to hold out. These consequences could extend to stewards as well: Baron N. G. Stroganov warned his stewards that for failure to collect obrok on time and send it to his home office in Orel "you will have cruel punishment without mercy and be put to work."[34]

Because supervision of labor and extraction of obrok were so problematical, the majority of pomeshchiki found themselves forced to pay some attention to regulating the lives of their peasants. There were enormous variations in the way noblemen faced this problem. Some prepared elaborate codes prescribing the behavior of their serfs; in 1838, when B. N. Iusupov appointed a new head steward for his Tula province holdings, two of thirty-eight points in his instruction established the steward's "full power and will" over the serfs, and virtually the entire document dealt with control of them. Other pomeshchiki, especially on obrok estates, were content to give their stewards vague directives "to watch over the peasants and not allow them to fall into laziness, drunkenness, and other debauchery." Most landowners, however, whether they spelled out the details or not, stressed the importance of strict controls over their serfs, believing such controls to be as necessary for the well-being of the peasants themselves as for the efficient functioning of estates.[35]

All noblemen, no matter how lenient on other matters, insisted on administrative control over peasant travel. Serfs required passes to leave their estates, and "unwarranted absences" were everywhere forbidden. Since serfs often had legitimate reasons for travel, monitoring their movement and determining who should be given permission to leave an estate proved a difficult task. Aside from those sent on special errands by their owners or stewards, peasants applied for permission to leave mainly for reasons of "business." In many cases such requests were for short-term absences—perhaps a day or two—in order to sell and buy goods at a local market. On obrok estates, however, serfs often applied for permission to leave for periods of three months to a year, so that they could engage in hired work elsewhere. Although all pomeshchiki required serfs to secure permission before leaving, they followed varying policies concerning the ease with which such permission was obtained and the authority for granting it. Usually only the steward could issue passes, but some owners distinguished between short-term passes for travel of small distances and authorization for more extended trips. Count Rumiantsev, for example, allowed his sotskie to give peasants permission to go to a nearby market to trade but required anyone wanting to go a distance of more than thirty *versty* (slightly more than thirty kilometers) to seek the approval of his seigneurial administration; house serfs needed the steward's approval for all absences.[36]

Noblemen strove to prevent all unexcused absences, using a variety of methods to dissuade would-be fugitives. Sotskie, desiatskie, and other specially designated "watchers" proved useful in keeping track of peasant movements. Count Rumiantsev instructed his stewards to select one peasant from every twenty households to be on the lookout for fugitives and "all suspicious matters." Many pomeshchiki relied on fear of swift retribution to discourage flight; Count Stroganov ordered his stewards to pursue and "cruelly punish without any mercy" all fugitives, warning that if they failed to do so they themselves would be "cruelly beaten with the knout." Not all noblemen, however, set such draconian standards. Many preferred to overlook short unexcused absences rather than create unnecessary trouble, and some followed a similar policy even with respect to purposeful flight. Count P. B. Sheremetev, like many other pomeshchiki, instructed stewards to take captured fugitives to the district capital for interrogation by local authorities but ordered that those who returned voluntarily should be spared any punishment whatsoever. Even those who were captured should have all their possessions returned to them after the interrogation, and only for a second offense should they receive corporal punishment.[37]

Controlling who came *onto* an estate was almost as important as keeping track of who left it, and many landowners devoted considerable attention to this question in their instructions. Fugitive serfs, runaway soldiers, thieves, brigands, and troublemakers threatened to steal a nobleman's property or harm his serfs—or, equally bad, corrupt them. Pomeshchiki therefore urged stewards and their assistants to be especially suspicious of all strangers and to refuse admission to all lacking appropriate passes. If caught, such persons should be turned over to authorities in the district capital. A related problem consisted of relations with neighboring noblemen's serfs, who might if unwatched poach on seigneurial or peasant land, cut down seigneurial trees, or steal from and pick fights with the peasants. Such trouble was especially common in the seventeenth and early eighteenth centuries when land boundaries and social relations were less clearly defined than later. Frequently pomeshchiki urged stewards to make sure that their serfs "live peacefully in the neighborhood" or "live peacefully with outsiders and do not cause them any kind of harm or bring on fights."[38]

Even when safely on the estate, noblemen believed, peasants were so lazy, careless, and improvident that they required constant direction both for their own good and for that of their owners. Essentially children at heart, they needed the guiding hand of the pomeshchik if they were not to lapse into drunkenness, sloth, debauchery, and immorality. For many owners, however, such supervision proved to be such a nuisance that they tended to abdicate their responsibility and not enforce proper standards of behavior. Some instructions, especially on obrok estates, made virtually no mention of this question. Perhaps pomeshchiki felt that firm guidance of peasant morality was implicit and did not need spelling out, but some made conscious decisions to ignore many or all of their estates with the important exception of extracting income from them. Prince F. N. Golitsyn, for example, turned over to his manager the task of preparing his 1796 instruction to the steward of his Tula province holdings. The instruction, although including the usual ritual directive to watch over the serfs and make sure that they behaved themselves, was almost wholly devoted to means of increasing estate income and contained virtually nothing on the lives of the peasants. Most pomeshchiki felt compelled, however, to pay some attention to regulating their serfs' lives because "the morals and virtue of our simple people demand this care." Some landowners went to great lengths to spell out the nature of such care.[39]

Peasants needed constant direction, pomeshchiki found, if they were to perform their tasks satisfactorily. Therefore, they often warned stewards to keep strict watch over them during their seigneurial labor, making use of sotskie, desiatskie, and other subordinates to "require the lazy to work, not permit anyone to loaf, and punish those not wanting to labor." Serfs were sometimes so "lazy" that they needed prodding to work on their own allotments, even though they themselves suffered the consequences. In 1811 pomeshchik Alekseev Gvozdev, noting that some of his peasants were not cultivating their garden plots, warned that in the future if he found anyone "from laziness and carelessness" neglecting his garden he would order not just the peasant and his wife but also the starosta beaten with birch switches, "for a peasant should not be without vegetables." The greatest cause of peasant misbehavior, however, was drunkenness, which led to idleness, sloppy work, thievery, fighting, and a general decline in morality. Few landowners missed the opportunity in their instructions to insist on the necessity of guarding against the evil of peasant carousing. Typical in this respect was the model instruction of Baron Wolf, who observed that it was important to keep serfs from drunkenness and punish the guilty as a deterrent to others, since "from drunkards are made in the end thieves and murderers."[40]

Noblemen usually advocated a policy of noninterference in the family lives of their serfs, with a couple of important exceptions. Pomeshchiki were anxious for their serfs to marry at a young age; they would thus be able to produce a maximum number of children and also would not be tempted to engage in nonmarital sex. As Count V. G. Orlov explained in 1796, marriage at an early age was "pleasing to God" because through it "morals are preserved and many vices are removed." Therefore, he ordered a fine imposed on all single women over twenty and all single men over twenty-five, ranging from twenty-five rubles for an average household to fifty for a rich one, with those too poor to pay subject to corporal punishment. Although he exempted anyone "unable" to marry, he warned his subordinates to be on the lookout for deception on this score and directed that in stubborn cases local peasant representatives should arrange marriage for the recalcitrant. A still more widely discussed problem, which landowners handled in varying ways, involved marriage off the estate. It was common practice, when serfs with different owners married, for the bride to join her husband after receiving the permission of her owner and paying him an exit fee; in effect, she was thus sold to her husband's owner. Most pomeshchiki condoned this practice, and a number established such fees in the instructions, often setting a sliding scale depending on the bride's ability to pay. Not all noblemen, however, were so accommodating; some, such as D. A. Shepelev and A. M. Cherkasskii, specifically barred their serf women from marrying off the estate, and others, such as Gvozdev, insisted that they secure "special written permission from me." Count Rumiantsev ordered his stewards not to interfere with peasant weddings—although he urged that priests make sure serfs were not marrying members of their own families—but made an exception, as did many other pomeshchiki, of house servants, who needed his permission to marry. Count Stroganov, on the other hand, required all his serfs to get their steward's written permission before marrying.[41]

Noblemen concerned with the moral order of their estates often felt that they had to prod serfs to attend church at the appropriate time. A surprising number of instructions included directives ordering stewards to insist that peasants attend church and refrain from work on Sundays and holidays, with recalcitrants to be punished corporally. Some pomeshchiki worked out complicated provisions so that church attendance would cause as little disruption as possible. Count Rumiantsev suggested that one person from each family be left home to prepare food and watch house and ordered that during Lent peasants' confessions be staggered so that everyone would not leave work at the same time. Special situations occasionally called for more extreme measures. In June 1652 B. I. Morozov wrote to several of his stewards ordering them to have priests conduct special masses and parade around the villages and fields with crosses "so that God will give rain on the land." When one of the stewards reported that the serfs refused to go to church and instead "work secretly for themselves," the nobleman directed that they be fined and beaten, for "nowhere on my estates do they work on Sunday." Nevertheless, the resistance continued, with several peasants refusing to go to church and harrassing the unhappy steward for insisting that they must.[42]

As should already be evident, pomeshchiki were especially interested in the punishment of their serfs who misbehaved; in fact, they devoted more attention in their instructions to this subject than to any other. This is hardly surprising, since there were so many opportunities for misbehavior and any violation of established rules seemed either a wilfull challenge to seigneurial authority or a sign of excessively lax seigneurial supervision. Speedy administration of justice was essential to serve as an example to other peasants and prevent the spread of criminal behavior. Peasants were like children, whom it was necessary to "hold in fear," pomeshchiki believed, because like children they would take any relaxation of discipline as a sign of weakness, and the peace and order of the estate would be threatened.[43]

Most noblemen gave their stewards the authority to try all but the most serious cases, usually by themselves but sometimes with the assistance of the "best and most honest" peasants. Very occasionally, reform-minded landowners allowed serfs to administer justice entirely on their own. In 1845, for example, Count Khreptovich set up a twenty-nine-point code and permitted his peasants to handle minor infractions themselves using a peasant court of judges, two of whom the serfs elected and one of whom his administration appointed. Such an arrangement was exceptional, however, and even Khreptovich felt compelled to warn his serfs that "since order cannot exist where there is not obedience," should they abuse the system it would be replaced by one "ensuring obedience and accepted on all neighboring estates." Elsewhere stewards were admonished to decide cases quickly, keeping careful records showing "who is innocent and who guilty, and why." Pomeshchiki usually desired to be kept abreast of the most serious cases and sometimes warned stewards not to decide these on their own but to write to the home office for advice. In the event of major crimes, such as murder, stewards were to turn to the appropriate authorities in the district city.[44]

Pomeshchiki prescribed punishment for a wide range of offenses, including drunkenness, laziness and bad work, theft, cutting seigneurial wood, trading forbidden products or trading without permission, nonpayment of obrok, unauthorized absence, flight, harboring fugitives, fighting, and disorderly conduct. Punishments varied considerably. Many noblemen insisted that for minor infractions, at least the first time they were committed, serfs should receive only verbal warnings or fines, and only for continued recalcitrance or more serious offenses should sterner measures be imposed. Thus, Count P. B. Sheremetev, in his detailed 1764 instruction, decreed that for drunkenness, "mischief and swearwords" his stewards should first try persuasion and then impose fines; if the miscreants persisted they should be placed "under guard on bread and water" for at least three days. Almost all noblemen relied on corporal punishment, however, for serious infractions and for repetitions of even minor mischief. Methods of inflicting corporal punishment included the use of birch switches, special sticks called *batogi,* whips, and in extreme cases the dread knout. Noblemen had differing favorites among these instruments. Count Orlov prescribed use of birch switches and batogi but forbade whippings, whereas Prince Cherkasskii insisted that batogi and the knout be avoided at all times. Countess Anna P. Sheremeteva ordered her stewards to "inflict cruel punishment, beat mercilessly with whips" those who stole, harbored thieves, or traded wine, beer, or tobacco. Even more brutal was D. A. Shepelev, who instructed his agents "to beat mercilessly with batogi" serfs catching seigneurial fish and to subject to the knout those cutting seigneurial wood. In general, punishments prescribed in the seventeenth and early eighteenth centuries tended to be more brutal than those decreed later, but there were numerous exceptions to this rule. And some noblemen, such as Count Orlov, discriminated in their punishments according to the wealth of the transgressor. "Rich peasants" should be punished first by fines, he ordered, "so as not to undermine their trade," although for repeated offenses they could be subjected to bodily punishment. The count then abruptly changed tack, however, and concluded that "the rich, by their good behavior, should serve as an example to others, and should be punished even more than the poor," who were often led to "bad acts" by their material deprivation.[45]

When peasants proved especially trying, a nobleman had two extreme solutions he could apply. He could, at will, sentence them to be exiled to Siberia, receiving in return a credit for the next recruit levy so that he would not suffer a financial burden for the loss. More prevalent was the practice of sending undesirable serfs into the army, thus at the same time helping to fill an estate's quota of recruits and eliminating troublemakers. This action represented an infringement on what was commonly regarded as the right of the peasant community to decide for itself who should serve as recruits, but it was an infringement often provided for in instructions, even by pomeshchiki who under normal circumstances followed other methods of choosing draftees. Thus, Count Rumiantsev, who prescribed that recruits should ordinarily be chosen by lot from the largest families, with anyone chosen permitted to buy a substitute, instructed his stewards "without any lot to mercilessly give away" those guilty of bad work or theft of seigneurial property. Some landowners were more explicit. P. M. Chenikova instructed her steward to choose for the army persons who were the most "unreliable, tipplers, fugitives," but not "a good person, of sensible conduct," and then write to her showing "that these people are bad people." [46]

Whatever their stress on exploitation, regulation, and punishment of serfs, these pomeshchiki did not see themselves as oppressive masters but rather as benefactors guiding their ignorant charges, providing them with the necessary direction and protecting them from adversity in time of trouble. Landowners had a personal interest in the well-being of their serfs if for no other reason than the desire to extract money from them: the hungry and impoverished made poor laborers and could not afford substantial obrok payments.

This concern of pomeshchiki for their peasants' welfare is evident in some—but by no means all—of their instructions. Noblemen urged stewards to see that land was not too unevenly distributed among serfs and ordered them to make sure that orphans and children of those unable to provide adequate support were cared for. Count Orlov instructed his steward to find homes for abandoned illegitimate children, adding that "this matter is pleasing to God" and promising that "for the support of such infants" the steward would "receive praise from me." Other landowners lectured stewards not to punish too severely and not to require overly burdensome labor; if peasants were worked so hard that "neither spring nor autumn nor winter do they have any rest," one pointed out, they would have no time for their own agriculture and would not be able to support themselves adequately. Several owners dealt in their instructions (as more did in practice) with giving relief to serfs who suffered from natural disasters. If a peasant's hut burnt down "from the will of God, and not from his own carelessness," wrote Count Sheremetev, he should receive a half-year immunity from seigneurial obligations; on the other hand, a peasant who lost a house through his own negligence should be punished both to promote greater care in the future and to serve as an example to others. Like several other landlords, G. I. Shipov linked the well-being of both his serfs and his estate with the fate of his steward: if he performed well he would be rewarded, "but for bad management and neglect of seigneurial interest and running the peasants" he faced "painful and merciless punishment."[47]

*   *   *

AMERICAN PLANTERS also sometimes issued written instructions for their overseers, most frequently upon their initial employment. For two principal reasons such instructions were less widespread than those issued by Russian pomeshchiki and less indicative of actual plantation management. First, most slaveowners did not have overseers, and many who did were resident planters themselves, able to give verbal directives on a continuing basis. The great majority of slaves, therefore, labored without the guidance of formal written rules. Second, since the administrative tasks of an overseer were usually simpler than those of a Russian steward, American instructions tended to be shorter than many of their Russian counterparts, with less specificity concerning problems of administration and finance. They were general guidelines for plantation management, typically ranging between one thousand and three thousand words in length. Nevertheless, because their main utility to us lies in their revelation of attitudes rather than their depiction of actual conditions, they are valuable for illustrating how slaveowners thought plantations should be run, what they thought their relations with slaves should be, and how they wanted those relations to appear to the world at large. This is especially true when these instructions are supplemented with model rules and descriptions of ideal management that appeared in the southern agricultural press. Both actual and model instructions were most common during the last thirty years of the slave regime— although they existed earlier too—because this was a time of great self-consciousness among southern slaveowners who, under pressure of criticism from the North, sought to rationalize to themselves and others the nature of their social system.[48]

Many of the themes contained in the planters' instructions were similar to those found in the rules of Russian pomeshchiki. Often they began with a general statement of the overseer's duties—to care for the planter's slaves and other property, produce a good crop, keep records—warning him to be obedient to his employer and diligent in his work or face immediate dismissal. Some planters enjoined their overseers not to drink and not to waste precious time visiting with friends because "subordination to the master is the first of an overseer's duties."[49]

Planters discussed the organization of agricultural labor in their instructions, but the perfunctory treatment that this basic subject often received suggests the degree to which these directives served as general guidelines rather than detailed descriptions of plantation operations. In most of the South plantation slaves worked under the gang system, in which groups of slaves labored together under the leadership of a driver, for a prescribed period of time each day. Often planters directed that slaves toil from sunrise to sunset, with a midday break for dinner that in the summer was sometimes extended to several hours so the hands could avoid working in the heat of the day. It was the overseer's task to give general supervision to this process, on many plantations blowing a horn for the slaves to rise in the morning and another for them to go to the fields and making sure that they performed their work with the requisite care and vigor. Constant supervision of slaves was necessary, "for when an overlooker's back is turned, the most of them will slight their work or be idle altogether." On the rice plantations of the Georgia and South Carolina lowlands, and occasionally elsewhere, the task system prevailed, with each slave assigned a job in the morning and free to stop work when he had completed it. This system required less direct supervision of labor and supposedly gave the hands an incentive to work as hard as possible so that they could maximize their free time. As one planter optimistically noted of his assignments, "all these tasks are light; and the negroes who industriously work from the time they go out . . . will finish their tasks and return to their houses between three and four o'clock."[50]

As in Russia, the personal lives of slaves received much attention. Although marriage and family were not legal institutions for slaves, some owners sought to promote monogamous matrimonial relations among them. Governor Hammond, who argued that "marriage is to be encouraged as it adds to the comfort, happiness & health of those who enter upon it, besides insuring a greater increase," provided unusually detailed rules for slave marriage. Like many masters, he required slaves to obtain his permission before marrying, paying newlyweds a five-dollar bounty to encourage wedlock. Unlike most, he also provided for divorces—although with a penalty. "The offending party must be severely punished" in cases of divorce, he wrote. "When both are in the wrong both must be punished, & if they insist on separating must have 100 lashes apiece"; neither party could then remarry for three years. Most planters were less specific, simply asserting that slaves should be encouraged to marry and lead moral lives, and some publicly despaired of inducing marital fidelity among their slaves: "As to their habits of amalgamation and intercourse, I know of no means whereby to regulate them, or to restrain them," lamented a Mississippi planter; "I attempted it for many years by preaching virtue and decency, encouraging marriages, and by punishing, with some severity, departures from marital obligations, but it was all in vain."[51]

Most planters were more concerned with regulating whom their slaves could marry than in prescribing fidelity. It was a common practice throughout the South for slaves to marry "abroad," that is, to marry slaves belonging to other masters. The practice was especially common on farms and small plantations, where the pool of available mates was small or nonexistent, but it occurred on larger holdings as well. There was, in contrast to the Russian custom, no automatic provision for such slaves to unite in one household, although occasionally a well-intentioned master would purchase the spouse of one of his slaves. Usually, however, such husbands and wives continued to live apart, with the man receiving weekend passes to visit his wife. Slaveholders were understandably unhappy with these arrangements, which provided slaves opportunities to leave home on a regular basis. Large planters, who had a sufficient number of young men and women to render off-plantation marriages unnecessary, were, unlike smaller holders, able to forbid the practice, and it is hardly surprising to find frequent proscriptions against it in their instructions. Some, such as Georgia's Robert Collins, discouraged such unions without actually banning them, but others, like Hammond, flatly prohibited them. Louisiana planter Bennet H. Barrow clearly explained the underlying reasons for refusing slaves permission to marry "abroad": noting that "negroes are verry much desposed to pursue a course of this kind," he warned that "it creates a feeling of independence, from being, of right, out of the control of the masters for a time," as well as exposing the parties to dangerous temptations. Such marriages were also risky for the slaves, since "when a man and his wife belong to different persons, they are liable to be separated from each other, as well as their children," by sale or the moving away of one of the owners.[52]

Some planters urged in their instructions that slaves engage in religious activity, although they were rarely so insistent on this matter as Russian pomeshchiki. Slaveowners who dealt with this question usually "encouraged" their slaves to attend church on Sunday but did not require such attendance or provide for punishment should slaves refuse to go. Hammond warned that although his slaves were "privileged & encouraged to go to Church on Sundays" religious meetings must not "conflict with the plantation hours." Why southern planters, most of whom were highly religious men and none of whom minded compelling their slaves to behave properly, were so casual on this question is not immediately apparent, but perhaps part of the explanation lies in their acceptance of nineteenth-century American voluntaristic ideas concerning religious behavior: church was something one chose, rather than was compelled, to attend. Perhaps, too, owners had trouble taking seriously the religious aspirations of their slaves; even those who encouraged religious instruction and church attendance frequently commented on what they considered the bizarre theology and religious style of blacks.[53]

Like Russian serfowners, slaveowners required their slaves to have passes in order to travel. Although a few slaves were allowed to seek employment on their own away from home, planters did not deal with this practice in their instructions. Indeed, Barrow strongly denounced the custom of giving "general Pass'es," whereby slaves could go where they wished, remarking that "no practice is more prejudicial to the community, and to the negros themselves." Planters varied in the generosity with which they awarded passes. Giving weekend permits to visit spouses was commonplace, but because most instructions forbade marriage "abroad" the question rarely emerged in them. Georgia planter Alexander Telfair instructed his overseer to give slaves passes to go "anywhere about the neighborhood," whereas J. W. Fowler of Mississippi decreed that since he had a large plantation with "a sufficient number of negroes . . . for society among themselves, they are not to be allowed to go off the plantation merely to seek society." Hammond ordered that no more than six people could leave the plantation at once, except to go to church. But however lenient or strict slaveholders were in awarding passes, all required their slaves to secure such passes—either from themselves, their overseers, or occasionally drivers—before leaving home. Many warned, too, against receiving "strange negroes" on the plantation.[54]

Slaves who transgressed required punishment, and virtually all planters gave their overseers the authority to "correct" malefactors, although not all agreed on what was an offense worthy of punishment. Among the most specific on the subject was Hammond, who listed nine crimes in descending order of seriousness, beginning with flight, absence without permission, stealing, and getting drunk and ending with uncleanliness and neglect of work or tools. Another of-

fense that planters sometimes singled out was fighting or raucous behavior: "If there is any fighting on the Plantation," one warned,
"whip all engaged in it—for no matter what the cause may have been,
all are in the wrong." But most instructions were vague on precisely
what infraction required what punishment, leaving it to the overseer's
discretion to let the punishment fit the crime within broad guidelines.
Rather than spelling out specifics, planters usually preferred to generalize about their approach to justice. Many stressed that it was essential to punish fairly—coolly rather than in anger—to avoid idle
threats, and to make sure that the guilty understood why they were
being chastised. "No person should ever be allowed to break a law
without being punished, or any person punished who has not broken
a well known law," explained South Carolina rice planter P. C. Weston in 1856. "Every person should be made perfectly to understand
what they are punished for, and should be made to perceive that they
are not punished in anger, or through caprice."[55]

Whipping was usually the prescribed method of punishment, but
planters varied considerably in their approach to the subject. Most
allowed their overseers broad discretion concerning the amount of
punishment to be applied in individual cases; indeed, masters seemed
more concerned with setting maximum limits to such punishment
than defining its exact nature, no doubt because there was usually
more danger that overseers would overpunish than underpunish.
Hammond set a maximum of one hundred lashes to be applied to a
slave in a single day but suggested that "in general 15 to 20 lashes
will be a sufficient flogging." Weston required his overseer to secure
his permission before administering more than fifteen lashes, and Telfair set a limit of fifty strokes. Other planters, too, cautioned against
excessive whipping. The influential manual *Affleck's Cotton Plantation and Account Book* suggested that putting troublesome slaves in
stocks was preferable to whipping them but that the most useful way
to promote harmonious relations was "rewarding good behavior." Of
course, antebellum planters were acutely conscious of public opinion,
and one may suppose that those who favored (or practiced) cruel and
unusual punishments would be wary of describing them in writing.
Several, however, did recommend treatment that they considered
more effective—because more unpleasant—than simple whipping.
Charles Manigault wrote the overseer of his Georgia plantation that
he should take any disorderly slave to jail in Savannah "& give him
prison discipline & by all means solitary confinement for 3 weeks,
when he will be glad to get home again." Then, the planter continued,

the refractory slave should be threatened with having his conduct reported to the owner and with being sold south to New Orleans. A small planter advised building a jail on the plantation instead and placing troublemakers in solitary confinement. "Negroes are gregarious," he explained; "they dread solitariness, and to be deprived from the weekly dances and chit-chat. They will work to death rather than be shut up." [56]

Although in many respects planters' instructions stressed the same general themes as did those of Russian pomeshchiki, two distinctive elements of importance can be seen in the American instructions. First, they contained far more material than their Russian counterparts on the care and protection of the slaves. Indeed, looking after the slaves was a subject that assumed considerable significance in most of the instructions. This was true regardless of the date composed, region of the South, or size of plantation. P. C. Weston summarized the sentiment found in many instructions: "The Proprietor, in the first place, wishes the Overseer most distinctly to understand that his first object is to be, under all circumstances, the care and well being of the negroes. The Proprietor is always ready to excuse such errors as may proceed from want of judgment; but he never can or will excuse any cruelty, severity, or want of care toward the negroes." Of course, Russian pomeshchiki, too, lectured stewards against oppressive conduct toward their charges, but such admonitions were usually perfunctory and did not begin to approach the directives of the Americans on this subject in either detail or depth of feeling. [57]

Planters devoted considerable attention in their instructions to the material needs of their slaves. They insisted on the importance of comfortable housing, with one family per house, and clothing, with most masters providing for the distribution of new outfits on a semi-annual basis. But they were especially concerned with the slaves' diet and medical care. The basic fare that they prescribed for working hands was remarkably similar: one peck of corn or meal per week and three to four pounds of meat (usually bacon). Children received smaller quantities. This basic ration was supplemented with various products, depending on the area and time of year, including vegetables, milk, sugar, coffee, and molasses. In addition, most planters assigned their slaves garden patches on which they could raise vegetables, tobacco, and chickens. Regardless of variety, what was most important was that the hands receive enough to eat; "in all cases of doubt," one planter noted, "it should be given in favor of the largest quantity." Masters were understandably concerned about their slaves' health, and most insisted that overseers take complaints of illness seriously, even though they were aware that many slaves shammed illness in order to avoid work. "Every reasonable complaint must be promptly attended to," ordered Hammond, "& with any marked or general symptom of sickness, however trivial, a negro may lie up a day or so at least." The method of caring for the sick varied. Many large planters had plantation hospitals—in charge of slave nurses—to which they consigned the ill, and most, whether or not they had such hospitals, instructed their overseers to send for doctors in all serious cases. Some slaveowners, however, had their overseers practice medicine, with the help of "a good book of Medical instruction," and Hammond, a strong believer in "homoeopathy," specifically barred doctors from his plantation—"there being no Homoeopathist convenient"—preferring to treat slaves himself.[58]

Often planters issued pointed reminders to overseers that their most important task was taking good care of the slaves. As early as 1759, Virginian Richard Corbin instructed his agent that "the care of negroes is the first thing to be recommended," enjoining him to "give me timely notice of their wants that they may be provided with all Necessarys." In the nineteenth century instructions commonly contained injunctions to protect the slaves, treat them "with kindness and consideration," and ensure that they lived in happiness and security. In addition to setting limits on the number of lashes overseers could apply, planters warned against "cruel or abusive" punishment. "Much whipping indicates a bad tempered, or inattentive manager, & will not be allowed," wrote Hammond. Similar admonitions warned against overworking hands, forcing them to work at night, or, if they labored under the task system, assigning excessively burdensome tasks. Emphasizing "the moral obligation of the master to attend to the comfort and happiness of his slaves," three planters argued in an 1846 essay, "Management of Slaves," that "whilst the slave is in theory in the closest bands [sic], in practice he has a friend and protector in his master." Because overseers lacked the planters' interest in the well-being of slaves, it was essential, the trio concluded, that planters keep careful tabs on their employees to make sure that the slaves were not being treated harshly or unfairly.[59]

Clearly, then, American instructions, which were less detailed than the Russian on purely administrative matters, placed a far greater emphasis on the protection, care, and needs of the slaves. This emphasis—especially in the published instructions—may in part have served a cosmetic purpose, designed to assure antebellum critics of slavery as well as slaveholders themselves that the peculiar institution was truly a benevolent system. But care of slaves was stressed in such a broad cross-section of instructions, unpublished as well as published, that it is hard to dismiss it as pure propaganda without arguing that so too were the instructions themselves. Instead, three other factors seem to be responsible for the contrast between American and Russian instructions on this question of protecting the bondsmen's well-being. In part, the contrast reflects the difference between a system in which masters provided the slaves' basic necessities and a serf economy in which peasants fended largely for themselves. There was no need for pomeshchiki to dwell on providing for the serfs' well-being because except in emergencies it was not their role to do so. In part, too, the contrast stemmed from differing perceptions of their functions held by pomeshchiki who were absent and planters who were resident—either in fact or in spirit. Whereas an absentee mentality led many Russian noblemen to care little what occurred on their estates so long as order was maintained and a healthy income produced, most southern slaveowners took a paternalistic interest in the lives of their slaves. Finally, many slaveowners felt that because slaves were black they were unable to manage their lives properly and needed the care and close supervision of their benevolent white masters. It is hard to avoid the conclusion that many of the planters' exhortations to protect their slaves reflected a belief in their innately childish nature.

This is clearly evident in the second major theme stressed in American instructions much more than in the Russian: the dependent nature of the slaves and the need to promote that dependence. Blacks were like children, unable to care for themselves and needing the protection and guidance of their superiors but at the same time constantly trying to test their patience and determination, seeking to escape the very dependence they required. The prudent master, therefore, realized that strict discipline and subordination of the slaves were essential for their own good. As Weston lectured his overseer, although his "first object" was the "care and well being of the negroes," to achieve this "it is absolutely necessary to maintain obedience, order, and discipline." Virginia planter Richard Eppes prescribed five to twenty-five lashes for most slave offenses in his 1858 "Code of Laws" but ordered that slaves who struck their overseer should receive 150 stripes for the first offense and 300 for the second; those who struck their master should receive 500 stripes "administered in five days one hundred a day." If for a moment the slaves were

allowed to escape their position of utter dependence, the whole master-slave relationship would be threatened.[60]

Planters went to great lengths to structure plantation management
so as to maximize this dependence. Take, for example, the question
of food rations. All agreed that slaves must receive a proper diet, but
this goal could be accomplished in various ways. Hammond ordered
food distributed to slaves weekly, explaining that because "Negroes
are improvident with a longer interval between allowances many will
consume, waste or barter their provisions before it closes." Others
considered even a weekly interval too long; as one slaveowner noted,
"some will steal the meat from others" and, like children, many
would eat their rations all at once. His solution was to dole out provisions daily, having a plantation cook prepare everyone's meals to
make sure that they were cooked properly. Although not all planters
used cooks to prepare slave meals, many agreed that such a system
was preferable to allowing families to cook on their own. As one
author explained in an essay entitled "The Health of Negroes," although the slaves "prefer to cook for themselves . . . there are always
some negroes on every place who are too careless and indolent to
cook their food in a proper manner." Of course, Russian pomeshchiki, too, insisted that their serfs were childlike and irresponsible,
but it would not have occurred to them to suggest that their peasants
were incapable of preparing their own food.[61]

A similar concern over the possible promotion of excessive independence led some slaveowners to reject the traditional practice of
giving slaves garden patches. A Mississippi planter explained that instead of providing such plots he would give each slave five dollars for
Christmas "and send them to the county town under the charge of
the overseer or driver, to spend their money." The advantage of this
system was that "the negroes are prevented from acquiring habits of
trading in farm produce, which invariably leads to stealing, followed
by whipping, trouble to the master, and discontent on the part of the
slave." Other masters, such as Bennet H. Barrow and Robert Collins,
followed a similar policy, giving their slaves Christmas money and
tobacco rather than letting them sell goods they raised in order to
prevent their acquiring "a spirit of trafficking." Some who allowed
slaves to have garden plots insisted that these be limited to providing
items for home consumption, not for sale.[62]

The problem, however, was more general than that of the proper
method of feeding slaves or whether they should be permitted to sell
the products that they raised: the ultimate goal was keeping slaves in

a state of complete dependence on their masters. Trading and cooking for oneself were not so much evils in themselves as opportunities for slaves to do things on their own, which were harmful, planters believed, to everyone concerned. Blacks were so irresponsible that they were not capable of doing anything without the proper direction. If a master failed to enforce curfew regulations, the "thoughtless" slaves would take advantage of his leniency and "sit up late at night." That was why strict discipline was necessary—as it was for children—for their own good. Barrow succinctly summed up the rationale for this paternalism in his "Rules": "You must," he enjoined, make the slave "as comfortable at Home as possible, affording him What is essentially necessary for his happiness—you must provide for him Your self and by that means creat in him a habit of perfect dependence on you." [63]

Here, too, is evident the resident mentality of the American planter, which contrasted so sharply with that of the Russian pomeshchik. The slaveowner was essential for the proper running of his estate; his slaves were dependent on him and must be kept so in virtually all respects. He could not, like his Russian counterpart, be concerned solely, or even primarily, with the financial rewards to be drawn from his plantation. As Barrow pointed out, "if a master exhibits no extraordinary interest in the proceedings on his plantation, it is hardly to be expected that any other feelings but apathy, and perfect indifference could exist with his negroes." The American instructions were designed to deal with plantations that constituted a planters' world, whereas the Russian ones were meant to impose some order on and extract money from a largely peasant world. [64]

* * *

PLANTERS AND POMESHCHIKI were rarely happy with the way their intermediaries managed their holdings. Too many things could go wrong, and overseers and stewards had to walk an impossibly thin line to avoid displeasing their superiors. If they applied regulations too strictly, the bondsmen complained of oppression; if they were excessively lax, serfs and slaves were likely to work poorly and manifest a generally disorderly spirit. It is thus no surprise that landowners usually found that their lieutenants were either too severe or too lenient and tended to be lazy, drunk, and irresponsible.

Absentee Russian lords were often dismayed when they or their representatives visited their estates or learned about actual conditions there. When Count P. I. Panin visited one of the estates belonging to his relative Princess Kurakina, he was shocked to find that "many of the young servants have fallen into drunkenness, self-willedness, ignorance, and rudeness," not just among themselves "but even to their mistress and the young princes," and that they thought nothing of leaving the seigneurial house on their own whenever they wished. The count warned that if such disorder and disrespect continued, the offenders "will be publicly whipped and transported to Siberian resettlement" and that for any theft the whole staff would be held accountable and whipped. An equally unhappy picture emerged from a report to Countess S. Bobrinskaia made by her head manager after visiting her estate in Simbirsk province in 1843. He found the estate in disorder, agricultural production hopelessly inefficient, and the administration at fault. "The steward has not the slightest moral influence on the peasants," he noted. "They do not respect him. The starosta and peasant representatives do not dare to know, and the steward does not want to know, what occurs on the estate, and affairs take their own course without a chief." Even more frustrating was the experience of Artemii Volynskii, who lived in St. Petersburg and was unable to secure from his stewards even basic information about his villages, such as how many serfs they contained. Although he sent forms for the stewards to fill out, he complained that these forms were never returned to him.[65]

Dissatisfaction with stewards was endemic among Russian landowners and those associated with them. Foreign travelers, who came in contact mainly with the upper ranks of society and therefore tended to see things through their eyes, were often sharply critical. Englishman Robert Lyall considered stewards "villains and robbers" who "seldom fail to enrich themselves" and noted the consequent existence of the adage "*Buy not a village, but buy a steward for yourself.*" Pomeshchiki, too, distrusted the performance and often the motives of their agents and were constantly checking up on them, corresponding with them, complaining to them, and threatening them. "Write to me what is going on," Bezobrazov would urge his stewards plaintively; upon finding out, he was often sorry he had asked. He consequently placed little trust in them. When he confronted one with a peasant's complaint that he drank too much and beat the serfs, the steward denied the accusation, but Bezobrazov chose to believe the peasant and severely reproached the steward. Even his four top stewards did not escape his wrath and received frequent beatings for dereliction of duty. Morozov's stewards, too, were in constant fear of beatings, and the nobleman did not hesitate to bypass his normal administrative hierarchy when he thought such punishment necessary. When seventy fish, sent to Moscow in a barrel by one of his stewards in Riazan district, arrived at Morozov's residence, forty of them were dead and most of the rest were too small to suit the nobleman's taste. He immediately wrote the local starosta to beat the steward mercilessly in front of the assembled serfs and threatened the starosta with a beating should he disobey the order. Morozov also had his stewards check up on each other and sometimes instructed one to punish another. In one instance he sent a steward to investigate charges that another had stolen some money and a bear from a traveling peasant, had pilfered grain from the seigneurial granary, and was generally uncooperative; when Morozov received a report corroborating some of the charges he ordered the miscreant beaten with sticks and replaced as steward.[66]

The slightest misfortune all too often seemed to pomeshchiki the consequence of malfeasance or conspiracy. In 1825 Count L. I. Salogubov's manager and steward in Riazan province reported that a serf had made a present to him of a grouse; the delighted count directed that the serf be given a fifty-kopek reward and that the bird be turned over to the glacier for later use. A week later the count ordered the bird prepared for the following day's dinner, but when the head chef went to fetch the grouse he found that it gave forth a "stinking odor" and was "partially damaged by mice." The next day the steward and manager reported the discovery to Salogubov, who replied, "I suspect abuse," and ordered an investigation of all those involved in the incident. Such distrust of stewards was clearly reflected in nineteenth-century literature. In Ivan Turgenev's masterful *Sportsman's Notebook,* the narrator tells of visiting an estate in Orel province which the steward treats "like his own property. The peasants are all around in his debt, they work for him as if they were his laborers." Of course, one can imagine that members of a nobleman's estate administration—who were constantly lectured, scolded, threatened, and punished—found the relationship at least as trying as their master did. "Working for a gentleman is dreadful!" the head clerk of an estate tells the narrator. "Nothing's ever right; this is badly done, that's all wrong."[67]

Southern planters, too, were constantly finding fault with their overseers, and many became convinced that overseers as a class were worthless. Landon Carter, noting their "disposition to untruth," speculated that they caught the trait from the slaves they supervised and declared that they simply could not be trusted. One half-century later

Barrow concurred that overseers were "a perfect nuisance," adding "I hope the time will come When every Overseer in the country will be compelled to addopt some other mode of making a living." Thousands of other slaveowners would have had little trouble agreeing that it was next to impossible to find a good, reliable overseer.[68]

The vagaries inherent in the master-overseer relationship are well illustrated by the correspondence between George Noble Jones and the overseers of his two adjacent plantations near Tallahassee, Florida. In October 1854 D. N. Moxley, the new overseer of El Destino plantation, wrote Jones expressing surprise when several slaves fled the plantation and sought refuge in the Tallahassee jail. "I have bin with Negroes for Somtime, and I never have knowne nor heard tell of thar running away to be put in Jail befor," he puzzled. One week later John Evans, long-time overseer of the neighboring Chemonie plantation, reported to his employer concerning Moxley. He described the newcomer as generally quite competent but found one shortcoming in his treatment of the slaves: "when he Flogs he puts it on in two Large doses. I think Moderate Flogings the best." Evans added that Moxley was upset and was threatening to quit but "I told him not to get disheartened for he would find you to be the Right kind of a man." Moxley himself expressed his anguish to Jones, who had evidently heard tales of the overseer's excessive severity from a Tallahassee lawyer, but then apologized for his "error"; the planter replied that he would accept the apology. Shortly thereafter the two overseers discussed the severity of whipping and came to an agreement that moderate chastisement was indeed preferable. Meanwhile Jones, bothered by complaints against Moxley, initiated his own investigation and concluded that the overseer was not guilty of excessive severity. "It has always been a source of great anxiety to me to protect my negroes from unnecessary punishment," he assured the Tallahassee lawyer who had complained. "I pay the highest wages in hopes of obtaining good overseers."[69]

Jones's overseer troubles, however, were not over. No sooner was the Moxley incident settled than the other overseer, Evans, announced that he was quitting. He denounced Jones for objecting when he and his new wife entertained friends and complained that "your Negroes behave badly behind my back and then Run to you and you appear to beleave what they say." Evans and his wife moved off the plantation, Jones hired a new overseer, and the matter appeared to be terminated. Half a year later, however, Evans's replacement died, and Evans, now sorry he had acted so rashly, wrote his former employer asking to have his old job back. Although Jones replied tersely, "I much regret that I can not employ you," the tenacious Evans informed Jones, who was conveniently vacationing in Switzerland and thus unable to act decisively, that he had returned to Chemonie "by the request of Mr. Moxley" and would very much like to oversee the following year. Evidently his persistence paid off, for two years later Evans was once again serving as Jones's overseer.[70]

Like Russian noblemen, countless southern planters were distressed by what they found when they checked up on overseers. When Virginian William Byrd visited his Falling Creek holding in 1709 he found the overseer, "Mr. G-r-l," drunk, "and the business not in so good order as I expected. I scolded at Mr. G-r-l till he cried," Byrd recorded in his diary, "and then was peevish." Later the same year he refused to pay another overseer who had "left everything in a sad condition." When Mississippi planter John C. Burruss returned home after an absence in 1850, he was shocked to find "my business in great disorder and much neglect" and the overseer badly wounded after engaging in a "drunken spree." "I discharged him at once," Burruss noted.[71]

Owners took various measures to remedy the situation. One of the most common in both Russia and the United States was to rely on the bondsmen as a source of information concerning estate managers' behavior. There were exceptions; Count Stroganov, for example, specifically forbade his serfs from coming to Moscow to present him with petitions, insisting instead that they go through channels and warning that those who violated his order "will be cruelly punished." Most pomeshchiki, however, saw peasant petitions as a useful way of gathering information and checking up on their stewards, about whom they were often ready to believe the worst in any case. Far more common than Stroganov's prohibition was Count Rumiantsev's encouragement of his serfs to report "to me personally without any fear" and his pledge that "for good will to me I promise a valuable reward." Many planters, too, actively encouraged slaves to inform on their overseers, a practice the latter naturally considered disruptive of plantation order and discipline. "My negroes are permitted to come to me with their complaints and grievances and in no instance shall they be punished for doing so," wrote one planter in his instruction. "On examination, should I find they have been cruelly treated, it shall be considered a good and sufficient cause for the immediate discharge of the Overseer." Hammond relied on his head driver to be "a confidential servant & . . . guard against any excuses or omissions of the Overseer."[72]

Planters continually sought to replace unsatisfactory overseers with diligent ones but were usually disappointed. In 1857 Georgia planter Louis Manigault became dissatisfied with his overseer for "placing himself on a par with the Negroes" and "breaking down long established discipline." After discharging the unsatisfactory overseer, he hired a new one for 1858, whom he enthusiastically described as "very highly recommended . . . & highly spoken of as a good planter and man of character." A year later, however, Manigault's hopes had been dashed. Upon returning from Europe he found that "there has been gross neglect & great want of attention on the part of the Overseer . . . For days [he] did not visit the plantation, neglecting all things." Manigault proceeded to fire him and find a replacement, "an Overseer of high rank & standing" who he optimistically predicted would manage much better.[73]

A similar pattern developed on numerous plantations: overseers who at first seemed perfect for the job soon proved gravely deficient and were dismissed, and the cycle would begin again. Although occasionally a planter was able to find an overseer he stuck with for years, overseers in general exhibited an impressive turnover rate. Between 1778 and 1806, for example, Thomas Jefferson employed thirteen men in succession as overseers at Monticello before finally hitting upon one whom he kept for the next sixteen years. Between 1849 and 1855 Alabama planter Hugh Davis went through eight overseers until, despairing of ever finding a satisfactory one, he determined to do without any; between 1857 and 1861 he employed a succession of eight more.[74]

In Russia an increasing number of landowners took part in a movement to secure professionally qualified stewards—who were free men and often foreigners, especially Germans—to put their estates in order. The idea of training professional stewards was broached as early as 1767 in an essay by Timofei Von Klingshtet. After pointing out that many pomeshchiki found it impossible to locate good stewards, he considered the utility of employing foreigners but concluded that because they were usually unfamiliar with local conditions they did more harm than good. His solution was to take youths between the ages of fifteen and twenty and send them to Latvia, where agriculture was more rationally organized than in Russia, for seven years of training after which they would be ready to upgrade the efficiency of Russian estate management. Interest in the training of a professional class of stewards spread in the nineteenth century. One author, writing in an agricultural paper in 1835, argued that long-term service was the key to the steward problem, suggesting that stewards' salaries be increased 10 percent each year so that they would have an incentive to stay with the same employer for a long time. Most noblemen, however, seemed to assume that hiring a foreigner guaranteed securing professional service, and during the last decades of serfdom it became fashionable to acquire stewards from Germany, the Baltic provinces, and occasionally England. Evidently these stewards did not always prove satisfactory to pomeshchiki either—one obvious disadvantage was that they could not be disciplined in the same manner that peasant stewards could—because there continued to be a brisk turnover in their employment, and the agricultural press regularly ran advertisements by foreigners boasting of their expertise and offering themselves for hire. A typical notice by a man named G. L. Mentsel described himself as a "village master from abroad, having a good theoretical and practical understanding of all branches of agriculture and having already managed for ten years several big estates in Podolia province"; a year-and-a-half later, still at the same address and this time calling himself "a German master thoroughly understanding agriculture," he was still seeking employment.[75]

The effort to procure professional stewards was part of a larger concern, manifested from the last third of the eighteenth century and accentuated in the first half of the nineteenth, with the proper running of landed estates. The publication of model instructions designed to inform noblemen of the most advanced methods of estate management was one sign of this concern, as was the organization by a group of noble intellectuals in 1765 of the Free Economic Society for the Encouragement in Russia of Agriculture and Household Management. During the first half of the nineteenth century various reform measures designed to rationalize agriculture through the application of "scientific" principles attracted increasing attention. In the 1830s two brothers from Saratov province tried to organize a "Society for the Improvement of Private Agriculture" that would act as a shareholders' corporation, amassing ten million rubles capital and running the estates of members, most of whom were pomeshchiki owning 500 or more souls. As one of the society's founders pointed out, although "agriculture demands the application of science ... the Russian nobleman, occupied exclusively in service, has neither the time nor the means to take the necessary care for the improvement of his property." Although the society never got off the ground, interest in more efficient organization of estates remained strong among a small minority of enlightened owners. The agricultural press reviewed a steady stream of booklets on how to manage estates and ran frequent

articles detailing the improved management of once poorly run establishments. The formula for such improvements was predictable: in
addition to purely technical innovations, such as better use of fertil-
izer, what was required was stricter supervision of the serfs, including
"a paternal guardianship" of their "moral and agricultural condition" so they would not only feel that "[our] lord is strict, so we have
order" but actually "from their souls love the order of their master."
In short, the suggestions were for more of the same.[76]

It is hardly surprising, then, that despite the upsurge of interest in
scientific estate management most pomeshchiki remained convinced
that their serfs and their stewards were responsible for whatever was
wrong with their estates. Even with professional stewards, the peasants remained lazy and uncooperative, and the stewards themselves
usually proved disappointing. The basic problem, of course, lay not
with the individuals involved but with the system as a whole. The
tasks of a steward—to keep order on an estate, produce a healthy
income for his employer, keep the peasants moderately prosperous,
administer justice strictly but fairly, maintain the goodwill and respect
of both serfs and nobleman—were virtually impossible to fulfill. Pomeshchiki, meanwhile, were caught between two incompatible impulses. On the one hand was their absentee mentality: not only were
they often forced to be away from their estates because of service or
ownership of multiple holdings, but there was a strong temptation to
leave all the harrowing worries of estate management to stewards,
who could be held strictly accountable should they fail to perform
properly. Estate management was a chore. On the other hand, noblemen wanted everything to be perfect and generally felt that they
themselves could do a much better job than their hapless administrators. Most pomeshchiki were unable or unwilling to live on their estates, but they were also unable or unwilling to leave those estates
entirely alone.

Some noblemen recognized the harmful impact of absenteeism. As
early as 1767 Count Roman Vorontsov lamented that when noblemen lived in Moscow or St. Petersburg they were obliged to leave
their estates with stewards who lacked a nobleman's sense of magnanimity and justice and often dealt unfairly with peasants. Nineteenth-century thinkers were equally concerned about the landowners' absence from their estates. One author, noting that "not many
Russian pomeshchiki live in their villages," asked, "who then runs
their vast estates?" and concluded that it was the peasants themselves.
"Who can be surprised, then," he added, "that many estates of absen-

tees are in such disorderly condition!" But such critics had no solution to the problem except to call for stricter supervision of serfs and the hiring of better stewards. In the same article in which he blamed stewards for dealing too harshly with serfs, Count Vorontsov argued that peasant "idlers" posed an increasing burden to pomeshchiki and had to be compelled to work harder. Pomeshchiki, forced to depend on intermediaries placed in an impossible situation, continued to blame inept and ill-intentioned individuals for their troubles rather than the system that produced them.[77]

Although overseers also posed a problem for southern planters, the problem was ultimately far less serious than was that of stewards for Russian pomeshchiki. The administrative tasks of overseers were less awesome than those faced by stewards; because the management hierarchy was simpler, the number of slaves to be supervised smaller, and communication with the master easier, there were fewer chances for things to go wrong. Furthermore, troubles with overseers affected only a small minority of slaveowners, because only a small minority used overseers in the first place. Many of those who did have overseers were still present on the plantations, able to make sure that operations progressed smoothly. The resident nature of the American planter class thus alleviated many of the worst problems associated with estate management.[78]

Indeed, there was a widespread tendency among planters to dispense with overseers altogether; as one slaveowner who did without them explained, "They are a perfect nuisance . . . I make better crops than those who employ them." Even among large planters their use was far from universal. According to calculations by Robert W. Fogel and Stanley L. Engerman, only one-quarter of all plantations with more than fifty slaves and one-third of those with more than one hundred slaves had hired white overseers during the late antebellum period. Even assuming that these figures represent underestimations—some overseers supervised more than one plantation, and others, as sons of owners, were not hired—it is clear that many substantial planters considered overseers more trouble than they were worth. "Never have an Overseer . . ." advised Barrow. "Never allow another man to talk to your negros."[79]

Doing without a white overseer on a large plantation often necessitated elevating the administrative authority of one or more black slaves, most often drivers. Some drivers, in the absence of their owners, were for all practical purposes overseers, as on the rice estates of the South Carolina and Georgia lowlands, although the term *overseer* was generally reserved for whites because it seemed to confer more dignity on blacks than was thought fitting. When North Carolina planter William S. Pettigrew took his annual summer vacation in Virginia during the 1850s, he left his adjacent estates in charge of two slaves, Moses and Henry, who, because they were illiterate, dictated weekly reports to their owner through a neighboring white farmer. John H. Cocke frequently left his Alabama plantation in the care of his literate slave Skipworth, who made periodic written reports to his owner during the 1840s and 1850s. "i have worked the people but not out of reason—and i have whiped none without a cause," he informed his master, proceeding to list the names of nine slaves whom he had found necessary to punish, together with "thir faults," all of which involved inattentive labor.[80]

Although in most states it was against the law in antebellum years to leave plantations untended by whites, these laws were enforced only sporadically, depending on the whim of individual judges as well as the state of public opinion. In 1835 a South Carolina planter whose overseer visited his plantation twice daily was convicted of violating an 1819 act requiring a white man to be in actual residence, but two decades later a Louisiana court ruled that an 1814 law requiring a white overseer for every thirty slaves "did not create an indictable offense" and dismissed charges against a planter accused of violating the act. Sometimes technicalities enabled slaveowners to escape penalties for not supervising their slaves carefully enough: the conviction of a Louisiana man for failing to have a white overseer spend the night on a farm separated by a forty-acre lot from his main holding was reversed on appeal because, the court ruled, "his two tracts . . . are cultivated as *one plantation.*" But the following year an Alabama court refused to accept an almost identical argument. The great majority of instances involving black overseers never reached court, however, and it remained a common practice for masters to entrust favored slaves with more authority than the law—or most southern whites—thought proper.[81]

Most often, however, planters who did without white overseers remained on their plantations and supervised operations themselves. Slave drivers and "overseers" on such estates assumed greater responsibility than they would have if white overseers had been present, but they usually did not receive the full authority of a white manager. In effect, such slaves shared with their owners the overseer's duties, but the ultimate responsibility rested with the planter who, in the absence of the overseer, became even more caught up in plantation administration. The elimination of a white overseer thus often represented an increase, not a decrease, in supervision of slaves, because the slaveowner himself took personal control of plantation operations. It was on these estates that the resident mentality of American planters achieved its fullest expression.

Alabama planter Hugh Davis, who experienced continual trouble with overseers on his River Bend plantation, decided in 1855 to dispense with them. He turned instead to two of his slaves, Wash, a carpenter and plow gang driver whom he made head driver, and Young Sol, a carriage driver and blacksmith who became his assistant. Davis himself remained in full authority, however, directing plantation affairs on a day-to-day basis. Bennet H. Barrow, who after 1838 also managed without an overseer, had a similar dispensation. Alfred, whom the planter praised as an "uncom-on good driver," was the head slave, but his powers were strictly limited—he did not, for example, have the right to punish other slaves—and Barrow himself served as overseer, insisting that it was a master's responsibility to manage his plantation personally. "It is wrong to allow a driver to use any authority . . ." he noted, for "negros are not Capable of self government." More than half a century earlier Landon Carter, who very carefully supervised his agricultural operations and despaired of finding honest and efficient white overseers—although he sometimes used them—relied on an old slave, Jack Lubbar, for various supervisory functions. Lubbar's duties, however, were limited, and Carter himself remained in full charge of his estates, keeping a tight rein on slaves and overseers alike. He railed at Lubbar as a "most lazy as well as stupid old fellow," but Carter was something of a misanthrope who railed at everyone, white and black, including members of his own family. His true feelings toward his black overseer were revealed when Lubbar was dying, years after he had been retired from all duties: "Farewell to as honest a human creature as could live," wrote Carter in his diary.[82]

The resident nature and mentality of the American slaveowning class, together with the small size of most holdings, thus obviated the most pressing problems connected with the management of slave labor. If on large plantations the number of slaves was rarely sufficient to create major administrative problems or to necessitate a substantial administrative hierarchy, among the great majority of small slaveowners there was little division of labor and no need for any management—white or black—aside from the owner himself. "I have no overseer, and do not manage so scientifically as those who are able to

lay down rules," asserted one such farmer, who admitted that his operations would be more efficient if he had enough slaves to differen-
tiate their tasks; "yet I endeavor to manage so that myself, family and
negroes take pleasure and delight in our relations." Such an expression typified the attitude of a large majority of southern slaveowners,
who felt at home—as most Russian noblemen did not—running their
farms and plantations.[83]

*   *   *

THERE WERE, THEN, both important similarities and differences in
the slaveowning experiences of the masters in Russia and the United
States South. The similarities stemmed from the nature of forced labor itself. American slaveowners and Russian serfowners lived primarily off the toil of their bondsmen and strove to maximize income
both by extension of their operations—acquisition of more land and
laborers, increase of area under cultivation—and by extracting the
maximum possible surplus from their bondsmen through strict control of their labor (and in Russia through the exaction of obrok payments). In both countries the owners sought to regulate the lives of
their charges in order to secure order, efficiency, and domestic tranquility. But in both countries the masters thought of themselves as
more than mere exploiters of human property: they were also guardians of public morality and protectors of the weak and ignorant who
needed the firm guidance they received not only to be productive laborers but also to be happy human beings. The masters knew, of
course, that bondage served their interests and that their well-being
depended on their slaves and serfs, but they also believed that bondage served the interests of society at large, including the bondsmen,
whose well-being depended on them. Such a view was self-serving,
but slaveowners and serfowners have hardly been unique in convincing themselves that what was in their own interest was in the broader
social interest as well.

The differences, which stemmed from specific historical conditions
in Russia and the United States, were equally great. Russian holdings
were large, pomeshchiki depended on a complex administrative hierarchy to manage them, and they tended toward absenteeism—both
in mentality and in fact. American holdings were comparatively
small, they required only minimal administrative organization, and
slaveowners were usually resident masters—both in mentality and in
fact. The American slaveowner was at home on his farm or plantation, whereas the Russian pomeshchik often felt like a visitor and

longed for the "society" of Moscow, St. Petersburg, or a provincial capital. The American farm or plantation was the slaveowner's world, but the Russian estate was the peasant's.

I have already explored several of the reasons for this contrast between Russian absenteeism and American residentialism. The large size and multiple nature of holdings in Russia encouraged the use of administrative bureaucracies. The high ratio of peasants to noblemen and the low ratio of blacks to whites meant that whereas Russian noblemen lived in a largely peasant environment in a numerical sense, American whites did not live in a correspondingly black environment. And the service obligations of noblemen led most to think of themselves not primarily as serfowners or managers of estates but as careerists who retired late in life to live on one of their holdings.

Other factors in the contrast relate to the two basic distinctions between Russian serfdom and American slavery outlined in the introduction. The serfs, unlike the slaves, were not outsiders deposited against their will in an alien environment, but Russians just as much as their owners. Although Africans and their descendants adjusted to America, they remained to most whites outsiders in a white America. Russian peasants, by way of contrast, "belonged" in their villages; their ancestors had usually lived there for generations, and they felt a strong sense of continuity. It was the pomeshchik who was often a stranger to his estate; his ancestors were not likely to have owned it as long as the peasants' ancestors had lived there, and he probably owned other holdings to which he was equally attached.

The political systems of the two countries accentuated this contrast in the degree of local attachments felt by the masters. In America these attachments were from an early date reinforced by the substantial degree of political power held by property-owning citizens on a local level. In the seventeenth century white colonists—at least those wealthy enough to meet the relatively low property requirements—were already electing delegates to their colonial legislatures to represent their interests and pass their colonies' laws; by the middle of the eighteenth century gentlemen in the southern colonies formed what amounted to a self-governing elite. Naturally, they associated their interests with those of the colony or county in question and came to feel a strong sense of attachment to both, a feeling that continued to flourish under the decentralized political system institutionalized by the United States Constitution. In the antebellum period, as in the colonial, southern whites saw themselves as citizens of North Carolina and Virginia, and later of Alabama and Mississippi, and saw the institutions of those states—and the particular counties in which they lived—as their own. Indeed, the South's minority status in an era of increasing sectional consciousness led southern politicians to emphasize all the more the importance of state and local power vis-à-vis the federal government. In short, southern slaveholders had a resident mentality when it came to politics too.[84]

Such sentiment was largely lacking among Russian pomeshchiki. The existence of numerous scattered holdings, which had its origin in the pomest'e system of the late fifteenth and sixteenth centuries, together with the service obligation that continued to prevail, made it difficult for noblemen to develop the kind of attachment to place that was common not just in the United States but also among western European aristocracies. A French or English nobleman had a local base; he was a duc d'Orleans or an earl of Nottingham. A Russian nobleman, however, was simply a nobleman, who might live in Moscow, St. Petersburg, or elsewhere and have holdings in several provinces. Local political attachments were correspondingly weak. A governor of a particular province—appointed by the tsar rather than elected by the people of the province—was not usually "from" the province at all; he served a term in much the same way that an ambassador serves a stint in a foreign country. He did not associate his interests with those of that province any more than those of another—indeed, he was likely some day to be stationed in another—and need not hold any property in it. Although the provincial reforms introduced by Catherine II in 1775 set up a perfunctory system of provincial and district "self-rule" among noblemen, noble assemblies never assumed the importance or the loyalties of their members that the empress hoped they would, for the good reason that everyone knew real power lay in St. Petersburg. The centralized political system thus strongly reinforced the pomeshchiki's absentee orientation.[85]

The role of race in contributing to the contrast is more problematic. Certainly, the existence of a racial distinction between master and slave was important in bringing southern whites to look on their slaves as outsiders, and to this extent it strengthened the notion that it was the slaves who lived in the masters' world and not vice versa. The racial component also appears to have contributed to the paternalistic feeling of many antebellum planters that their slaves needed care and protection, which it was their Christian duty to provide. Because "the Negroes are in a degraded state" and "living in manifold and gross sins," explained South Carolina missionary slaveholder Charles C. Jones, it was the obligation of slaveholders to upgrade them, offering moral and religious instruction. "We cannot disregard this obligation thus *divinely imposed*, without forfeiting our humanity, our gratitude, our consistency, and our claim to the spirit of christianity itself." Blacks' very racial inferiority demanded a concerned benevolence on the part of slaveowners. Yet one must be careful in accepting at face value the racially inspired motives of southern humanitarians. Russian noblemen were also convinced of the inherent inferiority of their serfs, and pomeshchiki were at least as vigilant as their American counterparts in insisting on the proper religious behavior of their peasants. Furthermore, in other countries where whites enslaved blacks—such as the Caribbean islands—race did not mitigate either the strongly absentee mentality held by most planters or the harshly utilitarian treatment meted out to their slaves. If race played a part in fomenting paternalistic ideals among American slaveholders, this was because of the existence of a particular set of racial attitudes among white Americans—attitudes not always shared by white slaveholders elsewhere—rather than because of the existence of racial distinction per se.[86]

A final factor of significance in explaining the contrast in mentality of American and Russian masters was the difference in the political economy of the two systems of bondage. Because there was a peasant as well as a seigneurial economy in Russia, with serfs providing for their own upkeep, it was possible for a pomeshchik—especially if his serfs were on obrok—to pay virtually no attention to them aside from enforcing the collection of rent. He could be essentially a rentier, living off the income they provided without concerning himself with their daily lives; he performed no necessary function on his estate and could be an absentee lord without abandoning his responsibility to his serfs. Such was not the case with the American slaveowner, who fed, housed, and clothed his slaves. It was part of his role to take care of his slaves' material needs, and if he failed to pay proper regard to them he was not, in fact, fulfilling his social responsibility. The relative independence enjoyed by many serfs thus encouraged an absentee mentality among their owners, while the dependence of the slaves required the attention of theirs.

A number of concrete historical conditions thus combined to produce significantly divergent attitudes toward their bondsmen among American slaveowners and Russian serfowners. Some of these conditions were demographic, as in the ratio of bondsmen to masters and the size of holdings; some were broadly social, as in the degree to which the bondsmen were outsiders in society at large; others were political, involving the amount of local power exercised by planters and pomeshchiki; still others stemmed from differences in the political economy of slavery and serfdom. The effect of all these was to produce a Russian master class that looked to their estates primarily for the income they generated, and a southern master class that, although not negligent of the financial benefits their holdings produced, regarded slaveholding as a way of life with nonpecuniary rewards of its own. This contrast in mentality had important implications for the treatment afforded the slaves and serfs, which is the main subject of the next chapter.

2

Planters, Pomeshchiki, and Paternalism

FOR SEVERAL REASONS it is a difficult task to generalize about the treatment the bondsmen actually received from their owners, and considerable confusion has characterized the efforts of historians to reach conclusions on this question. Some have depicted slavery in the United States South as the cruelest, most degrading form of servitude; others have more recently seen it as relatively lenient in comparison to the slave regimes of Brazil and the West Indies; and still others have stressed the high level of material comfort enjoyed by most American slaves. Ideological uniformity has rendered Soviet historians less willing to disagree over the basic character of serfdom—none questions its cruelly exploitative nature—but travelers to Russia in the eighteenth and nineteenth centuries differed widely in their evaluations of how masters treated their peasants, and current historians disagree sharply concerning the serfs' standard of living. Thus, although modern historians are united in condemning slavery and serfdom as brutal relics of the past, they have been unable to agree on many of the essential characteristics of the institutions.[1]

As Eugene D. Genovese has pointed out, one cause of this diversity of interpretation has been confusion concerning the concept of *treatment.* By *treatment of slaves,* he suggests, historians have meant three very different things: "day-to-day living conditions," including material well-being and conditions of labor; "conditions of life," or the quality of the bondsmen's family, religious, and cultural existence; and "access to freedom and citizenship." Because slaves in a given country might enjoy mild treatment according to one of these meanings while suffering severe treatment according to the others, it is necessary to define carefully what one is discussing before reaching conclusions concerning their condition. In this chapter I will deal with the bondsmen's physical treatment and material well-being, deferring until later the character of their internal lives as well as their access to freedom which, as Genovese points out, bears "no organic connection" to their condition under bondage.[2]

Another distinction must be made if confusion about *treatment* is to be avoided: that between those elements of the bondsmen's condition resulting from their bondage itself and those incidental to it. For example, hunger might be the consequence of crop failure and a poor diet generally prevailing in a region, or it might be the consequence of niggardliness on the part of a master in the face of agricultural plenty. Of course, to the slave hunger was hunger in either case, but one's evaluation of an owner who provided insufficient food in time of plenty must surely be different from that of an owner whose slaves suffered from prevailing conditions along with everyone else. Similarly, a high mortality rate can properly be regarded as one index of bad conditions, but it makes a difference for our appraisal of a system of bondage whether this high mortality rate stemmed from conditions imposed by owners—such as overwork—or from conditions existing in society at large, such as low level of medical knowledge. Neither good nor bad material conditions necessarily tell us much about the nature of a slave regime; if the slaves of a "poor" owner lived less well than those of a rich one, it was not necessarily because the poor owner was less solicitous of their welfare than the rich.

A final complication stems from the variability of slavery and serfdom. Some variations resulted from differentiation among the bondsmen themselves: the experiences of a house servant or blacksmith were likely to be quite different from those of a field laborer, and—especially in Russia—a significant amount of economic stratification distinguished the bondsmen's lives (see Chapter 6). Slaves and serfs were engaged in a wide variety of activities and hence experienced a wide range of slaveries and serfdoms. Other variations were consequences of differing characteristics of the owners and their surroundings. The life of a bondsman on a holding with only five or ten others was usually very different from that of one on an estate of two hundred; similarly, life on a cotton plantation in Alabama was likely to be different from that on a tobacco farm in Virginia, as was serfdom in the fertile, newly colonized lands of "New Russia" from that in the barren reaches of the far north. The degree of market orientation substantially influenced the treatment of the bondsmen. So did the system of estate management: serfs on obrok lived different lives from those on barshchina, and slaves who worked under overseers had experiences that were often dissimilar from those who labored under the task system or next to their owners. There were also changes over time in the treatment of slaves and serfs. Finally, one must take account of the whim and character of the owners, who ranged from sadists and psychopaths to gentle humanitarians.

Because of such variations, it is easy to find at least some evidence to support virtually any generalization one wants to make about slavery and serfdom, and one is tempted to assert that the only conclusion about bondage that makes any sense is an assertion of its diversity. This would be unsatisfactory, however; it is the task of the historian to weigh and make sense of conflicting evidence, to generalize on the basis of admittedly only partial information, to impose pattern upon chaos. In this chapter I shall try to make sensible generalizations about dominant trends in the treatment of the slaves and serfs, keeping in mind the diversity that existed and comparing treatment in the two countries along the way.

It is important to begin with the assertion of an obvious truth that is too easily obscured by arguments about specifics: the inherent injustice of slavery and serfdom as systems of labor. Two basic ingredients of this injustice inhered in bondage no matter what the specific attributes of the owners and their relations with their bondsmen: (1) the exploitation of labor, or appropriation by the owners of the surplus created by the bondsmen, and (2) the compulsion, or restriction of freedom, necessary to achieve this exploitation. Because these attributes inhered in bondage itself, the benevolence of individual owners could not make slavery and serfdom any less unjust as systems of labor. In this sense there could be no such thing as a "good" master. Such benevolence could, however, make the lives of the slaves and serfs less unpleasant, for there *were* good men and women who were masters.

*　　*　　*

IT IS APPROPRIATE to begin with the bondsmen's work, for slavery and serfdom remained, most fundamentally, systems of labor exploitation. Work constituted the primary experience of the slaves and serfs, as it did for most of humanity. The nature of their work and work relations helped to define the character of much of their lives.

During optimal conditions, as their instructions indicated, slaveowners expected their hands to work from dawn to dusk, with brief breaks for meals and often, during the summer, an afternoon siesta. Convinced that blacks were naturally lazy and would shirk their labor duties at every opportunity, slaveowners devoted a great deal of their attention—whether personally or through overseers and drivers—to making sure that their slaves worked diligently. For their part, ex-slaves often recalled backbreaking work as a central feature of their lives. This was especially true of those hired out and those under the supervision of overseers, because neither hirers nor overseers had the direct interest that owners did in avoiding injury to slaves through overwork. But even blacks who had relatively positive recollections of their masters not infrequently testified to the toil required of them; as one former slave put it, "dey treated us purty good, but we hab to work hard."[3]

The demands pomeshchiki placed on their serfs were equally burdensome, especially for the majority on barshchina, whose owners also expected a day's labor to stretch from sunup to sundown. Although custom stipulated that serfs should not be required to toil more than three days per week for their owners, barshchina of more than three days was widespread. Replying in 1767 to a survey conducted by the Free Economic Society, nobleman Petr Rychkov reported that in Orenburg province, although a three-day barshchina was the norm, many serfs were subjected to a work routine as long "as the pomeshchik wishes." An 1858 survey revealed a similar situation: in Tula province barshchina of more than three days prevailed on 18.7 percent of private estates, while on an additional 31.3 percent the amount of seigneurial labor required was unknown. Serfs commonly complained of overwork. In 1797 a peasant noted that his owner of 301 souls in Saratov province forced everyone but the youngest children to engage in constant barshchina, requiring them to leave these youngsters without supervision, from which neglect one had drowned. The women were subjected to "any work, light and heavy, until the last hour of childbirth"; as a consequence many had given birth to "dead babies," and in one summer alone ten women had miscarried and three died. Although in extreme cases such as this noblemen put their serfs on full-time barshchina, taking away their landed allotments and doling out to them monthly rations, the practice was highly unusual because it would have required a resident attitude lacking in most pomeshchiki. But if full-time seigneurial labor was rare, four-day and five-day barshchina was not, especially on the most fertile lands whose commercial potential noblemen were anxious to exploit to the fullest.[4]

Although work was the central feature of bondage, one must be careful about accepting the image of slavery and serfdom as untremit-

ting toil. Like all agricultural labor, that of slaves and serfs was subject to the rhythmic constraints of season and climate. If at harvest
time they often worked fourteen or more hours per day, during much
of the year—particularly the winter months—the workday was relatively abbreviated. Not only were there fewer hours of daylight but
also fewer chores required attention. Such seasonal variations were
especially extreme in Russia, because of its northerly latitude. On two
estates in Riazan province, for example, nineteenth-century serfs
toiled from 4 A.M. to 9:30 P.M. during June and July, with three hours
of midday rest, for a total of fourteen-and-one-half hours; in December and January, however, they worked only seven hours—from 8
A.M. to 4 P.M. with an hour's break—and one suspects that the pace
of their efforts was reduced as well. Similarly, in Tver province a typical workday varied from six hours in winter to twelve in the summer
and fifteen at harvest time. Although the southern United States did
not experience the extreme seasonal variations of Russia, in winter
the tempo of agricultural activity slackened considerably. Even in the
summer, bad weather often forced a halt to work, and illness or
feigned illness sharply depleted the workforce of almost all slaveowners. Of thirty-one working hands on George Noble Jones's Chemonie
plantation, only one did not miss any labor as a result of illness in
1841, and twenty-three hands missed ten or more days each.[5]

Even when climate and illness did not conspire against masters, all
was not work. Almost all slaves and serfs had Sundays off, and many
slaveowners required only half a day's labor, conditions permitting,
on Saturdays. Equally significant were the numerous holidays that the
bondsmen so eagerly looked forward to throughout the year. Virtually all slaveholders made it a practice to give slaves Christmas holidays of several days, in part, as Frederick Douglass theorized, as
"safety valves, to carry off the rebellious spirit of humanity," and in
part because they could easily be spared from physical labor at that
time of year. Shorter holidays were often given at other times, such as
after the harvest was in or even simply on the spur of the moment to
improve morale. "I gave my people a holiday this day, notwithstanding my work is so backward," Landon Carter noted in May 1772.
"The drowth seems to have affected them, and a play day may raise
their spirits." In Russia tradition dictated an even greater number of
occasions on which work stopped in a typical village, from elaborate
wedding and funeral ceremonies to religious holidays and birthdays
of the imperial family. In his mid-eighteenth-century instruction,
Count P. A. Rumiantsev listed forty-seven such holidays per year

when no work was to be performed; a mid-nineteenth-century description of social life in Tver province similarly noted that there were ninety-five Sundays and holidays per year—subtracting fifty-two Sundays yields forty-three holidays—and that a three-day per week barshchina thus in fact included only 135 workdays per year.[6]

There is considerable evidence that even on the job the pace of labor was often less than frantic. Planters and pomeshchiki, of course, *desired* their laborers to work quickly, steadily, and tirelessly, but their standards were rarely met. "I find it almost impossible to make a negro do his work well," complained Landon Carter in a typical statement. "No orders can engage it, no encouragement persuade it, nor no Punishment oblige it." Serfs were equally maddening. Travelers to both Russia and the South commented with interest on the lackadaisical pace and disorderly nature of labor, noting that without constant prodding the bondsmen would not work satisfactorily. If the masters ascribed this to the innate laziness of their charges, contemporaries opposed to bondage more often put the blame on a system of labor that provided no incentive for the laborer to work well; more recently, historians have also seen careless work as part of a secret effort to sabotage the routine of agricultural operations. And Genovese has put the question of "laziness" in new perspective by suggesting that American slaves shared with peasants of other countries a preindustrial sense of time, just as early industrial laborers resisted the efforts of their employers to make good clock-punchers of them. It was not that slaves and serfs were unwilling to work hard—like agricultural workers everywhere they accepted backbreaking labor as a normal component of life—but rather that they were unwilling to accept the masters' discipline of routinized labor.[7]

Despite these qualifications there can be little doubt that through physical compulsion masters were able to force more work from their bondsmen than they could have elicited through economic constraints and incentives alone. Serfs who performed three or more days of barshchina per week often had so little time to work on their own allotments that they used Sundays and holidays not to celebrate or rest but to work for themselves. Slaves, too, frequently devoted Sundays to tending their garden plots. Two econometricians have calculated that in the cotton-producing areas of the South emancipated blacks worked on the average between 28 and 37 percent fewer hours in 1879 than slaves had in 1859.[8]

As the bondsmen's desire to use their spare time to work on their own allotments makes clear, it was not so much hard work per se as the character of that work that made slavery and serfdom oppressive in their eyes. They expected to work hard, but they objected to two interrelated attributes of their work: exploitation and compulsion. Although one can debate the degree to which slaves and serfs understood the nature of class exploitation, there can be little doubt of their widespread recognition of the injustice of having to labor for the well-being of someone else. Frederick Douglass recalled a slave song that graphically expressed this sense of injustice:

> We raise de wheat,
> Dey gib us de corn;
> We bake de bread,
> Dey gib us de cruss;
> We sif de meal,
> Dey gib us de huss;
> We peal de meat,
> Dey gib us de skin,
> And dats de way
> Dey takes us in.

Serfs expressed a similar sense of outrage at owners who imposed such heavy barshchina obligations that they did not have time to work on their own allotments; "she deprives . . . us of all means of attaining our daily sustenance," one group of peasants noted of their owner in a typical complaint. There is also evidence that the very remoteness of many pomeshchiki led to a heightened sense of exploitation on the part of serfs who resented working for someone they rarely or never saw. Occasionally serfs coupled complaints of overwork with expressions of doubt that they legitimately belonged to their owners; in the case just cited, for example, the peasants insisted that "our present mistress does not have any documents or papers on our possession" and questioned whether they were really hers.[9]

Far stronger and more elemental than their sense of exploitation, however, although often confused with it, was the bondsmen's resentment of the compulsion that accompanied it. If bound labor was oppressive because the bondsmen were forced to work for another, it was the force rather than the working for another that seemed heinous to most contemporary critics of slavery and serfdom and to the bondsmen themselves. And indeed, it was not exploitation, which has been present in one guise or another in labor relations throughout history, but the denial of freedom that set slavery and serfdom apart from other labor systems. It is hardly surprising, then, that what the

bondsmen most hated about their work and strove hardest to minimize was the element of compulsion.[10]

Slaves and serfs had similar hierarchies of labor preferences that
reflected their desire to minimize the compulsion they experienced.
Serfs preferred to be held under obrok rather than barshchina, because the former tenure allowed them to escape much of the day-to-
day control of seigneurial authority and thus permitted them to secure substantially more control of their own lives. If they had to be
on barshchina, at least they might hope for a master who did not
impose more than three days seigneurial labor and a steward who
was relatively lenient about allowing them a large measure of self-
rule. The most fortunate slaves were those allowed to hire their own
time, earning money as they wished with a minimum of supervision
and turning over a prearranged amount to their owners, much like
serfs on obrok. Others might hope for a "good" master who relied
chiefly on trust, rewards, and his presence rather than strict regulation and punishment to induce good work from his hands. But what
slaves and serfs sought most of all was to escape their thralldom entirely; although free Negroes and state peasants did not always enjoy
a higher level of material prosperity than the bondsmen, they were
free from much of the regimentation that was such a central part of
the bondsmen's experience.

Despite the fears of planters and pomeshchiki, freedom to the
slaves and serfs did not mean freedom from work but freedom from
the many elements of compulsion that accompanied their work. They
objected to having to work when and where their owner dictated,
under his supervision or that of his subordinate, at a pace over which
they had little control, in constant fear of physical chastisement. This
is why even slaves and serfs who enjoyed relatively benign treatment
longed for freedom, why an ex-slave who described his master as "so
good ter us" could also remember that when he and his co-slaves
heard about emancipation they "jus' clap us hands en sing en dance,
en tank de Lawd dat us is free." For although the bondsmen were
poor, exploited, and overworked, so too were most of the world's free
population; the particular oppressiveness of slavery and serfdom
stemmed from the deprivation of freedom, the physical compulsion
that the masters deemed necessary to secure their labor.[11]

*   *   *

THE COMPULSION PRESENT in bondage took many forms aside
from that of work. Slaves and serfs could not travel freely. They usu-

ally could not choose their occupations. Their social and economic mobility, although not totally nonexistent, was severely limited. Many of them rose, worked, ate, rested, played, and slept when they were told. Although all of these limitations were galling, two elements of physical compulsion were especially important as indices of the bondsmen's treatment, because both they and their contemporaries considered them so: interference in their family lives and punishment.

Slaves and serfs often faced substantial limitations on when and under what conditions they could marry. Masters were anxious for their bondsmen to marry young—both to encourage "morality" and to produce many children—and many, recognizing that excessive restrictions on the bondsmen's right to choose their mates were likely to be counterproductive, allowed them considerable freedom of choice; even marriage with outsiders, although generally discouraged, was common in both Russia and the South. But the ultimate right to approve or disapprove marriages rested with the owners, and in both countries there were those who countermanded proposed marriage partners and even a few who denied some bondsmen—usually domestic servants—permission to marry at all.[12]

Other masters compelled reluctant youths to marry against their will. V. S. Suvorov ordered marriages to be arranged for all his male serfs who were still single at age twenty and all his females at age fifteen, and the grandfather of S. T. Aksakov, author of a compelling portrait of frontier life entitled *The Family Chronicle,* rewarded an ugly servant woman by marrying her to a man ten years her junior who "turned cold with horror" when introduced to his bride. Exslaves, too, occasionally recalled being assigned mates; as Katie Darling explained, under slavery "niggers didn't court . . . like they do now. Massa pick out a portly man and a portly gal and just put 'em together. What he want am de stock." If slaveowners and serfowners considered such interference a natural component of their paternal relationship with their bondsmen—after all, parents in the eighteenth and early nineteenth centuries could normally expect to have considerable influence over the marriage choices of their children—the slaves and serfs could hardly be blamed for viewing it in a somewhat different light.[13]

Once established, families faced the threat of two particularly blatant forms of interference. Most controversial and elusive is the subject of sexual exploitation of slave and serf women. Abolitionists, shocked (and perhaps titillated) by tales of sexual abuse, and recognizing the potential value to their cause of such tales, commonly portrayed slavery and serfdom as monstrous prisons of debauchery in which no woman was safe from the lecherous advances of her owner or his henchmen. "In the eyes of all old and young nobles alike," wrote Russia's foremost literary abolitionist A. N. Radishchev, serf women "are simply creatures for their lordly pleasure." Occasionally, concurring opinions came from the masters themselves, although most considered slavery and serfdom to be bastions of family morality. Perhaps the most biting comment from within the slaveowning class came from the pen of South Carolina's patrician diarist Mary Boykin Chesnut, who asserted that under slavery "we live surrounded by prostitutes . . . Like the patriarchs of old our men live all in one house with their wives and concubines, and the mulattoes one sees in every family exactly resemble the white children." [14]

Actual evidence concerning the incidence and character of sexual relations between masters and bondsmen, however, is disappointingly scarce. Despite an occasional comment like Chesnut's, the masters were understandably reticent on the subject. So too were the bondsmen. Serfs sometimes complained of sexual abuse—one wrote his owner, for example, denouncing a steward who "demands young girls for himself and has deprived many of their maidenhood"—but their complaints were typically vague and lacking in detail. The same was true of slave autobiographies, no doubt in part because they had to conform to prudish nineteenth-century standards. When slaves referred to interracial unions in such accounts, they usually did so in highly stylized fashion, as in Elizabeth Keckley's brief notation that because she was attractive a white man "persecuted me for four years, and I—I—became a mother." Other authors, such as Frederick Douglass, mentioned that their fathers were white, denounced the system that could produce such an abomination, and quickly dropped the subject. [15]

Nevertheless, certain generalizations may be hazarded. It is clear that interclass sexual contacts were widespread and spanned a full range from voluntary long-term liaisons to violent, resisted rapes. Exotic relations, although attracting considerable attention, were far from typical. A few pomeshchiki kept harems: P. A. Koshkarov, for example, a wealthy bachelor from Nizhnii Novgorod province, placed "12–15 young and beautiful girls" under the care of a trusted female servant and situated them in one whole wing of his seigneurial residence, and General L. D. Izmailov retained thirty young servant girls at his Tula province mansion for the amusement of himself and his guests. But although many masters dallied with attractive servants and some purchased girls for their physical charms, the keeping of formal harems was uncommon in Russia and virtually unknown in the United States South, where it would have necessitated an investment in conspicuous consumption beyond the reach of all but a tiny fraction of slaveowners and where it would have constituted too flagrant a violation of community standards. More common but still unusual were long-term love affairs between masters and favored bondswomen. Although these existed, they were sharply curtailed by racial taboos in most of the United States and the great gulf—physical and mental—that separated nobleman from peasant in Russia.[16]

Most sexual contacts between masters and bondswomen were of a more mundane variety and elicited little comment. Although few masters were as forthright as eighteenth-century planter William Byrd, who succinctly recorded in his diary, "I committed folly with F-r-b-y, God forgive me," there is a good deal of circumstantial evidence that slaveowners and serfowners, their sons, and their employees fairly routinely took advantage of women who attracted them. Indeed, South Carolina polemicist William Harper actually argued that the access of white men to black women in the South was a prime contributor to the purity of white women and the low incidence of prostitution. Sometimes masters used force to have their way with recalcitrant women, as did Smolensk province pomeshchik Pastukhov, who over a prolonged period "forcibly compelled peasant women and servant girls to engage in lecherous relations with him." Often, however, the very subordinate position of the bondswomen obviated the need to use violence against them; as one black man put it, slave women "know better than not to do what [their masters] say." Either way, however, the relationship was an unequal, exploitative one in which the potential use of force lurked in the background.[17]

Although precise data on the incidence of sexual relations between masters and bondswomen are lacking, there can be no doubt that such relations occurred far more frequently in the United States South than in Russia. This was true for three reasons, two of which were demographic. If in both countries a high proportion of the masters had sexual relations with at least one of their bondswomen at some point in their lives, the effect on the slaves and serfs differed. In the South the small size of holdings and the low ratio of slaves to owners meant that a woman's chance of being approached by her owner or overseer was extremely high, whereas in Russia the large size of holdings and high ratio of serfs to owners served to isolate most women from this risk. Equally important, because most pomeshchiki had little day-to-day contact with their serfs, they simply had less opportunity to become involved with their bondswomen than did resident American slaveowners. The vast majority of liaisons between noblemen and serfs occurred with house servants, the one group of serfs most noblemen saw on a regular basis. Finally, slaveowners generally took a more cavalier attitude toward their people's families than did serfowners. It made little sense for a planter to agonize over the effects of his advances toward a slave woman if he believed all blacks were naturally promiscuous; indeed, those southern whites who worried about interracial sex were usually more concerned about its impact on white families than on black.[18]

An equally sharp contrast between Russia and the American South was evident in the forced separation of bondsmen from members of their own families. Such separations constituted a particularly heart-rending component of slavery and serfdom, one that critics of the two institutions were quick to denounce. Even many defenders of bondage, while minimizing the frequency of forced separations, lamented the practice, urged steps to curtail it, and conceded that it provided a powerful argument to abolitionists. The issue was especially explosive in the United States, both because abolitionists operated more freely there and because American slaves were in fact separated from their loved ones more often than were Russian serfs. It is significant that professional slave traders acquired an unsavory reputation not only among critics of slavery but also among its most ardent supporters.[19]

Many well-disposed slaveowners tried to keep families together. Not only did such masters stress in their instructions the importance of encouraging family life among slaves, but they sometimes purchased spouses in order to keep families together. In 1807, for example, Thomas Jefferson, explaining that "nobody feels more strongly than I do the desire to make all practicable sacrifices to keep man & wife together," bought from his nephew the wife and two young sons of his slave Moses. In 1834, before moving all his slaves from Tennessee to a new plantation in Mississippi, James K. Polk arranged for the purchase of a slave's husband, so they would not be separated by the move. Ex-slave H. C. Bruce recalled that when his owner moved from Virginia to Missouri in 1844 no families were broken and the trip was a "wonderful experience"; he described Missouri slaveowners as strong promoters of family unity who "believed in having their slave women lead a virtuous life." Historians Robert W. Fogel and Stanley L. Engerman have concluded that slaveowners were "averse to breaking up black families" and that, even when moving slaves from the settled states along the Atlantic to the newly opened lands of the deep South, planters almost always kept families together.[20]

The evidence does not support such an interpretation. One cannot infer actual behavior of slaveowners from the statements of a few asserting the desirability of maintaining families, especially since even those few usually qualified their statements. Hammond, for example, although urging the encouragement of family life and deploring forced separations, added that "Negroes are themselves both perverse and comparatively indifferent about this matter," insisting on marrying off the plantation while fully aware of the risks entailed. "It is, therefore, impossible to prevent separations sometimes," he concluded. Men like Hammond tried to keep families together, but believing that blacks were "indifferent" to separations, they had few scruples against occasionally disrupting families, especially if their own financial interests were at stake.[21]

Even the most benevolent master was capable of taking action that resulted in the separation of his slaves. No better illustration can be found than in the behavior of South Carolina's Reverend Charles C. Jones, who exemplified the planter-paternalist who looked after his people. In 1856 Jones reluctantly decided to get rid of a family of seven slaves—mother, father, and five children—as quickly as possible; although the whole family was "unprincipled," the worst offender was eighteen-year-old Jane, who gave "constant trouble," culminating in her flight to Savannah where she hired herself out as a house servant, pretending she had Jones's permission. Insisting that "we could not conscientiously part the family," Jones determined that they should be "sold out of the city, all together, to one owner (not a speculator)." Soon General Harrison, "a gentleman of high respectability," agreed to purchase six of the slaves for between $4,200 and $4,250; twelve-year-old Titus would remain with the Joneses. Ten days later, however, a different purchaser acquired the six for $4,500, because Harrison's "offer in the end [was] not as advantageous." Jones assured his wife that he could have sold the family separately for even more money, but "conscience is better than money." Three months later the Joneses learned that the purchaser was in fact a slave trader who had taken the family for sale to New Orleans where Jane had died. "The revelation confirms me in the hitherto unshaken conviction that no confidence whatever can be placed in the word of a Negro trader," Jones's son wrote sanctimoniously, without any apparent recognition of the irony in his remarks. "It is the lowest occupation in which mortal man can engage." [22]

If humanitarians such as Jones found it necessary on occasion to separate slave families, one can imagine how common the practice was among less high-minded slaveholders. In a recent study of large planters in antebellum North Carolina, Jane Turner Censer found that family separations were common upon the deaths of owners; indeed, "only eight planters out of ninety-two, approximately nine percent, urged the executors of their wills to respect slave family relationships." A perusal of slave autobiographies and recollections also reveals the pervasive nature of forced separations: hardly a narrative of length fails to mention one, and many slaves described them as their most harrowing memory. Some separations were associated with the settling of the new states of the southwest, a process that according to one estimate involved the migration of 835,000 slaves and was especially traumatic because it uprooted slaves from their homes and friends as well as families. Sometimes slaves were sold as punishment. Most often, however, sales were dictated by economic constraints, such as liquidation of an estate following a slaveowner's death. Whatever the reasons for separations, some idea of their impact is evident in the assertion of an old Virginia woman three-quarters of a century after the end of slavery that "no white ever been in my house. Don't 'low it. Dey sole my sister Kate. I saw it wid dese here eyes. Sole her in 1860, and I ain't seed nor heard of her since. Folks say white folks is all right dese days. Maybe dey is, maybe dey isn't. But I can't stand to see 'em. Not on my place." [23]

Although it is impossible to determine precisely how frequently slave separations occurred, three statistical samples suggest that they were common enough to be a matter of intense concern to all slaves. A survey of 8,717 former Mississippi slaves registering marriages with Union army clergymen in 1864–65 revealed that 17.4 percent had had previous marriages broken by force; of those who had previously been married, 40.8 percent listed force as the cause of the marriage's termination. An analysis of postwar marriage records from Mississippi, Tennessee, and Louisiana yielded a similar result: 32.4 percent of 2,888 unions had been forcibly ended by masters. And of 2,358 ex-slaves interviewed by the Federal Writers' Project in the 1930s, 499 (21.2 percent) reported forced separations within their own families. Even these figures understate the incidence of forced separations: the first two samples indicated only separations of husbands from wives, not parents from children or siblings from each other, and the third consisted only of young slaves, who had not yet experienced all the separations possible over a full life cycle (and may not always have chosen to reveal them to white interviewers in any case). In addition, some slaves were torn from loved ones for prolonged periods without sale, most often by being hired out; Henry Bibb, for example, remembered being "taken away from my mother, and hired out to labor for various persons, eight or ten years in succession."[24]

Although forced separations of bondsmen occurred in Russia, they were less common than in the United States. Russians on the whole took serf families far more seriously than Americans took slave families. American slave marriages had no standing before the law, but marriages of serfs received full legal recognition (as had those of kholopy in Muscovy). Like other Russians, serfs had their marriages performed by priests and sanctified by the church, and they were expected to take their family responsibilities seriously. Elsewhere in the world, legal recognition of slave families has not always been a good indication of the treatment those families actually received; in Russia, however, it reflected a substantial degree of reality.[25]

Russian custom, unlike American, acted to minimize the number of family separations. Since serfs provided for their own sustenance, pomeshchiki had a strong interest in their family cohesion and hence their economic viability. Whereas in America when slaves with different owners married the ensuing marriage entailed weekend visits for the couple who remained separate during the week, in Russian off-estate marriages the bride invariably joined her new husband in exchange for an exit fee paid to her owner. Similarly, when a nobleman exiled a serf to Siberia he had to send the victim's wife (although not necessarily his children) into exile with him. As in America, separating families violated widely accepted standards of decency, but unlike American officials, Russian rulers not only condemned the practice but took repeated (although ineffective) action aimed at stopping it. As early as 1721 Peter I decreed that family members must not be sold apart from each other, and in the nineteenth century Nicholas I twice forbade selling unmarried children away from their parents.[26]

Nevertheless, forced separations continued, although more often of children from parents than husbands from wives. Owners with far-flung estates sometimes separated serfs from their families without formal sale, most often by taking young boys and girls into their own households to serve as domestics. On holdings of wealthy pomeshchiki separations even occurred through accident or inadvertence.

Ekaterina Petrova, for example, received the permission of her owner B I. Morozov to wed one of his serfs who resided on a different estate; when she joined him, however, the steward of her original estate kept her son. In this instance the story had a happy ending—in response to the woman's entreaties, Morozov ordered the boy returned to her—but not all pomeshchiki were receptive to even the most impassioned parental pleas. When pomeshchik Dmitrii Martinov died, his heirs "separated distant and near relatives, and even children." Until the end of serfdom the sale of children apart from their parents was a continuing, if not common, occurrence despite imperial prohibitions. Indeed, the need for numerous government decrees on the subject is an indication of their general ineffectiveness.[27]

The major occasion for men being forcibly separated from their wives and families was selection for military service. Indeed, to be sent into the recruits was regarded as almost certain perpetual separation from one's loved ones, because the chances of returning from twenty-five years in the army were slim. Russia's leading modern folklorist noted the striking similarity between traditional peasant recruiting and funeral lamentations, because to his village the recruit was for all practical purposes dead. As Englishman Robert Lyall observed in 1825, "when a new levy of men takes place . . . nothing is to be seen among [the peasants] but agitation and misery"; those chosen "take an everlasting farewell of their children, brothers, relations, and friends, and consider their entrance into the army as their *moral* death." Soldiers' wives were in an especially unfortunate position, since despite their husbands' long-term absence they were still legally married and hence forbidden to take up with other men. Indeed, some serfowners had soldiers' wives carefully watched and prevented from receiving male visitors, and pomeshchik V. L. Demidov actually ordered delinquent soldiers' wives expelled from his Nizhnii Novgorod estate. In 1809, for example, his estate-book noted that "soldatka" Katerina Il'ina was driven off "for bad conduct" and told not to return; when later she secretly visited the homes of three men, each was fined ten rubles. Because being drafted had such severe repercussions on one's family members, many pomeshchiki instructed their subordinates to choose unmarried men for military service.[28]

More common than forced separations of family members was the forced resettlement associated with populating new lands to the south and east, a process in many ways similar to the westward movement of slaves in the United States. Although most serfs moved in family groups or even whole estates, hundreds of thousands were uprooted from their homes and forced to start anew in a different—and often difficult—environment. The anguish that peasants felt at being torn from their ancestral villages is illustrated by a petition that serf Ignatii Ivanov sent to the governor of Vologda province in 1858. Ivanov complained that his owner personally came to the village of Chash-nikovo, which was composed of ten families who had resided there "since ancient times," to effect their expulsion. When Ivanov's father refused an order to tear down his house, the nobleman beat him. "At the urging of all my neighbors," Ivanov begged the governor "to leave us at our permanent place of residence," but no doubt anticipating the inevitable refusal, he concluded by imploring him to order the move delayed to "enable us first to supply ourselves with provisions." Sometimes resettlement also led to family separations: when in the 1820s and 1830s Prince M. S. Vorontsov moved many of his serfs from Vladimir province to his new holdings in the Crimea, they made the lengthy trip on foot and on arriving at their destination "lived torn from their families, because as a rule they were not resettled with families, since only the work force was needed there." [29]

Slave families faced forced separations more often than serf families, not so much because of the good or bad intentions of the owners but because of differing customs stemming from two very different historical experiences. American slavery was rooted in family separations: Africans brought to America were invariably torn not just from their homes and culture but also from their loved ones. As outsiders in an alien land, they and their descendants lacked any rights that society was bound to respect, and although well-meaning masters during the last century of slavery tried to keep families together, they did this because benevolence prompted it rather than because equity required it. The enserfment of Russian peasants in their own land, by contrast, did not involve their wholesale separation from homes, culture, or families, and even as serfs they continued to have certain rights that society recognized, whether by law or tradition. Although noblemen sometimes bought and sold individual serfs, more often they purchased populated estates whose composition they left unchanged; owners came and went, but the peasant community usually remained intact.

Of course, sexual exploitation of women and separation of families were only the most blatant ways in which bondage impinged on slave and serf families. In a more general sense the very fact of being owned, of lacking ultimate authority over themselves and their children, had a corrosive impact on the family lives of the bondsmen. [30]

Nor can the effects of sexual abuse and family separations be measured by their incidence alone, because they were part of a power relationship between masters and bondsmen; the possibility of this abuse was always present, as were the bondsmen's knowledge and fear of it.

But although interference in the bondsmen's family lives occurred in both Russia and the United States South, it was clearly more pervasive in the latter. This was true of both direct abuse and the more subtle impact that stemmed from frequent contact between master and slave. Pomeshchiki exercised rigid control over the behavior of their house servants, with whom they dealt on a daily basis, but often intervened little in the family lives of their village serfs except to set broad guidelines for them to follow. American slaveowners also came in contact most often with their servants, who consequently faced the greatest likelihood of owner meddling, but they also interfered more routinely in the lives of their field hands than did their Russian counterparts. Here is evident one of the most significant consequences of the contrast between the resident approach of the American masters and the absentee mentality of the Russian.

*   *   *

LIKE INTERFERENCE in their family lives, physical punishment of the bondsmen was a salient sign of their subordinate status and aroused their bitter resentment. Serfs complained both to their owners of undue punishment by stewards and other administration members and to government authorities of cruel treatment by owners. In 1841, for example, serfs of Moscow province pomeshchik Chulkov petitioned the chief of the Corps of Gendarmes, describing twenty-eight years of "tyranny" to which they had been subjected, including constant beatings with the knout and batogi that left them "at the point of complete physical exhaustion." Of 195 petitions that serfs from Saratov province sent to various officials between 1826 and 1860, 77 dealt with excessive punishment and cruelty. American slaves also complained to their owners of brutal overseers, and although they were not able to petition government officials, they bitterly complained among themselves about cruel owners. Indeed, slaves' narratives and autobiographies leave little doubt that their unhappiest recollections of bondage usually involved physical punishment. Ex-slaves who described their owners as cruel or mean almost always emphasized the whippings they or their overseers administered, and those who recollected their masters as "good" invariably associated that characteristic with an absence of corporal punishment. "You say how did our Marster treat his slaves? Scandalous, dey treated us jes' like dogs," recalled one woman, who immediately launched into a description of whippings doled out by the overseer. These were sometimes for a specific cause, as when she was whipped "till de blood dripped to de ground" for stealing a pig, but few excuses were needed for a whipping. "If dey beat our husbands and we looked at dem dey would beat us too," she remembered. Hundreds of other blacks told similar stories.[31]

Russian noblemen found corporal punishment essential for a broad range of offenses from trivial to serious. Casual beatings were probably most prevalent in the seventeenth and early eighteenth centuries, when the modern notion of humaneness was nonexistent and violence against subordinates virtually taken for granted. As one of A. I. Bezobrazov's stewards explained, "one must beat these peasants, sir, to keep them in control." (Stewards, too, received frequent beatings at Bezobrazov's order.) When peasant Mironko Ivanov was caught in theft and cursed his owner B. I. Morozov, the latter instructed his steward to beat him with a knout, jail him, and then beat and jail him again "to keep him from thus stealing and uttering slanderous words." Later in the year, despite Ivanov's personal appeal in which he admitted his guilt and begged for release so that he would not "starve to death," the angered nobleman ordered him held in jail until further notice.[32]

But harsh punishment for drunkenness, theft, disobedience, immorality, poor work, and nonpayment of dues, as well as for simply displeasing owners, continued to be commonplace in the late eighteenth and nineteenth centuries. V. L. Demidov, for example, continually punished his Nizhnii Novgorod province serfs for minor acts of misbehavior as well as for more serious derelictions such as theft and cutting seigneurial wood. In April 1812 he fined, corporally chastised, and assigned extra work to thirty peasants caught playing pitch-and-toss during Easter; eighteen years later he ordered similar treatment of fourteen serfs committing the same act and warned that if he discovered them at it again he would choose one by lot to send into the army. Demidov also strictly disciplined serfs for sexual misconduct; when two peasants were caught in the shed of a third, "where they had come for fornication," the male, whose offense was his second, was fined thirty rubles and forced to sit "two days in *repentance,* with his head half shaved," and the shed owner was fined a like amount and forced to sit in repentance for one-and-a-half days for helping arrange the rendezvous. General L. D. Izmailov, who presided over unusually cruel discipline of offending servants and peasants on his Khitrovshchina estate, succinctly explained its necessity: "Where in the state," he asked rhetorically, "are there not applied correctional and incentive measures to produce obedience to established authorities, restraint of vice, arrest of depravity peculiar to youth—in a word, to inculcate in all, as much as possible, good morals?"[33]

American slaveowners found physical chastisement an equally essential element of the maintenance of good morals. Colonial planters repeatedly recorded in their diaries accounts of their retribution against slave malefactors. "I beat my man Hampton for lying and other transgressions," noted William Byrd in 1739. "Manual a villain and must be whipped," asserted Landon Carter three decades later, proceeding to describe his faulty work. "Whipped he shall be." Nineteenth-century slaveowners also described punishment of slaves with repetitive frequency. "I corrected Enoch by giving him a few lashes," wrote one. Another, noting that "Uncle Duncan has been annoyed by fresh discoveries of rascality among his negroes," told how two slaves suspected of theft were put in stocks until one "confessed his guilt." Former slaves confirmed the prevalence of such punishments: of 2,358 interviews with ex-slaves conducted by the Federal Writers' Project, 688 touched on the question of physical abuse. Only 34 asserted the absence of such abuse on their holdings, with the rest detailing a variety of punishments, the most common of which by far was whipping.[34]

Nevertheless, although it is easy to document the widespread existence of punishment, it is more difficult to generalize about its frequency. American historians of slavery have differed sharply on the subject, because the evidence appears contradictory. Some slaves described constant abuse, but others told of owners who rarely or never resorted to the lash; although she had heard of whippings elsewhere, a Virginia woman reported that "Massa Scott never had non dat kinder stuff on his place." Many blacks, whether antebellum autobiographers or twentieth-century interviewees, apparently adjusted their testimony to meet the expectations of their audiences.[35]

Even in those few cases where the statistical evidence seems clear, historians have subjected that evidence to widely varying interpretations. Consider Bennet H. Barrow's Louisiana plantation, for which we have the best statistical information about punishments over a sustained period of time. Barrow's diary is filled with descriptions of whippings, jailings, and other corrections of recalcitrant slaves, and a casual perusal would convince most readers that abuse of slaves on the estate was a constant occurrence. Sometimes he punished individuals for misbehavior; his diary entry for 26 December 1836, for example, noted that "House Jerry and Israel [were] chained during Christmass" for "bad conduct." Often, however, Barrow "whiped all my ploughers—for shallow ploughing" or "whiped every hand in the field this evening commencing with the driver." According to the diary's editor, who did not consider Barrow a cruel master, there were 156 whippings on the plantation during 1840 and 1841, for a total of 331 offenses, most of which involved bad work.[36]

Historians, however, have reached conflicting conclusions on the basis of the Barrow diary. Fogel and Engerman, counting 160 whippings over a two-year period and estimating the plantation's workforce at 120, calculated an average of only "0.7 whippings per hand per year" and concluded that Barrow's diary showed how rarely most slaves were whipped. Gutman, in a lengthy rebuttal, argued that Fogel and Engerman ignored "whipping frolicks" in which most or all of Barrow's slaves were subjected to the lash, and that in any case to ask how often the average slave was whipped was to ask the wrong question. "It is much more relevant to know how often the whip was used," he explained, adding that a whipping took place "every 4.56 days." Suggesting that Barrow was probably typical of large planters, Gutman concluded that his diary showed how often slaves were punished. Still other historians then joined the fray. One insisted that Fogel and Engerman overestimated the number of Barrow's slaves and undercounted the number of whippings and that in fact the average slave was whipped 1.0, not 0.7, times per year. Another maintained that far from being typical, Barrow was "one of the most sadistic masters of whom there is any record," and thus whippings on his plantation were hardly indicative of the general plantation regime. In short, the availability of detailed statistical information concerning punishment on one plantation has done little to foster historical consensus.[37]

Still, on the basis of existing evidence the following generalizations seem warranted. A small number of antebellum slaveowners rarely or never physically punished their slaves; although other slaves envied those held under such a regime—"folks called us 'McCullough's free niggers,'" recalled one slave whose master spared the lash—neighboring planters considered excessively lenient masters subversive of local order. Perhaps an equally small number of owners resorted to sadistic tortures of a pathological nature; when uncovered, these excesses received even sharper community criticism. Most masters fell well between these two extremes: they or their subordinates resorted frequently to the lash—as well as to milder forms of discipline such as deprivation of privileges—but not uniformly for each slave. Some slaves were punished often and severely, but others escaped physical chastisement. House servants, who had the greatest contact with their masters and were constantly subject to their evaluation, were most likely to suffer the consequences of arousing their ire. The "average" slave was whipped relatively infrequently, although it is impossible to specify whether this means once a year, twice a year, or once every two years. On large plantations, however, the whip was typically in use every few days. (On very small holdings weeks or months could pass between whippings.) Most slaves were not punished often, but most slaveowners did punish often.[38]

It is, if anything, even more difficult to come to a conclusion concerning the frequency of punishment endured by a "typical" serf because of exceptionally wide variations in their treatment. Most subject to punishment were those who came in closest contact with their owners. Thus, Iaroslavl province pomeshchik Dmitrii Saltykov, a bachelor who in the early nineteenth century lived an isolated rural life whose boredom he relieved with "an occasional inclination to drunkenness" as well as "a tendency to excessive power which he exercises continually over his peasants," treated his 281 souls remarkably unevenly. Those fortunate enough to live some distance from his house were held on obrok and suffered little seigneurial interference, but those who lived near their owner endured oppressive labor obligations and frequent physical abuse. Worst off were the several dozen house servants, who bore the brunt of his irascible temper. Saltykov "continually beats his peasants who come before him for some reason or work in his home," reported a government investigator, "for either insignificant or nonexistent faults"; many of the victims eventually resorted to flight. Elsewhere, house serfs and those with special skills that brought them in touch with their owners were also at greatest risk of suffering seigneurial retribution. At General Izmailov's house virtually no servant escaped a wide variety of sadistic punishments imposed for minor offenses; during a twelve-year period valet Nikolai Ptitsin underwent beatings with birch switches more than one hundred times. When a girl from P. A. Koshkarov's harem was caught running away with a groom, "after a severe thrashing she was forced to sit on a chair for a whole month"; attached to her neck was an iron collar from which protruded iron spokes, which made it impossible for her to turn her head "so that the unfortunate girl had to sit without moving." The groom suffered a merciless beating from which he may have died.[39]

Historians of Russian serfdom, like those of American slavery, have reached differing conclusions concerning punishment. Most have been led by numerous heartrending cases to stress the unbearable physical abuse that serfs suffered. Some, however, have recognized the widespread variations that existed, and at least one has concluded that despite "isolated instances of cruelty" serfs were subjected to little physical abuse; "foreign travelers to Russia—unlike visitors to the slave plantations of the Americas—" he asserted, "hardly ever mention corporal punishment."[40]

Although this view represents a considerable exaggeration, it is clear that on the whole serfs suffered owner-imposed punishments less often than did American slaves. Pomeshchiki ordered severe retribution imposed on recalcitrant serfs, but they relied less extensively than most planters on routine use of physical coercion, for the simple reason that most noblemen concerned themselves relatively little with day-to-day estate management. The major exception was in their treatment of house servants, who felt the full brunt of their masters' displeasure on a daily basis.

An examination of punishments imposed on Count N. P. Sheremetev's Ivanovskaia estate over a twenty-year period (1790–1809) illustrates this trend. At first glance the situation appears remarkably similar to that on Barrow's plantation. Sheremetev's peasants underwent a steady stream of punishments, including beatings with birch switches, whippings, assignment to extra work, official scolding as well as occasional more stringent measures such as confinement in chains, arrest, and torture. By far the most common offense for which serfs were corrected was drunkenness, followed by various forms of mischief, fighting, and swearing, and then by theft, disobedience, absence at night, and a variety of other actions. Over the twenty-year period 109 serfs experienced 847 punishments, and 31 of the serfs received punishment more than ten times each. A punishment occurred, on the average, every 8.6 days—somewhat less often than on Barrow's plantation but on the same general order of frequency.

Closer examination, however, reveals striking differences in the way such punishments affected the bondsmen. Sheremetev's estate contained a total of 6,624 peasants; over the twenty-year period, therefore, there was on the average only one punishment for every 7.8 serfs, or one punishment for every 156 peasants per year. Even this average figure exaggerates the number of individuals punished, because many of those disciplined received more than one correction; only 5 percent of serfs on the estate suffered formal punishment during the twenty years. Under Barrow and Sheremetev punishments were meted out with comparable frequency, but whereas most of the former's slaves received chastisement over a two-year period, the vast majority of the latter's escaped it over a twenty-year period. Sheremetev's instructions to his stewards provided detailed descriptions of how and why his serfs should undergo correction, but the size and far-flung nature of his holdings, together with his absentee orientation, guaranteed that most of his serfs would never face administrative discipline.[41]

Of course, frequency of punishment alone does not indicate its full impact on the bondsmen: one must also consider its severity. As will become evident in the next two sections, those serfs who were punished were likely to undergo a more brutal regimen than were the slaves. The very pervasiveness of punishment in America encouraged the use of "moderate chastisement," because with most slaves undergoing corporal punishment, the effect of excessive severity would have been devastating to both economic and social order. In Russia, by contrast, a small enough proportion of serfs endured punishment that they could be effectively singled out for more drastic treatment. Although the dichotomy is too neat, one might suggest that punishment served two major overlapping functions, one of which was dominant in the South and the other in Russia: through their use of punishment the slaveowners sought primarily to influence the future behavior of those punished, whereas the pomeshchiki expected the example of brutal retribution to serve as a deterrent or object lesson to others. In both countries owners recognized that corporal punishment had an impact far wider than suggested by its frequency, because its very presence served as a constant reminder of what awaited those who displeased their master or one of his representatives. Most owners did not physically abuse most of their slaves and serfs most of the time, but both bondsmen and masters knew that such abuse was possible at any time.[42]

*   *   *

THUS FAR, our picture of the treatment that the bondsmen received has been largely static and hence incomplete. In both countries, especially the United States, an examination of the long term reveals substantial evolution of the bondsmen's treatment over time. Exploration of these changes is important because it shows the variability of slavery and serfdom under the impact of specific conditions. It also clarifies basic distinctions between the way those conditions shaped bondage in Russia and in the South.

During the century preceding emancipation in the United States South, slaveowners showed increasing concern over the treatment of their slaves, whom they more and more came to see as objects of their benevolence. This development did not necessarily mean that antebellum slavery was "better" than its colonial predecessor or that the typical bondsman in the 1840s was happier than his or her great-grandparents had been in the 1740s. Indeed, in some respects slaves clearly suffered from their masters' heightened interest in their well-being. On a purely physical level, however, there can be little doubt that the lot of most slaves improved substantially. Equally important were changes in relations between masters and slaves and in the way both sides conceptualized those relations.

It was easy during the seventeenth and early eighteenth centuries for slaveowners to take an essentially instrumental attitude toward their slaves, who were usually first-generation imports brought over for only one purpose—their labor-power. To the colonists, themselves often new settlers aggressively clearing the land and building their fortunes, African slaves seemed less objects of compassion or interest than of utility. Planters sought strong young men for field labor and showed remarkably little interest in them as human beings. Masters frequently resorted to draconian measures in order to break the independence and spirit of recalcitrant slaves and teach them who was in control. Brandings, mutilations, and other practices that would later be considered cruel and unusual were common occurrences, and slaveowners regularly devised imaginative punishments for slaves who displeased them. Virginia planter William Byrd, far more enlightened than most colonists of his day, scolded his wife when "against my will" she "caused little Jenny to be burned with a hot iron," but he too was constantly beating, boxing, whipping, and threatening troublesome slaves; when three of them left the plantation without permission he gave them "a vomit . . . which did more good than whipping." [43]

Such treatment must be seen in the context of the widespread acceptance in the seventeenth and early eighteenth centuries of physical chastisement of the poor and powerless in order to keep them in line. Indentured servants, vagrants, and those guilty of minor offenses regularly endured corporal punishment, and as late as 1766 Landon

Carter thought nothing of giving his own grandson a "cut over the left arm with the lash of my whip" when the child displeased him. (Carter's grandson was not poor, of course, but as a child he shared with the lower classes a lack of power which rendered him equally subject to physical correction.) It is not surprising that slaves, the most dependent and powerless of all, should suffer physical abuse in an age when the whip and the stocks were widely perceived as appropriate methods of handling troublesome behavior among the dependent and powerless.[44]

But because they were most vulnerable and because they were seen as different, black slaves not only received such abuse in more massive doses than others; they also continued to receive it when corporal punishment of whites was becoming less widespread and less acceptable than previously. Travelers to the eighteenth-century South were often shocked by the treatment they saw meted out to slaves. Reverend Charles Wesley described in disbelief how a South Carolina planter he met boasted that he would "first nail up a negro by the ears, then order him to be whipped in the severest manner, and then to have scalding water thrown over him, so that the poor creature could not stir for four months after." "Good God! Are these Christians?" asked New Jersey–born tutor Philip Fithian in 1773 after learning of the punishments devised by a Virginia overseer. The law provided little protection against such abuse. Although there were statutes against murder and torture of slaves, cases rarely came to court, and when they did conviction was uncertain at best. In South Carolina in 1799, for example, a man was indicted "for branding a negro with a hot iron," but although at first he was fined £100, the conviction was reversed on a technicality.[45]

During the late eighteenth century and especially during the first two-thirds of the nineteenth, many slaveholders exhibited a new sense of responsibility for their slaves. In instructions, private correspondence, and public appeals they showed an intense interest in their material well-being, stressed the importance of treating them humanely, and expressed forcefully the notion that they were guardians of a simple, trusting, but ignorant people who needed their moral stewardship in order to flourish. As Thomas Jefferson put it in 1814, "we should endeavor, with those whom fortune has thrown on our hands, to feed & clothe them well, protect them from ill usage, require such reasonable labor only as is performed voluntarily by freemen, and be led by no repugnancies to abdicate them, and our duties to them." Even northern travelers predisposed to be critical of what they found in the South were sometimes struck by the concern of slaveholders for the welfare of their "people." In 1826, for example, Presbyterian minister Timothy Flint noted the "growing desire among masters, to be popular with their slaves"; he attributed this trend to the calculated self-interest of slaveowners, "who have finally become impressed, that humanity is their best interest, that cheerful, well fed and clothed slaves, perform so much more productive labour, as to unite speculation and kindness in the same calculation."[46]

Flint was no doubt partially correct about the motivation of slave-owners. Clearly many saw the carrot as a more effective incentive than the stick, although most considered a combination of the two best of all. There is also reason to believe that the ending of slave imports in 1808 and the ensuing rise in the price of slaves that accelerated during the last years of the slave regime played their part in convincing slaveowners of the value of human life. Comparative evidence as well as common sense tell us that when labor is dear and cannot easily be replenished, management will be more solicitous of workers' welfare than when it is cheap and replacements are readily available.[47]

But interacting with crude self-interest were other factors that promoted the growth of slaveowner paternalism. Two of these dated largely from the eighteenth century. That century witnessed a fundamental change in attitudes toward cruelty, violence, punishment, rights, fairness—in short, how people may legitimately treat others—that led to developments as varied as a sharp decline in the use of corporal punishment on free citizens, the growth of the concept of natural rights, and the spread of a humanitarianism that brought with it the notion of the desirability of humane treatment of slaves. The emergence of a resident mentality among slaveowners had a similar effect. Planters who were still Englishmen at heart, as early settlers were in the mainland South and as West Indians continued to be in the eighteenth century, regarded slaves largely as means to wealth, especially when most of those slaves were new imports. The growth of local ties and commitments naturally led slaveowners to take a more active and permanent interest in their communities and property—including their human property, the majority of whom were now second-generation and third-generation Americans themselves. Their slaves became their "people" rather than simply their investment. The growth of a resident mentality thus combined with the growth of humanitarianism to affect profoundly the way masters thought about their slaves. A final factor reinforcing this trend in the nineteenth century was a conscious movement to strengthen slavery by making it more humane—to counter the abolitionist onslaught by ridding slavery of its abuses and making the peculiar institution as benevolent as proslavery ideologues were already insisting that it was.[48]

Concern for slaves took numerous forms, ranging from increased emphasis on their material comfort to efforts to promote their family lives. One of its most striking manifestations during the antebellum period was in the movement to convert slaves and instruct them in Christian doctrine. Motivated in part by a sincere concern for the salvation of their souls and a conviction that their religious instruction was an "obligation . . . *divinely imposed*" and in part by a belief that it would make them more obedient, this mission movement accelerated from the 1820s through the 1850s, when hundreds of thousands of slaves became formal members of southern religious denominations—especially Baptist and Methodist—and most others were exposed to regular Sunday church services, special sermons designed for slaves, or Bible readings by masters and mistresses. The contrast with the colonial period was striking: then, despite the efforts of organizations such as the Society for the Propagation of the Gospel in Foreign Parts, most masters had paid little attention to the religious lives of their slaves and the few ministers actively interested in reaching blacks had despaired of success. It became a stock argument of nineteenth-century defenders of slavery that one of the peculiar institution's major virtues was its exposure of formerly heathen blacks to Christianity.[49]

An equally significant index of new slaveowner attitudes was a decrease in the worst forms of physical abuse practiced against slaves. Of course, brutality remained far from nonexistent. Bennet H. Barrow, for example, in addition to whipping troublesome slaves liberally, invented a wide range of punishments designed to pain and humiliate them, including confinement to a special plantation jail, making men wear women's clothes, and putting them in chains; when a particularly persistent fugitive was caught, Barrow decided to exhibit him "during Christmas on a scaffold in the middle of the Quarter & with a red Flannel cap on." Occasionally, slaveowners resorted to sadistic tortures and murders. In 1811 Lilburne and Isham Lewis, nephews of Thomas Jefferson, dismembered an unruly servant with an axe as a lesson to their other slaves and scattered the pieces of his body over a blazing fire. But murders of slaves were extraordinary acts—if for no other reason than the folly of destroying valuable property—and maimings, amputations, brandings, and castrations became exceptional rather than commonplace occurrences, everywhere violating both the law and community standards of morality. Barrow was hardly a gentle man, but he bitterly denounced his neighbor as "the most cruel Master I ever knew of" for castrating three of his slaves and physically abusing others. Such social disapprobation of masters who severely mistreated their slaves exerted increasing pressure on slaveowners to avoid—or at least hide—excessive cruelty. Instructions, plantation correspondence, and public appeals all enjoined southerners to limit physical punishment to moderate whippings and to regard slaves as childlike dependents who needed their masters' love and protection. Although one must be skeptical of taking such propaganda at face value, abundant evidence confirms that an increasing number of slaveholders—although by no means all— came to see themselves as benevolent patriarchs who ruled firmly but fairly, taking loving care of all members of their "families," black as well as white.[50]

Such attitudes were also reflected in antebellum legal practices. Most southern states substantially strengthened their slave codes during the last half-century of bondage, making it illegal to teach slaves to read and write, restricting the ability of masters to free their slaves, and tightening provisions of slave patrols to guard against mischief and rebellion. But at the same time these states also acted to strengthen slavery by providing increased protection for slaves against abuse of their dependent position, thus refuting northern charges that slaves were defenseless against virtually any degradation to which southern whites might subject them. Not only did most states pass laws increasing penalties for serious physical mistreatment of slaves, but some judges showed an increased determination to see to it that these laws were enforced. As North Carolina's Chief Justice explained in 1823 in ruling that a white man could be indicted on assault charges for severely beating a slave, "mitigated as slavery is by the humanity of our laws, the refinement of manners, and by public opinion, which revolts at every instance of cruelty toward them, it would be an anomaly in the system of police which affects them, if the offence . . . were not indictable." The notion that slaveowners could commit virtually any act against slaves with impunity is not borne out by the willingness of courts to convict whites accused of murdering or severely mistreating blacks. Of course, slaves did not receive the same protection from the law as free persons. They could not testify against whites, and convicted murderers of slaves, although occasionally sentenced to death, usually received ten-year prison terms. Furthermore, slaves received almost no legal protection from acts committed by other slaves, which were commonly regarded as private matters not subject to the law. In 1859 the conviction of a Mississippi slave for raping a ten-year-old black girl was reversed by a court that ruled his act had violated no law.[51]

In any event, the vast majority of cases involving slaves never came to trial and indeed never came to light. Those most likely to be prosecuted pitted whites on opposing sides, as when a slaveowner charged an overseer or hirer with mistreating his property. When owners mistreated their own slaves, unless the action was so severe as to result in death or so notorious as to arouse widespread repugnance among neighbors, there was little likelihood of their being taken to court. Similarly, when slaves committed minor offenses on their own farms or plantations, their owners invariably handled the matter informally themselves. Most slaves depended for protection not on the courts but on the goodwill and paternalism of their masters.

Use of the term *paternalism* with reference to slavery has recently aroused considerable controversy among historians. The suggestion by several scholars—most notably Genovese—that antebellum–United States slaveowners exhibited a paternalistic attitude toward their slaves has seemed to some an effort to deny the horror of slavery by portraying the masters in a favorable light. Such criticism is based on the erroneous notion that paternalism implies a "good" slavery under which the bondsmen suffered little exploitation or oppression. Although some writers, especially during the first half of the twentieth century, have presented such a picture of benevolent slavery, one need hardly accept this judgment to argue that southern slaveowners tended toward paternalism. Their paternalism had to do not with a painless slavery but with their idea of reciprocal relations between themselves and their bondsmen, under which they owed their slaves support, protection, and even love in exchange for hard work, obedience, and even love. (Whether or not the slaves accepted this formula is a different question, to be treated in Part II.)[52]

The key to southern slaveholders' paternalism lies in their resident mentality. For them, slavery was not just an investment to be measured by profit and loss (although that was obviously important) but a way of life that provided unique pleasures as well as tribulations, both associated with the active management and care of slaves. Masters took an intense interest not just in the labor but also in the lives of their people. The small size of most holdings enabled owners to know their slaves personally and to intervene in their affairs on a day-to-day basis.

When such interaction became widespread is impossible to establish with precision (and may have varied in different regions), but evidence suggests that it was generally lacking in the seventeenth century, increasingly evident in the eighteenth, and pervasive in the nineteenth. During the first half of the colonial period both masters and slaves were usually new to America and, more important, to each other; bonds between them were few, and most planters probably looked upon Africans as a useful source of labor and little more than that. William Fitzhugh's letters from the last quarter of the seventeenth century, for example, show almost no interest in the lives of his black slaves (although he did express such interest in those of his white servants). In contrast, records of eighteenth-century planters reveal not only a real concern for the well-being of their slaves, most of whom were born in America, but also a knowledge of individuals and an assumption of substantial interest in their lives. William Byrd's diaries are filled with entries like "I went to visit a negro of Mr. Custis' who was very sick" and "I talked with my people." His interaction with them was not always benevolent. Equally often one reads entries such as "I threatened Anaka with a whipping if she did not confess the intrigue between Daniel and Nurse" or "I caused L-s-n to be whipped for beating his wife and Jenny was whipped for being his whore." Landon Carter, although complaining constantly about his slaves' laziness and thoughtlessness, personally attended those who were sick, as did George Washington when he was home. South Carolinian Eliza Lucas wrote her future husband in 1741 that she was kept busy by "a Sister to instruct and a parcel of little Negroes whom I have undertaken to teach to read." [53]

Slaveowners' interest and interference in the lives of bondsmen grew in the nineteenth century, with many masters and mistresses personally ministering to the ill and needy. "I walked over to the quarters this morning before breakfast, to see a sick woman, found her quite sick," wrote Mississippian Eliza L. Magruder in 1846; a few days later she noted, "I vaccinated 8 or 10 little darkies this morning." Other slaveowners, too, tended to the sick, comforted the ailing, and sent for physicians to treat their slaves; in 1853 South Carolina planter Robert F. W. Allston paid $390.21 for a doctor's numerous visits to his Waverly estate. Such concern was reinforced in the antebellum period by an increasing commitment of slaveowners to provide their slaves with material comfort and religious instruction. Masters read the Bible to their slaves, arranged special services for them, gave parties for them, and bombarded the reading public with admonitions to feed, clothe, and house them well. They expressed their "love" for them both in their public defenses of the peculiar institution and, sometimes, in their private behavior toward them. Almost all had personal favorites on whom they showered special rewards. At the same time they scolded, nagged, chided, punished, and insisted that blacks were incapable of managing without the care and direction of their superiors.[54]

The essence of this paternalism was to treat the slaves as permanent children, who on the one hand needed constant protection but on the other needed constant direction and correction. It is these two elements that rendered paternalism such a double-edged sword: continuous supervision and punishment constituted the other side of the coin of continuous love and protection. Because blacks were like children, they were—and must be kept—totally dependent on their masters. A good argument can be made that this kind of paternalism was more debilitating to the slaves and their culture than benign neglect would have been—that from the slaves' point of view the protection they received from their masters was not worth the constant meddling in their lives that necessarily went along with it.[55]

Slaveowners' paternalism found clear manifestation in the material care they provided their slaves. As early as the 1770s Englishman Alexander Hewatt, who deplored slavery for leaving its victims "defenceless to the insolence, caprice, and passions of owners, obliged to labour all their life without any prospect of reward," conceded that "comparatively speaking, [South Carolina slaves] are well clothed and fed . . . When they happen to fall sick, they are carefully attended by a physician; in which respect their condition is better than that of the poorest class of labourers in Europe." He proceeded to compare their treatment favorably to that of West Indian slaves. Of course, American slaves did not live in luxury; their lives were hard, and many suffered great cruelty. On a purely material level, however, most lived well not only in comparison with slaves of other countries but also in comparison with most of the world's population. Their relative material comfort reflected both the care they received and the generally high standard of living that prevailed in the United States.[56]

Housing and clothing provided for slaves were by most accounts crude but adequate. The South's temperate climate meant that even spartan accommodations were usually sufficient to protect slaves from the rigors of inclement weather; unlike Russia, the South required its inhabitants to spend relatively little time and effort keeping warm. Still, there was a marked tendency for slaveowners over the course of the last century of bondage to pay increasing attention to the slaves' shelter. Not only did authors bombard the reading public with admonitions to provide their laborers with tidy houses of sufficient size, but most masters made at least some effort to adhere to such standards. Of course, there were exceptions; Frances Kemble found slave cabins on her husband's rice plantation "filthy and wretched in the extreme." But whereas in the colonial period many owners had paid little attention to slaves' housing, finding space for them in barns, lofts, sheds, or even out in the open, in the nineteenth century masters typically supplied each family with a wooden cabin of 16 by 18 feet and insisted that it be regularly cleaned and maintained. Northern travelers critical of slavery were often surprised at these "well-made and comfortable" dwellings, and ex-slaves, too, testified to the rustic but generally satisfactory nature of slave housing. As fugitive Charles Ball recalled, slave cabins on his South Carolina plantation were "dry and comfortable"; he added, "in this practice of keeping their slaves well sheltered at night, the southern planters are pretty uniform." Antebellum slave clothing, too, was simple but adequate. Slaveowners typically issued field hands four coarse suits per year—pants and shirts for the men, dresses for the women, and long shirts for the children—plus one or two pairs of shoes that rarely fit comfortably and were often left unworn.[57]

The most important ingredient of the slaves' material well-being was their diet, and it was here that they fared best in comparison with most other laborers, bound and free, the world over. Aided by a mild climate and bountiful soil that yielded a ready agricultural surplus, slaveowners had little trouble providing their bondsmen with a large—and under optimal conditions varied—supply of food.

The basic allowance that most antebellum slaveowners allotted to their slaves was remarkably uniform: it centered on two staples, cornmeal and fat pork. Even in the eighteenth century these had usually formed the basis of slave diet (and southern diet in general), but in the nineteenth century a peck of cornmeal and two-and-one-half to four pounds of pork or bacon per week became the widely accepted standard for the healthy adult. Many owners supplemented this allowance with various regional and seasonal items. Those who lived near the coast, for example, often provided fish; Thomas Jefferson's "Ration list for 1796" included fish instead of pork, and Austin Steward remembered his Virginia owner supplying "a few herrings" in

addition to the ration of corn. In the summer masters commonly provided fruits and vegetables; one noted in his diary that he "gave the
negroes 108 water-melons and kept 18 for ourselves." Many owners
also dispensed occasional luxuries, such as molasses, sugar, coffee,
and even whiskey, and most made an effort to supply young children
with milk.[58]

If this basic allowance had constituted the sole fare of the slaves,
their diet would have been not only monotonous but also nutrition-
ally deficient. Indeed, some historians have argued that slave diet was
so unvaried that it left most bondsmen lacking basic vitamins and
seriously prone to illness. Even if true, this would say little about the
intentions of slaveowners, who had never heard of vitamins; the evidence suggests, however, that although some slaves subsisted largely
on pork and corn, for most these constituted only the core items,
which were supplemented by a wide range of additional products.
The majority of masters allowed their slaves small garden plots on
which they grew vegetables and raised chickens and which also often
provided them with petty cash to buy sugar, coffee, tobacco, and
other luxuries. In much of the South slaves could supplement their
diet with fish and shellfish caught from the teeming coastal waters
and inland rivers, and elsewhere they hunted and trapped small game
from wild turkeys to possums. In the summer there were other delicacies: "Plums, peaches, pears and apples; strawberries, blackberries,
raspberries and cherries . . . all these we are about to leave to our
negroes," wrote South Carolina's William Gilmore Simms in 1839 as
he prepared to depart his Woodland plantation for the summer.
"These poor devils, whom you northern abolitionists so greatly pity,
will have, for the gathering, constantly within their reach, dainties
which you and I would purchase with difficulty and at great price in
New-York and Charleston markets." In short, the basic allowance
provided only the "meat and potatoes" of the slave diet; the slaves
themselves—in cooperation with a generous environment—added
richness and variety to it.[59]

Despite the near ubiquity of the basic allowance, therefore, slaves'
diets varied considerably according to seasonal and regional constraints as well as the liberality of their owners in providing garden
plots and luxuries. Although some slaves were unable to partake of
these supplemental items and a few went to bed hungry, most had
diets that ranged from sufficient in quantity but lacking in diversity
to abundant and varied. As Frederick Douglass noted, "Not to give a
slave enough to eat, is regarded as the most aggravated development

of meanness even among slaveholders." Indeed, ex-slaves often had particularly fond memories of food under the peculiar institution, memories apparently partially colored by the deprivation many had since suffered. "Sumtimes, I wishes dat I c'uld be back ter de ol' place, 'cayse us did hab plenty ter eat an' 'specially at hog killin' time," declared one; another noted that although under slavery "us had a plenty ter eat . . . us don't always do dat now" and fondly remembered "bread, cake, greens, peas, and best er evything," adding, "I show did lak black-eyed peas and dem ash-cake." Black interviewers elicited much the same sentiment as white: in interviews conducted by whites, 87.9 percent of blacks who described the food they received as slaves rated it as "good," "adequate," or the same as their masters', while only 12.1 percent rated it as "bad" or "inadequate"; in interviews conducted by blacks, the corresponding figures were 80.0 percent and 20.0 percent.[60]

Indicative of the level of material care afforded antebellum southern slaves is evidence showing that they were considerably healthier than slaves elsewhere in the New World. Mortality rates of Caribbean slaves in the half-century before emancipation were 10 to 40 percent higher than those of southern bondsmen.[61] Recent research on height—historically closely related to nutrition—has revealed that southern slaves were more than two inches taller on the average than both Trinidad-born slaves and nineteenth-century Englishmen (although they were an inch shorter than American whites). The estimated life expectancy at birth of thirty-two to thirty-six for antebellum southern slaves was lower than that of white Americans overall (about forty) but higher than that of most people in the world, including those in northern cities such as New York and Boston, and probably close to that of southern whites.[62]

A final element of the slaves' material care was the medical treatment they received. Among both blacks and whites diseases—some diagnosed and others of vague nature—were rampant, because until the late nineteenth century medical knowledge was so primitive that the ability to prevent or contain illnesses was severely limited. Slaveowners' records from the colonial and antebellum periods alike are filled with comments such as "Nancy, Molly & Betty have the measles, & about ten of the negroes" or "11 sick now on hand." In a typical letter George Noble Jones's overseer reported that he was sick and "the black People has not bin so well of Late Either." He attributed the illness to "a heap of wet weather" but noted proudly that "Most Every Large Plantation in this Settlement has got the Measles

Except your Plantations." Bennet H. Barrow complained succinctly that "it seems I am never to escape the *Epidemics*."[63]

Although it probably made little difference, most sick blacks received considerably more medical attention than most sick whites, because slaveowners were constantly ministering to their ill slaves, both personally and through doctors. When William Byrd heard that ten nearby slaves had distemper, he "gave a vomit to six of my people by way of prevention." Two weeks later, when his maid Anaka became ill, he "gave her a vomit that worked very well and she was better the next day." Perhaps so, but he immediately added, "then I had her sweated and bled which gave her some ease. However, her fever continued violently." Nineteenth-century masters, too, frequently practiced home cures, from vomits and bleeding to medical concoctions; Barrow noted that although most doctors demurred, "Bleeding when first taken and Euretics immediately" thereafter would cure colds and scarlet fever "in ninety nine cases in one hundred." Nevertheless, like other planters he usually turned to trained physicians when serious illness struck. In certain instances—such as vaccinating for smallpox—doctors' attention proved beneficial, but in most cases their prescriptions differed little from those of slaveowners who treated their own slaves, and it is unlikely that the medical care that slaves received substantially promoted their health. Such care is significant not because it improved their health but because it indicated their owners' concern for their health.[64]

Of course, it is one thing to say that slaveowners cared for their slaves and spoke often of their affection for them; the question still remains to what extent the slaves themselves recognized such care and affection—that is, to what extent slaveowner paternalism was actually put into practice. There is a great deal of conflicting evidence on this issue. Some ex-slaves spoke only of oppression, exploitation, and misery when describing slavery. "I kin tell you things about slavery times dat would make yo' blood bile, but dey's too turrible. I jus' tries to forgit," declared one, who launched into a tale of whippings and tortures before stopping abruptly with the statement, "I ain't never tol' nobody all dis an' ain't gwine tell you no mo'." "Dem days was hell," asserted another succinctly.[65]

But others had different recollections. A few defended slavery as better than freedom: "People has the wrong idea of slave days," declared ex-slave Simon Phillips. "We was treated good." Although such advocates of slavery were rare among ex-slaves, the testimony of most contained abundant evidence of mixed and even positive feelings toward particular owners, together with assertions of good treatment, protective masters, and close ties between slaveowner and slave. (Such feelings for overseers, hirers, and patrollers were largely absent.) This is true of autobiographies written before the Civil War as well as those written later, of interviews conducted by blacks as well as those conducted by whites. A survey of ex-slaves who discussed their treatment in FWP interviews found that white interviewers were only slightly more likely than black to elicit favorable comments about slaveowners: in 795 interviews conducted by whites, 73.4 percent of the respondents expressed either "very favorable" or "favorable" attitudes toward their masters, while in 267 interviews conducted by blacks 59.5 percent did. More surprising than such views, which were colored by the passage of three-quarters of a century, were professions of profoundly ambivalent attitudes toward slaveowners by slave autobiographers who had fled the South and were directing their words to the northern public. Solomon Northup, for example, a free Negro who was kidnapped into slavery and who had three different masters, described two of them as cruel and abusive but the other as a "kind, noble, candid, Christian man" who was "a model master." Even Frederick Douglass, one of the most passionate critics of slavery among the fugitives, described an institution that was extremely variable, with pleasure and kindness coexisting with suffering and brutality.[66]

An extraordinary number of ex-slaves described their *own* masters as good while denouncing most others and slavery in general as cruel and inhuman. "Our marster wuz sho good to all his niggers," declared one ex-slave, immediately adding that "there wuz plenty white folks dat wuz sho bad to de niggers, and especially dem overseers." Another related that "I lived with good people; my white folks treated us good. There was plenty of em' that didn't fare as we did ... Dats why we loved, 'spected master, 'course he was so good to us." Similar stories were told by fugitives who escaped to Canada and were interviewed in 1863 by members of the American Freedmen's Inquiry Commission. Over and over, ex-slaves contrasted their own kind masters with cruel ones on adjacent holdings or with brutal overseers, hirers, and patrollers.[67]

In part, perhaps, such recollections may represent a psychological defense mechanism. Like other people, ex-slaves liked to remember their own position as especially favored, and many slaves evidently took real vicarious pleasure in the wealth, power, prestige, and kindness of their masters. As Douglass explained, slaves would frequently fight each other over whose master was kinder, smarter, or richer: "they seemed to think that the greatness of their masters was transferable to themselves." No doubt, too, many slaves, whose knowledge of the world was limited, were so impressed with their owners' wealth and power that they exaggerated their greatness in their own minds. A former slave from Alabama remembered that "ev'y body thought dey Marsta waz de bes', didn't know no better." (He himself called his owner "good ter us" but then mentioned that his earliest memory was of his mother being whipped.)[68]

But in a broader sense these recollections are surely an indication of the intense relationship that existed between many masters and slaves, a relationship that encompassed respect and affection as well as fear, hatred, and brutality. Virtually all blacks remembered slavery in the abstract as dreadful, and most could tell heartrending tales of horrors they had witnessed under it. Yet a substantial number had fond memories too, and warm personal feelings toward at least some of those who held them in bondage. They did not entirely share their masters' idea of what slaveholder paternalism was all about—they did not, for example, accept the notion of themselves as a simple, ignorant people who needed constant direction—but along with their bitterness they often shared at least some of the feelings of warmth that their masters expressed for them. That these feelings of affection could flourish between individual masters and slaves even within the exploitative, oppressive institution of bondage is a significant sign of the nature of social relations under American slavery, because such feelings have by no means been universal between class enemies in other times and places. Indeed, they were largely absent in pre-reform Russia.

*　　*　　*

IN RUSSIA, TOO, a movement toward amelioration in the treatment of serfs took place during the century preceding emancipation. The government took a number of steps to reduce the worst excesses of arbitrary pomeshchik authority over peasants, and some noblemen showed a heightened interest in the well-being of their serfs. This apparent parallel with developments in the United States South, however, was largely illusory. Although the government endeavored to eliminate abuses in serfdom, the various reforms failed to affect substantially the treatment of most serfs, who unlike American slaves did not see any improvement in their material standard of living. Equally important, few noblemen developed the kind of paternalistic ethic that was so widespread in the antebellum South.

As in America, harsh and arbitrary treatment of bondsmen was routine in seventeenth-century and eighteenth-century Russia. In their instructions to stewards pomeshchiki regularly prescribed "cruel punishment" and "merciless beatings with the knout" for peasants who disobeyed orders, just as the government did for those who disobeyed laws, and stewards regularly applied such treatment on their own when they deemed it necessary. The assertion of one of A. I. Bezobrazov's head stewards in 1686 that "one must beat these peasants, sir, to keep them in control" reflected a widely shared attitude among estate administrators, an attitude confirmed by the behavior of their employers. When one of Bezobrazov's peasants complained of steward-imposed beatings and whippings "in the field and on the threshing floor," Bezobrazov reproached the steward, but on numerous occasions the nobleman had both serfs and stewards beaten for minor offenses. Indeed, peasants rarely complained about routine physical correction, probably because both they and their owners took it for granted; only unusual brutality was worth noting.[69]

From the second half of the eighteenth century, there is evidence of mounting concern, especially at the governmental level, about the treatment of serfs. During the reign of Catherine II (1762–96), under the influence of Enlightenment thought, the "peasant question" emerged as a lively topic of debate in upper government and noble circles. The thrust of reform sentiment involved not the abolition of serfdom but rather methods of limiting the worst abuses associated with arbitrary power of pomeshchiki over peasants. Suggestions included setting limits to the amount of work that could be required of serfs, limiting the punishment to which they could be subjected, prohibiting their sale apart from the land, and providing for their ownership of property. Catherine herself expressed the physiocratic thought inherent in much of this reform sentiment when she noted in her famous "Instruction" of 1767 that agriculture, "the first and principal Labour, which ought to be encouraged in the People," could never flourish where producers were denied the right to their own property, for "Every man will take more Care of his own Property, than that which belongs to another." Government concern with the arbitrary nature of pomeshchik authority continued during the reigns of Alexander I (1801–25) and even conservative Nicholas I (1825–55), who established no fewer than ten secret governmental committees to consider the peasant question. Nicholas clearly expressed the dominant if vacillating sentiment that reforms were essential in an 1842 speech to the State Council. Noting that "serfdom . . . in its present form is perceptibly and obviously harmful for everyone," the monarch at the same time warned that "to touch it now would be even more disastrous." Still, "the present situation cannot continue *forever,*" he admitted; while "we cannot give freedom," we can, he suggested, "open the door to a different, transitional status" under which serfs would have rights—perhaps even including landowner-ship—clearly spelled out.[70]

Prompted by this new concern, the government took a series of measures designed to make serfdom more humane. As early as 1719 an imperial instruction to military governors referred to "some inde-cent people" who "beat and torment" their peasants, imposing on them "all sorts of unbearable burdens," thus forcing them to flee their homes and depriving the government of its legitimate tax revenue, and ordered intervention when necessary to prevent such abuse. In general, however, it was not until the late eighteenth century that the government took much action on behalf of mistreated serfs. Well into that century the bulk of laws and government decrees on the peasant question were aimed at restricting serf mobility, punishing fugitives, and strengthening the authority of pomeshchiki, but beginning in Catherine's reign an increasing number were designed to protect peas-ants against seigneurial abuse, improve their condition under serf-dom, and encourage private manumissions.[71]

The protective legislation, which increased in volume during the last years of serfdom, included both frivolous and serious measures. Several acts were aimed at the sale and separation of serfs. A law of 1771 prohibited the auctioning of individual serfs apart from the land, but when this proved too hard to enforce, it was superseded by one of 1792 that simply forbade use of a hammer by the auctioneer. Imperial ukazes of 1833 and 1841 repeated previous admonitions against separating family members by sale. Another group of laws sought to protect serfs from physical mistreatment. In 1797 Emperor Paul forbade Sunday barshchina and noted that a seigneurial work-load of three days per week was normal, although he did not actually prohibit barshchina of more than three days; a government circular of 1853 urged noblemen not to require more than the customary three days' labor. An act of 1827 provided that if sale of land left a pomeshchik with less than 4.5 desiatiny (1 desiatina = 2.7 acres) of land per soul, his serfs could petition to become state peasants. The legal codes of 1845 and 1857 set new restrictions on punishment of serfs: a maximum of forty blows with birch switches and fifteen with a stick. And the 1803 Free Cultivators Act—reinforced by legislation of 1842 and 1847—allowed noblemen to free both individuals and groups, in exchange for their self-purchase, setting them up as independent proprietors.[72]

The government also manifested its concern about abuse of seigneurial power through the practice of confiscating the estates of malefactors and putting them under the temporary control of guardians, who ran them until the owners were deemed fit to resume authority (or until they died and their heirs inherited the property). Although Peter I had ordered the confiscation of estates of owners who mistreated serfs as early as 1719, the practice was extremely rare until the nineteenth century. In 1802 Alexander I sent a secret circular to governors noting that "some pomeshchiki, forgetting their fear of God, their own honor, and their obligation to humanity, treat their peasants . . . cruelly and inhumanely." The emperor ordered governors to conduct investigations when they heard of seigneurial abuses—"especially cruelty and excessive punishments"—and then report immediately to him and await word on what action to take, adding that in order not to arouse the peasants the investigations should be conducted "in secret." Over the following decades an increasing number of noblemen faced such investigations and, in extreme cases, confiscation of their estates. In 1836, for example, when an investigator discovered "dissolute behavior" on the part of a serf-owner as well as "his cruelty to peasants, whom he reduced to such an impoverished condition that they lived on communal charity," the emperor ordered the estate put into guardianship, had the serfowner and his family exiled to Kostroma, allowed a serf who had been unjustly sent to Siberia to return home, and prescribed a "severe reprimand" for a local official who had ignored the situation. In another instance, in 1844, the estate of a pomeshchik who "forcibly seduced two underaged peasant girls of his and punished one of them for refusing to continue illegitimate relations with him" was placed under guardianship. In 1838, 140 estates were being run by guardians as a result of owner mistreatment of serfs; by 1854 their number had increased to 193 and they contained a total of 28,508 peasants.[73]

A final form of government action was confined to the empire's western provinces, where religious and nationality differences between serfs and owners frequently added to the complexity of peasant-noble relations. Reform measures began during the years 1816–19 with the landless emancipation of the serfs in the isolated Baltic provinces, where many noblemen, convinced that they would be better off economically as employers of hired labor without the burdens of serfdom, requested the transformation. More closely watched in the rest of Russia were the "inventory reforms" introduced in the western Ukraine, Belorussia, and Lithuania between 1845 and 1848, whereby peasant obligations to owners were spelled out—and limited—in agreements drawn up by committees of local officials. The practice of drawing up inventories had long been a customary feature of serf relations in the western provinces, but the introduction of mandatory inventories in the late 1840s cheered reformers and alarmed most pomeshchiki—even though the inventories did not appreciably lighten the burden of serfdom—because they signified government acceptance of the idea of imposing legal restraints upon arbitrary authority of masters over serfs.[74]

Nevertheless, for several reasons the impact of government efforts to ameliorate the serfs' condition was limited and did not turn serfdom into a version of paternalistic slavery. First, most of the reforms were more cosmetic measures than serious efforts to restrain the authority of pomeshchiki over their serfs. Although many high-ranking government officials were truly bothered by what they came to view as an anachronistic institution, they repeatedly shied away from far-reaching reforms that might alienate the nobility and risk provoking disorders among the peasantry. Equally significant, most of the new measures were either not enforced or enforced so lackadaisically as to vitiate their intent. Finally, the reform spirit was primarily governmental and did not spread to the bulk of pomeshchiki who, unlike most American slaveowners, remained little concerned about their serfs except as sources of income. The reform measures were significant as evidence of a new attitude on the part of the government and brought real benefits to a small number of serfs; their impact on serfdom as a whole, however, was relatively slight.

The inventory reforms must be seen as part of an exceptional policy designed to deal with specific regional peculiarities rather than as part of a general program to reform serfdom. The most salient feature of labor relations in the western provinces was that Orthodox Russian and Ukrainian peasants often belonged to Catholic or Protestant noblemen of Polish or Germanic nationality. The Russian government thus had two major reasons for concern. First, the nationalism of the Polish nobility—which flared into the open in 1831 and continued to smolder thereafter—rendered Russian authorities uniquely unsympathetic to the position and interests of pomeshchiki in the western Ukraine and Belorussia and anxious to secure the loyalty of the peasantry there in case of any nationalist revolt. Equally significant, the government viewed with a jaundiced eye ownership of Orthodox peasants by non-Orthodox landowners, a situation it faced only along the empire's borders. In such areas the government often appeared unusually solicitous of the peasants. The report of the Third Department (political police) for 1838, for example, noted that noblemen would be allowed to resettle Orthodox serfs in the western provinces "only where there would be Greco-Russian churches a short distance from the new settlement, or if pomeshchiki made a commitment to build churches in the new settlement and to provide at their own expense all necessary religious ceremonies." The same policy applied along Russia's southeastern border, where "the transfer of Russian peasants is absolutely forbidden into the trans-Volga region until its final organization, with the aim of saving Orthodox peasants from the power of noblemen of the Mohammedan faith, by whom they were often sold for resettlement in Transcaucasia." In any case, not only was inventory reform limited to areas where Polish or German noblemen predominated; it also failed to improve the condition of the serfs, whose initial joy quickly turned to dismay when they learned the nature of the inventories prepared for them by committees of noble officials. In some cases this dismay produced substantial peasant unrest and violence.[75]

The various acts designed to free or facilitate the freeing of serfs represented the most important of the government's reform measures. The vast majority of emancipated serfs—more than four hundred thousand souls—were in the Baltic provinces, where, as in the western Ukraine and Belorussia, most noblemen were non-Russians whose relations with their peasants constituted a special case. Within Russia proper, most significant were the laws of 1803 and 1842 designed to facilitate private manumissions, although fewer serfs were able to benefit from them than reformers originally hoped, because to do so necessitated the completion of voluntary agreements between serfs and their owners, agreements that usually required the serfs to offer substantial redemption payments to achieve their freedom. During the more than half-century under Alexander I and Nicholas I, 114,302 male souls received their freedom under the Free Cultivators Act of 1803 through 411 voluntary agreements; by far the largest of these involved the purchase of freedom by 13,371 serfs of Prince Alexander Golitsyn in 1807 for 5,424,168 rubles. Even more disappointing was the effect of the 1842 act, under which only 24,708 souls, all belonging to three serfowning families, were freed. Most noblemen were simply not interested in freeing their serfs.[76]

For the great majority of serfs who were *not* emancipated the impact of government-sponsored efforts at amelioration was slight. The number of serfs protected by guardianships was tiny. Indeed, most estate confiscations were for offenses other than abuse of serfs. In 1840, for example, 305 estates were placed under the care of guardians, but only 23 of these were for owner mistreatment of serfs; the bulk—270—was for owner indebtedness. Within individual provinces the same pattern held: of 283 noble estates under guardianship in Kaluga province in 1860, only 7 involved charges of cruelty to peasants; 155 were for underaged owners, 60 for excessive indebtedness, and 29 for unsettled disputes among heirs. Nor were serfs always satisfied with the administration of guardians, who were after all themselves noblemen sharing the basic attitudes toward peasants of the temporarily deposed owners. Guardianships were important not because they directly improved the lot of many serfs—they did not—but because the threat of their imposition hung over pomeshchiki and thus served to some extent to limit indirectly their abusive behavior.[77]

The governmental goal of softening serfdom was not entirely unfulfilled. Prominent individuals urged noblemen to treat their serfs humanely, and some nineteenth-century observers detected increased solicitude on the part of Russian masters for their charges. One Riazan province nobleman, for example, later recalled that by the 1840s serfdom had become "incomparably more tolerable than it previously was," not only because the government acted to prevent abuses but also because pomeshchiki themselves undertook "a lightening and improvement in the use of their authority." In 1844 the Third Department's "Moral-Political Report" was cautiously optimistic on the treatment of serfs. "Unfortunately, many of our noblemen," it noted, "especially the small landowners, as a result of insufficient education and a coarse lifestyle . . . do not understand that one may succeed better by means of gentle reprimands than constant severity, and know of no other way to discipline except corporal punishment." Nevertheless, conditions were improving, "for formerly cruel treatment of serfs was universal, but now it produces indignation even among noblemen, and the government takes measures as soon as a pomeshchik takes excessive or unjust action toward his peasants."[78]

Such judgments were overly optimistic. Although there was apparently some reduction in the incidence of extreme brutality, legislation designed to limit mistreatment of serfs was most notable for being ignored by pomeshchiki and unenforced by local authorities. Despite governmental admonitions, sale of serfs apart from land continued unabated, barshchina in excess of three days remained commonplace, and harsh physical punishment was so widespread that it would have been almost impossible for the government to intervene successfully against it. The juridical softening of serfdom evident from the late eighteenth century was only slightly translated into a softening of the actual serf regime.[79]

One reason for this is that officials charged with maintaining order and supervising relations between serfs and owners—from the lowest authorities at the district level to provincial governors—were themselves usually serfowners who shared the class attitudes of other noblemen. Such officials were inclined to be extremely suspicious of peasant complaints against owners and to give pomeshchiki the benefit of the doubt in all but the most flagrant cases of abuse. As a government report recognized in 1835, "the local police in many provinces are not only worthless but harmful; they not only do not stop abuses, but by their groundless and illegal actions frequently engender them."[80]

The government in St. Petersburg itself sent contradictory signals to these officials. It exhorted pomeshchiki to practice humanity, but its actions were unlikely to convince noblemen and local officials to take such exhortations seriously. Under the "enlightened" rule of Catherine II the government showed more interest in repressing serfs than in protecting them; during the first six (most "reform-minded") years of her reign alone, two hundred and fifty acts were passed imposing new restrictions on peasants and strengthening noble prerogatives over their human property. Meanwhile, she and her successor Paul transferred hundreds of thousands of state peasants to the ranks of privately held serfs. Although such grants were not continued in the nineteenth century and Alexander I and Nicholas I talked privately of the need for reform, both indicated by their actions an obsession with the maintenance of order, authority, and obedience that overwhelmed their reformist impulses. Occasionally they ordered confiscations of estates and imposition of guardianships, but more often they accepted the word of pomeshchiki and local officials that peasants had no cause for dissatisfaction and ordered severe chastisement of troublemakers. When the goal of protecting serfs from arbitrary treatment conflicted with the government's concern for order, the former almost always yielded precedence to the latter.[81]

If official Russia did not take seriously its own admonitions to protect serfs from mistreatment, it can hardly be surprising that such mistreatment remained widespread. Indeed, only the most exceptional cases came to authorities' attention. In its annual report for 1851 the Third Department listed twenty-five pomeshchiki and ten stewards who had caused the death of sixty-eight serfs through excessive punishment. But for every such disclosure, hundreds of less extreme examples of severity were ignored. Torture and sadistic cruelty, although common enough to cause official concern, did not typify the behavior of most pomeshchiki and stewards; a callous disregard for the humanity of their serfs, however, did.[82]

There is little evidence for the development among Russian pomeshchiki of the kind of paternalistic regard for their people that flourished among antebellum American planters. Of course, defenders of serfdom insisted that such paternalism existed; a Riazan province nobleman, for example, recalled from his childhood "a true patriarchal situation" and denied witnessing among the serfs poverty or "any kind of seigneurial oppression or tyranny." Most observers, however, recognized the shallowness of noble paternalism. Reform-minded nobleman A. P. Zablotskii-Desiatovskii argued in 1841 that although a small number of pomeshchiki provided for the well-being of their serfs, the typical nobleman was so different from his peasants that he was unable to develop any kind of empathy for them. To the serf, he noted, the nobleman "in a sense has the character of a foreign order, with strange, alien beliefs, habits, and customs." Nicholas Turgenev, a former Decembrist, put the same sentiment more bluntly from exile: "En Russie," he wrote, "noblesse *n'oblige* pas."[83]

The key to this lack of paternalism was the absentee mentality of most pomeshchiki. Serfowners who infrequently saw their serfs were not in the same position as most American slaveowners to care for their people, and even resident noblemen rarely knew and took an immediate interest in the lives of most of their serfs. When in Tolstoy's semiautobiographical short story "A Russian Proprietor" (1852) the nineteen-year-old hero Prince Nekliudov leaves the university to devote himself to improving the condition of his 700 serfs, his aunt is shocked by his peculiar behavior. "I am now in my fiftieth year, and I have known many fine men," she lectures; "but I have never heard of a young man of good family and ability burying himself in the country under the pretext of doing good." Few pomeshchiki read the Bible to their serfs, personally administered medicine to the sick, invited them to parties, or generally took any kind of delight in relations with them. The absentee mentality of pomeshchiki did not necessarily mean that Russian serfs fared worse than their American counterparts; indeed, from their point of view there were some real advantages to the seigneurial neglect they enjoyed. Absenteeism did, however, generally preclude the development of warm personal relations between master and serf.[84]

A graphic example is provided by developments on Countess S. Bobrinskaia's absentee holding in Simbirsk province during the years 1832–53. The estate, evidently never visited by the countess, contained more than six hundred male and female serfs who over the years stubbornly resisted efforts to rationalize their management and succeeded in frustrating a series of stewards sent to tame them. At the same time the peasants flooded the seigneurial home office with dozens of complaints of mistreatment and poverty. A special report, made in 1843 by the countess's head manager who came to the estate to find out what was wrong, pinpointed the problem. The semiliterate steward was totally incompetent, his reports were "impenetrable," the peasants paid no attention to his directives, and the fawning starosta answered every question with "I don't know, master, it's written down there." "The situation of this estate can be expressed in one word," complained the exasperated investigator: "it is a neglected orphan." Seven years later a new head manager found that nothing had improved; the starosta was "illiterate" and "untrustworthy," but "aside from him there is nobody." An unsatisfactory steward—not the same one as in 1843—had recently been removed, and the serfs refused to recognize the starosta's authority; in fact, "they are not in submission to him, but he to them." The head manager concluded sadly that "we need a local steward" but "it is difficult to find a steadfast and conscientious person."[85]

The lack of paternalistic care for Russian serfs was reflected in their material condition, which on the whole contrasted unfavorably with that of American slaves. In approaching this question, one must note at the start two important consequences of the fact that serfs usually provided their own sustenance rather than receiving periodic doles from their owners. First, the system as a whole lacked the paternalistic potential present in American slavery: even had pomeshchiki developed more benevolent feelings toward their peasants, such feelings would not necessarily have resulted in improved material conditions for them. Second, variations in standard of living were greater among the serfs than among the slaves. A small but highly visible fraction of serfs—almost all on obrok—lived in relative comfort, and a tiny number enjoyed real opulence. I shall examine property stratification among the bondsmen in Chapter 6; here generalizations refer to the great mass of serfs.

The serfs' material condition has been a subject of considerable interest to—and debate among—Soviet historians. Debate has focused on the status of obrok peasants, whose income and obligations are most easily measured, with most historians arguing that a progressive increase in obrok rates reflected a rising rate of exploitation that caused acute hardship for the majority of serfs. I. D. Koval'-chenko and L. V. Milov have shown, for example, that in four sample provinces average obrok payments per soul increased from a range of 4–4.8 rubles in the late eighteenth century to a range of 11.4–13.1 in the mid-nineteenth and that obrok payments as a percentage of peasant income increased from a range of 18–20.9 to 29.2–37.9. A few historians have challenged the thesis of increasing serf destitution. P. G. Ryndziunskii has drawn very different conclusions from those of Koval'chenko and Milov on the basis of the same statistics. Conceding that obrok rose faster than peasant income and that thus the rate of exploitation increased, Ryndziunskii maintained that in *absolute* terms peasants had more money left over after paying their obrok in the mid-nineteenth century than they had in the late eighteenth and thus could be considered better off (see Table 7).[86]

Similarly, some scholars have challenged the prevailing view that serfs suffered from increasing land deprivation as pomeshchiki increased seigneurial cultivation at the expense of peasant allotments. B. G. Litvak insisted that the size of these allotments, rather than progressively diminishing, showed contradictory trends, with obrok serfs in some sample districts actually having larger holdings in the mid-nineteenth century than their ancestors had in the late eighteenth. The existence of large tracts of unused land meant that in many areas noblemen could increase seigneurial cultivation without impinging directly on that of peasants. Litvak noted that although serfs often protested seigneurial exploitation, few complained of having their land appropriated.[87]

If there is some question about whether serf exploitation was increasing as systematically as most Soviet historians claim, there is little doubt that the vast majority of serfs lived in abject poverty and that many faced a constant struggle to avoid hunger. What is more, evidence suggests that conditions may actually have deteriorated during the first half of the nineteenth century when the swelling population strained the ability of Russia's unproductive agricultural system to produce a surplus for market while at the same time providing for the peasants' dietary needs. For most pomeshchiki the former assumed priority over the latter.

Table 7
Level of exploitation of obrok serfs in four provinces

	Serf income per soul (rubles)	Obrok per soul (rubles)	Obrok as % of income	Income minus obrok (rubles)
MOSCOW				
Late eighteenth century	23.0	4.8	20.9	18.2
Mid-nineteenth century	39.0	11.4	29.2	27.6
increase (%)	69.6	137.5	39.7	51.6
TVER				
Late eighteenth century	25.0	4.5	18.0	20.5
Mid-nineteenth century	40.5	13.1	32.3	27.4
increase (%)	62.0	191.1	79.4	33.7
OREL				
Late eighteenth century	21.0	4.0	19.1	17.0
Mid-nineteenth century	33.0	12.5	37.9	20.5
increase (%)	57.1	212.5	98.4	20.6
RIAZAN				
Late eighteenth century	23.0	4.5	19.6	18.5
Mid-nineteenth century	32.0	11.8	36.3	20.2
Increase (%)	39.1	162.2	85.2	9.2

Source: Based on statistics in I. D. Koval'chenko and L. V. Milov, "Ob intensivnosti obrochnoi ekspluatatsii krest'ian tsentral'noi Rossii v kontse XVIII-pervoi polovine XIX v.," *Istoriia SSSR,* 1966, no. 4, 67.

Unlike American slaves, serfs had to contend with a brutal and capricious climate that imposed severe hardships on them in two ways. First, the bitter Russian winter required peasants to spend a substantial portion of their time trying to keep warm. Although there were regional variations, peasant huts were typically designed with this above all else in mind: they were small, and their dominant feature was the stove that served not only as a place to prepare food but more important as a source of heat near—and on—which family members huddled and slept. In summer peasants often escaped their teeming quarters to sleep out of doors "in hay lofts, in sheds, in the yard," but most of the year they crowded together for warmth. "The peasant family in the winter lives in the same hut as its cattle," wrote one observer, who noted the prevalent "dampness and stench" as well as smoke that emanated from chimneyless fires. "The stove occupies ⅙ or ⅐ the area of the hut," wrote another, adding that "the pregnant, sick, old, and young" rarely ventured far from it.[88]

Second, and more important, serfs did not enjoy nature's bounty in the same way American slaves did. Because of the harsh climate and poor soil that prevailed in much of Russia, it was a constant struggle for peasants to secure an adequate supply of basic food items and difficult to supplement these with fruit, vegetables, fish, and small game. Although peasants enjoyed traditional delicacies such as *piroshki* and *bliny* on holidays and a small number of prosperous families were able to partake of such fare on a more regular basis, most serfs had an extremely limited diet that revolved around grain—from the bread (rye in the northern two-thirds of the country) that formed the heart of the meal to *kasha,* a cereal product made from groats, and *kvas,* a widely consumed beverage made from fermented bread. Cabbage was the most prevalent vegetable, whether consumed plain or in soup (*shchi*), supplemented by onions, beets, and cucumbers. Potatoes, first introduced on a widespread basis in Russia in the 1840s, became a staple only in the second half of the nineteenth century.

Even in the best of times crop yields were low and the peasant diet was precarious. During the first half of the nineteenth century grain yields differed little from those of the past: despite some regional variations, average yields for European Russia only slightly exceeded the abysmal level of three times the seed sown, less than half the prevailing yields in western Europe. As the population increased during the century preceding emancipation, per capita production declined precariously, even while yields per unit of land remained more or less constant and aggregate production increased as more land was brought under cultivation. During the 1840s and 1850s alone, the per capita grain harvest in European Russia declined 8 percent; per capita livestock holdings also fell. Crop failures occurred with increasing severity and frequency. Although occasional failures had been endemic throughout Russian history—in the eighteenth century hardship due to bad weather was especially marked in 1721–24, 1732–36, 1747–49, and 1780–81—in the 1830s and 1840s such disasters became routine, occurring on the average close to every other year and bringing in their wake widespread hunger, suffering, and even death, the latter a consequence of lowered resistance to disease as well as actual starvation.[89]

It is not surprising, then, that serfs were increasingly unable to meet their seigneurial obligations. Even in the seventeenth and eighteenth centuries hard times had commonly led impoverished peasants to seek temporary exemptions from obrok payments, and many had simply reneged on them. The 734 serfs on Baron P. P. Shafirov's Arzamasskii district estate, for example, owed the nobleman annually 110 rubles as well as a broad range of payments in kind, including pigs, geese, ducks, butter, eggs, chickens, sheep, and grain. In 1722 and 1723, however, "they paid him nothing, because of their poverty," explaining that "by the will of God" 173 of "their brother peasants" had died during the two years "from a failure of the grain crop and from the plague." During the nineteenth century the inability of serfs to fulfill obligations—and the resulting mounting arrears in their payments—became chronic and pervasive. Just as noblemen were increasingly in debt to their creditors, so too were their peasants ever more heavily "in debt" to their owners. In many cases such debt reached astronomical figures that could never conceivably be paid off. In the early 1820s, 862 souls owned by Prince Vorontsov in northwestern Russia were 50,830 rubles 15 kopeks in arrears. When in 1823 the prince began taking extreme measures to induce payment, including selling some of the debtors, the serfs managed to pay off 15,562 rubles of the debt, but by 1830 their arrears had reached 41,274 rubles 28 kopeks, or 45 rubles per soul.[90]

The precarious level of the serfs' material existence had a severe—and apparently increasing—impact on their health. Widely scattered statistics from the first half of the nineteenth century point to an average death rate in excess of 40 per 1,000, a figure more than one-third higher than that of southern slaves and similar to that of Caribbean slaves. Especially appalling was the mortality of young children. Frenchman Chappé d'Auteroche's observation in 1761 that although Russian peasants had many children, because of epidemics of smallpox, venereal disease, scurvy, and other illnesses few survived to adulthood, was echoed by official statistics from Orel province almost a century later; 60.9 percent of the province's recorded deaths in 1858 were of children five and under. Inaccurate but suggestive parish statistics indicate an increase in mortality rates beginning in the 1830s and accelerating in the 1840s, a trend confirmed by scattered statistics for individual estates as well.[91]

Of course, much of the material hardship endured by serfs was a consequence of a harsh environment and low level of agricultural technology rather than serfdom itself: serfs faced greater material deprivation than American slaves because the Russian standard of

living was in general lower than the American. But although pomeshchiki were not directly responsible for the harsh economic conditions that produced so much suffering among their serfs, they were
often responsible for exacerbating rather than alleviating that suffering. The way noblemen dealt with their serfs' misery demonstrates
the lack of paternalism that was so striking a feature of Russian
serfdom.

Pomeshchiki were "supposed" to look after their people in time of
disaster; indeed, such protection was an essential rationale for serfdom. And some did. Intelligent owners realized that their own well-
being depended on that of their serfs, that starving peasants could
neither labor effectively nor pay their monetary dues. Many owners,
therefore, strove to prevent their serfs from suffering undue hardship
as a result of natural disasters such as fire, epidemic, or crop failure,
and they responded to pitiful petitions from their peasants with temporary exemptions from obligations or even with small grants of aid.
Because of such largesse, a British traveler argued that "as regards the
rigid necessary—the bare elements of food, covering, and shelter—
the nobility's serfs have decidedly the same advantage over the twenty
million or so of crown slaves (facetiously termed free peasants) as Mr.
Legree's negroes have over free-born British paupers." [92]

This was not, in fact, the case. American slaves were fed by their
masters; where plantations were not self-sufficient in food, owners
purchased needed items for their slaves. Serfs, on the other hand,
were self-supporting; in hard times they had to suffer, turn to the
peasant community, or rely on their owners' charity. Although such
charity was sometimes forthcoming, it was not a routine feature of
master-serf relations. Whereas slaves' dependence on their owners for
food encouraged slaveowner paternalism, the serfs' self-sufficiency
discouraged the emergence of similar benevolent attitudes among
serfowners. Pomeshchiki typically showed more concern with
whether peasants would pay their dues in full than whether they
needed help in time of crisis. Noblemen who rarely knew their serfs
tended to assume that peasants who flooded seigneurial offices with
complaints of distress and requests for special exemptions were loaf-
ers evading their responsibilities. This was all the more so because of
the sheer volume of these petitions in many cases: during the decade
1826–36 Prince Vorontsov's serfs sent some two thousand complaints—about steward abuse, excessive obligations, and inability to
meet those obligations—to the prince's central office in Moscow. The
normal responses to such pleas therefore included accusations of

peasant laziness and deceitfulness and strictures to stewards to make sure that serfs met their obligations.[93]

In April 1842, for example, Countess Bobrinskaia's Simbirsk province serfs wrote to her head manager complaining of their "extreme destitution," accusing their steward of being unwilling to help them, and begging for a handout of grain for spring sowing. The steward, however, blamed the serfs for their own misery, noting that some had squandered their money on drink and others, "from laziness, carelessness in domestic science, and inclination to drunkenness," had ceased cultivating the land to take on hired work, forcing their wives and children to rely on communal charity for subsistence. The following month the head manager strongly reprimanded the unhappy serfs, warning that those who continued to make trouble would be sent into the army if fit or otherwise resettled in Siberia. Eight years later the steward had been promoted to head manager himself and had to deal with renewed complaints of poverty and inability to perform obligations. His response was angrily to denounce the peasants' impertinence: "I personally informed them all, in a communal gathering . . . that except through you they must not come to me with petitions," he reminded the estate starosta. "Therefore, declare to them that they absolutely must not dare to breach established order." The hapless serfs continued to petition various authorities, however, including even on occasion their owner, in vain attempts to secure relief.[94]

This tendency to dismiss desperate appeals for assistance as evidence of laziness and troublemaking was a reflection of noblemen's inclination to ignore their serfs—except as laborers to be exploited. Of course, American slaveowners regarded their slaves as sources of income too, but they *also* looked upon them as wards who needed care and protection and as individuals with personalities of their own. Pomeshchiki, despite lip service to their role as patriarchs, usually approached their serfs as absentee owners even when they actually lived on their estates. Their peasants reciprocated: evidence of affection for owners, widespread among bondsmen in the southern United States, is almost totally absent for Russia. Serfs looked upon their owners as aliens for whom they labored but whom they rarely knew. Indeed, some serfs were not even sure to whom they belonged.[95]

*   *   *

THUS, although American slavery and Russian serfdom were both preeminently systems of labor exploitation designed to support a dominant class of landowners through the toil of their human property, the treatment that property received diverged significantly during the century preceding emancipation. American slaveowners were largely resident, both physically and mentally, and expressed an increasingly paternalistic concern for the lives of their people. Russian serfowners usually approached their serfs as absentee lords, even when physically present, ignoring them except to extract income from them. The contrast was not, of course, absolute: in both countries there were exceptions to the pattern. Furthermore, in both countries most masters showed more interest in the lives of some of their bondsmen—usually servants—than others. Still, the tendencies of the two systems were prevalent enough to justify the generalization that on the whole antebellum southern slavery produced a paternalistic master class, whereas prereform Russian serfdom engendered one of rentiers.

Because the concept of planter paternalism has generated considerable confusion, it is important to emphasize that paternalistic bondage was not necessarily a "better" bondage. American slaves did enjoy a higher material standard of living than their Russian (or Latin American) counterparts, but they also suffered from much greater day-to-day interference in their lives. Although the slaves enjoyed greater protection and sometimes a warmer personal relation with their owners, the serfs were usually subject to less regulation and were therefore freer to lead their lives as they wished. The essence of slaveowner paternalism was to treat slaves as children who needed constant guidance because they could not manage on their own. Pomeshchiki, too, often spoke of their serfs as children, but their actions suggest either that they were guilty of child abuse or that they regarded them as someone else's children toward whom they owed little responsibility. As Countess Bobrinskaia's head manager suggested, Russian serfs were "neglected orphan[s]."

3

Ideals and Ideology

IN RUSSIA and the United States South bondage created master classes that despite numerous differences shared in many respects a similar outlook on the world. In both countries the masters expressed aristocratic pretensions, seeking to lead lives of genteel elegance and seeing themselves as purveyors of all that was virtuous, including honor, duty, courage, manliness, courtesy, and tradition. Of course, most masters failed in various respects to live up to their self-created standards—there were few perfect aristocrats—and many failed to meet any of them. Furthermore, these aristocratic pretensions did not go unchallenged: in the United States they were partially checked by the democratic spirit that swept the young republic in the forty years preceding the Civil War, and in Russia they were undermined by the nobility's absentee mentality. Nevertheless, both planters and pomeshchiki aspired to this ideal, and their spokesmen insisted that it was the true essence of the social orders they headed. Slaveowners and serfowners saw themselves as bastions of morality in an increasingly decadent era, and were convinced that their world was far preferable to the one that reformers were so persistently trying to foist on them.

Ultimately, however, Russian and American masters found themselves drawn in very different directions. The strength and independence of the southern slaveowning class reinforced its commitment to a world view and a social system increasingly at odds with those of the North, a commitment only heightened by attack from without, whereas the dependent position of Russian pomeshchiki rendered them unable to resist effectively the mounting calls for reform. In the end the Russian masters made an uneasy peace with a changing world, in the process ensuring that they would help to direct the institution of the new order and thereby preserve as much as possible of their way of life. The American masters, on the other hand, were determined to resist change to the death and thus guaranteed its triumph.

*   *   *

CENTRAL to the world view of slaveowners and serfowners was the aristocratic ideal. Significantly, the stereotype of master as aristocrat was also held—although often with very different overtones—by much of the outside world. It was a stereotype that the magnates tried to live up to, the lesser masters aspired to, and the ideologues of bondage insisted was characteristic of the social systems they defended.

To outside observers the most striking features of the aristocratic character fostered by slavery and serfdom were a series of traits stemming from the habit of command that was a natural by-product of owning human beings. Planters and pomeshchiki were widely seen as self-confident, impetuous, impulsive, undisciplined, self-indulgent, and arrogant toward those they considered their social inferiors. Englishman William Coxe found himself coldly received by the governor of Smolensk in the late 1770s because his plain dress created the impression that he was a tradesman, but on learning that he was dealing with an English gentleman the governor became a model of civility. A half-century later, when another English traveler told a nobleman "that some of our blood royal associate with commoners, and even preside at public festivals ... he appeared altogether overwhelmed with astonishment, considering it an act of degradation on the part of persons of such rank." Frenchman Alexis de Tocqueville observed that "the citizen of the Southern states becomes a sort of domestic dictator from infancy; the first notion he acquires in life is that he is born to command." As a result he had "the character of a haughty and hasty man, irascible, violent, ardent in his desires, impatient of obstacles." De Tocqueville added that southerners were "fond of grandeur, luxury, and renown, of gayety, pleasure, and, above all, of idleness." In this last observation he was not alone: visitors commonly noted among the masters a strong aversion to work, which they associated either with their bondsmen or with a mean, money-grubbing mentality of which they wanted no part. In both countries fictional stereotypes emerged of the lazy, idle, foppish, indecisive master, a cipher exclusively concerned with his own amusement.[1]

Slaveowners and serfowners did not so much reject the major components of these unflattering characterizations as shift their emphasis.

Laziness became an ability to relax and enjoy life without constant preoccupation with material gain, and haughtiness became a legitimate pride in the honor of one's family—a pride reflected in the intense interest the masters showed in lineage, rank, and title. Self-indulgence was easily transformed into a commendable passion for cultivating the higher things in life. Outdoor physical activity, horsemanship, and hunting came to assume inordinate importance for many planters and pomeshchiki; General L. D. Izmailov maintained 673 hunting dogs at his home estate, which consumed annually 1,640 sheep and required the attendance of 38 kennel keepers, and Alabama polemicist D. R. Hundley ascribed innumerable aristocratic virtues to the hunt, not the least of which was the "faultless physical development," "the good size and graceful carriage of the Southern Gentleman."[2]

Indeed, planters and pomeshchiki saw themselves as upholders of the best that civilization had to offer, aristocrats in the true sense of the word. Ownership of slaves and serfs, ideologues stressed, provided the masters an independence that enabled them to do their duty in a disinterested fashion, without being corrupted by the need to earn a living or curry favor with an employer or business associate. They were, consequently, in a position to uphold old-fashioned morality: they were courteous and generous to a fault; they were hospitable, honest, straightforward, and loyal; they valued above all home and hearth, family and religion; they prized their "manly" courage and decency and treated their women like ladies. They were patriarchs who governed their own "people" strictly but with justice and affection and who patriotically guarded the well-being of community and country.[3]

An essential element of these aristocratic pretensions was an ornate life-style. Few travelers to the slave South or imperial Russia failed to comment on the conspicuous consumption they witnessed. "Mrs. *Carter* informed me last Evening," marvelled Philip Fithian, a young New Jersey–born tutor who in 1773–74 sojourned on the estate of Virginia planter Robert Carter III, "that this Family one year with another consumes 27000 Lb of Pork; & twenty Beeves. 550 Bushels of Wheat. besides corn—4 Hogsheads of Rum, & 150 Gallons of Brandy." Russian noblemen, like American planters, flaunted their wealth and breeding with classically designed mansions, formal gardens, fancy balls, imported wines, strict etiquette, and a seemingly endless round of entertaining. Although the grandeur and elegance were seductive, many visitors found them troubling as well, suspecting that they represented "a love of display, rather than real taste and knowledge." American ambassador James Buchanan concluded that the Russian nobility had "acquired all the vices of French civilization in it's [sic] highest state without any of it's redeeming qualities, except politeness." Alexis de Tocqueville, no stranger to aristocratic foibles, saw in southern slaveholders "the tastes, the prejudices, the weaknesses, and the magnanimity of all aristocracies."[4]

Indicative of their life-style were the retinues of domestic servants with which wealthy planters and pomeshchiki surrounded themselves. Although no precise statistics exist on what proportion of American slaves were domestics, historians have commonly estimated that one-quarter of antebellum slaves "worked in and around the house rather than in the fields." If this estimate is accurate, there was an average of about two house slaves per slaveowning family, a relatively unimpressive figure until one recalls that most slaveowners possessed only a few slaves of any sort. Large planters invariably detailed a considerable number of slaves—usually including several children and old persons not fit for strenuous labor—to serve as cooks, butlers, valets, washers, maids, nurses, grooms, coachmen, gardeners, and the like. George Washington's 1786 list of slaves showed that of a total of 216, 67 resided at his "Home House" where no agricultural cultivation was practiced; 41 of these were adults, and although a few engaged in general labor or were idle because they were "old and almost blind," most were servants. Thomas Jefferson's Monticello slaves were divided into three categories: "house," "tradesmen," and "farm"; in 1810 about half of them—37 of 78—were house slaves. On John Tayloe's Mount Airy, Virginia, estate, 106 of 384 slaves in 1809 lived on his home plantation where no cultivation occurred and all the slaves were either domestics or skilled workers. Frederick Douglass remembered that his Maryland owner "kept a large and finely cultivated garden, which afforded almost constant employment for four men, besides the chief gardener." Because they already owned their slaves and the cost of keeping them at unproductive labor was therefore hidden, and because a substantial number of slaves were not suited for hard physical work anyway, planters easily fell prey to the temptation to use more servants than they "needed." In cities the majority of slaves performed domestic duties. The 105 planters who resided in Charleston in 1860 had an average of 10.1 and a median number of 9.8 slaves with them in the city, most of whom were servants.[5]

Wealthy Russian noblemen went further still. "A Russian seigneur feels himself forced to have eight and ten times more domestics than a Frenchman with the same income," noted a French observer. Servants constituted a smaller proportion of Russian serfs than of American slaves, but because Russian noblemen had far larger holdings than their American counterparts they were able to have more domestics as well. Dvorovye—serfs who did not have their own households but were part of the households of their masters—constituted a special category of serfs enumerated separately in national censuses. Although not all dvorovye were domestic servants—they could occupy such diverse positions as gardeners, musicians, stewards, and even agricultural laborers—most were engaged in making the lives of their owners more pleasant rather than producing income for them, and their numbers are broadly indicative of the level of conspicuous consumption enjoyed by pomeshchiki. In 1851 the ninth census counted 1,035,924 dvorovye, who formed 4.8 percent of the serf population; there was an average of about seven house serfs for every noble family.[6]

This figure, however, hides enormous disparities. The great magnates maintained armies of servants whose excessive numbers meant that many of them had little to do much of the time. In 1765 Prince P. B. Sheremetev, who owned 73,500 male souls, maintained 1,099 of them as dvorvye. Although he was clearly a man of unusual wealth, other prosperous pomeshchiki also kept huge household staffs; General Izmailov, who at the time of his death in 1834 owned some eleven thousand souls, maintained about eight hundred dvorovye on his home estate alone. A partial listing of their jobs reveals much about their owner's life: there were 50 grooms, 36 kennel keepers, 10 laundresses, 7 dairymaids, 11 waiters, 4 footmen, 2 valets, 5 chefs, 7 gardeners, 8 blacksmiths, 7 tailors, 7 saddlers, 6 infirmary workers, 5 scribes, 2 treasurers, and a steward. Although house serfs were most numerous on the holdings of the wealthiest noblemen, they constituted a higher proportion of the serfs owned by lesser pomeshchiki. Prince Sheremetev's 1,099 dvorovye, for example, constituted only 1.5 percent of his serfs, whereas among noblemen of more modest means the proportion of house serfs sometimes reached 20 percent. Although the very richest noblemen boasted private orchestras, acting troupes, or harems made up of house serfs, most pomeshchiki contented themselves with personal servants. But whatever tasks they assigned to their domestics, noblemen with few exceptions agreed that a large staff was essential. As Prince A. B. Kurakin, who kept three hundred servants at his home estate at Saratov province, wrote to his brother, who had evidently suggested that he had an unnecessarily large retinue, "I know what you think of excess of any sort; and I sincerely approve of this repugnance, but . . . many things, my friend, are easier to say than to do; if you could be here, I would be curious to see what reductions you would decide to make."[7]

In both Russia and the American South the aristocratic ideal was tempered by what was all too often a rather grubby reality. Sophisticated life-styles were usually late developments. The pomeshchik of the seventeenth century was likely to be a coarse fellow, scarcely distinguishable in physical appearance from his peasants, often illiterate and rarely showing the slightest interest in intellectual or cultural endeavors. Similarly, landowners in seventeenth-century Maryland and Virginia were on the whole unpretentious men seeking to build their fortunes in a rough frontier environment and wasting little effort at developing cultivated tastes. In both countries moderately wealthy men lived in rude wooden houses with few amenities and generally displayed manners and interests that little distinguished them from the masses around them.[8]

Only in the eighteenth century did a self-conscious master class begin to develop in either country. In Russia this involved the emergence of the nobility as a privileged order whose members, at first under the impetus of prodding from above, increasingly set themselves off from other Russians by adopting the form—and occasionally the content—of western European culture. By the third quarter of the eighteenth century the great magnates—families such as the Kurakins and the Vorontsovs—formed a small aristocracy within the nobility, conversing with each other in French and looking with contempt at the cultural primitiveness of life in the provinces. In 1789 Count D. P. Buturlin wrote to his uncle Count S. R. Vorontsov—in French—deploring Moscow's lack of culture and contrasting that city with the more sophisticated St. Petersburg, which excelled in "spirit, manners, conception, even opinion." In Moscow, he declared, "*theater* is a disgrace."[9]

Buturlin and Vorontsov were, of course, highly unusual men, but noblemen as a whole in the eighteenth century were increasingly conscious of themselves as a distinct group, who differed from other Russians in appearance, dress, manners, language, and interests. Noblemen of middle rank aped the behavior and aspired to the life-style of their wealthier brothers. For example, the diary of I. P. Annenkov, a pomeshchik from Kursk province who in the middle of the eighteenth century owned a thousand souls, reveals a new concern for the cultural achievements of his sons, whom he sent to the nearby cities of Kursk and Belgograd to study French, German, arithmetic, geometry, and science. When the eldest son, Aleksandr, wrote home in 1758 from wartime service in Brandenburg, his first letter was in French and his next in German, although the proud father replied to them in Russian. (Annenkov expressed his love for his daughters differently; when eighteen-year-old Anna married in 1746, her dowry included "silver, dresses and other things worth 1500 r[ubles]" as well as a village containing one hundred souls.)[10]

The process was similar in eighteenth-century America, where as settled life replaced raw frontier and as slavery became an entrenched institution wealthy planters of the Chesapeake colonies and South Carolina increasingly modeled themselves after English gentlemen. The history of the Carter family over four generations illustrates the triumph of this aristocratic ethos. John Carter, who arrived in Virginia in 1649, was a sharp businessman who aggressively built up his landholdings—in 1665 he received a headright of four thousand acres for transporting eighty indentured servants to the colony—most of which he left in 1669 to his son and sole surviving male heir, Robert. Soon known as "King" Carter because of his wealth and prominence, he too showed a strong acquisitive spirit. His correspondence was largely business-oriented, dealing with tobacco growing, prices, and marketing as well as acquisition of land and slaves. By the time of his death in 1732 he owned three hundred thousand acres and more than seven hundred slaves and was probably the richest man in Virginia. But he was also interested, especially in his later years, in enjoying the fruits of his success: he imported elegant manufactured items and artwork for his handsome mansion at Carotoman, drank French margaux, sent his son Landon to England and then to William and Mary College for a proper education, and served in various colonial governmental offices.[11]

The next two Carter generations brought a clear shift of focus. Landon Carter, who inherited nine plantations from his father in 1732, continued to add to his holdings—in good part through his three marriages—but he was less an empire builder than a consolidator and manager. Like others of his class he served as justice of the peace and delegate to the colonial assembly, but he was most noteworthy as a planter, patriarch, and supervisor of agricultural operations. A highly skeptical man convinced that all around him was weakness, he dabbled in science, religion, and philosophy but spent most of his time supervising plantation life, coping the best he could with lazy slaves, incompetent overseers, and ungrateful members of his own family, stressing always the need for discipline, moderation, diligence, and restraint in pursuit of pleasure. Landon's nephew, Robert Carter III, moved still farther away from the acquisitive spirit of the dynasty's founders. He bought neither land nor slaves and rented out the bulk of his seventy-thousand-acre holdings, concentrating his attention on his home plantation, Nomini Hall, where he presided over a life of refinement, entertainment, and sophisticated discourse. Philip Fithian, who came there to tutor the seven Carter children, was utterly charmed by what he found—although shocked by the waste and dissipation—from the elegance and fine manners to his employer's library of fifteen hundred books, his collection of musical instruments, and his "vastly delicate Taste." Robert III even shared the political and philosophical unorthodoxy that gained widespread currency among upper-South aristocrats of the Revolutionary era, rejecting the Anglicanism that all previous Carters had taken for granted to embrace, successively, Deism, Baptism, and Swedenborgianism, and providing in 1791 for the gradual manumission of his five hundred slaves.[12]

Although this four-generation sequence was not universal—in some families the same process took three generations and in others it did not occur at all—the Carters were typical of many wealthy colonial families in their progression from acquiring and building in early years to consolidating, managing, consuming, and in some cases dissipating in later years. A similar pattern, although partially cut short by the Civil War, is evident in the antebellum deep South—from inland South Carolina and Georgia to new southwestern states such as Alabama and Mississippi—where the sons of hardy pioneers who hacked plantations out of the wilderness began to discard their fathers' crude manners and cultivate a life-style of what they considered properly aristocratic caliber. Everywhere, once their operations were well established, planters sought to give legitimacy to their undertakings by becoming more than just agricultural entrepreneurs.[13]

Of course, even during the century before emancipation relatively few masters in either Russia or America approached the aristocratic gentility they sought. Because most foreign travelers came in contact mainly with the wealthiest planters and noblemen, they tended to exaggerate the grandeur of the masters' life-style, assuming that their hosts were typical of slaveowners and serfowners in general. Historians of both countries have been at pains to correct this notion, pointing out that because of sharp property stratification within the master class only a tiny fraction of planters and pomeshchiki were able to live fabled lives of leisure. In the South about three-quarters of all slaveowners possessed fewer than ten slaves and could frequently be found toiling in the fields alongside them. Few such farmers had elevated tastes, refined manners, sophisticated interests, or opulent lifestyles. Landscape architect Frederick Law Olmsted provided a graphic portrait of these lesser slaveowners in his famous travel accounts of the 1850s. He found that they enjoyed little material comfort, lacked basic amenities such as clean sheets, and displayed coarse manners, little generosity, and an appalling ignorance of the outside world. Although Olmsted stayed in the best homes he could find, except among the great aristocrats who were few and far between he saw "no garden, no flowers, no fruit, no tea, no cream, no sugar, no bread . . . no couch—if one reclined in the family room it was on the bare floor—for there were no carpets or mats. For all that the house swarmed with vermin." [14]

Although Russian serfowners generally owned more bondsmen than did American slaveowners, the majority were equally unable to enjoy the extravagant life-style that so impressed foreigners. To judge by their own complaints, they were virtually mired in poverty. According to standards widely accepted by the early nineteenth century, a nobleman needed to own at least a hundred male souls to live in moderate comfort and five hundred or even a thousand to be considered rich; three-quarters of them, however, possessed a hundred or fewer souls, and almost half had no more than twenty and were regarded as impoverished. One recent author has gone so far as to conclude that 98 percent of all noblemen had too few serfs "to be able to rely on their labour and rents for a decent living." Although this is clearly an exaggeration, most noblemen, like most American slaveowners, faced a constant struggle to earn enough to live in the style they judged fitting. Indebtedness grew alarmingly among pomeshchiki during the last century of serfdom, until on the verge of emancipation two-thirds of all serfs were mortgaged to government credit bureaus created expressly to loan money to needy noblemen. [15]

Although these intraclass divisions were significant, they did not vitiate the aristocratic pretensions of the master class as a whole. This was true for two main reasons. First, one must be careful about accepting too uncritically contemporary assertions of slaveowner and serfowner poverty. The wealthy—whether planters, noblemen, or capitalists—have throughout modern Western history complained of insufficient funds and found it necessary to borrow money, whether to finance further investment, tide them over periods of temporary shortage, or maintain an appropriate life-style. In the South such debtors included large planters such as Bennet H. Barrow; in Russia they included Count N. P. Sheremetev, owner of more than two hundred thousand serfs. If nineteenth-century noblemen considered anyone with fewer than one hundred souls poor, there is no reason for us to accept this judgment except in the sense that they were poorer than those owning a thousand souls and poorer than they would like to be. Similarly, one should not take Olmsted's judgments on the South at face value, valuable as his descriptions are, because his travel accounts were in part works of political propaganda designed to show the harmful effects of slavery. Unused to southern ways, he took unfamiliar patterns of behavior as evidence of ignorance, degradation, and poverty.[16]

Although small serfowners and slaveowners were hardly Croesuses and at the very bottom a few had real difficulty making ends meet, the poverty of most must be seen in relative terms. A Russian estate with twenty souls was worth, on the average, 3,000 to 4,000 rubles in the 1850s and one with one hundred souls would bring 15,000 to 20,000 rubles, far from trifling sums when a typical peasant family of eight got by on 75 to 100 rubles per year. A nobleman often received a salary for state service in addition to the income generated by his estate and the privileged order's immunity from state taxes. In the antebellum South slaves had become so expensive by the 1840s that they were increasingly out of reach of most southern whites—the proportion of white families owning slaves declined from 36 percent in 1830 to 25 percent in 1860—and ownership of even five slaves put one among the economic elite. Although the economic gap between large and small slaveholders was great, it was less significant than that between owners and nonowners; the wealth of the "average" slaveowner in the cotton South in 1860—$24,748—was 13.9 times that of the "average" nonslaveholder and more than five times that of the "average" northerner.[17]

Even more important, despite the stratification among the masters there was much that united them as a class. Not only were they wealthier than the vast majority of the population; they were also members of a social elite—the beneficiaries of forced labor—and were likely, whatever their differences with each other, to share certain assumptions about the way people should behave and society should be ordered. If wealthy planters and pomeshchiki were a minority of slaveowners and serfowners, they nevertheless dominated

society both economically and socially and set the tone for the aspirations of their less prosperous neighbors.

It was not the reality so much as the ideal of a particular life-style
that constituted the essence of the masters' aristocratic pretensions.
No matter how crude their actual existence, slaveowners and serfowners developed an aristocratic self-image, one that like most myths
was based on a small parcel of reality interwoven with large doses of
pure fantasy. Although the myth of the aristocrat was by no means
an accurate reflection of reality, it was a *part* of that reality, because
people are characterized by their values and self-image as well as by
the more tangible attributes of their existence; attitudes and beliefs
are as "real" as material goods. A group that sees itself as uncom-
monly generous or chivalric or hospitable—and that places exceptional stock in those traits—is in an important sense different from
one that does not. It is for this reason that the aristocratic ideal of the
masters was so important: it represented a dominant ethos sharply
divergent from the bourgeois ethos increasingly prevalent in the
northern states and parts of western Europe, one that stressed the
dignity of labor, the importance of constant striving for material self-
improvement, the availability of middle-class respectability to all willing to sacrifice for it, and a glorification of human progress and the
spread of democracy. Indeed, the masters' self-image is best understood in the context of their increasingly jaundiced view of the North
and western Europe, a view that led them to see themselves as a beleaguered minority, the last bastions of order and morality in a world
gone mad.[18]

Although the reality of life that was in most cases far from genteel
did not seriously undercut the masters' aristocratic pretensions, those
pretensions did face in each country a more serious obstacle. In the
United States the chief challenge came from the vibrant political democracy that swept South as well as North during the half-century
before the Civil War, bringing with it an egalitarian ideology inhospitable to anything that smacked of elitism. As early as 1776 Landon
Carter bitterly complained of being defeated for reelection to the Virginia legislature because "I did not familiarize myself among the
People." Later, he noted, the same thing happened to his son even
though he "kissed the arses of the people." Such "is the nature of
Popularity," he concluded. "She I long discovered to be an adultress
of the first order." Many others would soon learn the same lesson,
because almost everywhere in the antebellum South, as property qualifications, indirect elections, and a deferential political system gave

way to a vigorous two-party system based on full white manhood suffrage, candidates for elective office found it necessary to portray themselves as men of the people and conduct themselves in a suitably rustic style. Especially in the newer deep-South states such as Alabama and Mississippi, politics assumed the form of pandering to the prejudices of the masses and convincing them that the opposing party represented elite or privileged interests.[19]

Although this ebullient political democracy modified the aristocratic character of southern society, that character nevertheless survived: throughout the antebellum period the South exhibited both democratic and aristocratic tendencies that coexisted in an uneasy but usually peaceful equilibrium. Despite the necessity of appealing to the white masses, planters continued to dominate the South politically as well as socially and economically, and in a curious way democracy actually served to strengthen rather than weaken the defense of planter interests. Because the bulk of the working class—slaves—was outside the body politic, southern democracy was largely a democracy of independent property holders, most of whom saw no basic conflict between their own interests and those of the planting elite. Small slaveowners and yeomen farmers who aspired to be slaveowners naturally turned for leadership to men who were most successful by southern standards—wealthy planters. A perceived commonality of interest—defense of slavery and the right of southerners to shape their own destiny—thus enabled the South to be democratic and aristocratic at the same time: in defending slavery and the way of life that went with it, planters were cast as community and sectional spokesmen, statesmen protecting their people, white and black, from outside attack. Even as southern politics became as rough-and-tumble as any in America, southern spokesmen continued to insist that their section had a near monopoly on principled republican statesmanship whereas in the North a leveling democracy threatened to undermine the social order. During the generation before the Civil War many prominent southerners flatly rejected the notion of equal rights upon which political democracy rested; "it is a wretched and insecure government," declared South Carolina's James H. Hammond, "which is administered by its most ignorant citizens, and those who have the least stake under it." Because planters were at the head of a powerful and increasingly self-conscious sectional culture whose defense required both the preservation of an aristocratic ethos and popular (white) support, southern aristocracy was tempered but not undermined by political democracy.[20]

In Russia aristocracy faced a different challenge—that of the nobility's absentee mentality and dependent status—that ultimately
proved more subversive. Whereas southern planters were local, state,
and sectional leaders, the same could hardly be said for Russian pomeshchiki—especially the most wealthy—among whom absenteeism
was rampant. The effect of this absenteeism on political and social
life was as great as it was on the management of estates. Noblemen
who had estates scattered over several provinces and only occasionally visited them had few community ties and did not consider themselves representatives of particular localities so much as servitors in
the government bureaucracy. Despite Catherine II's highly touted provincial reforms, noblemen on the whole continued to lack any kind
of corporate spirit or local political identification. Although they
hoped that the government would serve their needs, it was no more
their representative than they were the political representatives of
their communities. The provincial and district noble assemblies established by Catherine quickly lost whatever limited authority she may
have intended for them. Real power continued to rest in the tsar and
his bureaucracy, and most noblemen shunned local elective office as a
nuisance to be imposed on unfortunate—often poor and ignorant—
resident pomeshchiki.[21]

The Russian nobility was thus a national service caste, fundamentally different from European aristocracies—or the American planter
class—whose loyalties, sympathies, and interests were firmly rooted
in a particular place. It lacked the independence, corporate spirit, local attachments—as well as the paternalism—of a landed ruling
class. Although noblemen had strong aristocratic pretensions, they
were often closer to rentiers living off the land than gentry living on
it. In a curious way Russian noblemen were less aristocratic than
American planters, and their sway over society was considerably less
extensive as well. Pomeshchiki thus constituted a peculiarly dualistic
class: on the one hand they were landowners and serfowners and
aspired to be a true landed aristocracy; on the other they were government bureaucrats and military servitors divorced both from their
estates and from the normal political power associated with landed
wealth. This dualism was clearly reflected in their ideology: their natural inclination, like that of American slaveowners, was to defend
their prerogatives when these came under attack, but their position
rendered them incapable—unlike American slaveowners—of developing a coherent argument against change or mounting a sustained
effort to prevent it.

* * *

AN EXAMINATION OF the arguments used to defend slavery and
serfdom reveals both striking similarities and an important difference.
American and Russian ideologues came up with many of the same
basic defenses of bondage, ranging from the practical to the theoretical, and in both countries linked bondage to a conservative social
order threatened by alien ideas. Russian thinkers, however, never
elaborated these themes with the same force, sophistication, or volume that the Americans did; whereas southern spokesmen put themselves at the head of a full-fledged proslavery movement, Russian proserfdom thought remained in embryonic form, largely undeveloped.
In the South, moreover, the defense of servitude flourished particularly during the thirty years preceding emancipation, but in Russia it
atrophied during those years until on the eve of emancipation virtually no one publicly called for the preservation of serfdom.

As one might expect, racial arguments in defense of slavery were
pervasive in the United States South. They were common, of course,
among "scientific" racists such as Josiah Nott and Samuel A. Cartwright, who concluded that blacks, with their smaller brains, sloping
foreheads, and deficient respiratory systems, were physiologically so
different from whites that they were fit only for slavery. But racial
arguments were common also among southerners who defended slavery primarily on other grounds. They were present early, as in Landon
Carter's casual entry in his diary that blacks "are devils and to make
them otherwise than slaves will be to set devils free," and late, as in
the insistence of James H. Hammond that emancipation was impossible because "the doom of Ham has been branded on the form and
features of his African descendants." Throughout the South whites
insisted that blacks were different, inferior, and suited for slavery.[22]

What is more noteworthy is that by the eighteenth century Russian
noblemen had come to regard themselves as so different from their
peasants that they were able to invent many of the same kinds of
racial arguments to defend serfdom that American slaveowners used
to justify their peculiar institution. The arguments were not as elabo-
rately worked out: one does not find tomes exploring the physiologi-
cal differences between peasant and nobleman (although some noble
spokesmen actually claimed that whereas they had white bones peasants had black bones). The basic assumptions, however, were similar;
they were "racial" in that they were predicated on the belief in inherent and immutable differences rather than in distinctions based on

particular social or environmental conditions. Peasants were just as intrinsically lazy, childlike, and requiring of direction as were blacks. In 1802 author N. M. Karamzin rebutted the environmentalist argument sometimes advanced by foreigners that the peasants were lazy *because* of serfdom; on the contrary, he insisted, "they are lazy from nature, from habit, from ignorance of the advantages of diligence." Just as defenders of slavery saw free blacks as an anomaly and insisted that all Negroes were better off as slaves, so too advocates of serfdom pointed to their "free" (state) peasants and maintained that they would be happier as serfs under the protection of pomeshchiki. During his short reign (1796–1801) Emperor Paul was able to act on his belief in the desirability of distributing "all state peasants to pomeshchiki" by awarding generous grants of state lands and peasants to deserving noblemen; he rejoiced in placing peasants under the supervision of "police masters" who would both care for them and guard the peace and security of the state.[23]

If racial arguments would seem to be particularly suited to the defense of black slavery, then surely "class" arguments would be the preeminent Russian defense of serfdom. And class arguments did abound. During the second half of the eighteenth century, as nonnoble traders and manufacturers began to challenge the economic supremacy of the nobility and to question their right to a monopoly of serfownership, noble spokesmen, led by Prince M. M. Shcherbatov, composed paeans to the virtue, honor, and service of the nobility, which they contrasted with the money-grubbing ways of the merchantry. If merchants deserved scorn, peasants required care and supervision. "The principal right of a Russian nobleman is to be a pomeshchik," wrote Karamzin in an essay extolling his own patriarchal regard for his "people"; "his principal duty is to be a good pomeshchik." Serfdom enabled noblemen to care for and protect their ignorant but well-meaning charges. Playwright and poet Ivan Boltin, emphasizing "the affection of the slaves [serfs] for their masters," noted that these masters "maintain their slaves as the duty of humanity demands" and contrasted the happiness of the Russian peasant with the misery of the poor in western Europe. Count D. P. Buturlin, writing in French to his uncle in 1803, succinctly expressed the paternalistic assumptions inherent in the defense of serfdom. "There is something paternal and gentle in the reciprocal relation between the master and his born servant, whereas this same relationship strikes me as purely mercenary between the hired servant and his master." In the latter case, he explained, "it is a free market, an exchange of his service for my money, and from that point it seems to me that I am finished with everything when I have paid him." [24]

But such arguments also abounded in the antebellum South. Indeed, a perusal of proslavery writings provides ample evidence that a paternalistic insistence on the humanity and harmony of slavery was as pervasive as the racial argument in its defense, especially during the last two decades before the Civil War. A host of polemicists developed detailed justifications centering on the humanity of slavery, the reciprocal relationship between master and slave, and the brutality of the free-labor system. As Baptist minister Thornton Stringfellow put it in an otherwise largely religious justification of the treatment of slaves, "their condition, *as a class,* is now better than that of any other equal number of laborers on earth, and is daily improving." [25]

Antebellum southerners recognized that many of their best arguments in defense of slavery were nonracial, and the less timid among them fully acknowledged this fact. They noted that throughout history slavery had been a prerequisite to civilization and pointed to the slave societies of antiquity and the unfree labor systems of medieval Europe as precedents for southern slavery. Occasionally they even used the precedent of Russian serfdom: Russian serfs, noted Thomas R. R. Cobb, "are contented with their lot and seek no change. They are indolent, constitutionally . . . They are mendacious, beyond the negro perhaps, and feel no shame at detection. Like him, too, they have no providence for the future, and no anxiety about it." [26]

These southerners were not stupid, and they realized that most of the slave systems they cited were not based on racial distinctions. The logic of their position, therefore, led them to broaden the defense of slavery to that of a superior social system, regardless of race. They extolled slavery for serving the best interests of all elements in society, without pitting class against class, while fostering all the tried and true social virtues. They did not deny that blacks were ideally suited for slavery, but they treated this predisposition as a fortunate accident rather than as the essential reason for slavery: had Africans not existed, other slaves would have been required in their place. As Hammond put it in his famous mud-sill speech, "In all social systems there must be a class to do the menial duties, to perform the drudgery of life. That is, a class requiring but a low order of intellect and but little skill. Its requisites are vigor, docility, and fidelity. Such a class you must have, or you would not have that other class which leads progress, civilization, and refinement. It constitutes the very mud-sill of society and of political government; and you might as well attempt to build a house in the air, as to build the one or the other, except on this mud-sill." The South was fortunate in having found blacks, but northern society also rested upon a mud-sill of workers who were "essentially slaves." [27]

During the 1840s and 1850s the boldest and most consistent of the proslavery advocates increasingly downplayed race as a justification for slavery and made explicit their belief that slavery was a superior social system regardless of race. This point of view never dominated the antebellum South's defense of slavery because of the political realities of appealing to a broad segment of nonslaveholding whites, but it was not limited to George Fitzhugh and a handful of eccentrics. "Pity it is," wrote author William Gilmore Simms, "that the lou'zy and lounging lazzaroni of Italy, cannot be made to labor in the fields, under the whip of a severe task-master!" Henry Hughes, in his highly abstract defense of "warranteeism," as he renamed slavery, noted that the "ethnical qualification" was "accidental." "Warranteeism without the ethnical qualification," he concluded, "is that to which every society of one race must progress." In his diary fire-eater Edmund Ruffin praised Fitzhugh's analysis of the "slavery of labor to capital" and ridiculed the notion that "Africans generally, or the negroes particularly, are descended from Ham." Fitzhugh's lead article in the October 1857 issue of DeBow's Review argued forcefully that even among whites free labor was inferior to slave and chided southerners for failing to carry proslavery arguments to their logical conclusion. "Domestic slavery must be vindicated in the abstract, and in the general," he asserted, "as a normal, natural, and in general, necessitous element of civilized society, without regard to race or color." [28]

Russians, then, developed an essentially racial argument in defense of serfdom, even though no racial distinction divided lord and peasant; at the same time Americans elaborated an ideology that stressed the virtues of aristocracy and noblesse oblige in an avowedly democratic society. Clearly, the master-bondsman relationship caused the owners to share certain common ideological assumptions, and the need to defend unfree labor had a logic of its own that propelled Russians and Americans to arrive independently at many of the same conclusions. The major difference was not so much in the arguments used as in their tone, depth, and subtlety. The Americans developed proslavery arguments with far greater detail and sophistication than the Russians. Although the masters' probondage arguments were by nature self serving, their self-serving character was far more evident in the Russian than in the American polemics.

Nowhere is this distinction clearer than in the religious justification of servitude, which was pervasive in the slave South but perfunctory in Russia. Volumes poured off the southern presses expanding on the themes that the ancient Hebrews had practiced slavery, that Jesus never condemned (and therefore implicitly condoned) it, that the curse of Ham marked blacks for slavery, and that slavery was in fact an enormous blessing to Africans because it entailed the conversion and religious elevation of an ignorant, pagan people. In addition, virtually every major work defending slavery incorporated the religious justification. Pomeshchiki, too, told their serfs that their status was ordained by God and regularly relied on priests to instill obedience in their peasant parishioners, and defenders of serfdom made passing references to it as part of a God-given order. But religious arguments were rarely central to formal writings advocating serfdom and never received the kind of elaboration that was common in the United States South. There were, no doubt, specific reasons for this contrast: unlike the Russian parish clergy, "a weak, tangential group lacking in influence and power," southern ministers constituted an independent-minded group that spoke out often on social issues and played a major role in defending the peculiar institution. Furthermore, the non-Christian status of Africans brought the question of slave conversion to the fore. But most of all the flourishing of religious justifications in the South and their abbreviation in Russia were extreme examples of the contrast in the sophistication of master-class ideology as a whole.[29]

In addition to racial and paternalistic arguments, two practical points received widespread circulation in both countries. The first was the economic necessity of forced labor. Americans and Russians recognized that their systems of bondage arose to meet a general labor shortage under conditions of relative population scarcity; both held out the prospect of economic disaster should unfree labor be abolished.[30] Even more widespread were dire predictions of social collapse—refusal to work, unrest, and rebellion—should slaves and serfs be emancipated. Russian polemicists could point to the degenerate condition of state peasants who were without proper seigneurial supervision, and their American counterparts had an even more compelling argument in the example of emancipation in the West Indies. The British colonies of Barbados and Jamaica showed how blacks, freed from the protective care of slavery, would revert to their primitive African ways, and Haiti held out the ultimate horror of revolution. A similar nightmare stalked the Russian gentry: the bloody Pu-

gachev rebellion of 1773–74, which for generations served as a
warning to pomeshchiki of just how precarious their position was.[31]

Russians and Americans even played the same word games, insisting that their particular form of bondage was the mildest or even that
it was not really bondage at all. Although Russians commonly used
the word *slavery* (*rabstvo*) to describe the status of their serfs, defenders of serfdom pointed out that their form of slavery was different
from others. "Between freedom and freedom, and between slavery
and slavery, there is a difference, and this difference is great and varied; a title means nothing," wrote Boltin. "There is freedom that is
worse, more intolerable, than slavery." Precisely the same kind of assertion was made in the United States: Henry Hughes's refusal to use
the word *slavery*, for which he substituted *warranteeism*, was unusual, but many held with Hammond that slavery was but a name
that meant little, because the working classes everywhere were really
slaves. "The difference between us," he lectured northerners, "is that
our slaves are hired for life and well compensated . . . Yours are hired
by the day, not cared for, and scantily compensated." Matthew Estes
agreed that the word *slavery* had given the South a bad name. "Theoretically, slavery has been abolished in most countries," he admitted;
"but practically, it exists almost every where—but without the responsibilities, interests, *humanities,* and sympathies of [southern]
slavery."[32]

Although probondage spokesmen used many different arguments
and their works often appear to consist of a jumble of different—even
conflicting—ideas appropriated because of their momentary utility, a
common thread runs through virtually all the defenses of servitude:
the assumption of natural human inequality. This assumption usually
appears only implicitly in arguments on behalf of forced labor, but at
times it is quite explicit. Prince Shcherbatov, for example, boldly refuted the concept of natural equality. "Not one person is completely
like another," he wrote; "and where this similarity is lacking, so too
is equality." Half a century later Admiral Mordvinov made the same
point. "Only disorganized, wild society offers equality of rights, conditions, and powers," he explained. "Such is the condition of all
Asiatic peoples." Nineteenth-century southerners were sometimes
even more explicit. "Man is born to subjection," wrote William Harper; "it is the very basis of his nature, that the strong should control
the weak and ignorant." Equally forceful was Hammond, who denounced as "ridiculously absurd that much lauded but nowhere ac-
credited dogma of Mr. Jefferson, that 'all men are born equal.'" Re-

gardless of the variety of ways used to support inequality (race, class, lineage, wealth, ability, intellect, or moral capacity), the essential premise of those who defended bondage was that all men were *not* created equal.[33]

Because the proponents of unfree labor defended inequality in an era of natural rights, they were compelled to challenge many of the dominant intellectual currents of their time, to reject the French Enlightenment, Jeffersonianism, and the very idea of progress. The defense of slavery thus led to reactionary views on most other social questions. Although some proslavery spokesmen in the United States South were able to stay in tune with the times by the simple expedient of excluding blacks from the realm of humanity and celebrating the equality of all whites, slavery left most ideologues uncomfortable with any talk of change or reform. For although planters and pomeshchiki were closely tied to the commercial economy and sometimes appeared indistinguishable from rural capitalists, their ideology was fundamentally different from that of the bourgeoisie. As bourgeois ideals gained increasing currency in western Europe and the northern United States, articulate slaveowners and serfowners became convinced that the societies they headed were last bastions of order and morality in an increasingly decadent and chaotic world. Russian and southern thinkers ridiculed notions of human progress and perfectibility, stressing instead man's innate depravity and need for order and authority; individualism, rationalism, free thought, and tinkering with the status quo could only lead to disaster. "Believe us, Sir, the fault is not in cities, nor yet in slavery, nor in marriage, nor religion," insisted Alabamian D. R. Hundley in explaining the futility of the reform impulse; "it is in MAN . . . Although you were to abolish every institution under the sun, so long as the human race continues mortal and frail as at present there will be no lack of sin and shame, sorrow and suffering."[34]

In 1857 British traveler Barbara Bodichon summed up in her diary a conversation she had with several southerners on a Mississippi River steamboat. "There is evidently a feeling," she wrote, "that Abolition and Woman's Rights are supported by the same people and same arguments, and that both are allied to atheism—and these slave owners are very religious people." Her observation was perceptive. Almost every major antebellum defender of slavery insisted on tying abolitionism to a host of other "isms"—heresies that threatened social peace and stability. George Frederick Holmes was typical in his suggestion that in the North, "where Fourierism, and Proudhonism,

Free Love, and Total Abstinence, and all the other forms of modern philanthropic innovation have found numerous and enthusiastic votaries, an exaggerated and distorted idea of the nature and functions of liberty has inspired the multitudinous heresy of Abolitionism." Rejecting the optimistic spirit of northern reform, Hammond deplored the democratic course of the nineteenth century, with the ascendance of "The MOB—THE SANS-CULLOTTES. Proclaiming as their watchword that now prostituted sentiment 'that all men are born free and equal,' they have rallied to their standard the ignorant, uneducated, semi-barbarous mass which swarms and starves upon the face of Europe!" Only one bulwark remained against this leveling surge: the slave South. Scoffing at abolitionist charges of a slaveowning aristocracy, Hammond replied, "I accept the terms. *It is a government of the best,* combining all the advantages of the old world." [35]

Russian defenders of serfdom denounced the democratic spirit in similar terms. Like their American counterparts, they saw themselves defending not simply an institution but a conservative regime, one threatened by equality, democracy, reform, and revolution. As early as the 1780s Count S. R. Vorontsov identified the main enemy as "this spirit of reform and universal equality preached for fifty years by the economists and encyclopedists in France." Half a century later Admiral Shishkov vigorously protested against the view that "the spirit of the times" demanded reform of serfdom. "By the term *spirit of the times,*" he asserted, "is often meant a general striving for willfulness and disobedience." Contrasting the social harmony of Russia with the turmoil of western Europe, he asked rhetorically, "why changes in laws, changes in customs, changes in manner of thought? And whence these changes? From the schools and philosophizing of those countries where these disorders, these insurrections, this insolence of thought . . . reign supreme." The only cure, he suggested, was strict censorship to guard against the spreading disease of free thought. In a fervent attack on the concept of a natural right to freedom Count F. V. Rostopchin explained that, although the term *freedom* was appealing, "it is not the natural condition of a person," because all members of society were dependent on one another. "The first consequence of freedom is willfulness," he noted, "the 2nd. is disobedience, and the 3rd. is revolt against all authority." In the first half of the nineteenth century Russians, like southerners, contrasted the harmony of their class relations with the chaos of the free-labor market in western Europe. For both, the defense of servitude was an integral part of the general defense of a world threatened by change.[36]

* * *

ALTHOUGH RUSSIAN and American ideologues made similar arguments in defense of forced labor, they developed and used those arguments very differently. The American arguments received greater elaboration and far surpassed the Russian in volume, subtlety, sweep, and abstraction. The Russian arguments were more obviously self-serving than the American and lacked their imagination and boldness. This difference became more marked over time until by the middle of the nineteenth century, when the proslavery movement in the South had acquired the character of a popular crusade, public commitment to serfdom in Russia had all but vanished.

The contrast was not at first apparent, because in the eighteenth century American and Russian thought on unfree labor followed remarkably similar paths. In both countries there was little discussion of bondage before the 1760s; challenges to slavery and serfdom were few, but so too were articulated defenses of institutions taken largely for granted. In both countries complacency and silence gave way to concern and debate during the last third of the century. Although those who raised the issue of forced labor rarely called for immediate abolition, they did broach the possibility of gradual emancipation in the future as well as discussing ways of more immediately limiting cruel and arbitrary treatment of the bondsmen. They also aroused the angry opposition of those who insisted that no change was needed.[37]

This parallel course came to an abrupt end in the nineteenth century. Cautious antislavery sentiment, common among spokesmen of the upper South, gradually evaporated and was replaced at first by an awkward, hesitant, even reluctant defense of slavery. As late as 1826 Presbyterian minister Timothy Flint was surprised to find that planters defended existing conditions primarily on the grounds of necessity, precedent, and the dangers of sudden emancipation, not the virtues of slavery. "I have never yet heard one," he exaggerated, "who does not admit that slavery is an evil and an injustice and who does not at least affect to deplore the evil." Then during the thirty years preceding the Civil War the South produced an extraordinary torrent of proslavery propaganda—propaganda that was for the most part bold, unapologetic, and insistent on the positive virtues of slavery. Whereas previous proslavery advocates had stressed the "practical" arguments of expedience, economy, and race, the new polemicists, who included many of the South's best minds, increasingly based their case on the higher ground of social theory: slavery was the best way to organize society. By the 1850s southern whites seemed so committed to their peculiar institution that a lone dissenter such as Hinton Helper found it expedient to leave the South altogether.[38]

In Russia, however, the trend that had begun in the eighteenth century continued in the nineteenth. Although some noblemen still spoke out in defense of serfdom and unarticulated sentiment in favor of maintaining the status quo remained strong, especially in the provinces, the balance gradually tipped in favor of those dissatisfied with the institution. By the 1840s free-labor ideas had spread widely among the educated nobility of Moscow and St. Petersburg, and public defense of serfdom became increasingly rare. "I have never been either an ultra-liberal or a carbonari . . . but I have always detested personal slavery, and I still detest it, and deplore its continuation among us and everywhere I see it," wrote Prince M. S. Vorontsov, whose father had defended serfdom. (Significantly, virtually all of the defenses of serfdom cited above date from before 1840.) Thus, Russia never experienced the kind of militant proslavery movement that swept the antebellum South.[39]

Whereas the entire American South seemed to rally around slavery, educated Russians became increasingly convinced that serfdom was a backward system that must somehow be abolished. Among the great Russian novelists of the nineteenth century Nikolai Gogol was virtually alone in his defense of serfdom (a defense that came late in his short life, when he had given himself over to a cranky mysticism), and some, like Ivan Turgenev, eluded heavy government censorship to criticize the institution. (In contrast, leading antebellum southern writers—one cannot call them great—commonly extolled the peculiar institution.) Government officials, too, often shared the dissatisfaction with serfdom. In 1839 the annual report of the Third Department suggested that the time had come for the government to begin preparing for eventual emancipation rather "than to wait until it begins from below, from the people." The report called for quiet deliberation, "without noise and without loud words," but concluded that "everyone is agreed" on the need for reform. When in 1857 Alexander II made public his decision to go ahead with emancipation, noblemen grumbled and dragged their feet, but there was no public opposition, no threat that serfowners might refuse to accept the reforms.[40]

Several specific factors contributed to the strength of probondage ideology in the American South and its weakness in Russia. The most obvious is that of race. Not only did proslavery spokesmen often couch their arguments in racial terms but southern whites were in general so imbued with the consciousness of race that they found it impossible to contemplate emancipation of blacks in a white society. Travelers in the antebellum South found that many whites who were distinctly unenthusiastic about slavery balked at the notion of turning blacks loose in the South. As one poor white told Olmsted, "I reckon the majority would be right glad if we could get rid of the niggers. But it wouldn't never do to free 'em and leave 'em here . . . Nobody couldn't live here then." That slavery in the United States was *racial* slavery clearly served to inhibit the growth of moderate opposition and to make southern whites more receptive to the proslavery appeal.[41]

Even though Russian defenders of serfdom invented essentially racial arguments to serve their cause and regarded peasants as a different people, a qualitative gap still separated both the perceptions of the difference between masters and bondsmen in the two countries and the perception of the threat inherent in emancipation. Blacks were not only different: they were outsiders in a country where everyone else was an insider or potential insider. (It is for this reason that free blacks seemed like such an anomaly.) Blacks were aliens—Africans deposited against their will in a foreign land—and despite protestations to the contrary most whites always regarded them as such. How else could one speak of sending "back" to Africa people who in most cases were third-generation and fourth-generation Americans? In a world where all free men were politically equal, the prospect of freeing black slaves alarmed slaveholders and nonslaveholders alike.[42]

Russian peasants, however, were not outsiders so much as the lowest level of a stratified society. White Americans could think of the United States as an all-white country, but Russia without the peasants was inconceivable. Not only did they constitute more than four-fifths of the population; they were also the essence of Russia. Their freedom seemed less threatening than did that of blacks in the southern United States, because Russia was a hierarchical society composed of legally established castes or estates without the slightest pretense to democracy or equal rights. An emancipated black in the United States was threatening because there was no perceived place for him except as a citizen; an emancipated serf, however, would still be a peasant, and no one imagined that emancipation would make a peasant the equal of a nobleman. Thus, the combination of race and democracy served to reinforce the commitment to slavery.

There was another way in which the lack of democracy served to undercut the Russian nobility's commitment to serfdom. Because

Russia had a bureaucratic government, organized on essentially military lines of command, the gentry was not in a position either to shape or to resist government policy. During the decades preceding emancipation the top ranks of government—the tsars and many of their closest advisors—flirted with adopting a policy of gradual reform. Southern whites would have elected new leaders, but Russian pomeshchiki had no such choice, because despite their government service the government was not theirs, and most of them remained totally ignorant of the deliberations conducted by successive secret government committees on how to handle the peasant question. Even when faced with emancipation in the late 1850s, reluctant noblemen did not actively resist; instead, they contented themselves with minor obstructions and delays and with insisting that the final settlement be as favorable as possible to their economic interests.[43]

Such was not, of course, the response of southern slaveholders when slavery was assaulted. Surely one important clue to the southern response lies in the nature of the challenge: it was open, and it came from without. Because the outspoken defense of slavery arose largely in response to attacks upon it, it is highly significant that opponents of slavery were able publicly—through meetings, petition drives, pamphlets, newspaper articles and editorials, and political speeches—to challenge both the legitimacy of slavery and the morality of slaveowners. Equally important was the sectional nature of the opposition: because antebellum slavery was southern and abolitionism northern, the attack on slavery appeared to be an attack on southern honor and on the South itself. There can be little doubt that the defense of slavery would have been very different but for the sectional character of the assault on it.[44]

Russia, however, was not divided into free and unfree sections, so there was no sectional attack upon serfdom. In fact, because of the nature of their government Russians never really conducted a public debate on the peasant question at all. Proposals for abolishing or modifying serfdom, although widely discussed in the highest circles, were confined to secret committees whose proceedings went unpublished. Heavy censorship meant that only the most Aesopian remarks critical of Russian institutions could appear in print, and nothing like the American abolitionists' denunciation of slaveholders as sinners was possible. As a result, serfowners never had—or got—to defend themselves as American slaveowners did. Even had they wanted to, they would not have been able to play the same ideological role as American proslavery spokesmen: there was no Russian "public" to appeal to, and censorship of arguments defending serfdom was almost as rigid as censorship of polemics against it. In short, the absence of a free press and of any tradition of democratic debate on policy precluded a full development of proserfdom thought.[45]

Thus, the flowering of the defense of bondage in the antebellum South, in contrast to its withering in prereform Russia, is partially explicable in terms of four characteristics present in the United States but absent in Russia: a racial distinction between owner and owned, a democratic political system, freedom of the press, and the sectional nature of servitude. These four are functionally related to a fifth, which subsumes the other four under it and is the most basic of all: the independence of the master class and the strength of its civilization. As I have argued throughout Part I, racial, political, cultural, and demographic differences acted to produce two different master classes. The southern was typically resident whereas the Russian was absentee-oriented; the southern was autonomous and dominant, both politically and culturally, whereas the Russian was weak and marginal. Planters were more independent than pomeshchiki in relationship to their property, their communities, and their government.

Although the logic of defending unfree labor produced similar arguments in Russia and the American South, the strength of the masters' ideology ultimately reflected their coherence as a class. Southern slaveowners, who constituted an independent ruling class at the head of a flourishing sectional culture, were able to sustain a proslavery ideology of considerable sophistication, whereas Russian noblemen, who formed a dependent group of state servitors with few ties to their peasants, their communities, or each other, put forth a world view without force or finesse, one that expressed little more than their desire to preserve as many of their privileges as possible. Pomeshchiki, unlike American planters, lacked the independence successfully to defend forced labor. They also lacked much of the incentive, because many of them were little more than rentiers, deriving an income from but otherwise relatively unconcerned about their estates. Whereas emancipation threatened the entire world of the southern slaveowners, it threatened the noblemen's livelihoods more than their lives. If a way could be found to safeguard their immediate economic interests, they had relatively little to lose from abolition. Therefore, during the preparations for emancipation in the late 1850s, they concentrated not on opposing the new order but on securing the best possible terms for themselves under it. And the terms they ultimately secured were generous indeed.[46]

We thus return to the question raised at the beginning of Chapter 1 concerning differences in the manner of abolition. Historians have devoted a great deal of attention to the coming of emancipation in the servile lands. They have meticulously traced the growth of abolitionist sentiment and vigorously debated the relative weight of specific factors in promoting government action against bondage. Historians of Russia have variously seen the decision to emancipate as the consequence of the perception that serfdom was an economic albatross around Russia's neck, the Crimean war's demonstration of Russia's military and economic weakness, fear of growing peasant unrest, or some combination of the three; historians of the United States have focused on Civil War causation and on the motives of Republicans in overturning southern institutions. Historians of both countries have grappled with the question of the compatibility or incompatibility of bondage with modern capitalism. All of these are important topics, and most will receive my attention in a subsequent volume.

But equally important in explaining the character and timing of emancipation—and much less studied—is the nature of the defense that bondage received. Such a defense existed wherever bondage came under attack, and the logic of defending unfree labor produced similar arguments—and similar assumptions about the nature of the good society—in countries as diverse as Russia and the United States. In short, one can see in the ideology of the master class certain important constants—shared assumptions—that cut across geographical, cultural, and economic variations. Nevertheless, these variations operated to accentuate the defense of unfree labor in the United States South and to undercut it in Russia. Because the former was a slaveholders' world and the latter a peasant world, the former produced a proslavery ideology unique in volume, subtlety, and abstraction while the latter saw arguments that were never as finely wrought lose all force and persuasiveness. It is worth noting that in this respect the United States, not Russia, was unusual among modern slaveholding societies: only in the South did such a potent proslavery crusade emerge, because only there did a resident slaveholding class acquire the independence and sectional hegemony that enabled it to fight its cause to the death.[47]

Although an elite can always be expected to defend its prerogatives—it is in the nature of kings to be monarchists, businessmen capitalists, and slaveholders supporters of slavery—the behavior of planters and pomeshchiki suggests that commitment to a social system will be greatest where an entire way of life rather than simply an economic interest is at stake. Evidence from other slave societies supports this conclusion: like the pomeshchiki, planters in the British West Indies, where plantations were preeminently speculations for absentee investors, offered little resistance to a compensated emancipation forced on them from above. As historian C. Vann Woodward has aptly written, "The end of slavery in the South can be described as the death of a society, though elsewhere it could more reasonably be characterized as the liquidation of an investment."[48] Ultimately, southern slaveowners rose to the defense of their peculiar institution—with both words and arms—because more than economic interest was at stake; Russian pomeshchiki failed to do so both because they lacked the means and because the threat raised by abolition was more to their pocketbooks than to their whole way of life. Given the balance of forces, they would soon find that even that threat could be successfully overcome.

*   *   *

WE ARE NOW in a position to return to the question of race and to attempt some generalizations concerning its significance for the masters' world view. This has been a subject of considerable interest to historians of the United States South, who have disagreed about the relationship between racial prejudice and slavery; it has also been a subject of great concern to historians of the Americas in general, who have vigorously debated the causes of variations in patterns of race relations and the connection between these and New World slave systems. Because Russian serfdom was a nonracial system of bondage, its comparision with American slavery sheds light on this issue.[49]

The initial demand for labor—the most basic cause of enslavement—was clearly color-blind. Elite groups with an abundance of land but insufficient hands to cultivate it forced whomever they could to work for them. In Russia this meant peasants; in America it included Indians, Africans, and white indentured servants. Of course, the Englishmen who settled the southern colonies were struck by the Africans' blackness (as well as by their heathenism and savagery) and, like most people coming in contact with others, assumed the superiority of their own ways. But colonial enslavers rarely expressed a belief in permanent, inherent black inferiority—they did not, for example, develop the Sambo stereotype that loomed so large in the nineteenth-century South—and in any case neither the Africans' color nor their other apparently distinctive attributes created either the need or the desire for slavery. The demand for labor was purely economic, and the color, religion, nationality, or culture of the laborers mattered little, except insofar as they affected their performance as laborers. (The same was true *after* emancipation as well, when a widespread movement swept the South to replace blacks—erroneously believed by many to be dying out—with white European immigrants and Chinese coolies, and when more successful efforts occurred in other American postemancipation countries to import European and East Indian laborers.)[50]

Given this demand for labor, however, the American settlers, like most other employers of unfree labor, found it easier to enslave outsiders than their own people, and indentured servitude did not degenerate into outright slavery. The Americans had both a specific and a general reason for this. The specific was the desire to encourage the continued voluntary migration of white immigrants, who would be understandably reluctant to commit themselves to a life of perpetual servitude. The general was the need that enslavers have commonly felt to find an objective basis for legitimizing their actions, a distinction between those whom it is legitimate to enslave—outsiders, inferiors, "them"—and those whom it is not. Throughout history enslavers have found it convenient to view their slaves as intrinsically different from themselves; the distinction has not always (or even usually) been racial—nationality, religion, or some other "ethnic" factor has often served as well—but slaves have traditionally been seen as outsiders different in some important respect from members of the body politic. Russian serfdom—and its predecessor kholopstvo—was unusual in lacking any such ethnic basis, and its absence produced a need to create social distance between master and bondsman sufficient to legitimize their relationship. It was the perception of difference rather than any particular somatic contrast that was crucial for establishing a proper we-they dichotomy.[51]

Once American slavery was established along racial lines, it became easy to confuse race with class, to assume that race was an essential rather than an incidental ingredient of slavery. Such confusion in fact made race an essential element of *American* slavery. Stimulated in part by egalitarian notions associated with the War for Independence and the subsequent spread of democracy, white racial consciousness increased markedly; if all men had equal rights, the only basis for holding slaves was that they were not quite men in the same sense others were. Even as the actual differences between the slaves and other Americans diminished—descendants of African captives

adopted the religion, language, and much of the culture of their owners, who in turn borrowed cultural traits from their slaves—the gap
between white and black seemed greater to most southern whites.
Slaveowners commonly referred to "my negroes" when they meant
"my slaves" and came to ascribe particular characteristics and personality traits to them as blacks rather than as slaves. Few southern
whites in the antebellum period would have agreed with Henry
Hughes that the "ethnical qualification" of American slavery was
"accidental." Far more typical was the assertion of "A Southern
Lady" that "the negro (as a people) *cannot* be free. He has not the
faculty of freedom. In no age and in no land has he lived free from
restraint, except as the savage." [52]

Because the Sambo stereotype appeared to be a reflection of the
racial nature of American slavery, it is highly significant that this
stereotype existed in Russia as well. Russian noblemen saw the peasants as inherently different from themselves, possessing the same lazy,
childlike character that American slaveholders ascribed to blacks.
That they did so clarifies the class nature of what appeared to be a
racial stereotype; although its manifestation in America was racial,
this stereotype was similar to that held by noblemen of peasants, rich
of poor, colonialists of subject peoples, native-born Americans of immigrants, insiders of outsiders. Americans developed the Sambo image not because their victims were black (although their color was an
extremely useful basis for their differentiation) but because they were
slaves; where somatic differences were lacking, masters were still able
to create the necessary social distance between themselves and their
bondsmen by acting as if they were present. The curse of Ham, which
many southern whites believed legitimized the enslavement of black
Africans, had previously been used to justify the bondage of a wide
variety of non-African peoples, beginning with the Canaanites held
by biblical Hebrews; throughout history enslaved peoples, of whatever race and nationality, have been seen as slavish by nature. [53]

Proslavery thought flourished in the antebellum South while the
defense of serfdom languished in prereform Russia less because of the
presence of physical differences between master and bondsman in
the former and their absence in the latter than of contrasting ways of
conceptualizing such differences. In Latin American slaveowning societies, where masters were white and slaves black, the ideological
defense of slavery was as perfunctory as in Russia and was rarely
based on the argument that blacks were inherently inferior to whites.
Although southern slavery shared a racial basis with that of other

New World countries, it alone developed a pervasive, militant pro-slavery movement in the first two-thirds of the nineteenth century. In short, racial distinctions between master and bondsman proved less significant in shaping owner ideology than how people looked at those distinctions.

For race was a subjective concept that some humans imposed on others; as sociologist Edgar T. Thompson has written, "races are made in culture, not found in nature." Within New World slaveown-ing societies racial definitions have varied substantially: in the United States persons with any measurable black ancestry were usually cate-gorized as Negroes, but elsewhere mulattoes were either classified as a group unto themselves or were further broken down into subgroups depending on their color and status. What makes someone "black," "white," "colored," "Negro," Afro-American," or "mulatto" is thus likely to tell us more about perceptions of dominant social groups than about the characteristics of those categorized. Even within a given society, racial conceptions can change markedly; although Af-rican slaves were to be found in the South from the first half of the seventeenth century, nineteenth-century racial stereotypes were largely new.[54]

The subjective nature of racial attitudes can be highlighted by an examination of how planters and pomeshchiki looked upon free blacks and state peasants. In both countries attitudes emerged that could not be predicted on the basis of existing racial configurations. The Russian view of "free" peasants as social misfits, who, lacking adequate supervision, allowed their natural inclination to laziness and debauchery to reign unchecked and were thus living proof of the necessity of bondage, was an essentially racial attitude paralleling the southern white image of free Negroes. If Russian noblemen expressed racial attitudes in the absence of racial distinction, southern whites were sometimes able to blur significantly the simple equation of color with degradation and slavery. In particular areas of the South—most notably southern Louisiana and Charleston—a three-tier color sys-tem prevailed, under which mulattoes were seen as possessing greater innate capacity for freedom than blacks and were allowed status and behavior that would have been unacceptable in a society in which all Negroes were deserving of slavery.

Even more remarkable were the occasional expressions of respect for free blacks revealed by antebellum trial records, expressions that suggest the kind of breach of white-black dichotomy more usually associated with Latin America. A Louisiana judge, in ruling that a free Negro could testify against whites, noted that the state had many freemen who were "respectable for their intelligence, industry and habits of good order," some of whom were "enlightened by education" and even "large property holders." To clinch the argument he pointed out that "the testimony of manumitted slaves was legal evidence under the Spanish and Roman laws." A South Carolina judge, in ruling that free blacks could own real estate, declared flatly, "it is certain that they are not aliens" and noted that some Negroes, "who have lost [their] distinctive mark, hold offices, as well as lands, and even seats in the legislature." He concluded that if free blacks were "not citizens, they are subjects." Perhaps most interesting was a South Carolina court's adoption of the concept widely held in Brazil that "money whitens." Ruling that a respectable man generally regarded as white could testify in court even in the face of conclusive proof that he had some black ancestry, the court declared that race "is not to be determined solely by . . . visible mixture . . . but by reputation." There were circumstances in which "a man of worth . . . should have the rank of a white man, while a vagabond of the same degree of blood should be confined to the inferior caste."[55]

Race, then, was clearly not an absolute. White racial views differed widely among slave societies, and even within individual societies— in this case the United States South—they were far from uniform and changed over time. In Russia, where no racial distinction existed between master and bondsman, essentially racial arguments were nonetheless invented to provide the distance between them necessary to justify bondage. Race was a device that dominant social groups found useful for legitimizing their treatment of others as outsiders, but it was by no means essential to that task. Throughout history religion, language, culture, and ostensibly criminal behavior have served as acceptable substitutes for race in giving sanction to slavery, and the Russian example—perhaps the most extreme in modern history for lack of ethnic distinction between masters and servants—illustrates the subjectivity of perceived human differences.

Nevertheless, race became so intertwined with slavery in the South, so confused with it in the minds of the participants, that it could not help but shape the particular nature of southern slavery. In conjunction with democracy, it strengthened the commitment to slavery of nonslaveholders, who shuddered at the thought of turning blacks loose in a white society. It facilitated the defense of slavery, because although race did not give rise to the proslavery movement, once that movement existed it served as a useful vehicle to promote the proslavery cause. And it accentuated the paternalism of slaveholders, who found it easier to view their slaves as in need of benevolent protection when they could be identified as members of a naturally childlike race. In short, the existence of racial distinction in a democratic environment facilitated the continued perception of slaves as outsiders who had no legitimate claim to participate as members of the body politic. Because Russian serfs were not such outsiders, the comparison of serfdom with American slavery underscores the degree to which race helped shape the particular character of slavery in the United States South.

Although both free blacks and state peasants were viewed as social misfits, this stereotype was far more pervasive in the United States than in Russia. In the antebellum South it expressed the conventional wisdom of a society determined to equate slave status with blackness; although fascinating examples of white racial ambivalence can be found, these were exceptions that proved the rule. The vast majority of southern whites regarded blacks as outsiders and free blacks as anomalous threats to the social order who by their very presence served to arouse false hopes of freedom in the slave population. Because free blacks were so few and rarely performed essential social functions, it was easy to argue that there was no place for them in the South, and the antebellum years saw—paralleling the rise of militant proslavery thought—a general tightening of laws designed to restrict their activities, limit individual manumissions, and drive away the manumitted. Such restrictive legislation was most severe in the deep South, where the absolute number of free blacks declined after 1840 and the proportion of blacks who were free fell from 3.1 percent in 1840 to 1.6 percent in 1860. Thus, antebellum southern whites not only equated blacks with slaves but acted to make that equation more nearly perfect.[56]

In imperial Russia state peasants, who formed a far larger proportion of the population than did free blacks in the South, were in a less anomalous position. Although proserfdom spokesmen argued that peasants were by their nature unfit for freedom and state peasants, too, should be turned into serfs, such arguments diminished in both frequency and persuasiveness during the first half of the nineteenth century, as proserfdom arguments themselves became increasingly rare. The reign of Paul witnessed the last major enserfment of state peasants through their distribution to noblemen.

Indeed, in the nineteenth century Russia saw the passage of a series of laws designed to encourage manumissions as well as a comprehensive reform of the administration of state peasants which aimed at improving what was widely regarded as their degraded condition. The reforms of 1837–41 reflected contradictory governmental thought in that they attempted to increase state peasants' civil rights while also increasing their supervision (and thus presumably improving their condition), and they aroused widespread protests from their supposed beneficiaries, who suspected a plot to take away their existing privileges and turn them into serfs. But the significant point here is that while in the South a major effort was under way to restrict the numbers, rights, and activities of free blacks, in Russia the opposite was occurring with respect to state peasants. It was in part as a result of efforts to facilitate manumissions and improve the condition of the state peasants—although there were other reasons as well—that the proportion of state peasants increased so dramatically in the years preceding emancipation, from 40.7 percent of the peasant population in 1795 to 53.1 percent in 1858. Unlike southern free blacks, who—except in Washington, D.C. and the border states of Maryland and Delaware—constituted a small, beleaguered, and marginal group, Russian state peasants during the last years of serfdom represented the majority of the peasant population. Whatever disabilities they suffered, they lived, according to the testimony of almost all foreign observers, far better than the serfs.[57]

Several factors contributed to this contrast in the position of free blacks and state peasants. It is easier to regard a tiny fraction than a substantial proportion of the population as an anomaly, so it is significant that state peasants were always far more numerous than free blacks. Equally important, the increasing commitment to slavery in the antebellum South made more tenuous the already less-than-secure position of those blacks who were not slaves, whereas the evaporation of proserfdom sentiment in Russia made state status for peasants seem a natural alternative. But surely contrasting racial patterns also played a major role in producing differing attitudes toward free blacks and peasants. Free blacks were misfits who theatened the social order because all blacks were outsiders who were "supposed" to be slaves rather than citizens; their color was a constant reminder of their alien nature. Peasants, however, were physically indistinguishable from their owners and, far from being outsiders, constituted the vast majority of the Russian population as well as the soul of the Russian nation. In the nineteenth century there gradually emerged a very different image of the peasant from that of the lazy, ignorant, coarse brute in need of constant seigneurial direction; the new stereotype, which received its most complete elaboration only in the last third of the century, was a positive one inconceivable of blacks in the slave South. A broad range of thinkers, from Slavophiles and romantic nationalists to populists, came to celebrate the peasants for epitomizing all the pastoral virtues of a simple, hardworking, patriotic, and honest people who knew little of and cared less for the corrupt and decadent life-style of "civilized" western Europeans and their Russian imitators.

Antebellum southern whites thus saw the descendants of Africans among them—both slave and free—as outsiders who could never truly be part of the body politic no matter how many generations were born on American soil. This conviction that blacks were outsiders strongly reinforced and became confused with the masters' belief that their slaves were inferior beings who needed their protection. Russian pomeshchiki shared many of the same attitudes toward their serfs that American slaveowners held toward their slaves, but these attitudes flourished best in an environment where they could appear directed at an alien race rather than merely at a subservient class. In short, racial distinction accentuated the class cohesion and hegemony of southern slaveowners; the racial nature of American slavery—although "accidental"—in conjunction with the egalitarian ethos of the antebellum South served to strengthen both the masters' paternalism and their commitment to slavery. It also affected the behavior and world view of the slaves, who were forced, unlike Russian serfs, to remain outsiders in their own country.

PART II

The Bondsmen and Their Masters

4

Community and Culture

IT WAS ONE THING for the masters to prescribe the nature of estate management and life but another to put those prescriptions into effect. In both Russia and the American South the bondsmen endeavored to follow their own customs, adhere to their own values, and develop their own style of life apart from—and largely unknown to—their owners. Perceptive observers noted that the bondsmen rarely revealed their feelings to outsiders. "Persons live and die in the midst of Negroes and know comparatively little of their real character," noted South Carolina minister and planter Charles C. Jones. "The Negroes are a distinct class in community, and keep very much to *themselves*. They are one thing before the whites, and another before their own color." Travelers to Russia, like those to the South, saw "cunning" and "deception" as prime traits of the bondsmen's character and attibuted it to their desire to keep their lives as free as possible of owner control. "The character of the peasant is a profound abyss, to the bottom of which no eye can pierce," asserted Frenchman Germain de Lagny. "Like the Negro . . . he practices the art of dissimulation to an extent of which it is perfectly impossible to convey an idea." Because absolute regulation of the bondsmen's lives was impossible, slaves and serfs were able, in slave quarters and peasant villages, to lead lives that were at least partially autonomous from the influences of their masters.[1]

The nature and degree of that autonomy, however, differed in the two countries. For a number of reasons the serfs found it easier than the slaves to achieve substantial independence from outside forces, and they were able to forge communal values, customs, and organizations based on centuries of tradition. Although the slaves, like the serfs, developed a culture that differed significantly from that of their owners, they found it more difficult to create their own collective forms and norms, and their communal life was more attenuated. Ultimately, slavery impinged to a greater degree and in a more corrosive manner on the independence of American blacks than serfdom did on that of Russian peasants.

*   *   *

STRIKINGLY DIFFERENT environments helped shape the lives of the Russian and American bondsmen. Most obvious was the contrast between the historical continuity experienced by the former and the discontinuity experienced by the latter. Slaves in the United States, as in the rest of the Americas, were the descendants of Africans uprooted from their homes and forced to live in an alien world, whereas serfs in Russia resided on their ancestral lands. The serfs, unlike the slaves, lived "at home" in a traditional world where customs had emerged over the centuries and changed but slowly.

Any examination of slave life in the American South must consequently begin by taking account of the foreign origins of the slave population. These origins were responsible for the particular complexity associated with the topic of American slave culture, because intertwined with the class dimension—the lives, values, and responses of slaves—is the ethnic dimension resulting from those slaves' distinctive background. Slave culture was at first also African culture; to the extent that slaves had ancient customs handed down from generation to generation, these were, perforce, of African origin. Yet subsequent generations of slaves in America were not themselves Africans but a new people, shaped by their new surroundings. This newness gives rise to a series of questions concerning slave culture: To what extent did the descendants of Africans transmit to their children the ways of their ancestors? What changes did those ways undergo under the influence of the dominant white society? How, in turn, did the dominant whites adapt to African influences? In short, what is the relationship between the culture of southern slaves and their peculiar background?

Although scholars have differed sharply on these questions,[2] there can be no denying the pervasive impact of historical discontinuity on the character of slave life in America. By the second half of the eighteenth century the slave population was already overwhelmingly creole or native rather than African-born, and after the ending of slave imports in 1808 the proportion of first-generation Americans in the slave population faded to insignificance. As a result the language, diet, religion, and most customs of the slaves became "American-ized," although, like other ethnic groups, blacks retained remnants of their traditional culture and in turn helped to shape the dominant culture, influencing a broad range of southern features from pronunciation of English to diet and agriculture. The strongest African survivals occurred in black music, which eventually exerted a powerful influence on American music in general, and in certain folk practices such as medicine and magic. In areas of especially heavy black concentration African influences were sometimes more persistent, and assimilation into the mainstream of American culture was slower and more tenuous; on the sea islands off South Carolina and Georgia, for example, blacks continued into the twentieth century to speak a "Gullah" dialect unintelligible to those unfamiliar with it. On the whole, however, African traditions were less persistent among slaves in the United States than in most of the Caribbean and Brazil, because African-born slaves in the United States quickly became a small and diminishing proportion of the black population, because in the South blacks lacked the numerical preponderance they enjoyed in many other New World slave societies, and because southern slaveowners impinged so greatly on the lives of their people. The forced migration of hundreds of thousands of slaves to the American South thus resulted in a cultural break of major proportions; the Afro-American descendants of early imports were less African in their beliefs and behavior than American.[3]

This discontinuity was evident in numerous social forms. The West African religious orientation, in which people lived in close proximity to gods personifying natural phenomena—trees, rivers, rain—and to spirits of ancestors who if properly propitiated watched over their descendants, was largely lost by the second generation. During the century preceding emancipation white southerners pressed with increasing vigor the conversion and religious instruction of their slaves, and John W. Blassingame has suggested that "the church was the single most important institution for the 'Americanization' of the bondsman." As one recent scholar put it, "in the United States the gods of Africa died." The same was true of traditional polygamous and extended family groupings. But perhaps most basic of all was the transformation of the West Africans' communal life-style. The ancestors of American slaves lived in villages that dominated virtually every aspect of life, from religious ritual to kinship and political relations. Lacking any concept of private property, they worked together, in communal groups, on communal land; tradition linked the individual—who counted for little—to family, clan, and village, and through these to ancestors and spirits. Because "the village was the family writ large," the slave trade to America not only tore apart families but also fragmented the communal identity and consciousness of their members. Africans survived in the United States, but their traditional way of life did not.[4]

Over the course of two and one-half centuries blacks in America developed customs and values different from those of both their African forebears and their white owners. Historical discontinuity interacted with the development of a distinctive Afro-American life-style to render southern slave culture a continually changing phenomenon. Some of its most widely noted attributes were most evident during the early colonial period but lost their salience as the African consciousness receded. Others were relatively late developments: black Christianity, for example, was largely a product of the century before emancipation and reached its apogee only during the last half-century. The slave experience, in short, was as subject to historical change as that of other Americans.

Although remnants of African tradition melded into this Afro-American culture and prevailing white mores strongly influenced it, its basis was the shared experience of blacks in American slavery, and the crucible in which it was forged was the slave quarters. Although blacks were unable to reproduce the African communities of their ancestors, the slave quarters facilitated the emergence of new communal standards and relationships. Although slaves held in very small units almost invariably lived in or near the houses of their owners, plantation hands usually resided in the quarters, a collection of huts grouped together in a semivillage some distance from the dwellings of owner and overseer. This relative isolation afforded millions of slaves a degree of independence and enabled them to enjoy a partially autonomous life-style.

In the quarters slaves prayed and partied, lived and loved, in great measure out of the control—and sight—of whites. As one historian has put it, "While from sunup to sundown the American slave worked for another and was harshly exploited, from sundown to sunup he lived for himself and created the behavioral and institutional basis which prevented him from becoming the absolute victim." To a degree slaveowner paternalism facilitated this independence, by providing the necessary breathing space for slaves to live their own lives as well as by giving them the frequent opportunity to hold dances, barbecues, celebrations, and prayer meetings. About ten

days after Charles Ball arrived on his new plantation in South Carolina, his owner arranged a huge feast for the slaves to celebrate completion of the harvest. "I doubt if there was in the world a happier
assemblage than ours, on this Saturday evening," Ball wrote later.
That night, they celebrated with dancing, singing, and storytelling,
and on Sunday afternoon "we had a meeting, at which . . . a man
named Jacob . . . sang and prayed"; meanwhile, "great many of the
people went out about the plantation, in search of fruits . . . With us,
this was a day of uninterrupted happiness." Numerous other blacks
had similar recollections. "Whoopee, didn' us have good Sa'dd'y
night frolics and jubilees," remembered one. "Some clap and some
play de fiddle, and, man, dey danced all night. Cornshucking was
'nother big frolic." [5]

Although slave communal life, for decades virtually ignored by historians, has in recent years received heavy emphasis from a new generation of scholars, the concept of the slave community has remained
vague and poorly defined. Indeed, despite pervasive use of the term
during the past decade and a half, the careful reader of recent historical literature is likely to remain confused about precisely what it was.
Some have used the term in a purely physical sense, as a synonym for
slave quarter; thus, Thomas L. Webber writes of the "slave quarter
community," by which he means simply the slave quarters. (The index
entry under *community* says "see quarter.") Similarly, John W. Blassingame, whose book is titled *The Slave Community,* nowhere defines
it, but his focus is so exclusively on slave culture that one is led to
conclude that he either sees culture and community as identical or
else uses *community* to refer to the people who lived under slavery as
a whole. (In this sense some people talk about the *black community,*
by which they mean, quite simply, blacks.) Other historians, however,
use the word in a very different way: Lawrence W. Levine refers to a
"sense of almost instant community" in slave singing, implying a particular relationship among people as the essence of community; in the
same sense he writes of the slaves' "communal consciousness."

Of course, the term *community* has several legitimate meanings.
Dictionary definitions include the purely physical—"a group of
people living in the same locality and under the same government" or
"the locality in which they live"—as well as the relational: "the quality of appertaining to all in common," or "society, the social state."
Surely, however, it is primarily the latter connotation that is significant to us; all people live in a locality, and to argue that slaves lived
in a community in this sense is a truism. The term has historical sig-

nificance in terms of relations among people and implies some form of social organization regulating shared standards of behavior. As Thomas Bender argues, "Community . . . is best defined as a network of social relations marked by mutuality and emotional bonds." Crucial to this definition is a sense of solidarity—Bender calls it "we-ness"—stemming from common values, perceptions, and interests as well as from a sense of mutual or collective responsibility. The concept of community overlaps but is distinct from that of culture; the bondsmen's communal organizations were both prime examples of their cultural activities and vehicles through which most of those activities were expressed, but at the same time *community* constituted a special cultural form that must be isolated in order to prevent its obscuration and mystification.[6]

When the slave community is seen in this way, an important observation concerns the rudimentary nature of its organization. Although the African community perished with the establishment of slavery in America, it was never fully replaced. The slave quarters functioned as a refuge from white control, but institutionally the slave community remained undeveloped, never assuming the concrete forms and functions that would enable it to serve as a basis around which the slaves could fully organize their lives.

An examination of communal organization among Russian serfs serves to clarify the nature of community as well as to underline its rudimentary development in the slave South. Like other peasants the world over, Russian serfs usually lived in villages. Although a small number of isolated rural homesteads persisted into the nineteenth century, especially in the sparsely settled north and on the southern borderland, as early as the sixteenth century these constituted a small minority of peasant dwellings; throughout the era of serfdom rural life meant village life (a fact underscored by the ability of both major words for *village* to mean "rural" as well). Villages ranged from populous establishments containing hundreds of households, shops, communal buildings, and a church down to tiny hamlets consisting of only a handful of huts. Frequently, a large village (*selo*) was surrounded by a number of satellite hamlets (*derevni*); in 1836, for example, the serfs in Riazan province inhabited 521 sela and 1,808 derevni, with an average of 37.7 serf households per village. Scholars have advanced varying reasons for the emergence of collective village life among the peasantry, from the need to cooperate in a harsh environment to the introduction of the three-field system, the desire of pomeshchiki to facilitate supervision of their serfs, and the policy of the government to deal with collective units instead of individuals for purposes of taxation and administration. For our purposes, however, the consequences of the village's dominance of rural life are far more important than the causes: serfs (and state peasants as well) spent their lives in the isolation of their villages, in an environment that was populated almost entirely by other peasants. The village was a world apart from the rest of Russia.[7]

The village constituted the peasants' world in a literal sense: its central institution, around which revolved their collective lives, was the peasant commune (*obshchina* or *mir; mir* also means "world"). A subject of intense ideological debate in Russian history—condemned by pro-Western modernizers for sapping individual initiative and celebrated by Slavophiles for its uniquely Russian character and by socialists for its protosocialism—the commune spread with villages during the early years of serfdom, existed throughout central and northern Russia by the early seventeenth century, and had acquired the sanction of tradition and custom by the early eighteenth. Receiving official government recognition and at least grudging seigneurial toleration, the mir constituted the political representative of the village, "the organizing basis of all village life," through which serfs ordered their lives and expressed their needs.[8]

The role and influence of the serf commune varied considerably, depending on the policies and residence of individual owners. Where pomeshchiki were resident owners, especially on relatively small estates, they often tried to keep virtually all authority in their own hands and minimize communal functions, whereas absentee owners were more likely to rely on the mir as an essential element of estate administration. Similarly, the mir usually had greater authority on obrok than on barshchina estates. Nevertheless, despite their legal right to do so, pomeshchiki almost never entirely dispensed with the commune, which virtually everywhere performed certain essential functions that changed little over the course of two centuries, functions that made it an integral part of peasant life, estate management, and rural government. The commune represented the lowest level of authority in a chain of command that linked the peasant to the tsar.[9]

The communal meeting or gathering (*mirskii skhod*) was the legislative expression of this basic level of government. The mir gathered at regular intervals for routine deliberations and elections as well as for exceptional debates when the situation warranted. A commune might represent a large village or more often several smaller ones. Usually all adult males were eligible to attend the meetings, but typically suffrage was limited to heads of families; on Prince Vorontsov's estates, only males over forty-five could vote. Sometimes, on a large estate consisting of many villages each village would send representatives to a general meeting. On the Sheremetev estates of central Russia there were two communal levels: the "simple" obshchina representing a single village and the "complex" representing several villages in an area (*volost'*). Whatever system of representation was used—a decision usually made by the serfs themselves unless their owners issued specific directives on the matter—records of the deliberations would be kept if possible by a peasant clerk, who was often the only literate serf on the estate.[10]

The most important routine function of the communal gathering was the election of peasant officials. Although some pomeshchiki insisted on appointing or having their stewards appoint these figures, most allowed their serfs a substantial degree of leeway in choosing their leaders, and some left local rule almost entirely in their hands. Typical noble instructions stipulated that peasant officials should be chosen at regular intervals—often annually—"by the whole mir from among good people," or even more specifically, that they be elected "among themselves, and the steward himself should not choose, but only make sure that good people are chosen." Sometimes, evidently, *good* was a code word for richest or most successful, but it also signified that peasants should select men who were trustworthy from their owners' point of view, "conscientious people who have not previously been under any kind of suspicion." Through such elections serfs usually chose the head of the commune—the starosta (or sometimes the burmistr)—as well as a number of assistants varying according to particular conditions and estate size. Often included were a clerk, one or more *tseloval'nik* (whose chief function was to watch over the treasury), sotskie and desiatskie, one or more obrok collector, and general "representatives" designed to assist in unspecified duties.[11]

The most obvious functions of these officials involved serving as the lowest level of seigneurial administration, helping the steward run the estate. The starosta and his assistants maintained order, often handled minor infractions of estate discipline themselves, and on barshchina estates helped supervise serf labor. Sotskie and desiatskie acted as policemen, keeping things running smoothly and reporting any problems to higher authorities. The tseloval'nik guarded the owner's treasury; the clerk kept his records; the obrok collector gathered his tribute. The starosta or burmistr acted as chief assistant to the steward and in his absence served as his lieutenant.[12]

As a result of these administrative functions, some historians have concluded that the mir, rather than representing a case of grass-roots democracy, acted as a tool of seigneurial exploitation—and sometimes as an agency of oppression of poor serfs by their richer, coopted brothers. Scholars have pointed to stipulations that only the "good" or "best" peasants be elected as evidence that communal officials were usually elite serfs who presumably cared little for the well-being of their poor neighbors; others have suggested—somewhat at cross purposes—that the "best" peasants usually avoided elective office, sometimes buying substitutes, leaving communal service to those most inclined to toady to seigneurial interests. A number of Soviet historians have been blunt in condemning the mir. "The representatives of the peasant obshchina composed one of the elements of estate rule," declared one typically. "Their actions were always first and foremost in seigneurial interests . . . not in the interests of the serf." [13]

In fact, although the mir was the lowest level of estate management, it was far more than this, and its leaders did not function simply as tools of class oppression. If it was convenient for absentee owners to allow their serfs a broad degree of local self-rule, it hardly follows that the serfs themselves had no interest in these activities. Abundant evidence suggests that pomeshchiki usually recognized the importance of maintaining a good working relationship with the commune precisely because it represented the prime medium through which peasants regulated their lives and expressed their social aspirations. Pomeshchiki expected the starosta and his assistants to keep serfs in line and maintain estate order, but peasants looked to them to handle internal civil relations among villagers as well as to represent their collective will in their dealings with their owner, the government, and the outside world. Historian V. A. Aleksandrov has perceptively noted "the dualism of the obshchina, as an instrument of estate administration and as an instrument of defense and preservation of peasant interests." [14]

The mir performed a host of functions on a regular basis that were of vital concern to the daily lives of the serfs. It exercised broad authority in internal village affairs, settling minor disputes among peasants, enforcing family morality, and maintaining a reserve of money and grain to help the needy in time of crisis. Tradition—together with noble instructions—gave the commune substantial power in selecting recruits to serve in the military levies the government periodically imposed. Although pomeshchiki had the ultimate right to send whomever they wanted into the army and availed themselves of this right by picking special troublemakers as well as by laying down general guidelines for the mir to follow in making their choices, most allowed the serfs themselves "to select . . . in the mir gathering whomever they sentence." The commune was thus able to take account of specific conditions, usually selecting for military service unmarried youths and those from large families, but sometimes resorting to lot.[15]

The obshchina's most important regular function, however, consisted of apportioning land and obligations among the village inhabitants. Because pomeshchiki typically cared little about the internal distribution of work and resources in their villages so long as those villages produced for them the requisite income, they usually assigned obligations to villages or estates collectively and allowed the commune to determine, on the basis of local conditions, who owed what. Of course, pomeshchiki laid down guidelines in their instructions, and resident owners of small estates often made decisions themselves; on large barshchina estates stewards generally organized and supervised seigneurial labor according to written instructions. Even when barshchina prevailed, however, pomeshchiki often set down only basic policy for how labor should be organized, allowing the mir to apply this policy as it saw fit. Where serfs worked "brother-for-brother" on a three-day-per-week barshchina, for example, they were usually able to decide for themselves who would perform seigneurial labor and who would cultivate peasant allotments. Where obrok prevailed, pomeshchiki typically stipulated the amount a village or estate owed but allowed the mir to determine how much each household should pay. Thus, A. M. Cherkasskii, in his 1719 instruction, ordered that reapportionment of obligations should be imposed "by determination of the mir itself . . . and the steward should not be involved in this reapportionment, but the reapportionment should be occasioned by petition of all the peasants every year or two." In reallocating obligations, the commune could operate on any basis it wanted, but the guiding principle was usually the relative ability of a family to pay or perform labor, based on its size, income, and any unusual circumstances (such as illness, weddings, or fires).[16]

The central feature of the reallocation process was the periodic redistribution of land allotments to peasant families; indeed, because of this centrality the obshchina was sometimes known as the "repartitional commune." Redistribution was a local phenomenon, encompassing individual villages or estates and occurring at varying intervals—ranging from a couple of years to several decades, but most often taking place every few years—depending on the will of the landowner as well as his serfs. Usually, however, pomeshchiki intervened little in the process, allowing serfs to elect surveyors and redivide their holdings whenever they deemed it appropriate. Conditions calling for such a repartition might include the taking of a new national census, dramatic changes in the population of a village or in the well-being of some families, or simply the passage of enough time to render previous arrangements inequitable. The main goal was to prevent the pauperization of families—and to maximize productive use of the land—by assigning plots to families on the basis of their ability to cultivate them. This did not require, either in theory or practice, equal division of the land among all families; indeed, large families and those with numerous livestock invariably received larger allotments than small families with few working hands or animals. It did restrain, however—in the interest of both pomeshchiki and their serfs—the emergence of vast disparities in peasant wealth that would place excessive burdens on some households (and thereby impair their ability to produce income for their owners).[17]

The practice of communal repartition served to fortify the collective mentality of the peasants. "Their" land was held collectively by the whole community rather than privately by individual peasants. Not only did periodic redistribution result in most serfs' having widely scattered strips of the land that they cultivated for their sustenance; it also meant that any individual parcel might well be assigned to someone else in the future. Critics of the communal system argued that it undermined individual initiative and inhibited the development of the concept of private property among the peasantry. But communal landholding and the communal responsibility engendered by the tendency of pomeshchiki to deal with the mir collectively through its leaders rather than with peasants individually also reinforced the serfs' sense of solidarity with each other, their recognition that their fate was bound up with that of their fellow villagers.[18]

This communal mentality and the degree to which serfs regarded the mir as their own are most evident in their behavior when dissatisfied with their treatment (see Chapters 5 and 6). When serfs felt the need for redress, they turned instinctively to the commune, collectively petitioning their owners, local government officials, or the tsar, and sometimes collectively going well beyond simple petitioning. Communal officials usually played leading roles in the process, organizing and running the mir gathering at which the proper course of action was discussed, helping draft petitions, and putting their names at the top of the list of subscribing peasants. If communal leaders refused to represent the villagers' interests, peasants often ignored them or replaced them with more cooperative leaders. In 1856, when serfs in Riazan province undertook a major confrontation with their owner Major-General P. E. Zavaritskii, their first act was to choose a new starosta, "who announced not only to the pomeshchik but also to the local police that he, elected starosta by the mir, would not recognize any authority except the will of the mir." Reproached by Zavaritskii for his disobedience, the peasant leader replied, "I am just as much a general as you, since the mir elected me." The mir's collective approval legitimized in the serfs' eyes virtually any behavior, and they expected their officials to defend them come what may.[19]

Seen in the light of the peasant obshchina, the absence of any communal organization among American slaves is striking. Of course, there were slaves who played managerial roles on southern plantations. A small number of planters allowed their slaves a substantial degree of self-rule; Mississippi planter Joseph Davis, for example, set up a plantation jury to determine the guilt or innocence of slaves charged with misconduct (although Davis himself sat as judge). More numerous were planters with slave drivers who were allowed to exercise considerable administrative authority, in some cases serving as virtual overseers. On the rice plantations of coastal South Carolina and Georgia, absentee owners commonly left their estates under the control of trusted black drivers who were only loosely supervised by white stewards. Like peasant officials in Russia, slave drivers were in an ambiguous position, both agents of plantation discipline and slaves who identified with the plantation labor force. One former slave recalled how "during my eight years' experience as a driver, I learned to handle the whip with marvelous dexterity and precision, throwing the lash within a hair's breadth of the back, the ear, the nose, without, however, touching either of them." He was thus able to spare his supposed victims who, "according to arrangement, would squirm and screech as if in agony, although not one of them had in fact been even grazed."[20]

Nevertheless, drivers hardly constituted the equivalent of serf officials. Except in isolated localities or on unusual, experimental plantations, drivers worked under the close supervision of owners and overseers and lacked the authority to serve the interests of the slaves. Indeed, many slaves looked upon drivers not as protectors or fellow bondsmen but as ruthless oppressors. But the essential point is that whether they identified with their charges or abused them, drivers were not, like serf officials, representatives of the slave community, nor were they seen as such by either slaves or planters. Drivers were invariably chosen by their masters, not by the other slaves; although individual blacks in positions of authority sometimes acted to protect individual slaves, they owed their positions of power to the trust of planters, not of slaves. Similarly, the Maryland slaves who according to Frederick Douglass eagerly sought the privilege of serving as "representatives" to run errands at the Great House Farm were selected by their overseers, not their peers: "the competitors for this office sought as diligently to please their overseers, as the office-seekers in the political parties seek to please and deceive the people." Of course, many plantations had informal slave leaders who served as true community representatives, but they were rarely recognized as such by whites, and their actual authority was correspondingly minimal.[21]

The slave community thus lacked the formal institutional basis of the peasant obshchina. Its absence did not, of course, preclude the existence of communal sentiment and behavior among the slaves; indeed, antebellum slaves had a strong sense of themselves as a people. It did, however, severely restrict the ability of slaves to express their communal feelings, in the process limiting the collective nature of their life and culture. The existence of communal forms of social organization in Russian villages and their absence on American plantations affected the ways in which the bondsmen related both to one another and to their owners. The former is the subject of this chapter; the latter is the subject of Chapters 5 and 6.

* * *

THE FAMILY was the most basic locus of the bondsmen's unsupervised lives. Both slaves and serfs found, in their families, a refuge in which their love and joy, jealousy and petty squabbling largely transcended their bondage. Through their families slaves and serfs were able to forge ties that were at least partially independent of the master-servant relationship that prescribed so much of their lives; in their families slaves and serfs were, like other people, husbands, wives, parents, children, lovers, friends, and rivals. Nevertheless, they remained bondsmen, and their families were never entirely free from owner influence. Although that influence manifested itself in numerous ways in both countries, it was more pervasive and confining in the American South than in Russia. A comparison of the family lives of the slaves and serfs reveals not only how both were sources of partial autonomy but also how both reflected the differing communal bases of the societies in which they existed. Here, as in many other areas, the question of historical continuity and discontinuity looms large:

Russian serf families rested on centuries of tradition and custom; American slave families, by contrast, had to be recreated in the New World.

The creation of basic family patterns among American slaves was largely an eighteenth-century phenomenon. The introduction of slavery into the mainland colonies involved widespread destruction of African families, whose members were routinely ripped from their kin and sold to planters interested in them almost exclusively for their labor-power. This interest also dictated that males heavily outnumbered females among imports—seventeenth-century planter William Fitzhugh instructed his "field representative" to purchase "what boys & men you possibly can [and] as few women as may be"—and consequently among the early colonial slave population as well. Newly imported Africans rarely enjoyed normal family relations—indeed, they often lived in sex-segregated barracks—and rarely had many children. Only through continued importation of new Africans did the slave population grow in the mainland colonies in the seventeenth and early eighteenth centuries. All of this changed markedly, however, in the eighteenth century, as an increasing proportion of American-born or creole slaves created greater equality between the number of males and females, a higher birthrate, and for the first time a possibility of family life for the majority of slaves. Evidence suggests that this crucial transition took place at somewhat varying times in the different mainland colonies but occurred in all of them during the second and third quarters of the eighteenth century. In All Hallow's parish, Maryland, for example, slave sex ratios declined from 1.59 in the 1720s to 1.11 in 1776; during the same period the ratio of adults to children dropped from 2.34 to 0.99. By the second half of the century American slaves were, to use Allan Kulikoff's apt phrase, "a prolifick people" and were, unlike slaves in most other New World regions, more than reproducing themselves through natural population growth.[22]

During the century preceding emancipation slave families were typically large, nuclear, and—unless broken by sale—relatively long-lasting. The even sex ratio made it possible for most American slaves to live in family units; the great majority lived in nuclear families— mother, father, and children—one family to a cabin. Widely scattered records suggest an average size of about seven children per completed slave family, with families of four to seven members prevailing at any given point in time. Research by Herbert Gutman has revealed not only that most slaves lived in families with two parents present but also that those same parents were likely to remain together over a prolonged period of time. Records from three Virginia counties, for example, show that upon emancipation more than three-quarters of sample slave families lived in a household consisting of either a husband and wife or husband, wife, and children; in three-fifths of the families on the Good Hope plantation in South Carolina, all the children in each family had the same father and mother.[23]

Families served as a major source of strength to antebellum slaves as well as vehicles for the propagation of community mores. Despite white assertions that "Negroes are themselves both perverse and comparatively indifferent about" family separations, abundant evidence exists of the slaves' defense of their families. Parents frequently named children—especially sons, who were more likely eventually to be separated from loved ones—after older relatives in order to assert kinship ties and facilitate their tracing in the face of potential disruption. For the same reason, as well as to assert their dignity, slaves sometimes took surnames unbeknownst to whites; when questioned in 1863, ex-slave Robert Smalls testified before the American Freedmen's Inquiry Commission that although "among themselves they use their titles [surnames] . . .[before] their masters they do not speak of their titles at all." But perhaps the clearest evidence of the importance of black families is the anguish of slaves—manifested both at the time and later in interviews and autobiographies—at the forcible separations that so many of them suffered. Moses Grandy was typical of many ex-slaves in his graphic depiction of the impact of such separations. When his younger brother was sold away, "my mother, frantic with grief, resisted their taking her child away. She was beaten and held down; she fainted; and, when she came to herself, her boy was gone." Later, Grandy and his wife were parted; "I have never seen or heard of her from that day to this," he related. "I loved her as I love my life."[24]

Slave families were able to play such an important role in the United States for a number of reasons. Favorable demographic conditions—a largely creole slave population with even sex ratios and a high reproductive rate—set the South off from most other New World slave societies. Equally important was the paternalistic attitude of many slaveowners, who sought to encourage family formation and avoid forced separations when possible. But most basic were the efforts of the slaves themselves, who overcame formidable odds by perpetuating family bonds under extremely adverse circumstances.[25]

That slave families were primarily the creation of slaves themselves and not simply replicas of white patterns made possible by owner benevolence is shown by the existence of family mores that differed in a number of significant respects from those prevalent in the dominant society. Unlike upper-class southern whites, for example, slaves practiced marital exogamy, avoiding marriage with first cousins. Slave sexual morality also differed from that of Victorian Americans: although marital fidelity was prescribed, premarital experimentation—not always with the ultimate marriage partner—was widespread and evidently widely tolerated. Gutman found a common pattern of a slave woman having all her children except the first by the same man. (Whether this constitutes promiscuity, as many observers traditionally argued, or a healthier attitude toward sex than was prevalent among "guilt-stricken" whites, as has been more recently asserted, is a subjective judgment.) Cheryll Ann Cody has suggested that naming practices indicate that most slaves "conceived of their families in a broad sense, including extended kin," whereas their masters "saw the nuclear family as the primary unit." (If so, this would accentuate the pain of forced separations, for even masters who kept nuclear families together sometimes broke extended ties.) The existence of autonomous patterns of family morality among the slaves is significant, both because it demonstrates the way in which they developed community standards different from those of their masters and because it suggests the key role of the family in promoting and supporting such standards.[26]

The evidence also suggests that antebellum slave society was an unusually female-centered world in which women played very different roles from those common in white America. They performed the kind of field labor that most free Americans considered a masculine preserve. More important was their prominent position within the family itself. Because slaves owned no property, their women were not subject to the control that property ownership traditionally enabled men to exercise. Furthermore, women experienced the kind of stability and continuity that enabled them to serve as the primary cultural carriers within the slave community. Young children were rarely sold apart from their mothers; the evidence uncovered by Gutman and others that slave boys were more often named after their fathers than were girls after their mothers indicates the fragility of male kinship ties, which had to be continually reasserted. When slaves married "abroad," it was invariably the men who were away visiting their families on weekends. In short, in an era that took male dominance and superiority for granted, the position of women within the slave family was one of unusual authority.[27]

Because historians, who once regarded the slave family as all but crushed under the oppressive weight of slavery, now commonly stress its strength and resiliency, it is necessary, as it would not have been a decade ago, to note the precariousness of slave families. Although well-intentioned owners tried to keep families together, forcible separations were a pervasive feature of slave life that had a devastating impact on their victims. Almost every major autobiography of an ex-slave testifies to the ubiquity of such separations. "My mother and I were separated when I was but an infant . . . I never saw my mother, to know her as such, more than four or five times in my life," recalled Frederick Douglass; "I received the tidings of her death [in his seventh year] with much the same emotions I should have probably felt at the death of a stranger." Henry Bibb never knew his father and at a young age "was taken away from my mother, and hired out to labor for various persons, eight or ten years in succession." William W. Brown had six brothers and sisters, but "no two of us were children of the same father." Similar stories were told time after time by other ex-slaves.[28]

Even when slaves were not separated from their loved ones, the impact of potential separation and of continued owner interference in their lives was often severe. It is difficult to evaluate the internal dynamics of slaves' family lives—how loving spouses were to each other, what kind of upbringing they gave to their children—because of the stylized nature of most of their recollections, but ritualistic expressions of love for mother should not lead us to underestimate the tremendous psychic damage imposed by slavery. Surely, one common assertion of ex-slaves is highly significant here: "No colored man wishes to live at home where his wife lives," observed Moses Grandy, "for he has to endure the continued misery of seeing her flogged and abused, without daring to say a word in her defense." Tom Epps later recalled a different reason that many slaves preferred to have wives who lived on different plantations: "cause dey could git a pass to go visit 'em on Saddy nights." Slave families showed tremendous vitality and resiliency, as recent research has demonstrated, but that husbands and wives often preferred to live apart from each other reveals a great deal about the impact of slavery on family life.[29]

The character of slave families is highlighted by their comparison with Russian serf families. As among the slaves, the family was the most important institution affecting the internal lives of the serfs. Families performed many of the same essential functions, providing a haven where bondsmen could live and love apart from the constraints their thralldom imposed upon them. At the same time, however, serf families differed from their American slave counterparts in several ways that reflected the contrasting nature of slave and serf life. Perhaps most important, the structure and character of serf families reflected and reinforced the largely communal life of the Russian peasant.

Unlike American slaves, Russian serfs did not have to reconstitute their families after a wrenching experience of being torn from their homeland and introduced into a strange new world. Serfs did not undergo a counterpart to the slave experience in the seventeenth and early eighteenth-century colonies, where disruption of previous family ties and uneven sex ratios severely limited the availability of normal family life. The numbers of male and female serfs were not precisely equal—there was a general surplus of about five females for every hundred males, and in specific localities the discrepancy was sometimes greater—but they were close enough to make marriage an almost universal institution among serfs. Because serfs never went through the trauma of the slave trade, their culture—and their families—exhibited far more continuity and was far more enmeshed in tradition than that of American slaves. The American roots of most nineteenth-century slave families went back barely a century, and few slaves, if one judges by narratives and autobiographies, were able to trace their ancestors back more than three generations; the roots of serf families extended for centuries, and generation after generation of peasants had frequently lived in the same village. In addition, the serf family as a rule faced less ongoing interference from owners than the slave family; forced separations of family members and sexual exploitation of women were far less common in Russia than in America (see Chapter 2, pages 114–19).[30]

Serf families, like those of slaves, were typically large. Early marriage—usually between the ages of sixteen and nineteen for women, seventeen and twenty-one for men—combined with little or no contraceptive knowledge and the desire in any case for additional hands to serve as added sources of family income, produced exceptionally high birthrates that were of the same order of magnitude as those prevalent among American slaves. Families with ten and twelve children were by no means unusual, and the average number of children born to serf families probably exceeded the mean of seven that prevailed among American slaves. Of course, at any given point in time most parents had fewer than seven children at home; some died in infancy, others reached adulthood before their youngest siblings were born, and many families were headed by parents who had not yet had all their children. Still, households were typically quite large. What is more, they grew larger over time: an abundance of evidence suggests that whereas in the sixteenth century the average peasant household contained no more than five persons, by the late seventeenth it contained more than eight, a figure that remained relatively constant throughout the serf era.[31]

As this growth in household size suggests, a substantial number of family residents under serfdom were persons other than a married couple and their children. Historians have established that throughout modern history the nuclear family has prevailed in western Europe and the United States including among slaves. Although paucity of research makes generalization risky, it is clear that small nuclear families were nowhere near so dominant within most of the Russian empire. Andrejs Plakans has recently shown, for example, that in the Baltic province of Kourland serf households at the turn of the nineteenth century typically consisted of huge "farmsteads" containing an average of some fifteen people each, only a third of whom were members of the head's conjugal family and only half of whom were even related.[32]

In Russia proper, serf households typically contained between six and twelve residents, but their structure varied considerably. Some consisted of nuclear families—a couple and their unmarried children—but on the same estate could often be found large extended families and various arrangements in between. The small estate owned by F. M. Bezobrazov in Brianskii district in the early eighteenth century, for example, contained a total of eight serf households. One of these was inhabited by Fedor Afonas'ev, his wife Varvara, and their two unmarried children. A neighboring household, however, contained thirty-one people spanning three generations. Eight of these were in a direct line—Filip Iakovlev, his wife Aksina, their two unmarried sons, a married son with a wife and two children—but the remainder consisted of Filip's five married brothers, their wives, and their unmarried children. Still a third neighboring household contained a total of nine persons, consisting of three generations in a straight line: Daniel Semenov and his wife Avdot'ia, three unmarried children, a married son with a wife and two children. It was this third or "joint family" pattern that seems to have been most prevalent. Married men typically brought their wives home with them, resulting in three and less often four generations in a straight line living together; less frequently, but by no means rarely, married men moved in with their brothers, leading to households with lateral kinships.[33]

Several causes contributed to the prevalence of the joint peasant household, but economic self-interest—of both peasants and po-meshchiki—was probably most basic. For serf families extra hands to perform agricultural labor and contribute to family income were always in demand, and the joint family allowed newly married sons to avoid the expensive necessity of setting up on their own. Because of economies of scale and the willingness of communes to grant them bigger allotments, large serf families were almost always in a better economic position than were smaller ones. Pomeshchiki, realizing that impoverished serfs were likely to be unproductive as well as un-able to pay substantial obrok dues, strove to promote big families and to prevent their members from leaving the joint unit to establish their own households; Prince A. M. Cherkasskii, in a typical instruction, ordered stewards to prevent family divisions so as to avoid "squalor." For much the same reason the peasant commune sought to promote large, economically viable families—sometimes even refusing serfs permission to leave joint families to set up on their own—because economically marginal serfs became a burden on the whole commu-nity. It is no accident, then, that household size increased dramatically during the seventeenth and early eighteenth centuries, a period of in-creasing seigneurial and communal authority (the household tax, im-posed on peasants in 1678 and replaced by the soul tax in 1719, also acted to boost household size during this formative period of serf-dom), stabilized during the last century of serfdom, and then declined sharply after emancipation. Nor is it surprising that households tended to be largest in the most fertile agricultural regions, where additional hands meant increased economic opportunity, and smallest in the north.[34]

As this suggests, the large joint or extended family was in part a reflection of the serf's communal life; indeed, it can be described as a communal family. Just as the village had its communal representative, so did each family have its leader, the *bol'shak* or head, who repre-sented the family in mir assemblies and traditionally ruled his brood with an iron hand, from deciding when sons and daughters should marry to imposing physical punishment on those who displeased him. The mir strongly supported the bol'shak's authority, not only by deal-ing with him as representative of the whole household and by resist-ing efforts to break up the family unit but also by backing up his physical authority. Peasant officials sometimes meted out corporal punishment to individuals at a bol'shak's request, although occasion-ally, if a family head abused his authority, the commune would inter-vene and even replace him with a different member of the family.

Physical chastisement of women and children was evidently pervasive and widely accepted. Although women's rights were rarely elevated anywhere in eighteenth-century or early nineteenth-century Europe, foreign travelers were struck by the way Russian peasants tyrannized their wives "whom they consider and treat as their slaves." The need to subjugate lazy or ungrateful wives is a frequent subject of Russian peasant folktales and songs. In one popular song a husband, disheartened when his kindness and presents produce in his wife only churlishness, finally buys her a "silken whip," which yields immediate results: she at once looks at him affectionately and after one stripe bows and kisses him. The position of women sharply differentiated the serf family from that of the American slave.[35]

The serf family reflected and reinforced communal life in its customs and culture as well as size and structure. Indicative of the subservience of the individual to the general good was the manner in which peasant marriages were contracted. In contrast to prevailing customs among American slaves, where prospective spouses courted and eventually married for love (or at least lust), traditional marriages among Russian peasants were arranged, at the peasants' behest, by matchmakers. In one of the rare memoirs written by an ex-serf, N. N. Shipov describes how, when he reached eighteen in 1820, his father decided to get him married. Because Shipov's family was unusually wealthy, there were only three eligible girls in his village, and his father called a family council to decide which one should receive the proposal. The young Shipov told his father that the choice was immaterial to him "since I do not know any of them," and when the decision was made an uncle was sent to conduct the elaborate negotiations that eventually resulted in a wedding.[36]

In more typical serf families, too, marriages were usually arranged not to suit the desires of the betrothed but to serve the economic and social well-being of their families, their community, and ultimately their pomeshchik. Prospective daughters-in-law were traditionally prized not for their charm or beauty but for their likely ability to work and bear abundant offspring; they were expected to "have the strength of an animal, and the endurance of a horse." Although there is evidence that young peasants engaged in widespread flirtatious games, many of which were associated with ritualized seasonal festivals and ceremonies, and some suggestion that premarital sexual activity was common, traditional weddings often carried more tragic than ecstatic overtones. The bride's family traditionally hired "chanters" or "weepers," poor women whose task it was to lament the lot of the gay young bride about to leave her loved ones forever to live among strangers; significantly, wedding lamentations bore striking resemblances to those sung at funerals and at the drafting of young men into the army. A number of unhappy stereotypes were associated with the peasant daughter-in-law, from the poor young girl overworked by unsympathetic—even jealous—parents-in-law whom she suddenly inherited to the girl, married off for economic reasons to an underaged boy, who becomes the mistress of her new father-in-law. Although couples produced by arranged marriages often came to love one another and sometimes the bride and groom themselves were eager participants of the marriage ceremony, from the peasant point of view marriage served primarily to fill certain familial and communal needs, not those resulting from the mutual attraction of two individuals.[37]

In numerous other respects, too, serf families were enmeshed in communal values, traditions, and customs handed down from generation to generation, which often retained only symbolic meaning. There were established and ritualized procedures for all stages of the family cycle. Unmarried girls and boys met each other and courted in the *khorovod* or circle dance, a highlight of village life in the warm months of the year, and in the *posidelka,* a winter party in which girls would first gather in a village hut spinning, combing, talking, and singing and then later in the evening entertain young men, with whom they danced and sang, usually while older people watched.[38]

The traditional wedding ceremony was equally ritualized, beginning with elaborate negotiations between members of the two families and containing formal gatherings and dinners in which family members got to know one another, continuing with the presentation of handmade dowry gifts by the bride to members of the groom's family as well as exchange of presents by other family members, the traditional bride's lament in which she would "entreat her relatives to break off the engagement," lamentations by hired chanters who bemoaned the hard fate the new bride faced, a formal church wedding conducted by a priest, display of the bride's blood-spattered shift on the day after the wedding, and postwedding family dinners and revelry. Although many of these stages were abbreviated or nonexistent among the poorest families—the bride's own lamentations, for example, often replaced those of hired chanters—ritual and tradition set the tone for courtship and marriage.

The same was true after marriage as well. Far more than American slaves, Russian serfs adhered to a rigid gender-based division of labor.

Although women performed heavy labor, it was not the same as men's: men ploughed and sowed, carted, chopped wood, constructed buildings, cared for horses; women raked hay, reaped grain, milked cows, and cared for chickens, in addition to the indoor work of caring for children, cleaning house, cooking, spinning, weaving, and sewing. Like weddings, other momentous events such as funerals (and the drafting of young men) required the following of traditional rituals, including formal lamentations consisting of "the most lamentable cries"—handed down over the generations—by hired mourners as well as family members.

In short, the peasant family was the lowest-level manifestation of the commune, and the commune was an extension of the family. The two institutions reinforced each other and were based on a common adherence to traditional values, beliefs, and customs. Although serfs' right to property had no basis in written statute, common law provided them with considerable de facto autonomy, regulating property relations among them in the interest of familial and communal felicity. The concept of family property was meaningless, however, apart from the obshchina; upon leaving it an individual "lost as well his family-property rights, which were transferred to his nearest relative." As one late nineteenth-century observer noted, the large peasant family produced communal cooperation and mutual responsibility and buttressed the "conviction that the mir is always just and reasonable, and that truth is nowhere to be found but in the unanimous opinion of the people." [39]

Of course, American slave families also reflected and helped shape communal standards and behavior. Southern blacks developed shared rituals (although these were much less elaborate than those of the serfs), from jumping the broom at marriage to engaging in funeral orations, songs, and shouts that may have had African origins. Although their households were usually composed of nuclear conjugal units, it does not follow that they were unaware of or unconcerned with broader kinship ties. Abundant evidence, from naming patterns to the rigid practice of marital exogamy, testifies to widespread and active interest among slaves in familial relations beyond those of the immediate kinship group. Furthermore, the common use of *aunt* and *uncle* as terms of respect or endearment for persons not actually related by blood suggests that on a more general level many slaves came to see *all* blacks as members of a giant extended family, brothers and sisters in their shared suffering. Ironically, forced separations may have acted to hasten the emergence of such a view for family members were in fact to be found scattered over wide areas of the South. As Gutman has argued, "sale and migration regularly broke up families and shattered kin networks but also spread a uniform Afro-American slave culture over the entire South."[40]

Nevertheless, although slave and serf families were both integrally part of communal life, they differed in part precisely because the two communal experiences were so different. This is evident both in the contrasting structures of families and in the differing degrees to which they faced forced separation and general owner interference. One reason for the attenuated nature of slaves' ceremonies was that their owners did not always allow them. Although recent historians have studied slave names as evidence of slave values, for example, it is clear that many masters personally named at least some of their slaves themselves, as the existence of "pet" names such as Pompey, Caesar, and Rastus suggests. "My name is Sarah now, but it was Annie until I was eight years old," recalled one ex-slave. "My old mistress' name was Annie and she name me that, and Mammy was afraid to change it until Old Mistress died."[41]

The bondsmen's families were products of sharply contrasting levels of social continuity as well as social control. Serf families evolved slowly in villages often inhabited by generation after generation of the same families, whereas slave families were reconstituted in the eighteenth and early nineteenth centuries in a new land along new lines and therefore lacked the accumulated trappings of centuries of tradition, custom, and ritual. Of course, serfdom exerted a powerful influence on the nature of peasant families, as the prevalence of large multigenerational households testifies. But individual serf families developed largely on "home turf" and were often able to exist with relatively minimal day-to-day meddling from above; slave families developed in a new land as a result of strenuous efforts on the part of the slaves themselves but encountered pervasive owner interference. The establishment and security of the one contrasted with the novelty and precariousness of the other.

*   *   *

A SECOND cultural manifestation of vital importance to the bondsmen was their religion. Here, as in their families, slaves and serfs found refuge from the rigors of the outside world. Here, too, there were significant differences in the experiences of the slaves and serfs. Christianity played a central role in the antebellum slave community in part because of the lack of other institutional outlets available to its members; among Russian serfs, by contrast, religion, although important, served less as a basic element of self-definition. Once again, the contrast in historical continuity was significant: for the serfs Orthodox Christianity was one of a myriad of cultural forms, one that continued to coexist with pre-Christian traditions, beliefs, and values, whereas for the slaves Protestant Christianity came to fill the void left by the weakening of traditional African ways. Antebellum slaves seized onto the religion of their masters and made it their own, in the process helping to forge themselves into a distinctive people; pre-reform serfs, however, continued to feel ambivalence about a church over which they had relatively little control. Both peasant and black "theology" contained elements of a religion of the oppressed, reminiscent of Christianity in its formative years, but those elements reached much greater fruition in the American South than in Russia.

The religion of American slaves, even more than their families, revealed the developmental nature of slave culture, because only during the half-century before emancipation did the "invisible church" come to play a central role in the slave quarters. During the seventeenth and first half of the eighteenth centuries most American blacks remained largely unexposed to Christianity. Slaves born in Africa usually clung to their native religions, both as part of their cultural identity and as a conscious means of rejecting their new situation. As late as 1837 Charles Ball remembered his grandfather, who had been born in Africa: "He never went to church or meeting," Ball noted, "and held, that the religion of this country was altogether false, and indeed, no religion at all"; he told instead of a true religion practiced at home, where everyone kept "a small book" which revealed the major tenets. Although this faith rarely survived the first generation—Ball observed that unlike African-born slaves, "the American[-born] negro . . . knows nothing of Africa, her religion, or customs"—Christianity was slow to spread among the slaves because their owners made little effort to propagate it. At first this was because of a lingering fear that conversion of slaves might require their emancipation, but during most of the colonial period it was the result of indifference together with concern about the impact of references to the spiritual equality of all before God. In the 1770s tutor Philip Fithian observed that in Virginia "the lower class of People, & the Servants, & the Slaves" considered Sunday "as a Day of Pleasure & Amusement," not prayer, and planter Landon Carter complained bitterly that one of his overseers had "turned a Baptist, and only wants to convert my People." He continued, "This is a strange year about my overseers; some [are] horrid hellish rogues and other[s] religious villains."[42]

By this time, in fact, an increasing number of slaves were being exposed to Christianity. Unlike the traditional churches of colonial America, the new evangelical sects—Baptists and Methodists—affected substantial numbers of blacks as well as whites. Whereas Landon Carter was disgusted with his overseer's proselytizing in 1776, his nephew Robert, who originally shared his skepticism, saw the light in 1778, converted to Baptism himself, and spent much of the next decade encouraging his slaves to follow suit—much to the annoyance of several of his overseers. Evangelicals differed from more traditional southern churchmen not only in actively seeking black converts but also in presenting an emotional "religion of the heart" that many blacks—and lower-class whites as well—found especially appealing. During the three-quarters of a century after the American Revolution the great majority of slaves converted to Christianity, most to Baptism and Methodism. They were subjected, during the thirty years prior to the Civil War, to an increasingly active mission movement of white churchmen to bring the word of God to the slaves, as ministers, planters, and proslavery ideologues reached a new consensus that religion produced more obedient rather than more rebellious slaves. On the eve of the war some half-million southern blacks—about one-eighth of the population—were formally enrolled in southern white churches, and most of the remainder were exposed to some form of Christian worship on a regular basis.[43]

The Christianity that whites preached to the slaves, however, was not precisely the same as the Christianity that the slaves themselves adopted. The religion that blacks heard from their owners—in white churches where they sat in segregated slave galleries, in sermons specially prepared for them by white ministers, and in Bible readings by members of slaveowning families—was heavily laced with admonitions to obey their masters and seek reward in the life after death. But many slaves took this message with a grain of salt. "Dat ole white preacher jest was telling us slaves to be good to our marsters," recalled one ex-slave from Virginia. "We ain't keer'd a bit 'bout dat stuff he was telling us 'cause we wanted to sing, pray, and serve God in our own way. You see, 'legion needs a little motion—specially if you gwine feel de spirret." When Presbyterian minister Charles C. Jones addressed a group of slaves in Liberty county, Georgia, on the Christian virtue of obedience, "one half of my audience deliberately rose up and walked off with themselves, and those that remained looked anything but satisfied, either with the preacher or his doctrine." Other slaves evidently agreed that the medium as well as the message they received was deficient; although the emotional character of Methodism and Baptism appealed to blacks, most slaves found even white evangelical Christianity to be excessively formal, while the more restrained practices of Episcopalians and Catholics hardly seemed to constitute religion at all. As one Louisiana black woman put it, in deriding the staid nature of white Catholicism, "the Lawd said you gotta shout if you want to be saved. That's in the Bible." [44]

In the quarters the slaves developed their own Christianity, the so-called "invisible church." Some masters permitted and even encouraged this development, as a healthy outlet for slaves' emotions, but many others opposed it as essentially seditious in nature. Slaves met in any case—openly when permitted, secretly in the quarters or in "hush arbors" when forbidden—to celebrate their own services, based on values quite different from those preached to them by whites. Not all slaves took part in these activities; as one ex-slave remembered, many instead "make no profession of religion" and on Sunday "resort to the woods in large numbers . . . to gamble, fight, get drunk, and break the Sabbath." But during the half-century before emancipation the slaves' particular form of Christianity was at the heart of their communal culture, serving as both a refuge from a hostile white world and a medium for affirming their own values, ideals, and life-style. The self-called black preachers who led the services came to occupy a central position of leadership among blacks both during the last years of slavery and after its abolition. [45]

There were a number of important features of slave religion in the antebellum South. Intensity and emotionalism were the most obvious characteristics. "The whole congregation kept up one loud monotonous strain, interrupted by various sounds: groans and screams and clapping of hands," wrote white Presbyterian minister R. Q. Mallard of a black revival meeting he observed in 1859. "Considering the mere excitement manifested in these disorderly ways, I could but ask: What religion is there in this?" Such complaints by whites—and even some blacks—were common, and there can be no doubt about the emotional nature of black religion. At the same time, however, it is important to remember the "enthusiasm" associated with lower-class white evangelical Christianity in the South as well. Bennet H. Barrow complained of the "rascality carried on" in black services, but he was equally harsh on the behavior of his poor white neighbors, noting in 1843 that "¼ of the White population are run crazy on the subject of the Miller prophesey [sic], that the world would come to an end some time this year." [46]

More distinctive—and the bases of many white attacks on black "superstition"—were the lack of formal theology among the slaves and the particular twist of their Christian message. Black parishioners turned to Christianity for solace from their suffering, but it is hardly suprising that, denied access to the Bible, they appropriated what they learned of the Christian message selectively, emphasizing most what would appeal to a downtrodden people. Instead of the injunctions to obey their masters, they talked of the justice that would be theirs in the life after death—in this sense their religion was reminiscent of that of slaves in the early Christian period—and of the love that Jesus had for them. Unlike traditional Protestants, they lacked a sense of depravity or personal unworthiness and saw God as an immediate being, a friend with whom they could communicate personally. They also accentuated the Old Testament over the New—much to the discomfort of theologically minded critics—rejoicing in Moses' delivery of his people from slavery and sometimes even confusing his role with that of Jesus. Most of these themes are reflected in the spirituals that the slaves continually created and recreated and that encapsuled the essence of their religious world view:

> In de mornin' when I rise,
> Tell my Jesus huddy [howdy] oh
> . . . . .
> Gwine to argue wid de Father and chatter wid de son,
> . . . . .
> Gwine to write to Massa Jesus,
> To send some Valiant soldier
> To turn back Pharoah's army, Hallelu![47]

Many of the distinctive features of antebellum slave religion appear in especially stark form when that religion is compared with that of the Russian peasants. Although the latter had been formally Christians since the end of the tenth century, Christianity played a much less central role in their lives than it did among the antebellum slaves. Of course, most peasants considered themselves good Christians, and foreign observers were sometimes struck by their extreme religiosity. But their religion, unlike that of the slaves, was of a predominantly formalistic nature. They kept icons in their huts and dutifully fulfilled the requisite church rituals, but they showed little of the slaves' spontaneous religious enthusiasm. Observers noted that the serfs, like the slaves, had little understanding of Christian theology and were mired in "superstition"; they did not note in them the same religious feeling or emotion, however, the same intense relationship between the individual and God. Rather, it was the "outward practices of devotion" that were most noteworthy. "The Russian thinks he perfectly understands and fulfills his religion, if he makes innumerable signs of the cross and genuflections before the smoky picture that adorns his isbas, and scrupulously observes those two commandments of the Church, to fast and make Lenten fare," wrote one nineteenth-century French traveler. The strong emphasis in Orthodox peasant Christianity on the fulfillment of ritual, the following of prescribed form, sharply differentiated it from antebellum black Christianity with its stress on feeling and the conversion experience.[48]

There were a number of reasons for this contrast. Most obvious were differences between Orthodox Christianity, which emphasized ceremony and ritual, and Protestantism, which exalted the relationship between the individual and God. But more important still was the particular nature of the Orthodox clergy and its relationship to the peasantry. Whereas the decentralized, individually oriented Protestant churches in the United States permitted the emergence of numerous self-called slave preachers who were able to minister to the slave community on its own terms, the Orthodox church provided the parish clergy to serve in villages and administer the sacraments to its inhabitants. The slaves were able to build their own "invisible church" that served as a focal point of their lives and enabled them to turn the religion of their masters into a source of independent communal cultural expression. The serfs, however, received their religion from above, and it consequently could not serve in the same way to unite them in opposition to their masters. (The exception—locally important but nationally relatively minor—was in those areas where serfs were of different religion from their owners. Where Orthodox peasants faced an upper class composed primarily of Lutherans, Catholics, or Moslems, and where "Old Believers"—Orthodox descendants who rejected minor church reforms undertaken in the seventeenth and eighteenth centuries and insisted that they alone followed the true path—prevailed among the peasants, religion performed some of the socially unifying functions that it did among American slaves.)[49]

The relationship between serfs and clergymen was complex and ambivalent and remains to be fully explored. Peasants sometimes seem to have resented priests as meddlers and to have ignored or even resisted their message. Noble instructions typically insisted that serfs go to church and perform the sacraments and threatened dire punishments to those who refused; the threats as well as scattered examples of peasant recalcitrance suggest that many peasants embraced those assigned to minister to them with considerably less than enthusiasm. Seventeenth-century pomeshchik B. I. Morozov was so enraged by his steward's reports that his serfs were disobeying his order to attend church and pray for rain, choosing instead to work Sundays on their plots, that he ordered offenders fined for the first two offenses and "beaten with batogi in front of the mir" for the third; when the steward read the order to the assembled serfs, several cried out in disrespect "with a loud noise," and noncompliance remained rife. Two centuries later a steward reported to his employer that "the peasants are careless about church, and fulfill its rites with reluctance." Observers commonly noted that "the Orthodox clergy, as a body, have no moral influence over the masses, and enjoy no confidence among them"; rather, many peasants regarded priests as exploiters living off exorbitant fees charged for performing religious rites.[50]

Considerable evidence supports this picture of tension between peasants and priests. The parish clergy had become, by the eighteenth century, a closed, largely hereditary caste, separated from the mass of the peasantry by the requirement (at least in theory) of formal seminary education, the right to which was passed on from father to son. "The formation of the clergy into a closed estate greatly reinforced the 'functionary' role conception of the clergy, whereby the priest was not so much a religious figure as a functionary performing rites and duties for a fee," writes Gregory Freeze, the most authoritative recent student of the subject. "Increasingly the cleric inherited his position as a kind of patrimony and source of income; he did not select church service as a 'calling' or claim a special religious inspiration." Contemporaries routinely deplored the character of the parish clergy, denouncing them as ignorant, venal, and prone to drink. Many of the same judgments are evident in folktales that peasants told about priests. Iu. M. Sokolov, a leading Soviet folklorist, collected many of these tales in a volume called *Priest and Peasant,* grouping them under headings that indicate their tone, such as "the greedy priest," "the priest lover," "the stupid priest." Perhaps their central theme is the depiction of priests routinely violating the Christian norms they supposedly upheld. "It is noteworthy," concluded Sokolov, "that peasant tales and proverbs sympathetically describing priests are totally lacking."[51]

Nevertheless, one must be careful not to overemphasize the antagonism between peasants and priests, because some evidence suggests a close—at times symbiotic—relationship between them. Although priests constituted a separate, closed estate, they were usually close to their parishioners in background, manner, and often outlook on life as well. "The young priest" typically "acquires the appearance, character, and even habits of the peasants surrounding him," noted a report of the Third Department in 1827. "In his thoughts and feelings he merges with the class that provides him with the means of existence." As a result "priests in the majority of cases spread harmful information and propagate among the people the idea of freedom. Good priests," the report concluded, "are a great rarity." [52]

Indeed, if priests depended on their parishioners for subsistence, peasants often relied heavily on their priests in dealing with the outside world. When serfs sent petitions to government officials, for example, they frequently turned for help—from moral support to the actual writing of their complaints—to their village priests. And in time of serf unrest priests played a complex and unpredicatable role. Pomeshchiki sent for priests to calm peasant turbulence but often got more than they bargained for. In 1797, when the 490 souls belonging to Moscow province pomeshchik P. P. Shakhovskii became unruly, a local official brought two priests with him to persuade the peasants to behave, but one of them instead expressed his solidarity with the serfs, declaring "to all the people that he would be glad to die for them, and at that all the peasants cried out to him in one voice that 'we will all die for you.'" After widespread disorders in 1826 Major-General G. I. Nostits traveled around Kiev province and reported to his superior that priests were under "great suspicion" and that although their role as ringleaders in serf disorders was often exaggerated, the province's "village priests differ little from the simple people in way of life and upbringing," while "they have few ties with the pomeshchiki, who are for the most part Catholic." Priests were likely, of course, to be especially supportive of the demands of Orthodox serfs owned by non-Orthodox noblemen, but even in the bulk of the empire, where no sectarian distinction separated owner from owned, priests were usually far closer in outlook to peasants than to noblemen. [53]

Even peasant folktales about priests are ambivalent and contradictory. Priests frequently appear as greedy, lazy, lecherous, or cunning, but rarely as villainous. There is evident in the tales delight in exposing priestly foibles and in showing priests as less saintly than they would like to appear, but one senses in them more humor than bitterness, more satisfaction in pricking bloated pretensions than anything else. Priests in peasant tales act as tricksters—or are themselves the object of peasant tricks—but not as oppressors, and the tales generally lack the hostility evident in many of those depicting noblemen and noble-serf relations. In "The Good Priest," for example, a priest feeds his hired worker breakfast, lunch, and supper all at once, to save time, before going off with him to cut hay, but the worker is then so full from the combined meals that he lies down and goes to sleep instead of working. In "The Buried Treasure" a priest dresses up as the devil, in a goatskin, in order to frighten a poor peasant out of the treasure he has found, but receives his comeuppance when the goatskin becomes attached to him and will not come off. In "Ivan and Mar'ia" a couple outwit a priest, deacon, and sexton who want to sleep with the wife, and then cheat them out of money to boot. Rather than portraying priests as evil, most of these stories show them as human beings—perhaps foolish—with the same kind of emotions and failings as other people. Such stories may be subject to conflicting interpretations, but one must be careful not to confuse a delight in the exposure of priests' human failings—common among many people of impeccably religious credentials—with prevalence of antireligious sentiments.[54]

Perhaps the most plausible conclusion is that when priests appeared as agents of outside—at worst pomeshchik—intervention, serfs wanted little to do with them, but when priests were willing to serve peasant interests and work with the mir, serfs often established close ties with them. Although some of Morozov's serfs refused to attend church when ordered, others displayed a very different attitude. Ninety serfs from the village of Liskovo sent the nobleman a petition relating that after being without a priest for some time as a result of the former priest's death, they had now been sent by the Church a priest, deacon, and church reader; the peasants begged Morozov to confirm their appointment so they could serve. Formal religion was a less central feature of serf culture than of antebellum slave culture, both because that religion was less their own—there were no serf preachers—and because it was less necessary to them politically. Because the invisible church was the one institution aside from the family that blacks could call their own, their religion functioned as an important means of defining themselves and their values; indeed, black preachers probably came closer than anyone else in the South to serving as the American equivalent of peasant officials. Serfs achieved self-definition in other ways, most notably through the obshchina. Like all premodern peoples, Russian peasants were religious—too much of their world was inexplicable to them without recourse to supernatural intervention—but their formal Christian religion was less central in defining what was unique about their lives than was the case among antebellum southern slaves.[55]

*   *   *

THE CHRISTIANITY of both slaves and serfs coexisted with a broad array of pre-Christian beliefs and customs. The relationship between these and formal Christianity was in both countries one of uneasy equilibrium: although churchmen denounced non-Christian religious remnants as superstition and educated bondsmen snickered at the ignorance of those who embraced them, most slaves and serfs saw little or no conflict between being good Christians and subscribing to elements of folk religion. Pre-Christian folkways were especially pervasive in the Russian villages. The cultural discontinuity experienced by American blacks, together with the intrusion of white norms and the zeal with which most slaves adopted Christianity in the antebellum years, weakened the persistence of African customs; among Russian peasants, however, ancient traditions and beliefs lingered on relatively undisturbed by the outside world and remained embedded in their communal consciousness.

Every large plantation (and many smaller ones) in the slave South had one or more conjurors known for their magical abilities, from putting curses on enemies to producing love potions and curing the ill. Ex-slaves who wrote autobiographies were almost invariably embarrassed about slave magic—especially about their own involvement in it—and decried it as a barbaric relic of a heathen past. Charles Ball, for example, lamented that slaves were "universally subject to the grossest and most abject superstition," and H. C. Bruce characterized conjurors as "a shrewd set of fellows" who "on that account alone were enabled to fool the less informed."[56]

Most slaves seem to have had a different view, however, putting equal stock in their magic and their Christianity. "I know all 'bout de conjer doctors," testified Nancy Bradford many years later. "Dey sho' kin fix you. Dey kin take yo' garter or yo' stockin' top and drap it in runnin' water and make you run de res' of yo' life, you'll be in a hurry all de time." Indeed, many slaves apparently saw little difference between their belief in Christianity and in conjurors, witches, and spirits. George White, whose father had been owned by a doctor, noted that "Papa was a kinda doctor too like his master, an' papa knowed all de roots . . . I know all de roots too . . . Dere's a root for ev'y disease an' I can cure most anything, but you have got to talk wid

God an' ask him to help out." Slave magic, like slave religion, was an expression of a premodern world view, one in which spirits intervened on earth on a daily basis and in which one could talk to God and the devil in a personal manner. Of course, this world view was by no means confined to blacks; indeed, some whites consulted black conjurors. A farmer named Reel, for example, consulted "Cato Sabo, the negro doctor," whenever he had troubles; "when Reel had corn to sell, he would refuse to dispose of it, until his negro told him he could spare it." [57]

In Russian villages pagan seasonal rituals persisted with only a thin veneer of Christian overlay. Perhaps the most widely commented upon of such festivals was the springtime Easter holiday, complete with painted eggs as symbols of fertility, a time of widespread popular reveling during which it was customary to give ubiquitous embraces without class or sexual discrimination. "If the red egg be offered, no magnate will refuse the solicited kiss to the vilest of the populace, no matron will excuse herself through modesty, no maiden out of bashfulness," wrote a foreign traveler with typical amazement. "Moreover, they celebrate with continual drunken orgies." Other traditional seasonal festivals that persisted with only slight modifications in deference to Christian sensibilities celebrated the winter solstice and the sun's rebirth, spring fertility, summer prosperity, and the autumnal harvest. [58]

Formal Christianity yielded, in everyday village life, to numerous magical "superstitious" practices. As among American slaves, fortune-telling and sorcery were widespread. Village doctors practiced divination—which persisted despite condemnation by the Church— by casting grain on ruled sheets of paper and reciting appropriate chants and formulas, cast spells that would relieve suffering, guarantee safe travel, or induce love, and put the evil eye on enemies. Some magic formulas even began with the ritual recital of "In the name of the Father, the Son, and the Holy Ghost." More than American slaves, Russian peasants continued to live with an extensive pantheon of spirits, witches, and magical figures who both personified various forces of nature and represented the spirits of the dead who watched over—and sometimes tormented—their descendants. "The Russian peasantry are still wallowing in superstitions," wrote a nineteenth-century observer. "With the advent of Christianity the heathen gods and goddesses were not annihilated, but only driven from heaven into hell." Forest spirits, water spirits, air spirits, and probably most important of all domestic spirits—who hid behind the stove by day but roamed the house and ate food left out for them by night—peopled the world of the peasants and were reflected in popular folktales and songs. So too were magical figures that personified natural character-istics such as rivers and frost, as well as forces of evil such as Koshchei the Deathless, Morskoi King of the Waters, Baba Yaga the hag, and both male and female snakes. Peasant tales frequently dealt with struggles between brave young men and these forces of evil who in-habited a land above the sky or below the earth, with both sides re-sorting to magic.[59]

The nature of the bondsmen's world view is perhaps nowhere bet-ter represented—or with greater difficulty understood—than in the stories they told. One encounters enormous problems in interpreting the significance of folktales. In both Russia and the United States most stories went unrecorded until the second half of the nineteenth century, and many surviving tales contain elements reflecting devel-opments that occurred after emancipation. Early recorders of folk-tales, such as Joel Chandler Harris and A. N. Afanas'ev, were heavily influenced by their sense of propriety, and they practiced considerable selectivity in their transcribing, toning down or ignoring stories that contained too much sex or that seemed to express excessive class an-tagonism and emphasizing instead magical, fairy, and animal tales. In Russia official government censorship prevented the publication of material deemed too critical of prescribed values. Even more serious are problems concerning the origins—and therefore the signifi-cance—of the tales. American folklorists have disagreed sharply over whether most black tales originated in Africa, as once seemed likely, or "are of demonstrably European origin," as more recent research suggests, but one might question the degree to which stories com-posed in either Africa *or* Europe can tell us much about slavery in the American South. Similarly, many Russian stories show remarkable similarity to western European ones, indicating a common remote ancestry of preserfdom days. In short, there is a serious question about the extent to which black and peasant folktales reflect condi-tions of slave and serf life.[60]

Nevertheless, recent scholars have tended—correctly I believe—to see in these tales broad evidence of the bondsmen's outlook and con-sciousness. Soviet folklorist Iu. M. Sokolov argued that despite the predilection of early recorders for magical tales, about 60 percent of peasant stories are realistic depictions of everyday life that reflect the peasants' attitudes toward their world, themselves, and their enemies. Similarly, in his important study of black folklore Lawrence W. Levine has insisted that the question of origins is largely irrelevant because "regardless of where slave tales came from, the essential point is that, with respect to language, delivery, details of characterization, and plot, slaves quickly made them their own and through them revealed much about themselves and their world." There is, perhaps, an element of exaggeration here, because the significance of a folktale will be somewhat different if that tale is told in numerous societies than if it developed under specific conditions of slavery or serfdom. Still, in a general sense Sokolov and Levine are surely right that the body of stories the slaves and serfs adopted and adapted came to reflect the concrete reality of the life they experienced and can therefore tell us much about their social attitudes.[61]

By the antebellum period southern slaves had a rich repertoire that, through telling and retelling, choice and alteration, they had shaped to serve the needs of an enslaved people. The most important body of these tales consisted of stories of trickery. In the animal trickster tales, by far the most well-known genre—and one existing in broad areas of Europe too, including Russia—a weak but wily animal, usually a rabbit, repeatedly outwits his stronger but less cunning rivals such as the bear and the wolf. It does not take great analytical sophistication to discern here a symbolic portrayal of slaves outwitting their masters and to recognize the slaves' identification with the animal trickster. This theme is even less disguised in another widely told group of stories, the John and Old Master tales, which depict a semiantagonistic, semifriendly rivalry between a slave and his owner in which the former usually gets the better of the latter—although the slave is not always the victor and both parties often appear ridiculous. Clearly, as recent scholars have argued, on one level the very existence of these tales represented an important sign of communal culture through which slaves were able to teach important moral lessons and also to triumph vicariously over their masters.[62]

But the message of these stories is complex and often ambiguous. Trickery enables the weak to outsmart the strong, but it also corrodes all relationships. The lesson most of the tales impart is of a cruel and compassionless world in which pity and friendship are signs of weakness. The trickster virtually never shows compassion for his hapless victims, who often do not appear to deserve the punishment they receive and whose fate—at least in the animal stories—is usually severe humiliation or violent death. Unlike the folklore of many other peoples, slave tales contain few depictions of courageous or noble behavior; there are no dragon slayers, giant killers, or defenders of the people—in short, no heroes. Instead, an individual usually tricks another individual; the principal virtues that emerge are cunning and winning. One can argue that this theme was a common-sense one for the slaves: that only through one's wits could one survive in a world as oppressive as theirs. If this was so, however, important implications follow that deserve to be explored in much greater depth than is possible here about the impact of slavery on the culture, values, and communal behavior of the slaves. "The recurring themes of these stories," Michael Flusche has cogently argued, "suggest that slavery tended to engender an atomistic individualistic world view among the slaves and that the slaves' sense of community was more complicated than simple unity in the face of white oppression."[63]

Russian peasant folktales performed many of the same functions as the slave stories. Two commonly told genres of tales were strikingly similar in Russia and the United States. Like blacks, peasants told animal trickster stories in which the weaker but smarter animal— usually the fox in Russia—outwits his strong but dumb tormentors. Indeed, in some instances Russian stories were virtually identical to their American counterparts, suggesting the likelihood of a common origin. In "The Little Fox Midwife," for example, the fox deceives the wolf into thinking she is being repeatedly called to assist at childbirths—"a firstling," "a middling," and "a lastling"—while she is really consuming their jar of honey; the wolf, on discovering the deception, insists that they both lie in the sun so the honey will show on the guilty party, but when he falls asleep the fox smears honey on him and makes him appear guilty. No one familiar with black tales will have much trouble recognizing the similarity between this story and "Who Ate Up the Butter?" in which the rabbit convinces his animal coworkers that his wife is giving birth to four successive babies— "Quarter Gone," "Half Gone," "Three Quarters Gone," and "All Gone"—meanwhile devouring their pound of butter; when the animals agree to jump over a fire to determine the guilty party, the rabbit tricks the bear into trying to cross his legs while jumping, he falls into the fire, and the other animals are convinced of his guilt.[64]

Similarly, tales of rivalry between peasant and lord—which pit the two in individual rivalry resulting in victory of sometimes one and sometimes the other—resemble the John and Old Master Tales told by southern blacks and indicate a similar impact of slavery and serfdom on the folk consciousness of the bondsmen. As with their American counterparts, some analysts have seen such tales as reflecting the peasants' "attitude toward serfdom, always hostile to pomeshchiki," but others have seen in them evidence of a pervasive peasant cunning and deceitfulness produced by the need to survive under serfdom. "The Russian is reproached with practising dissimulation, but his position as a slave obliges him to do so," wrote a French traveler in a typical comment reminiscent of similar suggestions made by travelers to the slave South. "Every individual who lives in perpetual fear of terrible and unmerciful punishment, at the caprice of his master, learns the logic of falsehood and dissimulation."[65]

In several important ways, however, Russian peasant folklore differed from that of southern blacks and expressed a very different kind of communal consciousness. Whole genres existed in Russia that were largely absent in the United States. Some of these reflected the historical continuity that underlay the peasant experience in contrast to that of Afro-Americans. Peasants continued, for example, to recite the *byliny* or ancient epics that dated from the period before serfdom and celebrated figures such as Prince Vladimir and Elijah of Murom, the "peasant knight" and "exponent of truth, patriotism, and love of mankind." Likewise, they sang historical songs dating from the sixteenth to early eighteenth centuries telling of Ivan the Terrible, the Time of Troubles, and especially the rebellion led by Stepan Razin.[66]

Even the tales that dated from the eighteenth and nineteenth centuries often expressed a communal solidarity lacking in the slave stories. Animal trickster tales that reflected a devil-take-the-hindmost amorality constituted a much smaller fraction in Russia—Sokolov estimated them at about 10 percent of the total—than in America. Other kinds of tales, meanwhile, reflected a different kind of consciousness. Mythological stories, pitting heroes—from a young prince to a simple peasant—against magical forces of evil threatening the nation or community, emphasized classical elements of heroism, self-sacrifice, and group solidarity rather than individual competition for wealth, food, or power. Utopian legends told of a golden age or mythical land where exploitation and oppression were unknown and celebrated a "returning deliverer"—often the "true tsar," beloved by the people but deposed by evil henchmen—who would liberate the masses from their oppressors and restore peace, harmony, and happiness to the land. (That the slaves' one returning deliverer was Moses again reveals the religious focus of their communality.) In short, peasant folklore, unlike that of American blacks, contained substantial elements of social consciousness expressing lofty ideals of heroism, generosity, and struggle for the common good.[67]

Although one must be careful about seeing precise social reality in

folklore—which is always a medley reflecting actual conditions, aspirations, previous conditions, and extraneous influences—peasant
communal consciousness was clearly of a more political nature than
that of American slaves. Black folktales illustrate the limitations as
well as the reality of the slave community. Slaves lived in a world that
was partially removed from that of their owners, and they were able
to develop their own unique culture that centered on their families,
their religion, and their lives in the quarters. At the same time, however, this community was a precarious institution, never secure from
the intrusion of white culture and the more damaging interference of
slaveowners. Planter paternalism (together with American prosperity
in general) not only gave southern slaves a material standard of living
rare among subject peoples; it also undercut their independence, autonomy, and collective consciousness. This is seen most clearly when
the slaves' mentality is compared with that of the Russian serfs. The
serfs' consciousness was in many ways profoundly conservative, centered on tradition, customs, and the mir—a local consciousness of
common ties and interests rather than a generalized class consciousness. Still, their outlook facilitated collective action to deal with common problems; as one observer put it, "The reliance shown by the
Russian peasant on the community, his conviction that the *mir* is always just and reasonable, and that truth is nowhere to be found but
in the unanimous opinion of the people have . . . helped to make the
Russian *moujik* a communist." [68]

*   *   *

WE HAVE THUS returned to the contrast between the slaves and the
serfs with respect to cultural autonomy and communal consciousness.
Earlier in this chapter I introduced the idea of geographical continuity
as a central ingredient of this question. Now I would like to expand
on this and to suggest a number of other factors that helped to
heighten the contrast.

Clearly, the cultural break resulting from the forced migration from
Africa to America fundamentally differentiated the experiences of
American slaves and Russian serfs. The serfs were held on their home
turf, where despite their bondage they could continue in many respects to live and act as their ancestors had; the slaves were torn from
their homeland and held in a new continent where inevitably, despite
strenuous efforts to preserve old ways, a drastic change in life-style
and consciousness ensued. Geographic continuity or discontinuity
was the most obvious single influence on the degree of cultural con-

tinuity among the bondsmen. In this respect the experience of serfs in Russia differed radically not only from that of slaves in the United States but also from that of slaves in other New World societies. The African diaspora was a fundamental fact of black slavery in the Americas, whereby black slaves became outsiders in white, European-derived societies.

There were a number of other significant causes, however, of the contrasting worlds and world views of the Russian and American bondsmen. Most of these have already been touched on and need only to be brought together, but a couple require slightly more elaboration. It is important to note that unlike the African diaspora these other elements did not separate the experience of Russian serfs from that of all New World slaves; concrete historical experiences differentiated the lives of Russian serfs and southern slaves, but the contrast was not one between slaves and serfs per se. Indeed, with respect to culture and community, Russian and American bondsmen stood at two extremes of a broad spectrum or continuum, on which slaves of other countries were fixed in varying more central locations.

Several demographic factors served to facilitate the development of autonomous communal behavior among the Russian serfs while severely restricting its potentiality among American slaves. Most obvious were the differing population mixes in the two countries. Whereas blacks were a minority in the South as a whole and about one-half of the population in the deep South, peasants constituted the overwhelming majority of Russians; similarly, the serfs were typically held in far larger units than the slaves.[69] As a consequence the serfs had far more opportunity to lead autonomous lives than did the slaves. Among slaves held in very small groups the chance to partake of communal activities was often virtually nonexistent, but even among most others simple population ratios meant that they came in contact with whites far more often than most serfs did with noblemen. The internal lives of bondsmen who were widely dispersed among many slaveholders in small units had to be very different from the lives of those who were concentrated among a tiny class of noblemen on large estates.

Even given the southern slaves' numerical disadvantage, an independent black culture could have been reinvigorated by a steady supply of new Africans keeping alive the memory of traditional ways and fostering resistance to European cultural penetration. Precisely this happened in some other New World slave societies.[70] It is therefore significant that the American slave population was largely creole from

an early date. In part, this was because alone among major slave societies the United States prohibited the importation of new slaves
more than half a century before it abolished slavery, but even more
important was the natural population growth that rendered American slaves overwhelmingly creole generations before the end of the
slave trade. By the American Revolution only about one-fifth of
American slaves were African-born, and during the first half of the
nineteenth century the proportion of Africans among southern slaves
was insignificant. In contrast to Brazil, Cuba, Haiti, and Jamaica,
where traditional African culture was continually buttressed from
without, in the United States during the century and a half before
emancipation an increasingly creole slave population became more
and more divorced from its ancestral roots.[71]

Differences in owner attitudes and behavior strongly reinforced the
dichotomy resulting from contrasting demographic patterns in Russia
and the United States. The absentee orientation of pomeshchiki allowed most serfs a substantial measure of freedom from direct, day-
to-day owner interference; even when serfs had resident owners,
those owners usually concerned themselves much less than most
American planters with the internal lives of their laborers. The absentee mentality of Russian noblemen thus served to strengthen the autonomy of peasant life. In the United States planter paternalism had
the opposite impact: the constant meddling that it engendered in
slaves' lives proved destructive of their communal independence. Paternalism not only provided antebellum slaves with one of the world's
highest material standards of living; it also subjected them to constant
white cultural penetration and thus seriously undermined their cultural autonomy. One might suggest that in a rough sense there was
an inverse relationship between the coherence of the masters' civilization and the autonomy of the bondsmen's communal culture:
where resident slaveowners took a lively interest in their communities
and their property, as southern planters did, that interest tended to
have a corrosive impact on the ability of the slaves to maintain their
own communal values and customs; where owners tended toward
absenteeism, the bondsmen were correspondingly freer to lead their
own lives and develop their own separate communal standards. (The
process worked the other way as well. Where the bondsmen were in
a huge numerical majority and showed strong communal solidarity,
their owners found it convenient to put an appropriate distance between themselves and their "brutish" property.)[72]

There was, finally, an economic basis for the serf community that

was largely lacking among American slaves: the existence of a secondary, peasant economy. Except for house servants, serfs grew their
own food on their landed allotments and were self-supporting; in addition many—especially those on obrok estates—raised goods for
market on "their" land as well as cultivating their owners' fields. Of
course, many southern slaves had garden plots whose produce they
used to supplement their diets and even to earn pocket money for
luxuries, and on the rice estates of coastal South Carolina and Georgia a real although limited slave economy developed as slaves raised
and sold their "own" provisions on their "own" time. Nevertheless,
the distinction was basic: the slaves received primary sustenance from
their masters for whom they worked full-time, and when allowed they
supplemented this by cultivating garden plots; the serfs were entirely
self-supporting and were increasingly engaged in their own commercial
operations. A major function of the commune was to regulate relations
inhering in economic independence, from dividing peasant landholdings equitably to adjusting the rent they paid their owners. In short,
communal independence rested on economic autonomy. In the slave
South, where many planters believed that allowing slave families to
cook their own meals promoted excessive independence, the slave community lacked any corresponding economic function.

Thus, a series of fundamental differences between the experiences
of American slaves and Russian serfs served to encourage autonomous communal life and culture among the latter and to restrict them
among the former. The slaves were physically torn from their African
roots, which grew increasingly remote as they became an almost entirely creole population; they constituted a minority of the southern
population, both numerically and in the sense of being outsiders; they
lived in relatively small groups on farms and small plantations, where
a resident slaveowning class interacted with them on a daily basis,
making every effort to limit their independence. The serfs lived on
their ancestral lands, where—together with state peasants—they constituted a large majority of the population; they lived isolated from
noblemen, whom they rarely saw, on large estates where, so long as
they made money for their owners, they were often left free to do
what they wanted; they were self-supporting and engaged in a flourishing, market-oriented economy of their own. The two groups were
both unfree peoples forced to labor for the well-being of a parasitic
class, but the environmental conditions of their bondage—conditions
that largely determined what kinds of lives they could lead—were in
many respects different.

Indeed, those environmental conditions can be placed at opposite ends of a spectrum, with those experienced by other slaves located at various points in between. Even though all New World slaves shared with those of the United States the geographic discontinuity produced by the forced migration of millions of Africans, the effects of this discontinuity on their lives and culture varied considerably, depending on concrete circumstances. In some slave societies demographic and social conditions were closer to those of Russia and favored the perpetuation of autonomous communal behavior; in others they more nearly resembled those of the United States, where close master-slave contact limited the emergence of an independent community. The United States and Russia, however, represented the two extremes, with other slave societies tending to share some features of the one and some of the other.

These variations can be clarified by considering briefly three other New World slave societies, those of Jamaica, Cuba, and Brazil. The Jamaican pattern—and that of several other Caribbean islands, especially St. Domingue—most closely resembled the Russian. True, Jamaican slaves did not experience the geographic continuity of Russian serfs. Other demographic and social characteristics, however, suggest greater similarity between the environments faced by Jamaican slaves and Russian serfs than between Jamaican and American slaves. Jamaican blacks outnumbered whites during the eighteenth and early nineteenth centuries by about ten to one, a figure analogous to the peasant/nobleman ratio in Russia. Furthermore, those slaves, the majority of whom were African-born until the abolition of the slave trade in 1808, typically lived on large plantations containing hundreds of laborers each; just as Russia was a peasant world, so was Jamaica a black—and in many ways an African—world. "The West Indian slave masters could not expect to assimilate or acculturate such a huge alien population," historian Richard Dunn has noted of Jamaican and other British island planters. "If they wished to preserve their own identity, they had to segregate themselves socially and culturally from the blacks." The vast majority of slaveowners, therefore—one expert has estimated 90 percent in the mid-eighteenth century—were absentee lords who rarely visited their estates and knew little of what occurred on them. They even provided their slaves with "provision grounds," plots of land with which, like Russian serfs, they were expected to provide their own sustenance; on Sundays slaves sold surplus goods in local markets, which came to play an important role both for the island's economy and for their own well-being. It is hardly surprising, then, that blacks in Jamaica "preserved more of their native culture than blacks in North America" and that they sometimes displayed the kind of communal solidarity when confronting their owners that was present among Russian serfs.[73]

Cuban conditions during the first half of the nineteenth century place that island somewhat nearer to the United States South than was Jamaica. Like slaves in the South, those in Cuba formed a large minority of the population—about two-fifths—although with free blacks they actually were in the majority. Most Cuban slaves lived on relatively small holdings—there was a mean of 7.59 slaves per owner in 1857—but in sugar plantation regions holdings were typically larger, and about one-quarter of all slaves were held in units of more than eighty. In contrast to the situation in the United States, however, continuation of the slave trade into the 1850s combined with a high mortality rate produced a heavy African component among Cuban slaves. Furthermore, Cuba's sugar planters were typically absentee proprietors who left estate management to hired overseers and their assistants, and nineteenth-century Cuban slavery showed little of the paternalism seen in the southern United States (or in Cuba itself in the eighteenth century).[74]

In some respects conditions in Brazil were closest to those in the United States. Throughout the first half of the nineteenth century slaves there constituted about one-third of the population, and as Stuart Schwartz has recently demonstrated, in the important northeastern sugar-producing region of Bahia province slaves were widely dispersed among a large, generally resident slaveowning population. The size of typical slaveholdings was remarkably similar in Bahia and the United States South: the former had an average of 7.2 slaves per owner in 1816, and the latter had an average of 8.7 in 1830. Genovese has suggested that, as in the United States, "the patriarchalism of the sugar-growing [Brazilian] Northeast constituted the most obvious feature of the social regime." Nevertheless, Brazilian conditions differed from those in the United States in a number of ways. First, as Genovese noted, Bahia was by no means the entire story; on the coffee plantations that developed in the south during the late eighteenth and early nineteenth centuries, hard-driving entrepreneurs showed little of the paternalism evident in the northeast. Equally important, the continuation of slave imports until the mid-nineteenth century, combined with a lack of natural population growth, meant that African-born blacks continued to constitute a large proportion of the slave population; geographic discontinuty was thus not translated into cultural discontinuity nearly so much as in the United States, and Brazil saw extensive survival of African traditions, notable especially in syncretic slave religion. Finally, many of Brazil's slaves supported themselves on their "own" plots of land, as in Jamaica and St. Domingue, and this economic autonomy, together with the substantial African legacy, encouraged a more collective response to servitude than was prevalent in the United States.[75]

The environments that the bondsmen faced thus varied widely, with the United States and Russia at opposite extremes. These variations dictated a diversity of slave experiences, encompassing substantial differences in the bondsmen's cultural activities, communal autonomy, and ultimately their world view.[76]

*   *   *

THE BONDSMEN's world view represents a subject of considerable complexity. Unraveling their attitudes, thoughts, and feelings is made especially difficult by the nature of the records they left, records that have lent themselves to varying interpretations. Recent historians have unanimously rejected the masters' belief in their charges' innate servility, but in doing so they have differed widely among themselves.

American scholars have engaged in an extensive debate over the nature of the antebellum slave character, a debate sparked by Stanley M. Elkins's controversial "Sambo" thesis. Southern slavery was such a brutal, "closed" institution, Elkins argued, that its victims were stripped of their individuality and transformed into infantile, docile, dependent "Sambos."[77] Subsequent historians have in general repudiated this interpretation, in the process devoting new attention to slave life and culture, but they have disagreed sharply over the precise nature of the slaves' personality and consciousness. Some have stressed their rebelliousness; others have suggested that they "fell into a paternalistic pattern of thought" or that they internalized the Protestant work ethic. Others still have maintained that slaves exhibited a broad variety of personalities and behavior and that any attempt to isolate a dominant pattern is doomed to failure.[78]

Soviet historians have usually formulated the question more in terms of thought than character. Some, such as B. G. Litvak, have lamented the peasants' inability to recognize their true interests and have criticized the "naive monarchism" that enabled them to have blind faith in the tsar's goodness despite all evidence to the contrary. Others have celebrated their antifeudal struggle and even insisted that there were "socialist ideas"—although of a "utopian" rather than a "scientific" variety—in their thought. The role of the serfs' ideology has received considerable attention. Some scholars have detected an increasing class consciousness among them, but others have stressed the primitive quality of peasant social consciousness under serfdom and questioned whether one can speak of such a thing as ideology among the serfs.[79]

If by *ideology* one means an articulated, carefully formulated philosophical position, then it is safe to say that most slaves and serfs had none. The bondsmen did, however, have a world view in the sense of a generalized social consciousness, a shared outlook on how things were, could be, and should be. Despite the intrusion of paternalism in the United States and naive monarchism in Russia, the bondsmen's social outlook was by no means simply a reflection of dominant ideologies in the two countries; although slaves and serfs did not always have a clear recognition of their "objective interests," their view of the world was in many ways distinctly different from that of their masters. The slaves' consciousness also differed substantially from that of the serfs, just as their lives did. The best way to elucidate the nature of the bondsmen's world view is through a careful examination of their resistance to what they regarded as unjust treatment. In both Russia and the United States South apparently servile beings engaged in a wide range of rebellious activity; how and under what conditions they chose to resist their oppressors reveal a great deal about the way the bondsmen thought of themselves and their world.

5

Patterns of Resistance

THROUGH A BROAD RANGE of activities the bondsmen made clear that they did not share—and were unwilling passively to accept—their owners' view of the proper social order. They dragged their feet in performing their daily chores, working slowly, feigning illness, and pretending to be so stupid that they could not manage the simplest tasks correctly. They stole from their owners. They balked at what they regarded as unjust treatment, complaining vociferously to their masters about the behavior of stewards and overseers. They ran away. They also physically confronted their tormentors, most often on a relatively small scale but occasionally in the kind of violent outbreak that went by various names such as revolt, insurrection, rebellion, and peasant war.

That the bondsmen resisted their debasement is clear; more interesting and significant are questions relating to how, when, and with what results they did so. Although American slaves and Russian serfs showed a common determination to protest against what they regarded as mistreatment, they did not always follow the same forms of protest. In this chapter I shall examine the basic types of resistance, analyze an important difference in the form that resistance took, and discuss the major consequences of the bondsmen's defiance. In the next I shall deal with the question of what produced resistance: under what conditions it was most likely and what an analysis of these conditions can tell us about the bondsmen's world view. We shall then be able to return, briefly, to the nature of the slave and serf community.

*   *   *

THE MOST PASSIVE TYPE of resistance employed by bondsmen consisted of a collection of acts that may conveniently be grouped together under the heading "silent sabotage." Although planters and pomeshchiki claimed that their laborers were lazy, stupid, and constitutionally incapable of getting things right on their own, recent historians have more often seen such behavior as constituting a conscious effort on the part of the bondsmen to get back at their oppressors. "The masses of slaves, for whom freedom could have been little more than an idle dream, found countless ways to exasperate their owners," noted Kenneth M. Stampp, including shoddy work, slowdowns, damaging property, feigning illness, petty theft, and testing new masters and overseers through minor acts of disobedience. Similarly, two leading Soviet historians noted the "pervasive and every-day character" of behavior by serfs "such as deliberately poor performance of barshchina, nonpayment of obrok, usurpation of seigneurial land, damage by cattle to pomeshchiki's meadows and fields, and so forth." As we have seen, masters were in fact rarely satisfied with the quality of their laborers' work; the slaves and serfs made running an estate an extremely trying business for owners and their administrative assistants.[1]

There is also abundant evidence that the bondsmen stole from their masters on a widespread basis, regarding such appropriation as "taking" or "using" what was rightfully theirs. "I was never acquainted with a slave who believed, that he violated any rule of morality by appropriating to himself any thing that belonged to his master, if it was necessary to his comfort," declared former slave Charles Ball. Planters' and pomeshchiki's instructions and correspondence as well as comments by other observers confirmed Ball's opinion. Frederick Law Olmsted noted the prevalence among slaves of "the agrarian notion . . . that the result of labour belongs of right to the labourer," a notion that received expression in Russia in the popular serf proverb "we are yours, but the land is ours." Nobleman reformer A. P. Zablotskii-Desiatovskii, noting the prevalence of "cunning and deception" among serfs, observed that where seigneurial authority was weak, serfs resorted to "deception of the pomeshchik, plunder of his property," whereas where it was severe "theft becomes a rule among his peasants."[2]

Although the ubiquity of silent sabotage is widely accepted, considerable disagreement exists as to how to interpret it. It is difficult to prove that less than perfect work or behavior constituted deliberate resistance to oppression unless one defines it as such a priori. Two American scholars have suggested that "malingering may have reflected no more than a disinclination to work, especially when the rewards were so meager. Likewise, what is taken for sabotage may have originated in apathy and indifference." Another has attributed what masters considered their slaves' shiftlessness to preindustrial work habits rather than either laziness or sabotage. And critics of forced labor in both Russia and the United States often blamed sloppy and inefficient work on a system of labor that provided few incentives for diligent work.[3]

Even if one assumes that silent sabotage constituted a form of resistance, the question remains, resistance to what? To bondage itself? How, then, does one account for similar behavior—from slowdowns to "sick-ins"—among a wide range of freely hired workers in the modern world? To unacceptable conditions within bondage? The problem here is that little apparent correlation can be demonstrated between silent sabotage and the severity of the slaveholding regime; it affected kind masters as well as severe ones, absentee proprietors as well as resident owners. Although silent sabotage is often categorized as a form of resistance, what is being resisted is rarely specified.

The situation may be clarified by considering a recent analogy. Absenteeism increased sharply among American automobile workers in the late 1960s and early 1970s, approximately doubling between 1965 and 1972; in the latter year an investigation revealed that "on Fridays and Mondays in many plants up to 15 per cent of the workers do not go in, causing some severe production problems." At a Ford plant over a four-year stretch 41 percent of disciplinary penalties imposed were for offenses against "time order." Will future historians interpret this absenteeism as a sign of protest against either capitalism in general or specific policies of the automobile companies? Or will they agree with the analyst who suggested "that perhaps the high absenteeism, the turnover and the shoddy work may be a way to express a deep and growing resentment towards boring, unfulfilling work"? Surely it is significant, too, that absenteeism among auto workers became especially pronounced during fishing and hunting seasons.[4]

Silent sabotage represented, then, an elusive, borderline type of behavior. Clearly slaves and serfs often felt dissatisfied with their working conditions and strove in various ways to make those conditions more tolerable. In doing so, they were taking part in a broad current of what may legitimately be regarded as primitive protest by alienated workers. But because sabotage was such a borderline form of protest, it is of limited utility to the historian of slave and serf resistance. Although antisocial behavior often represented either conscious or unconscious acts of defiance, these acts are difficult to analyze because they are virtually impossible to isolate. Day-to-day "resistance" was so ambiguous in nature that it is hard to determine when—and to what—it actually constituted resistance.

* * *

THIS WAS NOT the case at the opposite extreme, with organized, armed rebellion. As the most dramatic and clear-cut form of resistance, servile rebellion has had a special interest to modern historians. Much of their work has exhibited a celebratory character: to a generation of modern scholars the great slave rebellions—from the ancient Spartacist revolt to the uniquely successful Haitian revolution under the leadership of Toussaint L'Ouverture—testify to the heroic determination of the enslaved to be free. Soviet scholars have probably written more on the four great "peasant wars" that swept across Russia in the seventeenth and eighteenth centuries than on any other aspect of serfdom; the study of slave revolts has been less extensive among American historians, but during the past two decades a new interest has developed in the several more localized outbreaks that erupted in the United States during the eighteenth and nineteenth centuries. A comparison of these Russian and American revolts reveals important differences in the ways that slaves and serfs responded to their conditions and thus helps to highlight certain basic features of the bondsmen's world.

During the seventeenth and eighteenth centuries, at approximately fifty-year intervals, four massive armed conflicts labeled peasant wars by Soviet historians engulfed the Russian countryside. The insurgencies, led by Ivan Bolotnikov in 1606–7, Stepan Razin in 1670–71, Kondratii Bulavin in 1707–8, and Emelian Pugachev in 1773–74, were part uprisings and part civil wars and were by no means entirely composed of peasants, let alone serfs. Cossacks played a major role in the conflicts, townsmen were active participants in those of the seventeenth century, and disaffected southern pomeshchiki joined the armies led by Bolotnikov. Nevertheless, although each of the outbreaks bore certain distinctive features, and most non-Soviet historians have eschewed the term peasant war, I will use it here because it is at least as accurate as revolt or rebellion to describe conflicts that shared enough basic characteristics to warrant common consideration.[5]

All of the peasant wars occurred in times of national crisis, during or immediately after a war, when tensions were high, material conditions depressed, and the government's ability to handle insurgency reduced. The setting for Bolotnikov's rising was the Time of Troubles, which included a dynastic crisis and internal struggle for power, a series of crop failures that created massive hunger and flight, foreign intervention from Poland, and the binding of peasants to the land. Razin's revolt came on the heels of thirteen years of war against Poland. The conflict led by Bulavin followed the drastic increase in taxes by Peter I to pay for his wars, as well as widespread government conscription of peasant labor to build St. Petersburg in the north and work on government military fortifications in the south. The Pugachev rebellion occurred during the Turkish war of 1768–74. In each case economic hardship and social dislocation combined with heavy government commitment of resources to make the setting for internal disruption ideal.[6]

The peasant wars were all protracted struggles, enveloping a huge territory in bloody conflict for months. Even using the briefest possible periodization, the average duration of the peasant wars was a year, with Bulavin's nine-month rising of 1707–8 the shortest and Bolotnikov's fifteen-month campaign of 1606–7 the longest. Their geographical scope was as broad as their chronological, with each encompassing an area that ultimately included much of Russia. These were not brief localized outbreaks easily put down but massive challenges involving hundreds of thousands and sometimes millions of participants.[7]

Despite their broad geographic scope the peasant wars did display a strong regional character: they were all in part civil wars between the borderland and the established center. It was among the cossack-frontiersmen of the south that the peasant wars began. Nomadic, independent-spirited horsemen continually reinforced by fugitive peasants, the cossacks became partially settled over the course of the seventeenth and eighteenth centuries and were enlisted by the Russian government as a sort of border military guard against enemies to the south; in the eighteenth century some even became serfholders themselves. Nevertheless, the majority remained free spirits, restless and intolerant of restrictions. Among those who settled along the Don River—the most fertile breeding ground for peasant wars—there gradually developed a split between the earlier established cossacks who had entered government service and the newer arrivals who settled upstream, faced more tenuous economic conditions, and maintained a considerable degree of sympathy for and identity with the Russian peasantry.

The uprisings that began among the cossacks quickly spread to include other Russians as well. Although townsmen, subject nationalities, religious dissidents, and in Bolotnikov's case even pomeshchiki took part on the side of the insurgents, the most important rebel component consisted of the peasants. Once aroused, serfs flocked to join cossack forces, wreaking vengeance on their owners as well as local authorities. This was especially true during the Pugachev rebellion, when, during the summer of 1774, three million peasants living in an area of six hundred thousand square kilometers centered along the Volga River rose up en masse, pillaging, plundering, and killing their enemies. The peasant wars were thus expressions of struggle between borderland and center, outs and ins, haves and have-nots. Originating as frontier skirmishes, they developed into full-scale class warfare.

A number of trends differentiated the later peasant wars from the earlier ones. Probably most basic was the general hardening of class lines, reflected in the changing composition of rebel forces. Bolotnikov's uprising was less strictly a peasant operation than the later conflicts, more a struggle for power between the ins and outs (see Introduction). By the time of the second peasant war, few noblemen were willing to join the rebels, and serfs formed a more central element of the struggle. Still, small urban centers along the Volga provided a crucial source of support, rising in revolt at the approach of Razin's forces and opening their gates to his army. The eighteenth-century revolts, by contrast, lacked a major urban dimension, and Pugachev's rebellion, especially, took the form of an uprising of peasants and peasant factory workers in the Urals and Volga region, heeding Pugachev's call "to put to death" pomeshchiki and "take for yourselves in reward their houses and all their property." In short, as serfdom became solidified and class lines hardened, the peasant wars increasingly took on the character of class warfare.[8]

Rebel forces also developed increasingly complex organization. Of course, any struggle involving tens of thousands of insurgents over a period of several months had to be more than a spontaneous outpouring of disaffected violence. Each of the wars was headed by a charismatic leader who spearheaded the movement, coordinated the activities of military commanders, and issued appeals to the population at large. It was during the Pugachev rebellion, however, that both vertical and horizontal organization reached its peak; written and oral communication, both military and political, with military commanders, regional chiefs, and village authorities was coordinated through a bureaucratically structured War College headed by a chief clerk and secretary. A flood of manifestoes, often read to assembled masses by literate house serfs and priests, emanated from the War College. The Pugachev rebellion had all the trappings of an organized military operation.[9]

As for the goals of the rebels, historians have disagreed sharply among themselves. Some Western scholars have seen the rebellions as conservative responses to government centralization and modernization, whose aim was the largely negative one of returning to earlier conditions. Some Soviet historians, too, have stressed the rebels' lack of revolutionary ideology, suggesting they knew more what they opposed than what they favored.[10] Most Soviet historians, however, although conceding some conservative elements in the insurgencies, have celebrated their revolutionary nature. "A peasant war is directed against the whole serfholding system, against the whole class of feudalists and the serfholding government that expresses its interests, not only against individual representatives of the ruling class," wrote V. V. Mavrodin, the leading Soviet authority on the Pugachev rebellion. "During peasant wars the peasantry struggles not for compromise, but for liquidation of the serfholding system." Others have noted a need to distinguish between the goals of the rebel leaders and the desires of the peasants as well as between the objective and subjective nature of the uprisings. "Objectively, of course, the peasant war was directed against feudalism as a social structure . . ." observed L. V. Cherepnin, "but the limited world view of the peasant did not allow him to recognize this as the task standing before him on a nationwide scope."[11]

The strongest argument for lack of revolutionary consciousness among the rebels and their peasant supporters lies in what Soviet historians term their "naive monarchism." Each leader claimed to be struggling not against but in support of the monarchy; each claimed to be fighting for the "true tsar"—in Pugachev's case himself—overthrown by evil noblemen who had placed a false tsar on the throne. The peasant wars were thus closely linked to two phenomena of seventeenth-century and eighteenth-century Russia: the existence of numerous pretenders to the throne and an abundance of legends among the populace of a "returning deliverer" who would overthrow the usurping monarch, punish his evil noble supporters, and restore the true tsar to his rightful position. It is no accident that the peasant wars occurred either in periods of dynastic crisis, as in 1606–7, when it was easy to claim that the true tsar still lived, or during reigns that aroused considerable opposition, when some questioned the monarch's legitimacy.[12]

The pretender phenomenon reached its peak under Catherine II—

a woman, a foreigner, a ruler who came to power following her husband's murder by disaffected noblemen, and a person whose rule coincided with substantial economic hardship for most Russians—during whose reign no fewer than twenty-six pretenders surfaced, each claiming to be the real Tsar Peter III. Pugachev was thus able to take full advantage of popular suspicions about the monarch; the rebel claimed to be the deposed Peter, who had miraculously escaped death and was now returning to restore rightful conditions and punish the conspirators who had overthrown him. Pugachev's numerous manifestoes were issued in the name of Peter III, and his lieutenants appealed to the populace "to believe really and truly in our true Sovereign," explaining that nobles were lyingly calling him the cossack Pugachev. Pugachev himself issued imperial ukazes explaining how "we were deprived of the throne" by the enemies of "the peace of all Russia." [13]

To what extent Russians actually believed the fiction of "rebels in the name of the tsar" is a difficult question to answer. One may safely assume that few noblemen were fooled; those who supported Bolotnikov did so in order to defeat their own political enemies, not in a mistaken belief that they were fighting for a martyred tsar miraculously resurrected. Whether a significant number of peasants and cossacks were taken in is less clear. No doubt many simply took advantage of an opportunity to seek vengeance on hated pomeshchiki, and it is hard to believe that close advisors to Pugachev really thought that the illiterate cossack was in fact Peter III. But the felt need of rebels from Bolotnikov to Pugachev to wage their struggles on behalf of a just tsar—as well as the pretender phenomenon in general—testifies to the widespread faith of the peasantry in the goodness of their rulers.

One should not conclude, however, that because the peasant wars were not directed at tsarist rule they lacked revolutionary goals. Indeed, naïve monarchism had considerable revolutionary potential in that it was predicated on the mistaken belief that the tsar was really on the side of the humble and oppressed—that he favored sweeping changes in the social structure and system but was stymied by evil advisors. Leaders of all the peasant wars advocated restoring to the peasants their rightful "land and liberty"—in short the abolition of serfdom and the institution of a kind of "cossack democracy" in which there would be no noble exploitation of peasants. On a practical level these goals were accompanied by the exaction of terrible vengeance—both planned and spontaneous—against pomeshchiki unfortunate enough to get in the way of the rebels. For many of the serfs formal revolutionary goals loomed less large than the opportunity to vent their fury on their oppressors. Nevertheless, the leaders of each peasant war saw fit to enumerate a program that had at its heart the peasant longing for freedom.[14]

The revolutionary nature of the insurgents' program became increasingly clear with each revolt, as class lines grew more solidified and the ideological underpinnings of the movement received fuller elaboration. In the first peasant war rebel slogans emphasized replacing the false, boiar tsar with the true monarch, Dmitrii. Clearly, many of the rebels—including evidently Bolotnikov himself—saw this as a double restoration: the true tsar would restore the true social order in which peasants were free to come and go without the new restrictions they faced, cultivating their own lands free of noble exactions. At the same time the presence among the rebels of a major contingent of noblemen served to limit the explicitly antinoble features of rebel propaganda, and Bolotnikov's program never received much elaboration. Razin's objectives were only slightly more clearly defined: in proclamations to the populace he promised freedom for serfs as well as just retribution against pomeshchiki, merchants, and local officials, a policy that resulted in widespread violence against captured class enemies as well as the establishment of liberated zones based on a "cossack" order, with local governments run by elected atamans.[15]

The revolutionary nature of the peasant wars received the clearest expression under Pugachev. His specific injunctions as well as their class basis were uniquely spelled out in a series of increasingly radical "imperial" manifestoes in which he called not just for punishment of bad noblemen but for abolition of the nobility. On 1 December 1773, after promising land and liberty to his supporters, he directed them to deal harshly with his enemies, pomeshchiki whom he labeled "real offenders against the law and general peace, miscreants and violators of my imperial will." "Deprive them of all life," he urged, "that is put them to death, and take their houses and all their estates in compensation." Half a year later he went further:

By this decree . . . we grant to all hitherto in serfdom and subjection to pomeshchiki the right to be faithful slaves [i.e., subjects] of our crown, and we award them the old cross and prayer, heads and beards, liberty and freedom always to be cossacks, without demanding recruit levies, soul taxes or other monetary obligations, possession of the lands, the woods, the hay meadows, the fisheries, and the salt lakes, without payment or obrok, and we free all those formerly oppressed by the villainous nobles and bribe-takers and

judges, all peasants and all the people oppressed by obligations and burdens
. . . [As for] those who hitherto were nobles, with their estates, those opponents of our power and disruptors of the empire and ruiners of the peasants,
catch, kill, and hang them, and treat them just as they, having no Christianity, treated you, the peasants. With the annihilation of these enemies and
miscreant-nobles, all may feel peace and a tranquil life, which will last
through the ages.

That summer millions of peasants along the Volga River heeded Pugachev's call, turning their fury on their erstwhile owners in the
bloodiest uprising of Russia's history, one that for the next century
and more would continue to haunt the nobility and government.[16]

Nothing like the peasant wars occurred in the American South. The
closest approximations were the so-called Seminole wars of 1817–19
and 1835–42 in which Florida's Seminole Indians and hundreds of
blacks, mostly fugitives from Georgia and Florida plantations, resisted American encroachments. Although some of these blacks were
formally slaves of the Seminoles, in fact they lived more as free people
in their own villages, giving small tribute to their Indian protectors
and serving as a major nuisance to nearby planters. In both the first
Seminole war, which ended in American annexation of Spanish Florida, and the second, which ended in removal of the Seminoles and
some of their black allies to Indian Territory, blacks fought side by
side with the Seminoles, causing considerable damage to the invading
troops and organizing partisan-type warfare among slaves on nearby
plantations. But these were small-scale operations compared with the
peasant wars. The number of blacks involved never exceeded several
hundred, and the struggle did not spread beyond Florida to the great
interior of the South where most slaves lived. The Seminole wars resembled the peasant wars in that they were struggles of the borderland against centralized consolidation; they differed vastly, however,
in their scope, impact, and significance.[17]

Actual slave rebellions within the United States were also small-
scale affairs compared with their Russian counterparts. Although historian Herbert Aptheker, in the most complete study of the subject,
counted 250 "revolts and conspiracies in the history of American Negro slavery" involving at least ten slaves, most of these were minor
incidents of unrest that were quickly put down with a minimum of
local force or were nipped in the bud before they even occurred.
Other historians have been more impressed with the paucity than the
ubiquity of American slave revolts.[18]

Only a handful of revolts and conspiracies reached more than tiny proportions. Two of these occurred in colonial New York city, the first in 1712 when twenty-five to thirty slaves set fire to a building, attacked and killed nine whites, and wounded a few others, before being quickly rounded up by local soldiers. The second took place in 1741, when a supposed slave conspiracy to burn down the city and massacre the white inhabitants led to mass arrests culminating in a trial that resulted in the execution of thirty-one blacks and four whites and the transportation to the West Indies of seventy slaves. Most of the other revolts of importance occurred in South Carolina and Virginia. In 1739 up to a hundred slaves near Charleston revolted and killed a number of whites before their band was routed by a contingent of armed planters that afternoon. In 1800 a more elaborate plot to attack Richmond, led by Gabriel Prosser, was foiled before it unfolded, as was the conspiracy led by free Negro Denmark Vesey in Charleston in 1822. In 1811 perhaps as many as two hundred slaves attempted to march on New Orleans, but they were quickly captured or dispersed by local forces. A number of insurrections were reportedly planned in 1856 in Louisiana, Tennessee, and Kentucky, but in each of these, too, authorities were able to arrest the would-be rebels before any violence occurred.[19]

The bloodiest antebellum slave revolt and the one that caused white southerners most anguish was that led by Nat Turner in Southampton county, Virginia, in 1831. Turner, a highly religious slave who became convinced that God had chosen him to rise up against the white oppressors, led a group of seventy slaves on a two-day rampage that resulted in the deaths of fifty-nine whites before local residents captured most of the rebels. Turner himself escaped and hid out in the woods for more than two months before being seized, tried, and hanged. Although the revolt lasted less than two days and was easily suppressed, it played much the same role as Pugachev's rebellion in instilling an abiding fear in the hearts of southern masters that no matter how calm things might appear, the danger of servile insurrection lurked just beneath the surface.[20]

Many of the intended American revolts, such as those of Gabriel Prosser and Denmark Vesey, never reached the rebellion stage but were merely conspiracies that were suppressed before any slave violence occurred. Indeed, there is considerable evidence that some presumed conspiracies, such as the New York city plot of 1741 and several of the 1856 plots, existed only in the panicked minds of whites always on the lookout for insubordinate behavior on the part of their slaves. Clearly, many whites saw rebellion where none existed. In

1837 a free black named McDonald was tried and convicted in Alabama for insurrection. A slaveowner testified that his slave had taken him to a spot where he could secretly hear McDonald tell the slaves they "ought to rise . . . that they must raise five hundred men, but he would start with three hundred." Because there occurred "no disturbance in the county among the slaves," however, an appeals court overturned the judgment against McDonald, holding that "the conviction of the prisoner was unauthorized." Many of the slave conspiracies that dot southern history appear to have been closer to the variety led by McDonald than that led by Turner.[21]

Even those risings that did exist were of a very different order from Russia's peasant wars or for that matter from slave rebellions that occurred in Haiti, Jamaica, and Brazil. They were all small: none embraced more than a few hundred rebels, and most had considerably fewer than one hundred. They were local affairs, with none involving more than a single town or county. They were short: the Stono rebellion, for example, lasted less than a day and the Turner rebellion less than two. As a consequence of these characteristics they necessitated a minimum of formal organization and displayed nothing like Pugachev's War College, military command, and propaganda network. Finally, they were easily put down with a minimum of local force; in no case did they require mobilization of new troops or even the dispatch of soldiers from surrounding areas. In short, these outbreaks were minor affairs that hardly seem to justify the terms *revolt* or *insurrection—disorder* might be more appropriate—let alone *rebellion*. A pervasive *fear* of slave rebellion certainly engulfed the white South, but the reality was quite different.[22]

Both the existence of massive uprisings in Russia and their absence in the United States were consequences of concrete historical conditions and should not be seen as implying that the serfs were either braver or less satisfied than the slaves. This point requires emphasis primarily because some historians have maintained that the lack of rebellions among American slaves reflected their fundamental docility while others, rejecting this position, have exhibited an extreme defensiveness about the slaves' failure to rebel. Thus, Stanley Elkins's argument that American slaves were docile, infantile Sambos who could not imagine standing up to their oppressors elicited the comment from Eugene D. Genovese that "the slaves of the Old South should not have to answer for their failure to mount more frequent and effective revolts; they should be honored for having tried at all." Neither blaming nor honoring rebels, however, helps to explain the nature of their rebelliousness. Put most simply, the slave South lacked most of the conditions that facilitated major revolts in Russia and some other slave societies.[23]

In a major contribution to the question of comparative slave rebellion Genovese recently outlined eight basic factors conducive to slave rebellion, factors present in Haiti, Jamaica, Guiana, and to a lesser extent in Cuba and Brazil but largely absent in the United States:

1) the master-slave relationship had developed in the context of absenteeism and depersonalization as well as greater cultural estrangement of whites and blacks; 2) economic distress and famine occurred; 3) slaveholding units approached the average size of one hundred to two hundred slaves, as in the sugar colonies, rather than twenty or so, as in the Old South; 4) the ruling class frequently split either in warfare between slaveholding countries or in bitter struggles within a particular slaveholding country; 5) blacks heavily outnumbered whites; 6) African-born slaves outnumbered those born into American slavery (creoles); 7) the social structure of the slaveholding regime permitted the emergence of an autonomous black leadership; and 8) the geographical, social, and political environment provided terrain and opportunity for the formation of colonies of runaway slaves strong enough to threaten the plantation regime.

The essence of these conditions, he noted, concerned "the military and political balance of power."[24]

With some appropriate adjustments this list suggests that Russia in the seventeenth and eighteenth centuries was ripe for insurrection. Absenteeism and economic hardship were widespread. Holdings were large by American standards, and peasants represented a huge majority of the population. They lived on their home turf and therefore enjoyed an even greater degree of cultural continuity than the heavy preponderance of African-born slaves provided in some New World slave societies. Peasants were able to develop their own autonomous organizations and leadership. External—and in the case of Bolotnikov's revolt internal—wars preoccupied the ruling class. Geographic and political conditions facilitated flight to the south where semi-independent groups of cossacks flourished. To these we might add that poor communication over a far-flung empire prevented speedy and effective governmental response to disorder. Many of these factors, significantly, were also responsible for the emergence of a strongly collective outlook on the part of the serfs, an outlook clearly related to the particular modes of resistance they embraced.

The slave South lacked these conditions to such an extent as to make organized rebellion virtually suicidal, especially during the century before emancipation. Creole slaves enjoyed relatively good material conditions and lived in small units among generally resident planters and a large, stable white population. Planter paternalism undermined the slaves' ability to develop autonomous communal organizations, and between the American Revolution and the Civil War masters were unburdened with major military conflicts. Finally, as the frontier receded and communication improved, the slaves' ability to form outlaw bands declined. The balance of forces was thus such as to render successful rebellion virtually impossible. The ease with which the few American slave revolts were suppressed and the savage retribution exacted on those few who dared to organize armed insurrection served to impress on the mass of slaves the conventional wisdom that discretion is the better part of valor.

In fact the odds against successful rebellion were so great that one may legitimately ask why any occurred and what their leaders hoped to accomplish. In an interesting article Marion Kilson divided forty-three revolts and conspiracies by American slaves into three broad categories. "Systematic" or "rational" revolts, such as those planned by Gabriel Prosser and Denmark Vesey, aimed at "overthrowing the slave system and establishing a Negro state" and were "characterized, therefore, by careful planning and organization." Significantly, of seventeen such planned revolts, only one—the New York rising of 1712—"went beyond the planning phase." "Unsystematic" or "vandalistic" revolts, such as Nat Turner's, had no positive goals but were expressions of fury directed toward the destruction of slaveholders and their property. "I heard a loud noise in the heavens," Turner testified after his capture, "and the Spirit instantly appeared to me and said . . . I should arise and prepare myself, and slay my enemies with their own weapons." Unsystematic revolts were far more likely than systematic ones to go beyond the planning stage; eight of fourteen such planned insurrections actually occurred. Finally, twelve "situational" or "opportunistic" revolts, of which eight went beyond planning, represented efforts by small groups to escape to free areas and were thus more attempts to flee than to rebel against slavery. The bulk of actual slave risings were elemental expressions of the hatred slaves felt for their oppressors and showed little of the programmatic nature of Russia's peasant wars.[25]

Virtually anything could set off such expressions of slave fury, and for this reason, even though the revolts had little chance of success, the slaveowners' fear of them represented far more than paranoia. Outside events sometimes triggered rebellion. The St. Domingue revolution of the 1790s, for example, which led to the resettlement on the American mainland of thousands of island slaves carrying news of the rising, apparently produced a marked increase in slave unrest in the South, culminating in Prosser's conspiracy of 1800. African-born slaves often played a disproportionate role in uprisings of the colonial era, dominating the New York revolt of 1712 and the Stono rebellion of 1739.[26]

As in Russia, slave revolts shared certain common features. They tended to occur when whites were either internally divided or preoccupied with foreign enemies. Thus, the Stono rebellion took place when South Carolina whites were trying to cope with hostile Indians and black maroons, the Prosser conspirators took advantage of a state of near war with France in which rebel leaders evidently expected French help, and the Turner insurrection had as a backdrop a state constitutional convention in which nonslaveholding delegates from western Virginia attacked the dominant eastern planters and called for the abolition of slavery. Each major nineteenth-century revolt was headed by a charismatic leader who was literate, skilled, and able to agitate among the masses. It also appears that rebels were able to take advantage of relaxation of the slave regime to plan their risings: far from being most prevalent in areas of greatest hardship, American slave rebellions were most common in areas displaying "an alleviation of the condition of slavery," as in Virginia's tobacco counties, where slavery lacked the regimentation of large plantations in the deep South, and in Charleston, where an urban environment mitigated many of the harshest features of the peculiar institution.[27]

As in Russia, there is evidence of increasing ideological content in the later rebellions. Prosser's men planned, according to one participant, to kill all whites "except the Quakers, the Methodists & Frenchmen," who "were to be spared on account of their being friendly to liberty." Genovese has argued that there occurred a fundamental shift in the nature of New World slave revolts at the time of the French and Haitian revolutions of the 1790s. Slave outbreaks that came before then were invariably "escapist," seeking "the restoration of as much of a traditional African way of life as could be remembered and copied"; those that came after, influenced by "a new bourgeois-democratic ideology," were truly revolutionary. Now "Afro-American slaves . . . consciously willed their own elimination as a class and consciously sought to rebuild society on a new property base."[28]

Applied to the United States, this assertion, although based on grains of truth, seems an exaggeration. One may readily accept the "restorationist" label for early revolts, but the idea that nineteenth-century slave rebellions were part of a broad Western current of egalitarian revolution is more problematical. True, scattered evidence indicates that some slaves were aware of St. Domingue, the fourth of July, and the contradiction between their status and their masters' democratic rhetoric. What is lacking, however, is much evidence that this awareness was a motivating force in most of the slave risings, which were as numerous before as after 1800. The "unsystematic" revolts that were most prevalent were more functions of hatred and anger than of any abstract idea of equal rights; Nat Turner's confession—and evidently his appeal to blacks as well—testified more to a belief in biblical vengeance called down on whites than a democratic world view. Even in the Prosser conspiracy the appeal to most slaves was more one of retribution than of ideology. When potential recruits were asked if they were willing to fight whites for their freedom, their responses emphasized their hatred of whites, not their belief in any kind of ideal society: "I could kill a white man as free as eat," one asserted coolly. Ultimately, the ideological content of the American slave revolts was peripheral if for no other reason than their brevity and hopelessness. There could be, in the South, no real hope for the creation of the equivalent of a cossack democracy, and the rebellions did not last long enough to develop much of a program or ideological content.[29]

Even in Russia there were no peasant wars after 1774. Their absence during the last century of serfdom helps to highlight the preconditions for such rebellion and suggests that even in Russia large-scale uprisings were of limited significance as indications of the bondsmen's mentality. During the late eighteenth and early nineteenth centuries seigneurial landholdings penetrated into the southern steppe region where all the peasant wars had begun. At the same time the cossacks were increasingly transformed from a seminomadic group that welcomed fugitives into a settled people, some of whom owned serfs themselves. Meanwhile, the government's military, police, and administrative apparatuses in the provinces were substantially strengthened, facilitating a speedier response to potential violence. In short, some of the most important preconditions for massive rebellion were removed during the half-century following Pugachev's rising. The absence of such rebellions after 1774 indicates the degree to which the peasant wars were dependent on cossacks operating in a sparsely settled frontier region and a government unable to respond quickly to trouble.[30]

Rebellion was not, then, characteristic behavior of most Russian serfs any more than it was of most American slaves. Of course, the atypical can sometimes be highly significant, and the story of the bondsmen's revolts will continue to interest historians. Still, although more useful to the analyst of servile resistance than silent sabotage, such uprisings are not, I would suggest, as revealing of the bondsmen's world view as certain other types of protest. If day-to-day resistance was too ambiguous in nature to permit ready analysis, large-scale revolts were too rare, too dependent on outside factors, and, in the case of the United States, too fleeting to provide many clues to the social attitudes of the slaves and serfs. The rest of this chapter, and much of the next, will be devoted to an examination of two intermediate forms of resistance—more clearcut than silent sabotage and more frequent than rebellion—which are, I believe, more analytically useful.

*　　*　　*

REBELLION was by no means the only form of physical conflict between the bondsmen and authorities; far more common were smaller confrontations that pitted the slaves and serfs against their owners, stewards, and overseers. Similarly, silent sabotage was not the only type of passive protest shown by the slaves and serfs; hundreds of thousands ran away from their masters, either temporarily or for good. Flight and small-scale confrontations offer exceptional opportunities for exploring the bondsmen's mentality, because unlike rebellion they occurred often enough to be representative forms of behavior subject to generalization and unlike silent sabotage they clearly involved deliberate, conscious acts of defiance on the part of the bondsmen.

The basic Russian confrontation was a *volnenie,* a term without a precise English equivalent that has been used by both contemporaries and historians to denote something smaller than a rebellion. Dictionary translations include "agitation," "unrest," "disturbance," and "commotion," but none of these quite captures the spirit of the word. Consequently, although I shall sometimes refer to unrest or disturbances, when trying to be more specific I shall use the term *volnenie* (pl.: *volneniia*). Since these volneniia are unfamiliar to most American readers, it is worthwhile first to outline their archetypal pattern and then to present concrete examples.[31] My focus is on the period from the 1790s through the 1850s. Volneniia existed before then, but they were most common during the two-thirds of a century before emancipation; equally important, documentary material is far more abundant for this period than for earlier.[32]

The typical volnenie began when a group of serfs, dissatisfied for some reason, decided on collective protest. They might number from a handful to thousands, but groups in the hundreds were most common: the usual unit of action was either a village or several villages belonging to the same estate. The initial cause of the serfs' discontent (explored in depth in Chapter 6) might be anything from an increase in the burdens imposed on them to oppressive treatment by a steward or sale to a new owner, but it most frequently involved either a change in their actual condition or a dashing of somehow aroused hopes.[33]

Often the serfs began their protest by sending a petition to their owner, a local official, the governor, or even the tsar. These petitions constituted an important type of passive resistance in their own right and will receive treatment later in this chapter. Here it is sufficient to note that the results of their efforts were usually disappointing to those who were convinced that they had legitimate grievances that only had to be revealed in order to be remedied.

The next step was for the serfs to refuse to recognize their owner's authority over them or to stop working for him—in short, to go on strike. The serfs were usually careful to refrain from major violence against their owners or their owners' highest representatives, although peasants who remained loyal to their masters sometimes received beatings and loyal starosty were sometimes replaced. Most serfs must have realized, however, that assaulting authorities would bring down upon themselves certain retribution. The volneniia, although containing elements of spontaneity, were less expressions of wild fury by serfs seeking vengeance on their owners than organized collective endeavors by peasants who retained some hope that in the end their efforts would be successful.[34]

In response to such disobedience, the pomeshchik or steward invariably sent for the *ispravnik*, a minor official who in every provincial district (*uezd*) served as a combination of sheriff and magistrate and headed a three-man board known as the lower land court (*nizhnii zemskii sud*). He would come to the estate, either alone or with other members of the court, and talk to the recalcitrant peasants, typically alternating between dire threats of punishment should the serfs continue their disobedience and promises that if they relented they would be spared serious harm and their complaints would be investigated. No doubt such urgings were sometimes sufficient to restore order, but in most cases for which records have survived—which naturally tend to be the most serious cases—the peasants ignored the ispravnik's pleas, sometimes threatening him with bodily harm if he did not leave the estate. The frightened official would then return to the district capital and write a report to the provincial governor, who in turn reported to authorities in St. Petersburg.[35]

The governor, upon receiving the ispravnik's report, usually ordered other officials to the scene. These could range, depending on the seriousness of the situation, from the district marshal of nobility to the provincial marshal of nobility and even the governor himself. Sometimes special officials from St. Petersburg and officers of the Corps of Gendarmes (who were under the control of the Third Department) were also sent. These officials, usually accompanied by a small military guard, would repeat in succession the efforts of the ispravnik, striving through threats and promises to put down the volnenie with a minimum of force. Frequently, officials tried to divide the peasants against each other or secretly arrest one or more of their leaders, but such efforts sometimes backfired and led to greater peasant unity, and more than once enraged serfs forced the release of their captured leaders. In some volneniia peasant determination gradually faded as the weeks wore on or as their representatives were arrested and promises given that their complaints would be investigated.

Ultimately, soldiers were needed to crush the most stubborn volneniia. Occasionally, such clashes led to substantial casualties, although the poorly armed and untrained peasants almost always suffered a far higher toll than the military. After the volnenie its ringleaders usually received harsh punishments: savage beatings with birch switches, whips, and worst of all the knout, followed by exile to penal servitude, were routine inflictions, and under Nicholas I running the gauntlet became a common sentence imposed by military courts set up to deal with leaders of the worst volneniia. Often the bulk of peasants suffered little or no immediate hardship, however, and in some cases the serfs won real gains in their defeat.[36]

Three specific examples should make clearer many of the points suggested in the above schematization. None of the three conforms in all details to the model presented, but together they illustrate the broad range of possible actions and responses that characterized the volneniia.

The first example is a protest that began with a petition from twenty-five serfs in Moscow province to the provincial governor, on behalf of themselves and thousands of other peasants living in eight villages and forty-eight hamlets. Dated 1823 and written for the illiterate serfs by a servant of a neighboring nobleman, the petition related that before their owner E. A. Golovkina died in 1821 they had been managed by her steward Petr Ivanovich Lapirev. The peasants complained that even though Golovkina had been dead for two years, Lapirev continued to collect twenty-six rubles obrok from each of 3,840 male souls; they begged for government intervention against the steward's gathering money for a nonexistent owner. Meanwhile, the district ispravnik reported his version of the story to the governor. He wrote that Lapirev had told him that more than 4,300 souls, led by starosta Timofei Fedorov and three other peasants, were refusing to pay their obrok obligations. According to the ispravnik, the peasants were told that they had two new owners, the underaged Counts Shuvalov, and had to obey their noble guardian as well as Lapirev and the head starosta of the area; at this they "announced in one voice that not personally seeing these pomeshchiki, they would not obey the steward and starosta or pay the obrok." [37]

In an effort to restore order the ispravnik went to the village of Vishegorod, where Lapirev kept his headquarters, together with a noble assessor and four invalid soldiers, and called for representatives from each village to assemble and hear that they must obey their owners. Instead, more than two thousand serfs descended on the seigneurial house and shouted to the ispravnik that they wanted to replace Lapirev with a *burmistr* (bailiff, manager) of their own choosing and to elect new starosty. They then proceeded to choose one of their leaders as burmistr, selected two starosty to assist him, and sent for two local priests to administer oaths to the new peasant officials. The ispravnik, however, sent the priests away and, unable to persuade the serfs to desist, returned to the district capital. Soon thereafter, he received a letter from the steward that the new burmistr had gone to the neighboring district to collect peasant reinforcements for a new gathering. The ispravnik summoned a guard to protect the seigneurial house and requested assistance from the Moscow governor. [38]

It was not until a month later, however, that a punitive expedition headed by a major arrived to suppress the volnenie. After futile efforts by the ispravnik, a noble assessor, and an adjutant to the governor-general of Moscow province to convince the serfs to yield, the soldiers went into action. In each village in succession they assembled the peasants, quartered some troops, and arrested the ringleaders; despite threats of resistance, the remaining serfs submitted without a struggle. Nine of their leaders were jailed for a year and then transported to Siberia.[39]

This case demonstrates several features common in serfs' *volneniia*—confusion about their status resulting from absentee ownership, resentment against a steward's administration, desire to run their own affairs as much as possible, and a substantial degree of communal solidarity. The second example shows many of the same qualities but with a different resolution. In October 1851 R. S. Kozitsyn, steward on Count P. D. Kiselev's estate of 350 souls in Penza province, reported to the nobleman that his serfs, in response to an ordered administrative reorganization of the estate, were disorderly and insisted on sending walkers to Kiselev with a petition. The petition, written for the peasants by the estate *kontorshchik* (office clerk, a serf himself), complained bitterly of the steward, whom the peasants accused of overworking them—even on holidays—subjecting them to cruel punishments, taking away their livestock, and worst of all seducing many young girls. The petitioners begged Kiselev to protect them from his tyrannical steward.[40]

A month later the provincial governor wrote to Kiselev, portraying the kontorshchik Fedor Maksimov as the chief culprit. According to the governor, Maksimov incited the serfs against Kozitsyn, claiming that he had for three years concealed a seigneurial directive to put all the serfs on obrok, and got them to agree "that they would stand together." When the frightened steward tried to flee the estate, the serfs apprehended him, together with three loyal peasants—including a clerk and a coachman who received beatings for trying to help Kozitsyn escape—and placed the four under guard. They also replaced the old starosta with a new one whom the steward recognized under duress, beat the deposed starosta, stole the office chest and trunk, and forced Kozitsyn to issue a pass for three of them to carry a petition to St. Petersburg. When the ispravnik arrived with other members of the lower land court, an angry mob prevented them from arresting the new starosta.[41]

After a few days the commotion died down, the serfs apparently resumed obedience of their own accord, and the governor appointed a special official to investigate the disturbance. He reported that kontorshchik Maksimov was chiefly to blame for the trouble, because he "lyingly assured the peasants" of the nonexistent seigneurial order, but that others were also guilty, including the rebel starosta, a gardener who "shouted loudest and most rudely of all" and threatened the life of a priest, and two peasants who tried to grab the ispravnik. All but the gardener, who was one of the three walkers who had left for St. Petersburg, were promptly arrested; the district court sentenced Maksimov to thirty lashes and resettlement in Siberia, the starosta to sixty blows with birch switches, and two other peasants to military conscription. The investigating official found that the charges of sexual abuse leveled against the steward "hardly could be proven." The incident seemed to be over.[42]

More than a year later, however, a house servant in the estate's seigneurial mansion wrote to Kiselev on behalf of the other peasants, corroborating their accusations against Kozitsyn. The servant noted that in addition to committing other "illegal acts," the steward "demands young girls for himself and has deprived many of their maidenhood"; he also ran the estate as his own, without regard to Kiselev's instructions, driving the serfs to "extreme misery and poverty." As a result of this complaint—and no doubt of the unrest before it— Kiselev replaced Kozitsyn as steward and made some administrative changes similar to those demanded by the serfs. Thus, although the leaders of the volnenie were made to suffer grievously, the bulk of the peasants not only went unpunished but succeeded in winning their original demand.[43]

The third volnenie involved a far more protracted struggle of serfs for what they considered their rights. Whereas in the preceding episode an apparent peasant defeat turned into a partial victory, in this case what at first seemed likely to result in a quick redress of grievances led in the end only to bloody repression. Early in 1852 Savelii Matveev, chosen representative of 576 souls in Tver province, petitioned Nicholas I on their behalf. He explained that until 1840 they had belonged to Admiral A. S. Shishkov, whose will leaving them to his wife stipulated that the estate could not be mortgaged, sold, or rented out and that the peasants should not be charged more than 12,000 rubles obrok per year. Madame Shishkova observed these conditions, but in 1848 she died, leaving the estate to her niece, N. D. Shishkova, who immediately increased the serfs' obrok dues and was now planning to impose on them barshchina obligations as well. Matveev implored the "merciful sovereign" to order that the owner not impose barshchina or excessive obrok levies, refrain from cutting down the peasants' timber, and "in general adhere to the will of her deceased uncle." The tsar forwarded the petition to the governor of Tver province for consideration.[44]

The governor reported back one-half year later that before seeing the petition he had received a complaint from the new owner that her serfs, "for an unknown reason," were seeking their freedom and refusing to pay their obrok. He ordered the district ispravnik "to take measures to restore peace to the estate of pomeshchitsa Shishkova, and also make an investigation of the causes of the disorders," but learned from him that the peasants' complaints were well founded. The serfs were not seeking their freedom, the ispravnik reported, and insisted they were not being disobedient; they merely objected to paying 21,275 rubles obrok rather than the prescribed maximum of 12,000 and to the refusal of two agents sent by Shishkova to count the money in front of priests and other witnesses or give the peasants receipts for it. The governor concluded that the owner's behavior "aroused the dissatisfaction of the peasants and gave them cause to make complaints about her actions." Moreover, in a private meeting with the governor she "showed an extremely resistant character." Nevertheless, he decided to pursue a cautious policy. Unwilling flatly to take the side of serfs in a dispute with their owner, he decreed their petition "unfounded" and ordered the marshal of nobility to explain to them that "it is much more advantageous" to have their obrok payments increased once than to have other obligations—namely barshchina—introduced as well. At the same time he instructed the ispravnik to be on the lookout for abuses of power by Shishkova and to report any misbehavior to the marshal of nobility.[45]

The peasants, however, were not satisfied with this arrangement and insisted on a response to their petition before accepting any obligations not stipulated in the will. "One should not suppose," noted the ispravnik, "that without special severe measures they will be obedient to the pomeshchitsa and carry out her demands." Despairing of a voluntary return to order, provincial authorities jailed the original petitioner, Matveev, together with two other troublesome serfs, and in July 1853 the governor reported that a punitive expedition had brought the peasants back into obedience. In August and December, however, another serf presented petitions to Nicholas I and to the head of the Third Department. The minister of internal affairs ordered the governor to determine whether outsiders were inciting the peasants, and the ispravnik informed the governor that they were once again refusing to pay the increased obrok, having promised to do so earlier only out of fear. The exasperated governor told Shishkova not to make excessive demands on her serfs and instructed the ispravnik to take down the names of unruly peasants.[46]

The tsar, too, was annoyed with this long-festering unrest and sent aide-de-camp N. T. Baranov to Tver province to handle the matter. Although he personally told the peasants that Nicholas deemed their complaint unfounded, they remained skeptical and still refused to pay more than 12,000 rubles obrok. When Baranov ordered a military command to the scene, the two hundred soldiers proved insufficient to keep the serfs from the nine villages comprising the estate from hiding in the woods, and three hundred more soldiers had to be sent. The infuriated tsar's order that the volnenie's ringleaders be forced to run a gauntlet of a thousand men three times and then be sent to penal servitude in Siberia proved easier to give than to execute. The two chief culprits underwent the prescribed treatment and many others received public chastisement with birch switches, but 157 of the 576 males disappeared into the woods, and Baranov had to be content with leaving a list of names with an adjutant-general with instructions that upon capture they be sent to the governor for punishment.[47]

Although the volnenie seemed to be over, as soon as the troops were removed the serfs resumed their objections to the excessive obrok levy. Soldiers were once again needed to restore order—in the process seventy-eight peasants were jailed—but this action led to renewed protest. In December 1854 another peasant representative, Aleksei Vasil'ev, petitioned the head of the Corps of Gendarmes, repeating the whole story of the unjust obrok and complaining of cruel treatment by police and soldiers. Fifty-four peasants remained in jail, he asserted, nine had been drafted into the army, two—including Kuz'ma Mikhailov, a church starosta and "an honest and sober person"—had run the gauntlet of 3,003 blows and been resettled in Siberia, others had died in irons, and six more awaited exile in Siberia. "And we must now spend our lives worse than unthinking cattle," he asserted poetically, "and suffer frost and hardship, cold and hunger."[48]

This petition was forwarded to the minister of internal affairs, who pronounced it "undeserving of any consideration," but the unrest continued. In August 1856 he ordered the governor to take "the most stringent measures for the restoration of order on the estate." Having determined that Osip Fedorov was now one of the peasant leaders, the ispravnik recruited a retired soldier to make friends with Fedorov in order to capture him by stealth. The ensuing ambush proved successful despite the efforts of other serfs to rescue the prisoner, and the exultant governor assured a new minister of internal affairs that calm would now return to the estate. Almost a year later, however, the governor's successor had to order 250 soldiers to the scene to catch fugitives. Finally, only one serf remained missing, but the ispravnik was certain he would soon return. The volnenie was at last over, five-and-a-half years after it had begun.[49]

*   *   *

ALTHOUGH THERE WAS no exact American equivalent to the volne-niia, small-scale confrontations between slaves and plantation authorities were common. These conflicts took the form of open resistance on the part of individual slaves who felt that they were being treated unjustly. It is more difficult to approximate the frequency of these confrontations than of the Russian volneniia (and most of them must go forever undiscovered), but there are abundant records of blacks who stood up to whites, with varying consequences.[50] As with the volneniia, documentary evidence is most readily available for nineteenth-century confrontations, at least in part because the best sources on them consist of the recollections of ex-slaves themselves. Nevertheless, scattered evidence indicates the existence of similar if less numerous confrontations in the eighteenth century as well.[51]

One of the best examples of these confrontations appears in the most famous of all slave autobiographies—that of Frederick Douglass. A Maryland black who had undergone a variety of slave experiences including the relative independence afforded by life in Baltimore, Douglass was hired out in 1834 to a "Negro breaker" named Edward Covey. For six months Douglass endured in silence a life of ceaseless labor and frequent whippings, but at last, when Covey tried once too often to punish him without cause, the slave decided to fight back. The astonished employer called for his cousin Hughes to help him subdue Douglass, but the latter, with a "kick which sent him staggering away in pain," drove off the assistant. A protracted fight between Douglass and Covey followed, during which two other slaves refused to help the white man subdue the black, but finally Covey "gave up the contest," proclaiming "I would not have whipped you half so much as I have had you not resisted." But as Douglass pointed out, "the fact was, *he had not whipped me at all.*" The struggle's effect on both men was remarkable. "During the whole six months that I lived with Covey, after this transaction, he never laid on me the weight of his finger in anger," Douglass recollected. "I was a changed being after that fight. I was *nothing* before; I WAS A MAN NOW." The lesson was clear: if a slave was willing to make himself difficult to punish, not only would he feel himself more a man but some whites might not bother to try.[52]

A similar story is told in the improbable autobiography of Elizabeth Keckley, a Virginia-born house servant who succeeded—with the help of white friends—in buying her freedom and making her way to Washington, where she became a dressmaker first for Mrs. Jefferson Davis and then for Mrs. Abraham Lincoln. Well before this exalted career began, when she was a young woman of eighteen, the village schoolmaster, Mr. Bingham, announced for no apparent reason that he was going to flog her and, despite her protestations, proceeded to do so. When she complained to her owner, Mr. Burwell, he hit her with a chair. "It seems," Keckley wrote, "that Mr. Bingham had pledged himself to Mrs. Burwell to subdue what he called my 'stubborn pride.'" The following week, when Bingham returned to punish her again, the indignant slave, convinced she had done nothing to deserve a whipping, determined to resist to the end. After a struggle in which the woman bit her tormentor's finger, he dealt her a severe beating. "I went home sore and bleeding," she recalled, "but with pride as strong as ever." Several days later the persistent teacher tried a final time to break Keckley's spirit. Once again she resisted, and once again she suffered "many savage blows" for her impertinence. This time, however, her defiance brought more positive results. "As I stood bleeding before him," she remembered, "nearly exhausted with his efforts, he burst into tears, and declared that it would be a sin to beat me any more. My suffering at last subdued his hard heart; he asked my forgiveness, and afterwards was an altered man. He was never known to strike one of his servants from that day forward." For her owner, too, resistance led to repentance. When Bingham failed to subdue Keckley, Burwell tried twice, but after the second failure "he told me, with an air of penitence, that he should never strike me another blow; and faithfully he kept his word."[53]

One may justifiably doubt whether Keckley had really worked the miraculous conversion of her white tormentors that she claimed. Not only does that part of her story sound implausible; it also has a stereotypic cast that characterized so much of the political and hortatory literature of the mid-nineteenth century. Similarly, it is questionable whether Douglass could have grappled with Covey for two full hours without either of them suffering more than bruises and scratches. These accounts highlight some of the problems as well as opportunities associated with the use of slave autobiographies. Even excluding those autobiographies that were apparent forgeries, concoctions, and ghostwritings, the remainder still contain an amalgam of sentiments reflecting on the one hand the hopes, aspirations, and recollections of individual slaves, but on the other the intrusion of ideas acquired after escape from slavery and the espousal of principles designed to appeal to potential supporters. And ex-slaves were as liable as others to exaggerate their own exploits.[54]

Nevertheless, the episodes that Douglass and Keckley described have a significance that should not be overlooked. Whatever the exaggeration, there is little reason to doubt that these confrontations and hundreds more like them did take place; not only do their stories resemble too many others told by ex-slaves to be written off as sheer fantasy,[55] but other records corroborate the existence of slave confrontations. Equally important, although the slave autobiographies, like all reminiscences, consisted of varying combinations of fact and fiction, the latter is by no means useless to the historian: how slaves saw and described their resistance can be as revealing of their attitudes and behavior as how they actually resisted. The unlikely contrition often ascribed to masters reflected the very real feeling of slaves that resistance in itself constituted a moral victory. It is not surprising that slaves sometimes embellished this victory by having the challenged white authorities admit their own defeat, any more than it is surprising that these whites, in their records, refused to acknowledge such defeat. What seemed a victory to the one may not have been recognized as a defeat by the other.

By no means all slave accounts tell of black triumphs in confrontations with whites. Although the autobiographies, usually written by elite slaves who had successfully escaped from bondage, tend to exhibit an optimistic tone, slave narratives collected by interviewers generally present a less sanguine picture of the efficacy of resistance. Many years later, in the 1930s, an old black woman from North Carolina recalled the time patrollers interrupted a secret dance the slaves were conducting in the quarters. "Uncle Joe's son he decide dey was one time to die and he sta't to fight," she remembered. "He say he tired standin' so many beatin's, he jes can't stan' no mo." It was a futile effort doomed from the start; whatever a slave's chances in one-to-one combat against a white, for an individual to fight back against a group was a costly expression of rage. Not only did their number make defeat certain; because the challenge was an affront witnessed by many whites rather than a private matter between master and slave, severe retribution was an essential response. In this case, after the whites had whipped the slave "for a long time, den one of dem

take a stick an' hit him over de head, an' jes bus his head wide open
... De paddyrollers jes whip bout half dozen other niggers an' sen'
em home and leve us wif de dead boy."[56]

Trial records from southern courts confirm that slave recollections
of plantation confrontations were far more than fantasy. Indeed, the
picture of the conflicts that emerges from court testimony is fully consistent with the descriptions given by the ex-slaves themselves. Although the great majority of confrontations were settled informally
without recourse to trial, judicial records contain evidence about their
existence and character and show that southern courts were forced to
grapple with the problem of how to handle them. Like planters and
overseers, judges reacted in varying ways.

Because of the inclination of slaveowners to handle confrontations
privately, the majority of court cases involved conflicts between slaves
and authorities other than their owners—overseers, hirers, patrollers—and many grew out of disputes between planters and other
whites. Probably the type of confrontation most often resulting in a
trial was that between a slave and his overseer. In the Alabama case
of *State v. Abram,* a struggle occurred when the overseer, a man
named Kirkendall, discovered Abram "loitering about the negro cabins" claiming to be sick. Kirkendall, suspecting an attempt to avoid
work, "felt his pulse, told him he was not sick, and again ordered him
to his work." When Abram "moved off slowly," Kirkendall lashed
him with his whip, whereupon Abram grabbed the whip, threw the
overseer to the ground, and knocked a gun from his hand. As the two
men struggled, "Abram bit off a piece of the upper part, or rim of
Kirkendall's ear, and received in his own side a severe cut from Kirkendall's knife." Sometimes confrontations brought overseers trouble
from their employers as well as from their charges. When overseer
Hooper decided to whip Harry, an "ungovernable" slave, the latter
"refused to submit" and the two men battled each other with hoes.
Hooper finally shot Harry as the slave was attempting to escape but
then faced a lawsuit from the owner seeking to recover the value of
the dead man.[57]

When a confrontation between a slave and his *owner* reached
court, it was usually because the case involved a charge of murder. In
Tennessee, for example, a farmer named Bradford reproached his
slave Jacob for playing while pulling fodder "and threatened to whip
and sell him." The slave replied "that he was as tired of him (Bradford) as he (Bradford) was of him." When the incensed owner reached
for his whip, Jacob grabbed and broke it and then fled. Upon his

return home the following day, he refused to be punished, and "Bradford then ordered him to go off until he was willing to be tied and
whipped." A few days later the slave again returned and again refused
to be whipped, whereupon his owner "told him to go to the smoke-
house and take out as much provision as would do him until he was
willing . . . and clear out, [for] he did not wish him to be pillaging his
neighbors." Evidently Bradford soon thought better of this injunc-
tion, because he set out with his brother to catch, tie, and whip the
recalcitrant slave. A struggle ensued in which Jacob stabbed his master to death with a butcher-knife and then escaped. Months later he
was caught "in an adjoining State," tried, and sentenced to hang.[58]

Of course, most slaves did not confront their owners any more
than most serfs engaged in volneniia; if either had done so, slavery
and serfdom would have been impossible to maintain. The majority
of slaves reluctantly came to terms with the system and found their
own endurable if less than ideal niche. But slave challenges to masters' authority were more widespread than most whites admitted.
Like volneniia, such challenges were common enough to be significant on two levels. Their greatest immediate impact was naturally on
the participants themselves (on both sides), but equally important
was their long-term effect on others. The slaves autobiographies and
narratives suggest that most slaves knew of cases in which blacks resisted whites, and the major role that such incidents play in the writings and reminiscences of many ex-slaves indicates the kind of symbolic significance they must have attached to them. Masters too,
whether they wrote about them or not, were all too familiar with the
existence of such conflicts. They were not constant occurrences on
most plantations, but they did both reflect and affect the everyday
lives of master and bondsman.

*   *   *

THE MOST OBVIOUS difference between the Russian and American
confrontations is the collective nature of the former and the individual character of the latter. The serfs' volneniia reflected the overwhelmingly communal nature of their life and organization, whereas
the slaves' protest confirms the relative lack of such communality in
the antebellum South.

The volnenie was by its very nature a group enterprise, an action
taken by decision of the communal gathering and sustained by the
common efforts of peasants who often showed an extraordinary solidarity in defying owners and officials. Time after time authorities

attempting to talk serfs into submission reported that they "all in one voice announced that they would not obey any authorities," or "all in one voice shouted, that they did not want to and would not submit." When officials tried to arrest troublemakers—often communal leaders—the mass of peasants typically interceded in their behalf. In one case, when an ispravnik selected a serf for punishment, a crowd rushed up shouting, "We are all guilty and will not give him over to be beaten"; in another, when an official ordered an ispravnik to record the names of two peasant leaders, "the whole crowd in one voice repeated, 'Write us all down, we all speak as one'"; in still another, when peasants were told that the instigators of their volnenie were to be arrested, "they all in one voice called themselves the instigators." Once the decision was made to resist, the peasant community stood as a unified group.[59]

Of course, the contrast between Russian collectivism and American individualism was not absolute. Serfs at times confronted their owners as individuals, engaging in actions ranging from verbal assault to murder. In Orenburg province in 1850, for example, a boy slapped twice by his owner responded by bashing him on the head with a wooden shovel. A small but significant number of serfs reacted to provocations by killing or attempting to kill their oppressors: in 1842 fifteen pomeshchiki and three stewards were murdered, and attempts were made on the lives of four pomeshchiki and one steward. (Even this violence, however, often involved groups of serfs. When Kostroma province nobleman Anton von Shults was murdered in 1842, an investigation revealed that four peasants had definitely taken part in the killing, but that two others knew of the plot and thirty-four more were under suspicion of complicity; indeed, von Shults's mistreatment of his serfs had produced such dissatisfaction among them that "they almost all wished to be rid of such a pomeshchik . . . about which they sometimes talked openly among themselves.")[60]

Individual serfs sometimes acted alone, as well, in nonviolent challenges to pomeshchiki and stewards. Occasionally individuals rather than the mir as a whole sent petitions to authorities, although such solitary petitioners were most often house servants far removed from the communal life of the mass of peasants. Individual serfs also sometimes *opposed* communal decisions to challenge pomeshchiki. In 1834, for example, when 1,299 souls in two villages in Iaroslavl province decided to protest the high obrok levies they were forced to pay, the burmistr, starosta, and clerk refused to go along—and were promptly deposed by the other peasants. Individual initiatives among serfs were not entirely lacking, but they were clearly subordinated in the vast majority of cases to collective action.[61]

Among American slaves, although individual initiatives predominated, the cooperative element was not absent. Occasionally a group, surprised in a forbidden act, combined to resist capture or punishment, as in the case described by Austin Steward when twenty-five slaves taking part in an illicit dance attacked the patrollers who arrived to break it up. "Hand to hand they fought and struggled with each other" until three patrollers and six slaves lay dead. Such resistance was usually a spontaneous response to an emergency, however, rather than a planned and coordinated undertaking. More significant were the numerous occasions when small groups of slaves conspired together against whites. Collaboration among two or more slaves was widespread in the petty pilfering of white property that was endemic under slavery. Similarly, although most murders of owners and overseers were individual acts, some were the product of several slaves working together, and in other instances slaves acted to conceal the identity of murderers of hated whites. "Marse Jim had 'bout three hundred slaves, and he had one mighty bad overseer," recalled an ex-slave from Alabama. "But he got killed down on de bank of de creek one night. Dey never did find out who killed him, but Marse Jim always b'lieved de field han's done it." In this and other cases in which the guilty party was never apprehended, groups of slaves were either involved in assaults or acted to protect those who were. Indeed, many of what Aptheker and others have categorized as slave revolts can more properly be seen as conspiracies by small groups of slaves—in some ways similar to very small volneniia—against white authorities.[62]

The question of cooperation among slaves is thus complex. Such cooperation clearly existed, both in resisting whites and in protecting comrades in distress. Abundant evidence confirms that slaves not only concealed the criminal activities of others but also intervened in small ways to help those in trouble. Former slave Susan Broaddus, a house servant to a Virginia planter, recalled how her master would spell out words when he and his wife discussed things she was not to understand; once he spelled out the names of two slaves he planned to sell the next day, and the agitated servant, after finishing her chores as usual, rushed to her father, who surreptitiously knew how to read, with the letters she had carefully memorized. "De next day Gabe and Rufus was gone—dey had run away." Numerous slaves protected fugitives, whether headed north or lurking in nearby swamps and woods. As one former slave put it after telling of a runaway who lived undetected in the woods for many years with his wife and two sons, "all us slaves knew whar he wuz but, in dem days . . . nigger didn't tell on each other." [63]

Such cooperation was qualitatively different, however, from the communal behavior of Russian serfs. For one thing, every example of slave solidarity can be matched with one of pettiness, deceit, and treachery. In Louisiana Lew Chaney organized a group of slaves to flee together, but on learning that the plan was discovered he falsely reported to his master that the others were engaged in a plot to murder all the local whites; they were rounded up and eventually hanged, while Chaney "was even rewarded for his treachery." William Wells Brown recalled tricking another slave into taking a whipping intended for him, explaining that "this incident shows how it is that slavery makes its victims lying and mean." A similar mentality was expressed in the widely known slave ditty,

> Please ol' moster don't whip me!
> Whip dat nigger behin' de tree!

Although some ex-slaves told of helping fugitives, at least one recalled his own fear of "outlyers" and commented on "the viciousness of those runaway Negroes." Virtually every slave rebellion was plagued by internal divisions and spies: the Gabriel Prosser and Denmark Vesey conspiracies were both abortive because of revelations by slave informers, and Nat Turner, too, was ultimately betrayed by slaves. In short, there is conflicting evidence concerning the solidarity slaves showed in confronting whites, and their behavior was ambiguous. [64]

More important than this ambiguity in underscoring the difference between the behavior of the slaves and serfs is the *nature* of the very real cooperation that did exist among the slaves. Joint action by small groups of slaves represented the collaboration of individuals with other individuals rather than the kind of collective effort so common among the serfs. Cooperation among southern slaves was marked by an absence of any ongoing institutional or organizational basis and was perforce ad hoc in nature. Whereas in Russia peasants sometimes acted alone despite the predominantly collective ethos, in the United States slaves interacted with each other—and with authorities—primarily as individuals, although those individuals often cooperated with each other. Virtually nowhere in the antebellum South did whole plantations confront owners and overseers as they did in Russia. [65]

This contrast receives clarification from an examination of the differing ways in which the bondsmen appealed for redress when dissatisfied with their conditions. Collective petitions, agreed upon at the mir meeting, constituted a major form of peasant protest in Russia. Such petitions sometimes, but by no means usually, developed into volneniia. Because they were so common and because they constituted written expressions of the peasants' sentiments, they provide an important indication of their mentality.[66]

Because the vast majority of serfs were illiterate, the petition was typically penned for them, in appropriately humble language, by whomever they could find who was literate and willing to cooperate. Sometimes this person was a serf himself, such as clerk or house servant; sometimes he was a sympathetic outsider, such as a priest or retired soldier. Thus, although the petitions' sentiments came from the serfs, often their actual wording did not. A petition might list the names of all the subscribers to it—usually the members of the mir gathering—or it might, especially if large numbers of serfs were involved, identify one or more leaders as particularly responsible but declare it "on behalf of" an entire village or estate. At their gathering the serfs would choose one or two "walkers" to carry the petition to the designated recipient and would levy a small tax on themselves to pay the walkers' expenses.

A wide variety of persons, including the tsar, received peasant petitions. Although the Code of 1649 forbade serfs from denouncing their owners except to present evidence of treason, and a series of rulers issued orders during the first half of the eighteenth century forbidding anyone from appealing directly to the tsar rather than going through appropriate channels, peasant complaints continued. In 1765 Catherine II, annoyed by a swelling number of peasant supplicants, issued an ukaz reiterating the prohibition on peasant petitions to the tsar and providing penalties ranging from one month of penal servitude for first offenders to public whipping followed by eternal banishment to hard labor in distant Nerchinsk for third-time miscreants. When peasants continued to deluge the monarch with complaints, she decreed in 1767 that "such petitioners, as well as composers of these petitions, will be punished with the knout and immediately sent to penal servitude in Nerchinsk." Although such extreme retribution was no longer exacted in the nineteenth century, petitioning the tsar remained forbidden, and an 1845 law provided that "for presenting illegal complaints against their pomeshchiki, serfs will be subjected to up to fifty blows with birch switches."[67]

Nevertheless, walkers continued to arrive in St. Petersburg, where they would lie in wait along routes the tsar was known to frequent and at the monarch's approach fall on their knees, bow their heads to the ground, and present their petitions. The known number of such complaints increased from an annual average of 14.5 during the years 1796–1825 to 21.2 during the period 1826–49, before settling back to 16.8 during the preemancipation years 1850–56. When serfs complained to the tsar it was because they felt enormous provocation. In 1797, for example, the 301 souls of Atrada village in Saratov province wrote Paul detailing the oppression they suffered under their new owner N. V. Smirnov. Having taken away all their land, he imposed continuous seigneurial labor on men, women, and children so that "we do not even have our holidays and Sundays." The petition went on to elaborate numerous abuses, including overwork of pregnant women to the extent that "many . . . gave birth to dead babies, and in one summer 10 women miscarried" and three died. "Have pity on us, great sovereign emperor," implored the desperate serfs.[68]

Curiously, although appeals to the tsar were illegal, they were routinely forwarded to provincial authorities for consideration; at the provincial level these complaints occasionally prompted investigations of abuses but were usually declared "unfounded" or were lost in the shuffle of official reports, inquiries, and memoranda. The walkers themselves were sometimes sent away but were more often detained briefly and then returned home under guard for local punishment. That peasants continued to appeal to the crown in the face of such response is powerful testimony to the strength of their naive monarchism. It is also indicative of the degree to which, unlike American slaves, the serfs considered themselves part of society; they seriously hoped their petitions would bring about redress of their grievances.

Only the most desperate peasants, however, went through the difficult (and often expensive) process of petitioning the tsar. More numerous were complaints to other officials, occasionally prominent national figures such as the minister of internal affairs but usually provincial or district authorities. In Saratov province, for example, serfs sent at least 198 collective petitions to provincial or local officials between 1826 and 1860; of these, the great majority went to the governor, provincial marshal of nobility, or district marshal of nobility. Questions of authority loomed especially large in such complaints. In July 1837 twenty-one serfs in Vologda province complained to the governor that their steward, F. A. Trubachev, treated them cruelly and "without the permission of our owner" forced them to perform continuous seigneurial labor; "he has not given us one day for ourselves to cultivate our own plots," they lamented. The petitioners were evidently mistaken, however, in their assertion that the steward was acting without seigneurial permission, for their owner, Varvara Petrova Auerbakh, sent the starosta a blistering reproach: "I told you, beast, about carrying out the orders of Fedor Aleksandrovich [Trubachev] as if they were my own, and for your disobedience you will be severely punished." Two years later Trubachev had somehow acquired the estate as his own and a new petition to the governor bitterly denounced the former steward, "however he became our master," for his many cruelties.[69]

Most common of all were petitions to pomeshchiki. Some of these consisted of individual requests for small favors. In 1660, for example, Frolko Anan'in, who had been selected for military service, petitioned his owner B. I. Morozov to have someone else chosen in his place, explaining that "I have an old mother, a brother without a leg, and another little one with no one to feed him"; the nobleman obliged by having someone else sent. House servants—who were more often literate than other serfs and were isolated from the peasant commune—were especially likely to send individual petitions.[70]

But most petitions to pomeshchiki were, like those to officials, communal ventures. Many noblemen encouraged such petitions—especially when the performance of stewards was at issue—and on some estates serfs responded with barrages of complaints. In 1850 a group of peasants in Simbirsk province, headed by their starosta, petitioned their owner Countess Bobrinskaia, complaining, as they not infrequently did, of poverty and crop failure and requesting permission to delay their obrok payments. They also asked her to standardize their obligations, promising that in turn they would "forever pay our obrok without arrears" and reassuring her that "if you are unsure of this we pledge together, one for another." They concluded, "Should we receive your favor we shall beg for your health from the highest creator." On some noblemen's holdings such petitions required considerable expenditures of time and effort on the part of the seigneurial administration; during the decade 1826–36 Prince Vorontsov's Moscow office received about two thousand formal complaints from his far-flung estates. Clearly, the serfs' naive monarchism was to some degree tempered by their recognition of where concrete power over their lives actually lay.[71]

Slaves in the United States South also complained about their treatment or condition. As in Russia, some planters explicitly encouraged their people to report on the activities of overseers, but pleas for protection against the arbitrary behavior of hirers and overseers were common whether or not slaveowners specifically allowed them. As in Russia, too, slave entreaties continued despite the generally negative response they received. Frederick Douglass, for example, fled to his owner from "slave breaker" Edward Covey, begging for protection from the overwork and beatings to which he was subjected, but his master promptly sent him back to Covey with a scolding. Similarly, in 1833 two slaves from James K. Polk's absentee-owned plantation in Fayette county, Tennessee, sought protection from a cruel overseer by seeking refuge with Polk's brother-in-law A. O. Harris, more than a hundred miles away in Columbia; one of them, Ben, refused to go home, insisting, as Harris reported to Polk, that "he relys on your promise of keeping him here, of selling or hireing him in this county." At first the prospects for Ben looked promising. Harris was sympathetic with his plight and believed his tales of abuse at the hands of overseer Ephraim Beanland; therefore, "sooner than send him back confined (where he would not have staid perhaps if we had got him there) I have hired him at the Iron Works at $100 per year." But when the semiliterate Beanland, understandably upset at the flouting of his authority, complained to Polk "I think that haris done rong," Polk backed up his overseer, ordering the unhappy slave returned home.[72]

There were basic differences, however, in the form of the complaints issued by American slaves and Russian serfs. The slaves rarely wrote formal petitions. True, there were a tiny number of written appeals, such as the one Caesar Brown sent to his new mistress in 1830. Brown asserted that his former owner had promised to free him and begged his new one to "consider my Master's promise which you know to be true"; at the very least, he urged, "I beg you so far to indulge me as to lower the price at which I am valued and I will try to purchase my own freedom." But such epistles were highly unusual, because most slaves not only were illiterate but also lacked access to a sympathetic person who could pen an appeal for them. Similarly, the slaves' complaints were almost always directed toward an owner or individual they hoped would intercede with an owner, not a government official (and certainly not the president). Outsiders to the body politic, American slaves lacked any equivalent of the serfs' naive monarchism that enabled them to believe that the tsar was really on their side.[73]

Southern slaves lacked any tradition associated with petitioning that gave it legitimacy as a form of protest deserving response from above. There was no mechanism such as the mir gathering whereby the slaves could formalize their complaints and no governmental body to which they could look for help. Slave petitions were thus largely informal complaints of individuals to owners or their representatives and usually dealt with individual problems. When Frances Anne Kemble, the English wife of Georgia rice planter Pierce Butler, spent a year on her husband's estate, she found herself besieged by humble petitioners—mostly female—begging small favors. Although Butler told her to stop bringing him complaints, "as the people had hitherto had no such advocate, and had done very well without," the entreaties continued: "*Fanny* has had six children; all dead but one. She came to beg to have her work in the field lightened . . . *Sophy,* Lewis's wife, came to beg for some old linen . . . The principal favor she asked was a piece of meat, which I gave her." And so on.[74]

The bondsmen's petitions thus confirm the contrast between forms of protest that were predominantly collective in Russia and individual in the United States. Although this contrast stemmed primarily from differences between the world of the slaves and that of the serfs, one might also suggest that it reflected more general cultural differences between America and Russia: the slaves' behavior was characteristic of an individualistic society in which local initiative was widespread, whereas that of the serfs was shaped by a bureaucratically organized society in which individual action was discouraged. Just as the slaves and serfs adopted very different forms of struggle, their owners—and the political authorities—met the challenges very differently too. The Russian reaction to a volnenie was at every step a bureaucratic one. The distressed pomeshchik or his steward turned for help to the district ispravnik, who in turn constantly reported to and received instructions from higher officials through a regular chain of command. An enormous amount of give-and-take—bargaining, threatening, and cajoling of peasants—occurred over a period that could last months or even years. Slave insubordination in the United States, on the other hand, called forth an immediate, on-the-spot response by planter, overseer, or slave patrol. Except in extreme cases governmental authorities were not even notified. It is highly unlikely that, had the slaves on a southern plantation staged the kind of strike that was so common in Russia, either slaveowners or governmental authorities would have tolerated a situation in which the confrontation remained unresolved for months. In short, for all their obvious differences, the bondsmen shared certain traits with the masters in each country that indicate the degree to which the slaves and serfs absorbed the dominant culture of the society in which they lived: in ways they might not have entirely recognized, American slaves were profoundly American and Russian serfs profoundly Russian.

*   *   *

MORE COMMON THAN small-scale confrontations—indeed, the most widespread and characteristic form of resistance on the part of the bondsmen—was flight. Giving the lie to all claims of their contentment in servitude, slaves and serfs "voted with their feet" for freedom. Like local confrontations, flight serves as an extremely revealing type of resistance, both because it occurred so often and because it constituted a clear repudiation of thralldom. And like the confrontations, the flight of slaves and serfs reveals a common determination to escape oppression as well as significant differences in the way they expressed that determination.

In Russia, as we have seen, peasant flight had gone hand in hand with the process of enserfment; indeed, the initial binding of peasants to the land was undertaken largely to maintain an adequate labor force in the face of the widespread depopulation of central Russia. The prohibition of movement, however, did not prevent peasants from running away. Absentee proprietors found it all but impossible to stem the exodus that enserfment was designed to prevent; a series of petitions from noblemen to the tsar in the second half of the seventeenth century reveals that those returning home from military service sometimes found their estates all but deserted. In 1657, for example, a group of close to one hundred pomeshchiki from Galich and nearby cities explained to the tsar that while they were serving him in wars against Poland and Lithuania, their serfs ran away, looting and pillaging as they went; the distressed landholders begged the "merciful lord tsar and great prince" to help them regain their fugitives, "so that we, your slaves, will not in the end perish from these ruiners and leave abandoned your royal service." To combat this monumental problem, the government responded by instituting a series of formal searches during the second half of the seventeenth and early eighteenth centuries, despatching officials on armed expeditions to track down fugitives and return them to their rightful owners.[75]

Although such searches succeeded in locating some missing serfs and no doubt intimidated others contemplating escape, large-scale flight continued. Inventories of noble estates in the early eighteenth century listed numerous peasant households as "empty" with the explanation that their inhabitants were "in flight." Although statistics on the number of fugitives are inevitably imprecise, those available suggest the extent of the problem: during the years 1727–42, 327,046 serfs fled their homes. On some estates most or even all of the peasants disappeared.[76]

An examination of flight among Prince A. M. Cherkasskii's serfs—based on a fascinating study by historian K. N. Shchepetov—graphically illustrates the scope and process of peasant flight during the first half of the eighteenth century. A wealthy nobleman with numerous far-flung estates, Cherkasskii was so plagued by runaways that he petitioned the Senate to create a special search commission to track them down; the commission, headed by an officer of the famed Preobrazhenskii regiment, was formed in 1732. By 1734 he had located 11,467 fugitives from Cherkasskii's holdings, who constituted more than 16 percent of the nobleman's serfs. Although they were forcibly returned home, most soon disappeared again, usually winding up in precisely the same places they had first sought shelter; in 1739, 5,861 were captured and sent home for a second time.[77]

Cherkasskii's fugitives almost invariably headed east and southeast, setting themselves up as state peasants in the sparsely settled lands of Kazan and Voronezh provinces. An extraordinary degree of organization surrounded their flight; not only did whole households flee together—significantly, the number of women almost matched the number of men among the fugitives, 5,446 to 6,021—but entire villages typically migrated en masse, leaving and settling together in new surroundings. Indeed, 8,481 of the runaways located themselves in three large villages in Kazan and Voronezh. The decision to flee was thus a communal not an individual one, and flight resulted in the reconstitution rather than the destruction of familial and communal ties. Although a few of Cherkasskii's escapees struck out on their own, hiring themselves out at various jobs, seeking refuge with other pomeshchiki, or merging with the state peasantry, 86.8 percent of the fugitives went in groups to previously selected villages, where advance parties had already prepared for their arrival, sometimes even buying land from nearby pomeshchiki. Most often, however, they settled on previously unused land, where they established new communities in which they passed as state peasants. Village leaders, headed by the starosta, usually organized the flight and continued to fulfill their traditional functions in the newly established communities.[78]

Although not all flight was so systematically organized, in general collective action was central to the process. In 1692–93 a search of a newly settled region revealed that of 480 fugitives, 89.3 percent had fled in families or larger groups and two-thirds had managed to elude their owners for more than ten years. A typical petition of noblemen to the tsar in 1681 complained that their serfs were fleeing to the borderlands in groups of "a hundred and more," leaving their villages deserted; "they go boldly day and night, gathering long trains of carts," complained the aggrieved landowners, who described the pillage that their estates suffered at the hands of the departing peasants.[79]

A number of factors facilitated massive group flight, especially in the seventeenth and eighteenth centuries. Most basic was the relative ease with which serfs could move in a largely peasant world, where authorities were few and far between and owners typically absent for long periods of time. The frequency with which noblemen's requests for searches began with assertions of how their serfs fled while they were away in military service indicates the impact of such absenteeism on peasant flight. Almost as important was the availability of unsettled land, mostly in the south and east, to which fugitives could flee. Tens of thousands joined the cossacks, and others settled as state peasants in the southern steppes and Siberia. This flight was greatly facilitated by divisions within the landowning class and the government itself, divisions that led southern pomeshchiki and government officials surreptitiously to welcome fugitive peasants well into the eighteenth century. In the western provinces serfs sometimes fled across the Polish border.[80]

Not all flight was to the borderlands. Some fugitives stayed relatively near their homes, finding odd jobs in nearby towns, working as barge-haulers on rivers, seeking protection from pomeshchiki in need of labor, or living on their own, undetected, for prolonged periods of time. In a search of one section of Vladimir district in 1665–66, more than two hundred armed guards rounded up fifty-five Old Believers—men, women, and children—who had taken to the woods and eked out a meager existence for themselves for years. Sometimes, too, serfs who were given passes to be away from their estates overstayed the time allotted to them, returning either late or never. An imperial decree of 1736, noting that Peter I had fifteen years earlier ordered all fugitives subjected to "cruel punishment with the knout," distinguished between long-term runaways and those who "instigated by foolishness flee for whatever small reason, but then repent and return within a short time"; the latter, "according to natural law, can be punished less." Still, the decree concluded, all fugitives should be "subjected to punishment with the knout or cat o'nine tails, whip or batogi."[81]

Fugitive serfs sometimes joined together in roving bands (referred to in government documents as "robbers," "villains," or "brigands") ranging from a handful to more than fifty persons, wreaking havoc on noble property and making life dangerous for merchants and other travelers. Usually heavily armed, they operated on "cossack" principles, under the leadership of an elected starosta or ataman, making their camps in the woods or other deserted locations and sallying forth at night to seek sustenance for themselves and mete out vengeance on hated pomeshchiki and officials. "Partisan detachments," as they have been termed by Soviet historians, spanned a broad spectrum, from groups of fugitives who defended themselves when pursued to rebels who consciously struck at the bases of the serf order by attacking noble property (and sometimes noblemen themselves) and destroying records, but their existence depended to some extent at least on the support they received from the peasant population at large. Often short-lived groups that came together in the spring and summer when living off the land was easiest, they were especially prevalent when and where government security was weakest—in thinly settled lands to the south and east, in time of war and famine—but no region was totally immune from them in the seventeenth and early eighteenth centuries. Brigandage declined in the late eighteenth and early nineteenth centuries, when government communication improved and administration strengthened, although even then there occurred numerous minor acts of "pillage and robbery" by small groups of peasants.[82]

During the last century of serfdom peasants continued to flee from their owners in massive numbers and continued to pursue an essentially collective strategy in the process. The destination of their flight was not precisely the same as earlier; some areas that had served as refuges for fugitives were now settled with landed estates, and the tightening of class lines sharply reduced the number of noblemen willing to shelter other landlords' escapees. Still, even in central Russia the terrain contained abundant woods, marshes, and rivers that beckoned unhappy serfs, and the sparsely settled southern and eastern periphery continued to provide rich opportunities for life on the run. Equally important, serfdom itself still generated the same kind of peasant flight that was largely communal in conception and execution.

Even as provinces such as Voronezh and Tambov, to which peasants had fled in the seventeenth and early eighteenth centuries, became settled with serf-run estates, other areas, such as Siberia, continued to receive runaways, and new territories opened up. One of the most important of these was "New Russia," bordering on the Black Sea in the far south. The male population of three New-Russian provinces of Ekaterinoslav, Kherson, and Tauride grew from 67,730 in 1763 to 1,127,904 in 1834. Although some of this increase was due to colonization of serfs by pomeshchiki as well as settlement by diverse nationalities including Bulgars, Moldavians, Greeks, Jews, and Germans, much of it stemmed from the flight there of serfs from the Ukrainian provinces immediately to the north, and throughout the late eighteenth and first half of the nineteenth centuries those held as serfs constituted only slightly more than one-third of New Russia's peasant population. Even many peasants who worked on seigneurial land there were able to maintain an unusual degree of personal freedom. In 1796 Emperor Paul, noting that "free movement of settlers from place to place" in New Russia was causing great disorder, decreed that "each settler stay in that place and rank under which he is listed in the current census," fixed financial penalties for harboring fugitives, and ordered runaway serfs found in state villages sent into the army. But the problem remained largely uncorrected. As the leading student of the region has noted, in the first quarter of the nineteenth century "the overwhelming majority of settlers did not allow themselves to be enserfed, kept their rights and even preserved for themselves . . . a real independence." [83]

Despite a vastly expanded administrative apparatus, the government was no more able to keep serfs at home during the century preceding emancipation than it had been earlier. In 1845 the Ministry of Internal Affairs introduced a policy of branding fugitives and vagrants "by special instruments (expressly ordered for this from England) with the mark of the letter B. (for *brodiaga* [vagrant] or *beglyi* [fugitive]) on the right hand"; in 1846, 939 persons were branded, and in 1847 the number swelled to 3,553. That year, the Ministry reported, spurred by "various lying stories and rumors," more than eleven thousand serfs fled from their owners, many "in flights of almost entire villages." This figure, however, counted only the most blatant cases of large-scale group flight; as before, many serfs engaged in temporary visits to the woods, and others overstayed terms of legitimate absences for which they had been given passes, sometimes returning late but often using the allowed absence—and the accompanying pass—to make good a permanent escape. Peasants even ran away from the army, an offense that the government regarded as particularly heinous and strove to combat in the 1830s by launching a propaganda campaign praising mothers for turning in their fugitive sons and awarding the informers special silver medals with the inscription "for diligence." "Honor and praise to the conscientious peasant woman," extolled a leading agricultural journal, "for carrying out the law and duty of their tsar!"[84]

In short, the original goal of enserfment—prohibition of peasant movement—remained as elusive as ever. In fact, during the last decades of serfdom, prompted in part by rumors and hopes of emancipation, organized peasant flight grew increasingly problematical for authorities. Ever since the seventeenth century legends of "distant lands" of freedom had circulated among the peasantry, based at least in part on the very real possibilities open to fugitives on the southern and eastern frontiers, but in the first half of the nineteenth century these took on an increasingly utopian—and urgent—character. In the spring of 1825, for example, thousands of serfs fled from their estates along the Volga River in search of a supposedly rich land at a nonexistent "Dar'ia River," where the government was said to be allowing free settlement. The legend spread quickly, carried by roving rumormongers, and soon streams of migrants—many evidently "scouts, commissioned by village communes, after whom their villagers were prepared to resettle"—headed east. It took seven 500-man regiments of soldiers to apprehend 2,813 fugitives in the Urals, but others doubtless escaped capture.[85]

Similar rumors and mass migrations reappeared with increasing frequency during the decades preceding emancipation. In 1837 a group of pomeshchiki from one district of Voronezh province complained to the minister of internal affairs that their serfs were escaping to Anapa, a newly annexed fortified city on the eastern shore of the Black Sea, where they expected—and evidently sometimes found—willing acceptance by local authorities. "These flights . . . threaten to devastate landed estates," wailed the alarmed noblemen. Special military barricades trapped more than fifteen hundred of the fugitives, but mass defections of serfs seeking freedom continued. A number of collective migrations occurred in 1847. In Vitebsk province, in the northwest, rumors spread that the tsar would free anyone reaching neighboring Pskov province, and ten thousand serfs eagerly set off in April and May; most were stopped by soldiers and eventually returned home. That same year rumors that the government had invited serfs to resettle as free peasants in the Caucasus led to large-scale flight—sometimes of entire villages—from Saratov, Kursk, and Voronezh provinces. When stopped by pursuing soldiers in Voronezh province, seventy-five fugitives from a common estate in Kursk prov-

ince teamed up with local serfs to attack their pursuers and then—
urged on by two priests—to demand "delivery to them of an ukaz
concerning freedom"; only through "severe measures" did a specially
despatched command subdue the resisters.[86]

Flight from Saratov province to the nearby Caucasus took on an
especially persistent character. Temporarily curtailed after a massive
breakout in 1847, peasant departures reerupted in strength in 1850,
fueled by stories that the Tsarevich Alexander planned to abolish serfdom when he inherited the throne and was in the meantime encouraging serfs to resettle in the Caucasus. "There are even some villages,"
reported an official sent to investigate, "where only decrepit women
and disabled old men remain," and these few remnants "stubbornly
refuse any information on their fugitive relatives"; all five hundred
serfs from the estate of one unfortunate nobleman disappeared.
Equally interesting were the "secrecy and continued success" of the
escapes, which were carried off "as if according to a systematic, well-
considered plan inaccessible to detection by the usual means at the
disposal of the local police." The provincial governor, also noting
considerable evidence of planning and coordination on the part of the
fugitives, reprimanded local landowners and their agents, suggesting
that they should have been able "through good peasants to learn of
the intentions and preparations" of the conspirators. Although such
discovery proved difficult, one policeman was finally able to secure
some information by bribing a serf.[87]

From the late 1840s mass migration of serfs grasping at rumors of
freedom grew so widespread as to suggest an impending breakdown
of the social order. This movement reached its culmination in 1854–
55, during the Crimean war, when tens of thousands of serfs left to
volunteer for military service under the belief that they and their families would be freed. The exodus, prompted by a combination of patriotism, a desire to escape serfdom, misunderstanding of an imperial
call for a general levy, and the spreading of "lying rumors" by peasants and priests, was especially widespread in the southern provinces
but occurred throughout the empire. Many serfs flocked to Moscow,
where they were detained and then sent home in large groups under
military guard, while others crowded the country's roads and descended on provincial capitals, seeking to enlist. Although officials
warned that instigators would be treated "with the full severity of the
law, and all others will be sent back to their place of residence," the
tide continued. In Tambov province the marshal of nobility reported
that the flight was not only "growing stronger day by day" but was

having "harmful consequences, as those families staying in their houses, declaring themselves free, refuse obedience to seigneurial authorities." In widely scattered localities in the 1850s serfs became convinced that they would soon be free and seemed ready to act on the basis of virtually any rumor promising that freedom. One official lamented, "It is incomprehensible how gullible our people are!"[88]

American slaves, too, showed from the beginning a strong determination to run away. Despite the passage of severe laws designed to discourage flight—laws that in eighteenth-century Virginia and South Carolina provided for bodily mutilation or castration of repeat offenders—numerous blacks ran away, sometimes receiving help from other slaves. Landon Carter was distressed to find that his trusted gardener Johnny had harbored two fugitives for whom he had been searching in vain; typically, Carter marveled at the duplicity of his apparently faithful slave, noting that although "John[n]y is the most constant churchgoer I have . . . he is a drunkard, a thief and a rogue." For Carter, as for so many slaveowners, flight was the most pervasive and troubling of the many annoyances that interrupted normal plantation routine.[89]

Fugitive slaves sought refuge in a wide variety of places. As in Russia, the sparsely populated countryside provided easy hiding for runaways, who took to the local forests and swamps in impressive numbers. Others sought out loved ones on neighboring holdings or escaped to urban areas where they could either temporarily or permanently merge with the free black population. Others still fled beyond their colony's borders. Hundreds of slaves from South Carolina and Georgia crossed into Spanish Florida, where they found haven either with the Spanish or the Seminole Indians, and others secured refuge among the Creeks. Thousands of slaves took advantage of the Revolutionary War to escape from bondage, many fleeing to the British, who—in order to strike at the base of the rebellion—encouraged precisely such desertion.[90]

In the antebellum period a new goal beckoned fugitives: freedom in the North (and beyond, in Canada). Although legends of the underground railroad, with "conductors" who guided the slaves on their trek and "stations" where sympathetic whites and blacks sheltered them along the way, have been greatly exaggerated, tens of thousands of slaves eluded pursuers and escaped the South during the half-century preceding emancipation, and tens of thousands more tried. Most of the successful fugitives settled in the northern free states, where they struggled to support themselves in the face of intense racial hostility. Some, especially after the passage of a more stringent fugitive slave law in 1850 propelled fears among northern blacks of forcible return to slavery, sought sanctuary in Canada. But however difficult life was for free blacks in the North and Canada, to them—and to the millions of blacks who remained in the South—it was far preferable to slavery. As fugitive Benedict Duncan put it, "I had rather have a day free, than a week of life in slavery: I think that slavery is the worst evil that ever was."[91]

Slaves used an ingenious variety of methods to escape. Perhaps the easiest was to forge, borrow, steal, or otherwise secure a pass. J. W. Loguen and a friend each paid a sympathetic nonslaveholding white $10 for free papers, stole horses, and took off from their Alabama plantation on Christmas eve, when they were least likely to be missed; they traveled as free blacks, sometimes even staying at inns, although they had to fight off two groups of hostile whites on their way to freedom. Frederick Douglass borrowed the sailor's papers of a friend and traveled as a free black, taking a train from Baltimore to Wilmington and a boat from there to Philadelphia. Charles Ball stowed away on a ship. Some slaves showed enormous ingenuity and persistence, escaping a number of times, either because their first attempt was unsuccessful or because they returned for loved ones. John Moore, for example, ran away twice from Kentucky, returning for his wife after the first flight, "declaring at the same time that he was sick of freedom" so as to conceal his intent from his master.[92]

But most fugitives escaped on foot, traveled by night and slept in the woods by day, and were properly leery of both whites and blacks. As William Wells Brown later explained, "the slave is brought up to look upon every white man as an enemy . . . and twenty-one years in slavery had taught me that there were traitors even among colored people." Although some runaways received help—food, lodgings, directions—from slaves and free blacks, others found, as did Douglass the first time he tried to escape, that insufficient caution led to betrayal and reenslavement. Many fugitives were forced, with widely varying results, to deal with pursuers; some were caught and returned home, but others convinced suspicious whites of their free status, physically repelled posses, or escaped again after being captured. James W. C. Pennington escaped twice after being captured by whites on his way to Pennsylvania. James Curry and his two brothers separated when they were pursued after fleeing from North Carolina; Curry succeeded in reaching Washington, D.C., but he never saw his brothers again.[93]

Despite the heroism of those who defied the odds and escaped slavery, relatively few fugitives were able to reach the North. The great majority of these were from the upper South, where the proximity of free states beckoned and rendered the perilous journey more feasible; Kentucky, which shared a long border with the North separated only by the Ohio River, saw an especially large number of runaways. But for the vast majority of slaves in the deep South and most in the upper South as well, the obstacles to successful flight were overwhelming. Southern slaves faced much less favorable conditions than Russian serfs when it came to running away. The low ratio of blacks to whites, the small and dispersed nature of slaveholdings, the resident character of the masters, and the firm political control exercised by the slaveholding regime all combined to restrict sharply the slaves' freedom of movement. It was easier for serfs who lived in a largely peasant world to elude would-be pursuers than it was for slaves who lived in a largely white world. During the late antebellum period perhaps one thousand slaves per year reached the North.[94]

The unfavorable conditions faced by southern fugitives did not eliminate the efforts of slaves to run away; these conditions did, however, shape the nature of their flight in two significant ways. First, because fleeing to the North was so difficult, most fugitives remained in the general vicinity of their homes. Although occasionally they were able to reach nearby cities or enjoy lengthy stretches at large, most returned home—voluntarily or not—after a relatively short time; the most prevalent type of flight was not only of a local but also of a temporary nature.

This basic pattern was set early. On 24 June 1710 Virginia planter William Byrd wrote in his diary that on returning home after a short absence "I found all well except that a negro woman and seven cattle were gone." The following day she was still missing, although other slaves "found her hoe by the church land," but on 28 June "the negro woman was found again." Three days later she disappeared once more, wearing a punitive bit that Byrd ordered fastened to the mouths of troublemakers; this time she was gone a week when Byrd reported that she "was found and tied but ran away again in the night." Not all fugitives were so persistent, but the diaries of other colonial planters, like Byrd's, reveal the widespread nature of this sort of local temporary flight. Time after time slaves would take to the woods, sometimes returning after a few days of their own accord and sometimes necessitating a search costly in time, effort, and aggravation.[95]

In the antebellum period this kind of temporary flight continued to be commonplace, and on some holdings so pervasive as to threaten the orderly conducting of plantation routine. Take, for example, Louisiana planter Bennet H. Barrow's diary, which is filled with entries such as the following:

[22 Sept. 1838] Tom Beauf picked badly yesterday morning[;] whiped him. few Cuts—left the field some time in the evening without his Cotton and have not seen him since—He is in the habit of doing so yearly.

[28 Sept. 1838] Dennis and Tom "*Beauf*" ran off on Wednesday—Dennis came in yesterday morning after I went hunting. "Sick"—left the Sick House this morning—if I can see either of them and have a gun at the time will let them have the contents of it—Dennis returned to the Sick House at dinner.

[12 Oct. 1838] Tom Beauf came up and put his Basket down at the scales and it is the last I've seen of him . . . .

Although not all slaveowners were so bloodthirsty as Barrow, most suffered from the same kind of truancy. "Notwithstanding the certainty of being captured, the woods and swamps are, nevertheless, continually filled with runaways," explained Solomon Northup. "Many of them, when sick, or so worn out as to be unable to perform their tasks, escape into the swamps, willing to suffer the punishment inflicted for such offences, in order to obtain a day or two of rest." Fifty-three slaves ran away from James H. Hammond's Silver Bluff plantation between 1831 and 1853, but none succeeded in securing more than temporary liberty; two-thirds were apprehended while one-third returned home on their own, after an average absence of forty-nine days.[96]

Less frequently, local flight resulted in long-term or even permanent freedom. A few slaves made their way to cities and merged with the free colored population there. Others hid out in woods and swamps for prolonged periods. An ex-slave from Virginia remembered how her father ran away after a beating and stayed in the woods, returning home surreptitiously on weekends: "never did ketch him, though ole Marse search real sharp." Others told similar stories of those who had eked out livings in the woods for years, hunting, trapping, and stealing from local farms, and sometimes slipping back home for regular visits. One recalled a runaway who built a "vault" in the forest and lived there until emancipation with his wife and two sons. "All us slaves knew whar he wuz," he related. "Yas, yas, I don' et many er good meal of victuals in Bob's den."[97]

Equally significant was the predominantly individual character of slave flight. Fear of capture dictated that it was safest to travel alone or in very small groups, revealing one's plans to no one unless necessary. The difficulty of movement for southern blacks thus served to reinforce their noncollective ethos.

Not all slaves traveled alone or shunned other slaves. Historian Gerald Mullin found that in eighteenth-century Virginia newly imported slaves, who had not yet lost their communal African culture, sometimes "ran off in groups or attempted to establish villages of runaways on the frontier," whereas those born in America "nearly always ran off alone," a finding generally confirmed by Philip D. Morgan for South Carolina. In times of disorder, such as the American Revolution (and later the Civil War), groups of slaves took advantage of white division and disorganization by fleeing en masse. Even in ordinary times small bands sometimes traveled together; historian Michael P. Johnson located 351 advertisements in Charleston newspapers for groups of two or more fugitives between 1799 and 1830. Sometimes husbands and wives fled together, occasionally even taking with them small children, and other fugitives joined one or more friends in their break for freedom. Very occasionally, slaves escaped in large groups, although such travel was feasible only when the distance to be traveled was extremely short; as a youth, Horace W. Hawkins escaped across the Ohio River with thirteen other slaves from two holdings in Kentucky. And individual runaways often received help from other slaves, who sheltered and fed them during their flight.[98]

Clearly, then, there was cooperation among slaves in their efforts to escape from bondage. In two important respects, however, their flight lacked the communal features displayed by fugitive serfs. The most obvious of these was the overwhelmingly individual and small-group character of slave flight. The majority of fugitives escaped alone; less often they traveled in pairs, and much less often in small groups. Daniel Meaders' study of newspaper advertisements for eighteenth-century South Carolina fugitives found 2,001 runaways listed in 1,806 notices, for an average of 1.11 fugitive per escape; Michael P. Johnson's study, which examined only groups of two or more fugitives from South Carolina between 1799 and 1830, found that 70 percent of these groups consisted of two slaves each. Unlike Russian serfs, who usually fled in families, southern slave runaways were typically single men between the ages of 16 and 35. Fully 76.6 percent of the fugitives listed in the South Carolina *Gazette* between 1730 and 1787 and 88.3 percent of those listed in the Virginia *Gazette* were males. Indeed, although slaves occasionally ran away in family groups, more often flight separated family members—a fact that no doubt served as a major deterrent to running away. A number of fugitives later described the anguish that their escapes caused them. As Henry Atkinson, who left a wife and child in Norfolk, Virginia, put it, "It went hard to leave my wife; it was like taking my heart's blood: but I could not help it—I expected to be taken away where I should never see her again, and so I concluded it would be right to leave her ... I never expect to see her again in this world—nor our child." [99]

Even more important, whether slaves ran away singly, in pairs, or in small groups, their flight was the result of individual, not collective, decision making. Virtually never did *all* the slaves on an estate flee together, as in Russia. Nor was there any equivalent to the kind of communal planning that was frequently an integral part of the serfs' flight. An examination of fugitives' autobiographies and narratives reveals the extent to which each regarded the choice to run away as that of an individual apart from, not in concert with, the slave community at large. "I really loved my master," wrote Charles Ball, "but I had already determined that as soon as he was in his grave, I would attempt to escape from Georgia." Because of cruel treatment he received as a house servant in Memphis, Louis Hughes related, "I made up my mind to try and run away to a free country." David Barrett made up his mind to flee when his master threatened him with a whipping, and James W. Sumler recalled that "after I got to years of maturity, and saw white people sitting in the shade, while I worked in the sun, I thought I would like to be my own man." [100]

Slave flight thus reflected the largely noncollective character of slave life evident in other forms of resistance. A final confirmation of this pattern is suggested by the relative insignificance of maroon colonies in the Old South. True, runaways did sometimes band together in efforts to live off the land. When Octave Johnson fled his Louisiana home he lived for one-and-a-half years with an unusually large group of "outlyers." "Before I left our number had increased to thirty," he later recalled, "of whom ten were women." Making camp only four miles from his master's estate, Johnson and his comrades stole most of their food and managed to elude capture even though "often those at work would betray those in the swamp, for fear of being implicated in their escape." Elsewhere, too, groups of slaves lived together in remote swampy areas, surviving on what they could hunt, trap, and pillage. [101]

Runaway colonies were never more than a minor irritant, however, to southern slaveholders. Usually located in isolated areas—such as the Dismal Swamp along the border between North Carolina and Virginia, the bayous of southern Louisiana, and the swamp lands of northern Florida—maroons were relatively inaccessible to most southern blacks (and far enough removed from most plantations to receive little attention). They declined in number during the antebellum years, as the South became more settled and once-remote areas felt the press of civilization. Even in the eighteenth century, however, they were almost always small and lacked both the organization and stability of maroons in other slave societies. As Genovese put it, "The runaways . . . typically huddled in small units and may be called 'maroons' only as a courtesy."[102]

The weakness of southern runaway colonies appears most starkly when they are contrasted with the maroon societies that existed in Brazil, Jamaica, Surinam, and to a lesser extent Spanish and French America. These colonies of fugitives were characterized first by their large size and long duration; although the Brazilian community Palmares was unusual in surviving for ninety years with a population that approached twenty thousand, maroons elsewhere contained hundreds of members who managed to fend off military attacks for decades, sometimes negotiating elaborate treaties with their would-be destroyers. Equally important was the complex political organization that these colonies developed, often based at least in part on traditional African practices, with their own kings, military discipline, and internal social stratification. In essence, they constituted nations in exile.[103]

Historians have usually explained the lack of major maroon colonies in the United States as a function of unfavorable terrain. This explanation, however, appears only partly satisfying, because in a purely physical sense the South, a relatively sparsely settled region with large wilderness areas, should have provided an environment by no means entirely hostile to the emergence of maroons. In short, the South's unfavorable environment was far more than just geographic. The limited character of southern marronage is but another indication of the difficult conditions faced by slaves seeking to engage in communal endeavors and of the generally noncollective manner in which they responded to their bondage.

*   *   *

ALTHOUGH DIFFERENCES in form are most striking when analyzing slave and serf resistance, equally significant are similarities in effect and implication. The bondsmen were not merely passive objects who suffered the brutalities imposed on them in silence; rather, on a continuing basis they challenged the actions and thereby the authority of their owners. In the process, they helped to define the nature of class relationships as well as the nature of their own society.

Of the major types of resistance, large-scale rebellions had the least salutary impact on the lives of the bondsmen—a fact that goes far toward explaining their relative infrequency. Because organized rebellions constituted threats not only to individual masters but to the social order at large, the responses they elicited showed little of the ambiguity that followed other forms of resistance. Revolts invariably met with brutal repression and led to the passage of stringent new legislation designed to forestall future outbreaks as well as to more rigorous enforcement of existing regulations. Although they did leave a legacy of pride among the bondsmen in the heroic deeds of their comrades and ancestors, their most immediate and concrete aftermath was repression and suffering.[104]

The consequences of flight and local confrontations, by contrast, were totally unpredictable. Fugitives found that running away could produce a broad range of possible results, from permanent escape to speedy capture and punishment. If those who managed to escape faced uncertain and varied futures, those who were unsuccessful or who sought only temporary respite from the rigors of bondage also found that their flight produced variable and unpredictable consequences. A few were killed in the process of recapture, and many more received corporal punishment or were sold. When Thomas Jefferson recovered Jame Hubbard, a slave who had repeatedly run away, he "had him severely flogged in the presence of his old companions, and committed to jail"; the former president then decided to sell the slave, since "the moment he is out of jail and his irons off he will be off himself." But such harsh retribution was by no means universal. Beverly Jones described his uncle as "one nigger dat was always runnin' away" but recalled him as a "favored nigger" who was rarely whipped for his escapades. Many other runaways, too, received only mild chastisement or none at all—especially if they returned home voluntarily—either because they were favored or because their masters or overseers considered punishing them not worth the effort. The same variation existed in Russia. Some pomeshchiki, like Bezobrazov, ordered their stewards to beat fugitives with the knout "in front of all the peasants," but others prescribed corporal punishment only for those who fled repeatedly, imposing fines or simple warnings on first offenders. In cases of massive group flight ringleaders were usually singled out for special interrogation and punishment, but the majority of serfs typically were sent home for less severe correction with birch switches or for verbal warnings alone.[105]

Flight also had a variable impact on those bondsmen who did not try to escape. Some owners, overseers, and stewards took out their anger at fugitives beyond their reach on slaves and serfs at hand; Barrow, for example, whose Louisiana estate was plagued by widespread temporary flight, habitually expressed his fury by holding "whipping frolicks" in which he whipped *all* his slaves. Serfs who remained behind when others fled were likely to suffer concrete economic hardship, resulting from reassignment to them of obligations formerly owed by their departed villagers. But in a more general sense all slaves and serfs benefited when some ran away, because such flight reassured those who remained that they were more than helpless objects of oppression and that they too could opt to depart should conditions warrant. It also served to restrain the conduct of the masters, who recognized, however much they might dissemble on this point, that flight stemmed at least in part from specific grievances and that exacerbating those grievances was only likely to increase their problems with runaways. In short, the very existence of widespread flight helped to modify relations between masters and bondsmen as a whole.[106]

The same was true of small-scale confrontations, which even more than flight revealed the slaves' and serfs' ability to influence their own lives. True, the immediate results of such confrontations were mixed. Bondsmen rarely won complete and decisive victories, and their ensuing treatment was unpredictable, ranging from cruel torture to real alleviation of hardships. But total defeat was never a certainty either; in many small but important ways those who challenged authority found their behavior rewarded. Indeed, as much as anything it was this unpredictability that characterized the confrontations: the same kind of challenge elicited varying responses that entailed for the challengers a wide range of consequences.

In the United States a slave who made too much trouble could find himself repeatedly whipped, sold to a new owner, even killed—or allowed to do pretty much as he pleased. "My father was sold five times," recalled one ex-slave. "Wouldn't take nothin'. So they sold him. They beat him and knocked him about. They put him on the block and they sold him 'bout beatin' up his master." Josiah Henson's father, who fought with an overseer assaulting the slave's mother, received one hundred lashes, had his "right ear nailed to the whipping-post, and then severed from the body"; when he became moody he was sold. Robert Falls also remembered his father as a "fighter" who was "so bad to fight and so troublesome he was sold four times to my knowing and maybe a heap more times." But finally one of his owners told him, "You so mean I got to sell you. You all time complaining about you dont like your white folks. Tell me now who you wants to live with. Just pick your man and I will go see him." The troublesome slave selected a man named Henry Falls (whose surname he also adopted), and "after that the white folks didnt have no more trouble with my father." [107]

Often slaveowners considered it a particular challenge to tame a "bad nigger." One method, used by Douglass's owner, was to hire the slave to a special "Negro breaker," but more often the effort was made on the plantation. William W. Brown remembered Randall, one of his master's best workers, who proudly proclaimed that no white man would ever whip him. For some time he succeeded in avoiding the lash, but one day when his owner was away the overseer and three friends cornered, shot, beat, tied, and whipped him. "When his master returned home," Brown recalled, "he was much pleased to find that Randall had been subdued in his absence." But truly "bad niggers" could rarely be tamed: they usually required constant attention, or humoring. Barrow was puzzled that the same slave family could produce four brothers, two of whom were compliant and two inveterate troublemakers; he built a special jail for the turbulent brothers (and other offending slaves) and resorted to frequent whippings and occasional more imaginative punishments, but he was never able to change their behavior.[108]

Although troublemakers often received extra punishment, abundant evidence indicates that they were frequently able to get away with a great deal, sometimes through luck, but often through working out informal agreements with their owners. One ex-slave described a fight between a master and his slave, "both recognized bullies." The owner set the ground rules: "if you lick me I'll take it as my share, and that will end it, but if I lick you, then you are to stand and receive twenty lashes." Although the master ultimately prevailed in the half-hour struggle, he "gave his whipped man but six light strokes over his vest" and "these men got along well afterwards without fighting." One of the most effective methods slaves used to gain their objectives was to play whites off against each other. After some minor unrest on one of George Noble Jones's two neighboring plantations, one overseer reported to Jones of the other that "when he Flogs he puts it on in two [*sic*] Large doses," adding, "I think Moderate Flogings the best." Before being exonerated, the criticized overseer was forced to apologize to Jones for the trouble and concede the desirability of moderate chastisement; although he remained in his position, he was no doubt careful, at least for a while, to avoid administering severe whippings.[109]

Although the tactic of playing whites off against each other did not always work, most owners were anxious to protect their slave property from mistreatment by overzealous hirers and overseers. The same concern that prompted some owners to encourage slaves to report on their overseers led others to tolerate slave defiance of abusive overseers. Martha Bradley remembered that "one day I wuz workin' in de field and de overseer he come 'roun and say sumpin' to me he had no bizness say. I took my hoe and knocked him plum down." Upon learning of her behavior, her master began to whip her, but when she told him "whut dat overseer sez to me . . . Marster Lucas didn' hit me no more. Marse Lucas wuz allus good to us and he wouldn' let nobody run over his niggers." Another ex-slave recalled an even more extreme case of resistance. After an overseer had bullwhipped an old man, the slave "got up and knocked the overseer in the head with a big stick and then took a ax and cut off his hands and feet. Massa said he didn't ever want another white overseer, and he made my cousin overlooker after that." Although it is not likely that slaves often got away with unconcealed murder, successful defiance of an overseer when the master disapproved of his management was not unusual.[110]

Even when slaves were brought to trial for resisting authorities, the outcome was uncertain and depended on the zeal, fairmindedness, and peculiarities of judges, juries, and lawyers. Usually courts were hard on blacks who resisted whites. "If the master exceed the bounds of reason . . . in his chastisement, the slave must submit, as the child submits . . . and trust to the law for his vindication," ruled a Georgia judge in 1854 in upholding the conviction of a slave who had murdered his overseer after the latter had attacked him with a maul. "He cannot, himself, undertake to redress his wrong, unless the attack . . . be calculated to produce death." But not all judges agreed. The conviction of an Alabama slave who bit off part of his overseer's ear was overturned by an appeals court that did not consider injuring an ear "mayhem" unless done willfully. "Slave though he be, and forbidden to resist," ruled the court, ". . . he is nevertheless a human being, and when engaged in mortal strife, his adversary armed with a mortal weapon, and he defenseless, the law . . . would attribute such a mutilation . . . to the instinct of self defense, in which the will did not cooperate." Sometimes, too, slaves were acquitted on technicalities, even though they were clearly guilty of serious offenses.[111]

In short, although resisting was a risky business, it often brought tangible rewards. This was recognized by (among others) two former slaves, Frederick Douglass and H. C. Bruce. "He is whipped oftenest, who is whipped easiest," wrote Douglass, "and that slave who has the courage to stand up for himself against the overseer, although he may have many hard stripes at the first, becomes, in the end, a freeman, even though he sustain the formal relation of a slave." Bruce noted the prevalence of independent-minded slaves, "industrious, but very impudent," who would not submit to external control. "There were thousands of that class," he concluded, "who spent their lives in their master's service, doing his work undisturbed, because the master understood the slave." Both Douglass and Bruce exaggerated the ease of the process; often confronting authority led not to semifreedom but to harsh repression. But in a general sense they were surely right. Not only did many slaves secure more independent lives for themselves, but because masters never knew when excessive demands placed on slaves would trigger defiance, those who challenged owners and overseers also helped set limits to the mistreatment of their fellow slaves.[112]

In Russia, because the confrontations were more complicated, so too were the solutions to them. Ringleaders of volneniia were usually brutally punished, but the mass of peasants faced a less predictable fate. Sometimes many or all of them received corporal punishment (usually with birch switches), and when troops were used to restore order, serf casualties could be high. But often most serfs escaped any immediate punishment whatsoever, if for no other reason than the administrative difficulty and risk of disciplining hundreds of persons, and in some cases peasants found that their actions resulted in specific improvements in their condition. Usually, these improvements consisted of changes introduced by owners anxious to avoid renewed trouble—for example bringing in a new steward or reducing workloads—and were independent of any government initiatives. Even when serfs won no administrative concessions, they could look forward following volneniia to a certain caution on the part of pomeshchiki and stewards.[113]

Sometimes, especially during the last decades of serfdom, volneniia led to serious governmental investigations of serf allegations of mistreatment. Such inquiries fully sustained the serfs' contentions only in exceptional circumstances and usually supported the position of the pomeshchiki, but official investigations had an impact that was far from negligible. It was not unusual for officials, in their reports, to criticize everyone involved in a disturbance—serfs, owner, steward, and local authorities—and order remedies designed to improve conditions and thus prevent a new outbreak of trouble. Even when officials reported no misuse of power, the very existence (or threat) of an investigation undoubtedly served to deter arbitrary behavior on the part of landowners. No nobleman wanted to arouse the suspicions of high officials, the way L. N. Markovnikova did during a volnenie of her serfs in Nizhnii Novgorod province in 1826. After the serfs had been restored to obedience, the minister of internal affairs noted on the governor's report that "here is not sufficiently related the pomeshchitsa's management of the peasants, who perhaps actually find themselves in a difficult position." [114]

More significant from the peasants' point of view was the official reaction to a half-year volnenie in 1853 by more than two thousand serfs who complained of overwork and insisted that they should be state peasants rather than serfs because their ancestors had enjoyed state status until 1787. After they were brought into submission, a military court handed down unusually heavy sentences: two leaders were ordered to run the gauntlet of five hundred men eight times and then be sent away for fourteen years of penal servitude; fifty-three serfs received sentences involving lesser degrees of corporal punishment combined with penal servitude; and 520 others were given sixty blows with birch switches. Although a special investigation into the affair blamed the peasants for the volnenie and endorsed the sentences, officials in St. Petersburg were not satisfied. The president of the Senate wrote to the minister of internal affairs that the serfowner had "allowed himself to load the peasants with excessive obligations and burdens," and the following day the minister issued a circular to all provincial marshals of nobility stating that the tsar found it "completely criminal and entirely in violation of the spirit of our beneficial laws" for serfs to be compelled to work for their owners more than three days per week, as had just occurred in "one" province. The circular ordered marshals to make sure that barshchina be limited to the customary three days per week. [115]

Peasant petitions met with similarly varied responses. Most pomeshchiki were instinctively suspicious of peasant complaints, assuming that their authors were trying to get away with something; when not ignored, these complaints often elicited warnings of severe retribution. But noblemen also had reasons to take petitions seriously. They were anxious to check up on their stewards, whom they rarely trusted, and hence often welcomed peasant reports of steward wrongdoing. They also had a vested interest in preventing their serfs from falling into total destitution and sometimes responded favorably to requests for small favors such as temporary reduction of obrok payments and distribution of seigneurial grain. Noblemen were especially prone to come to the aid of their serfs in the wake of "acts of God" such as fires, epidemics, and crop failures, although even then peasants could never be sure of seigneurial generosity.[116]

Even illegal petitions to the tsar occasionally produced serious investigations. A petition to Alexander I in 1819 from serfs representing 327 souls in Iaroslavl province complaining that their owners Ivan and Dmitrii Kaftirev required them to perform excessive seigneurial labor led eventually to the creation of a commission of district noblemen that formulated guidelines spelling out relations between the Kaftirevs and their serfs. When more than a hundred house serfs of the notoriously sadistic General L. D. Izmailov wrote to Nicholas I in 1826 detailing brutal tortures on the nobleman's Tula province estate, district officials first tried to ignore the evidence, but pressure from St. Petersburg finally led to an inquiry that resulted in Izmailov being brought to trial.[117]

The reluctance and lethargy with which complaints to the tsar were investigated—but also the occasional victories serfs won through them—are illustrated by an examination of the consequences of a petition sent by serfs of Khristinovka village, in Kiev province, to Alexander I in 1817. The petition asserted that over a period of nine years their owner Ivan Stakhurskii had subjected them to cruel punishments and excessive barshchina, "not giving us rest for either Sundays or holidays." The complaint was forwarded to the governor of Kiev province, but by the time he sent an official to investigate, Stakhurskii had died and his two sons inherited the estate; the official conducted a perfunctory investigation and concluded that the various complaints were either groundless or unproven. Soon after this the brothers sold the estate to a new owner, Krasitskii, who was evidently as oppressive as Stakhurskii had been. In August 1820 the serfs sent a new petition to the tsar, repeating their original charges and criticizing the official who had supposedly investigated their situation for having "in no way made an inquiry of us." They complained that Krasitskii forced them to engage in continuous seigneurial labor and begged relief from both this overwork and "various punishments, imposed on us by pomeshchik Krasitskii without any humanity." When conditions did not improve, the persistent peasants sent the tsar still another petition in October 1823. At first this missive too seemed to bring little relief; indeed, in August 1825 a Kiev court ordered one of the petitioners punished with twenty-five lashes as an example. On 27 November 1826, however, the tsar's Committee of Ministers sent a directive to both the Kiev and district marshals of nobility, ordering them to make sure Krasitskii did not oppress his serfs. Nine years after the serfs of Khristinovka first petitioned the tsar, their complaints had finally met with a response.[118]

Petitions to provincial and district officials on the whole produced more favorable (and speedier) action than those to the tsar. The very process of petitioning these officials often entailed certain benefits for the serfs. Whereas petitions to the tsar were invariably presented by one or two walkers, large groups of peasants were able to deliver appeals to governors, marshals of nobility, and local authorities. Indeed, the governor of Smolensk, although conceding that pomeshchiki "often are not entirely correct in their actions concerning managing their peasants," suggested that one of the main reasons for the proliferation of petitions was that presenting them gave serfs the opportunity to leave their estates en masse. This suggestion, in turn, drew a sharp response from the minister of internal affairs, who criticized the governor for *allowing* large groups of peasants to present petitions to him. "Unwarranted absence of a whole crowd to present a petition against a pomeshchik," he stated, "already constitutes the beginning of disorder and volnenie."[119]

Although petitions to provincial and district officials often received perfunctory treatment, they were more likely to lead to investigation and even alleviation of seigneurial abuses than were those sent to St. Petersburg. The nature of these investigations is indicated by a study of Saratov province, where between 1826 and 1860 officials received 198 serf petitions. They judged forty-four of these to be totally unfounded, and the disposition of seventy-eight others remains unknown, but in seventy-six cases investigations convinced authorities that peasant complaints were at least partially justified. Usually the official response to these justified complaints was limited to reprimanding pomeshchiki or warning them that if they did not mend their ways they would face further consequences. In thirty-six instances, however, more extreme action ensued, including removal of stewards (six cases), countermanding seigneurial orders (three cases), securing written statements from pomeshchiki promising relief (six cases), putting estates under police supervision (four cases), taking legal action against owners (four cases), and initiating action to put estates under the control of legal guardians (ten cases).[120]

Such protective measures were both less and more effective than one might suppose. Even with the best of intentions officials were often unable to intervene effectively to protect mistreated serfs, as demonstrated by events on the Lopatino estate in Saratov province. Colonel Afanasii Pribytkov, upon acquiring the holding in 1849, immediately increased the serfs' obligations, reduced their allotments, and complained to district marshal of nobility Kozhin of their unruly behavior. After investigating the situation, Kozhin found the serfs blameless and fixed responsibility for the trouble squarely on the new owner's shoulders, noting that he wrote the village burmistr "only of punishment and of exacting arrears without mercy." During the following months Kozhin repeatedly urged Pribytkov to treat his people more humanely and sent reports to provincial authorities. As a result of these reports, in September 1850 the governor summoned a meeting of all the province's district marshals of nobility to consider Pribytkov's behavior; they concluded that he had "shattered the condition of the peasants and reduced them to an impoverished position" and recommended to the Senate that the estate be put into guardianship. The Senate took no action, however, and the situation continued to deteriorate in 1850 and 1851. Pribytkov complained bitterly to the provincial marshal of nobility about Kozhin's interference on his estate, charging that the official "has already totally destroyed my domestic peace and even security, and is completing my ruin."

The nobleman's concern for his security turned out to be well founded: in 1853 he was shot to death in his garden in the presence of his children and a number of servants. The district marshal reported that although five persons, including the burmistr, were personally involved in the murder, "there can be no doubt that all his peasants in general knew about the plot," and he observed with alarm that several other pomeshchiki in the district had perished in attacks "carried out by general conspiracy of [their] peasants." Given the circumstances, Kozhin, who had previously tried to protect the serfs from Pribytkov's excesses, now sharply changed his stance, urging the governor quickly to convene a military court to try and punish the guilty. "Without imposition of the strictest measures of punishment as an example for the future," he warned, "what will serve to guarantee the personal security of any nobleman?"[121]

Still, governmental action had an impact that was far from totally negligible. Although estates were put into guardianship only for the most flagrant cases of cruelty and the vast majority of abuses went unredressed, the effects of such guardianships were not limited to the serfs and owners directly involved and cannot be measured by their numbers alone. Confiscation of an estate was significant primarily because it was a threat always hanging over pomeshchiki, thus serving to deter repeated acts of extreme brutality, not because it directly rescued a large number of peasants.

Although Russian serfs most often confronted authorities collectively whereas American slaves typically did so individually, their resistance shared a common consequence: it enabled them to gain, in at least some small measure, more control over their own lives. In this respect the psychological impact on the slaves and serfs of their decisions to stand up to their masters was far from negligible. Frederick Douglass's description of his fight with Covey as "the turning point in my 'life as a slave'"—"I was *nothing* before. I WAS A MAN NOW"— and the announcement of an insurgent starosta that he was a general "since the mir elected me" testify to the degree that bondsmen felt transformed by self-assertion. In confronting their owners, they became not helpless objects of exploitation but shapers of their own destiny. The decision to resist represented an assertion of identity that was keenly felt by planters and pomeshchiki, who complained constantly of "insubordination," "disobedience," and "impudence." Doubtless one reason slaves and serfs continued to risk the savage reprisals to which they were often subjected was that their challenge of authority, whether successful or not, made them feel like independent men and women rather than the servile beings their owners insisted they were.[122]

6

Protest, Unity,
and Disunity

MASTERS IN RUSSIA and the United States typically saw their bondsmen's resistance as unprovoked and unjustified. When Vladimir province pomeshchik G. A. Vladykin's serfs began a volnenie in 1797, the unhappy owner complained that his people had become disobedient "for who knows what reason"; an official involved in the suppression of three volneniia in Riazan province in 1849 later expressed his puzzlement at these "somewhat strange" outbreaks, noting that their "general cause" was "not entirely clear." Southern whites showed similar bewilderment at slave ingratitude: Thomas Jefferson complained that his runaway slave Joe took off "without the least word of difference with any body, & indeed having never in his life recieved [sic] a blow from any one," and the overseer on James K. Polk's Mississippi plantation described the flight of a slave in 1839 as being "without any cause whatever." From the masters' point of view, the leading cause of servile unrest appeared to be an insubordinate spirit that could strike virtually anywhere without rhyme or reason.[1]

In fact, resistance was by no means so random or irrational. Although most bondsmen chafed under the oppression they experienced and would eagerly have grasped for freedom were it within reach, slavery and serfdom did not in themselves produce continuous generalized resistance. The kinds of resistance that were most prevalent—small-scale confrontations and flight—were almost always associated with particular incidents that served to set them off and legitimize them to the bondsmen.

An analysis of the specific grievances that triggered resistance on the part of slaves and serfs reveals much about their world view and about the character of their culture and community. Despite the existence of certain centrifugal forces among them, the bondsmen devel-

oped common notions—not always the same in the two countries—
of what was proper within the generally despised systems of forced
labor in which they were held. So long as the behavior of their masters (and their representatives) conformed to these notions of propriety, the bondsmen by and large made their peace with conditions that
seemed, although in an abstract sense unjust, as good as could likely
be obtained. When authorities violated the bondsmen's sense of what
was acceptable, however, reaction became probable. Slaves and serfs
suffered an enormous amount of abuse in silence, but when owners,
overseers, and stewards pushed too far, their actions lost all legitimacy in the bondsmen's eyes and hence justified physical resistance.

*   *   *

RUSSIAN SERFS resorted to protest when they felt that their collective "rights" were being violated. A wide variety of actions on the
part of authorities could give birth to this feeling, but all in one way
or another represented breaches of established norms. The serfs possessed a common sense of what was right, desirable, and tolerable,
and when faced with circumstances that appeared sufficiently unjust,
undesirable, or intolerable, they usually sought redress of grievances.
So long as such redress seemed feasible—as it did far more often than
it was—they largely engaged in protest within the system, sending
petitions and taking part in nonviolent volneniia; a sense of desperation and hopelessness, by contrast, could lead to flight or violence.

Economic hardship was a major cause of dissatisfaction and protest. Although serfs knew that poverty and toil were their fate, they
expected their owners to allot them sufficient land and time for their
own cultivation and to show a sensitivity to their plight by relaxing
obligations in times of special difficulty (such as crop failure). Petitions to authorities often complained of owners and stewards who
imposed excessive economic burdens, detailing specific acts of exploitation and concluding with a general statement of their miserable economic state; in a typical complaint to Emperor Paul a group of peasants from Vladimir province declared that their owner had "caused
us the most extreme harm and reduced us to total poverty and ruin."
In a study of 195 petitions to officials of Saratov province between
1826 and 1860, L. N. Iurovskii found that at least 106 included complaints of some form of economic oppression. Unanswered petitions
sometimes led to volneniia; serfs engaged in confrontations with authorities often protested excessive seigneurial labor requirements,
heightened obrok dues, insufficient time to work on their own allot-

ments, and a general condition of "complete ruin." Historian V. A. Fedorov's computations show that owner-imposed economic hardship—especially increase of obrok and barshchina obligations—contributed to 42.7 percent of the volneniia in the central-industrial region between 1801 and 1860.[2]

Extreme physical mistreatment was a second major complaint of serfs. Of 195 Saratov province petitions, 120 listed cruel treatment, a slightly larger number than mentioned economic oppression. Significantly, forty-three of these petitions indicted owners or stewards for both cruelty *and* economic deprivation. Indeed, peasants frequently linked the two kinds of abuse in their complaints, and no doubt in their minds as well. When Ivan Stakhurskii's serfs in Kiev province petitioned Alexander I against their owner, they combined charges of physical brutality, including beating two domestics to death for impudence, and of overwork, "not providing rest even on Sundays and holidays." Similarly, 375 souls involved in a volnenie in Moscow province in 1841 denounced their master's "tyranny," charging that he worked them incessantly and beat them with "a heavy-strapped knout and batogi . . . until complete exhaustion." Because many serfs had absentee owners, protests against physical mistreatment were often directed at stewards (as in the case of P. D. Kiselev's serfs discussed in Chapter 5). In 1852, for example, Countess Bobrinskaia's Simbirsk province serfs complained that their steward had "oppressed us to such an extent that we have lost all patience." His misdeeds including placing peasants who had formerly enjoyed obrok status on barshchina, assigning obrok dues that could not possibly be fulfilled, administering savage beatings, threatening to send whoever displeased him into the army, and cursing during Easter church services.[3]

But although serfs engaged in volneniia commonly told of economic and physical mistreatment, unless this mistreatment was of an unusually extreme and persistent nature it was rarely enough *in itself* to trigger active resistance. Indeed, several Soviet historians have recently disputed the widespread assumption that the mounting level of peasant unrest during the first half of the nineteenth century stemmed primarily from increased exploitation. Iu. Iu. Kakh and Kh. M. Ligi, after examining forty-three estates in the Baltic province of Lifland, found virtually no correlation between volneniia and the level of seigneurial exploitation. In a quantitative study of 2,342 serf volneniia between 1796 and 1856, B. G. Litvak found only twenty-six in which demand for larger landed allotments was the main cause. Nor did physical abuse always produce protest; serfs engaged in volneniia often complained of cruel treatment, but many others suffered brutal punishments in silence. It was less the fact than the circumstances of mistreatment that led serfs to resist.[4]

Circumstances producing resistance typically involved some sort of change in established relations, usually (but not always) to the serfs' detriment. When peasants objected to economic hardship or physical mistreatment, it was often to *new* hardship or mistreatment. An increase in obrok or labor obligations was far more likely to produce unrest than a continued high level of exploitation; so too were reduction in size of landed allotments, employment of a new steward, and efforts to reduce existing privileges. That almost any kind of change on an estate was likely to cause trouble is a clear indication of the conservative nature of the serfs' mentality. While detesting bondage abstractly, on a practical day-to-day level they adjusted to the reality of their situation—as most people do—accepting their obligation to conform to the requirements imposed on them and looking forward to the small pleasures and privileges that were theirs. The very stability and continuity of things were reassuring: serfs knew what was expected of them, what they could get away with, what life was like. Any change that disrupted that stability inevitably was troubling; it not only implicitly called into question the legitimacy of what had gone before and raised the possibility that existing relations were not immutable but also required a readjustment to a new reality.

Any kind of administrative reorganization of an estate or forced change in the peasants' status or routine was likely to produce discontent. The inventory reforms introduced in the western provinces between 1845 and 1848, although designed to prevent arbitrary treatment of serfs by spelling out the nature—and limits—of their obligations, sparked widespread peasant protest. Perhaps this was in part because the reforms, by setting limits to seigneurial authority, weakened the serfs' "respect" for their owners, but even more basic was the peasants' elemental suspicion of anything that upset established procedures. Many evidently believed that the inventories were designed to bind them even more tightly than before in servitude, and they refused to accept the inventory booklets listing their obligations. On one estate in Kiev province the serfs adamantly maintained that somewhere else in the Ukraine "those peasants who accepted the booklets remained peasants [i.e., serfs], but those who did not accept them received freedom and became cossacks." When officials tried to reason with them, peasant leaders responded rudely and warned the crowd, "Don't listen, this is all a lie"; the assembled serfs, in turn, refused to allow the arrest of their leaders, even when a squadron of lancers arrived, shouting "We did not give them up to the police, we will not give them up to soldiers either." [5]

Unfamiliarity with owners could be a prime source of disquiet among serfs. Indeed, confusion about the identity, status, and legitimacy of owners—and the proper relationship of serfs to them—was the most important single ingredient in producing peasant protests. Many developments could give rise to such confusion, but a change in ownership was the most common. Although Fedorov, in his categorization of 793 volneniia in the central-industrial region, listed 156 (or 19.7 percent) as caused by change in owner (second after 163 caused by high obrok and just ahead of the 125 caused by onerous barshchina and 117 by rumors of freedom), this total is far from complete because he assigned only one cause to each volnenie even though the causes were hardly mutually exclusive. Many volneniia listed by Fedorov as motivated by resentment of economic exploitation also represented reactions to new owners, and it is safe to say that in far more than one-fifth of all volneniia—probably in a majority—change of ownership was a significant factor. Because changed ownership represented the ultimate challenge to established procedures, over and over again serfs with new masters complained about them, detailed the hardships suffered at their hands, and even questioned their right to proprietorship. [6]

An illustrative case occurred in 1817 when Major Ivan Viridov sold his estate of more than five hundred souls in Kursk province to Petr Ammosov. Since Viridov had lived in Moscow and allowed the estate considerable self-management, the serfs were understandably upset by the change and refused to recognize their new owner's authority over them. As they explained in 1817 in one of several petitions they sent to the tsar, they had heard that Ammosov had never received "a legal deed of purchase"; nevertheless, "he came onto our estate as if by a legal deed" and immediately instituted oppressive measures, taking children from their families and sending them to work in distilleries "located in other villages of his where, in addition to being exhausted by heavy labor, they were punished and tormented brutally." The desperate serfs groped for an alternative, first offering to buy their freedom for the staggering sum of 245,000 rubles to be paid in installments over a protracted period, then hoping to return to their former owner Viridov, and all the time begging for imperial clemency. Above all, they entreated, do not make us "be the property of the greedy new pomeshchik Ammosov, who has oppressed and weighed down with burdens his other peasants as well." The emperor turned a deaf ear on the peasants, however, and the volnenie finally petered out in 1821 after the villagers were subjected to extensive whippings, jailings, and quartering of troops on their estate.[7]

As this example indicates, serfs were likely to be especially upset when new owners instituted changes in estate routine. An unknown master was disturbing enough, but one who began his tenure by demonstrating insensitivity to the concerns of his acquired people was asking for trouble. In 1843 Prince Leonid Mikhailovich Golitsyn inherited an estate in Riazan province from his grandfather and immediately antagonized the peasants by transferring them from obrok to barshchina, taking their best land for seigneurial use, and reorganizing the estate's administrative hierarchy. Four years later, when he visited the holding for the first time, the serfs surrounded him and begged for relief, humbly calling themselves his "children" and adding "we consider you forever as our father." Unwisely rejecting their efforts to establish a bond with him, Golitsyn became incensed, responding, "How are you my children? How am I as a father to you? . . . I am just your pomeshchik, I have legal authority over you, and you are my serfs, duty bound to obey me. But you do not obey, you all want things your own way . . . You have annoyed me so much now that I am even ready to renounce you." The offended serfs told their steward that "as a result of their pomeshchik's renouncing them, they also renounce him" and promptly refused to perform any seigneurial labor.[8]

Perhaps the most drastic assault an owner could make on traditional village order was to transfer some or all members of a newly acquired estate to a new locality, and it is not surprising that such action often elicited substantial resistance. When two pomeshchiki who purchased the village of Voskresenovka in Voronezh province in 1810 found the 208 souls "lazy" and inclined to "drunkenness," they determined to transfer them to holdings in the Don region. The serfs, used to considerable economic independence as salt-carriers, offered to buy their freedom; when this offer was refused, they became disobedient, shouting down efforts by the district ispravnik and other officials to reason with them and resisting a detachment of cossacks—in the process suffering nine killed and twenty-nine wounded—before finally yielding. Pomeshchitsa Kronshteinova faced a similar problem when, upon acquiring a Riazan province estate with insufficient land to support its 260 souls, she sold 101 of them to Nikolai Durasov for

transfer to an estate in Moscow province. Assured by a local towns-
man that an ukaz of 1816 forbade the sale of peasants without land,
the serfs sent walkers to the tsar with a petition offering to pay Durasov for their freedom; the walkers returned with a certificate indicating that their petition had been received, which the illiterate peasants evidently took as documentary evidence of their right to
freedom. When local authorities ignored their pleas, those sold to
Durasov again petitioned the tsar, complaining that their new owner
had torn down their houses and was planning to send them to work
in his paper mill. Some fled, but most stayed on Kronshteinova's estate, yelling at the ispravnik and his assistants that "if anyone appeared to take them away, they would beat him to death." It took a
squadron of hussars to round up and remove the determined villagers. Sometimes resettled serfs attempted to return to their original
homes. Prompted by heavy seigneurial labor, "unfamiliarity with the
locality, and a completely different kind of agriculture," fifty-five
serfs who had been moved to Ekaterinoslav province in New Russia
decided to return to their former owner in Orel province. Although
they went to work obediently after being tracked down and sent back
to their new estate, they steadfastly refused to reveal the identity of
their leaders.[9]

Serfs thus combined resistance to new owners with an impressive
defense of their "rights" as they understood them. Among the most
assertive of their rights were those peasants who considered themselves to be legally state peasants rather than privately owned serfs.
Until the end of the eighteenth century tsars regularly rewarded
noblemen with gifts of state peasants, who then became their serfs;
many of these newly enserfed peasants and their descendants resisted
their new status for years, insisting that their former freedom rendered them immune to bondage. In 1834 forty serfs from a village in
Viatka province began a volnenie; when the governor personally tried
to talk them into obedience, "they all in one voice shouted that they
. . . would not submit, considering themselves descendants of strel'tsy
[free musketeers in the sixteenth and seventeenth centuries] and therefore free." A decade later, serfs in Mogilev province refused to acknowledge the authority of their new owner, complaining of harsh
oppression; the key consideration in their resistance, however, was
their belief that the nobleman "acquired us illegally" because sixty
years earlier they—or for most of them their ancestors—had been
state peasants. In 1804 seventeen hundred souls inhabiting a number
of villages in Voronezh province refused to recognize the authority of
their owner, Semen Alekseev Vikulin, until they were subdued by

troops and seven of their leaders given fifty blows with the knout and banished to Siberia; 328 of them vanished in the woods. Although the provincial governor heard only "unfounded" complaints of oppression, the serfs themselves explained in a petition to Alexander I that they had formerly been state peasants, after which they had been given to a succession of pomeshchiki culminating in Vikulin, whose steward imposed savage beatings and excessive labor obligations on them. "However this master acquired us, we have no repose from his labor either day or night," they lamented, appealing for a return to their former happy condition.[10]

Those serfs whose owners had promised to manumit them also believed that they were entitled to freedom. As a secret Ministry of Internal Affairs report stated in 1843, "the most stubborn disobedience occurred on those estates where information spread among the peasants that their pomeshchiki had willed their freedom, which they did not receive on their owner's death." That issue was the cause of a volnenie that broke out in 1812 among 312 souls living in two districts of Vologda province. Refusing to acknowledge the legitimacy of their new owner, A. I. Iakovlev, they claimed that their earlier owner's deceased mother had intended to free them. The serfs from one of the villages got together and issued a "declaration," charging that on acquiring them Iakovlev had sent his representative to the estate to move them away, burn down their houses, and sell their land, as a consequence of which "we, all the peasants of the said estate, are unanimously agreed, from young to old, not to obey the aforementioned Mr. Iakovlev"; instead, they decided to appeal to the tsar to let them enter military service to defend the motherland. More than a year later, with the volnenie crushed, three peasant ringleaders were sentenced to receive 150 to 200 blows with the knout, have their nostrils slit, be branded on the forehead and cheek, and be sent to penal servitude in Nerchinsk; one other leader escaped with 100 blows of the knout and resettlement in Siberia. The ninety-five souls bought by N. P. Miliukov in 1833 were equally sure of their right to freedom, because their previous owner had promised to release them for 20,000 rubles. When the Tver province peasants refused to obey their new owner, however, he raised their obrok dues and took away some of their land. The determined peasants insisted that they were not being rebellious but only wanted to become state peasants, as was their due. "We cannot and do not want in any way to resist legal authority," they explained, "only to be protected by justice and defended in our prosperity and tranquility."[11]

As these examples suggest, many serfs who resisted their masters questioned the legality—or at least the propriety—of their owner-ship. A wide variety of situations, aside from former state status and promises of freedom, could give rise to this questioning. The eighteen hundred souls who lived in Maslov Kut in Stavropol province chafed for years under serfdom because their ancestors had been state peas-ants until 1787. Having to submit to an Armenian Moslem owner, however, was the last straw. In 1853 they refused to recognize his authority over them, reprimanding three priests who tried to per-suade them into obedience: "Your duty, fathers, is to defend us, not the accursed Armenian, our master." The next day they explained to an archdeacon sent by the governor that their master was a "heretic" whom they could not obey: "What justice is there in a government," they queried, when such heretics "are allowed to rule over Orthodox Christians?" The peasants were so convinced that right was on their side that military force was needed to subdue them; they suffered 124 killed and 114 wounded, and 54 of their leaders received severe cor-poral punishment. But serfs also challenged the authority of Ortho-dox masters who seemed to violate moral or legal standards. Relying on their understanding of an 1842 law stipulating that a pomeshchik could not sell land from an estate if less than 4.5 desiatiny (12.15 acres) per soul would remain, P. E. Zavaritskii's serfs in Riazan prov-ince insisted that they should become state peasants, because their estate had only 520 desiatiny for 262 souls. "We have the right to avail ourselves of our lawful freedom," they declared. A group of serfs in Tambov province refused to acknowledge their owner, even though according to the governor they lived "in the best condition," arguing that their previous owner had no right to sell them since they had been granted to him "until death."[12]

No serfs had better grounds for questioning the legitimacy of their owners than those who were not even sure who their owners were. Because pomeshchiki were so often distant, shadowy figures virtually unknown in their villages, there was considerable opportunity for this kind of confusion. When F. S. Turchaninova died, her Perm province serfs were employed for a while in mining before reverting, without their knowledge, to private ownership. The serf women, unused to seigneurial labor, vigorously resisted efforts to impose a three-day barshchina on them; when the district ispravnik arrived and ordered the estate office to summon all the women, only forty-four appeared, each carrying a child and insisting "that their husbands work for them, and that the female sex is not obliged to work." To the isprav-nik's assertion that they must obey the will of their new owner, their leader Dari'ia Potapova angrily replied that their owner had no heirs and they were managed by a guardian; despite the efforts of the assembled crowd to protect her, she was arrested and eventually, along with two other women and two men, sent to Siberia. In 1823 peasants of Ivanovskoe village in Nizhnii Novgorod province complained of being cruelly treated by their new owner, L. N. Markovnikova, and questioned whether they really belonged to her. "We entered her possession completely illegally, since our present mistress has neither documents nor deeds concerning our ownership," they declared, adding that because she was of peasant rather than noble descent "we have doubts about recognizing her as our legal pomeshchitsa and mistress." Concluding their petition, they inquired of the minister of internal affairs, "Ought we to belong to Mrs. Markovnikova, or should we acquire a different status?" In numerous other cases serfs unsure of their rightful owners sought clarification from officials, disputed the authority of pomeshchiki and stewards, and sought to have their status altered.[13]

Although serfs ran away for the same basic reason they confronted authorities—perceived violation of traditional rights—specific causes of flight were not always the same as those of other forms of resistance. True, fugitive serfs were sometimes motivated by the same concerns as those who staged volneniia or drafted petitions. Runaways complained of material hardship and physical mistreatment and spread rumors of impending emancipation or "free lands" where all were welcome. And often serfs engaged in temporary flight during volneniia, taking to the woods in order to avoid reprisals. But flight had some distinctive features that differentiated it from more active forms of resistance. Whereas volneniia and petitions were overwhelmingly communal endeavors, small groups of serfs with private grievances often ran away. Those given passes to trade or hire themselves out sometimes failed to return on time—or at all. House servants, who because of close contact with pomeshchiki had complaints not shared by the mass of serfs, often fled individually or in small groups. Family relations also impelled flight. A survey of one area revealed that in the late seventeenth century, in 139 of 302 cases in which causes of flight could be determined, serfs held by separate owners sought to join spouses or other relatives, and in another 23 serfs ran away from relatives.[14]

When flight was a communal affair, it generally represented feelings of greater hopelessness on the part of serfs than did petitions or volneniia. The latter, after all, were not acts of total desperation; serfs who appealed to authorities and engaged in confrontations had serious grievances, but they believed that there was a chance that those grievances could be redressed. Running away, by contrast, indicated a belief that such satisfaction was unlikely. Serfs whose petitions were rejected and whose volneniia were suppressed frequently fled their villages to escape the brutal punishments so often imposed on troublemakers. Economic distress was an especially potent cause of massive group flight from the late sixteenth century when many estates of central Russia suffered depopulation and abandonment to the end of serfdom. Regions affected by severe crop failure could expect increased flight, as peasants searched for ways to support themselves. In Vitebsk province, for example, three successive years of poor harvests led to widespread peasant departures in 1847, with serfs striving to settle on better land "and at the same time to free themselves from dependence on their owners."[15]

Despite these differences, flight represented, like direct confrontation, perception on the part of serfs that masters had somehow failed to fulfill their obligations. Pomeshchiki were "supposed" to provide for their people in time of distress; those unwilling or unable to do so were not performing their role as protectors and from the serfs' point of view had no right to expect them to perform theirs as laborers. Similarly, owners who physically mistreated serfs, interfered in their family lives, meddled excessively in communal affairs, or unilaterally introduced drastic changes in estate order were violating long-standing social norms. In all these areas the peasants had a sense of how things should be—based largely on tradition—and reacted strongly to defend what they regarded as their legitimate rights when they appeared threatened.

This basically conservative goal receives confirmation from a brief examination of resistance among state peasants. State peasants engaged, as one would expect, in far fewer volneniia than privately held serfs; although their economic condition was generally precarious, they did not usually have to deal with pomeshchiki and their subordinates, and they faced far less interference in their personal lives. Thus, although state peasants were about as numerous as serfs, between 1796 and 1856 they produced about one-sixth as many volneniia (and about one-fifth as many petitions to the tsar); on the whole, they simply had less to complain about. But like serfs, they strongly protested the violation of common values. In the western provinces such protest often occurred when state peasants were hired out to landlords and essentially treated like serfs.[16]

But the most persistent and revealing unrest among state peasants occurred as a response to the governmental reforms sponsored by Count P. D. Kiselev between 1837 and 1844. Although these reforms were designed to improve the condition of the state peasants by regularizing their administration, improving agricultural productivity, and providing them with very limited civil rights, they reacted with hostility to the bureaucratically imposed changes. Many evidently feared that they were about to be made serfs or court peasants, while others resented the way the reforms infringed on traditional village life. Several specific irritants ignited what a Ministry of Internal Affairs report for 1842 called "extremely serious disorders among state peasants," but almost all were related to "the introduction of various new agricultural measures and changes in the previous order of village administration."

A major object of resistance, especially in the Volga and Ural regions, was the government's effort—begun in the early 1830s and accelerated as part of the Kiselev reforms—to induce state peasants to grow potatoes, a crop with which they were hitherto unfamiliar; the result was a series of stubborn volneniia known as the potato riots. When an official in Viatka province tried to enforce governmental decrees on growing potatoes, he was told that "the potato is a descendant of that sacred apple for which original man was denied bliss, and that when it was abandoned with a curse on the ground from it was born the potato, and consequently, these seeds are antichrist." Although this official believed the peasants were just playing dumb, peasants elsewhere shared the notion that potatoes were not just new but actually immoral. In Osinskii district of Perm province state peasants beat the few who heeded government admonitions to grow the hated vegetable and dug up their gardens; when a district official tried to reason with them, they shouted, "Send us to Siberia, but we will not plant potatoes." Like privately held serfs, in short, state peasants strongly resisted attempts—however well-intentioned—to interfere with their traditional mode of life and to infringe on what they regarded as their rights. As a Third Department report noted in 1837, in warning of the need to proceed cautiously with the Kiselev reforms, "The state peasants, accustomed to an entirely free and loose life, to uncontrolled disposition of their activities and property, look with displeasure on any change in their condition that restricts or limits their freedom." So too did serfs.[17]

*　　*　　*

FLIGHT AND CONFRONTATIONS perpetrated by American slaves also occurred primarily in response to violations of accepted standards of treatment. Although the slaves usually acted as individuals or in very small groups and their actions lacked the organized element of Russian protest, their resistance nevertheless indicated the existence among them of common ideas of what was tolerable under slavery. Slave resistance thus represented individual manifestations of broadly shared communal standards.

By far the most common cause of resistance among the slaves was physical punishment or mistreatment. Because most slaves lived in close proximity to their owners and overseers and came in frequent contact with them, the threat of chastisement—most often in the form of whipping—hung over them at all times. Their most basic definition of a "good" master was one who did not whip his people much (or better yet, at all), and it is not surprising that whippings and fear of whippings led more slaves to run away and to confront whites than all other specific causes of resistance combined.[18]

Slaves who engaged in temporary local flight most often did so as an impulsive response to punishment. Planters themselves clearly recognized this; their diaries are filled with entries such as that of William Byrd (1741): "my Tom got drunk and did not what I bade him; so I beat him and he marched off." Ex-slaves confirmed the pattern; as H. C. Bruce noted, frequently, especially in the summertime when living off the land was easy, "slaves when threatened or after punishment would escape to the woods or some other hiding place." Both slaves and masters were well aware of the frequency with which hands responded to punishment by disappearing for a few days until they had cooled down, become hungry, missed loved ones, or for some other reason decided to return home.[19]

Although everyone recognized the ubiquity of temporary flight as a response to punishment, slaveowners were loathe to admit the existence of confrontations, and it is primarily to the ex-slaves and court records that one must turn to learn when blacks physically resisted white authorities. These sources indicate that, like flight, such resistance occurred most often in response to punishment. Solomon Northup resisted his Louisiana owner's effort to whip him for poor work, seizing the whip from the enraged master's hand and applying it to him instead. In Georgia a slave named Jim hit his overseer with a stick when the latter tried to whip him for playing cards; he was then whipped to death. Time after time slaves such as Frederick Douglass and Elizabeth Keckley, who physically confronted authorities, later described the struggle as stemming from their determination to resist punishment.[20]

Slaves who balked at punishment often combined confrontation *and* flight. When Louis Hughes's wife, Matilda, refused to allow her mistress to whip her, the incensed lady called for her husband, who choked and threatened the recalcitrant slave, prompting her to run away. Bluford, a Missouri slave, responded to a flogging from his master by returning the favor and then fleeing; when his owner tracked him down, Bluford stabbed him to death and escaped to the North. An ex-slave in Virginia recalled that when her master tried to whip his sister "she beat him an' den broke out of de room an' ran away an' stayed all night an' came back de next day." In 1834 Ephraim Beanland, James K. Polk's overseer, reported that when he started to "correct" Jack, the slave "curste me verry much" and ran off, later breaking a stick over the pursuing overseer's head before being caught, chained, and eventually sold. Because impulsiveness was such a major element in both flight and confrontation by slaves resisting punishment, the two forms of resistance appeared as almost interchangeable responses; sometimes one and sometimes the other might ensue and sometimes both together, depending on the individual slave's personality and on the specific circumstances surrounding the attempted chastisement. But when resistance resulted from fear or anticipation of whipping rather than actual punishment, it usually took the form of flight, as slaves sought to avoid angered authorities until passions cooled and intended whippings were forgotten.[21]

Central to the whole process of resisting punishment was the slaves' belief that the intended disciplining was unjust and undeserved. True, some slaves, with differing consequences, made it clear that they would never allow themselves to be whipped, no matter what the circumstances. But for most it was the injustice of the punishment rather than the physical pain it produced that provoked fury and resistance. (Slaves who determined to resist all efforts at chastisements may be viewed as having a more abstract sense of master-slave relations, seeing any punishment as an unjustified earmark of their bondage.) Solomon Northup resisted a whipping because he believed he "was guilty of no wrong whatever, and deserved commendation rather than punishment." Jeff refused a whipping by his Mississippi overseer in 1859, insisting "that he had done nothing to be whipped for." After six months of relentless abuse from Edward Covey, Frederick Douglass resolved "to obey every order, however unreasonable, if it were possible, and, if Mr. Covey should then undertake to beat me, to defend myself and protect myself to the best of my ability." Like other slaves who confronted authorities, Douglass was convinced he was being treated unfairly. This sense of legitimacy in resisting mistreatment had a dualistic impact on the slaves' consciousness: it enabled them to draw the line against extreme abuse, but it also implied—although they may not have recognized this—a tacit acceptance of slave relations short of that extreme. In this sense confrontations in the United States South, as in Russia, represented a conservative defense of perceived rights within bondage rather than a revolutionary effort to overthrow it.[22]

Although unjust punishment was the most widely perceived violation of acceptable white behavior, other kinds of mistreatment also led to resistance. Interference in slaves' family lives was the most important. Unwanted sexual advances sometimes led to physical resistance, as in the case of Josiah Henson's father, who fought with an overseer assaulting his mother.[23] Running away in order to visit or join relatives was more common still. In 1839 the overseer on Polk's Mississippi plantation reported that Charles had fled "without any cause whatever," but added as an afterthought that he suspected "he has goun back to Tennessee where his wife is."[24] But virtually any action that seemed arbitrary, unwarranted, and unfair could trigger resistance. Jake Williams ran away when his Alabama owner threw a stone at his dog Belle; when the overseer tracked Jake to a tree and tried to dislodge him, the slave "kicked de oberseer raght in de mouf, an' dat white man went a tumblin' to de groun!" The dogs, led by Belle, "pounced on him . . . and to' dat man all to pieces," whereupon Jake and the dog escaped. On a number of occasions slaves attacked patrollers who discovered surreptitious nighttime dances in the quarters.[25]

Mistreatment usually seemed worst to slaves when they were unused to or unprepared for it, and it is no accident that slaves who resisted were often those subjected to abuse after previously being treated relatively well. Because slaves, like serfs, adjusted to existing conditions and came to look on the little privileges they enjoyed as theirs by right, they tended to see a change for the worse as more intolerable than continued bad treatment. Whites noted that slaves accustomed to loose controls were especially difficult to tame. When Ephraim Beanland took over the task of overseeing Polk's plantation in Fayette county, Tennessee, in 1833, he found the hands wild and unmanageable, because they had "traded with white people and bin let run at so lose rained that I must be verry close with them." James H. Hammond experienced similar difficulties in 1831 when he acquired Silver Bluff, a South Carolina estate whose 147 slaves were used to living in considerable independence without a resident owner and bitterly resented his effort to run their lives. A Louisiana judge commented that "there is nothing extraordinary in the fact of a negro coming from Kentucky, where they are treated almost on an equality with their master, running away in Louisiana"; although he exaggerated the leniency of slave treatment in Kentucky, he correctly perceived the incitement to flight present in a suddenly imposed restriction on someone who had previously enjoyed a degree of autonomy.[26]

Ex-slaves provide equally clear testimony on this pattern. Lenient treatment, rather than promoting contentment, often made them long all the more for freedom. As William W. Brown noted in explaining his decision to run away from the Missouri tailor who had acquired him, although his new master treated him better than his previous one, "instead of making me contented and happy, it only rendered me more miserable, for it enabled me better to appreciate liberty." Other ex-slaves, such as Frederick Douglass and Austin Steward, made similar statements about the unsettling nature of mild treatment. This was especially true, however, when leniency was followed by severity. Isaac Throgmorton, sold to a Louisianan after enjoying considerable freedom as a barber in Kentucky, "saw so many cruelties that it sickened my heart"; finding that "all the privileges were taken from me," he decided to escape to the North. Frederick Douglass's abuse at the hands of Edward Covey was especially unbearable because the slave had formerly enjoyed a privileged life as a house servant in Baltimore.[27]

The destabilizing impact of change and the perceived threat it entailed to enjoyed privileges were often key factors in the decision to attempt to escape slavery. Long-term directional flight shared many features with local temporary flight and confrontations: like them, it was the result of largely individual decisions and occurred most often in response to punishment or other mistreatment seen as unjust and unbearable. Unlike them, however, it was often less impulsive than carefully deliberated and planned. Slaves usually thought long and hard before deciding to flee to the North, because they realized the consequences of a decision to run away: if successful, they would face separation, perhaps permanent, from all they had known, including home, friends, and relatives; if unsuccessful, they would face the likelihood of far more stringent reprisal than slaves who merely sulked in the woods for a few days.

Ex-slaves who wrote of their escapes often spoke of their general desire for freedom but usually described their actual decisions to flee as responses to particular grievances or provocations. Henry Bibb claimed to have had "a longing desire to be free" which "seemed to be a part of my nature" but noted that he first ran away in 1835 when his Newcastle, Kentucky, mistress began to abuse him physically: "She was every day flogging me, boxing, pulling my ears, and scolding," he related, "so that I dreaded to enter the room where she was." Every time he suffered a whipping he thought more about Canada, until he eventually decided to escape. Other fugitives described their decisions to run away in similar terms. James W. C. Pennington decided to run away from Maryland in 1828, when still a youth, after first his father and then he received undeserved beatings; he had previously received training as a mason, blacksmith, and carpenter and had enjoyed relatively kind treatment. Louis Hughes, a house servant in Memphis, first thought of heading for Canada after hearing his owner read about fugitives in the newspaper; he made the first of several attempts to escape when threatened with a flogging. David Barrett, whose Kentucky owner "was not so cruel as many others," was "determined not to be whipped"; when threatened with a whipping in 1818 he fled, crossing the Ohio River to freedom.[28]

As many of these examples suggest, house servants and artisans were prominently represented among the fugitives. Indeed, reliance on fugitives' autobiographies alone would lead one to conclude that elite slaves constituted a substantial majority of those who succeeded in escaping the peculiar institution. Autobiographies exaggerate this preponderance because skilled slaves were more likely than others to leave records of their exploits, but there is little doubt that elite bondsmen far exceeded their proportion of the slave population in the ranks of the fugitives, especially those who reached the North. In part, this was because they had greater opportunity to escape: they were more likely than most to be aware of alternatives to their current situation and of how to go about fleeing the South, and the masters' trust that some of them enjoyed enabled them to run away without immediate detection. But equally important, they often had greater motivation to escape. Partial exposure to freedom caused their unfree status to rankle all the more, as did the realization that they possessed the skills to prosper in a free society. Servants were frequently subject to closer, more galling supervision than the mass of field hands; charged with pleasing their masters, not just making money for them, their tasks were much more difficult to fulfill satisfactorily. As Douglass noted of "Old Barney," the groom on the plantation on which he grew up, "His office was by no means an enviable one. He often got presents, but he got stripes as well; for in nothing was Col. Lloyd more unreasonable and exacting, than in respect to the management of his pleasure horses ... No excuse could shield Old Barney, if the colonel only suspected something wrong about his horses; and, consequently, he was often punished when faultless." Elite slaves were also more likely than others to experience the kind of changes that so often proved unsettling: they were hired out, brought from the quarters to the big house, sent from the country to the city (and back again), promised and then denied freedom, and given extensive privileges that often proved only temporary.[29]

Among the kinds of changes likely to induce flight, few were as feared as change of ownership. As in Russia, this proved to be an extraordinarily disturbing experience, because slaves were never sure what they could expect. Not only were new owners likely to alter the routine to which everyone had grown accustomed; far more often than in Russia they were likely to divide holdings and even families. Forced separations were especially common following a slaveowner's death, when his or her property was often willed to several heirs or auctioned to cover debts. Most slaves consequently viewed their owners' impending deaths with trepidation even when they felt little fondness for them, and bondsmen with true affection for their masters sometimes felt cast asunder on their demise. "I felt that I had lost the only friend I had in the world," wrote Charles Ball of his master's death. "Had he lived, I should have remained with him and never left him ... but when he was gone, I felt the parting of the last tie that bound me to the place where I then was."[30]

As in Russia, the apparent violation of a former owner's will produced disquiet among slaves and led some to take matters into their own hands. David Holmes grew up in Mecklenburg county, Virginia, with a kind owner who, rumor had it, provided in his will for his slaves' emancipation. But his son, who inherited the plantation, was a cruel man with no interest in freeing his new property; when Holmes overheard him discussing his impending sale, he decided to escape, following the North Star to freedom. George P. Custis's seventy slaves also thought they were to be freed on their owner's death; when the Virginian died and his heir Robert E. Lee insisted that they were now his property, Wesley Norris ran away with his sister and cousin. Upon capture they told Lee, who demanded an explanation of their behavior, that "we considered ourselves free." The master, who obviously disagreed, had them severely whipped and then hired out to work on a railroad.[31]

Slaves who fled to the North, unlike those who engaged in temporary flight and confrontation, were obviously attempting to escape from bondage altogether, not merely to insist on their rights within it. Nevertheless, their actions too were usually sparked by perceived violations of traditional relations. American slaves, like Russian serfs, resisted authorities who breached their notion of what they had a right to expect. In both countries substantial change, especially change of ownership, was likely to foment dissatisfaction, and in both the bondsmen reacted defensively to protect their interests when they saw them under attack. This does not imply that they accepted the general principle of servitude or their owners' definition of what it entailed; it does mean, however, that they usually came to terms with the reality of their situation and strove to carve within it a tolerable niche for themselves. The resulting set of social relationships was extremely precarious; virtually any change could upset the equilibrium. Such destabilization, were it to occur often enough, promised to threaten the social order itself.

*   *   *

THIS KIND of general social destabilization did not occur in the United States South. Until the outbreak of the Civil War aroused new hopes among slaves for an imminent release from bondage, only one major event, the American War for Independence, came close to upsetting the southern social order. Taking advantage of wartime chaos and the proximity of British troops, tens of thousands of slaves fled their homes, sometimes in large groups. In 1781 Thomas Jefferson's Farm Book recorded at least thirty slave defectors who "joined [the] enemy" or "fled to the enemy & died" or "caught smallpox from [the] enemy & died." On one South Carolina plantation in 1779 "sixty four negroes went away in one night," and the next three years in the neighborhood "were years of general . . . calamity . . . in which, all but the particular friends of the British thought themselves fortunate if they could raise provisions, and save their negroes from being carried off." The disruption caused by the Revolutionary War underlines the tenuousness of master-slave relations; for the next three-quarters of a century, however, no outside event disturbed the basic equilibrium of those relations. Although most antebellum slaves longed for freedom, they had little reason to believe that it was attainable. Their confrontations and temporary flight were therefore aimed not at achieving liberation from slavery but at making life more endurable within it, and even their flight to the North entailed escape for individuals rather than an assault on the system as a whole.[32]

An examination of the dynamics of volneniia during the same period suggests very different conclusions concerning Russian serfs. Of course, precise figures on the number of volneniia will always be elusive. The Ministry of Internal Affairs and the Third Department both compiled statistics on them, but the latter's figures consistently exceeded the former's; neither body, however, was aware of all the peasant outbreaks that occurred, and subsequent research has revealed the existence of numerous volneniia not included in their listings. Still, these disturbances are amenable to quantitative analysis, even if scholars continue to differ on their exact numbers, because their collective character rendered them highly visible. Unlike individual confrontations in the old South, most of which went unrecorded, volneniia usually generated a great amount of paperwork, as government authorities reported to their superiors on efforts to restore order. The editors of the three volumes of *Krest'ianskoe dvizhenie* that cover the years 1796–1856 have consequently been able to put together good basic figures on the incidence of volneniia (see Table 8). Although more recent researchers, mining local archives, have uncovered still additional volneniia not included in these totals, the *Krest'ianskoe dvizhenie* statistics remain the most useful for establishing general trends and patterns.[33]

These statistics reveal, among other things, a significant and growing impact of outside events on master-serf relations. Despite fluctuations in the number of volneniia per year, four years—1797, 1826, 1848, and to a lesser extent 1812—stand out as having many more volneniia than those immediately preceding or following. In each of these years major events occurred, news of which quickly filtered down to the village level, although not always with equal impact in all parts of the Russian empire. By creating among the serfs expectations of important change, these events upset the precarious balance of forces that maintained social order.

On 6 November 1796, Catherine II died and her son Paul became tsar. Rumors had circulated among the peasants during the unpopular empress's reign that the tsarevich was sympathetic with their plight—one story even had him secretly helping Pugachev in 1773. His accession to the throne, therefore, aroused their hopes, present in at least latent form at each new coronation, that at long last their sufferings were to be relieved. In fact, Paul followed contradictory policies with respect to serfdom during his erratic five-year reign. He awarded hundreds of thousands of state peasants to favored noblemen in the last major act of enserfment by a Russian monarch; at the same time, however, he took other measures that led serfs to believe

Table 8
Peasant volneniia, 1796–1855, by year[a]

Year	No. of estates	Year	No. of estates	Year	No. of estates	Year	No. of estates
1796	55	1811	30	1826	104	1841	31
1797	119	1812	60	1827	33	1842	53
1798	10	1813	19	1828	15	1843	34
1799	7	1814	15	1829	20	1844	40
1800	12	1815	29	1830	44	1845	73
1801	5	1816	24	1831	32	1846	37
1802	18	1817	34	1832	19	1847	52
1803	18	1818	40	1833	24	1848	161
1804	18	1819	39	1834	36	1849	34
1805	26	1820	22	1835	15	1850	61
1806	14	1821	16	1836	65	1851	60
1807	11	1822	46	1837	21	1852	68
1808	28	1823	39	1838	36	1853	59
1809	20	1824	27	1839	47	1854	55
1810	16	1825	37	1840	33	1855	45

1796–1810   377 (annual average: 25.1)
1811–1825   477 (annual average: 31.8)
1826–1840   544 (annual average: 36.3)
1841–1855   863 (annual average: 57.5)

1796–1855 2,261 (annual average: 37.7)

Sources: KD-1, 18; KD-2, 817; KD-3, 732–33.

a. Figures are for number of estates on which volneniia occurred and include outbreaks among state peasants as well as serfs.

he was on their side. Of these the most important were a call to serfs as well as other orders to take the oath of allegiance, an ukaz of 12 December 1796, that allowed individual peasants—although not groups—to present petitions to the crown, and a decree of 5 April 1797, prohibiting seigneurial labor on Sundays so serfs could work three days for themselves and three for their owners. Many bondsmen evidently believed that these were only the first of a series of sweeping changes designed to free them entirely from seigneurial authority; indeed, the inevitable rumors spread that Paul had already issued an emancipation proclamation that was being suppressed by evil noblemen and corrupt officials.[34]

The response was immediate. Serf petitions to the tsar—often signed by one person on behalf of many, so as to conform to the letter of the law—soared from two in 1796 to fifty-seven in 1797, the largest number for any year on record. More ominous from the government's point of view was the unrest among serfs that became evident in December 1796 and exploded in January 1797. Peasants, sometimes encouraged by local priests, protested against pomeshchiki who seemed in violation of the imperial will, refusing to perform more than three days barshchina and in extreme cases denying their owners' authority over them. The situation became so threatening that on 29 January Paul issued a manifesto ordering serfs to obey their owners under risk of severe reprisal and chiding the parish clergy for their role in fanning discontent. "The clergy, especially parish priests, have the duty to warn their parishioners against lying and harmful talk," the monarch declared, "and to keep them in good conduct and obedience to their owners." At the same time he put Prince Nikolai Repnin in charge of suppressing the spreading unrest, a task he energetically fulfilled, noting in his journal that when he informed peasants of the tsar's true wishes they "thanked me for telling them the truth, and promised at once to be orderly and obey their pomeshchik." Although restoring calm was not always as easy as he suggested, by mid-year the worst was over. The pattern of seizing on the inauguration of a new tsar, however, would be repeated in the future.[35]

The Napoleonic invasion of 1812 disrupted the lives of many serfs, aroused among them widespread hopes for emancipation, and hence led to a resurgence of disorder. The serfs' response to the invasion was complex. Some, placing undue trust in the French rhetoric of "liberty, equality, and fraternity," harbored early expectations that Napoleon would free them; in September peasants belonging to several pomeshchiki in Moscow province's Volokolamskii district refused to obey seigneurial authorities, "saying that they are now French," and ransacked their owners' property. Many others displayed a characteristic patriotism, rushing to defend the motherland against infidel invaders and hoping that the tsar would reward their valor with liberty. Such patriotism rarely extended to the defense of noble interests, which serfs clearly differentiated from those of Russia and the government, and sometimes serfs combined declarations of eagerness to serve their country with acts of disobedience against pomeshchiki. Aleksandr Ivanovich Iakovlev's 319 souls in Vologda province, for example, rejected the nobleman's authority over them, claiming their previous owner had intended to free them; at the same time they declared their ardent desire "to enter military service for the motherland of Orthodox Christian faith." By creating confusion and dislocation, the invasion disrupted the normal routine of landed estates, especially in areas occupied by the French during the march to Moscow, and led to heightened peasant unrest. After the war returning soldiers, their horizons widened and then their hopes for change dashed, became leading agents of antiserfdom agitation.[36]

Alexander I's death on 18 November 1825, the ensuing unsuccessful attempt at a coup d'état by a group of liberal noblemen (Decembrists), and Nicholas I's accession to the throne led to major peasant disturbances in early 1826. Unrest was especially rampant near the capital cities of Moscow and St. Petersburg, where news of the remarkable events penetrated most quickly; indeed, more than half the volneniia that occurred in 1826 were located in the three provinces of Moscow, St. Petersburg, and Pskov (neighboring Petersburg). Ironically, serfs did not view the Decembrists as apostles of liberty but rather as a group of noblemen trying to usurp the true tsar's rightful place; in a supreme manifestation of naive monarchism they put their hopes for freedom in the martinet Nicholas, not in those who sought to reform Russia.

As in 1796, rumors quickly circulated that the new ruler intended to free the serfs—or had already done so—but was being stymied by the conniving noblemen who surrounded him. Even an imperial manifesto on 12 May rebutting these rumors had no discernible effect; as an official reported from St. Petersburg province, "The peasants, blinded by an imaginary freedom, do not want to believe that it [the manifesto] is the will of the Sovereign Emperor, but suppose that it is the intrigue and cunning of pomeshchiki." Major-General G. I. Nostits, commissioned to make a special investigation of sentiment in Kiev province, reported a similar state of mind. Panic reigned among local officials and noblemen, while peasants were mouthing expressions such as "Kill the pomeshchiki and Jews" and listening to wild rumors; a soldier on furlough was seized after passing himself off as a special official "sent by the Sovereign Emperor to arrest the pomeshchiki and announce to the peasants freedom from obligations." At the same time Nostits observed that the peasants' hostility was directed not at the government but at local noblemen, many of whom were Catholics of Polish ancestry. When a spy was sent to test public sentiment by talking against the government, enraged peasants apprehended and beat him. "It is in the nature of the Ukrainian peasant to obey the government completely," the general concluded, "although he has it in his character to stand on his own, and hates the 'pan' ['gentleman,' a Polish landowner]."[37]

The impact of outside events on local serf relations is finally evident in the unrest of 1848, a year that saw the greatest number of volneniia of any during the 1796–1856 period. While much of Russia suffered from serious crop failure in 1848, a number of developments conspired to create especially widespread disorders in the southwestern provinces; more than half the volneniia, petitions, and murders of authorities in that year took place in the three provinces of Volhynia, Podolia, and Kiev. Bordering on the Austro-Hungarian empire, these provinces were more likely than those in the interior of Russia to be influenced by revolutionary events in western and central Europe. Probably more important still was resistance that peasants in the southwest showed to the newly introduced inventory reforms. In addition, a major cholera epidemic swept the region, creating widespread suffering as well as rumors that the disease was being spread by "disloyal people, but especially the Poles." The volneniia of 1848 demonstrated once again that serfs were most likely to resist authorities when normal routine was disrupted and alternatives to it appeared before them.[38]

Although particular events triggered unusual numbers of outbreaks in specific years and regions, a more general pattern is also evident: the increasing incidence of volneniia. Despite annual fluctuations, the long-term trend was toward greater and greater unrest. If one ignores exceptional years such as 1797, 1826, and 1848, the trend was more or less continuous; what is more, it accelerated during the last two decades. By the middle of the nineteenth century serfs were engaging in volneniia more than twice as frequently as they had fifty years earlier (see Table 8).

This trend was indicative of a deterioration in the serfs' willingness to accept the legitimacy of their position in society or of serfdom itself. By the 1850s the social order seemed on the verge of collapse. Not only were serfs challenging authorities at a consistently high rate, but less and less provocation was necessary to set off volneniia. Most ominous of all, from the government's point of view, more and more serfs, convinced that emancipation was imminent, seemed to be seeking not just rectification of specific wrongs, but freedom. As the governor of Voronezh province noted in 1855 in a report on volneniia, their "chief cause" was the serfs' "one single desire, frequently expressed by them openly, to receive freedom."[39]

Significantly, this sharp rise in the number of volneniia was not matched by an increase in the number of peasant petitions to the crown, which peaked in the decade 1816–25 at an annual rate of 30.3 and by the decade 1846–55 had sagged to a rate of 19.3. Here too is evidence of the changing nature of serfs' consciousness. Peasants who sent petitions to the tsar were usually protesting specific grievances that they were hopeful of seeing redressed. More and more, however, the resistance that serfs displayed during the last two decades of serfdom was aimed not at alleviating wrongs or hardships within the general confines of existing relations but at fundamentally changing those relations. As an official from Riazan province later recollected, "the serf population began to develop a general unwillingness to endure any longer serf dependence, even though it had become much less oppressive than before." In short, the social order entered a period of crisis, as serfs sensed for the first time the impending abolition of serfdom and acted to make their dreams come true.[40]

One of the most noteworthy elements of this process is the awareness serfs showed of "outside" affairs. In protesting against mistreatment, they possessed a strong sense of their legal as well as customary rights, objecting to what they regarded as illegal practices such as compelling them to work more than three days per week on barshchina or disregarding a previous owner's will. They followed national events that might affect their status, such as the accession to power of a new tsar or the issuing of an imperial ukaz. In defending their interests, they demonstrated an impressive awareness—although not always accurate knowledge—of what was going on in the country, an awareness that suggests the degree to which they felt a part of society at large. Their naive monarchism was simply the clearest expression of this sense of belonging.

American slaves, by contrast, lacked this sense. Although slaves often knew more about specific developments than they let on, they generally lacked the kind of broad concern with national events evident among serfs; as outsiders they had little reason to believe that such events were likely to affect them. They did not look forward eagerly to the inauguration of a new president or expect that his election would mean deliverance for them. Because they were outside of society, they were in a peculiar sense also outside that society's history. Indicative of this ahistorical quality is the basically unchanged nature of their social consciousness during the half-century before the Civil War, a period when American politics increasingly revolved around debate over slavery. While the serfs were becoming convinced that freedom was finally within their grasp, the slaves saw little prospect for change. Unlike the serfs, whose struggle was increasingly transformed into one against serfdom as a whole, most slaves continued to strive for attainment of the best possible conditions within slavery (or to run away from it).

There is a certain irony in this. A number of recent scholars have been critical of the static approach usually taken to southern slavery, and it has become commonplace to call for greater attention to the way the institution evolved over time.[41] It should be clear that I share this concern, because American slavery in the seventeenth century was very different from what it would become in the nineteenth. Still, in one important sense time *did* stand still for the slaves: as outsiders they had little reason to believe that what happened in the country at large mattered to them, and they strove therefore to make the best of their world, not to change it. Only the Civil War was an event big enough to upset the equilibrium of master-slave relations. Within two years of its outbreak the South would see massive flight by slaves to Union lines, growing insubordination among slaves who remained at home, a sense that freedom *was* in fact attainable, and the emergence of a distinctively American equivalent to the peasants' naive monarchism: faith in Father Abraham Lincoln as returning deliverer.

*　　*　　*

WE ARE NOW in a position to return to the question of the bondsmen's culture. In both countries they developed their own behavioral norms distinct from those of their owners. But whose culture was it? Was the South home to attitudes and life-style that should be termed *black* or *slave*? To what extent were the actions of the Russian serfs determined by their serfdom and to what extent by their being peasants? In short, what was the relative impact of class versus caste in defining the world of the bondsmen? This is a question of considerable complexity. As we have seen, the masters often confused ethnic with class characteristics, ascribing the behavior of slaves and serfs to innate features. Outside observers were less consistent: although some shared the masters' views concerning the inherent laziness and dependence of blacks and peasants, others took pains to attribute such traits to their servile status rather than their nature. "The guile, the baseness, and rugged ferocity attributed to slaves, and men overwhelmed with oppression, are chiefly owing to their oppressors," explained an English traveler to late eighteenth-century Russia. "Exposed to corporal punishment, and put on the footing of irrational animals, how can they possess that spirit and elevation of sentiment which distinguish the natives of a free state? Treated with so much inhumanity, how can they be humane?" But what of the bondsmen themselves? Was their primary identity as slaves or blacks, serfs or peasants?[42]

An initial distinction must be made between the character of the bondsmen's culture and their subjective view of it. Objectively, the behavior of southern slaves was more shaped by slavery than that of Russian serfs was by serfdom. Although the vast majority of blacks in the antebellum South were slaves and hence slave culture appeared virtually synonymous with black, its most distinguishing features were largely consequences of *slave* relations, not ethnic traditions. Not only was the developing slave culture clearly distinct from ancestral black (African), but concrete slave conditions shaped many of that culture's noteworthy characteristics from family relations to religious behavior. It was the *slave* quarters that permitted the flowering of this culture. Although there were many exceptions, most free Negroes—who as Ira Berlin has noted generally "lived on the periphery of the South" and "worked on the margins of the Southern economy"—had little access to that environment. (With emancipation, of course, slave culture became black culture, even though most of its original essence was slave, not black; in turn, that culture was transformed by the end of slavery.)[43]

In Russia, by contrast, the bondsmen's culture was as much peasant as distinctively serf. Unlike slaves, who constituted the vast bulk of southern blacks, serfs were only about half of Russian peasants during the century before emancipation; they shared with state peasants traditions of a common culture whose roots in Russia antedated serfdom. Of course, bondage shaped the behavior of the serfs; testifying to this were the changes in their life-style that followed emancipation, such as the widespread rejection by ex-serfs of the large communal family. "Along with the bond between master and serf, that between father and son—the family bond, has been slackened," commented one observer a generation after emancipation. "They have tasted of freedom, and now, in the same way that the serf is rid of the master's yoke, the son strives to rid himself of the yoke of paternal authority, almost absolute until now." Many couples abandoned the joint or extended families that had prevailed under serfdom, and the average size of peasant households tumbled from 4.18 males in 1858 to 3.0 by the end of the century. But serfdom shaped the behavior of the serfs less than slavery did that of the slaves, both because of the existing cultural continuity the serfs enjoyed and because they faced substantially less owner interference. The serfs' life-style was thus part of a broader peasant life-style; the mir, for example, was a basic institution among state peasants as well as serfs. (Contrast this with the free Negroes' isolation from the slave quarters.) Ultimately, slave life was far more defined by slavery than was serf life by serfdom.[44]

From the bondsmen's point of view the situation was somewhat different. The South did see some division among Negroes according to status. "Free coloreds," most notably in lower-South cities such as New Orleans, Mobile, and Charleston, strove mightily to set themselves off from the mass of black slaves, especially if as was often the case they could show off a relatively light complexion. Light-skinned Negroes sometimes succeeded in hiding their ancestry and "passing" into the dominant white population, and occasionally groups of elite free coloreds were able to win acceptance from whites of their special status. In the Cane River country of northwest Louisiana a group of "creoles" descended from an eighteenth-century French settler and his African slave flourished in antebellum years as a prosperous, self-contained colony of slaveowning free mulattoes who prided themselves on their color, success, and "southern" culture. Even less unusual free Negroes sometimes displayed a distinct pride in their status, and in subsequent interviews such free blacks commonly stressed their superior position. "My muma and papy was free niggers," one explained typically; "I ain't no slave—ain't never bin one." Although there is little evidence of slave resentment against such ordinary free blacks, a great deal indicates that the snobbery of elite Negroes who scorned the slave masses elicited corresponding hostility from slaves. Such feelings remained strong even in post–Civil War days, when ex-slaves ridiculed the aristocratic pretensions of groups such as Mobile's Creole Fire Company Number 1 and New Orleans' quadroons.[45]

In general, however, antagonism between slaves and free blacks seems to have been overshadowed by feelings of common identity and interest in the face of white oppression. Except in a handful of deep-South cities few free blacks expressed elitist pretensions, and in the upper South, where more than 85 percent of the South's free blacks lived, most were poor farmers, hired hands, and domestic servants whose material standard of living was not far removed from that of the slaves. When such free Negroes and slaves came into contact with each other, they were more likely to display camaraderie than hostility or jealousy. In the cities, to the dismay of whites, they rubbed shoulders almost everywhere, from places of employment to churches, markets, "grog shops," and gambling halls. In the country such mingling was more difficult, because of the slaves' restricted lives, but it was not unusual for them to work together, socialize with each other, and even marry. The existence of kinship ties between slaves and free blacks and of a small amount of mobility between them in both directions—some slaves were manumitted or purchased their freedom, and some free blacks were kidnapped into slavery—were powerful forces making for close racial ties between slave and free, as were the increasing restrictions imposed on free blacks by white southerners during the last decades of slavery. Although the fears of many whites that free blacks were a dangerous source of rebellion among the slave population were on the whole unfounded, such whites were correct that more served to unite than to divide the two groups.[46]

In short, racial identification proved stronger than class among most slaves. The vast preponderance of slaves in the black population, together with the ease of somatic identification and the fact that whites seemed united to oppress them, led to the same widespread confusion between race and class among slaves as existed among their masters. Slaves referred to themselves in racial terms—as "colored" or "niggers" rather than "slaves"—and saw their oppressors as whites in general rather than slaveowners in particular. "White folks jes' naturally different from darkies," explained one ex-slave. "We's different in color, in talk, and in 'ligion and beliefs. We's different in every way and can never be spected to think or to live alike." Such racial loyalty was facilitated by the virulent racism of many nonslave-holding whites as well as by the absence in the South of any appreciable body of white abolitionists. Within the South, lines in fact appeared to be drawn according to race.[47]

Such racial identity needs to be clearly distinguished from local or communal solidarity with which it is sometimes confused. The African slave trade served from the beginning to fragment this kind of sentiment by breaking up communal and family units and thrusting together those who had different nationalities, spoke different languages, and followed different customs. The domestic slave trade continued this atomization: slaves were regularly taken from their communities, their friends, their relatives—from everything they knew—and reintegrated into new groupings of people with whom their major immediately recognizable bond was their color. Very few slave autobiographers were born, grew up, and lived (until escaping slavery) in one place, which came to encompass their world. Take, for example, Charles Ball, born in Maryland about 1780 to parents with different owners. Separated from his mother by sale at age four, Ball had five consecutive masters in Maryland and Washington, D.C., before being taken south when a young man. During the next few years in South Carolina and Georgia he had four more masters, the last two of whom he served as driver. After escaping to Maryland, he was kidnapped and returned to Georgia and then sold again, before he escaped a second time, made his way to Savannah, and stowed away on a ship headed for Philadelphia. Although not all autobiographers had as many owners as Ball, the vast majority were sold, inherited, or hired out more than once. It was a rare slave who lived out his years in the same place his parents and grandparents had before him, as did most serfs (or, for that matter, most peasants in other preindustrial societies). Under such circumstances local loyalties and attachments became at least partially superseded by a more generalized racial identity.[48]

The same forced movement that served to weaken local bonds thus fostered broader racial bonds, for the corollary of a weak sense of communal identity was a willingness to regard all blacks as one's brothers and sisters. (The practice of calling all older blacks "uncle" and "auntie" is indicative of this notion of all blacks as members of a giant extended family.) Although slaves did not display the kind of group solidarity common among peasants, they also lacked the sense of local chauvinism or hostility to outsiders that usually went with it. Even as they responded to the conditions they faced largely as individuals rather than as a collective, they identified with other black individuals across geographic and occupational lines. The word *community*, therefore, is best applied to the slaves in a somewhat unusual way, connoting a shared sense of brotherhood with others in like circumstances; their community was with all other slaves, indeed all other blacks, not with those who happened to live on the same farms and plantations.

Russian serfs, too, felt a considerable sense of "peasantness." Just as slaves and free blacks shared a common appearance, so too serfs and state peasants were physically indistinguishable from each other, while both looked strikingly different from noblemen. The common culture, life-style, and traditions of serfs and state peasants facilitated the emergence of a broad peasant identification. Serfs usually referred to themselves as peasants in much the same way that American slaves referred to themselves as blacks.

Nevertheless, the primary loyalty of the serfs was local—to group, village, and commune, rather than to class or caste. Serfs, who more often than not lived in the ancestral villages where their parents and grandparents had lived before them and where indigenous local institutions—the mir, the family—cemented communal relations, developed a strong collective feeling, a strong group identification with other villagers. Pomeshchiki might come and go, but the village, the mir, and the feelings the serfs had for them remained.

This kind of local identification had both positive and negative manifestations. The former was most evident in the extraordinary group solidarity serfs displayed when confronting their owners or authorities. Individual villagers took their cue from the commune; in a typical case, when a provincial governor singled out a young man from a large crowd of assembled serfs and asked him whether he would obey his master, the youth replied, "As the mir goes, so will I," giving the same response even after being punished for his insolence with twenty-five blows with birch switches. But the reverse side of this local identification and solidarity was a pervasive distrust of outsiders that was also largely absent among American slaves and that served to impede the development of a broad class consciousness among the serfs. Serfs were intensely suspicious of strangers of any kind, whether these be noblemen (including their owners), government officials, or foreign travelers; such suspicion extended sometimes to priests and usually to Jews in areas where they existed. It even extended to would-be supporters: a decade after emancipation populist agitators who went "to the people" to spread their revolutionary message were dismayed to find that peasants often looked on them as troublemakers rather than as friends. (Contrast this reaction to the enthusiasm southern blacks showed during Reconstruction when northern "carpetbaggers" came south to open schools among them and press for their political rights.)[49]

What is most remarkable, however, is the degree to which this suspicion extended to outside *peasants*. As we have seen, pomeshchiki sometimes found it necessary in their instructions to warn stewards about serfs' fighting with neighboring villagers, and such disputes—over land, animals, wood—were not uncommon. In 1648, for example, B. I. Morozov's serfs in Arzamasskii district engaged in a number of confrontations over land and crops with nearby peasants owned by other pomeshchiki; in one of these altercations six of Morozov's serfs were beaten and six horses were seized, but soon thereafter Morozov's peasants reciprocated, inflicting the same penalty on their rivals. In 1813, when M. A. Obreskov acquired the village of Chekashevi Poliani with 382 souls in Penza province, he decided that the peasants had too little land for their own needs, so he abolished seigneurial cultivation and reassigned each family an equal amount of land, expecting thus "to gain from them the diligence and obedience which the peasant owes his pomeshchik"; instead, however, they fought bitterly with the neighboring peasants—also owned by Obreskov—continuing a long-standing dispute that had evidently led to numerous violent altercations in the past.[50]

This suspicion of the outside world, a source of major village solidarity during volneniia, also enabled authorities to use divide-and-conquer tactics in suppressing them. Provincial officials sometimes brought in "witnesses"—serfs or state peasants from nearby villages—to help restore order on an estate. This tactic did not always work, any more than bringing in priests did; in 1855, for example, when the governor used twenty-five hundred state peasants to help put down a volnenie in Voronezh province, they refused to perform their assigned task, and a staff-officer of the Corps of Gendarmes secretly criticized the governor's action, stating that "in my opinion, use of large masses of witnesses to suppress turbulent peasants is a mistake." More often, however, especially before the very last years of serfdom when expectations of impending change affected peasant behavior, witnesses served to intimidate serfs engaged in volneniia, and their continued use indicates the extent to which authorities expected to be able to play off one group of peasants against another. The ultimate preserver of order, the army, was also largely a peasant force, made up of serf and state-peasant recruits, and it is significant that these recruits, when called on to put down volneniia, seem never to have hesitated to take action against fellow peasants. In short, peasant solidarity, so powerful a force *within* the local community, was relatively weak without. Although evidence suggests an increase in class consciousness during the 1850s, when rumors of a general emancipation ran rampant, the mir remained, in a literal sense, the world of the serfs.[51]

Clearly, slave and serf identity, ties, and loyalties were complex and partially overlapping. There is no necessary conflict among attachments to self, family, community, group, and class. Nevertheless, conditions bred among the serfs a much stronger sense of local community than among the slaves, who seemed at the same time to be both more individualistic and more willing to see themselves as part of a broader category of oppressed people. The race consciousness of southern slaves, which approached a general class consciousness, in turn produced far less collectivity than the more localized communal consciousness of the Russian serfs. Among both there existed a sense of unity—shared values, perceptions, and loyalties—but the nature of that sense differed markedly. For the serfs it meant attachment to village and commune; for the slaves it entailed a feeling of oneness with blacks in general.

* * *

POTENTIALLY the greatest countervailing force to this unity was the socioeconomic diversity that existed among the bondsmen. Although the great majority of them performed agricultural labor, a significant number spent some or all of their work time in ventures that required the application of various specialized talents. Occupational diversity in turn produced economic stratification that raised questions about the unity of the bondsmen's interests, attitudes, and values.

Such stratification was especially significant in Russia, where most serfs had opportunities to engage in their own economic activities, sometimes supplementing their meager incomes with various kinds of nonagricultural employment. This was particularly true in areas that were the least fertile, where pomeshchiki allowed most of their serfs to work on obrok; by the second half of the eighteenth century a national division of labor had emerged that in rough terms saw the fertile south concentrate on agriculture while elsewhere an increasing proportion of the population supplemented or even replaced agricultural employment with other means of support. But wherever obrok existed, serfs were able to produce their own goods, agricultural and nonagricultural, for market. By the late eighteenth century commercial activity among peasants—both state and serf—had reached considerable proportions, with the proliferation of local and regional fairs and markets. Beginning in 1812, the government began selling peasants four categories of licenses that authorized them to engage in trade of varying magnitude; in 1816, 5,126 such licenses were issued, and by 1852 their number had risen to 7,450. These traders, however, represented only the tip of the iceberg: the licenses were required only of peasants whose annual sales exceeded two thousand rubles (four thousand after 1821), and hundreds of thousands of serfs whose level of commercial activity was less than this were able to bring goods to market on their own. Indeed, Soviet historians have seen the main origins of Russian capitalism in this small-scale peasant commerce rather than in that of merchants and noblemen.[52]

Serfs engaged in a broad range of market-oriented activities. On a nationwide level agriculture maintained its primary importance. By the late eighteenth century serfs and state peasants were selling more grain on the domestic market than were pomeshchiki, and peasants had a virtual monopoly on sale of specialized agricultural products such as hemp, flax, and tobacco. But an increasing number of serfs sought to add to their meager earnings by engaging in various kinds of skilled trades (*promysli*) such as woodworking, carpentry, and tailoring, and others served the country's growing commercial needs by working in river transport. Sometimes whole villages specialized in promysli. As early as the first half of the seventeenth century Morozov had two large villages along the Volga River, Lyskovo and Murashkino, where skilled trades were prevalent; in Murashkino in 1625, 114 of 454 heads of households were artisans, including 10 blacksmiths, 10 sheepskin workers, 9 carpenters, 9 potters, 7 tanners, 7 silversmiths, 4 distillers, 4 carriers, 4 butchers, 4 tailors, and 4 shoemakers. Such specialization became more common during the last century of serfdom. On the far-flung Sheremetev holdings the village of Ivanovo in Vladimir province became known as a weaving center, where by 1800 178 shops sold cloth and other items twice weekly; in the first half of the nineteenth century the "village" became a major manufacturing and trading center, employing thousands of peasants—both from the estate and outsiders—in factory work, and boasting 66 stone and 111 wooden shops. Other Sheremetev villages specialized in metalwork, wooden handicrafts, and livestock raising, and in 1800 the family's various estates held twenty annual fairs and sixteen weekly or semiweekly markets. During the first half of the nineteenth century handicraft work, trading, and factory employment became extensive among serfs of the central-industrial and north-western regions of the country, especially near Moscow and St. Petersburg, and an increasing number of men left their estates on passes to earn a living elsewhere.[53]

The practice of receiving a pass to work for a stipulated time period away from one's estate—known as *otkhodnichestvo* (those who took advantage of it were *otkhodniki* or "departers")—became increasingly widespread as economic development created new kinds of employment opportunities. Even in the eighteenth century serfs on obrok often received permission from owners to leave home to work in factories, urban construction, river transport, and salt mines, as well as to make short trips to engage in small-scale commerce; an English traveler in the late eighteenth century noted "the frequent migration of country-people to towns" where "the boor in a short time becomes any thing, in which he can find employment: peddlar, footman, mechanic, artist, merchant." But in the nineteenth century, as the national division of labor reduced the need for agricultural manpower in north and north-central Russia, millions of male serfs left their villages to earn money elsewhere. In 1856, 1,354 men from Sheremetev's Iukhotskaia estate—almost one-half the estate's male population—received passes to work away from home, the great majority in St. Petersburg and Moscow. Hundreds of Prince Vorontsov's serfs from the central-industrial region also went to Moscow, St. Petersburg, and other towns where they found employment as carpenters, masons, painters, factory workers, laborers, and servants. By 1840, 136,000 otkhodniki were working in Moscow and 228,847 in St. Petersburg; in the latter city they constituted almost one-half the total population (which was, consequently, overwhelmingly male). In the late 1850s, 887,000 peasants (all but a small fraction men) from seven central-industrial provinces, the equivalent of more than one-quarter of the region's male peasants, were spending at least part of the time away from home on passes. Although many of these were state peasants, who not having owners found it easier to secure permission to leave their villages, serfs did not lag far behind; in Vladimir province, for example, 26.8 percent of the male state peasants were otkhodniki at some time in 1854, compared with 19.3 percent of the male serfs. Most received short-term passes of one to four months, but a significant minority were for periods of up to a year and longer.[54]

One consequence of this economic development was the emergence of increasing economic stratification within serf villages that, had it progressed far enough, might have served seriously to undermine prevailing communal values and solidarity. Soviet historians have focused a great deal of attention on the growth of economic differentiation among the peasantry, seeing it as a key sign of the breakdown of the feudal order and the emergence of capitalist relations, and they have engaged in extensive debates about the nature, timing, and extent of serf stratification as well as the criteria for measuring it. Some scholars have seen the existence of sharp "bourgeois stratification of the peasantry" as early as the seventeenth century; others have maintained that such stratification, although increasing, remained relatively slight even in the first half of the nineteenth. Still others have distinguished between "property differentiation," which existed early, and "social [or bourgeois] stratification," which involved actual class divisions among the peasantry in which the rich exploited the labor of the poor; the latter reached significant proportions only during the nineteenth century, leading finally (after emancipation) to "decomposition" of the peasantry into rural bourgeoisie and proletariat.[55]

Despite continuing disagreement among historians, a number of conclusions seem warranted. Differences in wealth among serfs on given estates clearly existed, even at an early date. Soviet scholars have typically followed Lenin in dividing peasant families into three categories—rich, middle, and poor—based most often on the number of horses they possessed but sometimes also on income, size of landholding, and ownership of other animals. Using such categorization, historians have had little trouble in demonstrating that virtually everywhere, some serfs were able to acquire more land and personal property, and consequently to live better, than others. For example, in an analysis of 185 families owned by P. P. Shafirov on an estate in central Russia in the early eighteenth century, Iu. A. Tikhonov found that ten families had no horses and were "on the edge of ruin," but thirty had four or more and lived quite comfortably; on the basis of ownership of horses and other animals as well as the amount of rye sown, he classified ten of the households as impoverished, ninety-one as poor, forty-nine as middle, and thirty-five as rich. Furthermore, there was a tendency—although it was not universal—for stratification to become more marked during the last century of serfdom, especially in the nonagricultural areas. E. I. Indova found that of 1,625 serf households on the Vorontsov holdings in Karelia province near St. Petersburg, the proportion of rich peasants increased slightly from 17.7 percent to 19.0 percent between 1812 and 1832, the proportion of poor surged from 49.4 percent to 66.6 percent, and the proportion of middle peasants declined sharply, from 32.9 percent to 14.4 percent. On the basis of numerous sample estates I. D. Koval'chenko concluded that the percentage of poor serfs increased significantly between 1800 and 1860, especially among those who lived in villages that were not totally agricultural.[56]

Serf stratification was usually greatest in the central-industrial and northwestern provinces, where obrok was prevalent and peasants had greater opportunity to pursue their own economic advantage, and in Belorussia and the western Ukraine, where communal redivision of peasant landholdings was less common. But even in Russia proper the repartitional commune did not come close to producing total economic equality among serfs. Some households were assigned more land than others because of their greater size and possession of livestock; furthermore, serfs were sometimes able to rent additional land, either from others within their village or from nearby outsiders, and even to purchase land (technically in the name of their owners). As Englishwoman Mary Holderness wrote of New Russia, where she spent four years in the early nineteenth century, "It always happens that some boors in every village, by superior industry and fortuitous circumstances, continue to be richer than the rest, and that others, by laziness, drunkenness, small families, and sundry accidents, remain in a state of comparative poverty." As a result, she noted, "one boor frequently serves another, letting out his own labour and land to his more fortunate neighbors."[57]

A few serfs became quite wealthy, occasionally even purchasing their "own" serfs. Noblemen were usually pleased to see their serfs acquire riches, because they could then be charged obrok dues many times as large as those most villagers paid. Count P. B. Sheremetev's 1764 instruction contained an entry entitled "on the purchase by peasants of workers" in which he stated that with the steward's permission his serfs were allowed to buy serfs from other pomeshchiki "in my name." The practice continued in the nineteenth century on the Sheremetev holdings: in 1810, 165 of the family's "capitalist" serfs on ten different estates owned a total of 400 male and 503 female serfs. A tiny number of serfs acquired enormous wealth, although legally it belonged to their owners, not to them. In the Sheremetevs' textile village of Ivanovo, a peasant named E. Grachev employed twenty-two workers in his calico-printing factory in 1789; six years later he became the first of Sheremetev's serfs to purchase his freedom, for the amazing sum of 130,000 rubles. Not all wealthy serfs found it easy to buy their freedom, however, because some noblemen enjoyed the prestige and power of owning rich persons. Nikolai Shipov, author of one of the very few narratives left by an ex-serf, related that his father, who had grown wealthy trading cattle in the southeast, was forced to pay his absentee owner more than 5,000 rubles per year in obrok dues in the early nineteenth century; although he and several other serfs tried to purchase their freedom, one even offering 160,000 rubles, the owner steadfastly refused. In a probably apocryphal story Count Sheremetev is said to have turned down an offer of 200,000 rubles from a serf named Shelyshin who sought his freedom, only to cheerfully manumit the enterprising peasant when he turned out to be the only person in St. Petersburg who could secure oysters for the nobleman's lunch.[58]

Serfs who acquired great wealth as traders or manufacturers rarely shared the social outlook of most villagers or partook of communal activities; although legally serfs, they were in fact merchants far removed from the collective world view of the mir. At the age of thirteen Nikolai Shipov accompanied his father on the first of what were to be many trading trips to the southeast steppes, leaving home in March and spending the summer purchasing horses and sheep from cossacks, hiring peasants to help drive the herds north, and selling them in markets of central Russia; his understanding of the world was predictably different from that of the serf who had never left his village and looked with distrust on everything outside it. The same was true to a lesser extent of ordinary otkhodniki. The narrator of *Vesti o Rossii (News of Russia)*, a semiautobiographical, semifictional poem-narrative written by an unknown peasant in the 1830s or 1840s, expressed the changed mentality of a young serf who returns to his native village after living for seven years in St. Petersburg. He laments:

> In the villages poor slaves
> Live half senselessly,
> Superstitious and coarse,
> As if waiting destruction.
> In worn and dirty attire
> Men and women are like shadows . . .
> I often thought with a shudder:
> "Can they live in such poverty from laziness?"

Upon returning home, his nostalgic memories of an idealized communal life quickly fade as he finds old village customs strange and depressing.[59]

Pronounced stratification could undermine the communal values and traditional behavior of an entire village, not just the few who left it. Folklorist Iu. M. Sokolov found that "in localities which had been more powerfully subjected to the penetration of capital and capitalist relations, the hand-made dowry quickly began to be replaced by the dowry of ready-made objects," and men sought wives who would be "of good figure and manner" rather than one who would be "a terrific worker." Where serfs worked for the well-being of their wealthier neighbors, the sense of mutual interest sometimes gave way to jealousy, recrimination, and an incipient notion of private property. "Stratification among the peasantry demolished the peasant 'mir,'" wrote historian E. I. Indova of the nineteenth-century Vorontsov holdings. "There occurred in it a bitter struggle between the poor and the well-to-do." Although the view that intraserf class conflict pervaded preemancipation villages represents a great exaggeration, scattered evidence indicates bad feelings between poor serfs and their more fortunate fellow-bondsmen. As a steward reported of an absentee-held estate in 1843, "Among the peasants there is a remarkable custom, clearly displaying their coarseness and ignorance: he who is somewhat poorer is obviously indignant and even threatens the well-to-do, so that in time he pays his obligation."[60]

Nevertheless, differentiation among serfs was on the whole not pronounced enough seriously to undermine communal solidarity. Very rich serfs were not only highly exceptional; they also operated largely outside the confines of the peasant commune. Their behavior therefore had relatively little impact on the collective mentality of most villagers. Although otkhodniki were numerous, most of them were less capitalist entrepreneurs than impoverished rural folk forced by the poor living they made in agriculture to seek whatever additional earnings they could scrape together from odd jobs and handicrafts; some were even hired out by their owners, like American slaves. The great majority of otkhodniki received short-term passes of one to four months; in seven central-industrial provinces only one-fifth of the otkhodniki in the middle of the nineteenth century received permission to stay away a year or longer, and most of these were state peasants. The mass of serf otkhodniki therefore maintained their basic village ties. Even serf entrepreneurs could be unexpectedly reminded of the bond they shared with other serfs. In 1831 Shipov, accustomed to coming and going as he pleased, suddenly found himself under house arrest, his pass confiscated by a jealous burmistr. Although he was released after a month, the reality of his status and the arbitrary treatment to which he could be subjected at any time convinced him of the need to escape.[61]

Individuals who temporarily left home were thus still essentially villagers at heart, and within the village itself stratification rarely proceeded far enough to undermine traditional attitudes and perceptions of common interests. Although most Soviet historians have stressed the increase of stratification, several have properly warned against the tendency to exaggerate it. As V. K. Iatsunskii put it, capitalist relations in the countryside "did not appear as early as is sometimes supposed, their proportion should not be exaggerated, and most important, they arose in the sphere of nonagricultural endeavors of the peasantry," not in the agricultural village itself. He concluded that "the majority of information on economic inequality among the peasantry of Russia in the first half of the nineteenth century gives no basis for asserting the presence at that time of capitalist stratification of the peasantry."[62]

Indeed, an examination of serf stratification in Russia should convince one of its limitations. Although it is easy to divide households into different categories of wealth, the gap separating one category from another was relatively slight; if one extreme among the serfs may conveniently be labeled poor, few among the other extreme would qualify by any but the most liberal standards as rich or well-to-do. Furthermore, because rich households were usually larger than poor, the common practice of categorizing serfs on the basis of *household* wealth substantially overstates the differences among them.

Take, for example, P. K. Alefirenko's study of stratification in the eighteenth century. Examining two estates owned by M. G. Golovkin in Moscow province where capitalist relations were supposedly pronounced, he divided the serf households into poor, middle, and well-to-do. Of the 104 households, 31 with no horses or one were poor, 59 with two or three horses were middle, and 14 households with four or more horses were well-to-do. But although a family with two horses was (other things being equal) likely to be better off than a family with one, the difference hardly seems such as to suggest that they had radically different outlooks on life or that they viewed each other as class enemies. Furthermore, the degree of stratification was less marked than it first appears, because although Golovkin's poor households had an average of 5.1 inhabitants, the middle had 6.5 and the rich 10.7. This was by no means unusual: both serfs and pomeshchiki recognized that economies of scale could be realized in large households, and they strove to prevent their division into smaller units; larger households almost always averaged more land, livestock, and income than their smaller neighbors. It did mean, however, that the gap between rich and poor was substantially smaller than the figures derived from using households as units of measurement suggest. The rich had 6.1 times as many horses as the poor measured by household, but only 2.5 times as many measured per capita (see Table 9). Equally interesting, the amount of rye cultivated per person varied little between rich and poor, averaging about 0.3 desiatina (1 desiatina = 2.7 acres) per person among all three categories. Rich households cultivated more rye than poor only because they contained more inhabitants.[63]

The situation was similar in the nineteenth century. On the Golitsyns' Muromskaia estate in Vladimir province the serfs were all on obrok, and many supplemented their agricultural income with outside labor, engaging in fishing, barge hauling, and various small handicrafts. As a result, R. M. Vvedenskii's study of their condition in 1829 appears to reveal considerable differentiation among the 244

Table 9
Stratification among serfs on two estates owned by M. G. Golovkin,
Moscow province, 1746

	Poor		Middle		Rich		
	No.	Percent	No.	Percent	No.	Percent	Total
Households	31	29.8	59	56.7	14	13.5	104
Persons	158	22.9	381	55.3	150	21.8	689
Persons/household	5.1		6.5		10.7		6.6
Horses	24	10.3	139	59.7	70	30.0	233
Horses/household	0.8		2.4		5.0		2.2
Horses/person	0.2		0.4		0.5		0.3

Source: P. K. Alefirenko, Krest'ianskoe dvizhenie i krest'ianskii vopros v Rossii v 30-50-kh godakh XVIII veka (Moscow: Izdatel'stvo Akademii nauk SSSR, 1958), 35.

households: 44 rich households had four or more horses and an average annual income of 73.2 rubles, 126 middle households had two or three horses and an average income of 39.7 rubles, and 74 poor households had no horses or one (only 2 households had no horses) and an average income of 22.0 rubles. Vvedenskii estimated that the annual expenditures (obrok and other obligations plus living expenses) of poor and middle families exceeded their incomes, and they were consequently forced to go ever deeper in debt, whereas the rich families ended the year with a small surplus. Clearly, the rich were better off than the poor. What is striking, however, is the small size of the gap separating them. Because rich households had substantially more inhabitants than poor, the average income per soul varied only from 8.6 rubles for the poor to 11.7 for the rich; the rich households were richer primarily because they had more workers, not because each of their workers made appreciably more (see Table 10).[64]

The level of inequality that these and other samples reveal, although real, is at the same time limited. With the exception of a tiny number of unusual "capitalist" serfs, the well-to-do lived a little better than the poor but can hardly be said, on the basis of their livestock holdings, income, or relationship to the means to production, to have constituted a separate class or even a separate social stratum with a distinctive social outlook. In fact, I. D. Koval'chenko has found considerable social mobility—upward and downward but especially downward—among serfs on sample estates during the first half of the nineteenth century. Of 304 rich households on eight agricultural estates, only 21 percent remained rich after half a century; 53 percent

Table 10
Stratification among serfs on the Golitsyns' Muromskaia estate,
Vladimir province, 1829

Type of household	Number	Income/ household (rubles)	Expenses/ household (rubles)	Surplus or deficit (rubles)	Souls/ household	Income/ soul (rubles)
Poor	74	22.0	28.6	−6.6	2.6	8.6
Middle	126	39.7	45.3	−5.6	4.2	9.5
Rich	44	73.2	69.3	3.9	6.3	11.7
Total	244	40.4	44.6	−4.2	4.1	10.0

Source: R. M. Vvedenskii, "Kharakter pomeshchich'ei ekspluatatsii i biudzhety obrochnykh krest'ian v 20-40-e gody XIX v.," Istoriia SSSR, 1971, no. 3, 48.

had fallen to middle status, 12 percent had skidded to poor status, and 16 percent had disappeared from the records altogether, either because they had left the estates or ceased to exist as families. Like the poor, well-to-do serfs toiled for the well-being of their owners and were subject to their arbitrary whims. Their elevated status must be seen in relative terms, as meaning that their material condition was slightly less desperate than that of most other serfs, but they were hardly rich by broader standards.[65]

Confirmation that this limited stratification did not in most cases come near to undermining the serfs' basic communal outlook, sense of shared values, and common interests is best seen in their behavior during volneniia. As we have seen, this behavior was highly collective and centered on the mir and its role as representative of the serf community. Although a few Soviet historians, seeking to accentuate the level of stratification and portray the serf village as plagued by incipient intrapeasant class conflict, have argued that rich peasants dragged their feet and sometimes even opposed their fellow villagers in volneniia, the most perceptive scholars have stressed instead the degree to which villagers united as a group to defend their common interests. The evidence on this score is overwhelming. The kind of solidarity and unity that serfs showed when confronting authorities is powerful testimony to the strength of their communal spirit and common identification.[66]

*   *   *

ALTHOUGH STRATIFICATION among American slaves has received insufficient attention from historians, it is safe to say that on the whole it was less marked than among Russian serfs. As in Russia, the bondsmen enjoyed considerable occupational diversity, with a significant proportion of them employed at some time in their lives in work other than basic field labor. For a variety of reasons, however, this diversity did not generally translate into broad socioeconomic stratification or into conflicting world views among the slaves.

Although Africans were imported for hard physical labor, from an early date some slaves demonstrated talents that led to their use in a variety of nonagricultural capacities. In colonial South Carolina, where blacks quickly came to constitute a majority of the population, their labor was needed not only to grow rice and other crops but also to serve as artisans, fishermen, sailors, hunters, lumberers, carriers, and guides. In a history of South Carolina and Georgia published in 1779, the author noted that "many negroes discover great capacities, and an amazing aptness for learning trades, where dangerous tools are used, and many owners, from motives of profit and advantage, breed them to be coopers, carpenters, bricklayers, smiths, and other trades." Although he and other whites deplored the independence that gave such slaves access to potentially dangerous information and weapons, skilled slaves served not simply the greed of white Carolinians but also very real societal needs, because as in other slave societies where blacks outnumbered whites—although to a lesser extent than in the Caribbean and Brazil—not enough skilled whites were available to fulfill all the middle-class jobs that had to be performed. The number of slave specialists consequently increased sharply during the second half of the eighteenth century: Philip D. Morgan has recently found that the proportion of skilled workers among inventoried South Carolina adult male slaves increased from 13.7 percent in 1750–59 to 28.6 percent in 1790–99. (Among women the proportion increased from 2.7 percent to 8.5 percent.)[67]

In the Chesapeake colonies, where blacks never formed a majority of the population, slaves' skills were less in demand, and in the seventeenth century almost all slaves found themselves relegated to field labor. By the first half of the eighteenth century, however, as the supply of white indentured servants dried up, slaves became numerically more significant, and a larger group of acculturated second-generation blacks emerged, opportunities for slaves to engage in skilled work increased markedly. Between 1658 and 1710 only four of 525 adult males (0.76 percent) listed in inventories in four Maryland counties were skilled craftsmen; between 1720 and 1730, however, thirteen of 213 (6.1 percent) were, with carpenters, coopers, and blacksmiths most numerous. Large planters in the late eighteenth century usually relied heavily on their own slaves for whatever skilled work they needed done and consequently had numerous black "tradesmen" or artisans; planters with more than one holding usually kept such slaves on their main or "home" plantation. In 1786, for example, George Washington had 216 slaves on six different holdings, of whom 67—41 adults—lived on the "Home House"; these Home-House slaves included 4 carpenters, 2 smiths, a waggoner, a carter, a gardener, 3 drivers and stablers, 2 seamstresses, and 4 spinners, as well as many domestic servants. (On a separate mill holding he had 3 coopers and a miller.) When Thomas Jefferson inherited 127 slaves from John Wayles in 1774, 8 of these were "tradesmen," including 3 watermen, 2 carpenters, 2 smiths, and a shoemaker. An 1810 listing of the 78 slaves on Jefferson's home plantation at Monticello divided them into 19 farm workers, 37 house slaves, and 22 tradesmen. Further north, in colonial New York, New Jersey, and New England, most slaves were either domestics or skilled artisans.[68]

Slaves continued to hold diverse occupations in the nineteenth century, although historians have disagreed on whether the number of skilled jobs for slaves was increasing or decreasing. Scholars such as Genovese have suggested that the number of slave craftsmen declined during the last seventy-five years of slavery, as the South came to rely more on skilled white workers and northern industry to provide essential nonagricultural items. In the deep South the intense demand for plantation hands to meet the surging world market for cotton limited the number of slaves available for other kinds of employment, especially in the 1840s and 1850s. At the same time, however, southern industries—although embryonic by northern standards—employed an increasing number of slaves. By the 1850s between 160,000 and 200,000 slaves—about 10 percent of the adult slave population—worked in textile, iron, tobacco, lumber, and grist mills, as well as in mines, on canals, on railroads, and in construction work; most of these were owned directly by industrialists, although some were hired. In cities such as New Orleans, Mobile, Charleston, Richmond, Baltimore, Louisville, and St. Louis, slaves worked as dockworkers, factory hands, mechanics, firemen, and odd laborers as well as domestic servants.[69]

In the countryside, where most slaves lived, occupational diversity persisted too. Olmsted visited a plantation in Mississippi that had 135 slaves, of whom 67 were field hands and 12 skilled workers (not counting house servants) including 2 seamstresses and one blacksmith, carpenter, wheelwright, slaves' cook, stable tender, cattle tender, hog tender, teamster, midwife, nurse, driver of the hoe-gang, and foreman of the plow-gang. In 1856, among the 96 slaves on George Noble Jones's El Destino plantation in Florida, 62 performed field labor while 7 had specialized jobs, mostly managerial and livestock tending; on his neighboring Chemonie plantation 7 of 44 working slaves had specialized tasks. Women had fewer opportunities to engage in skilled work (aside from domestic service). Large plantations often had nurses to care for young children and cooks to prepare slaves' food, and a South Carolina doctor noted in 1858 that in the Columbia region "on every plantation the sick nurse, or doctor woman, is usually the most intelligent female on the place." Fogel and Engerman, who have done the only thorough statistical work on the subject, estimated that during the last years of slavery 7.0 percent of the rural male adult slaves were engaged in managerial work, 11.9 percent were skilled craftsmen, and an additional 7.4 percent were semiskilled or domestics; leaving aside the domestics, close to one in five males performed a skilled job. (Among women 20 percent were domestic servants.) Even granting the imprecision of such estimates, it is clear that antebellum slaves worked in a broad range of occupations.[70]

Many skilled slaves—and some unskilled as well—were hired out to employers willing to pay their owners for their services. Slave hiring existed to some extent in the colonial South but expanded considerably in the antebellum period, especially in urban areas, where close to one-third of all slaves may have been held on hire, and in the upper South, where the shortage of labor was less pressing than in the cotton-producing states and more slaves were consequently available for hire. During the late antebellum years Virginia iron manufacturer William Weaver owned thirty-one slaves but annually rented ninety to one hundred more, paying their owners fees of up to $150. In Elizabeth City county, Virginia, on the western shore of the Chesapeake, *most* slaves experienced hire during the late eighteenth and early nineteenth centuries, when the decline of tobacco cultivation created a surplus of hands; only 39 percent of those sampled during the years 1784–87 "lived in the same household for three consecutive years." Hire was not always beneficial to the slave, who could easily draw an undesirable master. As Moses Grandy, who was hired out as a youth first to a kind man and then to a cruel one, noted, "In being hired out, sometimes the slave gets a good home, and sometimes a bad one: when he gets a good one, he dreads to see January come; when he has a bad one, the year seems five times as long as it is."

Furthermore, hirers lacked the incentive owners had to care for slaves. Hiring did, however, greatly increase the diversity of slaves' experiences and occupations.[71]

Self-hire, a special form of slave hiring limited almost entirely to a small number of skilled slaves, was the American equivalent of otkhodnichestvo. Slaves allowed to hire themselves out found employment on their own, paying their owners stipulated weekly or monthly fees for the privilege. Roundly criticized by whites for allowing slaves too much independence, the practice persisted on a modest scale despite legal prohibition and public condemnation, because it was to the mutual advantage of slave and master. As critics noted, however, it was hardly conducive to the stability of the slave system. Frederick Douglass remembered the time when he was permitted to hire on his own in Baltimore: "It was not long before I began to show signs of disquiet with slavery, and to look around for means to get out of that condition by the shortest route. I was living among *freemen;* and was, in all respects equal to them by nature and attainments. *Why should I be a slave?*" It is understandable, then, that slaveowners reserved the privilege of self-hire to a small number of trusted slaves with marketable skills.[72]

The occupational diversity that prevailed among slaves sometimes led to the kind of material differentiation that existed among serfs in Russia. Slaves allowed to hire their own time were often able to accumulate considerable sums of money (sometimes enabling them to purchase their freedom). So too, on occasion, were those hired out to work in industrial enterprises. Virginia iron manufacturer William Weaver established a system whereby his workers were paid bonuses for producing more than a standard quota; most were able to earn $10 to $15 per year, and skilled artisans made up to $50.[73]

Rural slaves also earned their "own" money. The practice was furthest developed on the lowland rice estates of South Carolina and Georgia where, under conditions of widespread owner absenteeism and the task system of labor, an internal slave economy developed, with slaves raising and selling their own provisions—and accumulating property—on their own time. Elsewhere, too, slaves raised produce on small garden plots not only to supplement their basic food allotment but also to trade for small luxuries such as tobacco and coffee. Masters contributed to differentiation among slaves by providing favored ones with cash bonuses, job promotions, and trading privileges; in his account book for 11 April 1811, Jefferson recorded that he gave carpenter "John Hemings 15 D. to wit the wages of one month in the year which I allow him as an encouragement." As a result real differences existed in the well-being of slaves on given holdings; as Charles Ball recalled of his South Carolina plantation, "although we were all slaves, and all nominally in a condition of the most perfect equality, yet there was in fact a very great difference in the manner of living, in the several families." Fogel and Engerman have estimated that although the slaveowner's average annual expenditure on a slave in 1850 was $48, unskilled hands were sometimes able to "earn" 2.5 times as much and skilled artisans up to 4.5 times as much.[74]

As in Russia, economic differentiation, if pronounced, could weaken the slaves' sense of common identity. The social outlook of an urban slave hiring his own time was bound to differ in some respects from that of a field hand. To a lesser extent, this was true in general of urban slaves, who enjoyed more flexible living arrangements, less supervision, and more numerous opportunities for social intercourse than their rural counterparts; as Douglass remarked, "[a] city slave is almost a free citizen, in Baltimore, compared with a slave on Col. Lloyd's plantation." In the countryside, too, occupational diversity sometimes led to differences in demeanor and attitude. An Alabaman given the job of driver later recalled, "I was proud of it 'cause I didn' have to work so hard no mo'. An den it sorta' made de other niggers look up to me." Whether slaves looked up to, envied, or resented those more fortunate than they, many observers noted an unusual spirit of independence among skilled slaves; significantly, most fugitive autobiographers had held some occupation other than field labor before their escape from bondage. Frances Kemble found the field slaves "stupid and brutish" on her husband's Georgia plantation; the coopers, blacksmiths, bricklayers, and carpenters, however, "exhibit[ed] a greater general activity of intellect, which must necessarily result from even a partial degree of cultivation."[75]

Nevertheless, stratification among American slaves was on the whole even more limited than among Russian serfs. There were several reasons for this, but the most basic was the total control that slaveowners sought to maintain over their slaves. Masters were never able entirely to shape their people's lives, but they did succeed in commanding almost all their labor. Unlike Russian serfs (or Jamaican slaves) who supported themselves, southern slaves with few exceptions received sustenance from their masters, for whom they worked full time. They had little occasion to engage in their own economic activity and found it correspondingly difficult to accumulate property.

Their economic equality was thus largely a function of their economic dependence.

The exceptions to this pattern were of limited scope. The internal economy that developed on South Carolina and Georgia rice plantations was confined largely to the coastal low-country, where a huge black majority and prevalent owner absenteeism rendered conditions closer than anywhere else in the United States to the Russian (or at least the Jamaican) model. (Even in the low-country, the most recent student of the subject has found, the slaves' economic activity was "on a much reduced scale" compared with that of Caribbean slaves.) Elsewhere in the South, where most slaves had resident masters who constantly meddled in their lives and strove to keep them in total dependence, garden plots were of minor economic importance and did not come close to providing the slaves with economic autonomy. The kind of peasant capitalism that existed in Russia did not emerge in the slave South.[76]

The privileged slaves of southern cities must be seen as exceptions that prove the rule rather than evidence of increasing slave stratification. Only a few unusual slaves were allowed to hire their own time; although 7.5 percent of all slaves were on hire in the late antebellum period, the vast majority of these were hired out by their owners to temporary masters rather than given the chance to find jobs on their own. And most urban slaves were domestic servants who suffered from the constant supervision to which domestics, whether urban or rural, were subject.[77]

During the antebellum period the limited autonomy that cities provided their slave inhabitants came under increasing attack from whites who lamented the corrupting impact that urban life had on blacks. Despite the dependent status of most urban slaves, it seemed to many white observers as if unrestrained licentiousness prevailed among them. As a prominent planter's son wrote from Savannah in 1856, "There are, you may say, hundreds of Negroes in this city who go about from house to house—some carpenters, some house servants, etc.—who never see their masters except at pay day, live out of their yards, hire themselves without written permit, etc. This of course is very wrong, and exerts a most injurious influence upon the relation of master and servant." He added, "Savannah is the last place in the world for servants inclined to evil." Determined to prevent the degradation of their charges by wicked city ways, slaveowners strove to keep the number of urban slaves to a minimum, an effort that in the deep South was aided by the heightened rural demand for labor.

Between 1840 and 1860 the proportion of slaves in the urban population declined in every major southern city; in 1860 only about 10 percent of all southerners and 6 percent of all slaves lived in towns of more than twenty-five hundred people.[78]

Two subsidiary factors further restricted differentiation among American slaves. The first was the small size of most southern holdings. On farms and plantations with fewer than fifty slaves, where three-quarters of all southern slaves resided, there was relatively little opportunity for the emergence of sharp social stratification. Masters could not spare slaves to engage solely in carpentry or smithing; they simply did not have enough building to do or horses to shoe. As a result slaves with skills frequently doubled (or tripled) in more than one capacity; it was not unusual to find a blacksmith who also performed field labor or a minister who was also a shoemaker. Small holdings thus dictated relatively homogeneous conditions on a given farm, and variations in the material well-being of slaves were more pronounced from owner to owner than among those held by any single master. Equally important, because there were numerous non-slaveholding whites, it was not essential that bondsmen in the South be trained to perform intermediate functions such as military defense or small-scale commerce, the way they were where blacks (and in Russia peasants) formed the bulk of the population. Russians and Brazilians found it necessary to arm their bondsmen, and slaves and free mulattoes controlled much of the commerce of Jamaica and St. Domingue, but southern slaveowners could insist that such activities were not appropriate for slaves because there were other people to perform them.[79]

As in Russia, therefore, stratification in the South rarely progressed far enough to divide slaves. Not only was property differentiation even more attenuated than among the serfs, but distinctions based on status were often temporary. Slaves who were especially diligent were sometimes promoted from field work to managerial positions and artisanry, while those who became too old or disabled to perform hard physical labor were assigned to domestic, mechanical, or gardening work. Slaves typically experienced one or more changes in status during their lifetimes, being hired out, receiving specialized training, moving with their owners from town to country or the reverse, being inherited or sold; in the course of these changes they saw a series of different occupations under a variety of conditions. (This was less true of female slaves, however, who were less often hired out, trained as skilled workers, allowed passes to leave home, and sold away from their families. Although historians have paid little attention to the subject and evidence is so far scanty, it may well be that slave women developed a different kind of community loyalty from the men, based on greater continuity and attachment to locality.) Because few slaves spent their lives with one master in one place, they rarely developed narrow identifications with locale, occupation, or status; the very diversity of experiences that individuals went through broadened their horizons and prevented the emergence of sharp social divisions among them.[80]

Slave autobiographies offer strong support for this generalization. Jacob Stroyer was born in 1846 near Columbia, South Carolina. Although his mother was a field hand, his father was a groom's assistant, and during his youth Jacob, too, learned to take care of horses, working under the authority of a demanding white groom who whipped and abused him. Upon his owner's death his widow sold the horses and assigned all who had formerly tended them to field work. Later Stroyer went to work as an assistant to a carpenter, whose trade he learned and was able to use during the war building Confederate fortifications. Jeremiah Loguen grew up in Kentucky, the pet of his white father-owner, and "the first ten years of Jarm's life was to him a period of much freedom." He was then abruptly sold away to Alabama, where he worked in the fields and "felt, for the first time, what it was to be a slave." He was presently hired out to kindly nonslaveholders, and upon returning to his owner three years later was "installed [as] the confidential servant and head man of the plantation." Other autobiographers, such as Frederick Douglass and H. C. Bruce, had equally varied careers.[81]

Under such circumstances it made little sense to pull rank or discriminate sharply on the basis of occupation or status; after all, who knew where he would live and what conditions he would face tomorrow? In a suggestive essay John W. Blassingame has argued that slaves rejected any system of stratification based on traditional occupational categories in favor of a very different subjective ranking of their own. Rather than considering artisans, drivers, and house servants the slave elite, "slaves reserved the top rungs of the social ladder for the blacks who performed services for other slaves rather than whites." Conjurors, preachers, folk doctors, midwives, teachers, and story-tellers qualified to be at the top of the slave hierarchy by these standards. Whether this thesis is fully sustainable is open to question, because it rests on few concrete data, but surely Blassingame is right to question whether a system of stratification based on economic function meant

much to the slaves themselves. Indeed, there is little evidence to suggest that such stratification caused basic divisions among them. The
artisans, preachers, drivers, and traders who sold products raised on
garden plots for small sums of money shared the basic values, aspirations, hopes, and fears of ordinary slaves, for the simple reason that
they *were* ordinary slaves. Like others, they sought to make life as
bearable for themselves as possible but resisted when pushed too far.
As in Russia, the harsh reality of bondage unified slaves in the South
far more than their rudimentary stratification divided them.[82]

*   *   *

HOUSE SERVANTS constituted a special case deserving separate consideration. Living and working apart from other bondsmen, servants
were the proverbial exception that proves the rule: their atypical experiences—and the prevalent images of those experiences—help
highlight normal patterns of community activities precisely because
their access to such activities was restricted. It is therefore significant
that historical stereotypes of servants in the antebellum South have
been strikingly different from those in prereform Russia.

Historians of American slavery have traditionally portrayed house
servants as the most fortunate of slaves, whose intimate association
with their owners presented them with numerous opportunities denied the mass of field hands. Such opportunities ranged from superior
material treatment—domestics typically ate scraps from their masters' tables, lived and slept in the "big house," and dressed in clothing
suitable for life among the whites they served rather than labor in the
fields—to exemption from backbreaking labor and, in many cases,
pampering by their owners. "Most domestics were proud of their positions of responsibility, of their fine manners and correct speech, and
of their handsome clothing and other badges of distinction," wrote
Kenneth M. Stampp in a typical evaluation. "Indeed, the domestics,
artisans, and foremen constituted the aristocracy of slave society."
Other historians have concurred in describing house slaves as "part
of the plantation elite," who looked down on common field laborers
and felt primary loyalty to and affection for their owners.[83]

It therefore comes as a surprise to the American reader to learn
that historians of serfdom have considered Russian house servants
among the *least* fortunate and most to be pitied of serfs. "Of all serfs,
saddest of all without doubt was the position of the dvorovye," wrote
V. I. Semevskii, explaining that they were subject to the unpredictable
whims of their owners, without whose approval they could hardly do

anything, including marry. Other historians have agreed, stressing the constant seigneurial interference, physical cruelty, and sexual abuse that servants suffered. Exceptionally skilled dvorovye, such as intellectuals, administrators, and performers appeared to be most miserable of all, their plight "truly horrible," for despite talents that exceeded those of their owners, such serfs still had to "submit to their whims, feel themselves in their complete power, and—most important—be conscious of this." [84]

Of course, the existence of these contradictory stereotypes does not in itself prove that they entirely reflected reality. Indeed, the very contrast—as well as other evidence—suggests that the status of servants was complex and full of ambiguities and traditional images in need of partial qualification. In the United States as well as Russia servants suffered more than other bondsmen from the capricious behavior of their masters and faced more interference in their daily lives, from sexual abuse of young women to punishment for not living up to exacting standards. Plantation diaries provide abundant evidence of the disadvantages of domestic status. William Byrd, in a typical entry for 1709, recorded that he "beat Anaka for letting the child piss in bed," while more than a century later Bennet H. Barrow constantly complained of his servants' thievery and "impudence," frequently punished them for minor acts of disobedience, and sometimes even "had a general whiping among the house ones." Ex-servants, too, recalled the abuse they suffered; Louis Hughes, for example, remembered his mistress as "naturally irritable" and noted that "servants always got an extra whipping when she had any trouble." As a result of such evidence, some historians have recognized the exaggerated nature of the traditional stereotype of the house servant as a member of the slave elite, and in a radical departure from his earlier view Blassingame has gone so far as to suggest that blacks considered "the position of the house servant at the very bottom of the slave's social ladder." [85]

In Russia, as in the United States, many house servants benefited materially from their status, appreciated not having to engage in ceaseless field labor, and looked on themselves as a cut above ordinary serfs. Nobleman A. P. Zablotskii-Desiatovskii noted that many peasants regarded house serfs as "something higher than themselves" and that serfs transferred out of dvorovyi status "always go to the field with indignation." In fictional accounts, too, "the Russian house-serf dressed in his master's cast-offs patronized the ragged peasants who worked the land." Whatever paternalistic relations existed

under Russian serfdom were confined almost entirely to those between master and servant; as one nobleman later recalled, during his
childhood the noble children not only thought of their dvorovye (unlike other peasants) as humans like themselves but even "lived one life
with them and ... entered into their lives with all our hearts and
understanding." Servants sometimes reciprocated such sentiments.
General Izmailov was a notoriously sadistic pomeshchik, but during
a judicial investigation of his treatment of serfs several members of
his house "aristocracy" testified that they were more than satisfied
with their care. "I cannot hear without sorrow," declared one, "of the
complaints against his excellency from these people for whom he did
so much, who enjoyed such paternal seigneurial favors." [86]

In short, in both countries house service provided bondsmen with
added hardships as well as special opportunities, and there is considerable evidence that servants—and other bondsmen too—had
strongly ambivalent feelings about their status. In the United States,
for every slave who testified that as a house servant he had borne the
brunt of planter irritability, there was another who recalled his situation as "preferable to that of a field hand" or who boasted, "Honey,
I wasn't no common eve'yday slave, I hoped [helped] de white folks
in de big house." Olmsted perceptively caught this varied attitude toward house service when he observed that those "brought up to
house-work dread to be employed at field-labour" whereas "those
accustomed to the comparatively unconstrained life of the negro-
settlement, detest the close control and careful movements required
of the house-servants." In Russia, too, attitudes varied. Some dvorovye loyally identified with their owners, but others had bitter memories of their service, as did the ex-servant who recalled serving as a
whipping-girl for the young girl she tended. The latter "did not like
to study and frequently did not know her lesson," remembered the
servant, "for which they did not punish her but me. The mistress
would clutch my head with her knees and whip me until blood came."
Peasant folklore suggests an ambivalent attitude toward house service
similar to that in the American South. In one lyric song a serf imagines:

> Oh, splendid is the life of a footman
> At the nobleman's court:
> They do not have to plow the land.

but is answered by a servant that life in the seigneurial mansion is not
so attractive:

Wherever they send you, you must run quickly, . . .
If you stand too long or loiter,
You have an interview with the mistress.
Look around behind you—
Someone is standing back of you, and threatening you with a stick.

In another a serf who imagines the luxury of house service is told:

Ah you stupid peasants,
Live a while with us!
There is surely nothing worse in the world,
Than a house serf's life.[87]

Still, despite the complexity of the question, there *was* ultimately a significant contrast in the way people looked at house service in the two countries. However exaggerated they may be, the conflicting historical stereotypes were not manufactured out of thin air or historians' fancy but were based upon equally prevalent stereotypes among contemporaries themselves. The most widespread image of dvorovye in eighteenth-century and nineteenth-century Russia was of serfs torn away from the village and forced to live under the watchful eye of demanding and arbitrary seigneurs; the most common image of house servants in the antebellum South was of slaves spared the rigors of field labor and allowed special favors by owners in the big house. Fictional portrayals closely reflected these stereotypes, as illustrated by two "abolitionist" pieces, both published in 1852: Harriet Beecher Stowe's *Uncle Tom's Cabin* and Ivan Turgenev's *A Sportsman's Notebook*. In the former, slaveowners manifest a "good-humored indulgence" of their servants: "Eliza had been brought up by her mistress, from girlhood, as a petted and indulged favorite"; Mrs. Shelby is "a woman of a high class, both intellectually and morally," to whom her husband gives "unlimited scope in all her benevolent efforts for the comfort, instruction, and improvement of her servants." Although many suffer cruel hardships, the villains are northerners, slave traders, and slavery as an institution, not southern slaveowners themselves. By contrast, Turgenev's Arina, a good, faithful maid, is hardly the beneficiary of a Mrs. Shelby's benevolence; rather, Madame Zverkova has "one firm principle: never to keep a married maid," and when the unfortunate girl seeks to marry, retribution is quick. "Of course I gave orders at once that her head should be shaved, that she should be put in sackcloth and sent home to the country," narrates the aggrieved master. "My wife lost an excellent maid, but there was nothing else to be done. Say what you like, you can't have laxity in your own house."[88]

The key to the contrasting stereotypes of servants—and the contrasting status that lay behind these stereotypes—lies in the nature of the slave and serf communities. What most distinguished the servants from other bondsmen was their relative distance from the village and quarters. The larger the holding, the greater this distance. Very wealthy masters usually had enough house servants so that they could form a society unto themselves, associating mostly with each other (and their masters) and having little to do with the mass of bondsmen. Such exclusivity was far more common in Russia than in the United States, because wealthy Russian noblemen owned many more people—and domestics—than their American counterparts, but it was by no means unknown in the South. Although only one-quarter of southern slaves lived on holdings of more than fifty, considerably more than one-quarter—probably a majority—of house servants did, since many small slaveowners could not afford the luxury of having domestics. Frederick Douglass described house servants on Colonel Lloyd's plantation as a "sort of black aristocracy" totally apart from other slaves, whom they resembled "in nothing, except in color." On smaller holdings servants were not numerous enough or isolated enough to form a separate caste, and often they associated freely with field hands—even to the point of marriage—serving as something of a cultural bridge between the big house and the quarters. Nevertheless, virtually everywhere servants were unable to partake of ordinary community life to the extent of most other slaves and serfs. They lived in their owners' houses, spent most of their time serving their masters, and were more subject than others to personal supervision. Although servants were by no means always isolated from other bondsmen, their separation from the village and quarters was inherent in their status.[89]

The essential question thus becomes the impact of this separation on the servants. Despite all the ambiguities involved, the answer is apparent: it was far greater in Russia than in the United States. The dvorovyi left the relatively autonomous world of the peasant village, where serfs rarely saw their owners, for one of close personal supervision; he lost his landed allotment, his personal "property," his right to work for himself three days per week (more if he was on obrok), and his ability to participate in mir gatherings and be a part of the peasant commune. The slave house servant was also deprived of full participation in community affairs, but the loss was less overwhelming because the slave community as a local entity was less all-embracing. Of course, house slaves in the South received closer personal supervision than field hands, but the matter was one of degree; most field hands, too, felt the watchful eye of a resident owner. The slave domestic did not give up the ability to engage in his own economic activities and participate in communal decision making because slaves as a whole lacked these prerogatives. Servants in both countries enjoyed certain material benefits as well as suffering from close contact with their masters, but removal from the community at large affected the condition of the slave less than that of the serf.

We are back, then, where we began Part II: the greater relative strength and autonomy of the serf community. Just as patterns of resistance provide important clues to the way the bondsmen related to each other in their villages and quarters, so too do attitudes about house service. Both are indicative of the very different kinds of social order that prevailed within the general system of human bondage that held sway in Russia and the United States South. By the middle of the nineteenth century another difference was evident as well: for a variety of reasons, Russian serfdom, unlike American slavery, seemed about to disintegrate of its own weight.

The Crisis of Unfree Labor

By the middle of the nineteenth century American slavery and Russian serfdom were labor systems in crisis. Although the crises they faced were not identical, both were based on the fundamental conflict between bondage and a modern world view consistent with the realities of nineteenth-century capitalism. At first simply two of many systems of unfree labor in the Western world, American slavery and Russian serfdom had become noteworthy as the most important remnants of an archaic social order, beleaguered outposts of servitude in an era that celebrated liberty and equality. What was true of the crises was also true of their resolution. In both cases, despite major differences in the way that participants responded to the pressure of events, the end result was the same: abolition of bondage. The legacy of slavery and serfdom, however, would persist for generations.

* * *

American slavery and Russian serfdom served similar socioeconomic functions. Emerging under conditions of labor scarcity on the periphery of a modernizing Europe, they constituted productive systems designed to support landholding elites. As such they shared ambiguous economic characteristics that have spawned considerable historical confusion.

On the one hand, both had strong commercial components. From the beginning American—indeed all New World—slaveholders formed a preeminently market-oriented class, living off the sale of goods produced by their chattel. Although the commercial orientation of most Russian serfowners was less pronounced and many small landowners lived in semi-impoverished autarchy, as a system serfdom too was predicated on the masters' appropriation and sale of goods produced by their bondsmen. Except on the smallest holdings, bar-shchina, which remained the dominant form of labor exploitation, implied seigneurial production for market. In the broadest sense both slavery and serfdom were labor systems that served to maximize the master class's access to market.

At the same time, slavery and serfdom were fundamentally noncap-italist productive systems, increasingly antagonistic to the emerging bourgeois world order, because they lacked capitalism's basic ingre-dient: a market for labor-power (that is, labor hire). The two systems of forced labor were thus marked by an essential contradiction be-tween the commercial orientation of the masters with respect to the *distribution* of their product and the noncapitalist nature of its *pro-duction*. This contradiction produced in both slavery and serfdom an incongruous mixture of characteristics, some of which engendered a distinctly capitalist tone; certainly, to take one example, slaveowners and serfowners were intensely interested in the price their crops would bring. Overall, however, the mode of production was more influential than that of exchange in shaping the nature of society in Russia and the United States South. The master-bondsman relation-ship was fundamentally different from that between employer and employee; so too was the social outlook of the master at odds with that of the bourgeois. In both countries bondage fostered distinctive societies that were increasingly out of step with the dominant course of the Western world.[1]

Ironically, this phenomenon was more pronounced in the United States South, where slavery was totally commercial in orientation, than in Russia, where market ties were less dominant. Here is persua-sive evidence that productive relations were more important than dis-tributive relations in shaping the nature of slave society, for nowhere was the contradiction between the two so great as in the Old South. Although the southern economy was pervasively commercial and his-torians such as James Oakes have seen antebellum slaveowners as businessmen par excellence, southern slavery was infused with a pa-ternalistic ethos shaped by the nonmarket relationship that existed between largely resident masters and their slaves.[2]

In Russia, by contrast, the market orientation of the masters was less pervasive but their treatment of their serfs was correspondingly more "capitalistic." Pomeshchiki who were generally absentee pro-prietors either physically or mentally took little interest in their peas-ants except as sources of income. Serfdom lacked the market for labor-power inherent in capitalism, but relations between nobleman and serf were often marked by quasi-capitalist features—payment of obrok fees, accumulation of arrears, rental of land—largely lacking in the slave South. The existence of a peasant economy in Russia in which serfs raised their own goods for sale meant that bondsman as well as master had market ties, and relations between the two inevitably reflected this reality.[3]

There were thus major differences between American slavery and Russian serfdom, differences that were based on specific demographic, socioeconomic, political, and cultural attributes of the two societies. (These differences were not, it should be clear by now, primarily based on the systemic distinction between slavery and serfdom, because in most respects Russian serfdom must be seen as a particular variety of slavery rather than a fundamentally distinct labor system.) Southern slaveowners were able to develop a far more cohesive civilization of their own than were Russian pomeshchiki. The rural South constituted a slaveholder's world in a way that rural Russia was not a serfholder's world; indeed, the Russian countryside belonged largely to the peasantry. Although slaves had their own lives, which did not entirely conform to the ideal prescribed for them by their masters, they were rarely able to develop the kind of economic, social, and even political autonomy enjoyed by most serfs.

An integral relation existed between the character of the bondsmen's lives and that of the masters'. The relative lack of communal autonomy among American slaves was in part a product of the slaveowners' cultural dominance: resident owners who took an active interest in running their estates and who maintained political and cultural hegemony within southern society impinged pervasively on the lives of their slaves and acted both consciously and unconsciously to undermine their communal independence. In Russia, not only did the absentee orientation and weak local ties of the nobility enable serfs to exercise much greater control over their lives than was enjoyed by the slaves; that autonomy in turn further undercut the nobility's interest in becoming a rural aristocracy. Just as Jamaican slaveowners felt uncomfortable among their slaves, who represented a culturally alien group that vastly outnumbered them, so too did Russian pomeshchiki; in very much the same way, they were outsiders in their own villages. There was thus an inverse relation between the dominance of the masters' culture and the autonomy of the bondsmen's.[4]

The coherence of both the masters' and the bondsmen's culture was related to the development of the labor systems in which they existed. The Old South, which saw the emergence of the least "capitalistic" form of slavery, spawned a master class that was uniquely dedicated to the preservation of a social order that it saw as the last bulwark against decadence, individualism, and greed. The antebellum South constituted, in the truest sense, a slave society, not just a society in which some people were slaves. It is for this reason that C. Vann Woodward has suggested that "the end of slavery in the South can be described as the death of a society, though elsewhere it could more reasonably be characterized as the liquidation of an investment." Although Woodward was writing only of New World slave societies, Russia clearly belongs with those he contrasted with the United States South. Like Caribbean slavery, Russian serfdom exhibited capitalistic features that ultimately sapped its ability to endure in a changing world.[5]

Ultimately, therefore, despite many similar features of Russian serfdom and southern slavery, there was a contrast in their viability. By the middle of the nineteenth century, as southern slavery was flourishing as never before, Russian serfdom constituted a bankrupt system widely recognized as on its last legs. The vitality of antebellum slavery was evident in the dynamic growth of the southern economy, the daily behavior of resident owners, and the burgeoning efforts of southern spokesmen to defend slavery as a noble institution essential to the preservation of a virtuous and harmonious society. This growing commitment to slavery, both as a practical way of life and as an abstract system, stands in stark contrast to the withering of noble support for Russian serfdom. Most pomeshchiki never really "lived" serfdom as southern planters did slavery; it served more as an investment for them, to use Woodward's terminology, than as an indispensable way of life. After the 1820s, when southerners were elaborating with increasing frequency and forcefulness their arguments in defense of the "peculiar institution," public defense of serfdom in Russia virtually disappeared. Informed noblemen realized that its demise was simply a matter of time.

So too did most serfs. Although bondsmen in both countries hated their servitude, most southern slaves saw little hope for an imminent end to slavery and continued to strive to make their lives as tolerable as possible within it (or to escape from it on an individual basis). In Russia, however, a spreading expectation of imminent emancipation fueled a growing unwillingness of serfs to tolerate continued bondage. The diminished provocation needed to ignite volneniia was a telling sign of a breakdown in the serfs' acceptance of the social order.

By midcentury, in short, Russian serfdom, unlike American slavery, was a system in internal crisis. It was not, in a literal sense, collapsing; it conceivably could have been maintained for years, perhaps even decades, but it had lost its long-term social viability. Informed noblemen, serfs, and government officials all expected its abolition. The question that remained to be determined was not whether emancipation would occur, but when and how.

*   *   *

A TELLING SIGN of the viability of unfree labor is provided by differing patterns of growth of the bound population. Historians of both New World slavery and Russian serfdom have recently paid considerable attention to demographic questions, and although they have not reached total agreement concerning the causes of variations in patterns of growth, they have established the existence of these variations. They are of interest to us here because of their indication of the general long-term health of unfree labor systems: a sharp decline in the proportion of bondsmen in the total population almost always signified serious problems for such a system and was followed within about a generation by its abolition.

In most New World slave societies slaves failed to reproduce themselves. The slave population grew rapidly, at least for a while, but only as a result of continued imports of new slaves from Africa. Because slave deaths exceeded births in countries as diverse as Brazil, Cuba, and Jamaica, the end of the slave trade led first to a leveling off and then to an outright decline in the number of slaves and, especially in Brazil and Cuba, a sharp decline in the proportion of the population that was unfree. In Brazil, for example, where importation of Africans ended in 1851, the number of slaves declined from about 2.5 million in 1850 to 1.5 million in 1872, and slaves as a proportion of the population fell from 32 percent to 15 percent. Although slaveowners fought rearguard actions designed to protect their investments, it was clear that the end of the slave trade doomed slavery in these countries; in all three, the beginnings of emancipation followed the cessation of large-scale African imports within about a quarter-century.[6]

Slavery in the United States constituted a major exception to this pattern. Although in the early colonial period the number of slaves increased only because of importation from Africa, in the eighteenth century slaves experienced natural population growth, with annual births continually exceeding deaths. There was some variation in the timing of this transition to natural population growth, which occurred earlier in the Chesapeake region than farther south; in all the southern colonies, however, slaves were more than reproducing themselves by the outbreak of the American Revolution, well before the end of the legal slave trade in 1808.[7] During the half-century after that, the number of American slaves more than tripled, from 1,119,354 in 1810 to 3,963,760 in 1860; with high birth rates (in excess of 50 per 1,000) and relatively low death rates (about 30 per 1,000), the black population—most of which was slave—grew naturally at an annual rate of more than 2 percent.[8]

Several specific factors, whose relative importance is still disputed by scholars, contributed to the unique natural population growth of American slaves. New patterns of lactation may have acted to boost fertility rates; as Herbert Klein and Stanley L. Engerman have pointed out, antebellum southern slaves generally followed American custom in breastfeeding their babies for about a year, whereas many West Indian women continued the African practice of nursing for two years. Absence of tropical diseases undoubtedly reduced mortality rates (although as Philip Curtin has noted, "the experience of Colombia, Panama, and Ecuador [where the black population grew far more rapidly than in most of Latin America] suggests that disease is not the only explanation" for high death rates.) The unusually high proportion of creoles among American slaves affected both fertility and mortality rates: everywhere native-born slaves tended to live longer and have more children than African imports because the Africans were both less resistant to New World diseases and more heavily male in composition.[9]

On a more general level, however, it is hard to avoid the conclusion that the relatively good material conditions under which most American slaves lived were central to their rapid population growth. The strength of their family life made possible a high birth rate, and it is surely no accident that the transition to natural population growth in the southern colonies coincided with the emergence of Afro-American families among second-generation slaves.[10] An abundance of food and the determination of resident owners to look after the welfare of their "people" was equally important in promoting the slaves' health and longevity. (In the Caribbean, by contrast, life was cheap and slaves were driven mercilessly, especially during boom times on the sugar islands. In Jamaica, pregnant women typically labored in the field even in their ninth month, a practice that both reduced the number of live births and increased the female mortality rate.) On the whole, slaves were simply healthier in the American South than elsewhere in the New World.[11]

If the growth of the bound population is an indication of the continuing vitality of American slavery, a final demographic contrast between the South and other New World slave societies underscores that vitality. As the southern commitment to slavery strengthened in the antebellum period, interest in private manumission of slaves waned, states took vigorous action to make the practice more difficult, and the number of slaves freed by their owners declined sharply. Although the number of free Negroes slowly increased, because like slaves they reproduced themselves, most were the descendants of those freed during the last quarter of the eighteenth century, and from 1820 to 1860 free Negroes declined as a proportion of the South's black population from 8.1 percent to 6.2 percent. Elsewhere, however, when it became clear that the end of the slave trade had doomed slavery, the number of manumissions—both private and government sponsored—increased dramatically. In Cuba, for example, although the slave population declined from 436,495 to 370,553 between 1841 and 1860, the number of free colored increased from 152,838 to 225,843. In Cuba and Brazil, and to a much lesser extent in the British West Indies, the freeing of slaves combined with the lack of natural population growth after the end of the slave trade to undermine slavery. The failure of slaves to reproduce themselves was a sign of the inability of slavery to survive without fresh supplies from Africa, and the freeing of large numbers of slaves was an index of the concomitant unwillingness of slaveholders to continue struggling for a lost cause. One way or another, abolition of the slave trade presaged the imminent end of slavery in all major New World slave societies except that of the United States.[12]

The growth pattern of the Russian serf population fell between the two extremes shown by American and Caribbean slaves. Births generally exceeded deaths, although by substantially smaller margins than among American slaves, and the number of serfs grew rapidly—primarily from natural increase but also from enserfment of state peasants and territorial expansion—in the eighteenth and early nineteenth centuries. The failure of the bound population to grow during the last years of serfdom, however, suggested a system unlikely to endure much longer.

The population of Russia, which was about 90 percent peasant, grew at a moderately rapid pace throughout the eighteenth and first half of the nineteenth century (see Table 11). Although some of this growth was the result of territorial expansion, within the area defined by Russia's 1719 boundaries the population increased at an annual rate of 0.81 percent between 1719 and 1858. This was considerably

Table 11
Male population of Russia, 1719–1858

Census	Year	Total population	Peasants	Serfs[a]	Serfs as percent of— Population	Peasants
I	1719	7,292,417	6,552,377	3,528,722	48.4	53.9
II	1744	8,600,954	7,793,776	4,348,873	50.6	55.8
III	1762	10,593,546	9,978,113	5,611,531	53.0	56.2
IV	1782	13,686,691	12,592,478	6,714,331	49.1	53.3
V	1795	18,168,574	16,321,984	9,787,802	53.9	60.0
VI	1811	20,232,352	18,217,744	10,455,986	51.7	57.4
VII	1815	20,911,493	17,849,543	9,987,997	47.8	56.0
VIII	1833	25,492,967	21,591,881	11,447,203	44.9	53.0
IX	1851	27,990,685	23,350,494	11,384,312	40.7	48.8
X	1858	28,935,190	24,015,651	11,338,042	39.2	47.2

Source: V. M. Kabuzan, *Izmeneniia v razmeshchenii naseleniia Rossii v XVIII-pervoi polovine XIX v.* (Moscow: Izdatel'stvo "Nauka," 1971), appendix 2.

a. Figures are for privately held serfs only and thus exclude clerical peasants.

less than the growth rate of southern slaves or that of the American population as a whole, but it was almost identical to the Italian growth rate between 1800 and 1871 of 0.8 percent and was substantially higher than the French rate of 0.4 percent.[13]

For most of the serfdom era serfs seem to have reproduced themselves at a rate at least as high as the population at large. With a high death rate (which despite widespread fluctuations averaged above 40 per 1,000 and was thus on the same order as that among Caribbean slaves) and an even higher birth rate (probably slightly in excess of the antebellum southern slaves' level of 50 per 1,000), the serf population grew rapidly in the eighteenth century. Swelled by the continuing enserfment of state peasants, the number of serfs increased as a proportion of both peasants and the total population.[14]

This situation changed in the nineteenth century: after peaking in 1795, the proportion of serfs declined steadily during the last half-century of serfdom; by 1858 serfs constituted only 39.2 percent of the population and a minority even of the peasants. What is more, after 1833 the serf population stopped growing and in fact declined slightly in absolute numbers as well. Between 1833 and 1858 the number of male serfs declined by 109,161 (or 1.0 percent), while all nonserf males increased by 3,551,384 (or 25.3 percent) (see Table 11).

Historians have put forward two different explanations for this decrease of the serf population during the last years of serfdom. Some, such as N. M. Shepukova, have argued that serfs experienced a sharp increase in mortality rates owing to increasing exploitation and a generally declining level of material well-being; the consequence was a serf population that was no longer reproducing itself. In a sharp response to this thesis, however, P. G. Ryndziunskii ridiculed the notion that serfs were "dying out" and suggested that the population stagnation was primarily the consequence of serfs' being freed by pomeshchiki who no longer valued their inefficient labor; the missing serfs had not died but had joined the ranks of state peasants. More recently two American historians have agreed with this contention, insisting that "with the exception of the effects of the cholera epidemic [of 1847–48], virtually all the net decline in the serf population was due to changes in legal status." Still other scholars have suggested a combination of the two arguments, maintaining that although some serfs were transferred to other population categories, such transfers were not numerous enough to explain the entire discrepancy between the population growth rates of serfs and state peasants.[15]

It is this last position that is most persuasive. A decline in the peasants' standard of living was apparently responsible for a decrease in the overall rate of population growth that was especially pronounced among serfs. Although birth statistics are not accurate enough to permit certainty, a small drop in fertility rates may have occurred owing to a slight increase in the average age of marriage and a substantial increase in otkhodnichestvo, which kept couples separated for prolonged periods of time.[16] Evidence for an increase in mortality rates is more clear-cut: during the 1830s, 1840s, and 1850s growing population pressure combined with a series of poor harvests to create widespread hunger, malnutrition, and disease; especially severe were the disastrous harvests of 1839 and 1843 and the cholera epidemic of 1847–48. State peasants suffered too, but because serfs in general lived more precarious lives, anything that tipped the balance even a little toward insufficiency was bound to affect them more seriously. The serfs were in no sense "dying out," but their natural growth rate slowed to a crawl; V. I. Krutikov's calculations for Tula province, for example, suggest a rate of 0.2 percent between 1833 and 1857. With such a pace, it would not require the freeing of many serfs to bring serf population growth to a complete halt.[17]

Many serfs did escape from bondage. These included those drafted into military service as well as their families; recruits and their sons together numbered more than half a million souls between 1833 and 1858. Also escaping serfdom were those who through self-purchase, owner manumission, government confiscation, and successful flight entered the ranks of state peasants. The precise number of serfs entering the state peasantry remains in dispute, but there is no doubt that it was quite substantial; the highest estimate to date is that of Steven L. Hoch and William R. Augustine, who suggest that as many as 1.7 million peasants may have escaped serfdom between the eighth and tenth censuses.[18]

Of course, such transfers did not represent an entirely new departure; peasants had all along escaped serfdom through military service, flight, and occasional manumission. What *was* new was the one-way nature of changes in peasant status, because prior to 1801 large numbers of peasants had *entered* serfdom as well through continuing enserfment of state peasants. The end of such large-scale enserfments represented the Russian equivalent of the end to the slave trade. With the low rate of natural increase and the substantial transfer of serfs to nonserf status, the serf population could not have continued to expand during the prereform period without a steady supply of new recruits. Like Caribbean slavery after abolition of the African slave trade, Russian serfdom on the eve of emancipation was a system of labor living on borrowed time.

Although historians continue to dispute the relative importance of a declining natural growth rate and freeing of serfs, both may be seen as signs of a crisis of the social order. The former points to a deterioration of the serfs' material condition that undermined the kind of population growth essential to serfdom's long-term survival; the latter indicates a reduction in pomeshchiki's commitment to that institution. Whether for economic self-interest, ideological qualms, concern for their own security, or a combination of these, public support for serfdom, unlike that of southerners for slavery, all but evaporated during the quarter-century before emancipation (see above, Chapter 3).

The absence of public defense does not mean that most pomeshchiki supported abolition; almost certainly the great majority—especially the less-educated small-scale landowners in the provinces—would have welcomed any delay in emancipation. Once the government made public its commitment to abolition in 1857, however, noblemen recognized the inevitability of change (and, equally important, were both unwilling and unable to take the kind of decisive action southern slaveholders were contemplating to prevent it). Thus, in the semimonthly *Landowners' Journal* (*Zhurnal zemlevladel'tsev*) in 1858 virtually all the articles took for granted the imminent abolition of serfdom (euphemistically termed "improvement of the peasants' way of life") and concentrated on defending the nobility's interests under the new order. In an essay warning of the dangers of "a *sudden* abolition of 'compulsory labor' " N. Danilov asserted that "not one well-thinking person, following impartial justice, would utter even one word in defense of that 'right' (the serf ownership of people) that constitutes *living* evidence of the remnants of *ancient* barbaric customs among *contemporary* citizenry." Like Danilov, pomeshchik Dmitrii Neronov did not bother to oppose abolition but expressed a lively concern for the fate of the nobles after emancipation; the "peasant question" was really a misnomer, he insisted, and was in fact a "pomeshchik question," because whereas peasants would remain peasants under the new order, pomeshchiki would lose the only distinctive privilege they enjoyed—ownership of settled estates.[19]

Noteworthy as an indication of this expectation of imminent emancipation was a sharp rise in the number of house serfs, as pomeshchiki took hundreds of thousands of serfs away from their villages and made dvorovye of them. The proportion of serfs who were dvorovye increased from 4.14 percent in 1833 to 4.79 percent in 1851 and then surged to 6.79 percent in 1858; between the latter two dates the number of house serfs of both sexes increased by 431,454—41.6 percent. These transfers of villagers to house status represented an effort by noblemen to maximize their own use of the increasingly valuable land and prepare for an emancipation that was widely (and correctly) expected to provide landed allotments for village serfs but not for dvorovye. Significantly, such transfers were especially numerous in the fertile provinces of the Ukraine and New Russia—in Kharkov province, for example, there was a 230.2 percent increase in the number of house serfs between 1851 and 1858, a figure exceeded in several other black earth provinces—whereas in much of northern Russia the proportion of dvorovye actually declined. In short, serfowners were not just expecting an imminent emancipation, they were jumping the gun by expropriating in advance the best land worked by their serfs. Whatever their personal preferences might have been, many pomeshchiki recognized that serfdom did not have long to survive, and instead of struggling to defend a nonviable system, they strove to safeguard their interests after its demise.[20]

* * *

THE SLAVE SOUTH did not face an internal crisis similar to that of prereform Russia. True, some historians have seen one; Charles W.

Ramsdell, for example, in an influential article published in 1929, argued that by the 1850s slavery had reached its natural limits in the United States and would inevitably have soon disappeared even had the Civil War not occurred. More recent research, however, has cast grave doubt on the idea that slavery as a system was in serious trouble in the late-antebellum South.[21]

In contrast to the widespread expectation of imminent emancipation in Russia, in the southern United States the 1850s was a time of general confidence among slaveholders. The southern economy, as a result of surging foreign demand for cotton, was booming, with per capita production actually increasing at a slightly faster pace than in the industrializing North. The recession that struck most of the United States in 1857 bypassed the South, where the price of cotton and other agricultural staples remained high, and planters strove to put as much land as possible under cultivation. Although the number of slaves continued to increase rapidly, demand for them grew at an even faster pace, leading to a sharp increase in slave prices and a vigorous although controversial movement to reopen the African slave trade. In short, although slavery impeded southern industrialization and mechanization, there is little evidence that as of 1860 it was producing the devastating effects on the southern economy that free-labor advocates insisted were inevitable.[22]

If objective conditions in the slave South suggested a healthy society, the subjective attitudes of slaveowners indicated widespread satisfaction with those conditions. Of course, rising slave prices represented an indirect vote of confidence by slaveholders in the system, but more direct testimony of that confidence may be seen in the pervasive celebration of the system by leading southern spokesmen. The militant proslavery movement, with its concomitant defense of the virtues of southern civilization and assault upon the alien values of the free-labor North, expressed the basic sanguinity of white southerners in a slave system that seemed to be flourishing. Southern whites were increasingly committed to their "peculiar institution," and all that it entailed. Unlike Russia (or other New World slave societies after the abolition of the slave trade), the South in the mid-nineteenth century did not face the imminent collapse of its labor system.

The South did, however, face a very real crisis. Unlike that of Russian serfdom, it was an externally generated crisis, because the slave South was increasingly a society different from and at odds with the rest of the world, including (most importantly) the northern United States. The crisis that this conflict created was ultimately as fatal to the social order of the South as was the internally generated crisis to that of Russia.

In the seventeenth and eighteenth centuries the South was simply one of numerous unfree societies, but by the second quarter of the nineteenth century it stood more and more isolated in the Western world, a bastion of slavery and conservatism in an era that celebrated liberty, fraternity, and equality. The triumph of the Haitian revolution in 1804, the winning of independence by the Spanish mainland colonies in the early nineteenth century, the abolition of slavery in the northern United States during the half-century following the American Revolution, and the British emancipation of 1833–38 left Brazil and Cuba as the only major slave societies in the New World aside from the United States South. During the generation preceding the Civil War southern whites were increasingly conscious that they lived in a distinctive society whose most salient features were shaped by the "peculiar institution."

Distinctiveness alone need not have produced a crisis for the slave South, but the multipronged massive assault on the very fabric of southern society that this distinctiveness generated could not fail to do so. From the 1820s on, abolitionists in the North and abroad condemned southerners as moral lepers who could only redeem themselves by the immediate and complete abandonment of slavery. More influential still, especially from the 1840s, were the free-labor spokesmen who painted the South as a backward and degraded land where slavery corroded everything it touched. The vigor of the proslavery movement during these years was a sign not just of an increasing commitment to slavery but also of the degree to which southerners felt themselves under attack. A siege mentality pervaded the late antebellum South.[23]

This mentality was by no means paranoid, because the South *was* under attack. History itself seemed on the side of the antislavery advocates, for the free-labor North was clearly pulling apart from and ahead of the slave South. Although the southern economy was expanding rapidly, it was not going through the kind of basic structural transformation that was occurring in the North (and here is a central blind spot of econometricians who stress the economic efficacy of antebellum slavery); as a result the South increasingly lagged behind the North not just in industrialization and urbanization but in many other indices of modernization, from transportation to mechanization, literacy, scientific endeavor, and education. Because relatively few immigrants wanted to settle where slavery prevailed, the southern population grew much more slowly than that of the North: between 1830 and 1860 the southern share of the total American population declined from 44.2 percent to 35.3 percent. Southerners had varying explanations for their section's backwardness: some turned it into a virtue, insisting that the South lacked the crude mercenary traits of the Yankees, others blamed the North for stealing the fruits of southern labor, and a few hardy souls like Hinton Helper saw slavery as the culprit. They were, however, acutely aware of the problem.[24]

The political assault on the South was most alarming of all. From 1789 to 1860 southerners dominated the federal government. Eight of the fifteen presidents who served during these years were southern slaveholders, and of the remaining seven, three were "doughfaces," northern men with southern principles. What is more, not one of the northern presidents served two terms, whereas four of the southerners did. Southern dominance of the executive branch of the government translated into southern ascendancy in the federal judiciary as well. Chief Justice Roger B. Taney, a former Maryland slaveowner who presided over the Supreme Court from his appointment by Andrew Jackson in 1835 until his death in 1864, enjoyed the company of a southern majority during most of his tenure; at the time of the Dred Scott decision in 1857, for example, five of the Court's nine justices were southern, and one of the northerners was a doughface. Southern interests were secure in the Senate too, because until 1850 half or more of the states (and hence of the senators) were southern, and even after 1850 southerners and doughfaces together formed a majority. Only in the House of Representatives, where the increasing northern majority of the population produced a corresponding northern majority of congressmen, were southerners not in command, and even there southern fears were assuaged until the mid-1840s by the gentlemen's agreement among Democrats and Whigs that agitation of the slavery issue was off limits; from 1836 to 1844, under the "gag rule," the House refused even to receive antislavery petitions. In short, southerners had come to expect the federal government to protect their interests—the most basic of which was slavery—from any and all attack; as long as it did so, it was performing an invaluable function and deserved full and enthusiastic support.[25]

That situation began to change dramatically during the 1840s and 1850s, when the prospect loomed that the federal government might soon challenge rather than safeguard southern interests. Whereas the abolitionists of the 1830s had seemed dangerous fanatics to most northerners as well as southerners, from the mid-1840s an increasingly vociferous free soil movement, grounded on the free-labor argument that slavery was a backward and inefficient system of labor, threatened to bar slavery's expansion into new western territories and thus consign it to gradual but ultimate extinction. The gentlemen's agreement to refrain from agitating the divisive issue of slavery broke down under this pressure, and by the mid-1850s, with the emergence in the North of the antislavery Republican party, national politics was hopelessly divided along sectional lines. Not only did the South face a new assault from without, but the changing balance of population held out the terrifying likelihood that this assault would soon be victorious. To the growing free-state majority in the House of Representatives was added, after 1850, that in the Senate, as well as the prospect of a "black Republican" president. It was this last prospect that was the most frightening, and with Abraham Lincoln's election to the presidency in 1860 the South's general crisis became the nation's secession crisis.[26]

The social isolation of the South and the economic, intellectual, and political assault upon it led, of course, to civil war and the overthrow of slavery. But it is not only because of this momentous objective change that one can legitimately assert a southern crisis, by taking advantage of historical hindsight to superimpose a theoretical construct upon the past. Abundant evidence suggests that politically aware southerners subjectively felt this crisis as well. It was not a narrowly defined economic (or cotton) crisis—the southern agricultural economy was booming in the 1850s and gave every indication that it would continue to do so in the immediately foreseeable future—but a general crisis of an entire social system. Southerners recognized that slavery—and with it their entire way of life—was under powerful attack from without; their increasingly shrill defense of it and the siege mentality that they exhibited during the last years of the old regime were indications of precisely how seriously they took this attack. As John C. Calhoun put it in 1850, the northern onslaught had already disrupted "the equilibrium between the two sections" and threatened the very existence of the Union, forcing the South soon "to choose between abolition and secession." Eloquently he concluded, "The South asks for justice, simple justice, and less she ought not to take." It was a sentiment that southerners widely shared.[27]

*   *   *

IN BOTH RUSSIA and the United States South unfree labor systems were abolished in the 1860s. Because of differences in the internal viability of those systems, however, as well as in the nature of their

crises, there were also fundamental differences in the course of abolition. Both slavery and serfdom were abolished from above, by governmental decree rather than popular upheaval. Nevertheless, the immediate consequences of the transformation were more far-reaching
in the South than in Russia.

In the United States slavery died violently, as the result of northern
military victory over a planter-led rebellion. Because southern slaveholders staked everything on preserving slavery—and lost—they
were in a poor position to influence the terms of the new settlement.
Viewed as traitors by an indignant northern population, they suffered
an immediate, uncompensated emancipation of their slaves (the only
large-scale confiscation of private property in American history), and
they were powerless to prevent the federal government from imposing
on the South a series of increasingly sweeping measures designed to
bring freedom in fact as well as in name to the ex-slave population.
Although historians continue to debate the degree to which "Radical" Republicans controlled the postwar Reconstruction process, in
comparison with developments in most other ex-slave societies there
can be little doubt about the radical nature of American Reconstruction. Through the Thirteenth, Fourteenth, and Fifteenth amendments
to the Constitution as well as the Reconstruction Acts of 1867 and
innumerable measures passed by the individual southern states, a major effort was undertaken to extend to the freedmen the full rights of
citizenship—redefined to include such new features as suffrage (at
least for males) and education—and indeed to make the ex-slaves the
backbone of political power in the South. The attempt was halting,
half-hearted, and ultimately unsuccessful, but even so the overthrow
of slavery constituted a revolution that brought fundamental changes
to southern life. In short, the continued internal viability of southern
slavery and the unique commitment to it of the master class produced
an emancipation that proved unusually radical in its social consequences.[28]

Emancipation in Russia, while momentous, represented less of a
break with the past. Abolition of serfdom occurred internally (although from above) rather than by imposition of outside force; unlike
southern planters, Russian pomeshchiki did not see their power and
influence crushed by military defeat. Indeed, once the inevitability of
change was clear to them, they played a major role in drafting and
implementing the provisions of the emancipation settlement. As a result, emancipation, although representing a significant new departure
for Russia, occurred within a broad framework of continuity. There

was no radical attempt to give sudden equality to the ex-serfs or to break the social and economic hegemony of the pomeshchiki; peasants were still peasants and noblemen still noblemen in a highly stratified society. Russian emancipation, unlike southern, was undertaken with the interests of the masters at heart and involved both financial compensation to owners and measures to ensure their continued authority in the countryside. In this respect the Russian experience was typical of the emancipation process in most slave societies, from the British West Indies and Brazil to the northern United States; the unusual vehicle of southern emancipation—Civil War—brought with it unusual revolutionary potential as well.[29]

But there was a common legacy of forced labor that Russia shared with the United States and with all other former slave societies as well. New forms of dependency that provided the ex-bondsmen with at best semifreedom became the rule. Exploitation, poverty, and bitterness endured, even as the freedmen struggled to take advantage of changed conditions. It proved far easier to abolish slavery and serfdom than to remove their influence: the "peasant question" in Russia and racial issues in the United States persisted as grim reminders of an earlier era. Although the world in the 1980s seems far removed from the one described in this book, it is well to remember the extent to which that earlier world has shaped our own.

Bibliographical Note

A complete list of the sources used to prepare this book would be excessive and redundant; full documentation appears in the notes. The reader does deserve, however, a brief explanation of the kinds of materials I have found useful. I have relied primarily on printed sources. *Printed* does not imply *secondary;* although I have made considerable use of the extensive secondary literature that exists on both American slavery and Russian serfdom, printed primary materials—some published contemporaneously and some collected by subsequent historians—form the foundation of this study. These materials are so abundant that the main difficulty the researcher encounters is not accumulating information but ordering and making sense of it. He or she also faces a decided lack of symmetry in some of the sources: although the information on both slavery and serfdom is voluminous, this information is not always of the same sort.

Most abundant of all, and most widely used by previous historians, are records left by the masters (and their allies). Diaries and reminiscences, plantation and estate records, and correspondence between owners and their administrative subordinates provide information on topics ranging from agricultural operations and treatment of the bondsmen to the masters' life-styles and attitudes.

Examples of such records left by American planters include Jack P. Greene, ed., *The Diary of Colonel Landon Carter of Sabine Hall, 1752–1778,* 2 vols. (Charlottesville: University Press of Virginia, 1965); John Spencer Bassett, ed., *The Southern Plantation Overseer as Revealed in His Letters* (Northampton, Mass.: Printed for Smith College, 1925); Ulrich B. Phillips and James David Glunt, eds., *Florida Plantation Records from the Papers of George Noble Jones* (St. Louis: Missouri Historical Society, 1927); and Edwin Adams Davis, ed., *Plantation Life in the Florida Parishes of Louisiana, 1836–1846, as Reflected in the Diary of Bennet H. Barrow* (New York: Columbia University Press, 1943). The second of these contains letters from the overseer of James K. Polk's absentee-held plantation in Mississippi; the last contains the "Rules" that Barrow composed for his Highland plantation as well as his diversely interpreted diary.

For two collections of correspondence between wealthy Russian noblemen and administrators on their absentee-held estates, one from the seventeenth century and one from the nineteenth, see A. I. Iakovlev, ed., *Akty khoziaistva boiarina B. I. Morozova,* 2 vols., (Moscow: Izdatel'stvo Akademii nauk SSSR, 1940, 1945); and I. Kuznetsov, ed., "Krepostnye krest'iane sela Barasheva-Usada v pervoi polovine XIX v.," *Krasnyi arkhiv,* 77 (1936), 117–50. The papers of the influential Vorontsov family are published as *Arkhiv kniazia Vorontsova,* 40 vols. (Moscow, 1870–97). Three recollections of a minor official in Riazan province detail aspects of serfdom there in the mid-nineteenth century, including the unmasking of an unusually sadistic pomeshchik; they are published together in S. T. Slovutinskii, *General Izmailov i ego dvornia; otryvki iz vospominanii* (Moscow: Academia, 1937).

Instructions on the running of plantations and estates, some intended only for the eyes of their recipients and others published as models, provide important insights into the ideals of the masters. Model instructions regularly appeared in *DeBow's Review,* the South's leading journal after 1846, as well as in agricultural magazines; 104 of these have been rearranged in a volume recently edited by James O. Breeden, *Advice among Masters: The Ideal in Slave Management in the Old South* (Westport, Conn.: Greenwood Press, 1980). For examples of previously unpublished instructions, see Ulrich B. Phillips, ed., *Plantation and Frontier,* vols. I and II of John R. Commons et al., eds., *A Documentary History of American Industrial Society* (Cleveland: Arthur H. Clark, 1910). See also Barrow's "Rules of Highland Plantation," cited above.

M. V. Dovnar-Zapol'skii assembled numerous Russian instructions in a series entitled *Materialy dlia istorii votchinnago upravleniia v Rossii* and published in successive issues of *Universitetskaia izvestiia,* 43–50 (1903–10). Model instructions sometimes appeared in the works of the St. Petersburg Free Economic Society, *Trudy Vol'nago ekonomicheskago obshchestva k pooshchreniiu v Rossii zemledeliia i domostroitel'stva,* which began publication in 1765. See also *Zemledel'cheskaia gazeta,* an agricultural journal that appeared twice weekly between 1834 and 1841.

Writings in defense of bondage are essential for unraveling the masters' ideology. Much of the most important southern proslavery propaganda, which reached its peak of intensity during the thirty years before the Civil War, was published in *DeBow's Review.* Leading proslavery pieces can also be found in two major collections, E. N. Elliott, ed., *Cotton Is King, and Pro-Slavery Arguments* (New York: Johnson Reprint Company, 1968; orig. pub. 1860); and Drew Gilpin Faust, ed., *The Ideology of Slavery: Proslavery Thought in the Antebellum South, 1830–1860* (Baton Rouge: Louisiana State University Press, 1981). Russian writings in defense of serfdom, never as numerous as American proslavery tracts, decreased in number while the southern crusade on behalf of slavery was cresting. For the most persistent voice in behalf of serfdom during the last third of the eighteenth century, see Prince M. M. Shcherbatov's collected works, *Sochineniia kniazia M. M.*

Shcherbatova, 2 vols., ed. I. P. Khrushchov (St. Petersburg: Izdanie B. S. Shcherbatova, 1896–98). Proserfdom writings also appeared in the Works of the Free Economic Society and, in passing, in the journal *Zemledel'cheskaia gazeta*. Other works are cited in the notes to Chapter 3.

Abundant evidence also exists for studying the lives of the bondsmen. For the antebellum slaves, who left more extensive documentary records than any other group of slaves in history, there are two major kinds of primary sources, autobiographies and interviews. Despite their often propagandistic nature, autobiographies, written either by fugitives who escaped to the North or by freedmen after the Civil War, represent the best direct testimony of the slaves' view of slavery. Among the most useful of dozens of such narratives are Charles Ball, *Slavery in the United States: A Narrative of the Life and Adventures of Charles Ball, a Black Man* (New York: John S. Taylor, 1837); Frederick Douglass, *Narrative of the Life of Frederick Douglass, an American Slave, Written by Himself* (New York: New American Library, 1968; orig. pub. 1845), the first of three autobiographies by Douglass; and Solomon Northup, *Twelve Years a Slave . . .* (New York: Miller, Orton & Mulligan, 1855). The largest collection of interviews with ex-slaves, invaluable for their sheer massiveness despite being recorded three-quarters of a century after emancipation, was undertaken under the auspices of the Federal Writers' Project in the 1930s. See George P. Rawick, ed., *The American Slave: A Composite Autobiography,* 19 vols. (Westport, Conn.: Greenwood Publishing Company, 1972); Rawick, ed., *The American Slave: A Composite Autobiography Supplement, Series 1,* 12 vols. (Westport, Conn.: Greenwood Publishing Company, 1977); and Charles L. Perdue et al., eds., *Weevils in the Wheat: Interviews with Virginia Ex-Slaves* (Charlottesville: University Press of Virginia, 1976).

There is no Russian equivalent to the Federal Writers' Project interviews, and only a handful of autobiographies were written by ex-serfs. See N. N. Shipov, "Istoriia moei zhizni: Razskaz byvshago krepostnago krest'ianina N. N. Shipova," *Russkaia starina,* 30 (1881), 133–48, 221–40, 437–78, 665–78; "Zapiska krepostnoi," *Russkaia starina,* 145 (1911), 140–51; and the anonymous poem-narrative, T. G. Snytko, ed., *Vesti o Rossii: Povest' v stikhakh krepostnogo krest'ianina, 1830–1840 gg.* (Iarolsavl: Iaroslavskoe knizhnoe izdatel'stvo, 1961).

Fortunately, however, much archival material shedding light on serf life and attitudes has been published, including petitions to owners and government authorities and resolutions ensuing from mir gatherings. This material appears in widely scattered sources, including estate records cited above. The best single source illustrating peasant attitudes and behavior is a multivolume collection of documents on peasant unrest entitled *The Peasant Movement in Russia,* under the general supervision of N. M. Druzhinin. I have used the first three volumes of this series: S. N. Valk, ed., *Krest'ianskoe dvizhenie v Rossii v 1796–1825 gg.: Sbornik dokumentov* (Moscow: Izdatel'stvo sotsial'no-ekonomicheskoi literatury, 1961); A. V. Predtechenskii, ed., *Krest'ianskoe dvizhenie v Rossii v 1826–1849 gg.: Sbornik dokumentov* (Moscow: Izdatel'stvo sotsial'no-ekonomicheskoi literatury, 1961); and S. B. Okun', ed., *Krest'ianskoe dvizhenie v Rossii v 1850–1856 gg.: Sbornik dokumentov* (Moscow: Izdatel'stvo sotsial'no-ekonomicheskoi literatury, 1963). When supplemented with similar materials published elsewhere, during both the Soviet and pre-Soviet periods, these documents provide considerable information on the serfs' world view, although not quite the same kind of information as is available on the outlook of American slaves.

Folklore provides important clues to the mentality of the slaves and serfs, although interpreting these clues is often tricky. Numerous collections of peasant and black songs and folktales exist. For two examples of folktales see Iu. M. Sokolov, ed., *Barin i muzhik: Russkie narodnye skazki* (Moscow: Academia, 1932); and Richard M. Dorson, ed., *American Negro Folktales* (Greenwich, Conn.: Fawcett Publications, 1967).

A wide variety of other collections shed light on the bondsmen as well as their masters. A few of these include *Materialy dlia istorii krepostnago prava v Rossii: Izvlecheniia iz sekretnykh otchetov Ministerstva vnutrennikh del za 1836–1856 g.* (Berlin: B. Behr's Buchhandlung, 1872), which contains reports from the Ministry of Internal Affairs; E. A. Morokhovets, ed., *Krest'ianskoe dvizhenie 1827–1869 godov*, 2 vols. (Moscow: Gosudarstvennoe sotsial'no-ekonomicheskoe izdatel'stvo, 1931), with similar reports from the political police; and Helen Tunnicliff Catterall, ed., *Judicial Cases concerning American Slavery and the Negro*, 5 vols. (New York: Octagon Books, 1968; orig. pub. 1926–37). For examples of documentary collections on revolts, see S. A. Golubtsov, ed., *Pugachevshchina*, 3 vols. (Moscow: Gosudarstvennoe izdatel'stvo, 1926–31); and Henry Irving Tragle, ed., *The Southampton Slave Revolt of 1831: A Compilation of Source Material* (New York: Random House, 1971).

Travel accounts provide a perspective different from those of both masters and bondsmen. For examples of many such accounts, see William Richardson, *Anecdotes of the Russian Empire* (London: Frank Cass, 1968; orig. pub. 1784); M. P. D. de Passenans, *La Russie et l'esclavage, dans leurs rapports avec la civilisation européene: ou de l'influence de la servitude sur la vie domestique des russes*, 2 vols. in 1 (Paris: Pierre Blanchard, 1822); Robert Pinkerton, *Russia: or Miscellaneous Observations on the Past and Present State of That Country and Its Inhabitants* (London: Seeley & Sons, 1833); Hunter Dickinson Farish, ed., *Journal & Letters of Philip Vickers Fithian, 1773–1774: A Plantation Tutor of the Old Dominion* (Williamsburg, Va.: Colonial Williamsburg, 1943); and Frederick Law Olmsted, *The Cotton Kingdom: A Traveller's Observations on Cotton and Slavery in the American Slave States*, 2 vols. (New York: Mason Brothers, 1861).

Population statistics provide important information on the worlds of both the masters and the bondsmen. Data from Russian censuses are available in Ia. E. Vodarskii, *Naselenie Rossii v konste XVII-nachale XVIII veka (chislennost', soslovno-klassovyi sostav, razmeshchenie)* (Moscow: Izdatel'stvo

"Nauka," 1977); V. M. Kabuzan, *Izmeneniia v razmeshchenii naseleniia Rossii v XVIII-pervoi polovine XIX v.* (Moscow: Izdatel'stvo "Nauka," 1971); and V. M. Kabuzan and S. M. Troitskii, "Izmeneniia v chislennosti, udel'nom vese i razmeshchenii dvorianstva v Rossii v 1782–1858 gg.," *Istoriia SSSR*, 1971, no. 4, 153–69. For more detailed statistics from the censuses of 1851 and 1858, see Petr Keppen, *Deviataia reviziia: Izsledovanie o chisle zhitelei v Rossii v 1851 godu* (St. Petersburg: V tipografii Imperatorskoi akademii nauk, 1857); and A. Troinitskii, *Krepostnoe naselenie v Rossii, po 10–i narodnoi perepisi* (St. Petersburg: Izdanie statisticheskago otdela tsentral'nago statisticheskago komiteta, 1861).

The best sources for American population statistics are the decennial census reports beginning in 1790; see, for example, U. S. Census Office, *Population of the United States in 1860* (Washington: Government Printing Office, 1864). For a collection of census material on the southern states, see Donald B. Dodd and Wynelle S. Dodd, comps., *Historical Statistics of the South, 1790–1970* (University, Ala.: University of Alabama Press, 1973). For population estimates before 1790 as well as statistics based on the decennial censuses, see *Historical Statistics of the United States: Colonial Times to 1957* (Washington: Government Printing Office, 1960).

A vast and rapidly growing historical literature exists on both American slavery and Russian serfdom. There is room here for mention of only a few of the most important books; other secondary works I have consulted appear in the notes. The following two lists are arranged alphabetically and are somewhat arbitrarily limited to seventeen books each.

Major Sources on Russia

Aleksandrov, V. A. *Sel'skaia obshchina v Rossii (XVII-nachalo XIX v.).* Moscow: Izdatel'stvo "Nauka," 1976.

Blum, Jerome. *Lord and Peasant in Russia from the Ninth to the Nineteenth Century.* Princeton: Princeton University Press, 1961.

Confino, Michael. *Domaines et seigneurs en Russie vers la fin du XVIIIe siècle: Etude de structures agraires et de mentalités économiques.* Paris: Institut d'études slaves de l'Université de Paris, 1963.

Fedorov, V. A. *Krest'ianskoe dvizhenie v tsentral'noi Rossii 1800–1860 (Po materialam tsentral'no-promyshlennykh gubernii).* Moscow: Izdatel'stvo Moskovskogo universiteta, 1980.

——— *Pomeshchich'i krest'iane tsentral'no-promyshlennogo raiona Rossii kontsa XVIII-pervoi poloviny XIX v.* Moscow: Izdatel'stvo Moskovskogo universiteta, 1974.

Field, Daniel. *The End of Serfdom: Nobility and Bureaucracy in Russia, 1855–1861.* Cambridge, Mass.: Harvard University Press, 1976.

Hellie, Richard. *Enserfment and Military Change in Muscovy.* Chicago: University of Chicago Press, 1971.

Ignatovich, I. I. *Pomeshchich'i krest'iane nakanune osvobozhdeniia,* 2nd ed. Moscow: I. D. Sytin, 1910.

Indova, E. I. *Krepostnoe khoziaistvo v nachale XIX veka po materialam votchinnogo arkhiva Vorontsovykh.* Moscow: Izdatel'stvo Akademii nauk SSSR, 1955.

Iurovskii, L. N. *Saratovskie votchiny: Statistiko-ekonomicheskie ocherki i materialy iz istorii krupnogo zemlevladeniia i krepostnogo khoziaistva v kontse XVIII i v nachale XIX stoletiia.* Saratov: Izdanie Saratovskogo instituta narodnogo khoziaistva, 1923.

Koretskii, V. I. *Zakreposhchenie krest'ian i klassovaia bor'ba vo vtoroi polovine XVI v.* Moscow: Izdatel'stvo "Nauka," 1970.

Koval'chenko, I. D. *Russkoe krepostnoe krest'ianstvo v pervoi polovine XIX v.* Moscow: Izdatel'stvo Moskovskogo universiteta, 1967.

Romanovich-Slavatinskii, A. *Dvorianstvo v Rossii ot nachala XVIII veka do otmeny krepostnago prava.* St. Petersburg: Tipografiia Ministerstva vnutrennikh del, 1870.

Rubinshtein, N. L. *Sel'skoe khoziaistvo Rossii vo vtoroi polovine XVIII v.* Moscow: Gosudarstvennoe izdatel'stvo, 1957.

Semevskii, V. I. *Krest'iane v tsarstvovanie Imperatritsy Ekateriny II,* 2 vols., 2nd ed. St. Petersburg: Tipografiia M. M. Stasiulevicha, 1901–3.

—— *Krest'ianskii vopros v Rossii v XVIII i pervoi polovine XIX veka,* 2 vols. St. Petersburg: Tipografiia tovarishchestva "Obshchestvennaia pol'za," 1888.

Shchepetov, K. N. *Krepostnoe pravo v votchinakh Sheremetevykh (1708–1885).* Moscow: Izdanie dvortsa-muzeia, 1947.

Major Sources on the American South

Blassingame, John W. *The Slave Community: Plantation Life in the Antebellum South.* New York: Oxford University Press, 1972; rev. ed. 1979.

Cooper, William J., Jr. *The South and the Politics of Slavery, 1828–1856.* Baton Rouge: Louisiana State University Press, 1978.

Escott, Paul D. *Slavery Remembered: A Record of Twentieth-Century Slave Narratives.* Chapel Hill: University of North Carolina Press, 1979.

Faust, Drew Gilpin. *James Henry Hammond and the Old South: A Design for Mastery.* Baton Rouge: Louisiana State University Press, 1982.

Fogel, Robert William, and Stanley L. Engerman. *Time on the Cross: The Economics of American Negro Slavery,* 2 vols. Boston: Little, Brown, 1974.

Genovese, Eugene D. *Roll, Jordan, Roll: The World the Slaves Made.* New York: Pantheon Books, 1974.

—— *The World the Slaveholders Made: Two Essays in Interpretation.* New York: Pantheon Books, 1969.

Gray, Lewis Cecil. *History of Agriculture in the Southern United States to 1860,* 2 vols. Washington: Carnegie Institution of America, 1933.

Gutman, Herbert G. *The Black Family in Slavery and Freedom, 1750–1925*. New York: Pantheon Books, 1976.

Joyner, Charles. *Down by the Riverside: A South Carolina Slave Community*. Urbana: University of Illinois Press, 1984.

Levine, Lawrence W. *Black Culture and Black Consciousness: Afro-American Folk Thought from Slavery to Freedom*. New York: Oxford University Press, 1977.

Morgan, Edmund S. *American Slavery, American Freedom: The Ordeal of Colonial Virginia*. New York: W. W. Norton, 1975.

Mullin, Gerald W. *Flight and Rebellion: Slave Resistance in Eighteenth-Century Virginia*. New York: Oxford University Press, 1972.

Oakes, James. *The Ruling Race: A History of American Slaveholders*. New York: Alfred A. Knopf, 1982.

Phillips, Ulrich B. *American Negro Slavery: A Survey of the Supply, Employment and Control of Negro Labor as Determined by the Plantation Regime*. Baton Rouge: Louisiana State University Press, 1966; orig. pub. 1918.

Stampp, Kenneth M. *The Peculiar Institution: Slavery in the Ante-Bellum South*. New York: Vintage Books, 1956.

Wood, Peter H. *Black Majority: Negroes in Colonial South Carolina from 1670 through the Stono Rebellion*. New York: Alfred A. Knopf, 1974.

Notes

Introduction

1. For the concept of a western European "core" versus the "periphery" to the east and west, see Immanuel Wallerstein, *The Modern World-System: Capitalist Agriculture and the Origins of the European World-Economy in the Sixteenth Century* (New York: Academic Press, 1974), esp. 86–102, 304–27. On the establishment of eastern European serfdom and its relation to the sixteenth-century economic renaissance, see László Makkai, "Neo-Serfdom: Its Origin and Nature in East Central Europe," *Slavic Review,* 34 (June 1975), 225–38; M. Malowist, "Poland, Russia and Western Trade in the Fifteenth and Sixteenth Centuries," *Past and Present,* 13 (1958), 26–33; Jerzy Topolski, "The Manorial-Serf Economy in Central and Eastern Europe in the Sixteenth and Seventeenth Centuries," *Agricultural History,* 48 (1974), 346–52; Jerome Blum, "The Rise of Serfdom in Eastern Europe," *American Historical Review,* 63 (1957), 807–36; and S. D. Skazin, "Osnovnye problemy tak nazyvaemogo 'vtorogo izdaniia krepostnichestva' v srednei i vostochnoi Evrope," *Voprosy istorii,* 1958, no. 2, 96–105. On the early spread of slavery in South and Central America, see, among others, Philip D. Curtin, *The Atlantic Slave Trade: A Census* (Madison: University of Wisconsin Press, 1969); Rolando Mellafe, *Negro Slavery in Latin America,* trans. J. W. S. Judge (Berkeley: University of California Press, 1975), 16–22, 29–31, 88–93; Richard S. Dunn, *Sugar and Slaves: The Rise of the Planter Class in the English West Indies, 1624–1713* (New York: W. W. Norton, 1973), esp. 46–83, 224–62; and Frederick P. Bowser, *The African Slave in Colonial Peru, 1524–1650* (Stanford: Stanford University Press, 1974), 1–124.

2. One historian has recently suggested that *kholop* is more appropriately translated *servant* than *slave.* See Herbert Leventer, "Comments on Richard Hellie's 'Recent Soviet Historiography on Medieval and Early Modern Russian Slavery,'" *Russian Review,* 36 (Jan. 1977), 64–67; and Richard Hellie's persuasive rebuttal in "A Reply," ibid., 68–75.

3. On kholopstvo, see V. M. Paneiakh, *Kabal'noe kholopstvo na Rusi v XVI veke* (Leningrad: Izdatel'stvo "Nauka," 1967); Paneiakh, *Kholopstvo v XVI-nachale XVII veka* (Leningrad: Izdatel'stvo "Nauka," 1975); E. I. Ko-

lycheva, *Kholopstvo i krepostnichestvo (konets XV–XVI v.)* (Moscow: Iz-datel'stvo "Nauka," 1971); Richard Hellie, "Recent Soviet Historiography on Medieval and Early Modern Russian Slavery," *Russian Review,* 35 (Jan. 1976), 1–32; and especially Hellie, *Slavery in Russia, 1450–1725* (Chicago: University of Chicago Press, 1982). Kholopstvo bears certain striking simi-larities to traditional African slavery, which contained both high and low status slaves and often served noneconomic functions; see Igor Kopytoff and Suzanne Miers, "African 'Slavery' as an Institution of Marginality," in *Slav-ery in Africa: Historical and Anthropological Perspectives,* ed. Miers and Kopytoff (Madison: University of Wisconsin Press, 1977), 12–14, 17–19, 55–59, 68–69.

4. There is no need here for detailed discussion of these terms. Among peasant categories were *starozhil'tsy* (sometimes *starinnye krest'iane*), *novo-poriadchiki* (sometimes *novoprikhodchiki,* or *prikhozhie krest'iane,* or *prishlye krest'iane*), *bobyli, serebreniki, polovniki, monastyrskie detenyshi;* among slaves there were *polnye kholopy, starinnye kholopy, sluzhilye liudi, delovye liudi, stradniki, dokladnye kholopy, zakladnye kholopy, kabal'nye kholopy,* and *dobrovol'nye kholopy.* For somewhat differing definitions and evaluations of these terms, see M. D'iakonov, *Ocherki iz istorii sel'skago naseleniia v Moskovskom gosudarstve (XVI–XVII vv.)* (St. Petersburg, 1898); B. D. Grekov, *Krest'iane na Rusi s drevneishikh vremen do XVII veka,* 2nd ed. (Moscow: Izdatel'stvo Akademii nauk SSSR, 1954), II, 76–209; Paneiakh, *Kholopstvo v XVI-nachale XVII veka,* 7–48; and Hellie, *Slavery in Russia,* 29–71.

5. V. I. Koretskii, *Zakreposhchenie krest'ian i klassovaia bor'ba vo vtoroi polovine XVI v.* (Moscow: Izdatel'stvo "Nauka," 1970), 11–47; Richard Hellie, *Enserfment and Military Change in Muscovy* (Chicago: University of Chicago Press, 1971), 77–92; Jerome Blum, *Lord and Peasant in Russia from the Ninth to the Nineteenth Century* (Princeton: Princeton University Press, 1961), 247–61; and Jack Marcellus Culpepper III, "The Legislative Origins of Peasant Bondage in Muscovy" (Ph.D. diss., Columbia University, 1965), 13–23. For charters to eight monasteries limiting peasant movement and for appropriate provisions of the codes of 1497 and 1550, see Richard Hellie, ed. and trans., *Readings for Introduction to Russian Civilization: Muscovite Society* (Chicago: University of Chicago, 1967), 97–105.

6. Hellie, *Enserfment and Military Change,* 21–47. For examples of land grants to pomeshchiki, see D. Ia. Samokvasov, ed., *Arkhivnyi material. No-vootkrytye dokumenty pomestno-votchinnykh uchrezhdenii Moskovskago gosudarstva XV–XVII stoletii* (Moscow: Universitetskaia tipografiia, 1905), I, pt. 2, 1–104 (quotation, 39).

7. Koretskii, *Zakreposhchenie krest'ian,* 11–14; R. G. Skrynnikov, "Kre-postnichestvo i stanovlenie barshchinnoi sistemy v Rossii v XVI veke," *Vop-rosy istorii,* 1976, no. 1, 33–50; N. Rozhkov, "Sel'skoe khoziaistvo Moskov-skoi Rusi v XVI veke i ego vliianie na sotsial'no-politicheskii stroi togo vremeni," in Rozhkov, *Istoricheskie i sotsiologicheskie ocherki. Sbornik sta-*

tei (Moscow: Izdanie I. K. Shamova, 1906), 57–59; D. P. Makovskii, *Razvitie tovarno-denezhnykh otnoshenii v sel'skom khoziaistve russkogo gosudarstva v XVI veke* (Smolensk: Smolenskii pedagogicheskii institut, 1960), 3–45; Richard Chancelour, "The Booke of the Great and Mighty Emperor of Russia," in *The Principal Navigations, Voyages, Traffiques & Discoveries of the English Nation,* ed. Richard Hakluyt (Glasgow: James MacLehose, 1903), II, 225 (quotation); and Thomas Randolphe, "The Ambassage of the Right Worshipfull Master Thomas Randolphe," ibid., III, 104.

8. Koretskii, *Zakreposhchenie krest'ian,* 13–46; Makovskii, *Razvitie tovarno-denezhnykh otnoshenii,* 89–113, 147–99; Skrynnikov, "Krepostnichestvo i stanovlenie barshchinnoi sistemy," 33–41, 50; Skrynnikov, *Rossiia posle oprichniny: ocherki politicheskoi i sotsial'noi istorii* (Leningrad: Izdatel'stvo Leningradskogo universiteta, 1975), 113–20, 141–45, 151–58. For a demurrer on the degree of seigneurial production in the Novgorod region, see G. V. Abramovich, "Novgorodskie pistsovye knigi kak istochnik po istorii barshchiny v pomestnom khoziaistve XVI veka," *Ezhegodnik po agrarnoi istorii Vostochnoi Evropy 1970 g.* (Riga, 1977), 14–30. For the contrast with the western borderlands of Russia, see Z. K. Ianel', "O nekotorykh voprosakh 'vtorogo izdaniia' krepostnogo prava i sotsial'no-ekonomicheskogo razvitiia barshchinnogo pomest'ia v Rossii," *Istoricheskie zapiski,* 78 (1965), 150–80.

9. Estimates of the Russian population in the sixteenth century vary widely, but even assuming the accuracy of the largest of these, population was extremely sparse. Perhaps the most reliable estimate for the middle of the century is 6.5 million persons; see Ia. E. Vodarskii, *Naselenie Rossii za 400 let (XVI-nachalo XX vv.)* (Moscow: "Prosveshchenie," 1973), 24–28. Hellie, *Enserfment and Military Change,* 305, mentions three population estimates for 1550, ranging from 2–3 million to 9–10 million. Assuming the accuracy of Vodarskii's figure, the population density in Russia would be about two persons per square kilometer, compared to about forty in France. Of course, in the central, most populated part of Russia the density was higher. More accurate population statistics exist for the late seventeenth century; see below, page 27.

10. On the major events of this period, see S. F. Platonov, *The Time of Troubles: A Historical Study of the Internal Crisis and Social Struggle in Sixteenth- and Seventeenth-Century Muscovy,* trans. John T. Alexander (Lawrence: University Press of Kansas, 1970; first pub. 1923); A. A. Zimin, *Oprichnina Ivana Groznogo* (Moscow: Mysl', 1964); Ruslan G. Skrynnikov, *Ivan the Terrible,* ed. and trans. Hugh F. Graham (Gulf Breeze, Fla.: Academic International Press, 1981); Skrynnikov, *Boris Godunov,* ed. and trans. Hugh F. Graham (Gulf Breeze, Fla.: Academic International Press, 1982); Skrynnikov, *Rossiia posle oprichniny;* George Vernadsky, *The Tsardom of Moscow: 1547–1682* (New Haven: Yale University Press, 1969); and V. I. Koretskii, *Formirovanie krepostnogo prava i pervaia krest'ianskaia voina v Rossii* (Moscow: Izdatel'stvo "Nauka," 1975).

11. Antonio Possevino, "The Missio Muscovitica," ed. and trans. Hugh F. Graham, *Canadian-American Slavic Studies*, 6 (Fall 1972), 469–70; Anthony Jenkinson, "A Note of the Proceeding of M. Anthonie Jenkinson," in Hakluyt, *The Principal Navigations*, III, 171; and Heinrich von Staden, *The Land and Government of Muscovy: A Sixteenth-Century Account*, ed. and trans. Thomas Esper (Stanford: Stanford University Press, 1967), 31, 33.

12. Koretskii, *Zakreposhchenie krest'ian*, 47–85, 161–81, 235–95; Koretskii, *Formirovanie krepostnogo prava*, 83–140, 192–222; Paneiakh, *Kabal'noe kholopstvo*, 33–36; Hellie, *Enserfment and Military Change*, 93–95; Vernadsky, *The Tsardom of Moscow*, 109–11, 139, 155–58, 216–19; Skrynnikov, *Rossiia posle oprichniny*, 160–67; Samokvasov, *Arkhivnyi material*, II, pt. 2, 1–344, 431–60 (quotations, 35, 302, 306); Giles Fletcher, "Of the Russe Commonwealth," in *Rude and Barbarous Kingdom: Russia in the Accounts of Sixteenth-Century English Voyagers*, ed. Lloyd E. Berry and Robert O. Crummey (Madison: University of Wisconsin Press, 1968), 170. See also *Akty feodal'nogo zemlevladeniia i khoziaistva XIV–XVI vekov*, ed. A. A. Zimin (Moscow: Izdatel'stvo Akademii nauk SSSR, 1956), II, 420–21.

13. On the flight of peasants to the south and their reception by local authorities, see Koretskii, *Formirovanie krepostnogo prava*, 88–116. Even southern pomeshchiki, however, were not immune from peasant flight; for a petition to the government from an Elets landholder seeking to regain fugitives, see G. N. Anpilogov, ed., *Novye dokumenty o Rossii kontsa XVI-nachala XVII v.* (Moscow: Izdatel'stvo "Nauka," 1967), 322–23.

14. Koretskii, *Zakreposhchenie krest'ian*, 97–160; Koretskii, *Formirovanie krepostnogo prava*, 148–91, 225–32; Hellie, *Enserfment and Military Change*, 96–113; R. G. Skrynnikov, "Zapovednye i urochnye gody tsaria Fedora Ivanovicha," *Istoriia SSSR*, 1973, no. 1, 99–129; and Culpepper, "The Legislative Origins of Peasant Bondage," 32–52, 78–82. For legal documents regulating peasant departure, see A. E. Vorms et al., eds., *Pamiatniki istorii krest'ian XIV–XIX vv.* (Moscow: Izdanie N. N. Klochkova, 1910), 41–50. For documents on peasant flight in the south, see Anpilogov, *Novye dokumenty*, 322–403, 425–26.

15. The quotation is from Hellie, *Readings*, 168–69, 171. For an example of the argument that Bolotnikov's revolt delayed the final enserfment of the peasantry, see A. Kh. Gorfunkel', "K voprosu ob istoricheskom znachenii krest'ianskoi voiny nachala XVII veka," *Istoriia SSSR*, 1962, no. 4, 112–18. On pomeshchik pressure to abolish the search period and on the code of 1649, see Hellie, *Enserfment and Military Change*, 123–40; Culpepper, "The Legislative Origins of Peasant Bondage," 89–116; Blum, *Lord and Peasant in Russia*, 260–65; A. G. Man'kov, *Razvitie krepostnogo prava v Rossii vo vtoroi polovine XVII veka* (Moscow: Izdatel'stvo Akademii nauk SSSR, 1962), 179–87; and Hellie, *Readings*, 127–232. Robert O. Crummey notes that the legislation of 1649 made little practical difference in the running of boiar estates, and that "landlords' attitudes and practices appear to have remained essentially unchanged throughout the period" 1613–89; see

his *Aristocrats and Servitors: The Boyar Elite in Russia, 1613–1689* (Princeton: Princeton University Press, 1983), 123.

16. E. A. J. Johnson, *American Economic Thought in the Seventeenth Century* (New York: Russell & Russell, 1961), 207–13; Richard B. Morris, *Government and Labor in Early America* (New York: Columbia University Press, 1946), 44–45, 52–90; Abbot Emerson Smith, *Colonists in Bondage: White Servitude and Convict Labor in America, 1607–1776* (Chapel Hill: University of North Carolina Press, 1947), 26–28. The quotation is from Gabriel Thomas, *An Historical and Geographical Account of the Province and Country of Pensilvania and of West-New-Jersey in America* (London, 1698), 28.

17. Almon Wheeler Lauber, *Indian Slavery in Colonial Times within the Present Limits of the United States* (New York: Columbia University Press, 1913); *Documents Relating to the Colonial History of the State of New Jersey* (hereafter cited as *New Jersey Archives*), XXX, "Calendar of New Jersey Wills, Administrations, Etc., Volume II—1730–1750," passim. See also Henry Scofield Cooley, *A Study of Slavery in New Jersey* (Baltimore, 1896), 11.

18. Lauber, *Indian Slavery,* 217–25, 283–88; Winthrop D. Jordan, *White over Black: American Attitudes toward the Negro, 1550–1812* (Baltimore: Penguin Books, 1969), 89–91; William Cronon, *Changes in the Land: Indians, Colonists, and the Ecology of New England* (New York: Hill and Wang, 1983), 42–44. The quotation is from Daniel P. Mannix and Malcolm Cowley, *Black Cargoes: A History of the Atlantic Slave Trade, 1518–1865* (New York: Viking Press, 1962), 61. According to Orlando Patterson, attempts to enslave conquered peoples have almost always been unsuccessful; see his *Slavery and Social Death: A Comparative Study* (Cambridge, Mass.: Harvard University Press, 1982), 110–13.

19. Morris, *Government and Labor,* 315–63; Edmund S. Morgan, *American Slavery, American Freedom: The Ordeal of Colonial Virginia* (New York: W. W. Norton, 1975), 3–130; Darrett B. Rutman and Anita H. Rutman, *A Place in Time: Middlesex County, Virginia, 1650–1750* (New York: W. W. Norton, 1984), 72, 130–38; Eugene Irving McCormac, *White Servitude in Maryland, 1634–1820* (Baltimore: Johns Hopkins Press, 1904); Warren B. Smith, *White Servitude in Colonial South Carolina* (Columbia: University of South Carolina Press, 1961); Cheeseman A. Herrick, *White Servitude in Pennsylvania: Indentured and Redemption Labor in Colony and Commonwealth* (New York: Negro Universities Press, 1969; first pub. 1926); and Lawrence William Towner, "A Good Master Well Served: A Social History of Servitude in Massachusetts, 1620–1750" (Ph.D. diss., Northwestern University, 1955). For an example of a servant separated from a loved one, see the plaintive request in the Pennsylvania *Gazette,* 31 Jan. 1760, of ex–New Jersey servant Andrew Konkel for information on the whereabouts of his brother, in *New Jersey Archives*, XX, "Extracts from American Newspapers Relating to New Jersey, Vol. IV, 1756–1761," 406.

The estimate on servants' death rate is from Lois Green Carr and Russell R. Menard, "Immigration and Opportunity: The Freedman in Early Maryland," in *The Chesapeake in the Seventeenth Century: Essays on Anglo-American Society*, ed. Thad W. Tate and David L. Ammerman (Chapel Hill: University of North Carolina Press, 1979), 208–10.

20. Thomas Jefferson Wertenbaker, *The First Americans, 1607–1690* (New York: Macmillan, 1927), 28–32; Wesley Frank Craven, *The Southern Colonies in the Seventeenth Century, 1607–1689* (Baton Rouge: Louisiana State University Press, 1949), 209–15; Aubrey Land, "The Tobacco Staple and the Planter's Problems: Technology, Labor, and Crops," *Agricultural History*, 43 (1969), 72–73; and Morgan, *American Slavery, American Freedom*, 297–304.

21. Christopher Hill, *The Century of Revolution, 1603–1714* (New York: W. W. Norton, 1961), 24, 247–87; Carl Bridenbaugh, *Vexed and Troubled Englishmen, 1590–1642* (New York: Oxford University Press, 1968), 355–56; Wallace Notestein, *The English People on the Eve of Colonization* (New York: Harper, 1954), 83–85; Keith Wrightson, *English Society, 1580–1680* (New Brunswick, N.J.: Rutgers University Press, 1982), 140–48; James Horn, "Servant Emigration to the Chesapeake in the Seventeenth Century," in Tate and Ammerman, *The Chesapeake*, 51–95; and David W. Galenson, *White Servitude in Colonial America: An Economic Analysis* (Cambridge: Cambridge University Press, 1981), 23–78.

22. For estimates of immigration to Virginia based on the number of headrights issued, see Wesley Frank Craven, *White, Red, and Black: The Seventeenth-Century Virginian* (Charlottesville: University Press of Virginia, 1971), 15–20; of 82,000 headrights issued in Virginia between 1635 and 1699, almost 47,000 (about 57 percent) were granted between 1650 and 1674. But for a warning that headrights are only a rough approximation to immigration because not all headrights were used, see Russell R. Menard, "Immigration to the Chesapeake Colonies in the Seventeenth Century: A Review Essay," *Maryland Historical Magazine*, 68 (Fall 1973), 324–25.

23. James A. Rawley, *The Transatlantic Slave Trade: A History* (New York: W. W. Norton, 1981), esp. 149–69; K. G. Davies, *The Royal African Company* (London: Longmans, Green, 1957), 7–15, 299; Edward D. Collins, "Studies in the Colonial Policy of England, 1672–1680: The Plantations, the Royal African Company, and the Slave Trade," *Annual Report of the American Historical Association for the Year 1900* (Washington: Government Printing Office, 1901), I, 142–57, 178–79; Pieter D. Emmer, "The History of the Dutch Slave Trade: A Bibliographical Survey," *Journal of Economic History*, 32 (1972), 728–47. On the proportion of slaves in New York and other colonies, see Table 1.

24. Land, "The Tobacco Staple and the Planter's Problems," 76–77; Gloria L. Main, *Tobacco Colony: Life in Early Maryland, 1650–1720* (Princeton: Princeton University Press, 1982), 54–55 (statistics); Wertenbaker, *The First Americans*, 130–33; Morgan, *American Slavery, American Freedom*, 297–304; and Rutman and Rutman, *A Place in Time*, 188–95.

25. Headright figures are from Craven, *White, Red, and Black,* 15–16.

26. Hill, *The Century of Revolution,* 206–8, 267–68; Menard, "Immigration to the Chesapeake Colonies," 326–28; Carr and Menard, "Immigration and Opportunity," 230–35. Although tobacco prices fluctuated wildly, the general trend was downward, from high prices until the 1660s to relatively low prices after 1680; see Russell R. Menard, "Farm Prices of Maryland Tobacco, 1659–1710," *Maryland Historical Magazine,* 68 (Spring 1973), 80–85.

27. The headright figures are computed from Craven, *White, Red, and Black,* 15–16. For estimates of immigration to Virginia and Maryland that vary slightly from Craven's but show the same trend, see Terry L. Anderson and Robert Paul Thomas, "The Growth of Population and Labor Force in the Seventeenth-Century Chesapeake," *Explorations in Economic History,* 15 (July 1978), 297. The decline in immigration after the 1670s was clearly not a consequence of decreased demand for servants, for as Menard has shown, prices for indentured servants in Maryland and Virginia rose from the mid-1670s to 1690; Menard, "From Servants to Slaves: The Transformation of the Chesapeake Labor System," *Southern Studies,* 16 (Winter 1977), 371–73.

28. Galenson has estimated that in the Chesapeake servant prices relative to slave prices increased 57 percent between 1675 and 1690; Galenson, *White Servitude in Colonial America,* 152–54. See also Main, *Tobacco Colony,* 100–3; and Richard N. Bean and Robert P. Thomas, "The Adoption of Slave Labor in British North America," in *The Uncommon Market: Essays in the Economic History of the Atlantic Slave Trade,* ed. Henry A. Gemery and Jan S. Hogendorn (New York: Academic Press, 1979), 377–98. For general treatment of the slave trade, see Curtin, *The Atlantic Slave Trade;* and Rawley, *The Transatlantic Slave Trade.* On the importation of slaves to Virginia, see Herbert S. Klein, *The Middle Passage: Comparative Studies in the Atlantic Slave Trade* (Princeton: Princeton University Press, 1978), 122–30.

29. For the transformation to natural population growth in the Chesapeake colonies, see especially Russell R. Menard, "The Maryland Slave Population, 1658–1730: A Demographic Profile of Blacks in Four Counties," *William and Mary Quarterly,* 3rd ser., 32 (Jan. 1975), 42–47; and Allan Kulikoff, "A 'Prolifick' People: Black Population Growth in the Chesapeake Colonies, 1700–1790," *Southern Studies,* 16 (Winter 1977), 391–403.

30. Smith, *Colonists in Bondage,* 264–70; McCormac, *White Servitude in Maryland,* 48–59; Raphael Semmes, *Crime and Punishment in Early Maryland* (Baltimore: Johns Hopkins Press, 1938), 116–18; and Harry B. Weiss and Grace M. Weiss, *An Introduction to Crime and Punishment in Colonial New Jersey* (Trenton, N.J.: Past Times Press, 1960), 71–78. The quotation is from *New Jersey Archives,* XIX, "Extracts from American Newspapers, Relating to New Jersey, Vol. III, 1751–1755," 163. For notices of fugitive slaves, see Lathan A. Windley, comp., *Runaway Slave Advertisements: A Documentary History from the 1730s to 1790* (Westport, Conn.: Greenwood Press, 1983).

31. Computed from *New Jersey Archives,* XIX, "Extracts from American Newspapers, Relating to New Jersey, Vol. III, 1751–1755," and XXXII, "Calendar of New Jersey Wills, Administrations, Etc., Vol. III—1751–1760." This figure is of course only a rough approximation; not all slaves and servants were listed in wills, and doubtless not all fugitives were advertised.

32. Colden to Micajah Perry, not dated but c. 1731, *The Letters and Papers of Cadwallader Colden,* II, in *Collections of the New-York Historical Society,* 51 (1918), 31–32.

33. H. L. Nieboer, *Slavery as an Industrial System: Ethnological Researches,* 2nd ed., revised (The Hague: Martinus Nijhoff, 1910) (quotation, 418–19); Eric Williams, *Capitalism & Slavery* (New York: Capricorn Books, 1966; first pub. 1944), 6–7; Evsey D. Domar, "The Causes of Slavery or Serfdom: A Hypothesis," *Journal of Economic History,* 30 (1970), 18–32.

34. Orlando Patterson, "The Structural Origin of Slavery: A Critique of the Nieboer-Domar Hypothesis from a Comparative Perspective," in *Comparative Perspectives on Slavery in New World Plantation Societies,* ed. Vera Rubin and Arthur Tuden, special issue of *Annals of the New York Academy of Sciences,* 292 (1977), 25, 15 (quotations); Patterson, *Slavery and Social Death,* passim; Frederic L. Pryor, "A Comparative Study of Slave Societies," *Journal of Comparative Economics,* 1 (March 1977), 25–49; Kopytoff and Miers, "African 'Slavery' as an Institution of Marginality," 68; R. Keith Aufhauser, "Profitability of Slavery in the British Caribbean," *Journal of Interdisciplinary History,* 5 (Summer 1974), 45–68; Roger Anstey, *The Atlantic Slave Trade and British Abolition, 1760–1810* (Atlantic Highlands, N.J.: Humanities Press, 1975).

35. Historians have noted the close connection elsewhere as well between increased agricultural demand and the spread of forced labor. Several recent historians of Africa, for example, have challenged the dominant interpretation of slavery there as primarily noneconomic, arguing that in much of the continent commercial agriculture transformed slavery from an institution of "marginality" into a mode of production. See especially Frederick Cooper, *Plantation Slavery on the East Coast of Africa* (New Haven: Yale University Press, 1977); and Paul E. Lovejoy, *Transformations in Slavery: A History of Slavery in Africa* (Cambridge: Cambridge University Press, 1983).

36. On agricultural production for the domestic market, see Percy Wells Bidwell and John I. Falconer, *History of Agriculture in the Northern United States, 1620–1860* (New York: Peter Smith, 1941), 138–40; Lawrence Henry Gipson, *The British Empire before the American Revolution* (Caldwell, Idaho: Caxton Printers, 1936), III, 76–79; and Marc Egnal, "The Economic Development of the Thirteen Continental Colonies, 1720 to 1775," *William and Mary Quarterly,* 3rd ser., 32 (April 1975), 198. On the share of tobacco and rice in exports to England, see James F. Shepherd and Gary M. Walton, *Shipping, Maritime Trade, and the Economic Development of Colonial North America* (Cambridge: Cambridge University Press, 1972), 38.

37. Population figures for most of the colonial period—especially the early years—are rough estimates and must be used with caution. For consistency and comparative purposes I have used figures contained in *Historical Statistics of the United States: Colonial Times to 1957* (Washington: Government Printing Office, 1960), which are as accurate as any overall estimates and are the most convenient to use because they exist for all the colonies at ten-year intervals. For average annual commodity export figures of the individual colonies, 1768–72, see Shepherd and Walton, *Shipping, Maritime Trade, and the Economic Development,* 47, which clearly demonstrates the connection between slavery and market-oriented production. Thus, in the upper South (Maryland and Virginia) the per capita value of exports was £1.82, and in the lower South (North Carolina, South Carolina, and Georgia) it was £1.78. The colonies where slavery was of minimal importance, however, had much lower figures: £1.03 for the middle colonies and £0.84 for New England.

38. On the minor role of Russian exports in the sixteenth and seventeenth centuries, see Wallerstein, *The Modern World-System,* 304–27; Malowist, "Poland, Russia, and Western Trade," 35–38; and N. N. Repin, "K voprosu o sviazi vneshnego i vnutrennego rynka Rossii vo vtoroi polovine XVII-pervoi chetverti XVIII v. (po materialam Arkhangel'skogo porta)," *Vestnik Moskovskogo universiteta,* ser. 9, istoriia, 1970, no. 5, 56–68. For crop yields on the holdings of one large seventeenth-century landowner, see D. I. Petrikeev, *Krupnoe krepostnoe khoziaistvo XVII v. po materialam votchiny boiarina B. I. Morozova* (Leningrad: Izdatel'stvo "Nauka," 1967), 93–98.

39. Koretskii, *Formirovanie krepostnogo prava,* 4–9 (quotation, 4); Koretskii, *Zakreposhchenie krest'ian,* 17–36; Skrynnikov, "Krepostnichestvo i stanovlenie barshchinnoi sistemy"; Iu. A. Tikhonov, *Pomeshchich'i krest'iane v Rossii: Feodal'naia renta v XVII-nachale XVIII v.* (Moscow: Izdatel'stvo "Nauka," 1974), 307. See also Blum, *Lord and Peasant in Russia,* 205–11, 224–28; Hellie, *Enserfment and Military Change,* 85; Daniel Chirot, "The Growth of the Market and Service Labor Systems in Agriculture," *Journal of Social History,* 8 (Winter 1975), 67–69; and Topolski, "The Manorial-Serf Economy in Central and Eastern Europe," 344–51. But for a note cautioning against exaggerating the role of barshchina in the sixteenth century, see A. L. Shapiro, "Barshchina v Rossii XVI veka (o metodakh ee izucheniia)," *Voprosy istorii,* 1978, no. 11, 33–50.

40. On Morozov's operations, see Petrikeev, *Krupnoe krepostnoe khoziaistvo,* 83–88, 112–50; and *Akty khoziaistva boiarina B. I. Morozova,* ed. A. I. Iakovlev (Moscow: Izdatel'stvo Akademii nauk SSSR, 1940, 1945), passim. For a more typical landholder, see A. A. Novosel'skii, *Votchinnik i ego khoziaistvo v XVII veke* (Moscow: Gosudarstvennoe izdatel'stvo, 1929), 91–122, 133–39, 158–59. On the widespread existence of barshchina on monastic holdings, see N. A. Gorskaia, *Monastyrskie krest'iane tsentral'noi Rossii v XVII v.: O sushchnosti i formakh feodal'no-krepostnicheskikh otnoshenii* (Moscow: Izdatel'stvo "Nauka," 1977), 234–39; and I. A. Bulygin, *Monastyrskie krest'iane Rossii v pervoi chetverti XVIII veka* (Moscow: Iz-

datel'stvo "Nauka," 1977), 161–73, 180–81, 203–38, 290–91, 306–7. On market-oriented seigneurial production in Belorussia, see Z. Iu. Kopysskii, "Rynochnye sviazi sel'skogo khoziaistva Belorussii XVI-pervoi poloviny XVII vv.," in *Ezhegodnik po agrarnoi istorii Vostochnoi Evropy 1962 g.* (Minsk, 1964), 141–51. On the growth of commercial agriculture in the eighteenth century, see Arcadius Kahan, *The Plow, the Hammer, and the Knout: An Economic History of Eighteenth-Century Russia,* with the editorial assistance of Richard Hellie (Chicago: University of Chicago Press, 1985), 57–59.

41. Tikhonov, *Pomeshchich'i krest'iane v Rossii,* 119, 172, 219–20, 292. See also his articles, "Feodal'naia renta v tsentral'noi Rossii (konets XVI-pervaia polovina XVII v.)," *Voprosy istorii,* 1972, no. 10, 41–57; and "Rost feodal'noi ekspluatatsii krest'ian posle Sobornogo Ulozheniia 1649 g.," *Istoriia SSSR,* 1973, no. 2, 155–65.

42. Philip Alexander Bruce, *Economic History of Virginia in the Seventeenth Century* (New York, 1896), I, 222 (quotation), 262; *Journal of Jasper Danckaerts, 1679–1680,* ed. Bartlett Burleigh James and J. Franklin Jameson (New York: Scribner's, 1913), 133; *Historical Statistics;* Aubrey C. Land, "Economic Behavior in a Planting Society: The Eighteenth Century Chesapeake," *Journal of Southern History,* 33 (1967), 469–85; Main, *Tobacco Colony,* esp. 16–47.

43. Craven, *White, Red, and Black,* 85–86 (statistics), 87 (quotation); Menard, "From Servants to Slaves," 360–61; Carville V. Earle, *The Evolution of a Tidewater Settlement System: All Hallow's Parish, Maryland, 1650–1783* (Chicago: University of Chicago Department of Geography Research Paper no. 170, 1975), 46–47. For adjustments to Craven's figures that do not alter his argument, see Anderson and Thomas, "The Growth of Population and Labor Force," 297.

44. Converse D. Clowse, *Economic Beginnings in Colonial South Carolina, 1670–1730* (Columbia: University of South Carolina Press, 1971); Peter H. Wood, *Black Majority: Negroes in Colonial South Carolina from 1670 through the Stono Rebellion* (New York: Alfred A. Knopf, 1974), passim; and Smith, *White Servitude in Colonial South Carolina.* On the value of rice as a proportion of exports to England, see Shepherd and Walton, *Shipping, Maritime Trade, and the Economic Development,* 38. For the establishment and early growth of slavery in Georgia, see Betty Wood, *Slavery in Colonial Georgia, 1730–1775* (Athens: University of Georgia Press, 1984), 1–109.

45. For a general treatment of slavery in the North, see Edgar J. McManus, *Black Bondage in the North* (Syracuse: Syracuse University Press, 1973); on the ending of slavery there, see Arthur Zilversmit, *The First Emancipation* (Chicago: University of Chicago Press, 1967). On Pennsylvania, see Herrick, *White Servitude in Pennsylvania,* and Allan Tully, "Patterns of Slaveholding in Colonial Pennsylvania: Chester and Lancaster Counties, 1729–1758," *Journal of Social History,* 6 (1973), 286–91.

46. Edgar J. McManus, *A History of Negro Slavery in New York* (Syra-

cuse: Syracuse University Press, 1966), 3–10, 23–24; Alexander C. Flick, ed., *History of the State of New York* (New York: Columbia University Press, 1933), I, 343–45, II, 266–67; Governor Cosby to the Board of Trade, in *The Documentary History of the State of New-York*, ed. E. B. O'Callaghan (Albany, 1849), I, 722–23. For a list of land grants, see Irving Mark, *Agrarian Conflicts in Colonial New York, 1711–1775* (New York: Columbia University Press, 1940), 21.

47. Bidwell and Falconer, *History of Agriculture*, 115, 133; Wertenbaker, *The First Americans*, 63–67; Lorenzo Johnston Greene, *The Negro in Colonial New England* (New York: Atheneum, 1968; first pub. 1942), 100–23; Towner, "A Good Master Well Served," 160–66; Robert C. Twombly and Robert H. Moore, "Black Puritan: The Negro in Seventeenth-Century Massachusetts," *William and Mary Quarterly*, 3rd ser., 24 (1967), 224–42.

48. Edward Channing, *The Narragansett Planters: A Study of Causes* (Baltimore, 1886), 6–10 (quotation, 10); Harry Lyman Koopman, *The Narragansett Country: Glimpses of the Past* (Providence: n.p., 1927), 25–28; William B. Weeden, *Early Rhode Island: A Social History of the People* (New York: Grafton Press, 1910), 143; and Elisha R. Potter, *The Early History of Narragansett*, in *Collections of the Rhode-Island Historical Society*, III (Providence, 1835), 114.

49. The term *slaves without masters* forms the title of the most recent comprehensive work on free blacks in the United States South; see Ira Berlin, *Slaves without Masters: The Free Negro in the Antebellum South* (New York: Pantheon Books, 1974). For works on state peasants in Russia, see note 70.

50. Ia. E. Vodarskii, *Naselenie Rossii v kontse XVII-nachale XVIII veka (chislennost', soslovno-klassovyi sostav, razmeshchenie)* (Moscow: Izdatel'stvo "Nauka," 1977). See also his articles, "Chislennost' naseleniia i kolichestvo pomestno-votchinnykh zemel' v XVII v. (po pistsovym i perepisnym knigam)," *Ezhegodnik po agrarnoi istorii Vostochnoi Evropy 1964 g.* (Kishinev, 1966), 217–30; "Razmeshchenie krest'ianskogo naseleniia v Rossii v poslednei chetverti XVII v.," ibid., *1966 g.* (Tallin, 1971), 137–46; and "Kolichestvo krest'ian, pomeshchikov i pashni na Smolenshchine vo vtoroi polovine XVII veka," in *Voprosy agrarnoi istorii tsentra i severo-zapada RSFSR: Materialy mezhvuzovskoi nauchnoi konferentsii* (Smolensk: Ministerstvo prosveshcheniia RSFSR, 1972), 79–87. In addition to works by Vodarskii, see N. M. Shepukova, "Izmenenie udel'nogo vesa chastnovladel'cheskogo krest'ianstva v sostave naseleniia Evropeiskoi Rossii (XVIII-pervaia polovina XIX v.)," *Voprosy istorii*, 1959, no. 12, 123–36; and V. M. Kabuzan, *Izmeneniia v razmeshchenii naseleniia Rossii v XVIII-pervoi polovine XIX v.* (Moscow: Izdatel'stvo "Nauka," 1971), appendix 2.

51. Vodarskii, *Naselenie Rossii v kontse XVII-nachale XVIII veka*, 102, 134, 192. The proportion of serfs was only slightly changed in 1719; see ibid. and Shepukova, "Izmenenie udel'nogo vesa," 126.

52. Joseph Marshall, *Travels through Germany, Russia, and Poland in the*

Years 1769 and 1770 (New York: Arno Press, 1971; first pub. London, 1772), 166–67.

53. Vodarskii, *Naselenie Rossii v kontse XVII-nachale XVIII veka*, 146–50. For a discussion of climatic and geographic conditions of Russia, see W. H. Parker, *An Historical Geography of Russia* (Chicago: Aldine, 1969; first pub. London, 1968), 13–29, 77–126.

54. Vodarskii, *Naselenie Rossii v kontse XVII-nachale XVIII veka*, 151–52, 180, 171. In his regional statistics Vodarskii excludes the *iasachnye* or fur-paying peasants of conquered nationalities in Siberia and the Urals. See also Shepukova, "Izmenenie udel'nogo vesa," 126–29. For a description of seventeenth-century colonization in the southeast, see E. A. Shvetsova, "Kolonizatsiia Tambovskogo uezda v XVII veke," *Ezhegodnik po agrarnoi istorii Vostochnoi Evropy 1964 g.* (Kishinev, 1966), 208–16.

55. In North America Samuel Sewall's booklet *The Selling of Joseph*, published in 1700, stands as the sole antislavery tract until the middle of the eighteenth century. With the exception of a small number of Quakers, few of whom were actively opposed to slavery until the second third of the eighteenth century, most colonists regarded the institution as so natural they did not even bother to defend it, let alone attack it. See David Brion Davis, *The Problem of Slavery in Western Culture* (Ithaca: Cornell University Press, 1966), 125–50; and Sydney V. James, *A People among Peoples: Quaker Benevolence in Eighteenth-Century America* (Cambridge, Mass.: Harvard University Press, 1963), chs. 7, 8. In Russia there was equally little articulated opposition to serfdom before the middle of the eighteenth century; see V. I. Semevskii, *Krest'ianskii vopros v Rossii v XVIII i pervoi polovine XIX veka* (St. Petersburg, 1888), I, 1–12.

56. For examples of whites sentenced to "slavery" in Massachusetts, see Helen Tunnicliff Catterall, ed., *Judicial Cases concerning American Slavery and the Negro* (New York: Octagon Books, 1968; first pub. 1926–37), IV, 469–70 (quotation, 469). On the lack of a clear distinction between slave and free among the early colonists, see Oscar and Mary F. Handlin, "Origins of the Southern Labor System," *William and Mary Quarterly*, 3rd ser., 7 (1950), 199–203. There is an extensive historical debate over the status of the few blacks in Virginia during the 1620s–50s; see, in addition to the Handlins' article, Carl N. Degler, "Slavery and the Genesis of American Race Prejudice," *Comparative Studies in Society and History*, 2 (1959), 49–66; Jordan, *White over Black*, 71–82; Alden T. Vaughan, "Blacks in Virginia: A Note on the First Decade," *William and Mary Quarterly*, 3rd ser., 29 (July 1972), 469–78; and T. H. Breen and Stephen Innes, *"Myne Own Ground": Race and Freedom on Virginia's Eastern Shore, 1640–1676* (New York: Oxford University Press, 1980). On planters' preferences among Africans, see Daniel C. Littlefield, *Rice and Slaves: Ethnicity and the Slave Trade in Colonial South Carolina* (Baton Rouge: Louisiana State University Press, 1981), 8–32 (quotation, 13).

57. Wood, *Black Majority*, 95–130 (quotation, 96); Kenneth W. Porter,

"Negroes on the Southern Frontier, 1670–1763," in Porter, *The Negro on the American Frontier* (New York: Arno Press, 1971), 157–60; and Ira Berlin, "Time, Space, and the Evolution of Afro-American Society on British Mainland North America," *American Historical Review*, 85 (Feb. 1980), 54–58.

58. Morgan, *American Slavery, American Freedom*, 154–57, 235–92, 316–37; T. H. Breen, "A Changing Labor Force and Race Relations in Virginia, 1660–1710," *Journal of Social History*, 7 (Fall 1973), 7–13; Breen and Innes, *"Myne Own Ground"*; Berlin, "Time, Space, and the Evolution of Afro-American Society," 67–69; Robert Beverley, *The History of Virginia, in Four Parts*, excerpted in *A Documentary History of Slavery in North America*, ed. Willie Lee Rose (New York: Oxford University Press, 1976), 26.

59. Breen, "A Changing Labor Force," 7–13. For a different discussion of the social composition of Bacon's Rebellion, see Bernard Bailyn, "Politics and Social Structure in Virginia," in *Seventeenth-Century America*, ed. J. M. Smith (Chapel Hill: University of North Carolina Press, 1959), 102–6; for a general account, see Wilcomb E. Washburn, *The Governor and the Rebel: A History of Bacon's Rebellion in Virginia* (Chapel Hill: University of North Carolina Press, 1957).

60. Breen, "A Changing Labor Force," 13–16; David W. Galenson, "British Servants and the Colonial Indenture System in the Eighteenth Century," *Journal of Southern History*, 44 (Feb. 1978), 41–66 (statistics); Morgan, *American Slavery, American Freedom*, 296; Beverley, *The History of Virginia*, 26.

61. Breen, "A Changing Labor Force," 16–17; Morgan, *American Slavery, American Freedom*, 316–69; Jordan, *White over Black*, 101–35; Wood, *Black Majority*, 150–55, 212–33; Klein, *The Middle Passage*, 122–30; Byrd letter in Elizabeth Donnan, ed., *Documents Illustrative of the History of the Slave Trade to America* (New York: Octagon Books, 1969; first pub. 1930–35), IV, 131–32.

62. A. Leon Higginbotham, Jr., *In the Matter of Color: Race and the American Legal Process, the Colonial Period* (New York: Oxford University Press, 1978), passim (quotation, 58); Wood, *Black Majority*, 271–77; Jordan, *White over Black*, 316–37; "An Act Concerning Negros and Other Slaves" (Maryland), in Rose, *A Documentary History of Slavery*, 24; "An act declaring that baptisme of slaves doth not exempt them from their bondage" (Virginia), ibid., 19; "An Act for the Encourageing the Importacion of Negros and Slaves into this Province" (Maryland), in Donnan, *Documents Illustrative of the History of the Slave Trade*, IV, 9–10. For other legislation, see Rose, *A Documentary History of Slavery*, 16–24.

63. *The Diary of Colonel Landon Carter of Sabine Hall, 1752–1778*, ed. and intro. Jack P. Greene (Charlottesville: University Press of Virginia, 1965), I, 429–30, II, 1148–49.

64. See sources cited in notes 4 and 13 above. On seventeenth-century peasant categories in general, see A. N. Sakharov, "Evoliutsiia kategorii

krest'ianstva v XVII v.," *Voprosy istorii,* 1965, no. 9, 51–67; and D'iakonov, *Ocherki iz istorii sel'skago naseleniia,* passim. On bobyli, see ibid., 206–40, and A. L. Shapiro, "Evoliutsiia bobyl'stva v Rossii v XVIII veke," in *Ezhegodnik po agrarnoi istorii Vostochnoi Evropy 1958 g.* (Tallin, 1959), 91–104.

65. N. P. Pavlov-Sil'vanskii, *Gosudarevy sluzhilye liudi: liudi kabal'nye i dokladnye,* 2nd ed. (St. Petersburg: Tipografiia M. M. Stasiulevicha, 1909), 34–208; A. M. Kleimola, "Up through Servitude: The Changing Condition of the Muscovite Elite in the Sixteenth and Seventeenth Centuries," *Russian History/Histoire Russe,* 6 (no. 2, 1979), 212–20; Crummey, *Aristocrats and Servitors.* Richard Hellie uses the terms *upper service class* and *middle service class* to distinguish between Moscow-based aristocrats and provincial pomeshchiki; see Hellie, *Enserfment and Military Change,* 22–24.

66. There is an extensive literature on Bolotnikov's uprising. For a sampling, see Paul Avrich, *Russian Rebels: 1600–1800* (New York: Schocken Books, 1972), 14–47; D. P. Makovskii, *Pervaia krest'ianskaia voina v Rossii* (Smolensk: Ministerstvo prosveshcheniia RSFSR, 1967); Koretskii, *Formirovanie krepostnogo prava,* 192–362; and V. I. Koretskii, "O formirovanii I. I. Bolotnikova kak vozhdia krest'ianskogo vosstaniia," in *Krest'ianskie voiny v Rossii XVII–XVIII vekov: problemy, poiski, resheniia,* ed. L. V. Cherepnin (Moscow: Izdatel'stvo "Nauka," 1974), 122–47.

67. Avrich, *Russian Rebels,* 23–26, 32–33, 90–92, 119–20 (quotation, 25); Makovskii, *Pervaia krest'ianskaia voina,* 24–29, 171–74, 463–82; A. L. Shapiro, "Ob istoricheskoi roli krest'ianskikh voin XVII–XVIII vv. v Rossii," *Istoriia SSSR,* 1965, no. 5, 63–65; L. V. Cherepnin, "Ob izucheniia krest'ianskikh voin v Rossii XVII–XVIII vv. (K teorii problemy)," in Cherepnin, *Krest'ianskie voiny v Rossii,* 12–13; V. V. Mavrodin et al., "Ob osobennostiakh krest'ianskikh voin v Rossii," *Voprosy istorii,* 1956, no. 2, 70–74.

68. D'iakonov, *Ocherki iz istorii sel'skago naseleniia,* 241–94; Novosel'skii, *Votchinnik i ego khoziaistvo,* 125–26, 271–74; Hellie, *Slavery in Russia,* 695–708; Blum, *Lord and Peasant in Russia,* 271–74; and E. V. Anisimov, "Izmeneniia v sotsial'noi strukture russkogo obshchestva v kontse XVII-nachale XVIII veka (Posledniaia stranitsa istorii kholopstva v Rossii)," *Istoriia SSSR,* 1979, no. 5, 35–51.

69. On Peter I's partial secularization of clerical holdings, see Bulygin, *Monastyrskie krest'iane,* 59–132. On Catherine II's full secularization, see Blum, *Lord and Peasant,* 362–66; and V. I. Semevskii, *Krest'iane v tsarstvovanie Imperatritsy Ekateriny II,* 2nd ed. (St. Petersburg: Tipografiia M. M. Stasiulevicha, 1901–3), II, 236–85.

70. The most complete work on state peasants, which concentrates on the first half of the nineteenth century, is N. M. Druzhinin, *Gosudarstvennye krest'iane i reforma P. D. Kiseleva* (Moscow: Izdatel'stvo Akademii nauk SSSR, 1946–58); see also Olga Crisp, "The State Peasants under Nicholas I," *Slavonic and East European Review,* 37 (June 1959), 387–412. For the

eighteenth century, see P. K. Alefirenko, *Krest'ianskoe dvizhenie i krest'ian-skii vopros v Rossii v 30–50–kh godakh XVIII veka* (Moscow: Izdatel'stvo Akademii nauk SSSR, 1958), 215–300; and Semevskii, *Krest'iane v tsarstvovanie Imperatritsy Ekateriny II*, II.

71. Pavlov-Sil'vanskii, *Gosudarevy sluzhilye liudi*, 137–259; A. Romanovich-Slavatinskii, *Dvorianstvo v Rossii ot nachala XVIII veka do otmeny krepostnago prava* (St. Petersburg, 1870), 2–285; M. Bogoslovskii, *Byt i nravy russkago dvorianstva v pervoi polovine XVIII veka* (Moscow: Tipografiia G. Lissnera i D. Sobko, 1906), 3–31; Blum, *Lord and Peasant in Russia*, 182–88, 308–17, 345–62. See also Brenda Meehan-Waters, *Autocracy and Aristocracy: The Russian Service Elite of 1730* (New Brunswick, N.J.: Rutgers University Press, 1982); and S. M. Troitskii, *Russkii absoliutizm i dvorianstvo v XVIII v.: Formirovanie biurokratii* (Moscow: Izdatel'stvo "Nauka," 1974).

72. V. M. Kabuzan and S. M. Troitskii, "Izmeneniia v chislennosti, udel'-nom vese i razmeshchenii dvorianstva v Rossii v 1782–1858 gg.," *Istoriia SSSR*, 1971, no. 4, 153–69.

73. Romanovich-Slavatinskii, *Dvorianstvo v Rossii*, 58–87; P. K. Alefirenko, "Russkaia obshchestvennaia mysl' pervoi poloviny XVIII stoletiia o sel'skom khoziaistve," *Materialy po istorii zemledeliia SSSR*, I (Moscow: Izdatel'stvo Akademii nauk SSSR, 1952), 545–47; M. M. Shcherbatov, "Razmyshlenie o dvorianstve," in *Sochineniia kniazia M. M. Shcherbatova*, ed. I. P. Khrushchov (St. Petersburg, 1896–8), I, 222; and Shcherbatov, "Zamechaniia Shcherbatova na bol'shoi nakaz Ekateriny," in M. M. Shcherbatov, *Neizdannye sochineniia* (Moscow: Ogiz-sotsekgiz, 1935), 56.

74. On the code of 1649 as it applied to serfs, see Man'kov, *Razvitie krepostnogo prava*, 179–87; and Blum, *Lord and Peasant in Russia*, 262–64. For a translation of the code's eleventh chapter, "Legal Procedure concerning the Peasants," see Hellie, *Readings for Introduction to Russian Civilization*, 215–32.

75. Man'kov, *Razvitie krepostnogo prava*, passim; Semevskii, *Krest'iane v tsarstvovanie Imperatritsy Ekateriny II*, I, 162–65, 178–90, 359, 379–80; Romanovich-Slavatinskii, *Dvorianstvo v Rossii*, 285–306; M. T. Beliavskii, *Krest'ianskii vopros v Rossii nakanune vosstaniia E. I. Pugacheva (formirovanie antikrepostnicheskoi mysli)* (Moscow: Izdatel'stvo Moskovskogo universiteta, 1965), 38–54, 266–77; and Blum, *Lord and Peasant in Russia*, 422–36.

76. William Richardson, *Anecdotes of the Russian Empire* (London: Frank Cass, 1968; first pub. 1784), 193; M. P. D. de Passenans, *La Russie et l'esclavage, dans leurs rapports avec la civilisation européene; ou de l'influence de la servitude sur la vie domestique des russes* (Paris, 1822), I, 79. For examples of numerous similar observations, see Johann-Georg Korb, *Diary of an Austrian Secretary of Legation at the Court of Czar Peter the Great*, ed. and trans. from Latin by Count MacDonnell (London: Frank Cass, 1968; first English ed. 1868, first Latin ed. 1700), II, 200; and Robert

Pinkerton, *Russia: Or Miscellaneous Observations on the Past and Present State of That Country and Its Inhabitants* (London, 1833), 285–86, 291.

77. Quotations are from I. I. Ignatovich, *Pomeshchich'i krest'iane nakanune osvobozhdeniia*, 2nd ed. (Moscow: I. D. Sytin, 1910), 22; A. V. Predtechenskii, *Ocherki obshchestvenno-politicheskoi istorii Rossii v pervoi chetverti XIX veka* (Moscow: Izdatel'stvo Akademii nauk SSSR, 1957), 30; Blum, *Lord and Peasant in Russia*, 422; and Alexander Gerschenkron, *Europe in the Russian Mirror: Four Lectures in Economic History* (Cambridge: Cambridge University Press, 1970), 93. For examples of similar statements, see V. V. Mavrodin, *Klassovaia bor'ba i obshchestvenno-politicheskaia mysl' v Rossii v XVIII v. (1725–1773 gg.)* (Leningrad: Izdatel'stvo Leningradskogo universiteta, 1964), 6; Beliavskii, *Krest'ianskii vopros v Rossii*, 32–34; and Terence Emmons, *The Russian Landed Gentry and the Peasant Emancipation of 1861* (Cambridge: Cambridge University Press, 1968), 19–20.

78. Patterson, *Slavery and Social Death*, 179, 178; Moses I. Finley, "The Idea of Slavery: Critique of David Brion Davis' *The Problem of Slavery in Western Culture*," in *Slavery in the New World: A Reader in Comparative History*, ed. Laura Foner and Eugene D. Genovese (Englewood Cliffs, N.J.: Prentice-Hall, 1969), 260.

79. Hellie, *Slavery in Russia*, 385–412, 710–13 (quotations, 711, 390). Patterson has delineated an "extrusive" concept of slave as "insider who had fallen" as well as the more familiar "intrusive" concept of slave as outsider; see his *Slavery and Social Death*, 38–44 (quotation, 41).

1. Labor Management

1. For a good, brief comparative treatment of the abolition of American slave systems, see Robert William Fogel and Stanley L. Engerman, *Time on the Cross: The Economics of American Negro Slavery* (Boston: Little, Brown, 1974), 29–38. On the abolition of eastern European serfdom, see Jerome Blum, *The End of the Old Order in Rural Europe* (Princeton: Princeton University Press, 1978), pts. 2 and 3.

2. For varying methods of emancipation, see Robert Brent Toplin, *The Abolition of Slavery in Brazil* (New York: Atheneum, 1972); C. L. R. James, *The Black Jacobins: Toussaint L'Ouverture and the San Domingo Revolution*, 2nd ed. rev. (New York: Vintage Books, 1963); William A. Green, *British Slave Emancipation: The Sugar Colonies and the Great Experiment, 1830–1865* (Oxford: Clarendon Press, 1976); Arthur F. Corwin, *Spain and the Abolition of Slavery in Cuba, 1817–1886* (Austin: University of Texas Press, 1967); John V. Lombardi, *The Decline and Abolition of Negro Slavery in Venezuela, 1820–1854* (Westport, Conn.: Greenwood Press, 1971); and Blum, *The End of the Old Order*, pt. 3.

3. Among numerous books on the subject the following are especially useful: Herman Belz, *A New Birth of Freedom: The Republican Party and*

Freedmen's Rights, 1861–1866 (Westport, Conn.: Greenwood Press, 1976); Michael Les Benedict, *A Compromise of Principle: Congressional Republicans and Reconstruction, 1863–1869* (New York: W. W. Norton, 1974); P. A. Zaionchkovskii, *Otmena krepostnogo prava v Rossii*, 3rd ed. (Moscow: Prosveshchenie, 1968); and Daniel Field, *The End of Serfdom: Nobility and Bureaucracy in Russia, 1855–1861* (Cambridge, Mass.: Harvard University Press, 1976).

4. See below, Epilogue, pages 363–68.

5. The best treatment of the Russian population in the eighteenth and nineteenth centuries, based on the ten censuses taken between 1719 and 1858, is V. M. Kabuzan, *Izmeneniia v razmeshchenii naseleniia Rossii v XVIII-pervoi polovine XIX v.* (Moscow: Izdatel'stvo "Nauka," 1971). See also N. M. Shepukova, "Izmenenie udel'nogo vesa chastnovladel'cheskogo krest'ianstva v sostave naseleniia Evropeiskoi Rossii (XVIII-pervaia polovina XIX v.)," *Voprosy istorii*, 1959, no. 12, 123–36; and V. M. Kabuzan and S. M. Troitskii, "Izmeneniia v chislennosti, udel'nom vese i razmeshchenii dvorianstva v Rossii v 1782–1858 gg.," *Istoriia SSSR*, 1971, no. 4, 153–69. More detailed work exists on the last two censuses, of 1851 and 1858: see Petr Keppen, *Deviataia reviziia: Izsledovanie o chisle zhitelei v Rossii v 1851 godu* (St. Petersburg, 1857); and A. Troinitskii, *Krepostnoe naselenie v Rossii, po 10-i narodnoi perepisi* (St. Petersburg, 1861).

The American population can be traced in the decennial published census reports. For a convenient compilation covering the southern states, see Donald B. Dodd and Wynelle S. Dodd, comps., *Historical Statistics of the South, 1790–1970* (University, Ala.: University of Alabama Press, 1973); for the number of slaveholders in 1860, see U.S. Census Office, *Agriculture of the United States in 1860* (Washington, 1864), 247; for an excellent discussion of the size of slaveholdings, see Lewis Cecil Gray, *History of Agriculture in the Southern United States to 1860* (Washington: Carnegie Institution of America, 1933), I, 529–39.

6. U.S. Census Office, *Agriculture of the United States in 1860*, 247; Troinitskii, *Krepostnoe naselenie v Rossii*, 45, 66. See Tables 5 and 6; for more on the wealth of the owners, see below, Chapter 3, pages 159–66.

7. Troinitskii, *Krepostnoe naselenie v Rossii*, 45; Gray, *History of Agriculture in the Southern United States*, I, 530. On the extensive Vorontsov holdings, see E. I. Indova, *Krepostnoe khoziaistvo v nachale XIX veka po materialam votchinnogo arkhiva Vorontsovykh* (Moscow: Izdatel'stvo Akademii nauk SSSR, 1955), 34–40.

8. U.S. Census Office, *Population of the United States in 1860* (Washington, 1864), 592–95; Gray, *History of Agriculture in the Southern United States*, I, 530, 531, 534; Troinitskii, *Krepostnoe naselenie v Rossii*, 49, 50, 45; Kabuzan and Troitskii, "Izmeneniia v chislennosti, udel'nom vese i razmeshchenii dvorianstva," 164–65.

9. Troinitskii, *Krepostnoe naselenie v Rossii*, 49, 45; Gray, *History of Agriculture in the Southern United States*, I, 531; Otto H. Olsen, "Historians

and the Extent of Slave Ownership in the Southern United States," *Civil War History*, 18 (June 1972), 101–16; Michael Craton, "Jamaican Slavery," in *Race and Slavery in the Western Hemisphere: Quantitative Studies*, ed. Stanley L. Engerman and Eugene D. Genovese (Princeton: Princeton University Press, 1975), 252, 254, 275. See also Richard S. Dunn, *Sugar and Slaves: The Rise of the Planter Class in the English West Indies, 1624–1713* (New York: W. W. Norton, 1973), 312.

10. A. Romanovich-Slavatinskii, *Dvorianstvo v Rossii ot nachala XVIII veka do otmeny krepostnago prava* (St. Petersburg, 1870), 115–208, 310–24, 490–500; S. A. Korf, *Dvorianstvo i ego soslovnoe upravlenie za stoletie 1762–1855 godov* (St. Petersburg: Tipografiia Trenks i Fiusno, 1906), 202, 212–14, 391–94, 436–59, 482–83; Robert David Givens, "Servitors or Seigneurs: The Nobility and the Eighteenth Century Russian State" (Ph.D. diss., University of California–Berkeley, 1975), 158–275, 367–520; Marc Raeff, "The Domestic Policies of Peter III and His Overthrow," *American Historical Review*, 75 (June 1970), 1291–94, 1302; Vorontsov letter, 9 Jan. 1797, in *Arkhiv kniazia Vorontsova* (Moscow, 1870–97), X, 5. For studies of the service bureaucracy, see Brenda Meehan-Waters, *Autocracy and Aristocracy: The Russian Service Elite of 1730* (New Brunswick, N.J.: Rutgers University Press, 1982); S. M. Troitskii, *Russkii absoliutizm i dvorianstvo v XVIII v.: Formirovanie biurokratii* (Moscow: Izdatel'stvo "Nauka," 1974); and P. A. Zaionchkovskii, *Pravitel'stvennyi apparat samoderzhavnoi Rossii v XIX v.* (Moscow: Izdatel'stvo "Mysl'," 1978).

11. L. N. Iurovskii, *Saratovskie votchiny: Statistiko-ekonomicheskie ocherki i materialy iz istorii krupnogo zemlevladeniia i krepostnogo khoziaistva v kontse XVIII i v nachale XIX stoletiia* (Saratov: Izdanie Saratovskogo Instituta narodnogo khoziaistva, 1923), 65–67.

12. See statistics presented above. For detailed information on the size of slaveholdings in different regions, see Gray, *History of Agriculture in the Southern United States*, I, 530–38. On the prevalence of resident owners, see Ulrich B. Phillips, *American Negro Slavery: A Survey of the Supply, Employment and Control of Negro Labor as Determined by the Plantation Regime* (Baton Rouge: Louisiana State University Press, 1966; first pub. 1918), 225–28; Kenneth M. Stampp, *The Peculiar Institution: Slavery in the Ante-Bellum South* (New York: Vintage Books, 1956), 35–44; and Eugene D. Genovese, *Roll, Jordan, Roll: The World the Slaves Made* (New York: Pantheon Books, 1974), 10–12.

13. Gerald W. Mullin, *Flight and Rebellion: Slave Resistance in Eighteenth-Century Virginia* (New York: Oxford University Press, 1972), 47–53; Gloria L. Main, *Tobacco Colony: Life in Early Maryland, 1650–1720* (Princeton: Princeton University Press, 1982), 128–37; Jackson T. Main, "The One Hundred," *William and Mary Quarterly*, 3rd ser., 11 (1954), 354–84; Louis Morton, *Robert Carter of Nomini Hall: A Virginia Tobacco Planter of the Eighteenth Century* (Williamsburg, Va.: Colonial Williamsburg, 1945), 83; Adam Gordon, "Journal of an Officer Who Travelled in

America and the West Indies in 1764 and 1765," in *Travels in the American Colonies*, ed. Newton D. Mereness (New York: Antiquarian Press, 1961), 397.

14. Genovese, *Roll, Jordan, Roll*, 11–12; James Herbert Stone, "Black Leadership in the Old South: The Slave Drivers of the Rice Kingdom" (Ph.D. diss., Florida State University, 1976), 9–16; William W. Freehling, *Prelude to Civil War: The Nullification Controversy in South Carolina, 1816–1836* (New York: Harper & Row, 1965), 9–17; Julia Floyd Smith, *Slavery and Rice Culture in Low Country Georgia, 1750–1860* (Knoxville: University of Tennessee Press, 1985), 7–8. On Polk's plantation management, see John Spencer Bassett, ed., *The Southern Plantation Overseer as Revealed in His Letters* (Northampton, Mass.: Printed for Smith College, 1925); on Jones's, see Ulrich B. Phillips and James David Glunt, eds., *Florida Plantation Records from the Papers of George Noble Jones* (St. Louis: Missouri Historical Society, 1927).

15. Genovese, *Roll, Jordan, Roll*, 11–12; Main, "The One Hundred," 357–64; Anton Chekhov, *The Three Sisters*, trans. Tyrone Guthrie and Leonid Kipnis (New York: Avon Books, 1965), 92; Margaret Mitchell, *Gone with the Wind* (New York: Macmillan, 1937), 583, 379; Edmund S. Morgan, *American Slavery, American Freedom: The Ordeal of Colonial Virginia* (New York: W. W. Norton, 1975), 367–68; Jane Turner Censer, *North Carolina Planters and Their Children, 1800–1860* (Baton Rouge: Louisiana State University Press, 1984), 6–10; Lowell Joseph Ragatz, *The Fall of the Planter Class in the British Caribbean, 1763–1833: A Study in Social and Economic History* (New York: Century, 1928), 3–80; Philip D. Curtin, *Two Jamaicas: The Role of Ideas in a Tropical Colony, 1830–1865* (Cambridge, Mass.: Harvard University Press, 1955), 15–16, 55; Eugene D. Genovese, *The World the Slaveholders Made: Two Essays in Interpretation* (New York: Pantheon Books, 1969), ch. 2, passim; Jones quotation in Robert Manson Myers, ed., *The Children of Pride: A True Story of Georgia and the Civil War* (New Haven: Yale University Press, 1972), 110. For a view of a Russian nobleman who did establish a resident regime, see S. T. Aksakov, *The Family Chronicle*, trans. M. C. Beverley (New York: E. P. Dutton, 1961; orig. pub. 1856).

16. Indova, *Krepostnoe khoziaistvo v nachale XIX veka*, 47–50. For other examples of such central offices, see D. I. Petrikeev, *Krupnoe krepostnoe khoziaistvo XVII v. po materialam votchiny boiarina B. I. Morozova* (Leningrad: Izdatel'stvo "Nauka," 1967), 56–61; K. N. Shchepetov, *Krepostnoe pravo v votchinakh Sheremetevykh (1708–1885)* (Moscow: Izdanie dvortsa-muzeia, 1947), 124–25; Count P. A. Rumiantsev, "Uchrezhdenie domovoe," in *Materialy dlia istorii votchinnago upravleniia v Rossii*, ed. M. V. Dovnar-Zapol'skii (published in *Universitetskaia izvestiia*, 43–50, 1903–10), 18–24; K. V. Sivkov, *Ocherki po istorii krepostnogo khoziaistva i krest'ianskogo dvizheniia v Rossii v pervoi polovine XIX veka: Po materialam arkhiva stepnykh votchin Iusupovykh* (Moscow: Izdatel'stvo Akademii nauk SSSR,

1951), 27–30; and Tatiana Bakounine, *Le domaine des Princes Koura-kine dans le gouvernement de Saratov* (Paris: Les presses modernes, 1929), 34–46.

17. A. A. Novosel'skii, *Votchinnik i ego khoziaistvo v XVII veke* (Moscow: Gosudarstvennoe izdatel'stvo, 1929), 50–65.

18. Several terms were used for those who managed the estates of pomeshchiki, the most common of which were *prikazchik, upravitel', upravliaiu-shchii,* and *burmistr.* Although these terms carry slightly varying connotations, I have for simplicity translated them all as *steward,* explaining distinctions when necessary. The American equivalent is *overseer.*

19. Michael Confino, *Domaines et seigneurs en Russie vers la fin du XVIIIe siècle: Etude de structures agraires et de mentalités économiques* (Paris: Institut d'études slaves de l'Université de Paris, 1963), 43–95; Petrikeev, *Krupnoe krepostnoe khoziaistvo XVII v.,* 61–70; Shchepetov, *Krepostnoe pravo v votchinakh Sheremetevykh,* 39–41, 124–26; Novosel'skii, *Votchinnik i ego khoziaistvo,* 52–54, 70–74; Indova, *Krepostnoe khoziaistvo v nachale XIX veka,* 52–59; and Bakounine, *Le Domaine des Princes Kourakine,* 102–9. The quotation is from the 1725 "Instruktsiia barona Nikolaia Grigor'evicha Stroganova votchinnym prikazchikam sela Rozhdestvenskogo Fedoru Klinovu i Danilu Chernikovu," in "Instruktsiia votchinnomu prikazchiku pervoi chetverti XVIII v.," ed. N. V. Ustiugov, *Istoricheskii arkhiv,* 4 (1949), 157.

20. See, especially, V. A. Aleksandrov, *Sel'skaia obshchina v Rossii (XVII-nachalo XIX v.)* (Moscow: Izdatel'stvo "Nauka," 1976); Aleksandrov, "Sel'-skaia obshchina i votchina v Rossii (XVII-nachalo XIX v.)," *Istoricheskie zapiski,* 89 (1972), 231–94; and L. S. Prokof'eva, *Krest'ianskaia obshchina v Rossii vo vtoroi polovine XVIII-pervoi polovine XIX v. (na materialakh votchin Sheremetevykh* (Leningrad: "Nauka" Leningradskoe otdelenie, 1981).

21. See Aleksandrov, *Sel'skaia obshchina v Rossii,* 69–78, 176–88, for a good discussion of the relative freedom allowed serfs on some obrok estates. On the Khreptovich experiment, see Adam Khreptovich, "Votchinnoe uchrezhdenie grafa I. Khreptovicha, dopolnennoe synom ego Adamom," in Dovnar-Zapol'skii, *Materialy dlia istorii votchinnago upravleniia,* 104–28, 129–38 (quotation, 134); and Count Ir. Khreptovich, "Pravila dlia sel'skago suda v Shchorsakh i Negnevichakh, izdannyia gr. Ir. Khreptovichem 1 iiunia 1845 g.," ibid., 45 (Dec. 1905), 139–46.

22. Confino, *Domaines et seigneurs en Russie,* 231–43; N. L. Rubinshtein, *Sel'skoe khoziaistvo Rossii vo vtoroi polovine XVIII v.* (Moscow: Gosudarstvennoe izdatel'stvo, 1957), 79–85; Jerome Blum, *Lord and Peasant in Russia from the Ninth to the Nineteenth Century* (Princeton: Princeton University Press, 1961), 572; Count Roman Vorontsov, "O sposobakh k ispravleniiu sel'skago domostroistva," *Trudy Vol'nago ekonomicheskago obshchestva k pooshchreniiu v Rossii zemledeliia i domostroitel'stva,* V (1767), 8. For examples of other lamentations over the inadequate supervision of

obrok peasants, see Aleksei Olishev, "Opisanie godovoi krest'ianskoi raboty v Vologodskom uezde, s primechaniiami," ibid., II (1766), 112–13; Timofei Von Klingshtet, "O neobkhodimoi nadobnosti v sredstvakh snabdit' zdeshnikh pomeshchikov sposobnymi i nadezhnymi prikashchikami ili upraviteliami," ibid., V (1767), 60–69; and Petr Ivanovich Rychkov, "Nakaz dlia upravitelia ili prikashchika, o poriadochnom soderzhanii i upravlenii dereven' v otsutstvie gospodina," ibid., XVI (1770), 35–37, 55–57.

23. For suggestions that the residence of owners and the size of their holdings influenced their decisions to use barshchina or obrok, see V. I. Semevskii, *Krest'iane v tsarstvovanie Imperatritsy Ekateriny II,* 2nd ed. (St. Petersburg: Tipografiia M. M. Stasiulevicha, 1901–3), I, 21–22, 30–31, 239–40; Blum, *Lord and Peasant in Russia,* 398–400; Indova, *Krepostnoe khoziaistvo v nachale XIX veka,* 29–30; William Tooke, *View of the Russian Empire* (New York: Arno Press, 1970; orig. pub. London, 1800), III, 210–11; and Mary Holderness, *New Russia* (New York: Arno Press, 1970; orig. pub. London, 1823), 201. The quotation is from N. Arnol'd, "Vred, proiskhodiashchii ot poseleniia krest'ian malymi derevniami," *Zemledel'cheskaia gazeta,* 15 Aug. 1839, 517.

24. Blum, *Lord and Peasant in Russia,* 394–97; Confino, *Domaines et seigneurs en Russie,* 187, 195; Rubinshtein, *Sel'skoe khoziaistvo Rossii,* 96–130; I. I. Ignatovich, *Pomeshchich'i krest'iane nakanune osvobozhdeniia,* 2nd ed. (Moscow: I. D. Sytin, 1910), 49–60, 199–207; Iurovskii, *Saratovskie votchiny,* 98–105; and Indova, *Krepostnoe khoziaistvo v nachale XIX veka,* 34–45. Figures on Bogorodskii district are from *Zemledel'cheskaia gazeta,* 31 July 1834, 65.

25. Regional statistics are from I. D. Koval'chenko, *Russkoe krepostnoe krest'ianstvo v pervoi polovine XIX v.* (Moscow: Izdatel'stvo Moskovskogo universiteta, 1967), 61. For other statistics, see Semevskii, *Krest'iane v tsarstvovanie Imperatritsy Ekateriny II,* I, 48–49; Ignatovich, *Pomeshchich'i krest'iane nakanune osvobozhdeniia,* 49; N. M. Shepukova, "K voprosu o chislennosti barshchinnykh i obrochnykh pomeshchich'ikh krest'ian Evropeiskoi Rossii vo 2-i polovine XVIII veka," *Ezhegodnik po agrarnoi istorii Vostochnoi Evropy 1964 g.* (Kishinev, 1966), 408; and V. A. Fedorov, "Barshchina i obrok v tsentral'no-promyshlennykh guberniiakh Rossii v pervoi polovine XIX v.," ibid. *1966 g.* (Tallin, 1971), 322–25. In fact, such a schematization is a slight oversimplification, because mixed obligations, in which peasants on a given estate owed both obrok and barshchina, were widespread. Mixed obligations could be of two types: sometimes the same serfs owed both, but more often some peasants on an estate were on barshchina while others on the same estate were on obrok. In the 1850s serfs were exclusively on barshchina on 44.5 percent of all estates with more than one hundred souls, exclusively on obrok on 18.5 percent, and on both on 37 percent; see Koval'chenko, *Russkoe krepostnoe krest'ianstvo,* 64–67.

26. William Kauffman Scarborough, *The Overseer: Plantation Management in the Old South* (Baton Rouge: Louisiana State University Press,

1966), 178–94; Stone, "Black Leadership in the Old South," 9–16; Morton, *Robert Carter of Nomini Hall,* 91–97; *Narrative of the Life of Frederick Douglass, an American Slave, Written by Himself* (New York: New American Library, 1968; orig. pub. 1845), 28.

27. Scarborough, *The Overseer,* passim; Genovese, *Roll, Jordan, Roll,* 13–25; Stampp, *The Peculiar Institution,* 38–44; Mullin, *Flight and Rebellion,* 47–53.

28. "Governor Hammond's Instructions to His Overseer," in *A Documentary History of Slavery in North America,* ed. Willie Lee Rose (New York: Oxford University Press, 1976), 347; Phillips and Glunt, *Florida Plantation Records,* 99–100, 150–51.

29. Genovese, *Roll, Jordan, Roll,* 365–88; Fogel and Engerman, *Time on the Cross,* 38–40, 200–1, 210–12; William L. Van Deburg, *The Slave Drivers: Black Agricultural Labor Supervisors in the Antebellum South* (Westport, Conn.: Greenwood Press, 1979); Leslie Howard Owens, *This Species of Property: Slave Life and Culture in the Old South* (New York: Oxford University Press, 1976), 121–35; James M. Clifton, "The Rice Driver: His Role in Slave Management," *South Carolina Historical Magazine,* 82 (Oct. 1981), 331–53; Stone, "Black Leadership in the Old South;" Smith, *Slavery and Rice Culture in Low Country Georgia,* 66–75. On the role of planters' wives in estate management, see Catherine Clinton, *The Plantation Mistress: Woman's World in the Old South* (New York: Pantheon Books, 1982), 7, 16–35.

30. Stampp, *The Peculiar Institution,* 38–44; Scarborough, *The Overseer,* 6–16; Fogel and Engerman, *Time on the Cross,* 200–1; Genovese, *Roll, Jordan, Roll,* 13 (quotation).

31. The best treatment of these instructions and the various forms of estate management that they represent is Aleksandrov, *Sel'skaia obshchina v Rossii,* passim; see also, Confino, *Domaines et seigneurs en Russie,* 40–95. Many of the surviving instructions have been published; the largest single collection of them is Dovnar-Zapol'skii, *Materialy dlia istorii votchinnago upravleniia.* For other citations, see below.

32. *Akty khoziaistva boiarina B. I. Morozova,* ed. A. I. Iakovlev (Moscow: Izdatel'stvo Akademii nauk SSSR, 1940, 1945), I, 146–47, 149–52; "Nakaz kn. A. M. Cherkasskogo prikazchiku sela Markova (Moskovskogo uezda)" (1719), in "Nakazy votchinnym prikazchikam pervoi chetverti XVIII v.," ed. I. F. Petrovskaia, *Istoricheskii arkhiv,* 8 (1953), 246–47; "Instruktsiia prikashchiku Muromskoi votchiny sela Karacharova, dannaia grafom Petrom Borisovichem Sheremet'evym" (1764), in Dovnar-Zapol'skii, *Materialy dlia istorii votchinnago upravleniia,* 79; Baron Vol'f, "Nakaz upraviteliu ili prikashchiku, kak upravliat' derevniami v otsutstvie pomeshchika," in *Trudy Vol'nago ekonomicheskago obshchestva,* XII (1769), 1–8; and Kapitan Bolotov, "Nakaz upraviteliu ili prikashchiku, kakim obrazom emu pravit' derevniami v nebytnost' svoego gospodina," ibid., XVI (1770), 80–86.

33. Novosel'skii, *Votchinnik i ego khoziaistvo v XVII veke,* appendix 2,

189; Rumiantsev, "Uchrezhdenie domovoe," 44, 49–69. See *Akty kho-ziaistva boiarina B. I. Morozova*, I, 207–8; "Nakaz D. A. Shepeleva prikaz-chiku sel'tsa Glinka (Mikhailovskogo uezda) Ivanu Balashevu" (1718), in Petrovskaia, "Nakazy votchinnym prikazchikam," 233–34; "Instruktsiia barona Nikolaia Grigor'evicha Stroganova," 170, 173–78; Aleksei Gvozdev, "Prikaznye punkty Kareevskomu i Barsukovskomu staroste, Timofeiu Pav-lovu" (1811), in "Prikazy starostam," ed. A. Cherepnin, *Trudy Vysochaishe uchrezhdennoi Riazanskoi uchenoi arkhivnoi komissii*, 19 (1904), 84–89, 92–93; and "Sel'tsa Koreeva i derevni Borshchov staroste Timofeiu Ivanovu. PRIKAZ!" (1855), ibid., 107–11. On the advantages of the task system, see F. Dikgof, "Vzgliad na khoziaistvennoe ustroistvo vvedennoe g. nadvornym sovetnikom Traubenbergom v imenii ego Nikol'skom, S. Peterburgskoi gu-bernii v Iamburgskom uezde," *Zemledel'cheskaia gazeta*, 22 Jan. 1837, 49–51; and Andrei Leopol'dov, "Ocherk khoziaistva Alekseia M. Sumarokova, Saratovskoi gubernii Serdobskago uezda v sele Aleksandrovke," ibid., 26 July 1838, 466. See also Blum, *Lord and Peasant in Russia*, esp. 444–48; Confino, *Domaines et seigneurs en Russie*, esp. 107–11; and P. K. Alefirenko, "Russkaia obshchestvennaia mysl' pervoi poloviny XVIII stoletiia o sel'skom khoziaistve," *Materialy po istorii zemledeliia SSSR*, I (Moscow: Izdatel'stvo Akademii nauk SSSR, 1952), 511–52.

34. *Akty koziaistva boiarina B. I. Morozova*, II, 545; "Instruktsiia barona Nikolaia Grigor'evicha Stroganova," 157. See also P. A. Rumiantsev, "Na-stavlenie, po kotoromu imeiut opravliatsa ot vsekh nizovykh nashikh votchin . . ." in Dovnar-Zapol'skii, *Materialy dlia istorii votchinnago uprav-leniia*, 7–8; *Arkhiv sela Voshchazhnikova: Bumagi Fel'dmarshala B. P. She-remeteva* (Moscow: A. V. Vasil'ev i K°, 1901), 96–99; B. P. Sheremetev, "In-struktsiia Iaroslavskoi moei votchiny iukhotskoi volosti prikashchiku . . ." (1764), in Shchepetov, *Krepostnoe pravo v votchinakh Sheremetevykh*, 277–78, 281; "Ulozhenie dlia Porech'ia, grafa Vladimira Grigor'evicha Orlova" (1796), in Dovnar-Zapol'skii, *Materialy dlia istorii votchinnago upravleniia*, 258–59; Gvozdev, "Prikaznye punkty Kareevskomu i Barsukovskomu sta-roste," 85–89; Gvozdev, "Prikaznye punkty nizhnemu Maslovskomu sta-roste Evteiu Kandrat'evu" (1811), in Cherepnin, "Prikazy starostam," 100; and "Sel'tsa Koreeva i derevni Borshchov staroste Timofeiu Ivanovu," 109–10.

35. Quotations are from Sivkov, *Ocherki po istorii krepostnogo prava*, 39, and the instruction written by Prince F. N. Golitsyn's manager, Mikhail Deriabin, "Prikazanie prikashchiku s. Liubashevki, Mikhailovskago tozh' (Efremovsk. u., Tul'skoi gub.) 1796 g.," in Dovnar-Zapol'skii, *Materialy dlia istorii votchinnago upravleniia*, 249. For examples of instructions allowing peasants substantial self-government, see "Instruktsiia Ober-kamergera Ivana Ivanovicha Shuvalova dlia upravleniia votchinoiu ego selom Myt s de-revniami (Vladimirskoi gub.) na r. Kliazme" (1795–97), ibid., 222–34; and Ir. Khreptovich, "Pravila dlia sel'skago suda." See also Aleksandrov, *Sel'skaia obshchina v Rossii*, 69–78, 176–88.

36. Rumiantsev, "Nastavlenie," 6 (quotation); Rumiantsev, "Uchrezhde-

nie domovoe," 42–43; *Akty khoziaistva boiarina B. I. Morozova,* I, 150–52; Anna Petrovna Sheremeteva, "Instruktsiia 1727 goda Grigoriiu Voroblevskomu, naznachennomu prikashchiku v iukhotskuiu volost'," in Shchepetov, *Krepostnoe pravo v votchinakh Sheremetevykh,* 266; "Nakaz kn. A. M. Cherkasskogo prikazchiku sela Markova," 252–53; "Instruktsiia barona Nikolaia Grigor'evicha Stroganova," 159–60; "Instruktsiia sotskomu pomest'ia Miloslavskoi, Demidova, Lopukhina i Barsheva v 1764 godu," in *Trudy Vladimirskoi uchenoi arkhivnoi kommissii,* 11 (1909), 26–27; Sheremetev, "Instruktsiia Iaroslavskoi moei votchiny," 273.

37. Rumiantsev, "Nastavlenie," 12; "Instruktsiia barona Nikolaia Grigor'evicha Stroganova," 160; Sheremetev, "Instruktsiia prikashchiku Muromskoi votchiny," 85–86. See also "Instruktsiia sotskomu," 28; Stepan Kashelov, "Punkty, po kotorym ispolniat' staroste Evseiu Ivanovu" (1760), in Cherepnin, "Prikazy starostam," 69; and "Nakaz kn. A. M. Cherkasskogo prikazchiku sela Markova," 251–52.

38. For examples of instructions dealing with outsiders coming onto estates, see *Akty khoziaistva boiarina B. I. Morozova,* II, 120–21; "Nakaz D. A. Shepeleva prikazchiku sel'tsa Glinka," 232; "Nakaz A. M. Cherkasskogo prikazchiku sela Markova," 250; Sheremeteva, "Instruktsiia 1727 goda Grigoriiu Voroblevskomu," 265–66; "Instruktsiia barona Nikolaia Grigor'evicha Stroganova," 158; and Gvozdev, "Prikaznye punkty Kareevskomu i Barsukovskomu staroste," 83. On relations with neighboring peasants, see *Akty khoziaistva boiarina B. I. Morozova,* I, 85, 89 (quotation), 93–95; Rumiantsev, "Nastavlenie," 10; and Sheremetev, "Instruktsiia prikashchiku Muromskoi votchiny," 88 (quotation).

39. Deriabin, "Prikazanie prikashchiku," 245–52; Bolotov, "Nakaz upraviteliu ili prikashchiku," 87. For other examples of instructions providing minimal direction on the supervision of peasants, see "Predpisanie kniagini Agrafeny Petrovny Volkonskoi, rozhd. Bestuzhevoi-Riumnoi, prikashchiku Ivanu Sidorovu v s. Kholopovitsy" (1728), in Dovnar-Zapol'skii, *Materialy dlia istorii votchinnago upraveleniia,* 210–12; "Instruktsiia Grigoriia Ivanovicha Shipova prikashchiku sela Liubashevki Mikhailovskago tozh, Efremovskago u., Tul'skoi gub. 13 dek. 1794 g.," ibid., 235–44; "Ukaz kniazia Alekseia Mikhailovicha Cherkasskago Abrosimu Semenovu" (1739), in *Russkii arkhiv,* 1889, nos. 7–8, 361–63; and "Instruktsiia Oberkamergera Ivana Ivanovicha Shuvalova," 222–34.

40. "Instruktsiia barona Nikolaia Grigor'evicha Stroganova," 170 (quotation), 172; Sheremetev, "Instruktsiia prikashchiku Muromskoi votchiny," 103; Gvozdev, "Prikaznye punkty Kareevskomu i Barsukovskomu staroste," 86, 91 (quotation); Bolotov, "Nakaz upraviteliu ili prikashchiku," 188–91; Vol'f, "Nakaz upraviteliu ili prikashchiku," 31 (quotation); "Nakaz kn. A. M. Cherkasskogo prikazchiku sela Markova," 254.

41. "Ulozhenie dlia Porech'ia, grafa Vladimira Grigor'evicha Orlova," 266; Rychkov, "Nakaz dlia upraviteliu ili prikashchiku," 33; Sheremetev, "Instruktsiia prikashchiku Muromskoi votchiny," 86, 98; "Nakaz D. A. She-

peleva prikazchiku sel'tsa Glinka," 234–35; "Nakaz kn. A. M. Cherkasskogo prikazchiku sela Markova," 252–53; Gvozdev, "Prikaznye punkty Kareevskomu i Barsukovskomu staroste," 84; Rumiantsev, "Uchrezhdenie domovoe," 46; "Instruktsiia barona Nikolaia Grigor'evicha Stroganova," 160–61.

42. Rumiantsev, "Uchrezhdenie domovoe," 42, 46–47; Andreev, "Nakaz votchinnika krest'ianam 1709 g.," 274; "Nakaz D. A. Shepeleva prikashchiku sel'tsa Glinka," 237–38; Vol'f, "Nakaz upraviteliu ili prikashchiku," 32; "Ulozhenie dlia Porech'ia, grafa Vladimira Grigor'evicha Orlova," 274; Gvozdev, "Prikaznye punkty Kareevskomu i Barsukovskomu staroste," 90–91; *Akty khoziaistva boiarina B. I. Morozova*, II, 26–36 (quotations, 26, 32, 34).

43. The quotation is from Gvozdev, "Prikaznye punkty Kareevskomu i Barsukovskomu staroste," 83.

44. Rumiantsev, "Uchrezhdenie domovoe," 48 (quotation); Sheremeteva, "Instruktsiia 1727 goda Grigoriiu Voroblevskomu," 265; Kashelev, "Punkty po kotorym ispolniat' staroste Evseiu Ivanovu," 69; "Nakaz kn. A. M. Cherkasskogo prikazchiku sela Markova," 255–57; Gvozdev, "Prikaznye punkty Kareevskomu i Barsukovskomu staroste," 83–84; Khreptovich, "Pravila dlia sel'skago suda," 139–41, 145 (quotation); "Ulozhenie dlia Porech'ia, grafa Vladimira Grigor'evicha Orlova," 254 (quotation), 262–63; "Instruktsiia barona Nikolaia Grigor'evicha Stroganova," 164–66; "Nakaz D. A. Shepeleva prikazchiku sel'tsa Glinka," 236–37.

45. Sheremetev, "Instruktsiia prikashchiku Muromskoi votchiny," 101; "Nakaz kn. A. M. Cherkasskogo prikazchiku sela Markova," 255–57; Sheremeteva, "Instruktsiia 1727 goda Grigoriiu Voroblevskomu," 265–66; "Nakaz D. A. Shepeleva prikazchiku sel'tsa Glinka," 234, 236–37 (quotation); "Ulozhenie dlia Porech'ia grafa Vladimira Grigor'evicha Orlova," 255, 263 (quotation). See also *Akty khoziaistva boiarina B. I. Morozova*, I, 149–52; "Instruktsiia barona Nikolaia Grigor'evicha Stroganova," 162; Rumiantsev, "Uchrezhdenie domovoe," 71–72; Rumiantsev, "Punkty, po kotorym imeiut vo vsekh nizovykh nashikh votchinakh upraviteli, prikashchiki, starosti za raznye prestuplenii krest'ian nakazyvat'" (1751), in Dovnar-Zapol'skii, *Materialy dlia istorii votchinnago upravleniia*, 2–3; "Instruktsiia Ober-kamergera Ivana Ivanovicha Shuvalova," 226; and Gvozdev, "Prikaznye punkty Kareevskomu i Barsukovskomu staroste," 84, 87. For the application of punishment, see Chapter 2, pages 120–26.

46. Rumiantsev, "Uchrezhdenie domovoe," 46 (quotation), 72; decree of pomeshchitsa P. M. Chenikova to steward Vas'ka Lintom of Kitaevo village, 1817, in *Russkaia starina*, 87 (1896), 82. See also Sheremeteva, "Instruktsiia 1727 goda Grigoriiu Voroblevskomu," 265–66; "Instruktsiia barona Nikolaia Grigor'evicha Stroganova," 170; Vol'f, "Nakaz upraviteliu ili prikashchiku," 29; "Instruktsiia Ober-kamergera Ivana Ivanovicha Shuvalova," 228.

47. "Ulozhenie dlia Porech'ia, grafa Vladimira Grigor'evicha Orlova,"

258–59, 264–65, 267 (quotation); "Instruktsiia barona Nikolaia Grigor'e-vicha Stroganova," 165–66; "Nakaz kn. A. M. Cherkasskogo prikazchiku sela Markova," 255; Bolotov, "Nakaz upraviteliu ili prikashchiku," 183 (quotation); Sheremetev, "Instruktsiia prikashchiku Muromskoi votchiny," 94; Rumiantsev, "Uchrezhdenie domovoe," 33–34, 73–74; "Instruktsiia Grigoriia Ivanovicha Shipova," 244.

48. For descriptions and evaluations of planter instructions, see Phillips, *American Negro Slavery*, 261–79; Scarborough, *The Overseer*, 68–74; and Fogel and Engerman, *Time on the Cross*, 110. Model instructions and descriptions of plantation management ran with great frequency in—among other journals—*DeBow's Review*, the most influential southern periodical of the 1840s and 1850s. For a collection of model instructions, see James O. Breeden, ed., *Advice among Masters: The Ideal in Slave Management in the Old South* (Westport, Conn.: Greenwood Press, 1980).

49. The quotation is from "Overseers at the South," *DeBow's Review*, 21 (Aug. 1856), 148. See also "Rules on the Rice Estate of P. C. Weston" (1856), in *Plantation and Frontier*, ed. Ulrich B. Phillips, vols. I and II of John R. Commons et al., eds., *A Documentary History of American Industrial Society* (Cleveland: Arthur H. Clark, 1910), I, 116; "Instructions by Alexander Telfair, of Savannah, Ga., to the Overseer of His Plantation Near Augusta" (1832), in Phillips, *Plantation and Frontier*, I, 126; "Governor Hammond's Instructions to His Overseer," 346–47; and Joseph A. S. Acklen, "Rules in the Management of a Southern Estate," *DeBow's Review*, 21 (Dec. 1856), 617–18.

50. For descriptions of the gang and task systems, see Phillips, *American Negro Slavery*, 247–49; Stampp, *The Peculiar Institution*, 54–56; Stone, "Black Leadership in the Old South," 17–38; Thomas F. Armstrong, "From Task Labor to Free Labor: The Transition along Georgia's Rice Coast," *Georgia Historical Quarterly*, 64 (Winter 1980), 432–37; Charles Joyner, *Down by the Riverside: A South Carolina Slave Community* (Urbana: University of Illinois Press, 1984), 43–59; Smith, *Slavery and Rice Culture in Low Country Georgia*, 45–63; and Philip D. Morgan, "Work and Culture: The Task System and the World of Lowcountry Blacks, 1700 to 1880," *William and Mary Quarterly*, 3rd ser., 39 (Oct. 1982), 563–99. For instructions concerning gang labor, see "Governor Hammond's Instructions to His Overseer," 351; A Small Farmer, "Management of Negroes," *DeBow's Review*, 11 (Oct. 1851), 370; St. George Cooke, "Management of Negroes," *DeBow's Review*, 14 (Feb. 1853), 177–78; "The Duties of an Overseer" (from *Affleck's Cotton Plantation Record and Account Book*), *DeBow's Review*, 18 (March 1855), 339 (quotation). For instructions concerning task labor, see "Rules on the Rice Estate of P. C. Weston," 117; and "Notes on the Management of a Southern Rice Estate," by the son of South Carolina Governor Allston, *DeBow's Review*, 24 (April 1858), 325 (quotation).

51. "Governor Hammond's Instructions to His Overseer," 352; Robert Collins, "Management of Slaves," *DeBow's Review*, 17 (Oct. 1854), 425; A

Mississippi Planter, "Management of Negroes upon Southern Estates," *DeBow's Review,* 10 (June 1851), 623 (quotation). For a similar declaration of the futility of teaching slaves morality, see A Small Farmer, "Management of Negroes," 372; for the argument that planters strongly promoted family formation among slaves, see Fogel and Engerman, *Time on the Cross,* 84–85.

52. Collins, "Management of Slaves," 425; "Governor Hammond's Instructions to His Overseer," 352; Bennet H. Barrow, "Rules of Highland Plantation" (1838), in *Plantation Life in the Florida Parishes of Louisiana, 1836–1846, as Reflected in the Diary of Bennet H. Barrow,* ed. Edwin Adams Davis (New York: Columbia University Press, 1943), 408–9; Agricola, "Management of Negroes," *DeBow's Review,* 19 (Sept. 1855), 362. On marriages off the plantation, see Genovese, *Roll, Jordan, Roll,* 472–75, and Herbert G. Gutman, *The Black Family in Slavery and Freedom, 1750–1925* (New York: Pantheon Books, 1976), 135–42.

53. "Governor Hammond's Instructions to His Overseer," 352; Collins, "Management of Slaves," 425; A Mississippi Planter, "Management of Negroes upon Southern Estates," 625; J. W. Fowler, "Rules for Plantation Management on a Cotton Estate in the Mississippi Bottoms" (1857), in Phillips, *Plantation and Frontier,* I, 114.

54. Barrow, "Rules of Highland Plantation," 406; "Instructions by Alexander Telfair," 126; Fowler, "Rules for Plantation Management," 114; "Governor Hammond's Instructions to His Overseer," 352–53.

55. "Governor Hammond's Instructions to His Overseer," 354; "Instructions by Alexander Telfair," 128 (quotation); "The Duties of an Overseer," 344; "Rules on the Rice Estate of P. C. Weston," 122.

56. "Governor Hammond's Instructions to His Overseer," 354 (quotation); "Rules on the Rice Estate of P. C. Weston," 117; "Instructions by Alexander Telfair," 126; "The Duties of an Overseer," 344 (quotation); "Overseers at the South," *DeBow's Review,* 21 (Sept. 1856), 279; Manigault letter, 1 March 1847, in Phillips, *Plantation and Frontier,* II, 32 (quotation); A Small Farmer, "Management of Negroes," 371 (quotation).

57. "Rules on the Rice Estate of P. C. Weston," 116.

58. On food, clothing, and housing, see "Rules on the Rice Estate of P. C. Weston," 116–17 (quotation); A Small Farmer, "Management of Negroes," 370; Fowler, "Rules for Plantation Management," 113–14; "Instructions by Alexander Telfair," 126, 129; "Governor Hammond's Instructions to His Overseer," 347–49, 353; "Management of Negroes," *DeBow's Review,* 10 (March 1851), 325–26; A Mississippi Planter, "Management of Negroes upon Southern Estates," 623–24; Cooke, "Management of Negroes," 177–78; Collins, "Management of Slaves," 422–24. On medical care, see "Governor Hammond's Instructions to His Overseer," 351 (quotations); "Contract between Charles Manigault and His Overseer, S. F. Clark" (1853), in Phillips, *Plantation and Frontier,* I, 124 (quotation); "Rules on the Rice Estate of P. C. Weston," 120; "Instructions by Alexander Telfair," 128; A Mis-

sissippi Planter, "Management of Negroes upon Southern Estates," 624. On actual material treatment of slaves, see Chapter 2, pages 134–38.

59. "Instructions Given by Richard Corbin, Esq." (1759), in Phillips, *Plantation and Frontier*, I, 109; "Contract between Charles Manigault and His Overseer," 123 (quotation); Fowler, "Rules for Plantation Management," 113 (quotation); "Governor Hammond's Instructions to His Overseer," 347; "Rules on the Rice Estate of P. C. Weston," 117; "Instructions by Alexander Telfair," 126; A Mississippi Planter, "Management of Negroes upon Southern Estates," 626; "The Duties of an Overseer," 344; "Overseers at the South," 279; John A. Calhoun, E. E. DuBose, and Virgil Bubo, "Management of Slaves" (1846), in *DeBow's Review*, 18 (June 1855), 714 (quotation); and Collins, "Management of Slaves," 116.

60. "Rules on the Rice Estate of P. C. Weston," 116; Michael L. Nicholls, "'In the Light of Human Beings': Richard Eppes and His Island Plantation Code of Laws," *Virginia Magazine of History and Biography*, 89 (Jan. 1981), 75.

61. Quotations are from "Governor Hammond's Instructions to His Overseer," 348; Agricola, "Management of Negroes," 359; and Ralph Butterfield, "The Health of Negroes," *DeBow's Review*, 25 (Nov. 1858), 571–72. On Hammond's only partially successful effort to create a dependent labor force on his South Carolina plantation, see Drew Gilpin Faust, *James Henry Hammond and the Old South: A Design for Mastery* (Baton Rouge: Louisiana State University Press, 1982), 72–104.

62. A Mississippi Planter, "Management of Negroes upon Southern Estates," 624; Barrow, "Rules of Highland Plantation," 409 (quotation); Collins, "Management of Slaves," 424.

63. Agricola, "Management of Negroes," 361 (quotation); "Rules on the Rice Estate of P. C. Weston," 116; Barrow, "Rules of Highland Plantation," 407.

64. Barrow, "Rules of Highland Plantation," 409–10.

65. Order of P. I. Panin to Egor Isakov, Ivan Solov'ev, and other peasants, 20 Jan. 1765, *Arkhiv kn. F. A. Kurakina*, V (Saratov, 1894), 255; I. Kuznetsov, ed., "Krepostnye krest'iane sela Barasheva-Usada v pervoi polovine XIX v.," *Krasnyi arkhiv*, 77 (1936), 132–33; "Perepiska Artemiia Volynskago s prikashchikami (1735 g.)," in Dovnar-Zapol'skii, *Materialy dlia istorii votchinnago upravleniia*, 217–20. See also Sivkov, *Ocherki po istorii krepostnogo khoziaistva*, 31–53.

66. Robert Lyall, *Travels in Russia, the Krimea the Caucasus and Georgia* (New York: Arno Press, 1970; orig. pub. London, 1825), I, 135; Petrikeev, *Krupnoe krepostnoe khoziaistvo XVII v.*, 55–56; Confino, *Domaines et seigneurs en Russie*, 74–80; Novosel'skii, *Votchinnik i ego khoziaistvo v XVII veke*, 85, 74, 61–65; *Akty khoziaistva boiarina B. I. Morozova*, I, 194, II, 151–52, 166, 172–74.

67. *Russkaia starina*, 25 (1879), 567–75 (quotation, 574–75); Turgenev, *A Sportsman's Notebook* (1852), trans. Charles and Natasha Hepburn (London: Cresset Press, 1950), 151, 159.

68. *The Diary of Colonel Landon Carter,* II, 628 (quotation), 682; "The Plantation Diary of Bennet H. Barrow," in Davis, *Plantation Life in the Florida Parishes of Louisiana,* 154. On relations between planters and overseers, see Scarborough, *The Overseer,* 102–37; and Genovese, *Roll, Jordan, Roll,* 13–25.

69. Moxley to Jones, 8 Oct. 1854, in Phillips and Glunt, *Florida Plantation Records,* 107 (quotation); Evans to Jones, 18 Oct. 1854, ibid., 111–12 (quotation); Moxley to Jones, 8 Nov. 1854, ibid., 116; Moxley to Jones, 8 Dec. 1854, ibid., 119–20; Jones to Moxley, 18 Dec. 1854, ibid., 120; Evans to Jones, 16 Nov. 1854, ibid., 117–18; Jones to W. G. M. Davis, 22 Jan. 1855, ibid., 123–24 (quotation).

70. Evans to Jones, 10 Jan. 1856, ibid., 150–51 (quotation); Moxley to Jones, 3 July 1856, ibid., 158–60; Evans to Jones, 2 Sept. 1856, ibid., 166–67; Jones to Evans, 2 Oct. 1856, ibid., 168 (quotation); Evans to Jones, 23 Oct. 1856, ibid., 169 (quotation); Evans to Jones, 3 May 1858, ibid., 173–74.

71. *The Secret Diary of William Byrd of Westover, 1709–1712,* ed. Louis B. Wright and Marion Tinling (Richmond, Va.: Dietz Press, 1941), 14, 89; John C. Burruss to his son John W. Burruss, 29 March 1850, John C. Burruss Family papers, microfilm of ms. at Louisiana State University Archives.

72. Quotations are from "Instruktsiia barona Nikolaia Grigor'evicha Stroganova," 165; Rumiantsev, "Uchrezhdenie domovoe," 48; Fowler, "Rules for Plantation Management," 113; and "Governor Hammond's Instructions to His Overseer," 352. See also "Ulozhenie dlia Porech'ia, grafa Vladimira Grigor'evicha Orlova," 256; Novosel'skii, *Votchinnik i ego khoziaistvo v XVII veke,* 50–52, 87–89; Confino, *Domaines et seigneurs en Russie,* 74–80; Thomas Fairfax to Bataile Muse, Dec. 1792, in *American Negro Slavery: A Documentary History,* ed. Michael Mullin (Columbia: University of South Carolina Press, 1976), 73; "Overseers at the South," 277; and Acklen, "Rules in the Management of a Southern Estate," 618.

73. Extracts from the Plantation Records of Louis Manigault, 20 Dec. 1858, 3 May 1859, in Phillips, *Plantation and Frontier,* I, 144–46. For another example of this pattern, see Bassett, *The Southern Plantation Overseer as Revealed in His Letters,* 54, 88–89.

74. Edwin Morris Betts, ed., *Thomas Jefferson's Farm Book with Commentary and Relevant Extracts from Other Writings* (Princeton: Princeton University Press, 1953), 148–50; Weymouth T. Jordan, *Hugh Davis and His Alabama Plantation* (University, Ala.: University of Alabama Press, 1948), 59–62, 65–73.

75. Von Klingshtet, "O neobkhodimoi nadobnosti," 60–69; K., "O luchshikh usloviiakh dlia naniatiia upravitelei," in *Zemledel'cheskaia gazeta,* 20 Aug. 1835, 530–35; Robert Sears, *An Illustrated Description of the Russian Empire* (New York, 1855), 515; *Zemledel'cheskaia gazeta,* 22 Jan. 1835, 56, and 1 Sept. 1836, 560. See also Sivkov, *Ocherki po istorii krepostnogo khoziaistva,* 31–37. For a few additional examples of numerous

advertisements placed by stewards, see *Zemledel'cheskaia gazeta,* 2 Feb. 1837, 80; 14 Jan. 1838, 32; 18 Feb. 1838, 112; 25 March 1838, 192; 2 Sept. 1838, 560; 11 Nov. 1838, 720; and 31 Jan. 1839, 72.

76. On the Society for the Improvement of Private Agriculture, see E. N. Kusheva, ed., "Proekt uchrezhdeniia aktsionernogo 'Obshchestva uluchsheniia chastnogo sel'skogo khoziaistva' 30-kh godov XIX v.," *Istoricheskii arkhiv,* 7 (1951), 46–95 (quotations, 60, 62). For a discussion of one manual, see Prince N. Volkonskii, "Usloviia pomeshchich'iago khoziaistva pri krepostnom prave," *Trudy Vysochaishe uchrezhdennoi Riazanskoi uchenoi arkhivnoi komissii,* 12 (1897), 125–47; for examples of reviews of others, see *Zemledel'cheskaia gazeta,* 22 Feb. 1838, 118, and 25 Feb. 1838, 125; for excerpts from one—appropriately translated from German—see ibid., 16 July 1837, 449–55. The quotations from articles on estate improvement are from Dikgof, "Vzgliad na khoziaistvennoe ustroistvo," 41–55 (quotation, 55), and Leopol'dov, "Ocherk khoziaistva Alekseia M. Sumarokova," 465–69 (quotation, 468–69).

77. Vorontsov, "O sposobakh k ispravleniiu sel'skago domostroistva," *Trudy Vol'nago ekonomicheskago obshchestva,* V (1767), 1–12; M., "Derevenskaia zhizn'," *Zemledel'cheskaia gazeta,* 16 May 1841, 307–8. For a semi-autobiographical treatment of a young nobleman who is stymied by the inertia of peasant ways when he returns from the university to his estate with grandiose ideas for improving conditions there, see Lyof N. Tolstoi, "A Russian Proprietor" (originally "Utro pomeshchika," 1852), in *A Russian Proprietor and Other Stories,* vol. XIII of *The Novels and Other Works of Lyof N. Tolstoi* (New York: Charles Scribner's Sons, 1911), 1–65.

78. For elaboration of this point, see Genovese, *Roll, Jordan, Roll.*

79. "The Plantation Diary of Bennet H. Barrow," 154; Fogel and Engerman, *Time on the Cross,* 200–1; Barrow, "Rules of Highland Plantation," 410.

80. Stone, "Black Leadership in the Old South," 9–55; Clifton, "The Rice Driver"; Frances Anne Kemble, *Journal of a Residence on a Georgian Plantation in 1838–1839* (Chicago: Afro-Am Press, 1969), 42–45; correspondence between William S. Pettigrew and his slaves Moses and Henry, 1856–58, in Robert S. Starobin, ed., *Blacks in Bondage: Letters of American Slaves* (New York: New Viewpoints, 1974), 12–35; George Skipworth to John H. Cocke, 8 July 1847, in *Slave Testimony: Two Centuries of Letters, Speeches, Interviews, and Autobiographies,* ed. John W. Blassingame (Baton Rouge: Louisiana State University Press, 1977), 66–67.

81. *State v. Elliott,* 2 Hill 617, May 1835, in Helen Tunnicliff Catterall, ed., *Judicial Cases concerning American Slavery and the Negro* (New York: Octagon Books, 1968; orig. pub. 1926–37), II, 359; *State v. Thompson,* 10 La. An. 122, February 1855, ibid., III, 634; *State v. Whetstone,* 13 La. An. 376, July 1858, ibid., III, 664; *Molett v. State,* 33 Ala. 408, Jan. 1858, ibid., III, 229–30. For the argument that slaves served as overseers on *most* plantations, see Fogel and Engerman, *Time on the Cross,* 210–12; for a more cautious evaluation, see Genovese, *Roll, Jordan, Roll,* 366.

82. Jordan, *Hugh Davis and His Alabama Plantation*, 62–65, 70–71; "The Plantation Diary of Bennet H. Barrow," 28 March 1843, 282 (quotation), 6 Aug. 1839, 156 (quotation); Barrow, "Rules of Highland Plantation," 409–10; *The Diary of Colonel Landon Carter*, 4 June 1766, I, 303, 25 June 1774, II, 834.

83. A Small Farmer, "Management of Negroes," 371.

84. On the development of self-government and attachment to local political institutions in the southern colonies, see Bernard Bailyn, "Politics and Social Structure in Virginia," in *Seventeenth-Century America*, ed. J. M. Smith (Chapel Hill: University of North Carolina Press, 1954), 90–115; Jack P. Greene, "Foundations of Political Power in the Virginia House of Burgesses, 1720–1776," *William and Mary Quarterly*, 3rd ser., 16 (1959), 485–506; Greene, *The Quest for Power: The Lower Houses of Assembly in the Southern Royal Colonies, 1689–1776* (Chapel Hill: University of North Carolina Press, 1964); Charles S. Sydnor, *Gentlemen Freeholders: Political Practices in Washington's Virginia* (Chapel Hill: University of North Carolina Press, 1952). The best treatment of the antebellum southern political system is William J. Cooper, Jr., *The South and the Politics of Slavery, 1828–1856* (Baton Rouge: Louisiana State University Press, 1978). On increasing southern antagonism to the federal government, see Jesse T. Carpenter, *The South as a Conscious Minority, 1789–1861* (New York: New York University Press, 1930).

85. Romanovich-Slavatinskii, *Dvorianstvo v Rossii*, passim, esp. 402–500; Korf, *Dvorianstvo i ego soslovnoe upravlenie*, passim, esp. 202–14, 287–363, 419–59, 635–51; Givens, "Servitors or Seigneurs"; P. A. Zaionchkovskii, "Gubernskaia administratsiia nakanune Krymskoi voiny," *Voprosy istorii*, 1975, no. 9, 33–51; Zaionchkovskii, *Pravitel'stvennyi apparat samoderzhavnoi Rossii v XIX v.* (Moscow: Izdatel'stvo "Mysl'," 1978), 142–78; and George L. Yaney, *The Systematization of Russian Government: Social Evolution in the Domestic Administration of Imperial Russia, 1711–1905* (Urbana: University of Illinois Press, 1973), 69–74, 193–227.

86. Charles C. Jones, *The Religious Instruction of the Negroes. In the United States* (New York: Negro Universities Press, 1969; orig. pub. Savannah, 1842), 145, 153, 165. For a thoughtful comparison of planter attitudes and behavior in the United States, Brazil, and the West Indies, see Genovese, *The World the Slaveholders Made*, 25–102.

2. Planters, Pomeshchiki, and Paternalism

1. For the view that United States slavery was uniquely oppressive, see Stanley M. Elkins, *Slavery: A Problem in American Institutional and Intellectual Life* (Chicago: University of Chicago Press, 1959), pts. 1, 2. A more balanced depiction of the harshness of antebellum slavery is Kenneth M. Stampp, *The Peculiar Institution: Slavery in the Ante-Bellum South* (New York: Vintage Books, 1956). For examples of numerous works questioning Elkins's conclusions from a comparative approach, see Eugene D. Genovese,

The World the Slaveholders Made: Two Essays in Interpretation (New York: Pantheon Books, 1969), ch. 2, and Carl N. Degler, *Neither Black nor White: Slavery and Race Relations in Brazil and the United States* (New York: Macmillan, 1971), ch. 2. Robert William Fogel and Stanley L. Engerman, *Time on the Cross: The Economics of American Negro Slavery* (Boston: Little, Brown, 1974), ch. 4, stress the relative material well-being of American slaves.

For diametrically opposite conclusions by British travelers concerning the treatment of late eighteenth-century Russian serfs, see William Richardson, *Anecdotes of the Russian Empire* (London: Frank Cass, 1968; orig. pub. 1787), 193–98; and William Tooke, *View of the Russian Empire* (New York: Arno Press, 1970; orig. pub. 1800), II, 144–45, 148. The prevailing Soviet view that serfs faced increasing exploitation and poverty is expressed by I. D. Koval'chenko and L. V. Milov, "Ob intensivnosti obrochnoi ekspluatatsii krest'ian tsentral'noi Rossii v kontse XVIII-pervoi polovine XIX v.," *Istoriia SSSR*, 1966, no. 4, 55–80; and challenged by P. G. Ryndziunskii, "Ob opredelenii intensivnosti obrochnoi ekspluatatsii krest'ian tsentral'noi Rossii v kontse XVIII-pervoi polovine XIX v. (o stat'e I. D. Koval'chenko i L. V. Milova)," *ibid.*, 1966, no. 6, 44–64.

2. Eugene D. Genovese, "The Treatment of Slaves in Different Countries: Problems in the Application of the Comparative Method," in *Slavery in the New World: A Reader in Comparative History,* ed. Laura Foner and Eugene D. Genovese (Englewood Cliffs, N.J.: Prentice-Hall, 1969), 202–18 (quotation, 203).

3. Stampp, *The Peculiar Institution,* 44–46, 75–85; Paul D. Escott, *Slavery Remembered: A Record of Twentieth-Century Slave Narratives* (Chapel Hill: University of North Carolina Press, 1979), 38; recollection of Walter Calloway (Alabama), in *The American Slave: A Composite Autobiography,* ed. George P. Rawick (Westport, Conn.: Greenwood Publishing Company, 1972), VI, 51 (quotation). For a good description of mistreatment at the hands of a hirer, see Frederick Douglass, *My Bondage and My Freedom* (New York: Dover Publications, 1969; orig. pub. 1855), 215–16.

4. Petr Rychkov, "Otvety na Ekonomicheskie voprosy . . . v razsuzhdenii Orenburgskoi gubernii," *Trudy Vol'nago ekonomicheskago obshchestva k pooshchreniiu v Rossii zemledeliia i domostroitel'stva,* VII (1767), 147; V. I. Krutikov and V. A. Fedorov, "Opisaniia pomeshchich'ikh imenii 1858–1859 gg. kak istochnik po istorii pomeshchich'ego khoziaistva i krest'ianstva nakanune reformy 1861 g. (po materialam Tul'skoi i Moskovskoi gubernii)," *Ezhegodnik po agrarnoi istorii Vostochnoi Evropy 1970 g.* (Riga, 1977), 144; *Krest'ianskoe dvizhenie v Rossii v 1796–1825 gg.: Sbornik dokumentov,* ed. S. N. Valk (Moscow: Izdatel'stvo sotsial'no-ekonomicheskoi literatury, 1961; hereafter cited as KD-1), 10 April 1797, 144–46. See also Jerome Blum, *Lord and Peasant in Russia from the Ninth to the Nineteenth Century* (Princeton: Princeton University Press, 1961), 444–48; N. L. Rubinshtein, *Sel'skoe khoziaistvo Rossii vo vtoroi polovine XVIII v.* (Moscow: Gosudar-

stvennoe izdatel'stvo, 1957), 160–63; I. I. Ignatovich, *Pomeshchich'i krest'iane nakanune osvobozheniia*, 2nd ed. (Moscow: I. D. Sytin, 1910), 123–25; and V. A. Fedorov, "Barshchina i obrok v tsentral'no-promyshlennykh guberniiakh Rossii v pervoi polovine XIX v.," *Ezhegodnik po agrarnoi istorii Vostochnoi Evropy 1966 g.* (Tallin, 1971), 325–27.

5. Prince N. Volkonskii, "Usloviia pomeshchich'iago khoziaistva pri krepostnom prave," in *Trudy Vysochaishe uchrezhdennoi Riazanskoi uchenoi arkhivnoi komissii*, 12 (1897), insert after 160; Vasilii Preobrazhenskii, *Opisanie Tverskoi gubernii v sel'sko-khoziaistvenom otnoshenii* (St. Petersburg, 1854), 99–101; Ulrich B. Phillips and James David Glunt, eds., *Florida Plantation Records from the Papers of George Noble Jones* (St. Louis: Missouri Historical Society, 1927), 539.

6. *Narrative of the Life of Frederick Douglass, an American Slave, Written by Himself* (New York: New American Library, 1968; orig. pub. 1845), 84; *The Diary of Colonel Landon Carter of Sabine Hall, 1752–1778*, ed. Jack P. Greene (Charlottesville: University Press of Virginia, 1965), 23 May 1772, II, 691; Count P. A. Rumiantsev, "Uchrezhdenie domovoe," in *Materialy dlia istorii votchinnago upravleniia v Rossii*, ed. M. V. Dovnar-Zapol'skii (published in *Universitetskaia izvestiia*, 43–50, 1903–10), 73–74; Preobrazhenskii, *Opisanie Tverskoi gubernii*, 99–101. Historian William K. Scarborough has suggested that "most slaves received annual holidays, amounting in the aggregate to from ten to fourteen days, exclusive of Sundays and partial holidays"; see his "Slavery—the White Man's Burden," in *Perspectives and Irony in American Slavery*, ed. Harry P. Owens (Jackson: University Press of Mississippi, 1976), 113. See also Eugene D. Genovese, *Roll, Jordan, Roll: The World the Slaves Made* (New York: Pantheon Books, 1974), 566–99.

7. *The Diary of Colonel Landon Carter*, 5 June 1773, II, 755. For two examples of contemporary analyses blaming bondage for killing the laborers' initiative, see A. P. Zablotskii-Desiatovskii, "O krepostnom sostoianii v Rossii. Zapiska A. Z-go D-go 1841 goda," in *Graf P. D. Kiselev i ego vremia. Materialy dlia istorii Imperatorov Aleksandra I, Nikolaia I i Aleksandra II*, ed. Zablotskii-Desiatovskii, IV (St. Petersburg, 1882), 271–344; and Frederick Law Olmsted, *The Cotton Kingdom: A Traveller's Observations on Cotton and Slavery in the American Slave States* (New York, 1861). On shoddy work as a form of resistance, see Chapter 5, pages 241–44. On the contrast between the slaves' concept of work and that of their masters, see Genovese, *Roll, Jordan, Roll*, 285–325.

8. For an example of a landowner objecting to his serfs' working their plots on Sundays—instead of resting and attending church—see *Akty khoziaistva boiarina B. I. Morozova*, ed. A. I. Iakovlev (Moscow: Izdatel'stvo Akademii nauk SSSR, 1940, 1945), II, 34. On reduced hours of black labor after emancipation, see Roger L. Ransom and Richard Sutch, *One Kind of Freedom: The Economic Consequences of Emancipation* (Cambridge: Cambridge University Press, 1977), 6–7, 232–36.

9. Douglass, *My Bondage and My Freedom*, 252–53; *Krest'ianskoe dvizhenie v Rossii v 1826–1849 gg.: Sbornik dokumentov*, ed. A. V. Predtechenskii (Moscow: Izdatel'stvo sotsial'no-ekonomicheskoi literatury, 1961; hereafter cited as KD-2), Aug. 1841, 638.

10. Generalizations in this and the next two paragraphs are based on analysis of numerous documents expressing the attitudes of slaves and serfs toward their work. For the United States these include slave autobiographies and interviews contained in Rawick, *The American Slave*, and Rawick, *The American Slave . . . Supplement, Series 1* (Westport, Conn.: Greenwood Publishing Company, 1977). For Russia they include peasant petitions contained in KD-1, KD-2, and *Krest'ianskoe dvizhenie v Rossii v 1850–1856 gg.: Sbornik dokumentov*, ed. S. B. Okun' (Moscow: Izdatel'stvo sotsial'no-ekonomicheskoi literatury, 1963; hereafter cited as KD-3).

11. Recollection of Levi Pollard, in *Weevils in the Wheat: Interviews with Virginia Ex-Slaves*, ed. Charles L. Perdue et al. (Charlottesville: University Press of Virginia, 1976), 228.

12. On marriage rules and off-estate marriages, see Chapter 1, pages 73–74, 79–80. For an example of a pomeshchik denying servants permission to marry, see S. T. Slovutinskii, *General Izmailov i ego dvornia; otryvki iz vospominanii* (Moscow: Academia, 1937), 137–41.

13. I. V. Chernyshev, *Agrarno-krest'ianskaia politika Rossii za 150 let* (Petrograd: Tipografiia Ministerstva putei soobshcheniia, 1918), 13–14; S. T. Aksakov, *The Family Chronicle*, trans. M. C. Beverley (New York: E. P. Dutton, 1961; orig. pub. 1856), 189; testimony of Silvia King, Jacob Branch, and Katie Darling, in *Life under the "Peculiar Institution": Selections from the Slave Narrative Collection*, ed. Norman R. Yetman (New York: Holt, Rinehart and Winston, 1970), 199, 39, 70 (quotation).

14. Aleksandr Nikolaevich Radishchev, *A Journey from St. Petersburg to Moscow*, ed. Roderick Page Thaler and trans. Leo Wiener (Cambridge, Mass.: Harvard University Press, 1958; orig. pub. 1790), 134; C. Vann Woodward, ed., *Mary Chesnut's Civil War* (New Haven: Yale University Press, 1981), 18 March 1861, 29. For the emphasis of sexual abuse by anti-bondage writers, see Hannah Stern Goldman, "American Slavery and Russian Serfdom: A Study in Fictional Parallels" (Ph.D. diss., Columbia University, 1955), 163–71; and Ronald G. Walters, "The Erotic South: Civilization and Sexuality in American Abolitionism," *American Quarterly*, 25 (1973), 177–201.

15. Petition of Denis Il'in to P. D. Kiselev, Penza province, 7 Dec. 1852, KD-3, 142; Elizabeth Keckley, *Behind the Scenes. Or, Thirty Years a Slave, and Four Years in the White House* (New York, 1868), 39; Douglass, *My Bondage and My Freedom*, 52.

16. "Stranitsa iz istorii krepostnago prava. Zapiski Ianuariia Mikhailovicha Neverova. 1810–1826," *Russkaia starina*, 40 (1883), 430–41 (quotation 433); Slovutinskii, *General Izmailov i ego dvornia*, 144–55. For examples of descriptions by ex-slaves of long-term affairs between slaveowners

and slave women, see Yetman, *Life under the "Peculiar Institution,"* 232; and John W. Blassingame, ed., *Slave Testimony: Two Centuries of Letters, Speeches, Interviews, and Autobiographies* (Baton Rouge: Louisiana State University Press, 1977), 360. See also Genovese, *Roll, Jordan, Roll,* 415–23. Relations between black men and white women, although far less common, also occurred; for an interesting case of a North Carolina man who unsuccessfully sued his wife for divorce when he found she was pregnant by a black, see *Walters v. Jordan,* 13 Iredell 361, 1852, in *Judicial Cases concerning American Slavery and the Negro,* ed. Helen Tunnicliff Catterall (New York: Octagon Books, 1968; orig. pub. 1926–37), II, 167–68. For a discussion of such cases, see Guion Griffis Johnson, *Ante-Bellum North Carolina: A Social History* (Chapel Hill: University of North Carolina Press, 1937), 588–89. On the widespread use of female slaves as concubines and wives in Africa, see Paul E. Lovejoy, *Transformations in Slavery: A History of Slavery in Africa* (Cambridge: Cambridge University Press, 1983), esp. 6–8, 17, 174–75, 214–16.

17. *Another Secret Diary of William Byrd of Westover, 1739–1741, with Letters & Literary Exercises, 1696–1726,* ed. Maude H. Woodfin (Richmond, Va.: Dietz Press, 1942), 18 Aug. 1740, 31; Harper, "Slavery in the Light of Social Ethics," in *Cotton Is King, and Pro-Slavery Arguments,* ed. E. N. Elliott (New York: Johnson Reprint Company, 1968; orig. pub. 1860), 580–85; Smolensk Governor Z. S. Kherkhenlidzev to Minister of Internal Affairs S. S. Lanskoi, 1851, KD-3, 205; testimony of W. L. Bost, in Yetman, *Life under the "Peculiar Institution,"* 37. On abuse of serf women, see V. I. Semevskii, *Krest'iane v tsarstvovanie Imperatritsy Ekateriny II,* 2nd ed. (St. Petersburg: Tipografiia M. M. Stasiulevicha, 1901–3), I, 318–19; A. Romanovich-Slavatinskii, *Dvorianstvo v Rossii ot nachala XVIII veka do otmeny krepostnago prava* (St. Petersburg, 1870), 314; and Blum, *Lord and Peasant in Russia,* 437. On abuse of slave women, see Stampp, *The Peculiar Institution,* 150–61; John W. Blassingame, *The Slave Community: Plantation Life in the Antebellum South* (New York: Oxford University Press, 1972), 82–83; and Genovese, *Roll, Jordan, Roll,* 413–27.

18. Robert William Fogel and Stanley L. Engerman have claimed, on the basis of the relatively slight increase in the number of mulattoes recorded in the federal censuses of 1850 and 1860—from 7.7 percent to 10.4 percent of the slave population—that interracial unions were rare and that only 1–2 percent of slave children were fathered by whites; see Fogel and Engerman, *Time on the Cross,* 130–33. Statistics on color, however, are highly inaccurate, and even if only 2 percent of slave children had white fathers, a much higher proportion of slave women would have had sexual relations with white men. In a harsh critique of Fogel and Engerman's argument, Richard Sutch has calculated that if "white men's sexual attentions were directed randomly at women between 15 and 30, each such slave woman had a 5.6% chance of being sexually approached by a white man each year, and a 58% chance of being approached at least once during the 15-year period of her

youth;"; Sutch, "The Treatment Received by American Slaves: A Critical Review of the Evidence Presented in *Time on the Cross*," *Explorations in Economic History*, 12 (Oct. 1975), 421–24 (quotation, 424).

19. For examples of proposals by probondage authors to prohibit the sale of serfs and slaves apart from land, see "Inalienability of Slaves," *DeBow's Review*, 23 (Aug. 1857), 211–13; and M. M. Shcherbatov, "Na chitannyi oktiabria 11 dnia golos Eletskoi provintsii gospodina deputata Mikhaila Davydova," in *Sochineniia kniazia M. M. Shcherbatova*, ed. I. P. Khrushchov (St. Petersburg, 1896–8), I, 115–16. From the last third of the eighteenth century proposals for ameliorating serfdom routinely included provisions barring peasant sales; see V. I. Semevskii, *Krest'ianskii vopros v Rossii v XVIII i pervoi polovine XIX veka* (St. Petersburg, 1888), passim. On proposals to protect slave families, see Genovese, *Roll, Jordan, Roll*, 52–53, 69.

20. Thomas Jefferson to Randolph Lewis, 23 April 1807, in *Thomas Jefferson's Farm Book with Commentary and Relevant Extracts from Other Writings*, ed. Edwin Morris Betts (Princeton: Princeton University Press, 1953), 26; Polk to his wife, 26 Sept. 1834, in *The Southern Plantation Overseer as Revealed in His Letters*, ed. John Spencer Bassett (Northampton, Mass.: Printed for Smith College, 1925), 77; H. C. Bruce, *The New Man. Twenty-Nine Years a Slave. Twenty-Nine Years a Free Man* (York, Pa., 1895), 16, 74; Fogel and Engerman, *Time on the Cross*, 44–52 (quotation, 52). Fogel and Engerman estimated that only "about 2 percent of the marriages of slaves involved in the westward trek were destroyed by the process of migration" (49).

21. "Governor Hammond's Letters on Slavery, 3," in *DeBow's Review*, 8 (Feb. 1850), 122. Hammond was, however, especially solicitous of two slave women with whom he had sexual liaisons and of their (and his) children. "Do not let Louisa or any of my children or possible children be the Slaves of Strangers," he wrote his son Harry in 1856. "Slavery *in the family* will be their happiest earthly condition." Drew Gilpin Faust, *James Henry Hammond and the Old South: A Design for Mastery* (Baton Rouge: Louisiana State University Press, 1982), 87.

22. Correspondence in *The Children of Pride: A True Story of Georgia and the Civil War*, ed. Robert Manson Myers (New Haven: Yale University Press, 1972), 183–84, 185 (quotation), 240–42, 243–44, 245–46, 255–56, 257–58 (quotation), 267 (quotation), 269, 270–71 (quotations), 309–10, 310 (quotation).

23. Jane Turner Censer, *North Carolina Planters and Their Children, 1800–1860* (Baton Rouge: Louisiana State University Press, 1984), 137–41 (quotation, 140); recollection of Anna Harris, in Perdue et al., *Weevils in the Wheat*, 128. Similar accounts abound in autobiographies and narratives; see, e.g., *An Autobiography of the Reverend Josiah Henson*, introd. Robin W. Winks (Reading, Mass.: Addison-Wesley, 1969; orig. pub. 1849), 14–18; *The Narrative of William W. Brown, a Fugitive Slave*, introd. Larry Gara (Reading, Mass.: Addison-Wesley, 1969; orig. pub. 1847), 7; *Narrative of*

the Life of Frederick Douglass, 22; Narrative of the Life and Activities of Henry Bibb, an American Slave (New York, 1849), 13–14; Austin Steward, Twenty-Two Years a Slave, and Forty a Freeman (Rochester, N.Y., 1859), 47–55; Narrative of the Life of Moses Grandy, Late a Slave in the United States of America (Boston, 1844), 5–6, 10–11; and hundreds of interviews in Rawick, The American Slave, and in Rawick, The American Slave . . . Supplement, Series 1. The estimate on interregional migration is from Fogel and Engerman, Time on the Cross, 44–47. For a recent study that stresses the frequency with which the interstate trade broke up slave families, see Donald M. Sweig, "Reassessing the Human Dimension of the Interstate Slave Trade," Prologue, 12 (Spring 1980), 5–19. See also Michael Tadman, "Slave Trading in the Ante-Bellum South: An Estimate of the Extent of the Inter-Regional Slave Trade," Journal of American Studies, 13 (Aug. 1979), 195–220.

24. The three samples are in Herbert G. Gutman, The Black Family in Slavery and Freedom, 1750–1925 (New York: Pantheon Books, 1976), 147; Blassingame, The Slave Community, 90; and Escott, Slavery Remembered, 48. These statistics differ sharply from those of Fogel and Engerman, Time on the Cross, 44–52, who deal only with separations resulting from the interregional slave trade and who base most of their conclusions on a faulty analysis of New Orleans slave sale invoices; see Sutch, "The Treatment Received by American Slaves," 396–411; and Herbert G. Gutman, Slavery and the Numbers Game: A Critique of Time on the Cross (Urbana: University of Illinois Press, 1975), 102–40. Bibb's statement is from Narrative of the Life and Activities of Henry Bibb, 14.

25. For a British traveler's observation on the contrast between the legal status of marriages of Russian serfs and that of American slaves, see Charles Henry Pearson, Russia, by a Recent Traveller: A Series of Letters (London: Frank Cass, 1970; orig. pub. 1859), 36. Historians of Latin America have noted a wide gap between law and reality with respect to slave families; see, e.g., David Brion Davis, The Problem of Slavery in Western Culture (Ithaca, N.Y.: Cornell University Press, 1966), 233–37; and Carl N. Degler, Neither Black nor White: Slavery and Race Relations in Brazil and the United States (New York: Macmillan, 1971), 36–37.

26. On exile, see Romanovich-Slavatinskii, Dvorianstvo v Rossii, 285–92; and Semevskii, Krest'iane v tsarstvovanie Imperatritsy Ekateriny II, I, 178–90. On government promulgations against family separations, see Blum, Lord and Peasant in Russia, 424, 428; Romanovich-Slavatinskii, Dvorianstvo v Rossii, 299–306; and Semevskii, Krest'iane v tsarstvovanie Ekateriny II, I, 170–71.

27. Petition of Ekaterina Petrova, 8 March 1660, in Akty khoziaistva boiarina B. I. Morozova, II, 122; petition to Alexander I from serf representatives of villages of Martinova, Gorodishchenskaia, and Orlova, Don region, 27 Aug. 1819, KD-1, 582; Semevskii, Krest'iane v tsarstvovanie Imperatritsy Ekateriny II, I, 162–69; Chappé d'Auteroche, A Journey into Si-

beria (New York: Arno Press, 1970; orig. pub. 1770), 316; Zablotskii-Desiatovskii, "O krepostnom sostoianii v Rossii," 292–93.

28. John S. Curtiss, *The Russian Army under Nicholas I, 1825–1855* (Durham, N.C.: Duke University Press, 1965), 232–37; Y. M. Sokolov, *Russian Folklore,* trans. Catherine Ruth Smith (New York: Macmillan, 1950), 235–40; Robert Lyall, *Travels in Russia, the Krimea, the Caucasus and Georgia* (New York: Arno Press, 1970; orig. pub. 1825), I, 139–42 (quotations 140, 142); Germain de Lagny, *The Knout and the Russians; or the Muscovite Empire, the Czar, and His People,* trans. John Bridgeman (London, 1854), 33; and V. Snezhnevskii, "Bykovskaia votchina Demidovykh (Materialy dlia istorii krepostnogo khoziaistva)," in *Deistviia Nizhegorodskoi gubernskoi uchenoi arkhivnoi komissii: Sbornik statei, soobshchenii, opisei, i dokumentov,* 7 (1906 or 1907), 123.

29. Petition of Ignatii Ivanov, 24 Sept. 1858, in "Dokumenty pomeshchich'ego proisvola," ed. K. V. Fedotov, *Vologodskii arkhiv: sbornik dokumentov i materialov* (Vologda: Vologodskoe knishskoe izdatel'stvo, 1961), 166–67; and E. I. Indova, *Krepostnoe khoziaistvo v nachale XIX veka po materialam votchinnogo arkhiva Vorontsovykh* (Moscow: Izdatel'stvo Akademii nauk SSSR, 1955), 42. See also L. N. Iurovskii, *Saratovskie votchiny: Statistiko-ekonomicheskie ocherki i materialy iz istorii krupnogo zemlevladeniia i krepostnogo khoziaistva v kontse XVIII i v nachale XIX stoletiia* (Saratov: Izdanie Saratovskogo instituta narodnogo khoziaistva, 1923), 86–94; and Aksakov, *The Family Chronicle,* 11.

30. For further treatment of this subject, see Chapter 4, pages 207–18.

31. Petition of M. Larionov and B. Sidorov, representatives of Chulkov's peasants, to A. Kh. Benkendorf, chief of the Corps of Gendarmes, 17 Sept. 1841, KD-2, 407; Iurovskii, *Saratovskie votchiny,* 155–59; recollection of Marinda Jane Singleton in Perdue et al., *Weevils in the Wheat,* 266–67.

32. A. A. Novosel'skii, *Votchinnik i ego khoziaistvo v XVII veke* (Moscow: Gosudarstvennoe izdatel'stvo, 1929), 163–66 (quotation, 163); and *Akty khoziaistva boiarina B. I. Morozova,* I, 128–29, 144–45.

33. Snezhnevskii, "Bykovskaia votchina Demydovykh," 123, 121; Slovutinskii, *General Izmailov i ego dvornia,* 135–36. For other accounts of punishment and brutality, see KD-1, KD-2, and KD-3, passim.

34. Quotations are from *Another Secret Diary of William Byrd,* 10; *The Diary of Colonel Landon Carter,* I, 495; John Blackford, *Ferry Hill Plantation Journal, January 4, 1838–January 15, 1839,* ed. and introd. Fletcher M. Green (Chapel Hill: University of North Carolina Press, 1961), 4; and Eliza M. Magruder Diary, 10 Feb. 1846, microfiche copy, original in Louisiana State University Archives. Statistics on slave narratives are from Escott, *Slavery Remembered,* 42–44. For accounts of punishment by ex-slaves, see Rawick, *The American Slave,* passim, and *The American Slave . . . Supplement, Series 1,* passim.

35. Recollection of Mrs. Candis Goodwin in Perdue et al., *Weevils in the Wheat,* 107. For the dominant historical assertion of the ubiquity of punish-

ment, see Stampp, *The Peculiar Institution,* 171–91; Blassingame, *The Slave Community,* 162–66; and George P. Rawick, *From Sundown to Sunup: The Making of the Black Community* (Westport, Conn.: Greenwood Publishing Company, 1972), 55–65.

36. See "The Plantation Diary of Bennet H. Barrow," in *Plantation Life in the Florida Parishes of Louisiana, 1836–1846, as Reflected in the Diary of Bennet H. Barrow,* ed. Edwin Adams Davis (New York: Columbia University Press, 1943), 69–285 (quotations, 85, 109, 140). For the editor's tabulation of whippings, see 431–40.

37. Fogel and Engerman, *Time on the Cross,* 145; Gutman, *Slavery and the Numbers Game,* 17–34; Sutch, "The Treatment Received by American Slaves," 339–42; Scarborough, "Slavery—The White Man's Burden," 123.

38. Recollection of Mandy McCullough Cosby in Rawick, *The American Slave,* VI (Alabama), 90. For further discussion of owner cruelty in the United States and changing attitudes toward it, see the following section.

39. Report of A. D. Stog to Minister of Internal Affairs A. B. Kurakin, 12 May 1808, KD-1, 237–42 (quotations, 239, 241); Slovutinskii, *General Izmailov i ego dvornia,* 117–35; Neverov, "Stranitsa iz istorii krepostnago prava," 438–41 (quotation, 439).

40. For traditional emphases on pomeshchik brutality, see Semevskii, *Krest'iane v tsarstvovanie Imperatritsy Ekateriny II,* I, 199–212; and Romanovich-Slavatinskii, *Dvorianstvo v Rossii,* 117–35. For more balanced judgments, see Blum, *Lord and Peasant in Russia,* 438–40; and V. A. Aleksandrov, *Sel'skaia obshchina v Rossii (XVII-nachalo XIX v.)* (Moscow: Izdatel'stvo "Nauka," 1976), 55–111. The assertion of relatively little brutality comes from Richard Pipes, *Russia under the Old Regime* (New York: Charles Scribner's Sons, 1974), 152.

41. The above analysis is based on information contained in K. N. Shchepetov, *Krepostnoe pravo v votchinakh Sheremetevykh (1708–1885)* (Moscow: Izdanie dvortsa-muzeia, 1947), 118–24.

42. Realization that abuse of power was an ever-present *possibility* under bondage proved more troubling to thoughtful slaveowners and serfowners than any other antibondage argument; for a good discussion of the problem this potential abuse of power posed for slaveowners—themselves acutely conscious of the corrupting nature of absolute power—and how some South Carolinians resolved it in their own minds, see Kenneth S. Greenberg, "Revolutionary Ideology and the Proslavery Argument: The Abolition of Slavery in Antebellum South Carolina," *Journal of Southern History,* 42 (Aug. 1976), 365–84. For Russian efforts to reduce the arbitrary power of pomeshchiki, see below, pages 140–44.

43. *The Secret Diary of William Byrd of Westover, 1709–1712,* ed. Louis B. Wright and Marion Tinling (Richmond, Va.: Dietz Press, 1941), 15 July 1710, 205; *Another Secret Diary of William Byrd,* 20 Dec. 1740, 123. On harsh punishment of slaves, see Winthrop D. Jordan, *White over Black: American Attitudes toward the Negro, 1550–1812* (Baltimore: Penguin

Books, 1969), 154–59; and Peter H. Wood, *Black Majority: Negroes in Colonial South Carolina from 1670 through the Stono Rebellion* (New York: Alfred A. Knopf, 1974), 277–84.

44. *The Diary of Colonel Landon Carter*, 27 June 1766, I, 310. On the prevalence of physical punishment among seventeenth-century and early-eighteenth-century Englishmen and Americans, see Lawrence Stone, *The Crisis of the Aristocracy, 1558–1641,* abridged ed. (London: Oxford University Press, 1967), 18–21, 108–9; Christopher Hill, *Society and Puritanism in Pre-Revolutionary England* (London: Secker and Warburg, 1964), 285–88; Richard Hofstadter, *America at 1750: A Social Portrait* (New York: Alfred A. Knopf, 1971), 46–47; Raphael Semmes, *Crime and Punishment in Early Maryland* (Baltimore: Johns Hopkins Press, 1938); and Richard B. Morris, *Government and Labor in Early America* (New York: Columbia University Press, 1946), 461–500.

45. *The Journal of the Rev. Charles Wesley, M. A.,* ed. Thomas Jackson (London, 1849), 2 Aug. 1736, I, 36; *Journal & Letters of Philip Vickers Fithian, 1773–1774: A Plantation Tutor of the Old Dominion,* ed. and introd. Hunter Dickinson Farish (Williamsburg, Va.: Colonial Williamsburg, 1943), 23 Dec. 1773, 51; *State v. Doctor James,* 2 Bay 215, 1799, in Catterall, *Judicial Cases concerning American Slavery,* II, 280. On the law and slaves in the colonial period, see A. Leon Higginbotham, *In the Matter of Color: Race and the American Legal Process, the Colonial Period* (New York: Oxford University Press, 1978).

46. Jefferson to Edward Coles, 25 Aug. 1814, in Betts, *Thomas Jefferson's Farm Book,* 39; Timothy Flint, *Recollections of the Last Ten Years,* ed. C. Hartley Grattan (New York: Alfred A. Knopf, 1923; orig. pub. 1826), 333. The best general treatments of the amelioration of slave handling in the antebellum United States are Genovese, *Roll, Jordan, Roll,* 49–70, and Willie Lee Rose, "The Domestication of Domestic Slavery," in Rose, *Slavery and Freedom,* ed. William W. Freehling (New York: Oxford University Press, 1982), 18–36.

47. On positive incentives held out to slaves, see Fogel and Engerman, *Time on the Cross,* 148–52, 239–43. For suggestions based on comparative evidence concerning the effect of ending slave imports on treatment of slaves, see Davis, *The Problem of Slavery in Western Culture,* 233; Genovese, *The World the Slaveholders Made,* 97–99; and Degler, *Neither Black nor White,* 74.

48. On the growth of humanitarianism in the eighteenth century and its effect on the treatment of slaves, see Jordan, *White over Black,* 365–68. On humane treatment of slaves as a partial response to abolitionism, see Genovese, *Roll, Jordan, Roll,* 56, and Rose, "The Domestication of Domestic Slavery."

49. The quotation is from Charles C. Jones, *The Religious Instruction of the Negroes. In the United States* (New York: Negro Universities Press, 1969; orig. pub. 1842), 165. On the antebellum mission movement, see Donald G. Mathews, "Charles Colcock Jones and the Southern Evangelical Cru-

sade to Form a Biracial Society," *Journal of Southern History*, 41 (Aug. 1975), 299–320; Erskine Clarke, *Wrestlin' Jacob: A Portrait of Religion in the Old South* (Atlanta: John Knox Press, 1979), 20–81; Albert J. Raboteau, *Slave Religion: The "Invisible Institution" in the Antebellum South* (New York: Oxford University Press, 1978), 152–75; Milton C. Sernett, *Black Religion and American Evangelicalism: White Protestants, Plantation Missions, and the Flowering of Negro Christianity, 1787–1865* (Metuchen, N.J.: Scarecrow Press, 1975), 41–81; and the revised edition of John W. Blassingame, *The Slave Community: Plantation Life in the Antebellum South* (New York: Oxford University Press, 1979), 70–104. On the lack of slaveowner interest in conversion in earlier times, see Raboteau, *Slave Religion*, 97–128, and Lester B. Scherer, *Slavery and the Churches in Early America, 1619–1819* (Grand Rapids, Mich.: William B. Eerdmans, 1975), 82–103.

50. "The Plantation Diary of Bennet H. Barrow," passim (quotations, 175, 174); Boynton Merrill, Jr., *Jefferson's Nephews: A Frontier Tragedy* (Princeton: Princeton University Press, 1976), esp. 257. On the decline of extreme forms of physical abuse and on community pressure to avoid them, see Jordan, *White over Black*, 265–68; Wood, *Black Majority*, 278; Genovese, *Roll, Jordan, Roll*, 49–70; and Scarborough, "Slavery—the White Man's Burden," 108–10.

51. Genovese, *Roll, Jordan, Roll*, 31–49; Stampp, *The Peculiar Institution*, 192–93, 218–19; Daniel J. Flanigan, "Criminal Procedure in Slave Trials in the Antebellum South," *Journal of Southern History*, 40 (Nov. 1974), 537–64; A. E. Keir Nash, "Fairness and Formalism in the Trials of Blacks in the State Supreme Courts of the Old South," *Virginia Law Review*, 56 (Feb. 1970), 64–100; Michael Stephen Hindus, *Prison and Plantation: Crime, Justice, and Authority in Massachusetts and South Carolina, 1767–1878* (Chapel Hill: University of North Carolina Press, 1980), passim; Mark V. Tushnet, *The American Law of Slavery: Considerations of Humanity and Interest* (Princeton: Princeton University Press, 1981); Edward L. Ayers, *Vengeance and Justice: Crime and Punishment in the Nineteenth-Century American South* (New York: Oxford University Press, 1984), 134–36. For the two cases discussed in this paragraph, see *State v. Hale*, 2 Hawks 582, Dec. 1823, in Catterall, *Judicial Cases concerning Slavery*, II, 45; and *George (a slave) v. State*, 37 Miss. 316, Oct. 1859, ibid., III, 363.

52. The concept of paternalism is developed most forcefully by Eugene D. Genovese, in *The World the Slaveholders Made*, and *Roll, Jordan, Roll*, 3–158. See also Rose, "The Domestication of Domestic Slavery." For two works that come close to arguing that slaveowner paternalism created a benign system of slavery, see Phillips, *American Negro Slavery*, esp. 306–8, 501–3, and Scarborough, "Slavery—The White Man's Burden," esp. 108–10. For sharp critiques of Genovese's argument, see Gutman, *The Black Family in Slavery and Freedom*, 309–18; James Oakes, *The Ruling Race: A History of American Slaveholders* (New York: Alfred A. Knopf, 1982), passim; and Censer, *North Carolina Planters and Their Children*, 135–49.

53. Richard Beale Davis, ed., *William Fitzhugh and His Chesapeake World*,

1676–1701: The Fitzhugh Letters and Other Documents (Chapel Hill: University of North Carolina Press, 1963), passim, and Davis's introduction, 43; *The Secret Diary of William Byrd,* 23 Nov. 1709, 109, 22 Feb. 1709, 7, 17 June 1710, 192; *Another Secret Diary of William Byrd,* 9 Aug. 1740, 110; *The Diary of Colonel Landon Carter,* passim; *The Diaries of George Washington, 1748–1799,* ed. John C. Fitzpatrick (Boston: Houghton Mifflin, 1925), I, passim, e.g., 4 Feb. 1760, 121, 8 Feb. 1760, 124, and 7 May 1760, 155–60; *The Letterbook of Eliza Lucas Pinckney, 1739–1762,* ed. Elise Pinckney (Chapel Hill: University of North Carolina Press, 1972), 6 Feb. 1741, 12.

54. Magruder diary, 31 Jan. 1846, 16 Feb. 1846; J. H. Easterby, ed., *The South Carolina Rice Plantation as Revealed in the Papers of Robert F. W. Allston* (Chicago: University of Chicago Press, 1945), 342–44. See Genovese, *Roll, Jordan, Roll,* 3–158 passim. For the argument that planters' wives were especially solicitous of slaves' welfare, see Catherine Clinton, *The Plantation Mistress: Woman's World in the Old South* (New York: Pantheon Books, 1982), 187–98.

55. For a fine account of a paternalistic planter's efforts to create slave docility, see Faust, *James Henry Hammond and the Old South,* 72–104.

56. Alexander Hewatt, *An Historical Account of the Rise and Progress of the Colonies of South Carolina and Georgia* (London, 1779), II, 93–95. For a strong but controversial assertion that antebellum slaves enjoyed a high level of material comfort, see Fogel and Engerman, *Time on the Cross,* 109–26. For evidence that many ex-slaves concurred in this judgment, see Escott, *Slavery Remembered,* 38–40.

57. Quotations are from Frances Anne Kemble, *Journal of a Residence on a Georgian Plantation in 1838–1839* (Chicago: Afro-Am Press, 1969), 30; Olmsted, *The Cotton Kingdom,* I, 152; and Charles Ball, *Slavery in the United States: A Narrative of the Life and Adventures of Charles Ball, a Black Man* (New York, 1837), 139. See Genovese, *Roll, Jordan, Roll,* 524–35, 550–52; Fogel and Engerman, *Time on the Cross,* 116–17; Weymouth T. Jordan, *Hugh Davis and His Alabama Plantation* (University, Ala.: University of Alabama Press, 1948), 82–85; Charles Joyner, *Down by the Riverside: A South Carolina Slave Community* (Urbana: University of Illinois Press, 1984), 106–26; and Julia Floyd Smith, *Slavery and Rice Culture in Low Country Georgia, 1750–1860* (Knoxville: University of Tennessee Press, 1985), 119–30. For more negative evaluations of slave housing and clothing, see Stampp, *The Peculiar Institution,* 289–95, and Blassingame, *The Slave Community,* 158–60.

58. Betts, *Thomas Jefferson's Farm Book,* 80–81; Steward, *Twenty-Two Years a Slave,* 111; Diary of Leonidas Pendleton Spyker, microfiche copy, original in Louisiana State University Archives, 30 Aug. 1857. See also Janet Schaw, *Journal of a Lady of Quality; . . . 1774 to 1776,* ed. Evangeline Walker Andrews (New Haven: Yale University Press, 1921), 176; Gregory A. Stiverson and Patrick H. Butler III, eds., "Virginia in 1732: The Travel Journal of William Hugh Grove," *Virginia Magazine of History and Biogra-*

phy, 85 (Jan. 1977), 32; Jordan, *Hugh Davis and His Alabama Plantation,* 83–84; Phillips and Glunt, *Florida Plantation Records,* 513–14; and Ball, *Slavery in the United States,* 42–43. Also, Stampp,*The Peculiar Institution,* 282; Fogel and Engerman, *Time on the Cross,* 110–11; Joyner, *Down by the Riverside,* 91–106; Leslie Howard Owens, *This Species of Property: Slave Life and Culture in the Old South* (New York: Oxford University Press, 1976), 50–51; and Kenneth F. Kiple and Virginia H. Kiple, "Black Tongue and Black Men: Pellagra and Slavery in the Antebellum South," *Journal of Southern History,* 43 (Aug. 1977), 413–17.

59. The quotation is from *The Letters of William Gilmore Simms,* ed. Mary C. Simms Oliphant, Alfred Taylor Odell, and T. C. Duncan Eaves (Columbia: University of South Carolina Press, 1952–56), 25 May 1839, I, 143. See also Stiverson and Butler, "Virginia in 1732," 32; Schaw, *Journal of a Lady of Quality,* 176–77; Bruce, *The New Man,* 84–85; Steward, *Twenty-Two Years a Slave,* 14; Solomon Northup, *Twelve Years a Slave . . .* (New York, 1855), 200–3; Ball, *Slavery in the United States,* 42–43, 166–67, 189, 204–5; Olmsted, *The Cotton Kingdom,* I, 251–52; and Easterby, *The South Carolina Rice Plantation,* 350. Also, Genovese, *Roll, Jordan, Roll,* 535–40; Fogel and Engerman, *Time on the Cross,* 110–15; Scarborough, "Slavery— The White Man's Burden," 113–14; and Todd L. Savitt, *Medicine and Slavery: The Diseases and Health Care of Blacks in Antebellum Virginia* (Urbana: University of Illinois Press, 1978), 86–103. For recent assertions that slave diet lacked balance and was deficient in protein and vitamins, see Owens, *This Species of Property,* 50–69; Kiple and Kiple, "Black Tongue and Black Men," 411–28; and Kenneth F. Kiple and Virginia Himmelsteib King, *Another Dimension to the Black Diaspora: Diet, Disease, and Racism* (Cambridge: Cambridge University Press, 1981), 79–95.

60. *Narrative of the Life of Frederick Douglass,* 65; Rawick, *The American Slave . . . Supplement, Series 1,* I (Alabama), 39, 365; Escott, *Slavery Remembered,* 10.

61. For estimates of mortality rates in Jamaica and Cuba, see Michael Craton, "Jamaican Slavery," in *Race and Slavery in the Western Hemisphere: Quantitative Studies,* ed. Stanley L. Engerman and Eugene D. Genovese (Princeton: Princeton University Press, 1975), 74; Richard S. Dunn, "A Tale of Two Plantations: Slave Life at Mesopotamia in Jamaica and Mount Airy in Virginia, 1799 to 1828," *William and Mary Quarterly,* 3rd ser., 34 (Jan. 1977), 41; B. W. Higman, *Slave Population and Economy in Jamaica, 1807– 1834* (Cambridge: Cambridge University Press, 1976), 106–8; Franklin W. Knight, *Slave Society in Cuba during the Nineteenth Century* (Madison: University of Wisconsin Press, 1970), 82; Jack Ericson Eblen, "On the Natural Increase of Slave Populations: The Example of the Cuban Black Population, 1775–1900," in Engerman and Genovese, *Race and Slavery in the Western Hemisphere,* 245. On the general malnutrition and sickliness of Caribbean slaves, see Kenneth F. Kiple, *The Caribbean Slave: A Biological History* (Cambridge: Cambridge University Press, 1984).

62. On slave height, see Robert A. Margo and Richard H. Steckel, "The

Height of American Slaves: New Evidence on Slave Nutrition and Health," *Social Science History*, 6 (Fall 1982), 516–38; and Gerald C. Friedman, "The Height of Slaves in Trinidad," ibid., 482–515. For slightly varying estimates of mortality rates and life expectancy among American slaves, see Reynolds Farley, *Growth of the Black Population: A Study of Demographic Trends* (Chicago: Markham Publishing Company, 1970), 35–36; Jack Ericson Eblen, "New Estimates of the Vital Rates of the United States Black Population during the Nineteenth Century," *Demography*, 11 (May 1974), 306–12; Edward Meekar, "Mortality Trends of Southern Blacks, 1850–1910: Some Preliminary Findings," *Explorations in Economic History*, 13 (Jan. 1976), 19–23; and Peter D. McClelland and Richard J. Zeckhauser, *Demographic Dimensions of the New Republic: American Interregional Migration, Vital Statistics, and Manumissions, 1800–1860* (Cambridge: Cambridge University Press, 1982), 11, 12, 74, 76, 77. In *Time on the Cross: Evidence and Methods—A Supplement* (Boston: Little, Brown, 1974), 125–26, Fogel and Engerman present higher figures than do other experts for American slaves' life expectancy and put these figures in comparative perspective. For evidence of unusually high—by southern standards—mortality rates in antebellum South Carolina, see Sherman L. Ricards and George M. Blackburn, "A Demographic History of Slavery: Georgetown County, South Carolina, 1850," *South Carolina Historical Magazine*, 76 (Oct. 1975), 215–24; and Faust, *James Henry Hammond and the Old South*, 76–83.

63. "Journal of Col. James Gordon, of Lancaster County, Va.," *William and Mary Quarterly*, 10 (Oct. 1902), 105; Diary of Leonidas Pendleton Spyker, 62; John Evans to George Noble Jones, 15 June 1852, in Phillips and Glunt, *Florida Plantation Records*, 71; "The Plantation Diary of Bennet H. Barrow," 2 April 1844, 321. See also Owens, *This Species of Property*, 19–49; and Kiple and Kiple, "Black Tongue and Black Men," 411–28.

64. *The Secret Diary of William Byrd*, 3 Jan. 1710, 126, and 20 Feb. 1710, 144; "The Plantation Diary of Bennet H. Barrow," 23 Aug. 1842, 269 (quotation), 321–24. For examples of medical care administered by both slaveowners and doctors, see *The Diary of Colonel Landon Carter*, I, 158; *The Diaries of George Washington*, I, 121, 124; Easterby, *The South Carolina Rice Plantation*, 342–44; Eliza Magruder Diary, 31 Jan., 16 Feb., 17 Feb. 1846. See also Savitt, *Medicine and Slavery*, 150–71; Kiple and King, *Another Dimension to the Black Diaspora*, 163–74; Stampp, *The Peculiar Institution*, 311–14; and Fogel and Engerman, *Time on the Cross*, 116–26.

65. The two quotations are from the recollections of Amy Chapman and Delia Garlic, both of Alabama, in Rawick, *The American Slave*, VI, 60, 129.

66. Testimony of Simon Phillips in Rawick, *The American Slave*, VI, 313; Escott, *Slavery Remembered*, 11; Northup, *Twelve Years a Slave*, 90; Douglass, *My Bondage and My Freedom*, passim. For other examples of ex-slaves defending slavery, see the recollections of Mary Rice and Mangan Shepherd in Rawick, *The American Slave*, VI, 329–30, 340.

67. Recollection of Martha Bradley in Rawick, *The American Slave*, VI,

46–47; recollection of Mrs. Mariah Hines in Perdue et al., *Weevils in the Wheat*, 139–40. For examples of similar testimony in AFIC interviews, see John W. Blassingame, ed., *Slave Testimony: Two Centuries of Letters, Speeches, Interviews, and Autobiographies* (Baton Rouge: Louisiana State University Press, 1977), 409–10, 418, 423, 430.

68. Douglass, *My Bondage and My Freedom*, 118; recollection of Oliver Bell in Rawick, *The American Slave . . . Supplement, Series 1*, I, 55–56.

69. Quotations are from "Nakaz D. A. Shepeleva prikazchiku sel'tsa Glinka (Mikhailovskogo uezda) Ivanu Balashevu" (1718), in "Nakazy votchinnym prikazchikam pervoi chetverti XVIII v.," ed. I. F. Petrovskaia, *Istoricheskii arkhiv*, 8 (1953), 234, 236; and Novosel'skii, *Votchinnik i ego khoziaistvo*, 163, 74. For graphic descriptions of mistreatment of serfs in the second half of the eighteenth century, see Semevskii, *Krest'iane v tsarstvovanie Imperatritsy Ekateriny II*, I, 199–212.

70. Quotations are from Catherine II, "The Instructions to the Commissioners for Composing a New Code of Laws," in *Documents of Catherine the Great: The Correspondence with Voltaire and the "Instruction" of 1767 in the English Text of 1768*, ed. W. F. Reddaway (Cambridge: Cambridge University Press, 1931), 264, 262; and Semevskii, *Krest'ianskii vopros v Rossii*, II, 60–61. See also Semevskii, *Krest'ianskii vopros v Rossii*, I, 38–43, 102–20, 228, 236–51, 467–500, and II, 3–17, 22–64, 109–46, 187–208, 529–70; M. T. Beliavskii, *Krest'ianskii vopros v Rossii nakanune vosstaniia E. I. Pugacheva (formirovanie antikrepostnicheskoi mysli)* (Moscow: Izdatel'stvo Moskovskogo universiteta, 1965), 8–10, 208–13, 252–53, 262–64; Robert E. Jones, *The Emancipation of the Russian Nobility, 1762–1785* (Princeton: Princeton University Press, 1973), 135–41; Isabel de Madariaga, *Russia in the Age of Catherine the Great* (New Haven: Yale University Press, 1981), 134–36, 175–78; Petr Bartenev, ed., *Deviatnadtsatyi vek: Istoricheskii sbornik* (Moscow, 1872), II, 145–208; and W. Bruce Lincoln, *Nicholas I: Emperor and Autocrat of All the Russias* (Bloomington: Indiana University Press, 1978), 185–95.

71. This change can easily be detected in the measures included in A. E. Vorms et al., eds., *Pamiatniki istorii krest'ian XIV–XIX vv.* (Moscow: Izdanie N. N. Klochkova, 1910), (quotation, 95–96). For restrictive legislation passed during the second half of the seventeenth century, see A. G. Man'kov, *Razvitie krepostnogo prava v Rossii vo vtoroi polovine XVII veka* (Moscow: Izdatel'stvo Akademii nauk SSSR, 1962).

72. Semevskii, *Krest'ianskii vopros v Rossii*, I, 253–81, II, 29–108, 152; Romanovich-Slavatinskii, *Dvorianstvo v Rossii*, 299–306; Ignatovich, *Pomeshchich'i krest'iane nakanune osvobozhdeniia*, 17–35; M. A. Rakhmatullin, "Zakonodatel'naia praktika tsarskogo samoderzhaviia: Ukaz ot 8 noiabria 1847 goda i popytki ego primeneniia," *Istoriia SSSR*, 1982, no. 2, 35–52; Blum, *Lord and Peasant in Russia*, 424–28, 445, 537–51; and Daniel Field, *The End of Serfdom: Nobility and Bureaucracy in Russia, 1855–1861* (Cambridge, Mass.: Harvard University Press, 1976), 40–50.

73. For Peter's instruction, see Vorms et al., *Pamiatniki istorii krest'ian*, 95–96; for Alexander's circular, see *Russkaia starina*, 6 (1872), 281–83; for statistics on confiscated estates, see *Materialy dlia istorii krepostnago prava v Rossii. Izvlecheniia iz sekretnykh otchetov Ministerstva vnutrennikh del za 1836–1856 g.* (Berlin, 1872), 31, 262–63. The quotations are from Third Department reports for 1836 and 1844, in *Krest'ianskoe dvizhenie 1827–1869 godov*, ed. E. A. Morokhovets (Moscow: Gosudarstvennoe sotsial'no-ekonomicheskoe izdatel'stvo, 1931), I, 22, 60.

74. N. P. Vasilenko, "Krest'ianskii vopros v iugo-zapadnom i severo-zapadnom krae pri Nikolae I i vvedenie inventarei," in *Velikaia reforma: Russkoe obshchestvo i krest'ianskii vopros v proshlom i nastoiashchem. Iubileinnoe izdanie*, ed. A. K. Dzhivelegov et al. (Moscow: Izdanie T-va I. D. Sytina, 1911), IV, 94–109; N. N. Ulashchik, "Vvedenie obiazatel'nykh inventarei v Belorussii i Litve," in *Ezhegodnik po agrarnoi istorii Vostochnoi Evropy 1958 g.* (Tallin, 1959), 256–77; V. V. Chepko, "Polozhenie krest'ian i klassovaia bor'ba v Belorusskoi derevne v pervoi polovine XIX veka," ibid., 178–79; Ignatovich, *Pomeshchich'i krest'iane nakanune osvobozhdeniia*, 164–73; Semevskii, *Krest'ianskii vopros v Rossii*, II, 481–513; Blum, *Lord and Peasant in Russia*, 542–44, 460–63; and Edward C. Thaden with the collaboration of Marianna Forster Thaden, *Russia's Western Borderlands, 1710–1870* (Princeton: Princeton University Press, 1984), 104–9, 133–37.

75. The quotation is from *Materialy dlia istorii krepostnago prava v Rossii*, 32.

76. Semevskii, *Krest'ianskii vopros v Rossii*, I, 253–81, II, 91–108, 209–38.

77. *Materialy dlia istorii krepostnago prava v Rossii*, 56; *Pamiatnaia knizhka Kaluzhkoi gubernii na 1861 god* (Kaluga, 1861), 347.

78. Quotations are from S. T. Slovutinskii, "Bunt i usmirenie v imenii Golitsyna (1847 g.)," in Slovutinskii, *General Izmailov i ego dvornia*, 252, and *Krest'ianskoe dvizhenie 1827–1869 godov*, I, 62. For examples of statements by individual noblemen advocating amelioration in treatment of serfs, see M. M. Shcherbatov, "Na chitannyi oktiabria 11 dnia golos Eletskoi provintsii gospodina deputata Mikhaila Davydova," 115–16; A. I. Polenov, "O krepostnom sostoianii krest'ian v Rossii" (1767), in *Russkii arkhiv*, 1865 (no. 3), 286–316; Prince M. S. Vorontsov to Count P. D. Kiselev, 17 Feb. 1837, in *Arkhiv kniazia Vorontsova* (Moscow, 1870–97), XXXVIII, 15–17. See also Semevskii, *Krest'ianskii vopros v Rossii*, I, 22–37, 57–87, 295–339, 369–92, II, 444–67.

79. Ignatovich, *Pomeshchich'i krest'iane nakanune osvobozhdeniia*, 34–45; Romanovich-Slavatinskii, *Dvorianstvo v Rossii*, 306; Semevskii, *Krest'ianskii vopros v Rossii*, I, 169; V. N. Bochkarev, "Byt pomeshchich'ikh krest'ian," in *Velikaia reforma*, III, 25–34; Blum, *Lord and Peasant in Russia*, 429.

80. *Krest'ianskoe dvizhenie 1827–1869 godov*, I, 18.

81. See Beliavskii, *Krest'ianskii vopros v Rossii*, 150–75, 266–79; Semev-

skii, *Krest'iane v tsarstvovanie Imperatritsy Ekateriny II*, I, 178–90; and Field, *The End of Serfdom*, 35–38, 45–50. For an unusual case involving the enserfment of several thousand Belorussian peasants in the early nineteenth century, see A. S. Kotsievskii, "Zakreposhchenie krest'ian-staroobriatsev Belorussii v kontse XVIII-nachale XIX vv.," *Voprosy agrarnoi istorii tsentra i severo-zapada RSFSR: Materialy mezhvuzovskoi nauchnoi konferentsii* (Smolensk: Ministerstvo prosveshcheniia RSFSR, 1972), 115–22.

82. *Krest'ianskoe dvizhenie 1827–1869 godov*, I, 97. For examples of exceptional cruelty on the part of serfowners, see S. T. Slovutinskii, "General Izmailov i ego dvornia," in Slovutinskii, *General Izmailov i ego dvornia*, esp. 117–36; Fedotov, "Dokumenty pomeshchich'ego proizvola," 147–68; and numerous cases scattered throughout KD-1, KD-2, and KD-3.

83. Quotations are from Slovutinskii, "Bunt i usmirenie v imenii Golitsyna," 252, 261; Zablotskii-Desiatovskii, "O krepostnom sostoianii v Rossii," 315; and N. Tourgueneff, *La Russie et les russes* (Brussels, 1847), III, 68. For other assertions of pomeshchik paternalism, see Robert Pinkerton, *Russia: or Miscellaneous Observations on the Past and Present State of That Country and Its Inhabitants* (London, 1833), 287; M. V. Dovnar-Zapol'skii, "Krepostniki v pervoi chetverti XIX v.," in *Velikaia reforma*, II, 134–35; and A. Povalishin, "Riazanskie pomeshchiki i ikh krepostnye: Usloviia normal'nago pomeshchich'iago khoziaistva," in *Trudy Vysochaishe uchrezhdennoi Riazanskoi uchenoi arkhivnoi komissii*, 14 (1899), 8.

84. Lyof N. Tolstoi, "A Russian Proprietor," in *A Russian Proprietor and Other Stories*, vol. XIII of *The Novels and Other Works of Lyof N. Tolstoi* (New York: Charles Scribner's Sons, 1911), 3.

85. I. Kuznetsov, ed., "Krepostnye krest'iane sela Barasheva-Usada v pervoi polovine XIX v.," *Krasnyi arkhiv*, 77 (1936), 117–50 (quotations, 132–33, 138).

86. For some of numerous works that portray a sharp decline in the serfs' material well-being during the century before emancipation, see Koval'chenko and Milov, "Ob intensivnosti obrochnoi ekspluatatsii krest'ian," 55–80 (statistics, 67); I. D. Koval'chenko, *Russkoe krepostnoe krest'ianstvo v pervoi polovine XIX v.* (Moscow: Izdatel'stvo Moskovskogo universiteta, 1967), esp. 259–71; 289–305, 316–30; V. A. Fedorov, *Pomeshchich'i krest'iane tsentral'no-promyshlennogo raiona Rossii kontsa XVIII-pervoi poloviny XIX v.* (Moscow: Izdatel'stvo Moskovskogo universiteta, 1974), 230–49; R. M. Vvedenskii, "Kharakter pomeshchich'ei ekspluatatsii i biudzhety obrochnykh krest'ian v 20–40-e gody XIX v.," *Istoriia SSSR*, 1971, no. 3, 44–57; and Ignatovich, *Pomeshchich'i krest'iane nakanune osvobozhdeniia*, 79–83, 139–42, 149. This view is criticized in Ryndziunskii, "Ob opredelenii intensivnosti obrochnoi ekspluatatsii krest'ian," 59–62. For a challenge to the usual assertion of grim conditions among serf ironworkers, see Thomas Esper, "The Condition of the Serf Workers in Russia's Metallurgical Industry, 1800–1861," *Journal of Modern History*, 50 (Dec. 1978), 66–79.

87. B. G. Litvak, "Ob izmeneniiakh zemel'nogo nadela pomeshchich'ikh krest'ian v pervoi polovine XIX v.," *Ezhegodnik po agrarnoi istorii Vostochnoi Evropy 1963 g.* (Vilnius, 1964), 523–34.

88. Quotations are from Zablotskii-Desiatovskii, "O krepostnom sostoianii v Rossii," 298; G. A. Masoedov, "Khoziaistvenno-statisticheskii obzor iuzhnoi chasti Tul'skoi gubernii . . . ," in *Trudy Vol'nago ekonomicheskago obshchestva,* 1849, pt. 1, section 1, 249; and Vasilii Preobrazhenskii, *Opisanie Tverskoi gubernii v sel'skom-khoziaistvenom otnoshenii* (St. Petersburg, 1854), 118, 119–20. For a description of peasant housing, see Mary Matossian, "The Peasant Way of Life," in *The Peasant in Ninteenth-Century Russia,* ed. Wayne S. Vucinich (Stanford: Stanford University Press, 1968), 4–8. On Russian climate and geography, see W. H. Parker, *An Historical Geography of Russia* (London: University of London Press, 1968), esp. 13–29.

89. For descriptions of peasant diet, see Preobrazhenskii, *Opisanie Tverskoi gubernii,* 149–52; Matossian, "The Peasant Way of Life," 12–14; and R. E. F. Smith and David Christian, *Bread and Salt: A Social and Economic History of Food and Drink in Russia* (Cambridge: Cambridge University Press, 1984), esp. 251–87. On crop yields, see Koval'chenko, *Russkoe krepostnoe krest'ianstvo,* 76–77, 298–305; Fedorov, *Pomeshchich'i krest'iane tsentral'no-promyshlennogo raiona Rossii,* 54–56; Pipes, *Russia under the Old Regime,* 5–8; Blum, *Lord and Peasant in Russia,* 329–32; and Arcadius Kahan, *The Plow, the Hammer, and the Knout: An Economic History of Eighteenth-Century Russia,* with the editorial assistance of Richard Hellie (Chicago: University of Chicago Press, 1985), 11–13, 48–50.

90. Excerpt from record book on the estate of Baron P. P. Shafirov, Arzamasskii district, 1723, in *Materialy po istorii krest'ianskogo i pomeshchich'ego khoziaistva pervoi chetverti XVIII v.,* ed. K. V. Sivkov (Moscow: Izdatel'stvo Akademii nauk SSSR, 1951), 21; E. I. Indova, *Krepostnoe khoziaistvo v nachale XIX veka po materialam votchinnogo arkhiva Vorontsovykh* (Moscow: Izdatel'stvo Akademii nauk SSSR, 1955), 122–27. See also ibid., 91, 114–15; Shchepetov, *Krepostnoe pravo v votchinakh Sheremetevykh,* 85–88, 170–77; Fedorov, *Pomeshchich'i krest'iane tsentral'no-promyshlennogo raiona Rossii,* 233–49; Vvedenskii, "Kharakter pomeshchich'ei ekspluatatsii i biudzhety obrochnykh krest'ian," 48, 54.

91. Chappé d'Auteroche, *A Journey into Siberia* (New York: Arno Press, 1970; orig. pub. London, 1770), 351–52; *Pamiatnaia knizhka Orlovskoi gubernii na 1860 god* (Orel, 1860), appendix, table 3, reverse side; S. Korsakov, "Zakony narodnaseleniia v Rossii," in *Materialy dlia statistiki Rossiiskoi imperii izdavaemye, s vysochaishago soisvoleniia, pri statisticheskom otdelenii soveta Ministerstva vnutrennikh del* (St. Petersburg, 1841), section 1, pt. 2, 222–301; A. G. Rashin, *Naselenie Rossii za 100 let (1811–1913 gg.): statisticheskie ocherki* (Moscow: Gosudarstvennoe statisticheskoe izdatel'stvo, 1956), 36–38; Georgii Nadezhdinskii, "Selo Golitsyno. (Istoricheskо-etnograficheskii ocherk)," in *Saratovskii sbornik. Materialy dlia*

izucheniia Saratovskoi gubernii (Saratov, 1881), I, pt. 1, 271. See also Kahan, *The Plow, the Hammer, and the Knout,* 7–15.

92. George Augustus Sala, *A Journey Due North: Being Notes of a Residence in Russia* (Boston, 1858), 229. See also *Akty khoziaistva boiarina B. I. Morozova,* I, 137–39, 166–67; Dovnar-Zapol'skii, "Krepostniki v pervoi chetverti XIX v.," 13–14; Indova, *Krepostnoe khoziaistvo v nachale XIX veka,* 165–66; and Ignatovich, *Pomeshchich'i krest'iane nakanune osvobozhdeniia,* 5–12, 118–23.

93. Indova, *Krepostnoe khoziaistvo v nachale XIX veka,* 105; Zablotskii-Desiatovskii, "O krepostnom sostoianii v Rossii," 315–20.

94. Kuznetsov, "Krepostnye krest'iane sela Barasheva-Usada," 126–28, 139, 135.

95. See Chapter 6, pages 310–11.

3. Ideals and Ideology

1. William Coxe, *Travels in Poland and Russia* (New York: Arno Press, 1970; based on 5th ed., London, 1802), I, 261; William Rae Wilson, *Travels in Russia* (New York: Arno Press, 1970; orig. pub. London, 1828), 360; Alexis de Tocqueville, *Democracy in America,* ed. Phillips Bradley (New York: Random House, 1945; orig. pub. in French, 1835, 1840), I, 410–11. See also Frances Anne Kemble, *Journal of a Residence on a Georgian Plantation in 1838–1839* (Chicago: Afro-Am Press, 1969), 75–77; and Robert Pinkerton, *Russia: or Miscellaneous Observations on the Past and Present State of That Country and Its Inhabitants* (London, 1833), 316–19. The classic Russian portrayal of the lazy nobleman is Ivan Goncharov's novel *Oblomov* (1859); for a discussion of this theme, see Hannah Stern Goldman, "American Slavery and Russian Serfdom: A Study in Fictional Parallels" (Ph.D. diss., Columbia University, 1955), 132–42; on the weak planter in American fiction, see William R. Taylor, *Cavalier and Yankee: The Old South and American National Character* (New York: Harper & Row, 1969; orig. pub. 1961), 153–61.

2. S. T. Slovutinskii, *General Izmailov i ego dvornia; otryvki iz vospominanii* (Moscow: Academia, 1937), 83–90; Daniel R. Hundley, *Social Relations in Our Southern States,* ed. and introd. William J. Cooper, Jr. (Baton Rouge: Louisiana State University Press, 1978; orig. pub. 1859), 28–29. For examples of intense pride in lineage, see Hundley, *Social Relations in Our Southern States,* 27–28; and M. M. Shcherbatov, "Na chitannye sentiabria 11-go dnia ukazy . . . ," in *Sochineniia kniazia M. M. Shcherbatova,* ed. I. P. Khrushchov (St. Petersburg, 1896–8), I, 56–61. "Wherever slavery became structurally very important, the whole tone of the slaveholders' culture tended to be highly honorific," noted Orlando Patterson in *Slavery and Social Death: A Comparative Study* (Cambridge, Mass.: Harvard University Press, 1982), 79. On the southern concept of honor, see Bertram Wyatt-Brown, *Southern Honor: Ethics and Behavior in the Old South* (New York: Oxford

University Press, 1982); and Edward L. Ayers, *Vengeance and Justice: Crime and Punishment in the Nineteenth-Century South* (New York: Oxford University Press, 1984), 9–33.

3. For an elaboration of master-class ideology, see the next section. Parallels in the character of Russian noblemen and American planters are briefly suggested in Roger Dow, "Seichas: A Comparison of Pre-Reform Russia and the Ante-Bellum South," *Russian Review*, 7 (1947), 13; and Clement Eaton, *The Growth of Southern Civilization, 1790–1860* (New York: Harper & Row, 1961), 22–24. On Russia, see A. Romanovich-Slavatinskii, *Dvorianstvo v Rossii ot nachala XVIII veka do otmeny krepostnago prava* (St. Petersburg, 1870), 57–87, 115–52; Marc Raeff, "State and Nobility in the Ideology of M. M. Shcherbatov," *American Slavic and East European Review*, 19 (1960), 364–71; and I. A. Fedosov, *Iz istorii russkoi obshchestvennoi mysli XVIII stoletiia: M. M. Shcherbatov* (Moscow: Izdatel'stvo Moskovskogo universiteta, 1967), 69–76. On the American South, see Eaton, *The Growth of Southern Civilization*, 113–24; Taylor, *Cavalier and Yankee*, 162–72, 201; and Rollin G. Osterweis, *Romanticism and Nationalism in the Old South* (Baton Rouge: Louisiana State University Press, 1967; orig. pub. 1949), esp. 16, 41–55, 82–102, 111–32. On the ideal of the leisured lady in the antebellum South, see Anne Firor Scott, *The Southern Lady: From Pedestal to Politics, 1830–1930* (Chicago: University of Chicago Press, 1970), 3–21; and Catherine Clinton, *The Plantation Mistress: Woman's World in the Old South* (New York: Pantheon Books, 1982), 87–109.

4. Quotations are from *Journal & Letters of Philip Vickers Fithian, 1773–1774: A Plantation Tutor of the Old Dominion*, ed. and introd. Hunter Dickinson Farish (Williamsburg, Va.: Colonial Williamsburg, 1943), 10 March 1774, 75; Robert Lyall, *Travels in Russia, the Krimea the Caucasus and Georgia* (New York: Arno Press, 1970; orig. pub. London, 1825), 53; *The Works of James Buchanan: Comprising His Speeches, State Papers, and Private Correspondence*, ed. John Bassett Moore (Philadelphia: J. B. Lippincott, 1908), II, 9 Aug. 1832, 229; and De Tocqueville, *Democracy in America*, I, 412.

5. *The Diaries of George Washington, 1748–1799*, ed. John C. Fitzpatrick (Boston: Houghton Mifflin, 1925), III, 15–17; Edwin Morris Betts, ed., *Thomas Jefferson's Farm Book with Commentary and Relevant Extracts from Other Writings* (Princeton: Princeton University Press, 1953), 128; Richard S. Dunn, "A Tale of Two Plantations: Slave Life at Mesopotamia in Jamaica and Mount Airy in Virginia, 1799 to 1828," *William and Mary Quarterly*, 3rd ser., 34 (Jan. 1977), 36–37; *Narrative of the Life of Frederick Douglass, an American Slave, Written by Himself* (New York: New American Library, 1968; orig. pub. 1845), 33–35; Richard C. Wade, *Slavery in the Cities: The South, 1820–1860* (New York: Oxford University Press, 1964), 32; Michael P. Johnson, "Planters and Patriarchy: Charleston, 1800–1860," *Journal of Southern History*, 46 (Feb. 1980), 53–54. The quotation on common estimates of the proportion of house slaves is from Eugene D. Genovese,

Roll, Jordan, Roll: The World the Slaves Made (New York: Pantheon Books, 1974), 328. Robert William Fogel and Stanley L. Engerman estimated that among agricultural slaves 26.3 percent of males were either skilled, semi-skilled, or managerial and that 20 percent of women were employed in household service; see their *Time on the Cross: The Economics of American Negro Slavery* (Boston: Little, Brown, 1974), 38–39.

6. The quotation is from M. P. D. de Passenans, *La Russie et l'esclavage, dans leurs rapports avec la civilisation européene: ou de l'influence de la servitude sur la vie domestique des russes* (Paris, 1822), I, 91. For statistics on the number of dvorovye in the eighth, ninth, and tenth censuses, see A. Troinitskii, *Krepostnoe naselenie v Rossii, po 10–i narodnoi perepisi* (St. Petersburg, 1861), 57–58. During the 1850s many pomeshchiki, anticipating emancipation and correctly supposing that they would not have to provide freed house serfs with land, transferred peasants from villages into their households, so that by the time of the tenth census in 1858 dvorovye constituted 6.8 percent of the serf population; figures from the ninth census therefore more accurately reflect the true proportion of dvorovye.

7. K. N. Shchepetov, *Krepostnoe pravo v votchinakh Sheremetevykh (1708–1885)* (Moscow: Izdatel'stvo dvortsa-muzeia, 1947), 288–93; Slovutinskii, *General Izmailov i ego dvornia*, 93–96; Tatiana Bakounine, *Le domaine des Princes Kourakine dans le gouvernement de Saratov* (Paris: Les presses modernes, 1929), 27 (quotation). In Chernigov province dvorovye made up 9.6 percent of all serfs in the late 1850s, but on estates with more than a hundred souls they made up only 4 percent; in Kharkov the corresponding figures were 24 percent and 11.3 percent; see I. I. Ignatovich, *Pomeshchich'i krest'iane nakanune osvobozhdeniia*, 2nd ed. (Moscow: I. D. Sytin, 1910), 210. See also V. I. Semevskii, *Krest'iane v tsarstvovanie Imperatritsy Ekateriny II*, 2nd ed. (St. Petersburg: Tipografiia M. M. Stasiulevicha, 1901–3), I, 141–56; and E. S. Kots, *Krepostnaia intelligentsiia* (Leningrad: Knigoizdatel'tsvo seiatel' E. V. Vysotskogo, 1926).

8. On Russia, see N. Chechulin, *Russkoe provintsial'noe obshchestvo vo vtoroi polovine XVIII veka* (St. Petersburg, 1889), 27–37, 53–54; Baron S. A. Korf, *Dvorianstvo i ego soslovnoe upravlenie, za stoletiia 1762–1855 godov* (St. Petersburg: Tipografiia Trenke i Fiusno, 1906), 1–2; and Marc Raeff, *Origins of the Russian Intelligentsia: The Eighteenth-Century Nobility* (New York: Harcourt, Brace & World, 1966), 31–32. On the Chesapeake colonies, see Louis B. Wright, *The First Gentlemen of Virginia: Intellectual Qualities of the Early Colonial Ruling Class* (San Marino, Calif.: Huntington Library, 1940), 40–62; Carville V. Earle, *The Evolution of a Tidewater Settlement System: All Hallow's Parish, Maryland, 1650–1783* (Chicago: University of Chicago Department of Geography Research Paper no. 170, 1975), 136–40; and Aubrey C. Land, "Economic Base and Social Structure: The Northern Chesapeake in the Eighteenth Century," *Journal of Economic History*, 25 (1965), 642–47.

9. Buturlin to Vorontsov, Moscow, 23 April 1789, in *Arkhiv kniazia Vo-*

rontsova (Moscow, 1870–97), XXII, 216–17. On the life-style and activities of the Vorontsovs and Kurakins, see *Arkhiv kniazia Vorontsova; Arkhiv kn. F. A. Kurakina* (St. Petersburg, Saratov, Astrakhan, and Moscow, 1890–1902); *Vosemnadtsatyi vek: Istoricheskii sbornik, izdavaemyi po bumagam famil'nago arkhiva kniazem Fedorom Alekseevichem Kurakinym*, ed. V. N. Smol'ianinov (Moscow: Tipo-litografiia N. I. Grosman i G. A. Vendel'shtein, 1904–5); and *Deviatnadtsatyi vek: Istoricheskii sbornik, izdavaemyi po bumagam famil'nago arkhiva kniazem Fedorom Alekseevichem Kurakinym*, ed. V. N. Smol'ianinov (Moscow: Tipo-litografiia N. I. Grosman i G. A. Vendel'shtein, 1903).

10. "Dnevnik Kurskogo pomeshchika I. P. Annenkova," in *Materialy po istorii SSSR, V: Dokumenty istorii XVIII veka*, ed. A. A. Novosel'skii (Moscow: Izdatel'stvo Akademii nauk SSSR, 1957), esp. 678 (quotation), 679, 683, 690–91, 749–53. See also Romanovich-Slavatinskii, *Dvorianstvo v Rossii*, 57–87, 211–85; Korf, *Dvorianstvo i ego soslovnoe upravlenie*, 3–4, 214–17; Chechulin, *Russkoe provintsial'noe obshchestvo*, 55–89; and M. Bogoslovskii, *Byt i nravy russkago dvorianstva v pervoi polovine XVIII veka* (Moscow: Tipografiia G. Lissnera i D. Sobko, 1904), 3–31.

11. On the Carters, see Wright, *The First Gentlemen of Virginia*, 235–85; Louis B. Wright, ed., *Letters of Robert Carter, 1720–1727: The Commercial Interests of a Virginia Gentleman* (San Marino, Calif.: Huntington Library, 1940); *The Diary of Colonel Landon Carter of Sabine Hall, 1752–1778*, ed. Jack P. Greene (Charlottesville: University Press of Virginia, 1965); Louis Morton, *Robert Carter of Nomini Hall: A Virginia Tobacco Planter of the Eighteenth Century* (Williamsburg, Va.: Colonial Williamsburg, 1945); and *Journal & Letters of Philip Vickers Fithian*.

12. The quotation is from *Journal & Letters of Philip Vickers Fithian*, 30. After Robert III's death in 1804, his son John contested the liberation of his slaves, and evidently few of them in fact received their freedom.

13. Louis Wright provided a different example of this pattern in colonial Virginia: "the first William Byrd, by shrewd business acumen, accumulated a fortune and established his family as a power in the land; the second William Byrd became an elegant ornament of that family, but inherited enough of his father's business judgment to hold onto his property and even to add to his possessions; the third William Byrd, by his vices and bad management, squandered the fortune"; Wright, *The First Gentlemen of Virginia*, 312. For a good description of a similar pattern of development in up-country South Carolina between 1790 and 1830, see William W. Freehling, *Prelude to Civil War: The Nullification Controversy in South Carolina, 1816–1836* (New York: Harper & Row, 1965), 17–21; on back-country Virginia, see Richard R. Beeman, *The Evolution of the Southern Backcountry: A Case Study of Lunenberg County, Virginia, 1746–1832* (Philadelphia: University of Pennsylvania Press, 1984), 60–229. On the aristocratic pretensions of South Carolina's rice planters, see Johnson, "Planters and Patriarchy."

14. Frederick Law Olmsted, *A Journey in the Back Country* (New York:

Schocken Books, 1970; orig. pub. 1860), 394. On the nonaristocratic life-style of most southern slaveowners, see James Oakes, *The Ruling Race: A History of American Slaveholders* (New York: Alfred A. Knopf, 1982). Although historians have disagreed over the precise degree of property concentration in the antebellum South, they are united in concluding that only a tiny minority were rich aristocrats. For differing approaches to this question, see Frank L. and Harriet C. Owsley, "The Economic Basis of Society in the Late Ante-Bellum South," *Journal of Southern History,* 6 (Feb. 1940), 24–45; Fabian Linden, "Economic Democracy in the Slave South: An Appraisal of Some Recent Views," *Journal of Negro History,* 31 (1946), 140–89; Gavin Wright, "'Economic Democracy' and the Concentration of Agricultural Wealth in the Cotton South, 1850–1860," *Agricultural History,* 44 (1970), 63–93; Randolph B. Campbell, "Planters and Plain Folk: Harrison County, Texas, as a Test Case, 1850–1860," *Journal of Southern History,* 40 (Aug. 1974), 369–98; and Albert W. Niemi, Jr., "Inequality in the Distribution of Slave Wealth: The Cotton South and Other Southern Agricultural Regions," *Journal of Economic History,* 37 (Sept. 1977), 747–53. For concentration of slaveholding, see Table 5, page 54.

15. For concentration of serfholding, see Table 6. The quotation is from Richard Pipes, *Russia under the Old Regime* (New York: Charles Scribner's, 1974), 179. For other categorizations of noblemen according to serfholding size, see Troinitskii, *Krepostnoe naselenie v Rossii,* 45, 66; L. N. Iurovskii, *Saratovskie votchiny: Statistiko-ekonomicheskie ocherki i materialy iz krupnogo zemlevladeniia i krepostnogo khoziaistva v kontse XVIII i v nachale XIX stoletiia* (Saratov: Izdanie Saratovskogo instituta narodnogo khoziaistva, 1923), 69; and Jerome Blum, *Lord and Peasant in Russia from the Ninth to the Nineteenth Century* (Princeton: Princeton University Press, 1961), 367–79. On noble indebtedness, see Blum, *Lord and Peasant in Russia,* 379–85.

16. On the indebtedness of Barrow and Sheremetev, see the editor's introduction to Edwin Adams Davis, ed., *Plantation Life in the Florida Parishes of Louisiana, 1836–1846, as Revealed in the Diary of Bennet H. Barrow* (New York: Columbia University Press, 1943), 19–23; and Shchepetov, *Krepostnoe pravo v votchinakh Sheremetevykh,* 80–85. Indebtedness was a traditional problem faced by European aristocracies; for a discussion of this problem among British gentry, see David Cannadine, "Aristocratic indebtedness in the Nineteenth Century: The Case Reopened," *Economic History Review,* 2nd ser., 30 (Nov. 1977), 624–50.

17. The value of estates is from Blum, *Lord and Peasant in Russia,* 372. For estimates of typical serf families' income, see I. D. Koval'chenko and L. V. Milov, "Ob intensivnosti obrochnoi ekspluatatsii krest'ian tsentral'nogo Rossii v kontse XVIII-pervoi polovine XIX v.," *Istoriia SSSR,* 1966, no. 4, 67; and R. M. Vvedenskii, "Kharakter pomeshchich'ei ekspluatatsii i biudzhety obrochnykh krest'ian v 20–40–e gody XIX v.," ibid., 1971, no. 3, 54. For salaries of various ranks of government servitors, see P. A.

Zaionchkovskii, *Pravitel'stvennyi apparat samoderzhavnoi Rossii v XIX v.* (Moscow: Izdatel'stvo "Mysl'," 1978), 74–77. On slave prices, see U. B. Phillips, "The Economic Cost of Slaveholding in the Cotton Belt," in Phillips, *The Slave Economy of the Old South: Selected Essays in Economic and Social History,* ed. Eugene D. Genovese (Baton Rouge: Louisiana State University Press, 1968), 124–28. Statistics on slaveholding wealth are from Gavin Wright, *The Political Economy of the Cotton South: Households, Markets, and Wealth in the Nineteenth Century* (New York: W. W. Norton, 1978), 34–42.

18. For a superb description of this bourgeois ideology, see Eric Foner, *Free Soil, Free Labor, Free Men: The Ideology of the Republican Party before the Civil War* (New York: Oxford University Press, 1970), esp. chs. 1, 2. For recent works that downplay—incorrectly I believe—the distinctiveness of southern values and ideology, see Oakes, *The Ruling Race,* esp. 69–95, 123–50, 227; and Jane Turner Censer, *North Carolina Planters and Their Children, 1800–1860* (Baton Rouge: Louisiana State University Press, 1984), passim, esp. 152–53.

19. *The Diary of Colonel Landon Carter,* 1 April 1776, II, 1008–9. On southern democracy, see Fletcher M. Green, "Democracy in the Old South," *Journal of Southern History,* 12 (1946), 3–23; J. Mills Thornton III, *Politics and Power in a Slave Society: Alabama, 1800–1860* (Baton Rouge: Louisiana State University Press, 1978), pt. 1, passim; and especially William J. Cooper, Jr., *The South and the Politics of Slavery, 1828–1856* (Baton Rouge: Louisiana State University Press, 1978), ch. 2. For development of the concept of "herrenvolk democracy," in which an egalitarian society for whites coexisted with the exclusion of blacks from the body politic, see George M. Fredrickson, *The Black Image in the White Mind: The Debate on Afro-American Character and Destiny, 1817–1914* (New York: Harper & Row, 1971), 61–64, 90–96. For the partial exception of South Carolina, which never established either a vigorous two-party system or a free-wheeling democratic style, see Kenneth S. Greenberg, "Representation and the Isolation of South Carolina, 1776–1860," *Journal of American History,* 64 (Dec. 1977), 723–43.

20. "Hammond's Letters on Slavery," in *The Pro-Slavery Argument; As Maintained by the Most Distinguished Writers of the Southern States* (Charleston, 1852), 110. The most cogent recent argument for the aristocratic character and planter domination of southern society is that of Eugene D. Genovese; see his *The Political Economy of Slavery: Studies in the Economy and Society of the Slave South* (New York: Vintage Books, 1965), esp. 28–34; *The World the Slaveholders Made: Two Essays in Interpretation* (New York: Pantheon Books, 1969), esp. 6, 138–43; and "Yeomen Farmers in a Slaveholders' Democracy," *Agricultural History,* 49 (April 1975), 331–42. On southern rejection of democratic egalitarianism, see W. G. Bean, "Anti-Jeffersonianism in the Antebellum South," *North Carolina Historical Review,* 41 (April 1935), 103–24. For an insightful discussion of the mu-

tually supporting relationship between aristocracy and republicanism in late eighteenth-century Virginia, see Edmund S. Morgan, *American Slavery, American Freedom: The Ordeal of Colonial Virginia* (New York: W. W. Norton, 1975), 363–87; for elaboration of a distinctive southern political culture rooted in slavery, see Kenneth S. Greenberg, *Masters and Statesmen: The Political Culture of American Slavery* (Baltimore: Johns Hopkins University Press, 1985).

21. See Romanovich-Slavatinskii, *Dvorianstvo v Rossii*, passim, esp. 402–10, 490–500; Korf, *Dvorianstvo i ego soslovnoe upravlenie*, 164–71, 202, 212–14, 225–63, 391–94, 431–51, 482–83, 631–51; Robert David Givens, "Servitors or Seigneurs: The Nobility and the Eighteenth Century Russian State" (Ph.D. diss., University of California–Berkeley, 1975); Pipes, *Russia under the Old Regime*, 98, 172–75, 179; Max Beloff, "Russia," in *The European Nobility in the Eighteenth Century: Studies of the Nobilities of the Major European States in the Pre-Reform Era*, ed. A. Goodwin (London: Adams and Charles Black, 1953), 172–73; Brenda Meehan-Waters, *Autocracy and Aristocracy: The Russian Service Elite of 1730* (New Brunswick, N.J.: Rutgers University Press, 1982), esp. 165–66; and Zaionchkovskii, *Pravitel'stvennyi apparat samoderzhavnoi Rossii.*

22. *The Diary of Colonel Landon Carter*, 31 Aug. 1778, II, 1148–49; and Hammond, "Speech on the Justice of Receiving Petitions for the Abolition of Slavery in the District of Columbia," in *Selections from the Letters and Speeches of the Hon. James H. Hammond, of South Carolina* (New York, 1866), 37–38. For Cartwright's argument, see his "Slavery in the Light of Ethnology," in *Cotton Is King, and Pro-Slavery Arguments*, ed. E. N. Elliott (New York: Johnson Reprint Company, 1968; orig. pub. 1860), 689–727. On southern white racism, see Winthrop D. Jordan, *White over Black: American Attitudes toward the Negro, 1550–1812* (Baltimore: Penguin Books, 1969); Fredrickson, *The Black Image in the White Mind*, chs. 2, 3; and William Stanton, *The Leopard's Spots: Scientific Attitudes toward Race in America, 1815–59* (Chicago: University of Chicago Press, 1960). Many of the leading antebellum defenses of slavery are reprinted in Drew Gilpin Faust, ed., *The Ideology of Slavery: Proslavery Thought in the Antebellum South, 1830–1860* (Baton Rouge: Louisiana State University Press, 1981).

23. Karamzin, "Pis'mo sel'skago zhitel'ia," in *Sochineniia Karamzina*, ed. Aleksandr Smirdin (St. Petersburg, 1848), III, 573; and N. M. Druzhinin, *Gosudarstvennye krest'iane i reforma P. D. Kiseleva* (Moscow: Izdatel'stvo Akademii nauk SSSR, 1946–58), I, 147. For other examples of the argument that the condition of state peasants proved peasants' unsuitability for freedom, see M. M. Shcherbatov, "Razsuzhdenie o nyneshnem v 1778 godu pochti povsemestnom golode v Rossii," in *Sochineniia kniazia M. M. Shcherbatova*, I, 645–47; A. I. Komissarenko, "Proekt vvedeniia lichnoi krepostnoi zavisimosti ekonomicheskikh krest'ian v Rossii v pervye gody posle sekuliarizatsii tserkovnykh imuchestv (60-e gody XVIII veka)," in *Ezhegodnik po agrarnoi istorii Vostochnoi Evropy 1970 g.* (Riga, 1977), 96 103; and

"Obozrenie raspolozheniia umov i razlichnykh chastei gosudarstvennogo upravleniia v 1835 godu," in *Krest'ianskoe dvizhenie 1827–1869 godov,* ed. E. A. Morokhovets (Moscow: Gosudarstvennoe sotsial'no-ekonomicheskoe izdatel'stvo, 1931), I, 18. On attitudes toward state peasants and their inadequate supervision, see Druzhinin, *Gosudarstvennye krest'iane i reforma P. D. Kiseleva,* I, 125–47; for the American equivalent, see Ira Berlin, *Slaves without Masters: The Free Negro in the Antebellum South* (New York: Pantheon Books, 1974), 316–80. On the development of nobles' views of themselves as inherently different from peasants, see Romanovich-Slavatinskii, *Dvorianstvo v Rossii,* 58–87.

24. Karamzin, "Pis'mo sel'skago zhitelia," 579; Ivan Boltin, *Primechaniia na Istoriiu drevniia i nyneshniia Rossii g. Leklerka (1788),* II, 243–44; Buturlin to his uncle S. R. Vorontsov, St. Petersburg, 30 July 1803, in *Arkhiv kniazia Vorontsova,* XXXII, 366. For other examples of paternalistic defenses of serfdom, see M. M. Shcherbatov, "Na chitannyi oktiabria 12 chisla golos gospodina deputata goroda Serpeiska, Rodiona Glinkova," in *Sochineniia kniazia M. M. Shcherbatova,* I, 128–29; Shcherbatov, "Primechanie na 13-iu stat'iu II glavy proekta pravam blagorodnykh," ibid., 195–96; "Memoires de la Princesse Dashkaw," in *Arkhiv kniazia Vorontsova,* XXI, 137; "Vozrazhenie grafa Rastopchina, na knigu, sochinennuiu grafom Stroinovskim, o usloviiakh s krest'ianami" (1811), in *Chteniia v Imperatorskom obshchestve istorii i drevnostei rossiiskikh pri Moskovskom universitete,* 30 (1859), no. 3, pt. 5, 40; and *Zapiski, mneniia i perepiski admirala A. S. Shishkova,* ed. N. Kiselev and Iu. Samarin (Berlin, 1870), II, 128–29. On Shcherbatov, see Fedosov, *Iz istorii russkoi obshchestvennoi mysli;* Raeff, "State and Nobility in the Ideology of M. M. Shcherbatov"; and Joan M. Afferica, "The Political and Social Thought of Prince M. M. Shcherbatov, 1733–1790" (Ph.D. diss., Harvard University, 1966). On noble efforts to resist merchant encroachments, see, in addition to the works on Shcherbatov, M. T. Beliavskii, *Krest'ianskii vopros v Rossii nakanune vosstaniia E. I. Pugacheva (Formirovanie antikrepostnicheskoi mysli)* (Moscow: Izdatel'stvo Moskovskogo universiteta, 1965), 87–88, 195–96, 239–43; Wilson Robert Augustine, "The Economic Attitudes and Opinions Expressed by the Russian Nobility in the Great Commission of 1767" (Ph.D. diss., Columbia University, 1969), 81–89; Paul Dukes, *Catherine the Great and the Russian Nobility: A Study Based on the Materials of the Legislative Commission of 1767* (Cambridge: Cambridge University Press, 1967), 113–15, 129–30; and Robert E. Jones, *The Emancipation of the Russian Nobility, 1762–1785* (Princeton: Princeton University Press, 1973), 64–67, 149–51.

25. Stringfellow, "The Bible Argument: or, Slavery in the Light of Divine Revelation," in Elliott, *Cotton Is King,* 491. Many of the best paternalistic defenses were reprinted in the 1850s in two large collections, *The Pro-Slavery Argument* and E. N. Elliott's much expanded volume, *Cotton Is King.* A fascinating and much-studied author not included in these two volumes is George Fitzhugh; see his *Sociology for the South: or, The Failure of*

Free Society (Richmond, Va., 1854), and *Cannibals All! or, Slaves without Masters,* ed. C. Vann Woodward (Cambridge, Mass.: Harvard University Press, 1960; orig. pub. 1857). For an analysis of his writings, see Genovese, *The World the Slaveholders Made,* pt. 2.

26. The quotation is from Thomas R. R. Cobb, *An Inquiry into the Law of Negro Slavery in the United States of America* (Philadelphia, 1858), cxviii. For arguments based on precedent, see Chancellor Harper, "Slavery in the Light of Social Ethics," in Elliott, *Cotton Is King,* 549–52, 574–75, 604–6; J. H. Hammond, "Slavery in the Light of Political Science," ibid., 634–37; Matthew Estes, *A Defence of Negro Slavery as It Exists in the United States* (Montgomery, Ala., 1846), 13–48; Fitzhugh, *Cannibals All!,* passim; and J. D. B. DeBow, "The Origin, Progress, and Prospect of Slavery," *DeBow's Review,* 9 (1850), 9–19. See also Edwin A. Miles, "The Old South and the Classical World," *North Carolina Historical Review,* 48 (1971), 258–75.

27. Hammond, "Speech on the Admission of Kansas . . . , March 4, 1858," in *Selections from the Letters and Speeches of the Hon. James H. Hammond,* 318–19. See also Hammond, "Slavery in the Light of Political Science," 643–46; Thomas R. Dew, "Professor Dew on Slavery," in *The Pro-Slavery Argument,* 325–26, 457–61; Cobb, *An Inquiry into the Law of Negro Slavery,* xxxvi, ccxvii–ccxviii; Fitzhugh, *Cannibals All!,* passim; Henry Hughes, *Treatise on Sociology, Theoretical and Practical* (New York: Negro Universities Press, 1968; orig. pub. 1854), passim; Edwin C. Holland, *A Refutation of the Calumnies Circulated against the Southern and Western States . . .* (New York: Negro Universities Press, 1969; orig. pub. 1822), 45–61; and Stringfellow, "Statistical View of Slavery," 533–34, 539. For an analysis of Hammond's conservative ideology, see Drew Gilpin Faust, *James Henry Hammond and the Old South: A Design for Mastery* (Baton Rouge: Louisiana State University Press, 1982), 260–83.

28. Simms, "The Morals of Slavery," in *The Pro-Slavery Argument,* 265; Hughes, *Treatise on Sociology,* 207; *The Diary of Edmund Ruffin,* ed. William Kauffman Scarborough (Baton Rouge: Louisiana State University Press, 1972), I, 240, 308; Fitzhugh, "Southern Thought," *DeBow's Review,* 23 (1857), 347. For the thesis that the paternalistic defense of slavery increasingly yielded to racist arguments, see John McCardell, *The Idea of a Southern Nation: Southern Nationalists and Southern Nationalism, 1830–1860* (New York: W. W. Norton, 1979), 49–90. Drew Faust has seen South Carolina's leading proslavery spokesmen as alienated intellectuals who through "their essays on slavery won recognition other intellectual endeavors failed to secure"; *A Sacred Circle: The Dilemma of the Intellectual in the Old South* (Baltimore: Johns Hopkins University Press, 1977), 113–31 (quotation, 116).

29. According to Drew Faust, "the Bible served as the core" of the "proslavery mainstream"; see her introduction to *The Ideology of Slavery,* 10. For examples of the many American writings defending slavery on religious grounds, see *Rev. Dr. Richard Furman's Exposition of the Views of the Bap-*

tists, Relative to the Coloured Population of the United States (Charleston, 1822); Charles Hodge, "The Bible Argument on Slavery," in Elliott, *Cotton Is King*, 841–77; Stringfellow, "The Bible Argument"; Albert Taylor Bledsoe, "Liberty and Slavery: or, Slavery in the Light of Moral and Practical Philosophy," in Elliott, *Cotton Is King*, 337–80; and Charles C. Jones, *The Religious Instruction of the Negroes. In the United States* (New York: Negro Universities Press, 1969; orig. pub. 1842). For a fascinating account of how the curse of Ham came to be applied to Africans, see William McKee Evans, "From the Land of Canaan to the Land of Guinea: The Strange Odyssey of the Sons of Ham," *American Historical Review*, 85 (Feb. 1980), 15–43. For the suggestion that the myth of Ham mediated between paternalistic and racial defenses of slavery, see Thomas Virgil Peterson, *Ham and Japheth: The Mythic World of Whites in the Antebellum South* (Metuchen, N.J.: Scarecrow Press and the American Theological Library Association, 1978).

For an example of the Russian argument that serfdom is God-given, see N. V. Gogol, "Russkii pomeshchik," in *Vybrannye mesta iz perepiski s druz'iami* (1847), reprinted in Gogol, *Sobranie sochinenii v semi tomakh* (Moscow: Izdatel'stvo "Khudozhestvennaia literatura," 1967), VI, 316–17. For a description of Russian religious justifications, see S. P. Mel'gunov, "Epokha 'ofitsial'noi narodnosti' i krepostnoe pravo," in *Velikaia reforma: Russkoe obshchestvo i krest'ianskii vopros v proshlom i nastoiashchem. Iubileinoe izdanie*, ed. A. K. Dzhivelegov et al. (Moscow: Izdanie T-va I. D. Sytina, 1911), III, 12–14. On the prominent role of southern clergymen in defending slavery, see H. Shelton Smith, *In His Image, But . . . : Racism in Southern Religion, 1780–1910* (Durham, N.C.: Duke University Press, 1972), 129–64; and Larry Robert Morrison, "The Proslavery Argument in the Early Republic, 1790–1830" (Ph.D. diss., University of Virginia, 1975), 30–59. On the weakness of the Russian parish clergy, see Gregory L. Freeze, *The Russian Levites: Parish Clergy in the Eighteenth Century* (Cambridge, Mass.: Harvard University Press, 1977), 179–217, 222 (quotation).

30. See, for example, M. M. Shcherbatov, "Zapiska po krest'ianskomu voprosu," in his *Neizdannye sochineniia* (Moscow: Ogiz-sotsekgiz, 1935), 8–9; Major General Afanasii Lavrent'evich Komarov's essay in *Trudy Vol'nago ekonomicheskago obshchestva k pooshchreniiu v Rossii zemledeliia i domostroitel'stva*, LXVI (1814), 128–61; and G. R. Derzhavin, *Sochineniia Derzhavina s ob'iasnitel'nymi primechaniiami Ia. Grota* (St. Petersburg, 1876), VI, 774–75; Chancellor Harper, "Harper on Slavery," in *The Pro-Slavery Argument*, 85–94; Estes, *A Defence of Negro Slavery*, 155–62; and J. D. B. DeBow, *The Interest in Slavery of the Southern Non-Slaveholder* (Charleston, 1860), 4–8.

31. See M. M. Shcherbatov, "Zamechaniia Shcherbatova na bol'shoi nakaz Ekateriny," in his *Neizdannye sochineniia*, 55–56; Shcherbatov, "Primechanie na 13-iu stat'iu," 196–97; "Mnenie ob osvobozhdenii krest'ian" (1767), in *Russkii arkhiv* (1871), 288–91; Komissarenko, "Proekt"; Karamzin, "Pis'mo sel'skago zhitelia," 569–74; "Zamechaniia grafa F. V. Ras-

topchina na knigu g-na Stroinovskago" (1811), in *Chteniia v Imperatorskom obshchestve istorii i drevnostei rossiiskikh,* 33 (1860), no. 2, pt. 5, 212–15; Fredericka Teute Schmidt and Barbara Ripel Wilhelm, "Early Proslavery Petitions in Virginia," *William and Mary Quarterly,* 3rd ser., 30 (1973), 138–40; Dew, "Professor Dew on Slavery," 437–40; Harper, "Slavery in the Light of Social Ethics," 617–23; Holland, *A Refutation of the Calumnies,* 61–85; and Estes, *A Defence of Negro Slavery,* 232–52.

32. Boltin, *Primechaniia,* 235–36; Hughes, *Treatise on Sociology;* Hammond, "Speech on the Admission of Kansas," 319; and Estes, *A Defence of Negro Slavery,* 130. See also Shcherbatov, "Zamechaniia Shcherbatova na bol'shoi nakaz Ekateriny," 55; Shishkov, *Zapiski, mneniia i perepiski,* II, 120–24; Cobb, *An Inquiry into the Law of Negro Slavery,* cxii–cxxxiii, ccix–ccxii; the editor's introduction to "Northern and Southern Slavery," *Southern Literary Messenger,* 7 (1841), 341; and Marcus Cunliffe, *Chattel Slavery and Wage Slavery: The Anglo-American Context, 1830–1860* (Athens: University of Georgia Press, 1979). On southern discomfort with the word *slavery,* see Kenneth S. Greenberg, "Revolutionary Ideology and the Proslavery Argument: The Abolition of Slavery in Antebellum South Carolina," *Journal of Southern History,* 42 (1976), 365–84.

33. Shcherbatov, "Razmyshlenie o dvorianstve," in his *Sochineniia,* I, 222; "Mnenie admirala Mordvinova po rabstvu krest'ian, v 1833 godu," in *Chteniia v Imperatorskom obshchestve istorii i drevnostei rossiiskikh,* 30 (1859), no. 3, pt. 5, 56; Harper, "Harper on Slavery," 8; and Hammond, "Slavery in the Light of Political Science," 637–38.

34. The quotation is from Hundley, *Social Relations in Our Southern States,* 149. Although the defense of serfdom was extremely useful to Russian supporters of the status quo, it was not absolutely essential. Under Nicholas I government spokesmen sometimes contrasted conservative Russia and the revolutionary West—using the official line of "Autocracy, Orthodoxy, and Nationality"—without reference to serfdom, and most Slavophiles, although contemptuous of western European decadence, were at least in theory critical of serfdom; see Edward C. Thaden, *Conservative Nationalism in Nineteenth-Century Russia* (Seattle: University of Washington Press, 1964), esp. 19–20; Nicholas V. Riasanovsky, *Nicholas I and Official Nationality in Russia, 1825–1855* (Berkeley: University of California Press, 1961), 84–101, 123, 134–40, 167–68; and Riasanovsky, *Russia and the West in the Teachings of the Slavophiles* (Cambridge, Mass.: Harvard University Press, 1952), 91–119, 136–40. On the reactionary course of antebellum southern thought, see Genovese, *The World the Slaveholders Made,* esp. 122, 152, 171, 196–202; Genovese, "Slavery—The World's Burden," in *Perspectives and Irony in American Slavery,* ed. Harry P. Owens (Jackson: University Press of Mississippi, 1976), 27–32, 40; James C. Hite and Ellen J. Hall, "The Reactionary Evolution of Economic Thought in Antebellum Virginia," *The Virginia Magazine of History and Biography,* 80 (1976), 476–88; Bean, "Anti-Jeffersonianism in the Antebellum South"; and Dickson D. Bruce, Jr.,

The Rhetoric of Conservatism: The Virginia Convention of 1829–1830 and the Conservative Tradition in the South (San Marino, Calif.: Huntington Library, 1982). But for the view that "herrenvolk democracy" enabled most southern whites to adhere to egalitarian tenets, see Fredrickson, *The Black Image in the White Mind,* 61–94.

35. Barbara Leigh Smith Bodichon, *An American Diary, 1857–8,* ed. Joseph W. Reed, Jr. (London: Routledge & Kegan Paul, 1972), 61; George Frederick Holmes, "Theory of Political Individualism," *DeBow's Review,* 22 (Feb. 1857), 134; Hammond, "Speech on the Justice of Receiving Petitions," 43–45. For other examples of proslavery denunciation of northern social trends, see Harper, "Slavery in the Light of Social Ethics," 580–85; Hammond, "Slavery in the Light of Political Science," 117, 149–50; Stringfellow, "Statistical View of Slavery," 524–28, 540–42; Simms, "The Morals of Slavery," 264; Fitzhugh, *Cannibals All!,* 6, 9–11, 85–106, 190–98, 213–16; and Hundley, *Social Relations in Our Southern States,* 14–17.

36. "Zapiska grafa S. R. Vorontsova o dvorianstve," in *Arkhiv kniazia Vorontsova,* XVI, 299–300; Shishkov, *Zapiski, mneniia i perepiski,* II, 121, 129; Shishkov to the Emperor, 12 Dec. 1836, in *Chteniia v Imperatorskom obshchestve istorii i drevnostei rossiiskikh,* 71 (1868), no. 3, pt. 2, 121–28; and "Zamechanie grafa F. V. Rastopchina na knigu g-na Stroinovskago," 204–5. See also Count D. P. Buturlin to S. R. Vorontsov, 22 Feb., 4 April, 30 July 1803, in *Arkhiv kniazia Vorontsova,* XXII, 334–36, 343–45, 364–66.

37. William Sumner Jenkins, *Pro-Slavery Thought in the Old South* (Chapel Hill: University of North Carolina Press, 1935), 3; David Brion Davis, *The Problem of Slavery in Western Culture* (Ithaca, N.Y.: Cornell University Press, 1966), 125–50, 365–445; Davis, *The Problem of Slavery in the Age of Revolution, 1770–1823* (Ithaca, N.Y.: Cornell University Press, 1975), 82–326; Jordan, *White over Black,* 287–304, 429–481; William W. Freehling, "The Founding Fathers and Slavery," *American Historical Review,* 77 (1972), 81–93; Larry Edward Tise, "Proslavery Ideology: A Social and Intellectual History of the Defense of Slavery in America, 1790–1840" (Ph.D. diss., University of North Carolina, 1975), 80–110; John Chester Miller, *The Wolf by the Ears: Thomas Jefferson and Slavery* (New York: Free Press, 1977); V. I. Semevskii, *Krest'ianskii vopros v Rossii v XVIII i pervoi polovine XIX veka* (St. Petersburg, 1888), I, 1–213; Beliavskii, *Krest'ianskii vopros v Rossii;* Jones, *The Emancipation of the Russian Nobility,* 135–42; Augustine, "Economic Attitudes and Opinions," passim; and A. I. Pashkov et al., *A History of Russian Economic Thought: Ninth through Eighteenth Centuries,* ed. John M. Letiche (Berkeley: University of California Press, 1964; orig. pub. in Russian, 1955), 475–575.

38. Timothy Flint, *Recollections of the Last Ten Years,* ed. C. Hartley Grattan (New York: Alfred A. Knopf, 1932; orig. pub. 1826), 329. For similar observations, see Morris Birkbeck, *Notes on a Journey in America, from the Coast of Virginia to the Territory of Illinois* (Ann Arbor, Mich.: Univer-

sity Microfilms, 1968; orig. pub. 1817), 16; Harriet Martineau, *Society in America*, ed. and abridged by Seymour Martin Lipset (Garden City, N.Y.: Doubleday, 1962; orig. pub. 1837), 189; and Kemble, *Journal of a Residence on a Georgian Plantation*, 130. On the triumph of militant proslavery thought, see Jenkins, *Pro-Slavery Thought*, 48–300; Genovese, *The World the Slaveholders Made*, pt. 2; Fredrickson, *The Black Image in the White Mind*, 43–96; Smith, *In His Image*, 129–64; and Ronald T. Takaki, *A Pro-Slavery Crusade: The Agitation to Reopen the African Slave Trade* (New York: Free Press, 1971). On the South as a closed society, see Clement Eaton, *The Freedom-of-Thought Struggle in the Old South* (New York: Harper & Row, 1964).

39. Vorontsov to P. D. Kiselev, Tiflis, 20 Oct. 1847, in *Arkhiv kniazia Vorontsova*, XXXVIII, 149–50. See Semevskii, *Krest'ianskii vopros v Rossii*, I, 336–end, and II, passim; Daniel Field, *The End of Serfdom: Nobility and Bureaucracy in Russia, 1855–1861* (Cambridge, Mass.: Harvard University Press, 1976), 6–7, 35–101, 359–60; Terence Emmons, *The Russian Landed Gentry and the Peasant Emancipation of 1861* (Cambridge: Cambridge University Press, 1968), 29–35; and Nicholas V. Riasanovsky, *A Parting of the Ways: Government and the Educated Public in Russia, 1801–1855* (Oxford: Oxford University Press, 1976), 262–63.

40. The quotation is from *Krest'ianskoe dvizhenie v Rossii v 1826–1849 gg.: Sbornik dokumentov*, ed. A. V. Predtechenskii (Moscow: Izdatel'stvo sotsial'no-ekonomicheskoi literatury, 1961), 344–45. For Gogol's defense of serfdom, see his essay "Russkii pomeshchik," 316–23; Turgenev's most damning portrait of serfdom is *A Sportsman's Notebook*, trans. Charles and Natasha Hepburn (London: Cresset Press, 1950; orig. pub. 1852); on Turgenev as an opponent of serfdom and autocracy, see Harry Hershkowitz, *Democratic Ideas in Turgenev's Works* (New York: Columbia University Press, 1932). For treatment of a prominent southern writer's proslavery convictions, see Jon L. Wakelyn, *The Politics of a Literary Man: William Gilmore Simms* (Westport, Conn.: Greenwood Press, 1973). Because most southern writers advocated slavery, Hannah Stern Goldman, who stressed the parallels between antibondage themes in American and Russian nineteenth-century fiction, was forced to compare Russian novels with those written in the *northern* United States; see her "American Slavery and Russian Serfdom."

41. Olmsted, *A Journey in the Back Country*, 203; he noted that "these views of slavery seem to be universal among people of this class. They were represented to me at least a dozen times." See also Fredrickson, *The Black Image in the White Mind*, 56–90.

42. Several authors have, in varying fashions, stressed the connection among race, democracy, and slavery in the South; see Carl N. Degler, *Neither Black nor White: Slavery and Race Relations in Brazil and the United States* (New York: Macmillan, 1971), 256–60; Degler, "The Irony of American Negro Slavery," in Owens, *Perspectives and Irony in American Slavery*, 3–

12; Morgan, *American Slavery, American Freedom*, 369–86; and Duncan J. MacLeod, *Slavery, Race and the American Revolution* (Cambridge: Cambridge University Press, 1975), 148–84.

43. Semevskii, *Krest'ianskii vopros v Rossii*, I, 336–end, and II, passim; Field, *The End of Serfdom*, 102–40, 172–232, 265–323, 359–60; P. A. Zaionchkovskii, *Otmena krepostnogo prava v Rossii*, 3rd ed. (Moscow: Prosveshchenie, 1968), 1–123; and W. Bruce Lincoln, *Nicholas I: Emperor and Autocrat of All the Russias* (Bloomington: Indiana University Press, 1978), 187–95.

44. Jenkins, *Pro-Slavery Thought in the Old South*, 65–66, 104; Fredrickson, *The Black Image in the White Mind*, 3; Ralph E. Morrow, "The Proslavery Argument Revisited," *Mississippi Valley Historical Review*, 48 (1961), 79–94; Barrington Moore, Jr., *Social Origins of Dictatorship and Democracy: Lord and Peasant in the Making of the Modern World* (Boston: Beacon Press, 1966), 121–22; Jesse T. Carpenter, *The South as a Conscious Minority, 1789–1861* (New York: New York University Press, 1930), 21–76, 173–220; and Cooper, *The South and the Politics of Slavery*, 58–65.

45. Semevskii, *Krest'ianskii vopros v Rossii*, I, 28–33, 393–410, 419–28, and II, 325–40, 349–61; and Field, *The End of Serfdom*, 39–40. For a contemporary observation on the contrast between Russian silence on the peasant question and an outspoken American abolitionism, see N. Tourgueneff, *La Russie et les russes* (Brussels, 1847), II, 113.

46. See, in addition to works cited in notes 39 and 43, B. G. Litvak, *Russkaia derevnia v reforme 1861 goda: Chernozemnyi tsentr, 1861–1895 gg.* (Moscow: Izdatel'stvo "Nauka," 1972); N. M. Druzhinin, *Russkaia derevnia na perelome: 1861–1880 gg.* (Moscow: Izdatel'stvo "Nauka," 1978), 3–83; and A. P. Korelin, *Dvorianstvo v poreformennoi Rossii, 1861–1904 gg.: Sostav, chislennost', korporativnaia organizatsiia* (Moscow: Izdatel'stvo "Nauka," 1979), 52–76, 179–232.

47. On common assumptions shared by slaveholders, see Genovese, *The World the Slaveholders Made*, pt. 1, esp. 3–7, 112; and Davis, *The Problem of Slavery in Western Culture*, 29–121, 222–61. For the suggestion that the antebellum South, as the most paternalistic of New World slave societies, produced the most elaborate and well-rounded defense of slavery, see Genovese, *The World the Slaveholders Made*, esp. 100–3; for the failure of Jamaican planters to develop the argument that slavery was a positive good, see Philip D. Curtin, *Two Jamaicas: The Role of Ideas in a Tropical Colony, 1830–1860* (Cambridge, Mass.: Harvard University Press, 1955), 62–69.

48. See Lowell Joseph Ragatz, *The Fall of the Planter Class in the British Caribbean, 1763–1833: A Study in Social and Economic History* (New York: Century, 1928), 3–80, 453–54; Curtin, *Two Jamaicas*, 15–18, 55, 62–69, 92–95; George M. Fredrickson, "After Emancipation: A Comparative Study of White Responses to the New Order of Race Relations in the American South, Jamaica, & the Cape Colony of South Africa," in *What Was Freedom's Price?*, ed. David G. Sansing (Jackson: University Press of Missis-

sippi, 1978), 76–80, 86; and Fredrickson, *White Supremacy: A Comparative Study in American and South African History* (New York: Oxford University Press, 1981), 163–64. The quotation is from Woodward, "The Price of Freedom," in Sansing, *What Was Freedom's Price?*, 97.

49. Differing views on the relationship between the origins of slavery and racial prejudice in the southern colonies are expressed by, among others, Oscar and Mary F. Handlin, "Origins of the Southern Labor System," *William and Mary Quarterly*, 3rd ser., 7 (1950), 199–222; Carl N. Degler, "Slavery and the Genesis of American Race Prejudice," *Comparative Studies in Society and History*, 2 (1959), 49–66; and Jordan, *White over Black*, pt. 1. For the view that race shaped the essential nature of southern slavery and white southern ideology, see Jordan, *White over Black*; Fredrickson, *The Black Image in the White Mind*, chs. 2, 3; and Degler, "The Irony of American Negro Slavery," 19–25. For the contrary view that class relationships and attitudes were most important, see Genovese, *The World the Slaveholders Made*, esp. 102–13, and Davis, *The Problem of Slavery in Western Culture*, esp. 30–31. There is a huge literature on comparative American race relations, for which the seminal work was Frank Tannenbaum, *Slave and Citizen: The Negro in the Americas* (New York: Alfred A. Knopf, 1946); for an attempt to put much of this literature in perspective, see H. Hoetink, *Slavery and Race Relations in the Americas: An Inquiry into Their Nature and Nexus* (New York: Harper & Row, 1973).

50. On the postemancipation search for alternatives to black labor in the South, see James L. Roark, *Masters without Slaves: Southern Planters in the Civil War and Reconstruction* (New York: W. W. Norton, 1977), 165–68; and Rowland T. Bertoff, "Southern Attitudes toward Immigration, 1865–1914," *Journal of Southern History*, 17 (Aug. 1951), 328–43. On the massive importation of indentured laborers—mostly East Indians—into postemancipation British Guiana, see Alan H. Adamson, *Sugar without Slaves: The Political Economy of British Guiana, 1838–1904* (New Haven: Yale University Press, 1972), 41–56, 104–16.

51. See Introduction, pages 43–45. As Orlando Patterson has shown, nonethnic systems of bondage were unusual but by no means nonexistent among slave societies; see his *Slavery and Social Death: A Comparative Study* (Cambridge, Mass.: Harvard University Press, 1982), 179.

52. On colonial efforts to set blacks apart legally, see A. Leon Higginbotham, Jr., *In the Matter of Color: Race and the American Legal Process, The Colonial Period* (New York: Oxford University Press, 1978). On the Revolution and democracy strengthening white racial consciousness, see Davis, *The Problem of Slavery in the Age of Revolution*, 303; Degler, "The Irony of American Negro Slavery," 12; MacLeod, *Slavery, Race and the American Revolution*, 183–84; and Fredrickson, *The Black Image in the White Mind*, ch. 2. The quotation by "A Southern Lady" is from "British Philanthropy and American Slavery," *DeBow's Review*, 14 (March 1853), 275.

53. On the slavish personality as a function of slavery, see Davis, *The Problem of Slavery in Western Culture*, 47, 59–60; and Genovese, *The World the Slaveholders Made*, 5–6. On similar stereotypes held by colonialists of natives and by American-born of immigrants, see Albert Memmi, *The Colonizer and the Colonized* (Boston: Beacon Press, 1965), 79–88; and John Higham, *Strangers in the Land: Patterns of American Nativism, 1860–1925* (New York: Atheneum, 1963; orig. pub. 1955), esp. 24–27, 131–57, 169–75. On varied uses of the curse of Ham, see Evans, "From the Land of Canaan to the Land of Guinea."

54. Edgar T. Thompson, "The South in Old and New Contexts" (1965), reprinted in Thompson, *Plantation Societies, Race Relations, and the South: The Regimentation of Populations* (Durham, N.C.: Duke University Press, 1975), 325. Numerous authors have written on variations in racial attitudes; see, e.g., Degler, *Neither Black nor White*, 92, 226–64; Hoetink, *Slavery and Race Relations in the Americas;* and Fredrickson, *White Supremacy.* On the contrast between southern white racial attitudes in the colonial and antebellum periods, see Jordan, *White over Black*, 388, 456, 528–29; and Fredrickson, *The Black Image in the White Mind*, 1–2, 71–90.

55. Quotations are from *State v. Levy and Dreyfous*, 5 La. An 64, Jan. 1850, in *Judicial Cases concerning American Slavery and the Negro*, ed. Helen Tunnicliff Catterall (New York: Octagon Books, 1968; orig. pub. 1926–37), III, 601; *Real Estate of Mrs. Hardcastle ads. Porcher, Escheater*, Harper 495, 1826, ibid., II, 334–35; and *State v. Cantey*, 2 Hill 614, May 1835, ibid., II, 358–59. On Louisiana's three-tier system in comparative perspective, see Laura Foner, "The Free People of Color in Louisiana and St. Domingue: A Comparative Portrait of Two Three-Tier Societies," *Journal of Social History*, 3 (1970), 406–30. For a fascinating study of a group of privileged free Negroes in Louisiana, see Gary B. Mills, *The Forgotten People: Cane River's Creoles of Color* (Baton Rouge: Louisiana State University Press, 1977).

56. The best general treatment of antebellum attitudes toward free blacks is Berlin, *Slaves without Masters*, 312, 316–40, 348–80. Statistics on the proportion of blacks who were free are from ibid., 137.

57. The best general work on the state peasants is Druzhinin's two-volume *Gosudarstvennye krest'iane i reforma P. D. Kiseleva.* On the reforms of 1837–41, see ibid., I, 476–572. On the peasants' negative responses to them, see ibid., II, 456–524; *Materialy dlia istorii krepostnago prava v Rossii. Izvlecheniia iz sekretnykh otchetov Ministerstva vnutrennikh del za 1836–1856 g.* (Berlin, 1872), 71–74, 93–99; and M. S. Valevskii, "Volneniia krest'ian v Zaural'skoi chasti Permskago kraia v 1842–1843 gg." (1844), in *Russkaia starina*, 26 (1879), 411–32, 627–46. On the changing proportion of serfs and state peasants, see N. M. Shepukova, "Izmenenie udel'nogo vesa chastnovladel'cheskogo krest'ianstva v sostave naseleniia Evropeiskoi Rossii (XVIII-pervaia polovina XIX v.)," *Voprosy istorii*, 1959, no. 12, 131. For two examples of numerous foreign comments on the relatively favorable

condition of state peasants, see Xavier Hommaire de Hell, *Travels in the Steppes of the Caspian Sea, the Crimea, the Caucasus, &c.* (London, 1847), 108–9; and Robert Pinkerton, *Russia: or Miscellaneous Observations on the Past and Present State of That Country and Its Inhabitants* (London, 1833), 281–82.

4. Community and Culture

1. Charles C. Jones, *The Religious Instruction of the Negroes. In the United States* (New York: Negro Universities Press, 1969; orig. pub. Savannah, Georgia, 1842), 110; and Germain de Lagny, *The Knout and the Russians; or the Muscovite Empire, the Czar, and His People,* trans. John Bridgeman (London, 1854), 155.

2. For opposing positions, see E. Franklin Frazier, *The Negro Family in the United States,* revised and abridged (Chicago: University of Chicago Press, 1966; orig. ed. 1939), 15; and Melville J. Herskovits, *The Myth of the Negro Past* (Boston: Beacon Press, 1958; orig. pub. 1941), 145–291. For a recent view, see David Roediger, "The Meaning of Africa for the American Slave," *Journal of Ethnic Studies,* 4 (Winter 1977), 1.

3. Allan Kulikoff, "The Origins of Afro-American Society in Tidewater Maryland and Virginia, 1700 to 1790," *William and Mary Quarterly,* 3rd ser., 35 (April 1978), 256–57; Peter H. Wood, *Black Majority: Negroes in Colonial South Carolina from 1670 through the Stono Rebellion* (New York: Alfred A. Knopf, 1974), 56–62, 168–91; Albert J. Raboteau, *Slave Religion: The "Invisible Institution" in the Antebellum South* (New York: Oxford University Press, 1978), 41–49; Lawrence W. Levine, *Black Culture and Black Consciousness: Afro-American Folk Thought from Slavery to Freedom* (New York: Oxford University Press, 1977), 19–25, 53–61; Leroi Jones, *Blues People: Negro Music in White America* (New York: William Morrow, 1963), 12–27; Eileen Southern, *The Music of Black Americans: A History* (New York: W. W. Norton, 1971), 135–38, 160–63, 215–23; Dena J. Epstein, *Sinful Tunes and Spirituals: Black Folk Music to the Civil War* (Urbana: University of Illinois Press, 1977), esp. 77–98, 343–48; Charles Joyner, *Down by the Riverside: A South Carolina Slave Community* (Urbana: University of Illinois Press, 1984), passim, esp. 58–59, 144–53, 194–224; John W. Blassingame, *The Slave Community: Plantation Life in the Antebellum South* (New York: Oxford University Press, 1972 [all references are to the first, 1972 edition of this book, except when otherwise indicated]), 17–75; Eugene D. Genovese, *Roll, Jordan, Roll: The World the Slaves Made* (New York: Pantheon Books, 1974), 209–32, 431–41; Gerald W. Mullin, *Flight and Rebellion: Slave Resistance in Eighteenth-Century Virginia* (New York: Oxford University Press, 1972), esp. 34–62, 83–98, 161–63; and Johnson Ajibade Adefila, "Slave Religion in the Old South: A Study of the Role of Africanisms in the Black Response to Christianity" (Ph.D. diss., Brandeis University, 1975), 78–96, 156.

4. John W. Blassingame, *The Slave Community: Plantation Life in the Antebellum South,* revised and enlarged ed. (New York: Oxford University Press, 1979), 98; Raboteau, *Slave Religion,* 5–86 (quotation, 86); Herskovits, *The Myth of the Negro Past,* 62–63; Nathan Irvin Huggins, *Black Odyssey: The Afro-American Ordeal in Slavery* (New York: Random House, 1977), 3–15 (quotation, 7); and Paul Bohannan, *Africa and African Forms* (Garden City, N.Y.: National History Press, 1964), 174–84. For works that emphasize the African roots of slave religion and customs, see Mechal Sobel, *Trabelin' On: The Slave Journey to an Afro-Baptist Faith* (Westport, Conn.: Greenwood Press, 1979); David R. Roediger, "And Die in Dixie: Funerals, Death, & Heaven in the Slave Community, 1700–1865," *Massachusetts Review,* 12 (Spring 1981), 163–83; and Joyner, *Down by the Riverside.*

5. Quotations are from George P. Rawick, *From Sundown to Sunup: The Making of the Black Community* (Westport, Conn.: Greenwood Publishing Company, 1972), xix; Charles Ball, *Slavery in the United States: A Narrative of the Life and Adventures of Charles Ball, a Black Man* (New York: 1837), 200–3; and Abraham Chambers, in *The American Slave: A Composite Autobiography Supplement, Series 1,* ed. George P. Rawick (Westport, Conn.: Greenwood Press, 1977), I, 87. For descriptions of the slave quarters, see Kenneth M. Stampp, *The Peculiar Institution: Slavery in the Ante-Bellum South* (New York: Vintage Books, 1956), 292–95; Thomas L. Webber, *Deep like the Rivers: Education in the Slave Quarter Community, 1831–1865* (New York: W. W. Norton, 1978), 324; and Frederick Law Olmsted, *The Cotton Kingdom: A Traveller's Observations on Cotton and Slavery in the American South* (New York, 1861), I, 237–38.

6. Webber, *Deep like the Rivers;* Blassingame, *The Slave Community;* Levine, *Black Culture and Black Consciousness,* 25, 29; Thomas Bender, *Community and Social Change in America* (New Brunswick, N.J.: Rutgers University Press, 1978), 7. For a recent work that combines geographic and relational meanings of *community,* see Joyner, *Down by the Riverside,* esp. 132. Dictionary definitions are from *The American Heritage Dictionary of the English Language* (New York: Dell Publishing Company, 1970), 146; and *The Oxford Universal Dictionary on Historical Principles,* 3rd ed., revised (Oxford: Clarendon Press, 1955), 352.

7. Jerome Blum, *Lord and Peasant in Russia from the Ninth to the Nineteenth Century* (Princeton: Princeton University Press, 1961), 504–5; Richard Pipes, *Russia under the Old Regime* (New York: Charles Scribner's, 1974), 16–19; George L. Yaney, *The Systematization of Russian Government: Social Evolution in the Domestic Administration of Imperial Russia, 1711–1905* (Urbana: University of Illinois Press, 1973), 129–43; Michael Confino, *Systèmes agraires et progrès agricole: L'assolement triennal en Russie aux XVIIIᵉ–XIXᵉ siècles* (Paris: Mouton, 1969), 92–127; Mary Matossian, "The Peasant Way of Life," in *The Peasant in Nineteenth-Century Russia,* ed. Wayne S. Vucinich (Stanford: Stanford University Press, 1969), 1–3. Statistics on villages in Riazan province are from *Materialy dlia statistiki*

Rossiiskoi imperii . . . (St. Petersburg, 1841), II, table insert after 18. *Derevnia* means both "small village" (or "hamlet") and "country"; *sel'skii,* or "rural," is the adjectival form of the noun *selo,* "village."

8. The best study of the serf commune is V. A. Aleksandrov, *Sel'skaia obshchina v Rossii (XVII-nachalo XIX v.)* (Moscow: Izdatel'stvo "Nauka," 1976) (quotation, 176), which contains (3–43) a lengthy historiographical treatment of the subject as well. See also his "Sel'skaia obshchina i votchina v Rossii (XVII-nachalo XIX v.)," *Istoricheskie zapiski,* 89 (1972), 231–94, and *Obychnoe pravo krepostnoi denevni Rossii XVIII-nachalo XIX v.* (Moscow: Izdatel'stvo "Nauka," 1984); L. S. Prokof'eva, *Krest'ianskaia obshchina v Rossii vo vtoroi polovine XVIII-pervoi polovine XIX v. (na materialakh votchin Sheremetevykh)* (Leningrad: "Nauka" Leningradskoe otdelenie, 1981); and E. N. Baklanova, *Krest'ianskii dvor i obshchina na russkom Severe: Konets XVII-nachalo XVIII v.* (Moscow: Izdatel'stvo "Nauka," 1976), 138–91.

9. On varying patterns of communal authority, see Aleksandrov, *Sel'skaia obshchina v Rossii,* 111–80, and Aleksandrov, "Sel'skaia obshchina i votchina v Rossii."

10. Aleksandrov, *Sel'skaia obshchina v Rossii,* 117–18, 151–65; Blum, *Lord and Peasant in Russia,* 524–25; V. I. Semevskii, *Krest'iane v tsarstvovanie Imperatritsy Ekateriny II,* 2nd ed. (St. Petersburg: Tipografiia M. M. Stasiulevicha, 1901–3), I, 288–89; E. I. Indova, *Krepostnoe khoziaistvo v nachale XIX veka po materialam votchinnogo arkhiva Vorontsovykh* (Moscow: Izdatel'stvo Akademii nauk SSSR, 1955), 61–62; Prokof'eva, *Krest'ianskaia obshchina v Rossii,* passim, esp. 21.

11. Quotations are from Anna Petrovna Sheremeteva, "Instruktsiia 1727 goda Grigoriiu Voroblevskomu, naznachennomu prikazchikom v iukhotskuiu volost'," in K. N. Shchepetov, *Krepostnoe pravo v votchinakh Sheremetevykh (1708–1885)* (Moscow: Izdanie dvortsa-muzeia, 1947), 266; "Nakaz kn. A. M. Cherkasskogo prikazchiku sela Markova (Moskovskogo uezda)" (1719), in "Nakazy votchinnym prikazchikam pervoi chetverti XVIII v.," ed. I. F. Petrovskaia, *Istoricheskii arkhiv,* 8 (1953), 250; and P. B. Sheremetev, "Instruktsiia Iaroslavskoi moei votchiny iukhotskoi volosti prikashchiku . . ." (1764), in Shchepetov, *Krepostnoe pravo v votchinakh Sheremetevykh,* 272. See also Aleksandrov, *Sel'skaia obshchina v Rossii,* 118–23; Prokof'eva, *Krest'ianskaia obshchina v Rossii,* 34–43; Michael Confino, *Domaines et seigneurs en Russie vers la fin du XVIIIᵉ siècle: Etude de structures agraires et de mentalités économiques* (Paris: Institut d'études slaves de l'Université de Paris, 1963), 82–85; Semevskii, *Krest'iane v tsarstvovanie Imperatritsy Ekateriny II,* I, 248–54, 290–92; Shchepetov, *Krepostnoe pravo v votchinakh Sheremetevykh,* 130–32; and Indova, *Krepostnoe khoziaistvo v nachale XIX veka,* 60–62.

12. In addition to sources in notes 8–11, see Chapter 1, pages 62–63.

13. D. I. Petrikeev, *Krupnoe krepostnoe khoziaistvo XVII v. po materialam votchiny boiarina B. I. Morozova* (Leningrad: Izdatel'stvo "Nauka,"

1967), 80. See also Indova, *Krepostnoe khoziaistvo v nachale XIX veka,* 59; I. V. Chernyshev, *Agrarno-krest'ianskaia politika Rossii za 150 let* (Petrograd: Tipografiia Ministerstva putei soobshcheniia, 1918), 27, 30; and Shchepetov, *Krepostnoe pravo v votchinakh Sheremetevykh,* 130–32.

14. Aleksandrov, *Sel'skaia obshchina v Rossii,* 178. See also Prokof'eva, *Krest'ainskaia obshchina v Rossii,* 45–53, 128.

15. "Nakaz D. A. Shepeleva prikazchiku sel'tsa Glinka (Mikhailovskogo uezda) Ivanu Balashevu" (1718), in Petrovskaia, "Nakazy votchinnym prikazchikam," 231 (quotation); Aleksandrov, *Sel'skaia obshchina v Rossii,* 243–73; Prokof'eva, *Krest'ianskaia obshchina v Rossii,* 151–57.

16. "Nakaz kn. A. M. Cherkasskogo," 253–54.

17. V. A. Aleksandrov, "Zemel'no-peredel'nyi tip sel'skoi obshchiny v pozdnefeodal'noi Rossii (XVIII-nachalo XIX v.)," *Voprosy istorii,* 1975, no. 10, 53–70; Baklanova, *Krest'ianskii dvor i obshchina na russkom Severe,* 144–54; Prokof'eva, *Krest'ianskaia obshchina v Rossii,* 56–93; Blum, *Lord and Peasant in Russia,* 508–23; Semevskii, *Krest'iane v tsarstvovanie Imperatritsy Ekateriny II,* I, 103–15; L. N. Vdovina, "Zemel'nye peredely v krest'ianskoi obshchine v 20–50-e gody XVIII veka (po materialam monastyrskikh votchin)," *Istoriia SSSR,* 1973, no. 4, 140–51; and I. I. Ignatovich, *Pomeshchich'i krest'iane nakanune osvobozhdeniia,* 2nd ed. (Moscow: I. D. Sytin, 1910), 149–51.

18. For an article attacking the harmful consequences of common landholding and frequent repartition, see Aleksandr Mishurinskii, "O vrednom obyknovenii krest'ian delit' ezhegodno luga i pashni," *Zemledel'cheskaia gazeta,* 26 April 1835, 271–72. Aleksandrov argues that serfs had a dualistic attitude toward the land, looking upon it as both communal and private, with a gradual evolution from the former to the latter; Aleksandrov, *Sel'skaia obshchina v Rossii,* 236–41.

19. Report of staff officer Ivashentsov to Chief of the Corps of Gendarmes V. A. Dolgorukov, Riazan province, 14 Nov. 1856, in *Krest'ianskoe dvizhenie v Rossii v 1850–1856 gg.: Sbornik dokumentov,* ed. S. B. Okun' (Moscow: Izdatel'stvo sotsial'no-ekonomicheskoi literatury, 1963), 555. For emphasis on the collective nature of serf protest, see B. G. Litvak, "O nekotorykh chertakh psikhologii russkikh krepostnykh pervoi poloviny XIX v.," in *Istoriia i psikhologiia,* ed. B. F. Porshnev and L. I. Antsyferova (Moscow: Izdatel'stvo "Nauka," 1971), 206–10.

20. The quotation is from Solomon Northup, *Twelve Years a Slave . . .* (New York, 1855), 226–27. On Davis's jury system, see Janet Sharp Hermann, *The Pursuit of a Dream* (New York: Oxford University Press, 1981), 12–13. On black drivers and overseers, see James Herbert Stone, "Black Leadership in the Old South: The Slave Drivers of the Rice Kingdom" (Ph.D. diss., Florida State University, 1976); James M. Clifton, "The Rice Driver: His Role in Slave Management," *South Carolina Historical Magazine,* 82 (Oct. 1981), 331–53; Julia Floyd Smith, *Slavery and Rice Culture in Low Country Georgia, 1750–1860* (Knoxville: University of Tennessee Press,

1985), 66–75; William L. Van Deburg, *The Slave Drivers: Black Agricultural Labor Supervisors in the Antebellum South* (Westport, Conn.: Greenwood Press, 1979); Eugene D. Genovese, *Roll, Jordan, Roll: The World the Slaves Made* (New York: Pantheon Books, 1974), 365–81; Leslie Howard Owens, *This Species of Property: Slave Life and Culture in the Old South* (New York: Oxford University Press, 1976), 121–35; Weymouth T. Jordan, *Hugh Davis and His Alabama Plantation* (University, Ala.: University of Alabama Press, 1948), 62–65; and Robert William Fogel and Stanley L. Engerman, *Time on the Cross: The Economics of American Negro Slavery* (Boston: Little, Brown, 1974), 38–39, 200–1, 210–12. For letters from black overseers to their masters, see Robert S. Starobin, ed., *Blacks in Bondage: Letters of American Slaves* (New York: New Viewpoints, 1974), 12–35, 42–56.

21. *Narrative of the Life of Frederick Douglass, an American Slave* (New York: New American Library, 1968; orig. pub. 1845), 30. Van Deburg notes that the slave narratives "contain certain data which could be used to support the stereotype of the slave supervisory elite as brutal, dehumanized tools of the white master class," but he dismisses these as exaggerated accounts designed to curry favor with whites by blaming blacks for the worst cruelties of slavery; Van Deburg, "The Slave Drivers of Arkansas: A New View from the Narratives," *Arkansas Historical Quarterly,* 35 (Autumn 1976), 238. For an ex-slave's recollection of a brutal driver, see the testimony of Henry Cheatam in Rawick, *The American Slave . . . Supplement, Series 1,* I, 89.

22. Fitzhugh to John Withers, 5 June 1682, in *William Fitzhugh and His Chesapeake World, 1676–1701: The Fitzhugh Letters and Other Documents,* ed. Richard Beale Davis (Chapel Hill: University of North Carolina Press, 1963), 119. On the eighteenth-century transformation of slave family life in the Chesapeake colonies, see Russell R. Menard, "The Maryland Slave Population, 1658 to 1730: A Demographic Portrait of Blacks in Four Counties," *William and Mary Quarterly,* 3rd ser., 32 (Jan. 1975), 42–47; Allan Kulikoff, "A 'Prolifick' People: Black Population Growth in the Chesapeake Colonies, 1700–1790," *Southern Studies,* 16 (Winter 1977), 391–412; Kulikoff, "The Origins of Afro-American Society in Tidewater Maryland and Virginia, 1700 to 1790," *William and Mary Quarterly,* 3rd ser., 35 (April 1978), 240–45, 249; Carville V. Earle, *The Evolution of a Tidewater Settlement System: All Hallow's Parish, Maryland, 1650–1783* (Chicago: University of Chicago Department of Geography Research Paper no. 170, 1975), 49–50; and Gloria L. Main, *Tobacco Colony: Life in Early Maryland, 1650–1720* (Princeton: Princeton University Press, 1982), 126–37. A somewhat different pattern for South Carolina is suggested by Wood, *Black Majority,* 145, 150–54. For the argument that the American slave family emerged in the eighteenth century, see Herbert G. Gutman, *The Black Family in Slavery and Freedom, 1750–1925* (New York: Pantheon Books, 1976), 327–57. On slave population growth, see Epilogue, pages 363–64.

23. Gutman, *The Black Family in Slavery and Freedom,* passim, esp. 11, 50–51. See also Richard S. Dunn, "A Tale of Two Plantations: Slave Life at

Mesopotamia in Jamaica and Mount Airy in Virginia, 1799 to 1828," *William and Mary Quarterly*, 3rd ser., 34 (Jan. 1977), 58–59; C. G. Holland, "The Slave Population on the Plantation of John C. Cohoon, Jr. Nansemond County, Virginia, 1811–1863: Selected Demographic Characteristics," *Virginia Magazine of History and Biography*, 80 (July 1972), 337–38; Melvin Zelnik, "Fertility of the American Negro in 1830 and 1850," *Population Studies*, 20 (July 1966), 82; Albert Virgil House, ed., *Planter Management and Capitalism in Ante-Bellum Georgia: The Journal of Hugh Fraser Grant, Ricegrower* (New York: Columbia University Press, 1954), 258–62; and Ulrich B. Phillips and James David Glunt, eds., *Florida Plantation Records from the Papers of George Noble Jones* (St. Louis: Missouri Historical Society, 1927), 329–31, 511–12, 537–38, 547–49, 551–52, 561–62, 566–71.

24. Quotations are from "Governor Hammond's Letters on Slavery, 3," *DeBow's Review*, 8 (Feb. 1850), 122; Robert Smalls, in *Slave Testimony: Two Centuries of Letters, Speeches, Interviews, and Autobiographies*, ed. John W. Blassingame (Baton Rouge: Louisiana State University Press, 1977), 373–74; and *Narrative of the Life of Moses Grandy, Late a Slave in the United States of America*, 2nd ed. (Boston, 1844), 5–6, 11. On naming practices among slaves, see Gutman, *The Black Family in Slavery and Freedom*, 186–256, 373–74; and Cheryll Ann Cody, "Naming, Kinship, and Estate Dispersal: Notes on Slave Family Life on a South Carolina Plantation, 1786 to 1833," *William and Mary Quarterly*, 3rd ser., 39 (Jan. 1982), 192–211.

25. For the view that slaves internalized their owners' morality and that strong slave families resulted primarily from the policies of slaveowners, see Fogel and Engerman, *Time on the Cross*, 78–86, 126–44. On black families as a source of emotional strength for slaves, see especially Gutman, *The Black Family in Slavery and Freedom*, and Genovese, *Roll, Jordan, Roll*, 443–523. Also see Justin Labinjoh, "The Sexual Life of the Oppressed: An Examination of the Family Life of the Ante-Bellum Slaves," *Phylon*, 35 (Dec. 1974), 375–97; Webber, *Deep like the Rivers*, 111–27, 157–79; Escott, *Slavery Remembered*, 47–51; and Owens, *This Species of Property*, 191–213.

26. Gutman, *The Black Family in Slavery and Freedom*, 86–95, 104–47, 155–68, 61–86; Cody, "Naming, Kinship, and Estate Dispersal," 193; and Genovese, *Roll, Jordan, Roll*, 458. See also Richard H. Steckel, "Slave Marriage and the Family," *Journal of Family History*, 5 (Winter 1980), 406–21. Catherine Clinton found cousin marriage rates of 12.4 percent and 12.3 percent among antebellum plantation owners and wives; see her book *The Plantation Mistress: Woman's World in the Old South* (New York: Pantheon Books, 1982), 233.

27. See especially Deborah G. White, "Female Slaves: Sex Roles and Status in the Antebellum Plantation South," *Journal of Family History*, 8 (Fall 1983), 248–61; and White, *Ar'n't I a Woman?: Female Slaves in the Plantation South* (New York: W. W. Norton, 1985). See also Jacqueline Jones, "My Mother Was Much of a Woman," *Feminist Studies*, 8 (Summer 1982), 235–69. On the prevalence of field work among slave women, see Carole

Shammas, "Black Women's Work and the Evolution of Plantation Society in Virginia," *Labor History*, 26 (Winter 1985), 11–20.

28. *Narrative of the Life of Frederick Douglass*, 22–23; *Narrative of the Life and Adventures of Henry Bibb, an American Slave* (New York, 1849), 14; *The Narrative of William W. Brown, a Fugitive Slave* ... (Reading, Mass.: Addison-Wesley, 1969; orig. pub. 1847), 1, 4. For other recollections of forced separations, see *An Autobiography of the Reverend Josiah Henson* (Reading, Mass.: Addison-Wesley, 1969; orig. pub. 1849), 13–18; Elizabeth Keckley, *Behind the Scenes. Or, Thirty Years a Slave, and Four Years in the White House* (New York, 1868), 22–30; *The Rev. J. W. Loguen, as a Slave and as a Freeman. A Narrative of a Real Life* (Syracuse, N.Y., 1859), 113–22; and Jacob Stroyer, *Sketches of my Life in the South*, pt. 1 (Salem, 1879), 28–31.

29. *Narrative of the Life of Moses Grandy*, 16; Epps testimony in Charles L. Perduc ct al., eds., *Weevils in the Wheat: Interviews with Virginia Ex-Slaves* (Charlottesville: University Press of Virginia, 1976), 89.

30. For sex ratios among serfs, see Petr Keppen, *Deviataia reviziia. Izsledovanie o chisle zhitelei v Rossii v 1851 godu* (St. Petersburg, 1857), 10; A. Troinitskii, *Krepostnoe naselenie v Rossii, po 10–i narodnoi perepisi* (St. Petersburg, 1861), 53–54; and *Materialy dlia statistiki rossiiskoi imperii*, I, 205–19. On the near universality of marriage among serfs, see Peter Czap, Jr., "Marriage and Peasant Joint Family in the Era of Serfdom," in *The Family in Imperial Russia: New Lines of Historical Research*, ed. David L. Ransel (Urbana: University of Illinois Press, 1978), 111, 114.

31. On age of marriage, see Czap, "Marriage and Peasant Joint Family," 108–14; and Steven L. Hoch, "Serfs in Imperial Russia: Demographic Insights," *Journal of Interdisciplinary History*, 13 (Autumn 1982), 229–30. Average sizes of peasant households are given in Ia. E. Vodarskii, *Naselenie Rossii v kontse XVII-nachale XVIII veka (Chislennost', soslovno-klassovyi sostav, razmeshchenie)* (Moscow: Izdatel'stvo "Nauka," 1977), 47–49, 114; V. D. Nazarov and Iu. A. Tikhonov, "Krest'ianskii i bobyl'skii dvor v svetskikh vladeniiakh tsentral'nykh uezdov pervoi poloviny XVII veka," *Istoriia SSSR*, 1977, no. 4, 159–60; Andrejs Plakans, "Peasant Farmsteads and Households in the Baltic Littoral, 1797," *Comparative Studies in Society and History*, 17 (Jan. 1975), 21–24; V. A. Aleksandrov, "Tipologiia russkoi krest'ianskoi sem'i v epokhu feodalizma," *Istoriia SSSR*, 1981, no. 3, 84–87; Aleksandrov, *Obychnoe pravo krepostnoi derevni*, 50–57; Hoch, "Serfs in Imperial Russia," 233; Peter Czap, Jr., "The Perennial Multiple Family Household, Mishino, Russia 1782–1858," *Journal of Family History*, 7 (Spring 1982), 11; and Michael Mitterauer and Alexander Kagan, "Russian and Central European Family Structures: A Comparative View," ibid., 109–10. Additional figures can be computed from data in K. V. Sivkov, ed., *Materialy po istorii krest'ianskogo i pomeshchich'ego khoziaistva pervoi chetverti XVIII v.* (Moscow: Izdatel'stvo Akademii nauk SSSR, 1951), passim; Shchepetov, *Krepostnoe pravo v votchinakh Sheremetevykh*, 286–87, 348–

53; Petrikeev, *Krupnoe krepostnoe khoziaistvo XVII v.*, 190–94; and *Materialy dlia statistiki rossiiskoi imperii*, II, insert after 18.

32. Plakans, "Peasant Farmsteads and Households in the Baltic Littoral," 21–24; Plakans, "Seigneurial Authority and Peasant Family Life: The Baltic Area in the Eighteenth Century," *Journal of Interdisciplinary History*, 5 (Spring 1975), 642–48, 654; and Plakans, "Parentless Children in the Social Revisions: A Study of Methodology and Social Fact," in Ransel, *The Family in Imperial Russia*, 80–86.

33. For household members on Bezobrazov's estate, see Sivkov, *Materialy po istorii krest'ianskogo i pomeshchich'ego khoziaistva*, 37–39. See also E. N. Baklanova, "K kharakteristike krest'ianskogo dvora kak khoziaistvennoi edinitsy v Vologodskom uezde v kontse XVII veka," in *Ezhegodnik po agrarnoi istorii Vostochnoi Evropy 1970 g.* (Riga, 1977), 87–88; Baklanova, *Krest'ianskii dvor i obshchina na russkom Severe*, 31–34; Czap, "Marriage and Peasant Joint Family," 118–21; Czap, "The Perennial Multiple Family Household," 12; Hoch, "Serfs in Imperial Russia," 230–39; Mitterauer and Kagan, "Russian and Central European Family Structures," 110–11; Rodney D. Bohac, "Peasant Inheritance Strategies in Russia," *Journal of Interdisciplinary History*, 18 (Summer 1985), 26–27; Aleksandrov, *Obychnoe pravo krepostnoi derevni*, 57–67; Aleksandrov, "Tipologiia russkoi krest'ianskoi sem'i," 88–92; Maxime Kovalevsky, *Modern Customs and Ancient Laws of Russia: Being the Ilchester Lectures for 1889–90* (London, 1891), 47–60; and Anatole Leroy-Beaulieu, *The Russia Peasant* (Sandoval, N.M.: Coronado Press, 1962; orig. 3 vols. in French, 1881–89), 92–102.

34. "Nakaz kn. A. M. Cherkasskogo," 254; Semevskii, *Krest'iane v tsarstvovanie Imperatritsy Ekateriny II*, I, 319–21; Chernyshev, *Agrarno-krest'ianskaia politika Rossii*, 20–21; Czap, "Marriage and Peasant Joint Family," 119; Czap, "The Perennial Multiple Family Household," 12, 17–18, 23–25; Hoch, "Serfs in Imperial Russia," 239–41; Bohac, "Peasant Inheritance Strategies in Russia," 30–42. On changes in family size over time, see Vodarskii, *Naselenie Rossii v kontse XVII-nachale XVIII veka*, 47–49. On the impact of the household tax, see Richard Hellie, *Slavery in Russia, 1450–1725* (Chicago: University of Chicago Press, 1982), 413, 705–6; and Baklanova, *Krest'ianskii dvor i obshchina na russkom Severe*, 16–17. For the persistence of somewhat smaller families in the north, see Aleksandrov, "Tipologiia russkoi krest'ianskoi sem'i," 84–87; Aleksandrov, *Obychnoe pravo krepostnoi derevni*, 55–57; Baklanova, *Krest'ianskii dvor i obshchina na russkom Severe*, 16, 39–40; and Mitterauer and Kagan, "Russian and Central European Family Structures," 109–10.

35. Chappé d'Auteroche, *A Journey into Siberia* (New York: Arno Press, 1970; orig. pub. London, 1770), 304; and W. R. S. Ralston, *The Songs of the Russian People, as Illustrative of Slavonic Mythology and Russian Social Life* (London, 1872), 9–10. See also Aleksandrov, *Sel'skaia obshchina v Rossii*, 294–310; Aleksandrov, *Obychnoe pravo krepostnoi derevni*, 174–86; Hoch, "Serfs in Imperial Russia," 237–39; Czap, "The Perennial Multiple

Family Household," 23–25; Matossian, "The Peasant Way of Life," 17–18; Leroy-Beaulieu, *The Russian Peasant*, 92–108; and Kovalevsky, *Modern Customs and Ancient Laws of Russia*, 44–47.

36. N. N. Shipov, "Istoriia moei zhizni: Razskaz byvshago krepostnago krest'ianina N. N. Shipova," *Russkaia starina*, 30 (1881), 141. For another peasant account of a courtship, see *Vesti o Rossii: Povest' v stikhakh krepostnogo krest'ianina, 1830–1840 gg.*, ed. T. G. Snytko (Iaroslavl: Iaroslavskoe knizhnoe izdatel'stvo, 1961), passim.

37. Y. M. Sokolov, *Russian Folklore*, trans. Catherine Ruth Smith (New York: Macmillan, 1950), 203. See also W. R. S. Ralston, *Russian Folk-Tales* (London, 1873), 299–300; Ralston, *The Songs of the Russian People*, 284–96; Matossian, "The Peasant Way of Life," 18; Sokolov, *Russian Folklore*, 515–17; Czap, "Marriage and Peasant Joint Family," 104–5; and Robert Johnston, *Travels through Parts of the Russian Empire* (New York: Arno Press, 1970; orig. pub. London, 1815), 189–90.

38. For this and the next two paragraphs, see Ralston, *The Songs of the Russian People*, 2–8, 32–39, 262–96, 314–44; Sokolov, *Russian Folklore*, 204–8, 213–40; Matossian, "The Peasant Way of Life," 26–28; Friedrich Christian Weber, *The Present State of Russia* (London, 1823), 121 (quotation). For a description of an elaborate wedding ceremony of a well-to-do serf, see Shipov, "Istoriia moei zhizni," 141–45.

39. V. A. Aleksandrov, "Semeino-imushchestvennye otnosheniia po obychnomu pravu v russkoi krepostnoi derevne XVIII-nachale XIX veka," *Istoriia SSSR*, 1979, no. 6, 37–54 (quotation, 45); Aleksandrov, *Obychnoe pravo krepostnoi derevni*, 137–249; Kovalevsky, *Modern Customs and Ancient Laws of Russia*, 47–61 (quotation, 61). See also Czap, "The Perennial Multiple Family Household," 23–25.

40. Roediger, "And Die in Dixie"; Genovese, *Roll, Jordan, Roll*, 194–202, 475–81; Gutman, *The Black Family in Slavery and Freedom*, passim (quotation, 165).

41. Testimony of Sarah Wilson in Norman R. Yetman, ed., *Life under the "Peculiar Institution": Selections from the Slave Narrative Collection* (New York: Holt, Rinehart and Winston, 1970), 325–26. James H. Hammond named at least some of his slaves, as part of his effort to establish total authority over them; see Drew Gilpin Faust, *James Henry Hammond and the Old South: A Design for Mastery* (Baton Rouge: Louisiana State University Press, 1982), 89. Gutman maintained that owners rarely named slaves; see *The Black Family in Slavery and Freedom*, 194–95.

42. Quotations are from Ball, *Slavery in the United States*, 23, 219; *Journal & Letters of Philip Vickers Fithian, 1773–1774: A Plantation Tutor of the Old Dominion*, ed. Hunter Dickinson Farish (Williamsburg, Va.: Colonial Williamsburg, 1943), 10 July 1774, 180–81; and *The Diary of Colonel Landon Carter of Sabine Hall, 1752–1778*, ed. Jack P. Greene (Charlottesville: University Press of Virginia, 1965), 13 July 1776, II, 1056–57. On African religion and its persistence among first-generation slaves, see Rabo-

teau, *Slave Religion*, 4–16; Kulikoff, "The Origins of Afro-American Society," 256–57; and Michael Bradley, "The Role of the Black Church in Colonial Slave Society," *Louisiana Studies*, 14 (Winter 1975), 413–15. On the reluctance of colonial slaveowners to proselytize among the slaves, see Winthrop D. Jordan, *White over Black: American Attitudes toward the Negro, 1550–1812* (Baltimore: Penguin Books, 1969), 180–93; David Brion Davis, *The Problem of Slavery in Western Culture* (Ithaca, N.Y.: Cornell University Press, 1966), 197–222; Lester B. Scherer, *Slavery and the Churches in Early America, 1619–1819* (Grand Rapids, Mich.: William B. Eerdmans Publishing Company, 1975), 82–103; and Raboteau, *Slave Religion*, 97–128.

43. Louis Morton, *Robert Carter of Nomini Hall: A Virginia Tobacco Planter of the Eighteenth Century* (Williamsburg, Va.: Colonial Williamsburg, 1945), 239–41; Donald G. Mathews, *Religion in the Old South* (Chicago: University of Chicago Press, 1977), 136–50, 188–97; Scherer, *Slavery and the Churches in Early America*, 143–49; Raboteau, *Slave Religion*, 128–37, 148–50, 212; Genovese, *Roll, Jordan, Roll*, 183–93; Milton C. Sernett, *Black Religion and American Evangelicalism: White Protestants, Plantation Missions, and the Flowering of Negro Christianity, 1787–1865* (Metuchen, N.J.: Scarecrow Press, 1975); Erskine Clarke, *Wrestlin' Jacob: A Portrait of Religion in the Old South* (Atlanta: John Knox Press, 1979), 20–81; and Dickson D. Bruce, Jr., *And They All Sang Hallelujah: Plain-Folk Camp-Meeting Religion, 1800–1845* (Knoxville: University of Tennessee Press, 1974), 74–75.

44. Quotations are from Cornelius Garner in Perdue et al., *Weevils in the Wheat*, 100; Clarke, *Wrestlin' Jacob*, 40; and Catherine Cornelius in Genovese, *Roll, Jordan, Roll*, 238. On white proselytizing of slaves and their responses to it, see especially Genovese, *Roll, Jordan, Roll*, 183–93, 202–9; Raboteau, *Slave Religion*, 213–19; and Stampp, *The Peculiar Institution*, 156–62.

45. On the centrality of religion in the slave community, see Genovese, *Roll, Jordan, Roll*, 236–38, 255–84; Rawick, *From Sundown to Sunup*, 30–51; Raboteau, *Slave Religion*; Owens, *This Species of Property*, 148–63; and Sernett, *Black Religion and American Evangelicalism*, 93–109; as well as numerous slave autobiographies and interviews cited elsewhere. On lack of religiosity among some slaves, see *Narrative of the Life and Adventures of Henry Bibb*, 21–23 (quotation); Charles Ball, *Slavery in the United States*, 162–65; and Raboteau, *Slave Religion*, 225.

46. Quotations are from Rev. R. Q. Mallard to his wife, Mary, Chattanooga, 18 May 1859, in Robert Manson Myers, ed., *The Children of Pride: A True Story of Georgia and the Civil War* (New Haven: Yale University Press, 1972), 483; and "The Plantation Diary of Bennet H. Barrow," in *Plantation Life in the Florida Parishes of Louisiana, 1836–1846, as Reflected in the Diary of Bennet H. Barrow*, ed. Edwin Adams Davis (New York: Columbia University Press, 1943), 14 May 1837, 91, and 2 April 1843, 283.

47. The quotation is from Levine, *Black Culture and Black Consciousness*,

36. On the distinctive nature of antebellum black religion, see especially Genovese, *Roll, Jordan, Roll*, 209–84; Levine, *Black Culture and Black Consciousness*, 25–55; Raboteau, *Slave Religion*, 239–65; and Mathews, *Religion in the Old South*, 214–36.

48. The quotation is from Hommaire de Hell, *Travels in the Steppes of the Caspian Sea*, 51. See also Weber, *The Present State of Russia*, 120–21; Stepniak, *The Russian Peasantry: Their Agrarian Condition, Social Life, and Religion* (New York, 1888), 218–28; and A. P. Zablotskii-Desiatovskii, "O krapostnom sostoianii v Rossii. Zapiska A. Z-go D-go 1841 goda" in *Graf P. D. Kiselev i ego vremiia. Materialy dlia istorii Imperatorov Aleksandra I, Nikolaia I i Aleksandra II*, ed. A. P. Zablotskii-Desiatovskii (St. Petersburg, 1882), IV, 312–14.

49. On the Russian parish clergy, see Gregory L. Freeze, *The Russian Levites: Parish Clergy in the Eighteenth Century* (Cambridge, Mass.: Harvard University Press, 1977); and Freeze, "Social Mobility and the Russian Parish Clergy in the Eighteenth Century," *Slavic Review*, 33 (Dec. 1974), 641–62. On Old Believers, see Michael Cherniavsky, "The Old Believers and the New Religion," *Slavic Review*, 25 (1966), 1–39.

50. Quotations are from *Akty khoziaistva boiarina B. I. Morozova*, ed. A. I. Iakovlev (Moscow: Izdatel'stvo Akademii nauk SSSR, 1940, 1945), II, 34, 35; I. Kuznetsov, "Krepostnye krest'iane sela Barasheva-Usada v pervoi polovine XIX v.," *Krasnyi arkhiv*, 77 (1936), 129; and Stepniak, *The Russian Peasantry*, 229. On nobles ordering church attendance by their serfs, see "Nakaz D. A. Shepeleva prikazchiku sel'tsa Glinka," 237–38; A. I. Andreev, ed., "Nakaz votchinnika krest'ianam 1709 g.," *Istoricheskii arkhiv*, 8 (1953), 274; Shchepetov, *Krepostnoe pravo v votchinakh Sheremetevykh*, 160–63; E. P. Shlossberg, "K voprosu ob izmenenii feodal'noi renty v Belorussii XVII-XVIII vekov (po dannym inventarei feodal'nykh vladenii)," *Ezhegodnik po agrarnoi istorii Vostochnoi Evropy 1958 g.* (Tallin, 1959), 123; and Zablotskii-Desiatovskii, "O krepostnom sostoianii v Rossii," 312–14. For an unusual pomeshchik who *prevented* his serfs from attending church, see S. T. Slovutinskii, *General Izmailov i ego dvornia; otryvki iz vospominanii* (Moscow: Academia, 1937), 141–44.

51. Freeze, "Social Mobility and the Russian Parish Clergy," 661 (quotation); and Freeze, *The Russian Levites*, passim. On the prevalence and character of seminary education for priests, see Gregory L. Freeze, *The Parish Clergy in Nineteenth-Century Russia: Crisis, Reform, Counter Reform* (Princeton: Princeton University Press, 1983), 103–7, 111, 118, 156, 159. On the degraded character of the clergy, see Johann-Georg Korb, *Diary of an Austrian Secretary of Legation at the Court of the Czar Peter the Great*, trans. from Latin and ed. by Count MacDonnell (London: Frank Cass, 1968; orig. pub. in English, 1868; in Latin, 1700), II, 181; Hommaire de Hell, *Travels in the Steppes of the Caspian Sea*, 51–52; Stepniak, *The Russian Peasantry*, 229–32; and Donald W. Treadgold, "The Peasant and Religion," in Vucinich, *The Peasant in Nineteenth-Century Russia*, 100–1. For folktales

dealing with priests' relations with peasants, see Iu. M. Sokolov, ed., *Pop i muzhik: Russkie narodnye skazki* (Moscow: Academia, 1931), which includes (9–34) the author's introduction (quotation, 19).

52. *Krest'ianskoe dvizhenie 1827–1869 godov,* ed. E. A. Morokhovets (Moscow: Gosudarstvennoe sotsial'no-ekonomicheskoe izdatel'stvo, 1931), I, 9–10.

53. Report of ispravnik V. D. Tolbuzin to Moscow Governor P. M. Kozlov, 12 May 1797, in *Krest'ianskoe dvizhenie v Rossii v 1796–1825 gg.: Sbornik dokumentov,* ed. S. N. Valk (Moscow: Izdatel'stvo sotsial'no-ekonomicheskoi literatury, 1961), 106; and report of Major-General G. I. Nostits to General Saken, 24 July 1826, in *Krest'ianskoe dvizhenie v Rossii v 1826–1849 gg.: Sbornik dokumentov,* ed. A. V. Predtechenskii (Moscow: Izdatel'stvo sotsial'no-ekonomicheskoi literatury, 1961), 43.

54. The stories mentioned are in Sokolov, *Pop i muzhik,* 43–44, 67–71, and 103–8. The argument in this paragraph, although based on the stories in Sokolov's collection, differs sharply from his own evaluation (18–31), which stresses class antagonism between priest and peasant; note the contrasting attitudes evident in this collection with those toward pomeshchiki revealed in Sokolov, ed., *Barin i muzhik: Russkie narodnye skazki* (Moscow: Academia, 1932).

55. Petition of peasants of Lyskovo, Nizhnii Novgorod district, to Morozov, 1660, in *Akty khoziaistva boiarina B. I. Morozova,* II, 137–38.

56. Ball, *Slavery in the United States,* 165; H. C. Bruce, *The New Man. Twenty-Nine Years a Slave. Twenty-Nine Years a Free Man* (York, Pa., 1895), 57.

57. Nancy Bradford in Rawick, *The American Slave,* VI, 44–45; George White in Perdue et al., *Weevils in the Wheat,* 310; *Reel v. Reel,* 2 Hawks 63, June 1822, in Helen Tunnicliff Catterall, ed., *Judicial Cases concerning American Slavery and the Negro* (New York: Octagon Books, 1968; orig. pub. Washington, 1926–37), II, 43. See also Escott, *Slavery Remembered,* 103, 108; Levine, *Black Culture and Black Consciousness,* 55–80; Genovese, *Roll, Jordan, Roll,* 209–32; Raboteau, *Slave Religion,* 275–88; Adefila, "Slave Religion in the Old South," 78–96; and Joyner, *Down by the Riverside,* 144–53.

58. The quotation is from Korb, *Diary of an Austrian Secretary of Legation,* I, 99–100. For a similar comment from a nineteenth-century traveler, see Hommaire de Hell, *Travels in the Steppes of the Caspian Sea,* 52–55. For descriptions of traditional ceremonies, see Ralston, *The Songs of the Russian People,* 2–39, 186–259; and Matossian, "The Peasant Way of Life," 32–39.

59. The quotation is from Stepniak, *The Russian Peasantry,* 218. See also Sokolov, *Russian Folklore,* 241–56; Ralston, *The Songs of the Russian People,* 80–160, 345–433; Ralston, *Russian Folk-Tales,* 63–324; Shchepetov, *Krepostnoe pravo v votchinakh Sheremetevykh,* 224; and Vasilii Preobrazhenskii, *Opisanie Tverskoi gubernii v sel'sko-khoziaistvenom otnoshenii* (St. Petersburg, 1854), 87–89.

60. The question of interpreting folktales is an extremely complex one that can only be touched on lightly here. On selective recording, see Michael Flusche, "Joel Chandler Harris and the Folklore of Slavery," *Journal of American Studies*, 9 (Dec. 1975), 349–56; Sokolov, *Barin i muzhik*, 9–13; and Sokolov, *Pop i muzhik*, 9–13. The quotation is from Richard M. Dorson, ed., *American Negro Folktales* (Greenwich, Conn.: Fawcett Publications, 1967), editor's introduction, 15–16; see also Dorson, "African and Afro-American Folklore: A Reply to Bascom and Other Misguided Critics," *Journal of American Folklore*, 88 (April-June 1975), 151–64. On Russian tales' similarity to those of western Europe, see Sokolov, *Russian Folklore*, 419–33; and Ralston, *Russian Folk-Tales*, 4–9.

61. Sokolov, *Russian Folklore*, 400–7, 439–40; Sokolov, *Pop i muzhik*, editor's introduction, 12; Levine, *Black Culture and Black Consciousness*, 82. See also, Joyner, *Down by the Riverside*, 172–73.

62. See Levine, *Black Culture and Black Consciousness*, 81–135; Sterling Stuckey, "Through the Prism of Folklore: The Black Ethos in Slavery," *The Massachusetts Review*, 9 (Summer 1968), 417–37; Dickson D. Bruce, Jr., "The 'John and Old Master' Stories and the World of Slavery: A Study in Folktales and History," *Phylon*, 35 (Dec. 1974), 418–29; Joyner, *Down by the Riverside*, 173–89; and Bernard Wolfe, "Uncle Remus and the Malevolent Rabbit," *Commentary*, 8 (1949), 31–41. For a good collection of tales, see Dorson, *American Negro Folktales*.

63. Flusche, "Joel Chandler Harris and the Folklore of Slavery," 349. For other views of the ambiguous implications of black folktales, see Levine, *Black Culture and Black Consciousness*, 113–33, and Joyner, *Down by the Riverside*, 194.

64. The most complete collection of peasant tales is A. N. Afanas'ev, comp., *Narodnyia russkiia skazki* (Moscow, 1855–64). For animal tales, see Adolph Gerber, *Great Russian Animal Tales: A Collection of Fifty Tales* (New York: Burt Franklin, 1970; orig. pub. 1891), 2–84; and Sokolov, *Russian Folklore*, 433–39. For "The Little Fox Midwife," see Gerber, *Great Russian Animal Tales*, 14; and for "Who Ate Up the Butter?" see Dorson, *American Negro Folktales*, 68–71.

65. For peasant and master tales, see Sokolov, *Barin i muzhik;* and N. L. Brodskii, "Krepostnoe pravo v narodnoi poezii," in *Velikaia reforma: Russkoe obshchestvo i krest'ianskii vopros v proshlom i nastoiashchem. Iubileinoe izdanie*, ed. A. K. Dzhivelegov et al. (Moscow: Izdanie T-va I. D. Sytina, 1911), IV, 1–33 (quotation, 2), both of which stress class antagonism. The quotation on peasant deceitfulness is from Germain de Lagny, *The Knout and the Russians; or the Muscovite Empire, the Czar, and His People*, trans. from French, John Bridgeman (London, 1854), 171. For similar comments by other Western observers, see Chappé d'Auteroche, *A Journey into Siberia* (New York: Arno Press, 1970; orig. pub. 1770), 315; William Richardson, *Anecdotes of the Russian Empire* (London: Frank Cass, 1968; orig. pub. 1784), 241; *Journey for Our Time: The Journals of the Marquis de Custine,*

ed. and trans. Phyllis Penn Kohler (New York: Pellegrini & Cudahy, 1951; orig. pub. Paris, 1843), 87; Robert Johnston, *Travels through Part of the Russian Empire* (New York: Arno Press, 1970; orig. pub. London, 1815), 275; and A. D. White, "The Development and Overthrow of the Russian Serf System," *Atlantic Monthly,* 10 (Nov. 1862), 548.

66. Sokolov, *Russian Folklore,* 291–334, 342–68 (quotation, 322–23); and Ralston, *The Songs of the Russian People,* 39–76. For the text of 127 songs celebrating Razin's rebellion, see A. N. Lozanova, *Narodnye pesni o Stepane Razine* (Nizhe-volzhskoe oblastnoe nauchnoe obshchestvo kraevedeniia, 1928). See also V. S. Sokolova, *Russkie istoricheskie predaniia* (Moscow: Izdatel'stvo "Nauka," 1970).

67. Sokolov, *Russian Folklore,* 381–495; Ralston, *Russian Folk-Tales,* 62–177, 230–324; K. V. Chistov, *Russkie narodnye sotsial'no-utopicheskie legendy XVII–XIX vv.* (Moscow: Izdatel'stvo "Nauka," 1967), 15–32, 220–326; A. I. Klibanov, "Narodnaia sotsial'naia utopiia v Rossii v XIX veke," *Voprosy filosofii,* 1972, no. 11, 108–21. For the estimate of the incidence of trickster tales, see Sokolov, *Russian Folklore,* 397–98. Richard Pipes has suggested that the trickery existing in some Russian tales reflects attitudes toward outsiders, whereas the solidarity and cooperative behavior noted by observers were reserved for members of the commune; see Pipes, *Russia under the Old Regime,* 159–60.

68. The quotation is from Kovalevsky, *Modern Customs and Ancient Laws of Russia,* 61.

69. See Chapter 1, pages 51–57.

70. For the impact of continued infusions of Africans on patterns of resistance, see Carl N. Degler, *Neither Black nor White: Slavery and Race Relations in Brazil and the United States* (New York: Macmillan, 1971), 51–62; and Eugene D. Genovese, *From Rebellion to Revolution: Afro-American Slave Revolts in the Making of the New World* (Baton Rouge: Louisiana State University Press, 1979), 28–32, 52–54, 61–62, 97–102. On African cultural influences in Jamaica, Brazil, and Mexico, see Orlando Patterson, *The Sociology of Slavery: An Analysis of the Origins, Development, and Structure of Negro Slave Society in Jamaica* (London: Associated University Presses, 1967), 273–83; Richard S. Dunn, *Sugar and Slaves: The Rise of the Planter Class in the English West Indies, 1624–1713* (New York: W. W. Norton, 1972), 250–52; Roger Bastide, *African Civilizations in the New World,* trans. from French, Peter Green (New York: Harper & Row, 1971); A. J. R. Russell-Wood, *The Black Man in Slavery and Freedom in Colonial Brazil* (New York: St. Martin's Press, 1982); and Colin A. Palmer, "Religion and Magic in Mexican Slave Society, 1570–1650," in *Race and Slavery in the Western Hemisphere: Quantitative Studies,* ed. Stanley L. Engerman and Eugene D. Genovese (Princeton: Princeton University Press, 1975), 311–28.

71. The estimate of the proportion of African-born slaves in the United States is from Fogel and Engerman, *Time on the Cross,* 23–24; see also Kulikoff, "A 'Prolifick' People," 406, 423. In Jamaica African-born slaves

formed more than two-thirds of the black population during most of the eighteenth century and a majority until British abolition of the slave trade in 1808; see Michael Craton, "Jamaican Slavery," in Engerman and Genovese, *Race and Slavery in the Western Hemisphere,* 284. In Cuba African natives constituted 45 percent of all blacks and a majority of slaves as late as 1841; see Jack Ericson Eblen, "On the Natural Increase of Slave Populations: The Example of the Cuban Black Population, 1775–1900," in Engerman and Genovese, *Race and Slavery in the Western Hemisphere,* 234.

72. See Chapter 2. On the ambiguous effects of slaveowner paternalism, see especially Genovese, *Roll, Jordan, Roll,* passim.

73. For demographic information on Jamaica, see Craton, "Jamaican Slavery," 252, 254, 275, 284; and B. W. Higman, *Slave Population and Economy in Jamaica, 1807–1834* (Cambridge: Cambridge University Press, 1976), 13, 70. The estimate on the rate of absenteeism is from Craton, "Jamaican Slavery," 262; the quotations are from Dunn, *Sugar and Slaves,* 237, 250; on black culture, community, and resistance, see Patterson, *The Sociology of Slavery,* 182–283. On the emergence of a self-supporting "protopeasantry" in Jamaica and Saint Domingue, see Sidney W. Mintz, "Was the Plantation Slave a Proletarian?" *Review,* 2 (Summer 1978), 92–96; Mintz, *Caribbean Transformations* (Chicago: Aldine, 1974), 180–206; Michael Craton, *Searching for the Invisible Man: Slaves and Plantation Life in Jamaica* (Cambridge, Mass.: Harvard University Press, 1978), 56, 161–62; and Gwendolyn Midlo Hall, *Social Control in Slave Plantation Societies: A Comparison of St. Domingue and Cuba* (Baltimore: Johns Hopkins Press, 1971), 66–68.

74. On Cuban population statistics, slaveholding size, and absenteeism, see Franklin W. Knight, *Slave Society in Cuba during the Nineteenth Century* (Madison: University of Wisconsin Press, 1970), 22, 134–35, 69–70. For the proportion of African-born blacks, see Eblen, "On the Natural Increase of Slave Populations," 234. On the transformation of Cuba's economy during the late eighteenth and early nineteenth centuries, see Knight, *Slave Society in Cuba,* 3–46, and Eugene D. Genovese, *The World the Slaveholders Made: Two Essays in Interpretation* (New York: Pantheon Books, 1969), 65–71. For an examination of eighteenth-century Cuban slavery, see Herbert S. Klein, *Slavery in the Americas: A Comparative Study of Virginia and Cuba* (Chicago: University of Chicago Press, 1967).

75. E. Phillip LeVeen, "A Quantitative Analysis of the Impact of British Suppression Policies on the Volume of the Nineteenth Century Atlantic Slave Trade," in Engerman and Genovese, *Race and Slavery in the Western Hemisphere,* 74; Stuart B. Schwartz, "Patterns of Slaveholding in the Americas: New Evidence from Brazil," *American Historical Review,* 87 (Feb. 1982), 55–86 (esp. table, 82); Genovese, *The World the Slaveholders Made,* 71–85 (quotation, 76). For an attack on the idea that Brazilian slaveowners were paternalistic, see Degler, *Neither Black nor White,* 67–75. For evidence that Brazilian slaves were often self-supporting, see Stuart B. Schwartz, "Resist-

ance and Accommodation in Eighteenth-Century Brazil: The Slaves' View of Slavery," *Hispanic American Historical Review,* 57 (Feb. 1977), 69–81; and Robert Edgar Conrad, ed., *Children of God's Fire: A Documentary History of Black Slavery in Brazil* (Princeton: Princeton University Press, 1983), 58, 60–62, 78, 160–62.

76. See also Peter Kolchin, "Reevaluating the Antebellum Slave Community: A Comparative Perspective," *Journal of American History,* 70 (Dec. 1983), 579–601. Significantly, where the environment southern slaves faced came closest to the Caribbean model—as in the South Carolina and Georgia low-country—so too did the slaves' society; see especially Joyner, *Down by the Riverside;* and Smith, *Slavery and Rice Culture in Low Country Georgia.*

77. Stanley M. Elkins, *Slavery: A Problem in American Institutional and Intellectual Life* (Chicago: University of Chicago Press, 1959), ch. 3. For a collection of early responses to the Sambo thesis, see Ann J. Lane, ed., *The Debate over Slavery: Stanley Elkins and His Critics* (Urbana: University of Illinois Press, 1971).

78. See, e.g., Herbert Aptheker, *American Negro Slave Revolts* (New York: International Publishers, 1969; orig. pub. 1943); Genovese, *Roll, Jordan, Roll,* 113–49 (quotation, 143–44); Fogel and Engerman, *Time on the Cross,* passim; Blassingame, *The Slave Community,* 132–53; 213–61; and Kenneth M. Stampp, "Rebels and Sambos: The Search for the Negro's Personality in Slavery," *Journal of Southern History,* 37 (Aug. 1971), 367–92.

79. B. G. Litvak, *Opyt statisticheskogo izucheniia krepostnogo dvizheniia v Rossii XIX v.* (Moscow: Izdatel'stvo "Nauka," 1967), 6–7; Litvak, "O nekotorykh chertakh psikhologii russkikh krepostnykh," 199–214; Klibanov, "Narodnaia sotsial'naia utopiia v Rossii," 108; V. A. Fedorov, "K voprosu ob ideologii krepostnogo krest'ianstva," in *Voprosy agrarnoi istorii tsentra i severo-zapada RSFSR: Materialy mezhvuzovskoi nauchnoi konferentsii* (Smolensk: Ministerstvo prosveshcheniia RSFSR, 1972), 140–51; M. A. Rakhmatullin, "K voprosu ob urovne obshchestvennogo soznaniia krest'ianstva v Rossii," ibid., 158–70; and P. G. Ryndziunskii, "Ideinaia storona krest'ianskikh dvizhenii 1770–1850–kh godov i metody ee izucheniia," *Voprosy istorii,* 1983, no. 5, 10–16.

5. Patterns of Resistance

1. Kenneth M. Stampp, *The Peculiar Institution: Slavery in the Ante-Bellum South* (New York: Vintage Books, 1956), 97–109, 334–35 (quotation, 97); and N. M. Druzhinin and V. A. Fedorov, "Krest'ianskoe dvizhenie v Rossii v XIX v.," *Istoriia SSSR,* 1977, no. 4, 108. For similar suggestions by other historians, see Raymond A. Bauer and Alice H. Bauer, "Day to Day Resistance to Slavery," *Journal of Negro History,* 37 (Oct. 1942), 388–419; Herbert Aptheker, *American Negro Slave Revolts* (New York: International Publishers, 1969; orig. pub. 1943), 141–49; Gerald W. Mullin, *Flight and Rebellion: Slave Resistance in Eighteenth-Century Virginia* (New York: Ox-

ford University Press, 1972), 53–62; K. V. Sivkov, *Ocherki po istorii kre- postnogo khoziaistva i krest'ianskogo dvizheniia v Rossii v pervoi polovine XIX veka: Po materialam arkhiva stepnykh votchin Iusupovykh* (Moscow: Izdatel'stvo Akademii nauk SSSR, 1951), 204; E. I. Indova et al., "Klasso- vaia bor'ba krest'ianstva i stanovlenie burzhuaznykh otnoshenii v Rossii (vtoraia polovina XVII–XVIII v.)," *Voprosy istorii,* 1964, no. 12, 28–29; and V. A. Fedorov, *Krest'ianskoe dvizhenie v tsentral'noi Rossii 1800–1860 (Po materialam tsentral'no-promyshlennykh gubernii)* (Moscow: Izdatel'stvo Moskovskogo universiteta, 1980), 41.

2. Charles Ball, *Slavery in the United States: A Narrative of the Life and Adventures of Charles Ball, a Black Man* (New York, 1837), 298–99; Fred- erick Law Olmsted, *The Cotton Kingdom: A Traveller's Observations on Cotton and Slavery in the American Slave States* (New York, 1861), I, 106; A. P. Zablotskii-Desiatovskii, "O krepostnom sostoianii v Rossii. Zapiska A. Z-go D-go 1841 goda," in *Graf P. D. Kiselev i ego vremia. Materialy dlia istorii Imperatorov Aleksandra I, Nikolaia I i Aleksandra II,* ed. A. P. Za- blotskii-Desiatovskii (St. Petersburg, 1882), IV, 312. On the legitimacy of theft from masters in slave culture, see Eugene D. Genovese, *Roll, Jordan, Roll: The World the Slaves Made* (New York: Pantheon Books, 1974), 599–609.

3. George M. Fredrickson and Christopher Lasch, "Resistance to Slavery," *Civil War History,* 12 (Dec. 1967), 328; Genovese, *Roll, Jordan, Roll,* 285– 324. For "free-labor" critiques of the inefficiency of slavery and serfdom, see, e.g., Olmsted, *The Cotton Kingdom;* Zablotskii-Desiatovskii, "O krepost- nom sostoianii v Rossii," 271–344; and M. P. D. de Passenans, *La Russie et l'esclavage, dans leurs rapports avec la civilisation européene: ou de l'influ- ence de la servitude sur la vie domestique des russes* (Paris, 1822).

4. Agis Salpukas, "Workers Rebel against Boredom on Assembly Lines," *New York Times,* 2 April 1972, N34 (quotations); Carl Gersuny, *Punish- ment and Redress in a Modern Factory* (Lexington, Mass.: D. C. Heath, 1973), 40.

5. The literature on the peasant wars is vast. L. V. Cherepnin, ed., *Kres- t'ianskie voiny v Rossii XVII–XVIII vekov: problemy, poiski, resheniia* (Moscow: Izdatel'stvo "Nauka," 1974), contains a bibliography listing more than seven hundred works appearing between 1953 and 1973 (400–44). For two brief general surveys, see B. I. Buganov, *Krest'ianskie voiny v Rossii XVII–XVIII vv.* (Moscow: Izdatel'stvo "Nauka," 1976); and Paul Avrich, *Russian Rebels: 1600–1800* (New York: Schocken Books, 1972). Other ma- jor works include D. P. Makovskii, *Pervaia krest'ianskaia voina v Rossii* (Smolensk: Ministerstvo prosveshcheniia RSFSR, 1967); V. I. Koretskii, *For- mirovanie krepostnogo prava i pervaia krest'ianskaia voina v Rossii* (Mos- cow: Izdatel'stvo "Nauka," 1975), 192–369; I. V. Stepanov, *Krest'ianskaia voina v Rossii v 1670–1671 gg.: Vosstanie Stepana Razina* (Leningrad: Iz- datel'stvo Leningradskogo universiteta, 1966, 1972); and V. V. Mavrodin et al., *Krest'ianskaia voina v Rossii v 1773–1775 godakh: Vosstanie Pugacheva*

(Leningrad: Izdatel'stvo Leningradskogo universiteta, 1961–70). For collections of documents, see E. A. Shvetsova, ed., *Krest'ianskaia voina pod predvoditel'stvom Stepana Razina: Sbornik dokumentov* (Moscow, 1954–62); A. N. Lozanova, *Narodnye pesni o Stepane Razine* (Nizhe-volzhskoe oblastnoe nauchnoe obshchestvo kraevedeniia, 1928); S. A. Golubtsov, ed., *Pugachevshchina* (Moscow: Gosudarstvennoe izdatel'stvo, 1926–31); and E. I. Indova et al., eds., *Krest'ianskaia voina 1773–1775 gg. v Rossii: Dokumenty iz sobraniia Gosudarstvennogo istoricheskogo muzeia* (Moscow: Izdatel'stvo "Nauka," 1973).

6. For the hypothesis that peasant wars "are most likely to occur in time of war which heightens discontent and creates a situation in which the state, preoccupied with external commitments, is less efficient than usual in maintaining internal order," see Philip Longworth, "The Last Great Cossack-Peasant Rising," *Journal of European Studies*, 3 (1973), 34. See also Avrich, *Russian Rebels*, 1.

7. Soviet historians disagree sharply over periodization of peasant wars. For example, some authors assign the years 1606–7 to the first peasant war, counting only the period of the actual rising led by Bolotnikov, but others include precursory and subsequent unrest and insist that the first peasant war, properly understood, lasted from 1603 to 1614. See, e.g., A. A. Zimin and A. A. Preobrazhenskii, "Izuchenie v sovetskoi istoricheskoi nauke klassovoi bor'by periody feodalizma v Rossii (do nachala XIX veka)," *Voprosy istorii*, 1957, no. 12, 142–44; "O krest'ianskoi voine v russkom gosudarstve v nachale XVII veka (obzor diskussii)," ibid., 1961, no. 5, 104–19; and A. P. Pronshtein, "Reshennye i nereshennye voprosy istorii krest'ianskikh voin v Rossii," ibid., 1967, no. 7, 156.

8. The quotation is from Pugachev's ukaz of 1 Dec. 1773, in Golubtsov, *Pugachevshchina*, I, 36. For the simplification of class alliances in the peasant wars, see Avrich, *Russian Rebels*, 25–26, 88–92, 119–20, 157–59, 215, 247–49; Makovskii, *Pervaia krest'ianskaia voina v Rossii*, 24–29, 171–74, 463–82; A. L. Shapiro, "Ob istoricheskoi roli krest'ianskikh voin XVII–XVIII vv. v Rossii," *Istoriia SSSR*, 1965, no. 5, 63–65; L. V. Cherepnin, "Ob izucheniia krest'ianskikh voin v Rossii XVII–XVIII vv. (K teorii problemy)," in Cherepnin, *Krest'ianskie voiny v Rossii*, 12–13; V. I. Koretskii, "O formirovanii I. I. Bolotnikova kak vozhdia krest'ianskogo vosstaniia," ibid., 133–46; B. I. Buganov and E. V. Chistiakova, "O nekotorykh voprosakh istorii vtoroi krest'ianskoi voiny v Rossii," *Voprosy istorii*, 1968, no. 7, 44–45; and M. A. Rakhmatullin, "Krest'ianskaia voina v Rossii 1773–1775 godov," *Istoriia SSSR*, 1973, no. 6, 43–48.

9. M. D. Kurmacheva, "Ob uchastii krepostnoi intelligentsii v krest'ianskoi voine 1773–1775 gg.," in Cherepnin, *Krest'ianskie voiny v Rossii*, 307–25; Longworth, "The Last Great Cossack-Peasant Rising," 29–33. For a collection of manifestoes, ukazes, and correspondence among Pugachev's forces, see Golubtsov, *Pugachevshchina*, I.

10. See, e.g., Avrich, *Russian Rebels*, 256–57; Longworth, "The Last

Great Cossack-Peasant Rising," 17–19; Roland Mousnier, *Peasant Uprisings in Seventeenth-Century France, Russia, and China,* trans. from French by Brian Pearce (New York: Harper & Row, 1970), 196–215, 327–48; Pronshtein, "Reshennye i nereshennye voprosy istorii krest'ianskikh voin," 154–55; Buganov and Chistiakova, "O nekotorykh voprosakh istorii vtoroi krest'ianskoi voiny," 45–46.

11. Quotations are from V. V. Mavrodin, "Po povodu kharaktera i istoricheskogo znacheniia krest'ianskikh voin v Rossii," in Cherepnin, *Krest'ianskie voiny v Rossii,* 36–38; and Cherepnin, "Ob izucheniia krest'ianskikh voin v Rossii," 8. For a criticism of the "schematization" of Soviet interpretations of peasant wars, see John T. Alexander, "Recent Soviet Historiography on the Pugachev Revolt: A Review Article," *Canadian Slavic Studies,* 4 (1970), 614.

12. On the general phenomena of pretenders, returning-deliverer legends, and naive monarchism, see K. V. Chistov, *Russkie narodnye sotsial'no-utopicheskie legendy XVII–XIX vv.* (Moscow: Izdatel'stvo "Nauka," 1967), 24–195, 220–36; Philip Longworth, "The Pretender Phenomenon in Eighteenth-Century Russia," *Past and Present,* 66 (Feb. 1975), 61–83; and Daniel Field, "The Myth of the Tsar," in *Rebels in the Name of the Tsar,* ed. Daniel Field (Boston: Houghton Mifflin, 1976), 1–29.

13. Appeal by Colonel [in Pugachev's army] Ivan Griaznov, 8 Jan. 1774, in Golubtsov, *Pugachevshchina,* I, 74; Pugachev's ukaz of 2 Dec. 1773, ibid., I, 37.

14. On the revolutionary goals of the rebels, see, e.g., Mavrodin, "Po povodu kharaktera i istoricheskogo znacheniia krest'ianskikh voin," 36–40; E. I. Indova, A. A. Preobrazhenskii, and Iu. A. Tikhonov, "Lozungi i trebovaniia uchastnikov krest'ianskikh voin v Rossii XVII–XVIII vv.," in Cherepnin, *Krest'ianskie voiny v Rossii,* 241–69; and V. I. Buganov, "Ob ideologii uchastnikov krest'ianskikh voin v Rossii," *Voprosy istorii,* 1974, no. 1, 44–60.

15. Indova, Preobrazhenskii, and Tikhonov, "Lozungi i trebovaniia uchastnikov krest'ianskikh voin"; Mousnier, *Peasant Uprisings in Seventeenth-Century France, Russia, and China,* 186–87, 223; Avrich, *Russian Rebels,* 92–97, 117–19; Koretskii, "O formirovanii I. I. Bolotnikova kak vozhdia," 133–46; A. N. Sakharov, "Stepan Razin—predvoditel' krest'ianskoi voiny," in Cherepnin, *Krest'ianskie voiny v Rossii,* 148–65; Buganov, "Ob ideologii uchastnikov krest'ianskikh voin"; Cherepnin, "Ob izucheniia krest'ianskikh voin," 13–16; and Buganov and Chistiakova, "O nekotorykh voprosakh istorii vtoroi krest'ianskoi voiny," 44–46.

16. For the ukazes of 1 Dec. 1773 and 31 July 1774, see Golubtsov, *Pugachevshchina,* I, 36, 40–41. See also Indova, Preobrazhenskii, and Tikhonov, "Lozungi i trebovaniia uchastnikov krest'ianskikh voin"; Longworth, "The Last Great Cossack-Peasant Rising," 17–23; and Mavrodin et al., *Krest'ianskaia voina 1773–1775 gg.,* II, 413–43.

17. The best work on the Seminole wars consists of a series of articles by

Kenneth Wiggins Porter, all reprinted in his volume *The Negro on the American Frontier* (New York: Arno Press, 1971). See especially the following: "Negroes and the East Florida Annexation Plot, 1811–1813" (1945), 183–204; "Negroes and the Seminole War, 1817–1818" (1951), 205–37; "Negroes and the Seminole War, 1835–1842" (1964), 238–61; "The Negro Abraham" (1946), 295–337; and "John Caesar: Seminole Negro Partisan" (1946), 339–57.

18. Aptheker, *American Negro Slave Revolts,* passim (quotation, 162). For examples of different views, see Winthrop D. Jordan, *White over Black: American Attitudes toward the Negro, 1550–1812* (Baltimore: Penguin Books, 1969), 113; M. Foster Farley, "The Fear of Negro Slave Revolts in South Carolina, 1690–1865," *Afro-American Studies,* 3 (Dec. 1972), 199; Genovese, *Roll, Jordan, Roll,* 587–96; and Ray Granade, "Slave Unrest in Florida," *Florida Historical Quarterly,* 55 (July 1976), 29.

19. Aptheker, *American Negro Slave Revolts,* 172–73, 192–95, 219–24, 267–76, 345–50; Ferenc M. Szasz, "The New York Slave Revolt of 1741: A Re-Examination," *New York History,* 28 (July 1967), 215–30; Peter H. Wood, *Black Majority: Negroes in Colonial South Carolina from 1670 through the Stono Rebellion* (New York: Alfred A. Knopf, 1974), 308–20; Mullin, *Flight and Rebellion,* 124–61; John Lofton, *Insurrection in South Carolina: The Turbulent World of Denmark Vesey* (Yellow Springs, Ohio: Antioch Press, 1964); Robert S. Starobin, ed., *Denmark Vesey: The Slave Conspiracy of 1822* (Englewood Cliffs, N.J.: Prentice-Hall, 1970); and Harvey Wish, "The Slave Insurrection Panic of 1856," *Journal of Southern History,* 5 (1939), 206–22.

20. Aptheker, *American Negro Slave Revolts,* 293–324; Stephen B. Oates, *The Fires of Jubilee: Nat Turner's Fierce Rebellion* (New York: Harper & Row, 1975). For a good collection of documents on the Turner rebellion, see Henry Irving Tragle, ed., *The Southampton Slave Revolt of 1831: A Compilation of Source Material* (New York: Random House, 1971). William Styron's novel *The Confessions of Nat Turner* (New York: Random House, 1967) created intense controversy over both Turner himself and slave rebelliousness in general. See John Henrik Clarke, ed., *William Styron's Nat Turner: Ten Black Writers Respond* (Boston: Beacon Press, 1968); and John B. Duff and Peter M. Mitchell, eds., *The Nat Turner Rebellion: The Historical Event and the Modern Controversy* (New York: Harper & Row, 1971).

21. *State v. M'Donald,* 4 Porter 449, January 1837, in Helen Tunnicliff Catterall, ed., *Judicial Cases concerning American Slavery and the Negro* (New York: Octagon Books, 1968; orig. pub. Washington, 1926–37), III, 141–42. For evidence that various slave conspiracies were mostly products of white imagination, see Szasz, "The New York Slave Revolt of 1741"; Philip D. Morgan and George D. Terry, "Slavery in Microcosm: A Conspiracy Scare in Colonial South Carolina," *Southern Studies,* 21 (Summer 1982), 121–46; Richard C. Wade, "The Vesey Plot: A Reconsideration," *Journal of Southern History,* 30 (May 1964), 143–61; and Charles B. Dew, "Black Ironworkers and the Slave Insurrection Panic of 1856," ibid., 41 (Aug.

1975), 321–38. For a rejoinder to Wade, see Robert S. Starobin, "Denmark Vesey's Slave Conspiracy of 1822: A Study in Rebellion and Repression," in *American Slavery: The Question of Resistance*, ed. John H. Bracey, August Meier, and Elliott Rudwick (Belmont, Calif.: Wadsworth Publishing Company, 1971), 142–57. In *Southern Honor: Ethics and Behavior in the Old South* (New York: Oxford University Press, 1982), Bertram Wyatt-Brown sees southern insurrection scares as a "form of mass ritual" (406), an exercise for "the restoration of order through the venting of society's worst fears" (431).

22. See sources cited in notes 19 and 20. For some of many studies of slave revolts in the Caribbean and South America, see C. L. R. James, *The Black Jacobins: Toussaint L'Ouverture and the San Domingo Revolution*, 2nd ed., revised (New York: Vintage Books, 1963; orig. pub. 1938); Stuart B. Schwartz, "The *Mocambo*: Slave Resistance in Colonial Bahia," *Journal of Social History*, 3 (Summer 1970), 313–30; R. K. Kent, "An African State in Brazil," *Journal of African History*, 6, no. 2 (1965), 161–75; Orlando Patterson, *The Sociology of Slavery: An Analysis of the Origins, Development and Structure of Negro Slave Society in Jamaica* (London: Associated University Presses, 1967), 260–83; Mary Reckord, "The Jamaican Slave Rebellion of 1831," *Past and Present*, 40 (July 1968), 108–25; Barbara Klamon Kopytoff, "The Early Political Development of Jamaican Maroon Societies," *William and Mary Quarterly*, 3rd ser., 35 (April 1978), 287–307; and Michael Craton, *Testing the Chains: Resistance to Slavery in the British West Indies* (Ithaca, N.Y.: Cornell University Press, 1982). For the contrast between the United States and other New World slave societies, see especially Eugene D. Genovese, *From Rebellion to Revolution: Afro-American Slave Revolts in the Making of the New World* (Baton Rouge: Louisiana State University Press, 1979), 1–50.

23. Stanley M. Elkins, *Slavery: A Problem in American Institutional and Intellectual Life* (Chicago: University of Chicago Press, 1959), ch. 3; Genovese, *Roll, Jordan, Roll*, 594.

24. Genovese, *From Rebellion to Revolution*, 11–12. See also John W. Blassingame, *The Slave Community: Plantation Life in the Antebellum South* (New York: Oxford University Press, 1972), 124–31; and Carl N. Degler, *Neither Black nor White: Slavery and Race Relations in Brazil and the United States* (New York: Macmillan, 1971), 47–61.

25. Marion D. de B. Kilson, "Towards Freedom: An Analysis of Slave Revolts in the United States," *Phylon*, 25 (1964), 175–80; Turner's confession to Thomas Gray in Tragle, *The Southampton Slave Revolt of 1831*, 310.

26. For the immediate impact of the St. Domingue revolution on American slaves, see Aptheker, *American Negro Slave Revolts*, 96–101; and Jordan, *White over Black*, 391–99. On the dominant role of African-born slaves in American risings, see Genovese, *From Rebellion to Revolution*, 42; and Wood, *Black Majority*, 301–3. For a very different conclusion, however, see Mullin, *Flight and Rebellion*, 121–58.

27. For the impact of depression and division among whites, see Genovese,

From Rebellion to Revolution, 42–49; Aptheker, *American Negro Slave Revolts,* 79–124, 139; Wendell G. Addington, "Slave Insurrections in Texas," *Journal of Negro History,* 35 (Oct. 1950), 410–11; and Wish, "The Slave Insurrection Panic of 1856," 206–7. For the suggestion that lenient treatment facilitated rebellion, see Kilson, "Towards Freedom," 179–83, 187 (quotation, 183); and Jordan, *White over Black,* 391–99.

28. Mullin, *Flight and Rebellion,* 155–61 (quotation, 158); Genovese, *From Rebellion to Revolution,* 82–137 (quotations, 82, 94, 118).

29. For the argument that southern slaves considered the Western revolutionary tradition their own, see Genovese, *From Rebellion to Revolution,* 126–37. For Turner's confession, see Tragle, *The Southampton Slave Revolt of 1831,* 306–18. The quotation is from Mullin, *Flight and Rebellion,* 145.

30. For a suggestive list of reasons for the absence of peasant wars after 1774, see Rakhmatullin, "Krest'ianskaia voina v Rossii 1773–1775 godov," 50–51.

31. The basic source for studying these volneniia is a massive, multivolume collection of documents under the general editorship of N. M. Druzhinin, entitled *Krest'ianskoe dvizhenie v Rossii v XIX-nachale XX veka,* containing peasant petitions, reports of local and provincial governmental officials, letters of pomeshchiki, and other material. For this study I have used the first three volumes of this series, *Krest'ianskoe dvizhenie v Rossii v 1796–1825 gg.: Sbornik dokumentov,* ed. S. N. Valk (Moscow: Izdatel'stvo sotsial'no-ekonomicheskoi literatury, 1961); *Krest'ianskoe dvizhenie v Rossii v 1826–1849 gg.: Sbornik dokumentov,* ed. A. V. Predtechenskii (Moscow: Izdatel'stvo sotsial'no-ekonomicheskoi literatury, 1961); and *Krest'ianskoe dvizhenie v Rossii v 1850–1856 gg.: Sbornik dokumentov,* ed. S. B. Okun' (Moscow: Izdatel'stvo sotsial'no-ekonomicheskoi literatury, 1963), hereafter cited as KD-1, KD-2, and KD-3. The secondary literature on the peasant movement is huge; for two historiographical surveys of recent works, see V. A. Fedorov, "Istoriografiia krest'ianskogo dvizheniia v Rossii perioda razlozheniia krepostnichestva," *Voprosy istorii,* 1966, no. 2, 148–56; and Fedorov, "Noveishaia sovetskaia literatura o krest'ianskom dvizhenii v Rossii pervoi poloviny XIX veka," ibid., 1977, no. 1, 140–48. Other secondary and primary sources are cited below, when appropriate.

32. On seventeenth-century and eighteenth-century volneniia, see V. I. Semevskii, *Krest'iane v tsarstvovanie Imperatritsy Ekateriny II,* 2nd ed. (St. Petersburg: Tipografiia M. M. Stasiulevicha, 1901–3), I, 412–56; V. V. Mavrodin, *Klassovaia bor'ba i obshchestvenno-politicheskaia mysl' v Rossii v XVIII v. (1725–1773 gg.)* (Leningrad: Izdatel'stvo Leningradskogo universiteta, 1964), 33–66; P. K. Alefirenko, *Krest'ianskoe dvizhenie i krest'ianskii vopros v Rossii v 30–50–kh godakh XVIII veka* (Moscow: Izdatel'stvo Akademii nauk SSSR, 1958), 136–50, 195–213; N. L. Rubinshtein, "Krest'ianskoe dvizhenie v Rossii vo vtoroi polovine XVIII veka," *Voprosy istorii,* 1956, no. 11, 34–51; E. S. Kogan, *Ocherki istorii krepostnogo khoziaistva po materialam votchin Kurakinykh 2–i poloviny XVIII veka* (Moscow: Go-

sudarstvennyi istoricheskii muzei, 1960), 76–100; K. V. Sivkov, "Iz istorii krest'ianskikh vosstanii v XVIII v. (Vosstanie 1744 g. v Pskovskoi provintsii)," *Izvestiia Tverskogo pedagogicheskogo instituta,* 2 (1926), 76–94; A. S. Orlov, *Volneniia na Urale v seredine XVIII veka (K voprosu o formirovanii proletariata v Rossii)* (Moscow: Izdatel'stvo Moskovskogo universiteta, 1979); and *Materialy po istorii volnenii krepostnykh manufakturakh v XVIII veke* (Moscow: Izdatel'stvo Akademii nauk SSSR, 1937).

33. For computations of the average number of peasants and villages participating in volneniia, see M. A. Rakhmatullin, "Krest'ianskoe dvizhenie v Rossii v 20–kh godakh XIX v.," *Ezhegodnik po agrarnoi istorii Vostochnoi Evropy 1965 g.* (Moscow, 1970), 326–31; V. A. Fedorov, "Krest'ianskoe dvizhenie v tsentral'no-promyshlennykh guberniiakh Rossii v 1800–1860–kh godakh," ibid., 312; and Fedorov, *Krest'ianskoe dvizhenie v tsentral'noi Rossii,* 49. On rare occasions volneniia encompassed thousands of peasants from many estates over a broad geographical area and approached full-scale revolts; for one such outbreak, see I. I. Ignatovich, *Krest'ianskoe dvizhenie na Donu v 1820 g.* (Moscow, 1937); and KD-1, 578–616.

34. For examples of volneniia beginning with replacement of starosty, see KD-1, 729–31, 741–44; KD-2, 287–89; KD-3, 138–39, 365, 371–72, 555. See also K. N. Shchepetov, *Krepostnoe pravo v votchinakh Sheremetevykh (1708–1885)* (Moscow: Izdanie dvortsa-muzeia, 1947), 150–52; Alefirenko, *Krest'ianskoe dvizhenie i krest'ianskii vopros v Rossii,* 139–40; Sivkov, "Iz istorii krest'ianskikh vosstanii v XVIII v.," 79; and I. Kuznetsov, ed., "Krepostnye krest'iane sela Barasheva-Usada v pervoi polovine XIX v.," *Krasnyi arkhiv,* 77 (1936), 125–28.

35. On the role of ispravniki and Russian rural administration in general, see George L. Yaney, *The Systematization of Russian Government: Social Evolution in the Domestic Administration of Imperial Russia, 1711–1905* (Urbana: University of Illinois Press, 1973), passim, esp. 69–71, 129–43, 218–19. For fascinating descriptions of authorities' responses to volneniia, see two reminiscences by Stepan Timofeevich Slovutinskii, a nobleman who served as an aide to the governor of Riazan province from 1847 to 1859, "Bunt i usmirenie v imenii Golitsyna (1847 g.)," and "Krest'ianskie volneniia v Riazanskoi gubernii (s 1847 po 1858)," both reprinted with other material in S. T. Slovutinskii, *General Izmailov i ego dvornia; otryvki iz vospominanii* (Moscow: Academia, 1937), 241–461.

36. Historians have offered varying estimates of how often soldiers were needed to put down volneniia. According to one analysis troops were used to restore order on 125 of 349 estates where volneniia occurred between 1844 and 1849; a more recent and comprehensive study of seven central-industrial provinces between 1801 and 1860 indicates that soldiers were used in only 162 of 1,119 volneniia. See Iu. I. Gerasimov, "Krest'ianskoe dvizhenie v Rossii v 1844–1849 gg.," *Istoricheskie zapiski,* 50 (1955), 266; and Fedorov, *Krest'ianskoe dvizhenie v tsentral'noi Rossii,* 46, 48.

37. Petition to Moscow Governor G. M. Bezobrazov, Vishegorodskaia vo-

lost', Vereiskii district, Moscow province, 1823, KD-1, 739–40; report of Vereiskii district ispravnik Bukolov to Moscow Governor Bezobrazov, 4 Nov. 1823, KD-1, 741.

38. Ibid., 741–44.

39. Report of Adjutant Baranov to Moscow Governor-General D. V. Golitsyn, 7 Dec. 1823, KD-1, 744–45.

40. Kozitsyn to Kiselev, Chembarskii district, Penza province, 27 Oct. 1851, KD-3, 135; petition to Kiselev, 30 Oct. 1851, KD-3, 135–37.

41. Governor A. A. Panchulidzev, Penza province, to Kiselev, 14 Nov. 1851, KD-3, 138–39.

42. Ibid., 140–42, and 621 (note 121).

43. Petition of Denis Il'in to Kiselev, 7 Dec. 1852, KD-3, 142–43, and 621 (note 123).

44. Petition of Savelii Matveev to Nicholas I, Bezhetskii district, Tver province, 29 Jan. 1852, KD-3, 266–68.

45. Tver Governor A. P. Bakunin to M. I. Leks, official of the Ministry of Internal Affairs, 17 July 1852, KD-3, 269–71.

46. Governor Bakunin to Minister of Internal Affairs D. G. Bibikov, 30 June 1853, KD-3, 273; Governor Bakunin to Minister of Internal Affairs Bibikov, 9 Feb. 1854, KD-3, 274–75.

47. N. T. Baranov to Nicholas I, 17 July 1854, KD-3, 276–77; Baranov to Nicholas I, 12 Aug. 1854, KD-3, 277–78. The tsar noted on Baranov's first report that severe punishment was necessary as an example.

48. Governor Bakunin to Minister of Internal Affairs Bibikov, 20–23 Aug. 1854, KD-3, 278–79, 636–37 (note 262); petition of Aleksei Vasil'ev to the head of the Corps of Gendarmes, A. F. Orlov, 21 Dec. 1854, KD-3, 282. The last phrase rhymes in Russian: "stuzhu i nuzhdu, kholod i golod."

49. KD-3, 637 (notes 265 and 266); Governor Bakunin to Minister of Internal Affairs S. S. Lanskoi, 9 Oct. 1856, KD-3, 283; Acting Governor P. E. Ivanov to Lanskoi, 23 July 1857, KD-3, 284.

50. Slave autobiographies, written either by fugitives who escaped to the North or by freedmen after emancipation, are the best sources of information on slave confrontations. Some of these are cited below. These can be supplemented by interviews with ex-slaves in George P. Rawick, ed., *The American Slave: A Composite Autobiography* (Westport, Conn.: Greenwood Publishing Company, 1972), and *The American Slave: A Composite Autobiography Supplement, Series 1* (Westport, Conn.: Greenwood Press, 1977). Also important are the trial records contained in Catterall, *Judicial Cases concerning American Slavery*. Plantation records are notably reticent on the subject of slave conflicts, although much can be gleaned by reading between the lines; planters often complained about insubordination but rarely discussed confrontations except in terms of complete slave subjugation, no doubt because to do so required admitting a degree of slave assertiveness that most planters were loathe to recognize.

51. For examples of eighteenth-century confrontations, see *The Diary of*

Colonel Landon Carter of Sabine Hall, 1752–1778, ed. Jack P. Greene (Charlottesville: University Press of Virginia, 1965), II, 754; Lathan Algerna Windley, "A Profile of Runaway Slaves in Virginia and South Carolina from 1730 through 1787" (Ph.D. diss., University of Iowa, 1974), 153; and Catterall, *Judicial Cases concerning American Slavery,* III, 415–16, 416–17, 423–25.

52. Frederick Douglass, *My Bondage and My Freedom* (New York: Dover Publications, 1969; orig. pub. 1855), 205–49 (quotations 243, 246).

53. Elizabeth Keckley, *Behind the Scenes: Or, Thirty Years a Slave, and Four Years in the White House* (New York, 1868), 36, 37–38.

54. For differing evaluations of slave autobiographies and interviews as sources, see John W. Blassingame, "Using the Testimony of Ex-Slaves: Approaches and Problems," *Journal of Southern History,* 41 (Nov. 1975), 473–92; David Thomas Bailey, "A Divided Prism: Two Sources of Black Testimony on Slavery," ibid., 46 (Aug. 1980), 381–404; and Norman R. Yetman, "Ex-Slave Interviews and the Historiography of Slavery," *American Quarterly,* 36 (Summer 1984), 181–210.

55. For examples of confrontations in the writings of other ex-slaves, see Solomon Northup, *Twelve Years a Slave . . .* (New York, 1855), 108–52; Austin Steward, *Twenty-Two Years a Slave, and Forty Years a Freeman* (Rochester, N.Y., 1859), 33–39, 56–61; H. C. Bruce, *The New Man. Twenty-Nine Years a Slave. Twenty-Nine Years a Free Man* (York, Pa., 1895), 34–36; and Louis Hughes, *Thirty Years a Slave: From Bondage to Freedom* (Milwaukee, 1897), 95–99.

56. Account of Fanny Moore in Rawick, *The American Slave,* XV, 132.

57. *State v. Abram (a slave),* 10 Ala. 928, January 1847, in Catterall, *Judicial Cases concerning American Slavery,* III, 162; *Martineau v. Hooper,* 8 Mart. La. 699, September 1820, ibid., 466.

58. *Jacob (a slave) v. State,* 3 Humphreys 493, December 1842, in Catterall, *Judicial Cases concerning American Slavery,* II, 516–17.

59. Commander of the 6th Bashkir regiment, Major Shaidarov, to Novgorod province Governor P. I. Sumarokov, 5 May 1813, KD-1, 291; Viatka province Governor K. Ia. Tiufiaev to Minister of Internal Affairs D. N. Bludov, 18 July 1834, KD-2, 257; report of Ol'gopol'skii district ispravnik I. Shumkevich to Governor-General D. G. Bibikov of Podolia and Volhynia provinces, 5 May 1848, KD-2, 617; report of staff-officer Ivashentsov to Chief of the Corps of Gendarmes V. A. Dolgorukov, Riazan province, 14 Nov. 1856, KD-3, 556; report of Esaul Rubanovskii to the chief ataman of the Don forces, A. K. Kireev, 7 Feb. 1811, KD-1, 269. For a similar incident among eighteenth-century serfs who worked in textile and paper factories owned by nobleman A. A. Goncharov in Kaluga province, see report of Voevoda Aleksei Khvoshchinskoi to the Manufaktur-Kollegiia, 10 Dec. 1752, in *Materialy po istorii volnenii krepostnykh manufakturakh,* 17. On the importance of the obshchina as the serfs' agency of social protest, see Fedorov, *Krest'ianskoe dvizhenie v tsentral'noi Rossii,* 50–51; and I. S. Prokof'eva,

Krest'ianskaia obshchina v Rossii vo vtoroi polovine XVIII-pervoi polovine XIX v. (na materialakh votchin Sheremetevykh (Leningrad: "Nauka" Leningradskoe otdelenie, 1981), 185–209.

60. Report of the director of the Department of Police, V. V. Orzhevskii, to Minister of Internal Affairs L. A. Perovskii, 1851, KD-3, 109; *Materialy dlia istorii krepostnago prava v Rossii: Izvlecheniia iz sekretnykh otchetov Ministerstva vnutrennikh del za 1836–1856 g.* (Berlin, 1872), 81–84; report of Kostroma province Governor N. I. Zhukov to Minister of Internal Affairs L. A. Perovskii, 16 Oct. 1842, KD-2, 443. For statistics on and brief descriptions of murders of serfowners and stewards, see the annual reports in *Materialy dlia istorii krepostnago prava,* and in *Krest'ianskoe dvizhenie 1827–1869 godov,* ed. E. A. Morokhovets (Moscow: Gosudarstvennoe sotsial'no-ekonomicheskoe izdatel'stvo, 1931), I. See also V. I. Krutikov, *Krest'ianskoe dvizhenie v Tul'skoi gubernii v kontse XVIII i pervoi polovine XIX veka* (Tula: Tul'skii gosudarstvennyi pedagogicheskii institut imeni L. N. Tolstogo, 1972), 40, 51.

61. Report of Iaroslavl province Governor K. M. Poltoratskii to Minister of Internal Affairs D. N. Bludov, 2 Oct. 1834, KD-2, 287–89. On the prevalence of house serfs among individual petitioners, see L. B. Genkin, "Krest'ianskie zhaloby pervoi poloviny XIX v. kak istoricheskii istochnik (po materialam Gosudarstvennogo arkhiva Iaroslavskoi oblasti)," in *Voprosy istorii sel'skogo khoziaistva, krest'ianstva, i revoliutsionnogo dvizheniia v Rossii* (Moscow: Izdatel'stvo Akademii nauk SSSR, 1961), 167–68.

62. Steward, *Twenty-Two Years a Slave,* 33–39 (quotation, 36); Michael S. Hindus, "Black Justice under White Law: Criminal Prosecutions of Blacks in Antebellum South Carolina," *Journal of American History,* 63 (Dec. 1976), 585; testimony of Anthony Abercrombie in Rawick, *The American Slave,* VI, 7. For examples of court testimony on group murders of whites, see Catterall, *Judicial Cases concerning American Slavery,* II, 60, 132–34, III, 200–1, 301–2, 342.

63. Quotations are from testimony of Susan Broaddus in Charles L. Perdue, et al., eds., *Weevils in the Wheat: Interviews with Virginia Ex-Slaves* (Charlottesville: University Press of Virginia, 1976), 55; and testimony of Ishrael Massie, ibid., 210. On slaves' protecting fugitives, see Allan Kulikoff, "The Origins of Afro-American Society in Tidewater Maryland and Virginia, 1700 to 1790," *William and Mary Quarterly,* 3rd ser., 35 (April 1978), 252–54; and Larry Gara, *The Liberty Line: The Legend of the Underground Railroad* (Lexington: University of Kentucky Press, 1961), 54–62.

64. Northup, *Twelve Years a Slave,* 247–48; *The Narrative of William W. Brown, a Fugitive Slave . . .* (Reading, Mass.: Addison-Wesley, 1969; orig. pub. 1848), 21–24 (quotation, 23–24); testimony of Father Baker in Rawick, *The American Slave . . . Supplement, Series 1,* I, 33; Bruce, *The New Man,* 34; Mullin, *Flight and Rebellion,* 152–53; Lofton, *Insurrection in South Carolina,* 138–54; Oates, *The Fires of Jubilee,* 115.

65. Latin American slaves engaged in collective acts of resistance more

than did North American; for an account of collective behavior by Brazilian slaves in some ways resembling a Russian volnenie, see Stuart B. Schwartz, "Resistance and Accommodation in Eighteenth-Century Brazil: The Slaves' View of Slavery," *Hispanic American Historical Review,* 57 (Feb. 1977), 69–81.

66. On serf petitions see, in addition to specific sources cited below, Genkin, "Krest'ianskie zhaloby pervoi poloviny XIX v."; E. S. Paina, "Zhaloby pomeshchich'ikh krest'ian pervoi poloviny XIX v. kak istoricheskii istochnik," *Istoriia SSSR,* 1964, no. 6, 110–17; G. A. Kavtaradze, "Zhaloby krest'ian pervoi poloviny XIX veka kak istochnik dlia izucheniia ikh sotsial'-nykh trebovanii," *Vestnik Leningradskogo universiteta,* 1968, no. 20, 54–61. Numerous examples of petitions can be found in KD-1, KD-2, and KD-3.

67. A. E. Vorms et al., eds., *Pamiatniki istorii krest'ian XIV–XIX vv.* (Moscow: Izdanie N. N. Klochkova, 1910), 139–41, 230; Isabel de Madariaga, "Catherine II and the Serfs: A Reconsideration of Some Problems," *Slavonic and East European Review,* 52 (Jan. 1974), 47–54.

68. Petition of peasants of Atrada village, Saratov province, to Paul I, 10 April 1797, KD-1, 143–46. Statistics on the number of petitions to the tsar are from KD-1, KD-2, and KD-3.

69. Petitions dated 31 July 1837 and 11 June 1839 in K. V. Fedotov, ed., "Dokumenty pomeshchich'ego proizvola," in *Vologodskii arkhiv: sbornik dokumentov i materialov* (Vologda: Vologodskoe knizhskoe izdatel'stvo, 1961), 155–57. Statistics on petitions in Saratov province are from L. N. Iurovskii, *Saratovskie votchiny: Statistiko-ekonomicheskie ocherki i materialy iz istorii krupnogo zemlevladeniia i krepostnogo khoziaistva v kontse XVIII i nachale XIX stoletiia* (Saratov: Izdanie Saratovskogo instituta narodnogo khoziaistva, 1923), 150–54.

70. Petition of Frolko Anan'in to Morozov, 2 March 1660, in *Akty khoziaistva boiarina B. I. Morozova,* ed. A. I. Iakovlev (Moscow: Izdatel'stvo Akademii nauk SSSR, 1940, 1945), II, 121.

71. Petition to Countess Bobrinskaia, 29 March 1849, in Kuznetsov, "Krepostnye krest'iane sela Barasheva-Usada," 136–37; E. I. Indova, *Krepostnoe khoziaistvo v nachale XIX veka po materialam votchinnogo arkhiva Vorontsovykh* (Moscow: Izdatel'stvo Akademii nauk SSSR, 1955), 105. On collective protests against hirers and stewards in Belorussia, see P. G. Kozlovskii, "Klassovaia bor'ba krest'ian v magnatskikh votchinakh Belorussii vo vtoroi polovine XVIII v.," in *Ezhegodnik po agrarnoi istorii Vostochnoi Evropy 1966 g.* (Tallin, 1971), 259–62.

72. Douglass, *My Bondage and My Freedom,* 226–32; A. O. Harris to Polk, 30 Dec. 1833, Harris to Polk, 3 Jan. 1834, Ephraim Beanland to Polk, 1 Feb. 1834, in *The Southern Plantation Overseer as Revealed in His Letters,* ed. John Spencer Bassett (Northampton, Mass.: Printed for Smith College, 1925), 55–65. For other examples of Polk's slaves complaining to whites about their overseer, see ibid., 145, 153–54.

73. Letter of Caesar Brown, 30 May 1830, in *Blacks in Bondage: Letters of American Slaves,* ed. Robert S. Starobin (New York: New Viewpoints, 1974), 102.

74. Frances Anne Kemble, *Journal of a Residence on a Georgian Plantation in 1838–1839* (Chicago: Afro-Am Press, 1969), 170, 190–91.

75. Petition of noblemen from Galich and other cities to Tsar Aleksei Mikhailovich, 1657, in A. A. Novosel'skii, ed., "Kollektivnye dvorianskie chelobitnye o syske beglykh krest'ian i kholopov vo vtoroi polovine XVII v.," *Dvorianstvo i krepostnoi stroi Rossii XVI–XVIII vv.: Sbornik statei, posviashchennyi pamiati Alekseia Andreevicha Novosel'skogo* (Moscow: Izdatel'stvo "Nauka," 1975), 304–8; for other petitions, see ibid., 308–43. On government efforts to combat flight in the decades after the establishment of serfdom, see A. G. Man'kov, *Razvitie krepostnogo prava v Rossii vo vtoroi polovine XVII veka* (Moscow: Izdatel'stvo Akademii nauk SSSR, 1962), 22–113; and N. V. Kozlova, *Pobegi krest'ian v Rossii v pervoi treti XVIII veka (iz istorii sotsial'no-ekonomicheskoi zhizni strany)* (Moscow: Izdatel'stvo Moskovskogo universiteta, 1983). For imperial decrees establishing searches, see Vorms et al., *Pamiatniki istorii krest'ian,* 76–90. On flight in the seventeenth and eighteenth centuries see, in addition to sources cited below, Semevskii, *Krest'iane v tsarstvovanie Imperatritsy Ekateriny II,* I, 395–412; Alefirenko, *Krest'ianskoe dvizhenie i krest'ianskii vopros v Rossii,* 94–114; Man'kov, *Razvitie krepostnogo prava v Rossii,* 122–78; and V. I. Meleshko, *Klassovaia bor'ba v Belorusskoi derevne vo vtoroi polovine XVII–XVIII v.* (Minsk: "Nauka i tekhnika," 1982), 103–26.

76. Statistics are from Indova et al., "Klassovaia bor'ba krest'ianstva," 29–30; and Mavrodin, *Klassovaia bor'ba i obshchestvenno-politicheskaia mysl' v Rossii,* 13–14. For listings of empty peasant households, see K. V. Sivkov, ed., *Materialy po istorii krest'ianskogo i pomeshchich'ego khoziaistva pervoi chetverti XVIII v.* (Moscow: Izdatel'stvo Akademii nauk SSSR, 1951), passim.

77. K. N. Shchepetov, "Beglye krest'iane kniazia A. M. Cherkasskogo v pervoi polovine XVIII v.," *Istoriia SSSR,* 1963, no. 6, 129–30.

78. Ibid., 130–36. Decades later, however, many of the successful fugitives once again found themselves serfs. In 1743 Count P. B. Sheremetev acquired most of Cherkasskii's holdings, and in the 1750s he established his control over Znamenskoe village in Kazan, where 4,849 of the original fugitives had fled; the inhabitants came under the authority of a steward and were forced to pay obrok dues (ibid., 136–37).

79. L. G. Zanicheva, "Krest'ianskie pobegi vo vtoroi polovine XVII v. (po materialam syska G. S. Isupova v Meshcherskom krae)," in *Ezhegodnik po agrarnoi istorii Vostochnoi Evropy 1964 g.* (Kishinev, 1966), 233; petition of noblemen of Novosil'skii district, 1681, to Tsar Fedor Alekseevich, in Novosel'skii, "Kollektivnye dvorianskie chelobitnye," 320. The diary of Kursk pomeshchik Ivan Petrovich Annenkov is filled with entries such as that of 20 Dec. 1757 in which he noted that "some peasants ran away"; although most

fled in groups, some went "leaving their husbands" or "leaving his wife." See "Dnevnik kurskogo pomeshchika I. P. Annenkova," in *Materialy po istorii SSSR*, V: *Dokumenty po istorii XVIII veka*, ed. A. A. Novosel'skii (Moscow: Izdatel'stvo Akademii nauk SSSR, 1957), 732. See also S. M. Kashtanov, ed., "Otdatochnye knigi Troitse-Sergieva monastyria 1649–1650 gg.," in *Istoricheskii arkhiv*, 8 (1953), 202; *Akty khoziaistva boiarina B. I. Morozova*, passim.; and Kozlova, *Pobegi krest'ian*, 55–57.

80. See Man'kov, *Razvitie krepostnogo prava v Rossii*, 27–29, 122–78; Alefirenko, *Krest'ianskoe dvizhenie i krest'ianskii vopros v Rossii*, 94–97, 107–12; Ia. E. Vodarskii, *Naselenie Rossii v kontse XVII-nachale XVIII veka (Chislennost', soslovno-klassovyi sostav, razmeshchenie)* (Moscow: Izdatel'stvo "Nauka," 1977), 155–56; E. A. Shvetsova, "Kolonizatsiia Tambovskogo uezda v XVII veka," in *Ezhegodnik po agrarnoi istorii Vostochnoi Evropy 1964 g.* (Kishinev, 1966), 209–12; S. Ia. Borovoi et al., "O nekotorykh zakonomernostiakh razvitiia agrarnykh otnoshenii v iuzhnykh koloniziruemykh okrainakh Evropeiskoi Rossii (vtoraia polovina XVIII-pervaia polovina XIX v.)," *Ezhegodnik po agrarnoi istorii Vostochnoi Evropy 1968 g.* (Leningrad, 1972), 8–11; Blum, *Lord and Peasant in Russia*, 552–53; and William H. McNeill, *Europe's Steppe Frontier: 1500–1800* (Chicago: University of Chicago Press, 1964), 192–93.

81. V. S. Rumiantseva, "O krest'ianakh-raskol'nikakh kanuna vosstaniia S. T. Razina (po dokumentam Prikaza tainykh del)," in Cherepnin, *Krest'ianskie voiny v Rossii*, 270–86; Vorms et al., *Pamiatniki istorii krest'ian*, 114. See also Man'kov, *Razvitie krepostnogo prava v Rossii*, 22–103; L. G. Zanicheva, "Sotsial'no-ekonomicheskoe polozhenie krest'ian shatskogo uezda v XVII v.," *Ezhegodnik po agrarnoi istorii Vostochnoi Evropy 1962 g.* (Minsk, 1964), 209–10; and Zanicheva, "Krest'ianskie pobegi vo vtoroi polovine XVII v.," 231–33.

82. See Denise Eeckaute, "Les brigands en Russie du XVIIᵉ au XIXᵉ siècle: mythe et réalité," *Revue d'histoire moderne et contemporaine*, 12 (July-Sept. 1965), 161–202; Alefirenko, *Krest'ianskoe dvizhenie i krest'ianskii vopros v Rossii*, 114–32; Mavrodin, *Klassovaia bor'ba i obshchestvenno-politicheskaia mysl' v Rossii*, 17–28; Mank'ov, *Razvitie krepostnogo pravo v Rossii*, 107–10. For examples of imperial decrees on brigands, see *Materialy dlia istorii Voronezhskoi i sosednikh gubernii. Voronezhskie akty*, I (Voronezh, 1887), 113–14; S. I. Volkov, ed., "Instruktsiia upravitelem dvortsovykh volostei 1731 g.," *Istoricheskii arkhiv*, 6 (1951), 196–97; and Vorms et al., *Pamiatniki istorii krest'ian*, 159–60. The quotation is from an 1839 report of the Ministry of Internal Affairs in *Materialy dlia istorii krepostnago prava v Rossii*, 37–38.

83. Quotations are from Vorms et al., *Pamiatniki istorii krest'ian*, 159–60, and E. I. Druzhinina, *Iuzhnaia Ukraina v 1800–1825 gg.* (Moscow: Izdatel'stvo "Nauka," 1970), 166. See also V. M. Kabuzan, "Krest'ianskaia kolonizatsiia severno prichernomor'ia (Novorossii) v XVIII-pervoi polovine XIX vv. (1719–1857 gg.)," *Ezhegodnik po agrarnoi istorii Vostochnoi Ev-*

ropy 1964 g. (Kishinev, 1966), 313–24 (population statistics, 323); Borovoi et al., "O nekotorykh zakonomernostiakh razvitiia agrarnykh otnoshenii," 8–11; and E. I. Druzhinina, *Iuzhnaia Ukraina v period krizisa feodalizma, 1825–1860 gg.* (Moscow: Izdatel'stvo "Nauka," 1981). For statistics on serfs as a proportion of New Russia's population, see N. M. Shepukova, "Izmenenie udel'nogo vesa chastnovladel'cheskogo krest'ianstva v sostave naseleniia Evropeiskoi Rossii (XVIII-pervaia polovina XIX v.)," *Voprosy istorii,* 1959, no. 12, 131.

84. Information on 1845, in *Materialy dlia istorii krepostnago prava v Rossii,* 141; information on 1846, ibid., 161; information on 1847, ibid., 177, 170; *Zemledel'cheskaia gazeta* (St. Petersburg), e.g., 6 Dec. 1835, 784, 24 April 1836, 263–64 (quotation), and 1 March 1840, 141. See also I. I. Ignatovich, *Krest'ianskoe dvizhenie v Rossii v pervoi chetverti XIX veka* (Moscow: Izdatel'stvo sotsial'no-ekonomicheskoi literatury, 1963), 443–48; Shchepetov, *Krepostnoe pravo v votchinakh Sheremetevykh,* 225–27; and Fedorov, *Krest'ianskoe dvizhenie v tsentral'noi Rossii,* 105–7.

85. A. V. Kleiankin, "S Volgi—na legendarnuiu 'Reku Dar'iu'," *Voprosy istorii,* 1971, no. 6, 146–53 (quotation, 152). On distant-land legends, see Chistov, *Russkie narodnye sotsial'no-utopicheskie legendy,* 239–327.

86. Message from pomeshchiki of Pavlovskii district, Voronezh province, to Minister of Internal Affairs D. N. Bludov, May 1837, KD-2, 330–31; information on 1847, in *Materialy dlia istorii krepostnago prava v Rossii,* 170–77; "List of Incidents throughout the Empire from 27 September to 4 October [1847]," in KD-2, 579–80; report on actions of the Third Department for 1847, in *Krest'ianskoe dvizhenie 1827–1869 godov,* I, 75 (quotation). For other incidents on mass flight, see ibid., 13–14, 72; *Materialy dlia istorii krepostnago prava v Rossii,* 138; KD-2, 223–26; and KD-3, 593–95.

87. See documents dating from the fall of 1850 in KD-3, 76–86. Quotations are from note of official A. G. Shcherbinin to Minister of Internal Affairs Perovskii, ibid., 76, and report of Saratov Governor M. L. Kozhevnikov to the head of the Third Department A. F. Orlov, ibid., 81.

88. On efforts of serfs to volunteer for military service, see KD-3, 431–516. Quotations are from report of Minister of War V. A. Dolgorukov to the head of the Third Department A. F. Orlov, 29 June 1854, ibid., 441; report of the head of the second district Corps of Gendarmes S. V. Perfil'ev to Orlov, ibid., 442; and letter of special official A. N. Leont'ev to Manager of the Third Department L. V. Dubel't, 24 Sept. 1850, ibid., 79. See also Fedorov, *Krest'ianskoe dvizhenie v tsentral'noi Rossii,* 126–32.

89. *The Diary of Colonel Landon Carter,* 27 April 1766, I, 291–92. On laws to combat flight, see Windley, "A Profile of Runaway Slaves," 15–62. On slaves' helping fugitives, see Kulikoff, "The Origins of Afro-American Society," 253–54.

90. On slave flight in the colonial South, see Windley, "A Profile of Runaway Slaves"; Daniel E. Meaders, "South Carolina Fugitives as Viewed

through Local Newspapers with Emphasis on Runaway Notices, 1732–1801," *Journal of Negro History,* 60 (April 1975), 284–319; Mullin, *Flight and Rebellion,* esp. 34–46, 94–121; Wood, *Black Majority,* 239–68; Robert McColley, *Slavery and Jeffersonian Virginia* (Urbana: University of Illinois Press, 1964), 91–101; Kenneth W. Porter, "Negroes on the Southern Frontier, 1670–1763," in *The Negro on the American Frontier,* 155–80; and Lathan A. Windley, comp., *Runaway Slave Advertisements: A Documentary History from the 1730s to 1790* (Westport, Conn.: Greenwood Press, 1983). On the impact of the Revolutionary War, see Chapter 6, page 320.

91. See Gara, *The Liberty Line,* which provides a useful corrective to overblown claims concerning the underground railroad; Stampp, *The Peculiar Institution,* 109–24; Genovese, *Roll, Jordan, Roll,* 648–57. On efforts by slaveowners and government officials to catch fugitives, see Stanley W. Campbell, *The Slave Catchers: Enforcement of the Fugitive Slave Law, 1850–1860* (Chapel Hill: University of North Carolina Press, 1968). On conditions among free blacks in the North, see Leon F. Litwack, *North of Slavery: The Negro in the Free States, 1790–1860* (Chicago: University of Chicago Press, 1961). For interviews taken in 1855 with fugitives in Canada, see Benjamin Drew, ed., *The Refugee: A North-Side View of Slavery* (Reading, Mass.: Addison-Wesley, 1969; orig. pub. Boston, 1856), quotation 77.

92. *The Rev. J. W. Loguen, as a Slave and as a Freeman. A Narrative of a Real Life* (Syracuse, N.Y., 1859), 260–341; *Life and Times of Frederick Douglass, Written by Himself* (London: Collier Books, 1962; orig. pub. 1881), 198–201; Ball, *Slavery in the United States,* 481–517; John Moore interviewed by Henry Bibb in *Voice of the Fugitive,* 4 June 1851, reprinted in John W. Blassingame, ed., *Slave Testimony: Two Centuries of Letters, Speeches, Interviews, and Autobiographies* (Baton Rouge: Louisiana State University Press, 1977), 275. For other examples of slaves' escaping more than once, see Ball, *Slavery in the United States,* 387–517; and Henry Bibb, *Narrative of the Life and Adventures of Henry Bibb, an American Slave* (New York, 1849), 46–174.

93. Gara, *The Liberty Line,* 2–18, 44–68; *The Narrative of William W. Brown,* 42; *Narrative of the Life of Frederick Douglass,* 91–99; James W. C. Pennington, *The Fugitive Blacksmith; Or, Events in the History of James W. C. Pennington,* 2nd ed. (London, 1849), 12–43; narrative of James Curry in *The Liberator,* 10 Jan. 1840, reprinted in Blassingame, *Slave Testimony,* 140–44.

94. For estimates of the number of fugitives, see Gara, *The Liberty Line,* 36–41; and Genovese, *Roll, Jordan, Roll,* 648. But see also Aptheker, *American Negro Slave Revolts,* 140–41, for much higher estimates.

95. *The Secret Diary of William Byrd of Westover, 1709–1712,* ed. Louis B. Wright and Marion Tinling (Richmond, Va.: Dietz Press, 1941), 24 June, 28 June, 1 July, 8 July 1710, 195, 196, 197, 199, 202. For similar examples, see *The Diary of Colonel Landon Carter,* esp. I, 289–92, 370–72, 389, 415,

II, 601, 777; Betts, *Thomas Jefferson's Farm Book*, 20–23, 34–35, 46; and *The Diaries of George Washington, 1748–1799*, ed. John C. Fitzpatrick (Boston: Houghton Mifflin, 1925), I, 155, II, 28.

96. "The Plantation Diary of Bennet H. Barrow," in *Plantation Life in the Florida Parishes of Louisiana, 1836–1846, as Revealed in the Diary of Bennet H. Barrow*, ed. Edwin Adams Davis (New York: Columbia University Press, 1943), 130–33; Northup, *Twelve Years a Slave*, 241; Faust, *James Henry Hammond and the Old South*, 94–95. See also Bassett, *The Southern Plantation Overseer*, passim; James Monette Day Book and Diary (microfiche copy, original in Louisiana State University Archives), 29, 30 Sept. 1848, 4; Jacob Stroyer, *Sketches of My Life in the South*, part 1 (Salem, 1879), 37–38; Gara, *The Liberty Line*, 19–23, 27–30; Escott, *Slavery Remembered*, 83–85.

97. Quotations are from recollections of Cornelia Carney and Ishrael Massie, both in Perdue et al., *Weevils in the Wheat*, 66–67, and 209–10. For a similar recollection from Alabama, see Anka Bishop in Rawick, *The American Slave: A Composite Autobiography*, VI, 35–36.

98. Mullin, *Flight and Rebellion*, 34–35; Philip D. Morgan, "Black Society in the Lowcountry, 1760–1810," in *Slavery and Freedom in the Age of the American Revolution*, ed. Ira Berlin and Ronald Hoffman (Charlottesville: University Press of Virginia, 1983), 138–39; Michael P. Johnson, "Runaway Slaves and the Slave Communities in South Carolina, 1799 to 1830," *William and Mary Quarterly*, 3rd ser., 38 (July 1981), 418–41; Samuel Ringgold Ward, *Autobiography of a Fugitive Negro: His Anti-Slavery Labours in the United States, Canada, & England* (London, 1855), 18–25; Horace W. Hawkins interview with the American Freedmen's Inquiry Commission in Blassingame, *Slave Testimony*, 442. See also Faust, *James Henry Hammond and the Old South*, 94.

99. Meaders, "South Carolina Fugitives"; Johnson, "Runaway Slaves and the Slave Communities in South Carolina," 420; Windley, "A Profile of Runaway Slaves," 65; Gara, *The Liberty Line*, 44–68; Genovese, *Roll, Jordan, Roll*, 648–57; Henry Atkinson in Drew, *The Refugee*, 56. For another example of how flight separated spouses, see *Narrative of the Life and Adventures of Henry Bibb*, 46–174.

100. Ball, *Slavery in the United States*, 385; Hughes, *Thirty Years a Slave* 80; Drew, *The Refugee*, 189, 68.

101. Octave Johnson interview with American Freedmen's Inquiry Commission in Blassingame, *Slave Testimony*, 395. For a description of a "village called *des Nantanapalle*," inhabited by fifteen fugitive slaves in colonial Louisiana, see *Re Indian Sansoucy*, 3 La. Hist. Q. 443, March 1727, in Catterall, *Judicial Cases concerning American Slavery*, III, 401. On American maroons, see especially Herbert Aptheker, "Maroons within the Present Limits of the United States," *Journal of Negro History*, 24 (1939), 167–84; Genovese, *From Rebellion to Revolution*, 68–81; and Porter, *The Negro on the American Frontier*, passim.

102. Genovese, *From Rebellion to Revolution*, 77.

103. See especially the essays in Richard Price, ed., *Maroon Societies: Rebel Slave Communities in the Americas*, 2nd ed. (Baltimore: Johns Hopkins University Press, 1979); Genovese, *From Rebellion to Revolution*, 51–81; Kopytoff, "The Early Political Development of Jamaican Maroon Societies"; and Craton, *Testing the Chains*, 61–96.

104. For recognition among Soviet historians that the consequences for serfs of large-scale revolt were at best ambiguous, see Shapiro, "Ob istoricheskoi roli krest'ianskikh voin," 61–63; Mavrodin, "Po povodu kharktera i istoricheskogo znacheniia krest'ianskikh voin," 45–51; and Rakhmatullin, "Krest'ianskaia voina v Rossii 1773–1775 godov," 51–55. Western historians have stressed the harsh repression the revolts engendered. See, e.g., Avrich, *Russian Rebels*, 47, 109–11, 117–18, 243, 247, 258. For accounts of repression following southern slave revolts, see Wood, *Black Majority*, 323–26; Darold D. Wax, "'The Great Risque We Run': The Aftermath of Slave Rebellion at Stono, South Carolina, 1739–1745," *Journal of Negro History*, 67 (Summer 1982), 136–47; Lofton, *Insurrection in South Carolina*, 155–239; and Oates, *The Fires of Jubilee*, 129–45. But for very different assessments, see Mavrodin et al., "Ob osobennostiakh krest'ianskikh voin v Rossii," 70; Cherepnin, "Ob izucheniia krest'ianskikh voin v Rossii," 19–20; and Genovese, *Roll, Jordan, Roll*, 596.

105. Jefferson to Reuben Perry, 16 April 1812, in Betts, *Thomas Jefferson's Farm Book*, 35; Beverly Jones's recollection in Perdue et al., *Weevils in the Wheat*, 181; A. A. Novosel'skii, *Votchinnik i ego khoziaistvo v XVII veke* (Moscow: Gosudarstvennoe izdatel'stvo, 1929), 128 (quotation); Shchepetov, *Krepostnoe pravo v votchinakh Sheremetevykh*, 148–49; "Nakaz kn. A. M. Cherkasskogo prikazchiku sela Markova (Moskovskogo uezda)" (1719), in I. F. Petrovskaia, ed., "Nakazy votchinnym prikazchikam pervoi chetverti XVIII v.," *Istoricheskii arkhiv*, 8 (1953), 252.

106. See "The Plantation Diary of Bennet H. Barrow," passim, e.g., 4 Jan. 1839, 140. For an example of a seigneurial instruction ordering the reassignment of fugitives' obligations, see "Nakaz kn. A. M. Cherkasskogo," 251. The process is described in Shchepetov, *Krepostnoe pravo v votchinakh Sheremetevykh*, 147–48.

107. Account of Lucretia Alexander in Rawick, *The American Slave*, VIII, 33; *An Autobiography of the Reverend Josiah Henson* (Reading, Mass.: Addison-Wesley, 1969; orig. pub. 1849), 14; account of Robert Falls in Rawick, *The American Slave*, XVI, Tennessee section, 13. For examples of brutal treatment of slaves who resisted authorities in the colonial period, see *Re Negro Pierrot*, 11 La. Hist. Q. 288, January 1742, in Catterall, *Judicial Cases concerning Slavery*, III, 415–16; and *Attorney General v. Overzee*, 4 Md. Arch. 190, December 1658, ibid., IV, 11–13.

108. *Narrative of the Life of Frederick Douglass*, 71–83; *The Narrative of William W. Brown*, 2–4; "The Plantation Diary of Bennet H. Barrow," 164, 191, and passim.

109. Bruce, *The New Man*, 37–38; Phillips and Glunt, *Florida Plantation Records*, 111, 113–14. On slaves' getting away with challenging owners and overseers, see Blassingame, *The Slave Community*, 212–13.

110. Account of Martha Bradley in Rawick, *The American Slave*, VI, 46, and account of John Walton, ibid., V, 129.

111. *Jim (a slave) v. State*, 15 Ga. 535, July 1854, in Catterall, *Judicial Cases concerning Slavery*, III, 36; *State v. Abram (a slave)*, 10 Ala. 1928, January 1847, ibid., III, 162. For examples of slaves being acquitted on technicalities, see *State v. King (a slave)*, 12 La. An. 593, July, 1857, ibid., III, 657; and *State v. Henderson (a slave)*, ibid., III, 667–68.

112. Douglass, *My Bondage and My Freedom*, 95; Bruce, *The New Man*, 36–37. For a similar statement, see J. W. Lindsay's testimony in Blassingame, *Slave Testimony*, 397–98. See also Owens, *This Species of Property*, 104.

113. For an example of serfs' wringing administrative concessions from their owners through volneniia, see the incident involving Kiselev's serfs discussed above, pages 261–62.

114. Notation of Minister of Internal Affairs A. L. Perovskii on report of Governor M. A. Orosov, 3 Oct. 1849, KD-2, 641. For the peasants' version, see petition of peasants of Ivanovskoe village to Perovskii, 1849, KD-2, 211, 638–39.

115. Letter of A. I. Chernishev, president of the Senate, to Minister of Internal Affairs Bibikov, 22 Oct. 1853, KD-3, 385; and circular of Bibikov to provincial marshals of nobility, 24 Oct. 1853, KD-3, 386. For the full story of this volnenie, see KD-3, 358–86.

116. For positive responses from noblemen to serf petitions reporting on stewards, see Novosel'skii, *Votchinnik i ego khoziaistvo v XVII veke*, 74; and Kozlovskii, "Klassovaia bor'ba krest'ian v magnatskikh votchinakh Belorussii," 259–62. For examples of owners granting small favors in response to peasant petitions, see *Akty khoziaistva boiarina B. I. Morozova*, I, 138, 167, 192, 205–6, 215–16, II, 31, 121; Indova, *Krepostnoe khoziaistvo v nachale XIX veka*, 165–66; and Kuznetsov, "Krepostnye krest'iane sela Barasheva-Usada," 122.

117. KD-1, 688–97; Slovutinskii, *General Izmailov i ego dvornia*, 163–238.

118. Petition of peasants of Khristinovka village, Kiev province, to Alexander I, 7 Sept. 1817, KD-1, 458–60 (quotation, 460); report of Kiev Governor F. V. Nazimov to Manager of the Ministry of Police S. K. Viazmitinov, 19 March 1819, KD-1, 460–64; petition of peasants of Khristinovka village to Alexander I, 8 Aug. 1820, KD-1, 465–68 (quotation, 467); and note, 796.

119. Head of the second district Corps of Gendarmes S. V. Perfil'ev to Chief of the Corps A. F. Orlov, 27 July 1851, KD-3, 200–1; and note, 629 (quotation).

120. Iurovskii, *Saratovskie votchiny*, 159–61. On putting estates under the control of guardians, see Chapter 2, page 143.

121. See documents in the appendix of Iurovskii, *Saratovskie votchiny,* 165–83 (quotations, 169, 174, 180, 183).

122. Douglass, *My Bondage and My Freedom,* 246, and KD-3, 555.

6. Protest, Unity, and Disunity

1. "Opis' del arkhiva Vladimirskago gubernskago praveleniia. Dela kantseliarii Vladimirskago gubernatora XVIII veka," in *Trudy Vladimirskoi uchenoi arkhivnoi kommissii,* 5 (1903), 29–30; S. T. Slovutinskii, "Krest'ianskie volneniia v Riazanskoi gubernii (s 1847 po 1858)," in *General Izmailov i ego dvornia; otryvki iz vospominanii* (Moscow: Academia, 1937), 344; Jefferson to Joseph Daugherty, Monticello, 31 July 1806, in *Thomas Jefferson's Farm Book with Commentary and Relevant Extracts from Other Writings,* ed. Edwin Morris Betts (Princeton: Princeton University Press, 1953), 22; and John I. Garner to Polk, 3 Nov. 1839, in *The Southern Plantation Overseer as Revealed in His Letters,* ed. John Spencer Bassett (Northampton, Mass.: Printed for Smith College, 1925), 129.

2. Resolution of serfs owned by M. F. Engalichev, Sviatovo village, Pereslavskii district, Vladimir province, Dec. 1796, KD-1, 34; L. N. Iurovskii, *Saratovskie votchiny: Statistiko-ekonomicheskie ocherki i materialy iz istorii krupnogo zemlevladeniia i krepostnogo khoziaistva v kontse XVIII i v nachale XIX stoletiia* (Saratov: Izadanie Saratovskogo instituta narodnogo khoziaistva, 1923), 159; petition of serfs owned by Lev and Leodor Mel'nitskii, Bezhetskii district, Tver province, to Minister of Justice V. N. Panin, 1851, KD-3, 224; V. A. Fedorov, *Krest'ianskoe dvizhenie v tsentral'noi Rossii 1800–1860 (po materialam tsentral'no-promyshlennykh gubernii)* (Moscow: Izdatel'stvo Moskovskogo universiteta, 1980), 48–50.

3. Iurovskii, *Saratovskie votchiny,* 159; petition of peasants of Khristinovka village, Kiev province, to Alexander I, 7 Sept. 1817, KD-1, 458–60 (quotation, 460); petition of peasant representatives, Gribanovo village, Volokolamskii district, Moscow province, to Chief of the Corps of Gendarmes A. Kh. Benkendorf, 27 Sept. 1841, KD-2, 406–7; petition of Countess Bobrinskaia's peasants to head steward P. Violev, 16 June 1852, in I. Kuznetsov, ed., "Krepostnye krest'iane sela Barasheva-Usada v pervoi polovine XIX v.," *Krasnyi arkhiv,* 77 (1936), 140–41. See also K. V. Fedotov, ed., "Dokumenty pomeshchich'ego proizvola," in *Vologodskii arkhiv: sbornik dokumentov i materialov* (Vologda: Vologodskoe knizhskoe izdatel'stvo, 1961), 147–68; and Slovutinskii, "General Izmailov i ego dvornia," in *General Izmailov i ego dvornia,* esp. 194–97.

4. Iu. Iu. Kakh and Kh. M. Ligi, "O sviazi mezhdu antifeodal'nymi vystupleniiami krest'ian i ikh polozheniem," *Istoriia SSSR,* 1976, no. 2, 86–91; B. G. Litvak, *Opyt statisticheskogo izucheniia krepostnogo dvizheniia v Rossii XIX v.* (Moscow: Izdatel'stvo "Nauka," 1967), 16–17.

5. Report of I. I. Funduklei, governor of Kiev province, to Nicholas I, 6 April 1848, KD-2, 610–11. For examples of resistance to inventory reforms

in Podolia province, see KD-2, 614–22. For other examples of resistance to administrative reorganization, see E. S. Kogan, *Ocherki istorii krepostnogo khoziaistva po materialam votchin Kurakinykh 2-i poloviny XVIII veka* (Moscow: Gosudarstvennyi istoricheskii muzei, 1960), 83–94; Slovutinskii, "Krest'ianskie volneniia v Riazanskoi gubernii," 353–55; report of A. F. Orlov, head of the Third Department, to Nicholas I, 20 Nov. 1847, KD-2, 598; and KD-3, 135–43 (on the volnenie of P. D. Kiselev's serfs discussed in Chapter 5).

6. Fedorov, *Krest'ianskoe dvizhenie v tsentral'noi Rossii,* 48–50. For recognition by historians of the major role played by change of ownership in producing serf unrest, see ibid., 53, 100–5; P. K. Alefirenko, *Krest'ianskoe dvizhenie i krest'ianskii vopros v Rossii v 30–50–kh godakh XVIII veka* (Moscow: Izdatel'stvo Akademii nauk SSSR, 1958), 142–50; V. V. Mavrodin, *Klassovaia bor'ba i obshchestvenno-politicheskaia mysl' v Rossii v XVIII v. (1725–1773 gg.)* (Leningrad: Izdatel'stvo Leningradskogo universiteta, 1964), 33–38; I. I. Ignatovich, *Pomeshchich'i krest'iane nakanune osvobozhdeniia,* 2nd ed. (Moscow: I. D. Sytin, 1910), 259; V. I. Krutikov, *Krest'ianskoe dvizhenie v Tul'skoi gubernii v kontse XVIII i pervoi polovine XIX veka* (Tula: Tul'skii gosudarstvennyi pedagogicheskii institut imeni L. N. Tolstogo, 1972), 45; and Reginald Zelnik, "The Peasant and the Factory," in *The Peasant in Nineteenth-Century Russia,* ed. Wayne S. Vucinich (Stanford: Stanford University Press, 1968), 172.

7. Report of Kursk province Governor A. I. Nelidov to St. Petersburg Governor-General S. K. Viazmitinov, 30 April 1817, KD-1, 501–3; report of Kursk province Governor A. S. Kozhukhov to Viazmitinov, 6 Oct. 1819, KD-1, 503–5; peasant petition to Alexander I, 29 July 1820, KD-1, 505–7 (quotations); and report of Governor Kozhukhov to Manager of the Ministry of Internal Affairs V. P. Kochubei, 2 Oct. 1820, KD-1, 507–8.

8. Slovutinskii, "Bunt i usmirenie v imenii Golitsyna (1847 g.)," in *General Izmailov i ego dvornia,* 262–68 (quotations 267, 268). For a different perspective on this volnenie, see KD-2, 597–99.

9. Report of Voronezh Governor A. B. Sontsov to Minister of Police A. D. Balashov, 18 Oct. 1810, KD-1, 265–67; report of Balashov to Alexander I, Nov. 1810, KD-1, 268–69; report of Esaul Rubanovskii to Don Forces Ataman A. K. Kireev, 7 Feb. 1811, KD-1, 269–70; report of Riazan province Governor I. I. Kniazev to Governor-General of St. Petersburg S. K. Viazmitinov, 12 April 1817, KD-1, 555–57; petitions to Alexander I of peasants sold to N. A. Durasov, 31 Dec. 1817 and Feb. 1818, KD-1, 557–60; report of Governor Kniazev to Viazmitinov, 4 July 1818, KD-1, 560–61 (quotation, 560); report of Acting Governor-General of Novorossia and Bessarabia P. I. Fedorov to Minister of Internal Affairs Bibikov, 29 Oct. 1852, KD-3, 235–36 (quotation).

10. Report of Viatka province Governor K. Ia. Tiufiaev to Minister of Internal Affairs D. N. Bludov, 18 July 1834, KD-2, 257 (quotation); report of the head of the fourth district Corps of Gendarmes Buksgevgen to Chief

of the Corps A. F. Orlov, 17 April 1845, KD-2, 536–37; petition of peasants owned by pomeshchik Tsekhanovetskii to Nicholas I, May 1847, KD-2, 538 (quotation); report of F. A. Pushkin, Governor of Voronezh province, to Alexander I, 19 April 1804, KD-1, 186–88; petition of peasants owned by Vikulin to Alexander I, June 1804, KD-1, 188–89 (quotation). On resistance of former state peasants to serfdom, see I. I. Ignatovich, *Krest'ianskoe dvizhenie v Rossii v pervoi chetverti XIX veka* (Moscow: Izdatel'stvo sotsial'no-ekonomicheskoi literatury, 1963), 42–50, 294–320, 323–51; and Fedorov, *Krest'ianskoe dvizhenie v tsentral'noi Rossii*, 79–86.

11. Information extracted from the report of the Department of Police for 1842, in *Materialy dlia istorii krepostnago prava v Rossii: Izvlecheniia iz sekretnykh otchetov Ministerstva vnutrennikh del za 1826–1856 g.* (Berlin, 1872), 77 (quotation); declaration of peasants of Kur'ianovskaia village, 2 Sept. 1812, KD-1, 285 (for the full story of this volnenie, see 282–95); report of Tver Governor A. P. Tol'stoi to Minister of Internal Affairs D. N. Bludov, 19 Dec. 1833, KD-2, 239–41; and petition of peasants' representative I. S. Zhuravlev to Nicholas I, July 1834, KD-2, 241–44 (quotations, 243).

12. Report of Archdeacon Vasilii Popov to Governor of Stavropol province A. A. Volotskii, 14 Jan. 1853, KD-3, 358–61 (for the suppression of this volnenie, see 362–85); petition of peasants of Churilovka village, Riazan province, to Alexander I, Dec. 1856, KD-3, 559; report of Aide-de-camp D. A. Sheping to A. A. Arakhcheev, 7 July 1816, KD-1, 403–6. On the destabilizing impact of an 1847 ukaz allowing serfs collectively to buy their freedom if their estate was sold at auction, see M. A. Rakhmatullin, "Zakonodatel'naia praktika tsarskogo samoderzhaviia: Ukaz ot 8 noiabria 1847 goda i popytki ego primeneniia," *Istoriia SSSR*, 1982, no. 2, 35–52.

13. Report of Ekaterinburg district lower zemskii court to Perm province Governor K. Ia. Tiufiaev, 12 Sept. 1828, KD-2, 119–23 (quotation, 120); petition of peasants of Ivanovskoe village, Kniagininskii district, Nizhnii Novgorod province, to Minister of Internal Affairs L. A. Perovskii, Aug. 1849, KD-2, 638. For other examples of confusion over ownership, see KD-1, 393–401, 739–41; KD-2, 96–99; KD-3, 421–23, 540–42.

14. Ignatovich, *Krest'ianskoe dvizhenie v Rossii v pervoi chetverti XIX veka*, 443–48; E. I. Indova, *Krepostnoe khoziaistvo v nachale XIX veka po materialam votchinnogo arkhiva Vorontsovykh* (Moscow: Izdatel'stvo Akademii nauk SSSR, 1955), 105; K. N. Shchepetov, *Krepostnoe pravo v votchinakh Sheremetevykh (1708–1885)* (Moscow: Izdanie dvortsa-muzeia, 1947), 225–27; L. G. Zanicheva, "Krest'ianskie pobegi vo vtoroi polovine XVII v. (Po materialam syska G. S. Isupova v Meshcherskom krae)," *Ezhegodnik po agrarnoi istorii Vostochnoi Evropy 1964 g.* (Kishinev, 1966), 234. For an example of flight by a cruelly abused servant girl in 1826, see Fedotov, "Dokumenty pomeshchich'ego proizvola," 151–55.

15. Information for 1847 in *Materialy dlia istorii krepostnago prava v Rossii,* 171. On economic distress as a major cause of flight to the middle

Volga region in the early eighteenth century, see N. V. Kozlova, *Pobegi krest'ian v Rossii v pervoi treti XVIII veka (iz istorii sotsial'no-ekonomicheskoi zhizni strany)* (Moscow: Izdatel'stvo Moskovskogo universiteta, 1983), 57–60.

16. Statistics on the relative prevalence of resistance among state peasants and serfs are from Litvak, *Opyt statisticheskogo izucheniia krepostnogo prava v Rossii XIX v.*, 10. On resistance of state peasants to renters in the western provinces, see N. M. Druzhinin, *Gosudarstvennye krest'iane i reforma P. D. Kiseleva* (Moscow: Izdatel'stvo Akademii nauk SSSR, 1946, 1958), I, 102–20; and V. I. Meleshko, *Klassovaia bor'ba v Belorusskoi derevne vo vtoroi polovine XVII–XVIII v.* (Minsk: "Nauka i tekhnika," 1982), passim. For examples of such resistance, see KD-1, 215–22; and KD-2, 310–12.

17. Information extracted from the report of the Department of Police for 1842, in *Materialy dlia istorii krepostnago prava v Rossii*, 71; report of A. P. Naidanov, manager of Viatka province Court lands office, 28 May 1834, KD-2, 251; report of Perm province Governor I. I. Ogarev to Minister of Internal Affairs A. G. Stroganov, 11 June 1841, KD-2, 409; and review of the popular mood in 1837, in *Krest'ianskoe dvizhenie 1827–1869 godov*, ed. E. A. Morokhovets (Moscow: Gosudarstvennoe sotsial'no-ekonomicheskoe izdatel'stvo, 1931), I, 24. On the Kiselev reforms and resistance to them, see Druzhinin, *Gosudarstvennye krest'iane i reforma P. D. Kiseleva*, I, 476–628, II, 8–290, 456–524; and P. G. Ryndziunskii, "Dvizhenie gosudarstvennykh krest'ian v Tambovskoi gubernii v 1842–1844 gg.," *Istoricheskie zapiski*, 54 (1955), 315–27. For an account by the chief forester of Shadrinskii district, Perm province, of attempts to suppress the potato riots, see M. S. Valevskii, "Volneniia krest'ian v Zaural'skoi chasti Permskago kraia v 1842–1843 gg.," *Russkaia starina*, 26 (1879), 411–32, 627–46.

18. For recognition among historians of the dominant role played by punishment in producing flight, see Peter H. Wood, *Black Majority: Negroes in Colonial South Carolina from 1670 through the Stono Rebellion* (New York: Alfred A. Knopf, 1974), 247; Lathan Algerna Windley, "A Profile of Runaway Slaves in Virginia and South Carolina from 1730 through 1787" (Ph.D. diss., University of Iowa, 1974), 164–71; Kenneth M. Stampp, *The Peculiar Institution: Slavery in the Ante-Bellum South* (New York: Vintage Books, 1956), 109–24; Larry Gara, *The Liberty Line: The Legend of the Underground Railroad* (Lexington: University of Kentucky Press, 1961), 23–26; and Eugene D. Genovese, *Roll, Jordan, Roll: The World the Slaves Made* (New York: Pantheon Books, 1974), 648–57.

19. *Another Secret Diary of William Byrd of Westover, 1739–1741, with Letters & Literary Exercises, 1696–1726*, ed. Maude H. Woodfin (Richmond, Va.: Dietz Press, 1942), 21 Jan. 1741, 129; H. C. Bruce, *The New Man. Twenty-Nine Years a Slave. Twenty-Nine Years a Free Man* (York, Pa., 1895), 32. See also "The Plantation Diary of Bennet H. Barrow," in *Plantation Life in the Florida Parishes of Louisiana, 1836–1848, as Reflected in*

the Diary of Bennet H. Barrow, ed. Edwin Adams Davis (New York: Columbia University Press, 1943), 22 Sept. 1838, 130; and Solomon Northup, *Twelve Years a Slave* . . . (New York, 1855), 241.

20. Northup, *Twelve Years a Slave,* 108–10; *Williams v. Fambro,* 30 Ga. 232, March 1860, in *Judicial Cases concerning American Slavery and the Negro,* ed. Helen Tunnicliff Catterall (New York: Octagon Books, 1968; orig. pub. Washington, 1926–37), III, 75–76; Frederick Douglass, *My Bondage and My Freedom* (New York: Dover Publications, 1969; orig. pub. 1855), 205–47; and Elizabeth Keckley, *Behind the Scenes. Or, Thirty Years a Slave, and Four Years in the White House* (New York, 1868), 33–38. See also Austin Steward, *Twenty-Two Years a Slave, and Forty Years a Freeman* (Rochester, N.Y., 1859), 58; and *State v. Abram (a Slave),* 10 Ala. 928, 1847, in Catterall, *Judicial Cases concerning American Slavery,* III, 162.

21. Louis Hughes, *Thirty Years a Slave. From Bondage to Freedom* (Milwaukee, 1897), 95–99; Bruce, *The New Man,* 34–36; testimony of Jeff Stanfield in *Weevils in the Wheat: Interviews with Virginia Ex-Slaves,* ed. Charles L. Perdue et al. (Charlottesville: University Press of Virginia, 1976), 280; Beanland to Polk, 1 April 1834, in Bassett, *The Southern Plantation Overseer,* 67.

22. Northup, *Twelve Years a Slave,* 110; *Jeff (a Slave) v. State,* 37 Miss. 321, Oct. 1859, in Catterall, *Judicial Cases concerning American Slavery,* III, 363; Douglass, *My Bondage and My Freedom,* 241.

23. *An Autobiography of the Reverend Josiah Henson* (Reading, Mass.: Addison-Wesley, 1969; orig. pub. 1849), 13–15. For another example, see George P. Rawick, ed., *The American Slave: A Composite Autobiography* (Westport, Conn.: Greenwood Publishing Company, 1972), VI, 47.

24. John I. Garner to Polk, 3 Nov. 1839, in Bassett, *The Plantation Overseer,* 129. For an example of slave children running away to visit their mother held on a nearby plantation in South Carolina, see *Reed v. Delmore,* 2 Brevard 76, May 1806, in Catterall, *Judicial Cases concerning American Slavery,* II, 287. Historians have generally emphasized the prevalence of local flight to visit relatives; see Wood, *Black Majority,* 253–54; Gerald W. Mullin, *Flight and Rebellion: Slave Resistance in Eighteenth-Century Virginia* (New York: Oxford University Press, 1972), 106; Windley, "A Profile of Runaway Slaves," 164–71; Stampp, *The Peculiar Institution,* 109–24; and Genovese, *Roll, Jordan, Roll,* 648–57. Gutman argued, however, that family ties more often impeded than caused slave flight; Gutman, *The Black Family in Slavery and Freedom,* 264–69.

25. Testimony of Heywood Ford in Rawick, *The American Slave,* VI, 124. For examples of confrontations with patrollers breaking up slave dances, see Steward, *Twenty-Two Years a Slave,* 33–39; and testimony of Fanny Moore in Rawick, *The American Slave,* XV, 132.

26. Beanland to Polk, 22 Dec. 1833, in Bassett, *The Plantation Overseer,* 54; Drew Gilpin Faust, *James Henry Hammond and the Old South: A Design for Mastery* (Baton Rouge: Louisiana State University Press, 1982), 69–

104; and *Nott v. Botts,* 13 La. 202, March 1839, in Catterall, *Judicial Cases concerning American Slavery,* III, 519. See also Charles C. Jones to his parents, Savannah, 27 Oct. 1860, in *The Children of Pride: A True Story of Georgia and the Civil War,* ed. Robert Manson Myers (New Haven: Yale University Press, 1972), 624.

27. *The Narrative of William W. Brown, a Fugitive Slave, and a Lecture Delivered before the Female Anti-Slavery Society of Salem, 1847* (Reading, Mass.: Addison-Wesley, 1969; orig. pub. 1847), 37; Douglass, *My Bondage and My Freedom;* Steward, *Twenty-Two Years a Slave,* 106–15; American Freedmen's Inquiry Commission interview with Isaac Throgmorton in *Slave Testimony: Two Centuries of Letters, Speeches, Interviews, and Autobiographies,* ed. John W. Blassingame (Baton Rouge: Louisiana State University Press, 1977), 434; and Douglass, *My Bondage and My Freedom,* 141–249. See also Charles Ball, *Slavery in the United States: A Narrative of the Life and Adventures of Charles Ball, a Black Man* (New York, 1837), 483.

28. *Narrative of the Life and Adventures of Henry Bibb, an American Slave* (New York, 1849), 17, 16; James W. C. Pennington, *The Fugitive Blacksmith; or, Events in the History of James W. C. Pennington,* 2nd ed. (London, 1849), 1–9; Hughes, *Thirty Years a Slave,* 80–86; interview with David Barrett in *Anti-Slavery Record,* 3 (July 1837), reprinted in Blassingame, *Slave Testimony,* 189. See also Ball, *Slavery in the United States,* 383–85.

29. Douglass, *My Bondage and My Freedom,* 112–13. Many historians have stressed the disproportionate number of skilled slaves among fugitives; see, e.g., Mullin, *Flight and Rebellion,* 94–97; Gara, *The Liberty Line,* 41–44; and Ira Berlin, *Slaves without Masters: The Free Negro in the Antebellum South* (New York: Pantheon Books, 1974), 45, 160. For a different view, see Wood, *Black Majority,* 240–41.

30. Ball, *Slavery in the United States,* 387. On the role of change in ownership in precipitating flight, see Wood, *Black Majority,* 253–54; Windley, "A Profile of Runaway Slaves," 164–71; Daniel E. Meaders, "South Carolina Fugitives as Viewed through Local Colonial Newspapers with Emphasis on Runaway Notices, 1732–1801," *Journal of Negro History,* 60 (April 1975), 298–99; Stampp, *The Peculiar Institution,* 109–24; and Gara, *The Liberty Line,* 23–26.

31. Interview with David Holmes in *Anti-Slavery Reporter,* 1 Feb. 1853, reprinted in Blassingame, *Slave Testimony,* 295–302; interview with Wesley Norris, 1866, ibid., 467.

32. Quotations are from Betts, *Thomas Jefferson's Farm Book,* 29; and *Webb v. Billinger,* 2 Dessaussure 482, May 1807, in Catterall, *Judicial Cases concerning American Slavery,* II, 290–91. For the Revolutionary War's impact on master-slave relations, see especially Jeffrey J. Crowe, "Slave Rebelliousness and Social Conflict in North Carolina, 1775 to 1802," *William and Mary Quarterly,* 3rd ser., 37 (Jan. 1980), 79–102; Sylvia R. Fry, "Between Slavery and Freedom: Virginia Blacks in the American Revolution," *Journal*

of Southern History, 49 (Aug. 1983), 375–98; Philip D. Morgan, "Black Society in the Lowcountry, 1760–1810," in *Slavery and Freedom in the Age of the American Revolution,* ed. Ira Berlin and Ronald Hoffman (Charlottesville: University Press of Virginia, 1983), 108–13; Alan Kulikoff, "Uprooted Peoples: Black Migrants in the Age of the American Revolution, 1790–1820," ibid., 144–45; and Benjamin Quarles, *The Negro in the American Revolution* (Chapel Hill: University of North Carolina Press, 1961), passim.

33. See KD-1, 18; KD-2, 817; and KD-3, 732–33. For higher figures based on more recent research in local archives, see Fedorov, *Krest'ianskoe dvizhenie v tsentral'noi Rossii,* 43–51; M. A. Rakhmatullin, "Krest'ianskoe dvizhenie v Rossii v 20-kh godakh XIX v.," in *Ezhegodnik po agrarnoi istorii Vostochnoi Evropy 1965 g.* (Moscow, 1970), 325; and V. D. Chernyshev, ed., "Dokumenty o krest'ianskom dvizhenii v 1826 godu," *Voprosy istorii,* 1975, no. 8, 102–11.

34. See E. P. Trifil'ev, *Ocherki iz istorii krepostnago prava v Rossii. Tsarstvovanie Imperatora Pavla pervago* (Kharkov: Tipografiia "Pechatnoe Delo" kn. N. N. Gagarina, 1904), 7–20, 284–316; and Litvak, *Opyt statisticheskogo izucheniia krepostnogo dvizheniia,* 7–9.

35. Trifil'ev, *Ocherki iz istorii krepostnago prava,* 284–336 (quotation, 331); and M. De-Pule, "Krest'ianskoe dvizhenie pri Imperatore Pavle Petroviche," in *Russkii arkhiv,* 1869, no. 3, 525–77 (quotation, 544). For examples of volneniia sparked by Paul's accession to the throne, see KD-1, 52–56, 88–90, 142–43.

36. Quotations are from the journal of the Committee of Ministers, 24 Sept. 1812, KD-1, 306; and declaration of peasants of Kur'ianovskaia village to Vologda province assessor G. A. Vakhrushev, 2 Sept. 1812, KD-1, 285 (for the full story of this volnenie, see 282–95). See also Ignatovich, *Krest'ianskoe dvizhenie v Rossii v pervoi chetverti XIX veka,* 76–100; and V. I. Babkin, "Spetsifika klassovoi bor'by v period Otechestvennoi voiny 1812 goda," *Istoriia SSSR,* 1972, no. 2, 111–21.

37. Quotations are from N. L. Manzei to P. V. Golenishev-Kutuzov, governor-general of St. Petersburg province, 23 May 1826, in Chernyshev, "Dokumenty o krest'ianskom dvizhenii v 1826 godu," 107; and Major-General G. I. Nostits to General Saken, 24 July 1826, KD-2, 37, 39, 41. See also M. A. Rakhmatullin, "Krepostnoe krest'ianstvo Rossii i dvizhenie dekabristov," *Istoriia SSSR,* 1977, no. 4, 127–51. Of 176 volneniia, petitions, and murders of pomeshchiki and stewards listed in KD-2 for 1826, 96 occurred in the three provinces of St. Petersburg, Moscow, and Pskov; see KD-2, 818–21.

38. The quotation is from information extracted from the report of the Department of Police for 1848 in *Materialy dlia istorii krepostnago prava v Rossii,* 192. For examples of disorders in conjunction with the introduction of inventory reforms, see KD-2, 609–11, 614–22. See also Iu. I. Gerasimov, "Krest'ianskoe dvizhenie v Rossii v 1844–1849 gg.," *Istoricheskie zapiski,* 50 (1955), 255–60; Rakhmatullin, "Zakonodatel'naia praktika tsarskogo

samoderzhaviia," 38–46; and Edward C. Thaden (with the collaboration of Marianna Forster Thaden), *Russia's Western Borderlands, 1710–1870* (Princeton: Princeton University Press, 1984), 133–43. Of 202 volneniia, petitions, and murders occurring in 1848, 112 took place in Volhynia, Podolia, and Kiev provinces; see KD-2, 818–21.

39. Report of Voronezh province Governor Iu. A. Dolgorukii to Minister of Internal Affairs D. G. Bibikov, 3 July 1855, KD-3, 475–76. On massive peasant flight during the Crimean war, see Chapter 5, pages 284–85.

40. Slovutinskii, "Bunt i usmirenie v imenii Golitsyna (1847 g.)," 256. Statistics on petitions to the crown are from KD-1, 18; KD-2, 817; and KD-3, 732–33. For suggestive but sketchy suggestions of a change in serf consciousness, see the editor's introduction to KD-3, 16–18; V. A. Fedorov, "K voprosu ob ideologii krepostnogo krest'ianstva," in *Voprosy agrarnoi istorii tsentra i severo-zapada RSFSR: Materialy mezhvusovskoi nauchnoi konferentsii* (Smolensk: Ministerstvo prosveshcheniia RSFSR, 1972), 150–51; Fedorov, *Krest'ianskoe dvizhenie v tsentral'noi Rossii*, 125–44; and M. A. Rakhmatullin, "Vozrastnoi sostav vozhakov krest'ianskogo dvizheniia v Rossii (1826–1857 gg.)," *Istoriia SSSR*, 1984, no. 4, 139–49.

41. See, e.g., Gutman, *The Black Family in Slavery and Freedom*, 33–34; and Willie Lee Rose, *Slavery and Freedom*, ed. William W. Freehling (New York: Oxford University Press, 1982), 35–36, 198–99.

42. The quotation is from William Richardson, *Anecdotes of the Russian Empire* (London: Frank Cass, 1968; orig. pub. 1784), 241, 196–97.

43. The quotation is from Berlin, *Slaves without Masters*, 217. Of 488,070 free blacks in the United States in 1860, only 46.3 percent lived in the South, and of these, 47.9 percent lived in the border region of Washington, D.C., Delaware, Maryland, and Kentucky. In short, only 27.9 percent of the nation's free Negroes lived in those states that contained 91.3 percent of its slaves; furthermore, in the deep South 53.2 percent of free Negroes lived in cities, but only 4.3 percent of slaves did. Statistics on free Negroes are from Berlin, *Slaves without Masters*, 136, 176; those on slaves are from *Slavery and the Southern Economy: Sources and Readings*, ed. Harold D. Woodman (New York: Harcourt, Brace & World, 1966), 14.

44. The quotation is from Anatole Leroy-Beaulieu, *The Russian Peasant* (Sandoval, N.M.: Coronado Press, 1962; orig. pub. in French, 1881–89), 62–63. Statistics on the size of peasant households are from Ia. E. Vodarskii, *Naselenie Rossii v kontse XVII-nachale XVIII veka (Chislennost', soslovno-klassovyi sostav, razmeshchenie)* (Moscow: Izdatel'stvo "Nauka," 1977), 48. On changes in family relations as a consequence of emancipation, see also Stepniak, *The Russian Peasantry: Their Agrarian Condition, Social Life and Religion* (New York, 1888), 74; and N., "O krest'ianskikh semeinykh razdelakh v Voronezhskoi gubernii," in *Voronezhskii iubileinyi sbornik v pamiat' trekhsotletiia g. Voronezha* (Voronezh, 1886), 331–35. On state peasants, see Druzhinin, *Gosudarstvennye krest'iane i reforma P. D. Kiseleva;* and Olga Crisp, "The State Peasants under Nicholas I," *Slavonic and East European Review,* 37 (June 1959), 387–412.

45. The quotation is from Sarah Wooden Johnson in Perdue et al., *Weevils in the Wheat,* 163. On relations between free Negroes and slaves in the antebellum South, see Berlin, *Slaves without Masters,* 56–58, 197–98, 269–83. On the Cane River Negroes, see Gary B. Mills, *The Forgotten People: Cane River's Creoles of Color* (Baton Rouge: Louisiana State University Press, 1977). For the story of a remarkable slaveowning free Negro family in South Carolina, see Michael P. Johnson and James L. Roark, *Black Masters: A Free Family of Color in the Old South* (New York: W. W. Norton, 1984). On postemancipation hostility between ex-slaves and elite Negroes, see Peter Kolchin, *First Freedom: The Responses of Alabama's Blacks to Emancipation and Reconstruction* (Westport, Conn.: Greenwood Press, 1972), 142–43; Joel Williamson, *After Slavery: The Negro in South Carolina during Reconstruction, 1861–1877* (Chapel Hill: University of North Carolina Press, 1965), 316–17; Leon F. Litwack, *Been in the Storm So Long: The Aftermath of Slavery* (New York: Alfred A. Knopf, 1979), 513–14; and Thomas Holt, *Black over White: Negro Political Leadership in South Carolina during Reconstruction* (Urbana: University of Illinois Press, 1977), 43–71.

46. Berlin, *Slaves without Masters,* esp. 136, 217–49, 284–380; Richard C. Wade, *Slavery in the Cities: The South, 1820–1860* (New York: Oxford University Press, 1964), 143–80, 248–52; and Genovese, *Roll, Jordan, Roll,* 398–413. For the story of a free black man kidnapped into slavery, see Northup, *Twelve Years a Slave.*

47. See Paul D. Escott, *Slavery Remembered: A Record of Twentieth-Century Slave Narratives* (Chapel Hill: University of North Carolina Press, 1979), 95–100 (quotation 95). For the argument, exaggerated I believe, that slavery gave birth to a protonationalism among blacks, see Genovese, *Roll, Jordan, Roll,* passim.

48. Ball, *Slavery in the United States.* For other examples, see Douglass, *My Bondage and My Freedom; The Narrative of William W. Brown;* Bruce, *The New Man;* Northup, *Twelve Years a Slave;* Keckley, *Behind the Scenes;* and *Narrative of the Life of Moses Grandy, Late a Slave in the United States of America,* 2nd ed. (Boston, 1844).

49. The quotation is from Slovutinskii, "Bunt i usmirenie v imenii Golitsyna," 322. On peasant reaction to the populists, see, e.g., Franco Venturi, *Roots of Revolution: A History of Populist and Socialist Movements in Nineteenth Century Russia* (New York: Alfred A. Knopf, 1964), esp. 498–506.

50. Exchange between K. Shanskoi, steward of Bogorodskoe village, Arzamasskii district, and Morozov, 9 July and 14 July 1648, in *Akty khoziaistva boiarina B. I. Morozova,* ed. A. I. Iakovlev (Moscow: Izdatel'stvo Akademii nauk SSSR, 1940, 1945), I, 93–95; M. A. Obreskov to Commander-in-Chief in St. Petersburg S. K. Viazmitinov, 11 Aug. 1814, KD-1, 325–26.

51. Letter of staff officer F. T. Zagorskii to Chief of the Corps of Gendarmes A. F. Orlov, 4 Aug. 1855, KD-3, 479–83 (quotation, 483). For an example of successful use of witnesses to put down a volnenie, see KD-1,

286–87. On the local character of the peasant movement and the absence of a broad peasant consciousness, see M. A. Rakhmatullin, "K voprosu ob urovne obshchestvennogo sosnaniia krest'ianstva v Rossii," in *Voprosy agrarnoi istorii tsentra i severo-zapada RSFSR*, 158–70. For the argument that peasant class consciousness developed during the late 1850s, see Fedorov, "K voprosu ob ideologii krepostnogo krest'ianstva," 150–51.

52. Soviet historians have engaged in lengthy debates about the timing of the genesis of Russian capitalism. For a good review of this literature, see Samuel H. Baron, "The Transition from Feudalism to Capitalism in Russia: A Major Soviet Historical Controversy," *American Historical Review*, 77 (1972), 715–29. For important works dealing with serfs' economic activities, see N. L. Rubinshtein, *Sel'skoe khoziaistvo Rossii vo vtoroi polovine XVIII v.* (Moscow: Gosudarstvennoe izdatel'stvo, 1957); I. D. Koval'chenko, *Russkoe krepostnoe krest'ianstvo v pervoi polovine XIX v.* (Moscow: Izdatel'stvo Moskovskogo universiteta, 1967); and V. A. Fedorov, *Pomeshchich'i krest'iane tsentral'no-promyshlennogo raiona Rossii kontsa XVIII-pervoi poloviny XIX v.* (Moscow: Izdatel'stvo Moskovskogo universiteta, 1974). On licenses for peasant traders, see N. S. Sviridov, "Torguiushchie krest'iane kontsa krepostnoi epokhi (po materialam pervoi poloviny XIX stoletiia)," *Istoriia SSSR*, 1969, no. 5, 48–55 (statistics, 53).

53. Rubinshtein, *Sel'skoe khoziaistvo Rossii*, 315, 424–25; V. Geiman, "Boiarin B. I. Morozov i krupneishie ego votchinnye sela Murashkino i Lyskovo, Nizhegorodskogo uezda," in *Khoziaistvo krupnogo feodala-krepostnika XVIII v.* (Leningrad: Izdatel'stvo Akademii nauk SSSR, 1933, 1936), II, 20–31; D. I. Petrikeev, *Krupnoe krepostnoe khoziaistvo XVII v. po materialam votchiny boiarina B. I. Morozova* (Leningrad: Izdatel'stvo "Nauka," 1967), 164–66; Shchepetov, *Krepostnoe pravo v votchinakh Sheremetevykh*, 44–49, 72–76, 93–95, 182–96, 354; and Koval'chenko, *Russkoe krepostnoe krest'ianstvo*, 86–90, 205–17. See also A. M. Shabanova, "Biudzhety krest'ianskikh khoziaistv Aleksandro-Svirskoi votchiny v srediny XVIII veka (iz opyta sostavleniia krest'ianskikh biudzhetov)," in *Ezhegodnik po agrarnoi istorii Vostochnoi Evropy 1970 g.* (Riga, 1977), 106–7; and Indova, *Krepostnoe khoziaistvo v nachale XIX veka*, 79–85.

54. William Tooke, *View of the Russian Empire* (New York: Arno Press, 1970; orig. pub. London, 1800), III, 201; Shchepetov, *Krepostnoe pravo v votchinakh Sheremetevykh*, 180–82; Indova, *Krepostnoe khoziaistvo v nachale XIX veka*, 85–88; and Fedorov, *Pomeshchich'i krest'iane tsentral'no-promyshlennogo raiona Rossii*, 205–9, 219. On otkhodnichestvo in the seventeenth and eighteenth centuries, see also A. N. Sakharov, *Russkaia derevnia XVII v.: po materialam patriarshego khoziaistva* (Moscow: Izdatel'stvo "Nauka," 1966), 73–84; Alefirenko, *Krest'ianskoe dvizhenie i krest'ianskii vopros v Rossii*, 44–52, 164, 171; and M. Ia. Volkov and S. M. Troitskii, "O burzhuaznom rassloenii krest'ian i skladyvanii rynka naemnoi rabochei sily v Rossii v pervoi polovine XVIII v.," *Istoriia SSSR*, 1964, no. 4, 90–105.

55. The quotation is from E. I. Indova et al., "Problema klassovogo rassloeniia krest'ianstva perioda pozdneva feodalizma v svete trudov V. I. Lenina o razvitii kapitalizma v Rossii," *Ezhegodnik po agrarnoi istorii Vostochnoi Evropy 1961 g.* (Riga, 1963), 24. On categorization of stages of stratification, see I. D. Koval'chenko, "Nekotorye voprosy genezisa kapitalizma v krest'ianskom khoziaistve Rossii," *Istoriia SSSR*, 1962, no. 6, 70; and Koval'chenko, *Russkoe krepostnoe krest'ianstvo*, 367–73. For a few examples of the extensive literature on the subject, see "Diskussiia o rassloenii krest'ianstva v epokhu posdnego feodalizma," *Istorii SSSR*, 1966, no. 1, 70–81; Volkov and Troitskii, "O burzhuaznom rassloenii krest'ian"; and N. A. Bogoroditskaia, "Rassloenie krest'ian v Simbileiskom imenii Nizhegorodskogo uezda v pervoi polovine XIX v.," *Ezhegodnik po agrarnoi istorii Vostochnoi Evropy 1965 g.* (Moscow, 1970), 265–79.

56. Iu. A. Tikhonov, "Krest'ianskoe khoziaistvo tsentral'noi Rossii pervoi chetverti XVIII v. (Po materialam podvornogo opisaniia imeniia P. P. Shafirova v Zhernovskoi volosti Kashirskogo uezda v 1716 g.)," *Istoriia SSSR*, 1971, no. 4, 169–78; Indova, *Krepostnoe khoziaistvo v nachale XIX veka*, 115–17 (also 100–5, 130–33, 147–48); Koval'chenko, *Russkoe krepostnoe krest'ianstvo*, 349 (also passim, 108–286, 342–64). But for evidence that stratification intensified little in two agricultural regions, see A. Z. Baraboi, "Rassloenie i nachalo razlozheniia krest'ianstva na pravoberezhnoi Ukraine v pervoi polovine XIX v.," *Ezhegodnik po agrarnoi istorii Vostochnoi Evropy 1960 g.* (Kiev, 1962), 38–52; and Bogoroditskaia, "Rassloenie krest'ian v Simbileiskom imenii."

57. Mary Holderness, *New Russia* (New York: Arno Press, 1970; orig. pub. London, 1823), 111–12. On stratification in the Ukraine, see I. D. Boiko, "K voprosu o rassloenii ukrainskogo krest'ianstva vo vtoroi polovine XVI–pervoi polovine XVII v.," *Ezhegodnik po agrarnoi istorii Vostochnoi Evropy 1960 g.*, 27–37; Baraboi, "Rassloenie i nachalo razlozheniia krest'ianstva"; and Ignatovich, *Pomeshchich'i krest'iane nakanune osvobozhdeniia*, 173–94. On serfs renting and purchasing land, see, e.g., Sakharov, *Russkaia derevnia XVII v.*, 119–47; Rubinshtein, *Sel'skoe khoziaistvo Rossii*, 38–49, 128; Semevskii, *Krest'iane v tsarstvovanie Imperatritsy Ekateriny II*, I, 335–59; and Koval'chenko, *Russkoe krepostnoe krest'ianstvo*, passim.

58. P. B. Sheremetev, "Instruktsiia Iaroslavskoi moei votchiny iukhotskoi volosti prikashchiku . . . ," in Shchepetov, *Krepostnoe pravo v votchinakh Sheremetevykh*, 273; ibid., 355; Henry Rosovsky, "The Serf Entrepreneur in Russia," *Explorations in Entrepreneurial History*, 6 (May 1954), 207–33 (215–19 on Grachev); N. N. Shipov, "Istoriia moei zhizni: Razskaz byvshago krepostnago krest'ianina N. N. Shipova," *Russkaia starina*, 30 (1881), 145–47; Blum, *Lord and Peasant in Russia*, 474. See also Sviridov, "Torguiushchie krest'iane kontsa krepostnoi epokhi"; Slovutinskii, "General Izmailov i ego dvornia," 45–48; and William L. Blackwell, *The Beginnings of Russian Industrialization, 1800–1860* (Princeton: Princeton University Press, 1968), 205–11.

59. Shipov, "Istoriia moei zhizni," 135–40, 221–26 (on trading operations); *Vesti o Rossii: Povest' v stikhakh krepostnogo krest'ianina, 1830–1840 gg.*, ed. T. G. Snytko (Iaroslavl: Iaroslavskoe knizhskoe izdatel'stvo, 1961), quotation, 31.

60. Y. M. Sokolov, *Russian Folklore*, trans. Catherine Ruth Smith (New York: Macmillan, 1950), 208; Indova, *Krepostnoe khoziaistvo v nachale XIX veka*, 105; Kuznetsov, "Krepostnye krest'iane sela Barasheva-Usada," 132. For views similar to Indova's, see Shchepetov, *Krepostnoe pravo v votchinakh Sheremetevykh*, 106–7; and L. S. Prokof'eva, *Krest'ianskaia obshchina v Rossii vo vtoroi polovine XVIII-pervoi polovine XIX v. (na materialakh votchin Sheremetevykh)* (Leningrad: "Nauka" Leningradskoe otdelenie, 1981), 164–65.

61. Sakharov, *Russkaia derevnia XVII v.*, 83–84; Rubinshtein, *Sel'skoe khoziaistvo Rossii*, 30; Fedorov, *Pomeshchich'i krest'iane tsentral'no-promyshlennogo raiona*, 208–9; Shipov, "Istoriia moei zhizni," 229–32.

62. V. K. Iatsunskii, "Genezis kapitalizma v sel'skom khoziaistve Rossii," *Ezhegodnik po agrarnoi istorii Vostochnoi Evropy 1959 g.* (Moscow, 1961), 45–46. For a similar warning, see P. A. Zaionchkovskii, *Otmena krepostnogo prava v Rossii*, 3rd ed. (Moscow: Prosveshchenie, 1968), 24.

63. See Alefirenko, *Krest'ianskoe dvizhenie v Rossii*, 33–36 (information for table, 35).

64. R. M. Vvedenskii, "Kharakter pomeshchich'ei ekspluatatsii i biudzhety obrochnykh krest'ian v 20–40-e gody XIX v.," *Istoriia SSSR*, 1971, no. 3, 46–48. See also I. D. Koval'chenko and L. V. Milov, "Ob intensivnosti obrochnoi ekspluatatsii krest'ian tsentral'noi Rossii v kontse XVIII-pervoi polovine XIX v.," *Istoriia SSSR*, 1966, no. 4, 64; and Koval'chenko, *Russkoe krepostnoe krest'ianstvo*, passim, esp. 288, 300, 349.

65. Koval'chenko, *Russkoe krepostnoe krest'ianstvo*, 357–64 (358–59 for the example given).

66. For a thoughtful essay on this subject, see M. A. Rakhmatullin, "K voprosu o vliianii rassloeniia krest'ianstva na kharakter ego bor'by (20-e gody XIX v.)," *Istoriia SSSR*, 1970, no. 4, 154–67. See also two historiographical articles by V. A. Fedorov, "Istoriografiia krest'ianskogo dvizheniia v Rossii perioda razlozheniia krepostnichestva," *Voprosy istorii*, 1966, no. 2, 153; and "Noveishaia sovetskaia literatura o krest'ianskom dvizhenii v Rossii pervoi poloviny XIX v.," ibid., 1977, no. 1, 142–43; and his *Krest'ianskoe dvizhenie v tsentral'noi Rossii*, 111–14.

67. Wood, *Black Majority*, 104–30, 196–210; Alexander Hewatt, *An Historical Account of the Rise and Progress of the Colonies of South Carolina and Georgia* (London, 1779), II, 97; Morgan, "Black Society in the Lowcountry," 99. For the argument that in slaveowning societies where whites constituted a small proportion of the population they commonly allowed privileged groups of mulattoes to serve essential economic, social, and military functions, see Harry Hoetink, *Slavery and Race Relations in the Americas: An Inquiry into Their Nature and Nexus* (New York: Harper & Row,

1973), 36–37; and Laura Foner, "The Free People of Color in Louisiana and St. Domingue: A Comparative Portrait of Two Three-Caste Societies," *Journal of Social History,* 3 (Summer 1970), 415.

68. Russell R. Menard, "The Maryland Slave Population, 1658 to 1730: A Demographic Profile of Blacks in Four Counties," *William and Mary Quarterly,* 3rd ser., 32 (Jan. 1975), 36–37, 51–53; Mullin, *Flight and Rebellion,* 83–91; *The Diaries of George Washington, 1748–1799,* ed. John C. Fitzpatrick (Boston: Houghton Mifflin, 1925), III, 15–17; Betts, *Thomas Jefferson's Farm Book,* 7–9, 128; Edgar J. McManus, *Black Bondage in the North* (Syracuse, N.Y.: Syracuse University Press, 1973), 41–45. On the increase in occupational diversity among slave women in late eighteenth-century and early nineteenth-century Virginia, see Carole Shammas, "Black Women's Work and the Evolution of Plantation Society in Virginia," *Labor History,* 26 (Winter 1985), 26–27.

69. Genovese, *Roll, Jordan, Roll,* 388–90; Robert S. Starobin, *Industrial Slavery in the Old South* (New York: Oxford University Press, 1970), 1–36; Charles B. Dew, "Disciplining Slave Ironworkers in the Antebellum South: Coercion, Conciliation, and Accommodation," *American Historical Review,* 79 (April 1974), 398–418; Wade, *Slavery in the Cities,* 28–46.

70. Frederick Law Olmsted, *The Cotton Kingdom: A Traveller's Observations on Cotton and Slavery in the American Slave States* (New York, 1861), II, 177; Ulrich B. Phillips and James David Glunt, eds., *Florida Plantation Records from the Papers of George Noble Jones* (St. Louis: Missouri Historical Society, 1927), 549–50, 515–16; Dr. R. W. Gibbes to South Carolina Governor R. F. W. Allston, Columbia, 6 March 1858, in *DeBow's Review,* 24 (April 1858), 321; Robert William Fogel and Stanley L. Engerman, *Time on the Cross: The Economics of American Negro Slavery* (Boston: Little, Brown, 1974), 38–40.

71. Dew, "Disciplining Slave Ironworkers in the Antebellum South," 395–405; Sarah S. Hughes, "Slaves for Hire: The Allocation of Black Labor in Elizabeth City County, Virginia, 1782 to 1810," *William and Mary Quarterly,* 3rd ser., 35 (April 1978), 260–86 (quotation, 265); *Narrative of the Life of Moses Grandy,* 7. See also Wade, *Slavery in the Cities,* 33–54. According to Fogel and Engerman, *Time on the Cross,* 56–57, in 1860, 31 percent of urban slaves and 6 percent of rural slaves were on hire.

72. Douglass, *My Bondage and My Freedom,* 319. On self-hire, see Wade, *Slavery in the Cities,* 48–54; Starobin, *Industrial Slavery in the Old South,* 135–37; and Edna Chappell McKenzie, "Self-Hire among Slaves, 1820–1860. Institutional Variation or Aberration?" (Ph.D. diss., University of Pittsburgh, 1973).

73. Dew, "Disciplining Slave Ironworkers in the Antebellum South," 405–11.

74. Betts, *Thomas Jefferson's Farm Book,* 34; Ball, *Slavery in the United States,* 275; Fogel and Engerman, *Time on the Cross,* 148. On low-country slave capitalism, see especially Philip D. Morgan, "Work and Culture: The

Task System and the World of Lowcountry Blacks, 1700–1880," *William and Mary Quarterly*, 3rd ser., 39 (Oct. 1982), 563–99; Morgan, "The Ownership of Property by Slaves in the Mid-Nineteenth-Century Low Country," *Journal of Southern History*, 49 (Aug. 1983), 399–420; Charles Joyner, *Down by the Riverside: A South Carolina Slave Community* (Urbana: University of Illinois Press, 1984), 129–30; and Thomas F. Armstrong, "From Task Labor to Free Labor: The Transition along Georgia's Rice Coast," *Georgia Historical Quarterly*, 64 (Winter 1980), 432–37.

75. Wade, *Slavery in the Cities*, 62–75, 81–93, 143–79; Douglass, *My Bondage and My Freedom*, 147; recollection of Rufus Dirt in Rawick, *The American Slave*, VI, 117; Genovese, *Roll, Jordan, Roll*, 392–94; and Frances Anne Kemble, *Journal of a Residence on a Georgian Plantation in 1838–1839* (Chicago: Afro-Am Press, 1969), 25.

76. The quotation is from Morgan, "Work and Culture," 597. See also Chapter 1, pages 85–87.

77. On domestic servants in southern cities, see Wade, *Slavery in the Cities*, 30–33.

78. The quotation is from Charles C. Jones, Jr. to Rev. C. C. Jones, Savannah, 1 Oct. 1856, in Myers, *The Children of Pride*, 241–42. On the decline of urban slavery, see Wade, *Slavery in the Cities*, 16–27, 243–46, 326–27 (population figures). For the argument that urban slavery suffered primarily because of the booming demand for labor on the deep South's cotton plantations, see Claudia Dale Goldin, *Urban Slavery in the American South, 1820–1860: A Quantitative History* (Chicago: University of Chicago Press, 1976).

79. Genovese, *Roll, Jordan, Roll*, 388–90; Hoetink, *Slavery and Race Relations in the Americas*, 36–37; Marvin Harris, *Patterns of Race in the Americas* (New York: Walker & Company, 1964), ch. 7. On the arming of slaves in Brazil, see Carl N. Degler, *Neither Black nor White: Slavery and Race Relations in Brazil and the United States* (New York: Macmillan, 1971), 76–82.

80. For the argument that slaveowners often changed the occupations of slaves to fit their capabilities at varying stages of the life cycle, see Fogel and Engerman, *Time on the Cross*, 75.

81. Jacob Stroyer, *Sketches of My Life in the South*, part 1 (Salem, 1879), 9–26; *The Rev. J. W. Loguen, as a Slave and as a Freeman. A Narrative of a Real Life* (Syracuse, N.Y., 1859), quotations 29, 93, 226; Douglass, *My Bondage and My Freedom*, 33–320; Bruce, *The New Man*, 11–87.

82. John W. Blassingame, "Status and Social Structure in the Slave Community: Evidence from New Sources," in *Perspectives and Irony in American Slavery*, ed. Harry P. Owens (Jackson: University Press of Mississippi, 1976), 137–51 (quotation, 142). On divisions and unity among slaves, see also Escott, *Slavery Remembered*, 59–69. In contrast to Blassingame, Charles Joyner found that "slaves generally seem to have shared a sense of status stratification ranging from house servants at the top through drivers and artisans on down to field hands"; Joyner, *Down by the Riverside*, 83–84.

83. Quotations are from Stampp, *The Peculiar Institution*, 337, and Blassingame, *The Slave Community*, 155. See also C. W. Harper, "House Servants and Field Hands: Fragmentation in the Antebellum Slave Community," *North Carolina Historical Review*, 55 (Jan. 1978), 42–54; Harper, "Black Aristocrats: Domestic Servants of the Antebellum Plantation," *Phylon*, 56 (June 1985), 123–35; and Wade, *Slavery in the Cities*, 114. On close ties between house servants and whites, see Genovese, *Roll, Jordan, Roll*, 343–61.

84. Semevskii, *Krest'iane v tsarstvovanie Imperatritsy Ekateriny II*, I, xv, 158–59 (quotation, 158); and Ignatovich, *Pomeshchich'i krest'iane nakanune osvobozhdeniia*, 235. See also A. Romanovich-Slavatinskii, *Dvorianstvo v Rossii ot nachala XVII veka do otmeny krepostnago prava* (St. Petersburg, 1870), 325–28; P. I. Sakulin, "Krepostnaia intelligentsiia," in *Velikaia reforma: Russkoe obshchestvo i krest'ianskii vopros v proshlom i nastoiashchem. Iubileinoe izdanie*, ed. A. K. Dzhivelegov et al. (Moscow: Izdanie T-va I. D. Sytina, 1911), III, 83–103; E. S. Kots, *Krepostnaia intelligentsiia* (Leningrad: Knigoizdatel'stvo seiatel' E. V. Vysotskogo, 1926), 31–42; Blum, *Lord and Peasant in Russia*, 455–60; and Marc Raeff, *Origins of the Russian Intelligentsia: The Eighteenth-Century Nobility* (New York: Harcourt, Brace & World, 1966), 110–14.

85. *The Secret Diary of William Byrd of Westover, 1709–1712*, ed. Louis B. Wright and Marion Tinling (Richmond, Va.: Dietz Press, 1941), 84 (quotation), 85, 112, 113, 337, 583; "The Plantation Diary of Bennet H. Barrow," 106, 173, 192 (quotation); Hughes, *Thirty Years a Slave*, 72–73; Blassingame, "Status and Social Structure in the Slave Community," 139. See also Mullin, *Flight and Rebellion*, 62–82; Genovese, *Roll, Jordan, Roll*, 327–37, 343–65; and Leslie Howard Owens, *This Species of Property: Slave Life and Culture in the Old South* (New York: Oxford University Press, 1976), 107–20.

86. Zablotskii-Desiatovskii, "O krepostnom sostoianii v Rossii," 308; Hannah Stern Goldman, "American Slavery and Russian Serfdom; A Study in Fictional Parallels" (Ph.D. diss., Columbia University, 1955), 182; P. D. Boborykin, "Krepostnye razvivateli," in *Velikaia reforma*, IV, 76–86 (quotation, 77–78); Slovutinskii, "General Izmailov i ego dvornia," 103–14 (quotation, 110).

87. *The Narrative of William W. Brown*, 2; testimony of Mollie Tillman in Rawick, *The American Slave*, VI, 381; Olmsted, *The Cotton Kingdom*, I, 236; "Zapiska krepostnoi," in *Russkaia starina*, 145 (1911), 149; Sokolov, *Russian Folklore*, 514; N. L. Brodskii, "Krepostnoe pravo v narodnoi poezii," in *Velikaia reforma*, IV, 14.

88. Harriet Beecher Stowe, *Uncle Tom's Cabin* (New York: New American Library, 1966; orig. pub. 1852), 19–21; Ivan Turgenev, *A Sportsman's Notebook*, trans. Charles and Natasha Hepburn (London: Cresset Press, 1950; orig. pub. 1852), 27, 29. See also Goldman, "American Slavery and Russian Serfdom," 182–92.

89. Douglass, *My Bondage and My Freedom*, 109. For a sensitive analysis

of the position of southern house slaves, see Genovese, *Roll, Jordan, Roll,* 327–65. See also Escott, *Slavery Remembered,* 59–67. On numbers of house servants, see Chapter 3, pages 160–62.

Epilogue

1. On the relationship between slavery and capitalism, see especially Elizabeth Fox-Genovese and Eugene D. Genovese, "The Janus Face of Merchant Capital," in *Fruits of Merchant Capital: Slavery and Bourgeois Property in the Rise and Expansion of Capitalism* (New York: Oxford University Press, 1983), 3–25.

2. James Oakes, *The Ruling Race: A History of American Slaveholders* (New York: Alfred A. Knopf, 1982). For the contrast between "paternalistic" southern slavery and "capitalistic" Caribbean slavery, see Eugene D. Genovese, *The World the Slaveholders Made: Two Essays in Interpretation* (New York: Pantheon Books, 1969), 21–102.

3. This in no way implies that pomeshchiki had a capitalist attitude toward their agricultural operations; with few exceptions they sought to maximize their income by squeezing more out of their serfs, not by rationalizing their operations or stimulating productivity. See Michael Confino, *Domaines et seigneurs en Russie ver la fin du XVIIIᵉ siècle: Etude de structures agraires et de mentalités économiques* (Paris: Institut d'études slaves de l'Université de Paris, 1963), 146–59.

4. See above, Chapters 1 and 4.

5. C. Vann Woodward, "The Price of Freedom," in *What Was Freedom's Price?,* ed. David G. Sansing (Jackson: University Press of Mississippi, 1978), 97.

6. Population figures on Brazil are from E. Phillip LeVeen, "A Quantitative Analysis of the Impact of British Suppression Policies on the Volume of the Nineteenth Century Atlantic Slave Trade," in *Race and Slavery in the Western Hemisphere: Quantitative Studies,* ed. Stanley L. Engerman and Eugene D. Genovese (Princeton: Princeton University Press, 1975), 74. See also Michael Craton, "Jamaican Slavery," ibid., 249–84; Richard B. Sheridan, "Mortality and Medical Treatment of Slaves in the British West Indies," ibid., 285–310; Philip D. Curtin, *The Atlantic Slave Trade: A Census* (Madison: University of Wisconsin Press, 1969), esp. 28–34; C. Vann Woodward, "Southern Slaves in the World of Thomas Malthus," in *American Counterpoint: Slavery and Race in the North-South Dialogue* (Boston: Little, Brown, 1971), 78–106; and Franklin W. Knight, *Slave Society in Cuba during the Nineteenth Century* (Madison: University of Wisconsin Press, 1970), 22, 47–58, 63, 137–53. For a dissenting view, see Jack Ericson Eblen, "On the Natural Increase of Slave Populations: The Example of the Cuban Black Population, 1775–1900," in Engerman and Genovese, *Race and Slavery in the Western Hemisphere,* 211–47.

7. See sources cited in Chapter 4, note 22.

8. For slightly varying estimates of rates of natural population growth, see Melvin Zelnik, "Fertility of the American Negro in 1830 and 1850," *Population Studies,* 20 (July 1966), 77–83; Reynolds Farley, *Growth of the Black Population: A Study of Demographic Trends* (Chicago: Markham Publishing Company, 1970), 22, 32; Jack Ericson Eblen, "New Estimates of the Vital Rates of the United States Black Population during the Nineteenth Century," *Demography,* 11 (May 1974), 307–9; Edward Meekar, "Mortality Trends of Southern Blacks, 1850–1910: Some Preliminary Findings," *Explorations in Economic History,* 13 (Jan. 1976), 14, 19–23; and Peter D. McClelland and Richard J. Zeckhauser, *Demographic Dimensions of the New Republic: American Interregional Migration, Vital Statistics, and Manumissions, 1800–1860* (Cambridge: Cambridge University Press, 1982), 11–16, 73–77, 81–83. For two exceptions to the typical American pattern in South Carolina, see Sherman L. Ricards and George M. Blackburn, "A Demographic History of Slavery: Georgetown County, South Carolina, 1850," *South Carolina Historical Magazine,* 76 (Oct. 1975), 215–24; and Drew Gilpin Faust, *James Henry Hammond and the Old South: A Design for Mastery* (Baton Rouge: Louisiana State University Press, 1982), 76–83. For a fine case study of the demographic contrast between the United States and Jamaica, see Richard S. Dunn, "A Tale of Two Plantations: Slave Life at Mesopotamia in Jamaica and Mount Airy in Virginia, 1799 to 1828," *William and Mary Quarterly,* 3rd ser., 34 (Jan. 1977), 33–65.

9. Herbert S. Klein and Stanley L. Engerman, "Fertility Differentials between Slaves in the United States and the British West Indies: A Note on Lactation Practices and Their Possible Implications," *William and Mary Quarterly,* 3rd ser., 35 (April 1978), 354–74; Curtin, *The Atlantic Slave Trade,* 93; Alan Kulikoff, "A 'Prolifick' People: Black Population Growth in the Chesapeake Colonies, 1700–1790," *Southern Studies,* 16 (Winter 1977), 396–403; Richard B. Sheridan, "Mortality and Medical Treatment of Slaves," 285–310.

10. Kulikoff, "A 'Prolifick' People"; Kulikoff, "The Origins of Afro-American Society in Tidewater Maryland and Virginia, 1700 to 1790," *William and Mary Quarterly,* 3rd ser., 35 (April 1978), 240–56; Russell R. Menard, "The Maryland Slave Population, 1658 to 1730: A Demographic Profile of Blacks in Four Counties," ibid., 32 (Jan. 1975), 38–47; Herbert G. Gutman, *The Black Family in Slavery and Freedom, 1750–1925* (New York: Pantheon Books, 1976), 327–57. See also above, Chapter 4, page 208.

11. John Campbell, "Work, Pregnancy, and Infant Mortality among Southern Slaves," *Journal of Interdisciplinary History,* 14 (Spring 1984), 793–812; Dunn, "A Tale of Two Plantations"; B. W. Higman, *Slave Population and Economy in Jamaica, 1807–1834* (Cambridge: Cambridge University Press, 1976), 75–76, 79, 108–9, 121–25; Knight, *Slave Society in Cuba,* 68–84; Sheridan, "Mortality and Medical Treatment of Slaves." For the recent argument that malnutrition and consequent high rates of infant and child mortality were far more important than low fertility rates in pre-

venting natural population growth among Caribbean slaves, see Kenneth F. Kiple, *The Caribbean Slave: A Biological History* (Cambridge: Cambridge University Press, 1984), esp. 110–34. See also Chapter 2, page 137.

12. On the decline of southern manumissions, see Ira Berlin, *Slaves without Masters: The Free Negro in the Antebellum South* (New York: Pantheon Books, 1974), 135–57 (statistics, 137). On the Cuban contrast, see Knight, *Slave Society in Cuba,* 86 (statistics), 137–78; and Rebecca J. Scott, "Gradual Abolition and the Dynamics of Slave Emancipation in Cuba, 1868–86," *Hispanic American Historical Review,* 63 (Aug. 1983), 449–78.

13. Population figures are from V. M. Kabuzan, *Izmeneniia v razmeshchenii naseleniia Rossii v XVIII-pervoi polovine XIX v.* (Moscow: Izdatel'stvo "Nauka," 1971), appendix 2, 10–15; these figures exclude the armed forces. Other scholars have presented statistics that vary slightly from these, either because of different boundaries (e.g., some examine only European Russia) or because of inclusion of military personnel. See N. M. Shepukova, "Izmenenie udel'nogo vesa chastnovladel'cheskogo krest'ianstva v sostave naseleniia Evropeiskoi Rossii (XVIII-pervaia polovina XIX v.)," *Voprosy istorii,* 1959, no. 12, 123–36; and, for the last two censuses, Petr Keppen, *Deviataia reviziia. Izsledovanie o chisle zhitelei v Rossii v 1851 godu* (St. Petersburg, 1857); and A. Troinitskii, *Krepostnoe naselenie v Rossii, po 10-i narodnoi perepisi* (St. Petersburg, 1861).

14. On serfs' death and birth rates, see above, Chapter 2 (sources listed in note 91) and Chapter 4 (sources listed in note 31).

15. Shepukova, "Izmenenie udel'nogo vesa chastnovladel'cheskogo krest'ianstva," 133–36; P. G. Ryndziunskii, "Vymiralo li krepostnoe krest'ianstvo pered reformoi 1861 g.?" *Voprosy istorii,* 1967, no. 7, 54–70; Steven L. Hoch and Wilson R. Augustine, "The Tax Censuses and the Decline of the Serf Population in Imperial Russia, 1833–1858," *Slavic Review,* 38 (Sept. 1979), 403–25 (quotation, 424); V. I. Krutikov, "Izmenenie chislennosti i sotsial'nogo sostava naseleniia Tul'skoi gubernii v kontse XVIII-pervoi polovine XIX veka," in *Voprosy agrarnoi istorii tsentra i severo-zapada RSFSR: Materialy mezhvuzovskoi nauchnoi konferentsii* (Smolensk: Ministerstvo prosveshcheniia RSFSR, 1972), 123–29.

16. Although between 1719 and 1858 the population grew at an annual rate of 0.81 percent within boundaries existing at the time of the first census, between 1833 and 1858 the rate was only 0.64 percent; after emancipation the population resumed its earlier rate of growth, increasing at an annual rate of 0.91 percent between 1858 and 1885. See Kabuzan, *Izmeneniia v razmeshcheniia naseleniia Rossii,* 10, 13–14. Hoch and Augustine, "The Tax Censuses and the Decline of the Serf Population," 424, suggest a decline in fertility owing to an increase in the age of marriage, a thesis that draws support from the finding of Peter Czap, Jr., that in two districts of Riazan province the mean age of serf women at first marriage increased from 17.5 in the mid-eighteenth century to 18.2 in the mid-nineteenth; most of this increase, however, was the result of the virtual elimination of *very* young

marriages, with brides of 13, 14, and 15, marriages that probably did not lead to immediate childbirth in any case. See Czap, "Marriage and Peasant Joint Family in the Era of Serfdom," in *The Family in Imperial Russia: New Lines of Historical Research,* ed. David L. Ransel (Urbana: University of Illinois Press, 1978), 111. For the suggestion that otkhodnichestvo may have reduced birth rates in the nineteenth century, see I. D. Koval'chenko, *Russkoe krepostnoe krest'ianstvo v pervoi polovine XIX v.* (Moscow: Izdatel'stvo "Nauka," 1967), 324–28.

17. Krutikov, "Izmenenie chislennosti i sotsial'nogo sostava naseleniia Tul'skoi gubernii," 126–29. For the argument that because of their slightly better economic position state peasants were less affected than serfs by conditions that produced increased mortality rates, see N. M. Druzhinin, *Gosudarstvennye krest'iane i reforma P. D. Kiseleva* (Moscow: Izdatel'stvo Akademii nauk SSSR, 1946–1958), II, 294–300. On mortality rates, see Chapter 2 (sources cited in note 91).

18. For differing estimates of the number of serfs entering the state peasantry, see Ryndziunskii, "Vymiralo li krepostnoe krest'ianstvo," 65; Shepukova, "Izmenenie udel'nogo vesa chastnovladel'cheskogo krest'ianstva," 133; Koval'chenko, *Russkoe krepostnoe krest'ianstvo,* 324–28; and Hoch and Augustine, "The Tax Censuses and the Decline of the Serf Population," 410. The argument that recruit levies were primarily responsible for the declining serf population was made as early as 1861 by Troinitskii, *Krepostnoe naselenie v Rossii,* 54–56.

19. N. Danilov, "Obzor statei, kasaiushchikhsia do uluchsheniia byta poselian," *Zhurnal zemlevladel'tsev,* no. 9 (Aug. 1858), 1–32 (quotations 31, 2); and Dmitrii Neronov, "Pis'ma Zvenigorodskago pomeshchika o sovremennykh voprosakh. Pis'mo vtoroe," ibid., no. 14 (Oct. 1858), 10–26.

20. Troinitskii, *Krepostnoe naselenie v Rossii,* 57–61.

21. Charles W. Ramsdell, "The Natural Limits of Slavery Expansion," *Mississippi Valley Historical Review,* 16 (Sept. 1929), 151–71; William J. Cooper, Jr., "The Cotton Crisis in the Antebellum South: Another Look," *Agricultural History,* 49 (April 1975), 381–91.

22. Although there has been an extensive and continuing debate about slavery's impact on the southern economy, recent scholars have generally agreed that the antebellum South enjoyed rapid economic growth. On the earlier debate, see Harold D. Woodman, "The Profitability of Slavery: A Historical Perennial," *Journal of Southern History,* 29 (Aug. 1963), 303–25; and Hugh G. J. Aitken, ed., *Did Slavery Pay? Readings in the Economics of Black Slavery in the United States* (Boston: Houghton Mifflin, 1971). On the rapid southern economic growth of 1840–60, see Robert William Fogel and Stanley L. Engerman, *Time on the Cross: The Economics of American Negro Slavery* (Boston: Little, Brown, 1974), passim, esp. 247–57. On the movement to restore the slave trade, see Ronald T. Takaki, *A Pro-Slavery Crusade: The Agitation to Reopen the African Slave Trade* (New York: Free Press, 1971).

23. For recent documentation of how defensiveness about slavery pervaded late antebellum southern thought, see John McCardell, *The Idea of a Southern Nation: Southern Nationalists and Southern Nationalism, 1830–1860* (New York: W. W. Norton, 1979); and William J. Cooper, Jr., *The South and the Politics of Slavery, 1828–1856* (Baton Rouge: Louisiana State University Press, 1978). For the argument that the conflict between North and South was rooted in the clash of two rival ideologies spawned by divergent socioeconomic systems, see Barrington Moore, Jr., *Social Origins of Dictatorship and Democracy: Lord and Peasant in the Making of the Modern World* (Boston: Beacon Press, 1966), 111–55.

24. See, e.g., Thomas Prentice Kettell, *Southern Wealth and Northern Profits* (New York, 1860); and Hinton Rowan Helper, *The Impending Crisis of the South: How to Meet It* (New York, 1857). Population statistics are from *The Statistical History of the United States from Colonial Times to the Present* (New York: Basic Books, 1976), 22. For recent treatments of southern economic backwardness, see Gavin Wright, *The Political Economy of the Cotton South: Households, Markets, and Wealth in the Nineteenth Century* (New York: W. W. Norton, 1978), esp. 89–127; and Fred Bateman and Thomas Weiss, *A Deplorable Scarcity: The Failure of Industrialization in the Slave Economy* (Chapel Hill: University of North Carolina Press, 1981). See also the perceptive essay by Harold D. Woodman, "Economic History and Economic Theory: The New Economic History in America," *Journal of Interdisciplinary History,* 3 (Autumn 1972), 323–50.

25. The best general treatment of southern efforts to use the federal government to safeguard slavery is Cooper, *The South and the Politics of Slavery.*

26. See Eric Foner, *Free Soil, Free Labor, Free Men: The Ideology of the Republican Party before the Civil War* (New York: Oxford University Press, 1970); Richard H. Sewell, *Ballots for Freedom: Antislavery Politics in the United States, 1837–1860* (New York: Oxford University Press, 1976); and Cooper, *The South and the Politics of Slavery.*

27. Calhoun speech, 4 March 1850, in *The Works of John C. Calhoun,* ed. Richard K. Crallé (New York, 1851–55), IV, 542–73 (quotations, 556, 571). For a skillful exposition of the thesis that the late antebellum South faced a general crisis, see Eugene D. Genovese, *The Political Economy of Slavery: Studies in the Economy and Society of the Slave South* (New York: Random House, 1965), esp. 13–39.

28. The literature on both "Radical" Reconstruction and the consequences of emancipation is immense and growing. For the suggestion that American Reconstruction, although woefully inadequate, was radical in comparison with emancipation elsewhere in the western hemisphere, see Eric Foner, *Nothing but Freedom: Emancipation and Its Legacy* (Baton Rouge: Louisiana State University Press, 1983), esp. 39–73.

29. For two recent works on peasants and noblemen in postemancipation Russia, see N. M. Druzhinin, *Russkaia derevnia na perelome: 1861–1880 gg.*

(Moscow: Izdatel'stvo "Nauka," 1978); and A. P. Korelin, *Dvorianstvo v poreformennoi Rossii, 1861–1904 gg.: Sostav, chislennost', korporativnaia organizatsiia* (Moscow: Izdatel'stvo "Nauka," 1979). For two important American works on the formulation and implementation of the emancipation settlement, see Daniel Field, *The End of Serfdom: Nobility and Bureaucracy in Russia, 1855–1861* (Cambridge, Mass.: Harvard University Press, 1976); and Terence Emmons, *The Russian Landed Gentry and the Peasant Emancipation of 1861* (Cambridge: Cambridge University Press, 1968).

Index

292, 302, 320; skilled slaves of, 345; provides bonuses, 347–348

Jews, Russian, 65, 282, 324, 332

Johnson, Michael P., 289

Jones, Charles C., 61, 100–101, 115, 195, 220

Jones, Charles, C., Jr., 115

Jones, George Noble: as absentee owner, 60; and overseers, 66–67, 90–91, 294–295; illness on plantations of, 107, 137–138; occupations of slaves of, 346

Kakh, Iu. Iu., 304

Karamzin, N. M., 171

Karelia province, 337

Kazan province, 279

Keckley, Elizabeth, 112, 266, 267, 314

Kemble, Frances, 135, 277, 348

Kentucky, 54, 251, 286, 287, 289, 317, 351

Kharkov province, 369

Kherson province, 282

Kholopy (slaves): described, 2–3, 385n2, 386n4; become serfs, 3, 37–38; marriages of recognized, 117; lack ethnic distinctiveness, 44–45, 185

Khreptovich, Adam, 63, 75

Khreptovich, I. M., 63

Kiev province, 225, 298–299, 304, 305–306, 324, 325

Kilson, Marion, 254

Kiselev, P. D., 261, 262, 304, 313

Klein, Herbert, 364

Klingshtet, Timofei von, 92

Kopytoff, Igor, 18

Koretskii, V. I., 22

Koshkarov, P. A., 112, 124

Kourland province, 213

Koval'chenko, I. D., 150, 151, 337, 342

Krest'ianskoe dvizhenie v Rossii, 321, 470n31

Krutikov, V. I., 367

Kulikoff, Allan, 208

Kurakin, A. B., 161–162

Kurakin family, 88, 162

Kursk province, 162, 283, 306–307

Labor shortage: as cause of forced labor, 2, 17–19; and origins of Russian serfdom, 4, 6, 8, 30–31; and origins of American slavery, 10, 12, 15, 16–17, 30–31, 184–

185; in British West Indies, 13; and pro-bondage arguments, 174

Lagny, Germain de, 195

Latvia, 92

Laws: codifying serfdom, 8–10, 41–42; codifying slavery, 35; on black overseers, 96; on slave and serf marriage, 117; protecting slaves, 128, 131–132; restricting slaves, 131; reforming serfdom, 142–144; and race, 187–188; and slave confrontations, 268–269, 295–296; and peasant petitions, 273

Lee, Robert E., 319

Legislative codes, Russian: (1497), 4; (1550), 4; (1649), 9, 10, 41, 273

Lenin, V. I., 43, 337

Levine, Lawrence W., 199, 229, 230

Lewis, Isham, 130

Lewis, Lilburne, 130

Lifland province, 304

Ligi, Kh. M., 304

Lincoln, Abraham, 373

Lincoln, Mrs. Abraham, 266

Lithuania, 6, 7, 144, 278

Litvak, B. G., 150, 239, 304

Livonian war, 6, 7

Loguen, J. W., 286, 351

Louisiana: size of slaveholdings in, 54; slave families separated in, 116; racial attitudes in, 187–188; slave rebellions in, 251; slave flight in, 272, 317; free blacks in, 329

Lucas, Eliza, 133

Lyall, Robert, 88, 118

Lyskovo (village), 226, 335

Magic: among slaves, 227–228; among serfs, 228–229

Magruder, Eliza L., 133

Mallard, R. Q., 221

Manigault, Charles, 82–83

Manigault, Louis, 92

Manumissions and self-purchase: in Russia, 142–143, 145, 189–190, 338, 367, 368; in America, 164, 330, 365; dashed expectations of, 309, 319; in Caribbean and Brazil, 365

Market, production for: and spread of slavery, 19–22, 23–26, 359–360, 392n35; and spread of serfdom, 22–23, 27–31, 359–360; and barshchina, 65,

Illustration on page 47 reprinted by permission of the Bettmann Archive
Illustration on page 193 reprinted by permission of Culver Pictures
Picture research by Pembroke Herbert/Picture Research Consultants

Printed in the USA
CPSIA information can be obtained
at www.ICGtesting.com
LVHW011756221123
764659LV00003B/43